# FAITH AGAINST REASON

*An exchange of views between Lord Jakobovits and Reform Rabbi Hugo Gryn as the 'bridges of understanding' came tumbling down (see Chapter 19).*

# FAITH AGAINST REASON

Religious Reform and the
British Chief Rabbinate, 1840–1990

## MEIR PERSOFF

VALLENTINE MITCHELL
LONDON • PORTLAND, OR

First published in 2008 by Vallentine Mitchell

Suite 314, Premier House,　　　　920 NE 58th Avenue, Suite 300
112–114 Station Road,　　　　　　Portland, Oregon,
Edgware, Middlesex HA8 7BJ　　　　97213-3786

www.vmbooks.com

Copyright © 2008 Meir Persoff
Meir Persoff has asserted his right under the Copyright, Designs and Patents Act 1988 to be identified as the author of this work.

British Library Cataloguing in Publication Data

Persoff, Meir
  Faith against reason : religious reform and the British
Chief Rabbinate, 1840-1990
  1. Chief Rabbinate - Great Britain - History - 20th century
  2. Judaism - Great Britain - History - 20th century
  3. Chief Rabbinate - Great Britain - History - 19th century
  4. Judaism - Great Britain - History - 19th century
  I. Title
  296'.0941

ISBN 978 0 85303 679 1 (cloth)
ISBN 978 0 85303 670 8 (paper)

Library of Congress Cataloging-in-Publication Data:
A catalog record has been applied for

*All rights reserved. No part of this publication may be reproduced, stored in or introduced into a retrieval system, or transmitted, in any form or by any means, electronic, mechanical, photocopying, recording or otherwise without the prior written permission of the publisher of this book.*

Typeset in 11/13pt Joanna MT
Printed by Biddles Ltd, King's Lynn, Norfolk

For Sharon
and Jonathan,
with love

'I believe with perfect faith'
Moses Maimonides (1135–1204)


'There is reason to believe'
Morris Joseph (1848–1930)

# Contents

| | |
|---|---|
| List of Plates | xi |
| Preface | xiii |
| Introduction by Todd M. Endelman | xxv |
| | |
| Prologue: The Great Secession | 1 |
| 1. Omens of Peace | 19 |
| 2. Under the Canopy | 39 |
| 3. Censure and Silence | 61 |
| 4. Bonds of Brotherhood | 79 |
| 5. Joseph's Coat | 99 |
| 6. Singer's Song | 116 |
| 7. A New Religion | 137 |
| 8. Holy War | 159 |
| 9. Strangled Spirit | 171 |
| 10. Traditional Judaism | 190 |
| 11. The New Paths | 211 |
| 12. Call and Recall | 225 |
| 13. Omens of War | 245 |
| 14. Scraps of Paper | 272 |
| 15. Jacobs' Ladder | 283 |
| 16. 'This is the Law' | 302 |
| 17. Heart Talks to Heart | 318 |
| 18. Tokens of Disunity | 343 |
| 19. Broken Bridges | 361 |
| Epilogue: Change or Die | 380 |

| | |
|---|---|
| Notes | 390 |
| Appendix I: The Present Position of Judaism in England | 434 |
| Appendix II: The Jewish Religious Union | 439 |
| Appendix III: Synagogue and Marriage Statistics | 446 |
| Bibliography | 449 |
| Index | 465 |

# Plates

1. Nathan Marcus Adler
2. Moses Montefiore
3. David Woolf Marks
4. Moses Gaster
5. Hermann Adler
6. Samuel Montagu
7. Claude Montefiore
8. Lily Montagu
9. Hermann Gollancz
10. Simeon Singer
11. Morris Joseph
12. Israel Abrahams
13. Joseph Hochman
14. Joseph Herman Hertz
15. Israel Mattuck
16. Victor Schonfeld
17. Yechezkel Abramsky
18. Robert Waley Cohen
19. Isaac Herzog
20. Solomon Schonfeld
21. Isidor Grunfeld
22. Harold Reinhart
23. Israel Brodie
24. Ewen Montagu
25. Louis Jacobs
26. Isaac Wolfson
27. Yaacov Herzog
28. Immanuel Jakobovits
29. Morris Swift
30. John Rayner
31. Sidney Brichto
32. Tony Bayfield

# Preface

During the autumn of 1844, at the height of the campaign to elect a successor to Chief Rabbi Solomon Hirschell (1762–1842) and in the aftermath of the Reform secession some thirty months earlier, 'A Friend of Truth' published 'a few words' to his coreligionists on the problems and challenges facing British Jewry and its future leader. It was 'the unanimous desire of all classes of the Israelites', he wrote, 'that only such men are in nomination for the office who are wholly of our own time, and not imbued with the prejudices and bigotry of the darker ages ... A Chief Rabbi of England will not exercise an influence over the Jews of Great Britain alone, but also over those in the English Colonies; and even, to some extent, over the Jews of every country, since England is admitted on all hands to be the great commercial and political centre of the Globe. A discreet choice may, consequently, lead to the most beneficial results to the whole Jewish race; whilst the reverse would produce the most injurious effects, not only for the present time, but also for future generations.'[1]

Outlining 'the real object of this important appointment', the campaigner asserted that a Chief Rabbi was 'not required for mere forms' sake, nor for the simple purpose of having the vacant seat refilled, nor yet for the vain gratification of showing to the world that the high title of Chief Rabbi has been conferred upon a learned man – to whom great honour and deference will be paid from all sides'. Rather was it to be presumed 'that he is to teach, guide and direct those under his care whose spiritual welfare is entrusted to him; – that he might encourage them to the pursuit of virtue and true piety; – that he might elevate their minds to an enlightened course; – free them from all irreligious prejudices, and promote the education of their children'.

As for the qualities required of the Chief Rabbi, 'pre-eminent over all the rest of his brethren', he had to be 'a hero in mind, and the characteristics of such are a calm, grave, mild and consistent disposition; a penetrating understanding; a comprehensive and quick conception; a rational, reflecting and discreet judgment; and an extensive and skilful experience in government'. Since England's Jews, declared 'A Friend of Truth', were descendants from many different countries and frequently entertained different opinions on the same subjects, 'it will not appear too much to expect that a Rabbi should unite all these qualities, in order to reconcile this diversity of opinion'. To that end, he would – 'recognising his own weakness and insignificance – emulate the attributes of the Most High, and endeavour to act towards his fellow-creatures with that mercy and tolerance which the Lord manifests unto him; and be generous, indulgent and compassionate'.

Three years before these admonitions, during the troubled twilight of Hirschell's Chief Rabbinate, the first public rumblings of strife, schism and secession began to surface in the London Jewish press, which had 'hitherto avoided direct reference to the attempt of a few gentlemen, at the West End of the town, to form a synagogue there, with certain omissions from the established liturgy, and in contravention of the regulations of one of the London congregations [Bevis Marks] of which they have been and are yet members'.[2] Despite ecclesiastical condemnation of these moves, and in the face of a 'caution' against the perpetrators and their supporters – the term *cherem* (excommunication) was still largely eschewed – hopes were widespread that

> nothing further may be required. There are rumours also that in the thin ranks of the disaffected, temperate expostulation on the prospective consequences of schism is even now inducing a return to conformity: and many appear to think that sufficient has not been tried of this milder and more efficacious remedy; but that the absence of experience (happily existing among Jews) of how schism is fostered has betrayed our leaders into the only policy likely to fan the flame. Those who entertain this opinion assert that while the almost universal feeling condemns this movement as the presumptuous attempt of a handful of laymen, and while therefore there need be no apprehensions of the evil spreading, the only wise policy would be to treat the attempt as neither formidable by numbers, by station (at least theological), nor otherwise possessing a single element of union, and therefore to withhold that most powerful element – the occasion for a common defence.[3]

As today's community knows only too well, the flame was fanned by its erstwhile leaders, the 'evil' spread, and the 'handful of laymen' grew into a formidable body of Progressive Jews, spawning Reform, Liberal and

Conservative constituents in increasing, and increasingly voluble, numbers. Some thirty years after the secession, the United Synagogue came into being, motivated by its founders' belief – so contends its present leader, Chief Rabbi Sir Jonathan Sacks – 'that it was possible to guide Anglo-Jewry in such a way as to preserve the great principles of Jewish life without at the same time closing oneself off from the unfolding possibilities of an open society, and without separating oneself from the majority of the Jewish people'.[4]

Sacks argues that, unlike the forces of dissent in Germany and the United States,

> the synagogue stood firm in Anglo-Jewry on its ancient religious foundations in a way that it did not elsewhere. Individual Jews in Britain had their differences with the community. They protested, they left, they disaffiliated, and in extreme cases they converted or married out of the faith, or both. They did so, as far as we can tell, not less and not more than Jews elsewhere. But they did so as individuals. They did not do so as a community. When they identified with the community, whatever their private doubts and hesitations, they respected its long history and religious integrity. They did not seek to reform or reconstruct it.[5]

Dismissing allegations of latitudinarianism or hypocrisy on the part of those who, over its history, remained within the United Synagogue and pledged allegiance to it, the Chief Rabbi asserts that they manifested a wish

> to be part of a community which embodies the Jewish faith of the generations. It was the classic gesture of *emunah*. Those who joined it were not necessarily strictly observant, nor did they thereby signal that they had through personal reflection arrived at all thirteen of Maimonides' principles of faith. But they were making a significant declaration none the less, that they wished to belong to a congregation which in its public and collective expressions remained loyal to the principles by which Jews had always lived, and whose faith they wished to see continued as a living possibility for those who came after them. It was not a personal profession of righteousness, but it was a decision to remain related to the community of faith. And it had significant consequences. It meant that, whether frequently or intermittently, they were in touch with the Judaism of the ages, performing its deeds, sharing its prayers and aspiring to its ideals. It meant that they had not foreclosed the possibility of a deeper engagement with tradition, whether for themselves or for their children or

grandchildren, for they had never institutionalised and thus perpetuated their private disagreements with it. It meant that they were open – and faith itself is a form of openness – to the voice of the Divine Presence as it spoke through the texts and laws and prayers that the Jewish people had always held holy, and even if they did not hear it now, they kept alive the possibility that they might one day. It meant that they were loyal – and *emunah* means loyalty – to the Judaism of all time, not just one time. The United Synagogue stayed open to them, and they stayed open to it. By drawing a distinction between the individual and the community, and protecting the latter against changes that might sever its connection with the 'congregation of Israel' extended through space and time, Anglo-Jewry was faithful to a fundamental of Judaism, that it is in community that faith must be kept alive.[6]

By the start of Sacks' Chief Rabbinate, four years before the above lines were written, the United Synagogue's own Review (let alone the evidence adduced by fifteen decades of Progressive Judaism) was telling a different story. Its very title – *A Time For Change*[7] – bespoke crisis, decline, failing goals and falling membership. The movement stood at a crossroads, wrote the Review's secretary, Simon Caplin. The nature of Jewish identity had changed as the range of Jewish choices had expanded radically; traditional ties no longer exercised a hold over the individual; new expressions of Jewishness were being heard. 'The conclusion to which we were driven was that the root cause of the United Synagogue's crisis was a drift away from the fundamental goals or "mission" of the organisation. This was the single factor common to all the symptoms.'[8]

Discussing the attractions of the 'new expressions of Jewishness', United Synagogue members surveyed by the Review were emphatic in their attitudes to the non-Orthodox bodies:

> The growing Masorti [Conservative] movement was considered to be a very attractive alternative to the United Synagogue. The Masorti was thought to provide just the right combination of respect for halachah with a modern outlook. Masorti was considered 'less bigoted, less reactionary and less hypocritical than the United Synagogue'. United Synagogue rabbis in comparison, it was felt, spent too much time 'looking over their shoulders' in fear of 'other rabbis" censure ... The temptation to join the Masorti movement, with its traditional service, greater community feeling and equal place for women, provided some of the respondents with deep feelings of inner conflict. Those

Preface xvii

respondents would clearly remain with the United Synagogue if only it could provide that feeling of progress within tradition that Masorti appears to generate.

Of the Reform community, there was 'considerable first-hand and second-hand experience' among those surveyed.

On the positive side, they like the orderly nature of the service, the togetherness that results from reciting in unison, the set and well-signposted text which makes the service easier to follow, the better decorum and the shorter length. On the negative side, many felt that the atmosphere was too church-like and Anglicised. Overall, most respondents preferred a United Synagogue service for providing a familiar and traditional service. Those respondents who attend irregularly feel more comfortable with the traditions that they remember from their childhood even if they cannot understand the content and feel somewhat removed. Nevertheless, it was felt that there were lessons that could be learned from Reform services that might improve aspects of United Synagogue services without detracting from tradition. For example, a straightforward text and guide to the text including the repetitions was suggested. More communal singing is often requested ... These aspects, in addition to being worthwhile in themselves, would automatically improve decorum.[9]

Asked to characterise their level of religious observance, the United Synagogue members in the survey labelled themselves as 'non-religious (secular) Jew', 4 per cent; 'just Jewish', 16 per cent; 'Progressive Jew (e.g., Reform)', 3 per cent; 'traditional (not strictly Orthodox)', 67 per cent; 'strictly Orthodox Jew (*shomrei Shabbat*)', 10 per cent. The Review commented: 'As expected, the great majority of the respondents identified themselves as "traditional" Jews. This represents the central block of nominally Orthodox members who, in their responses to open-ended questions, frequently describe themselves as "middle-of-the-road" Jews.' High on the list of reasons given by former US members for leaving the organisation were their preference for Reform or Masorti and their perception of the United Synagogue as being 'too blinkered/right wing' or 'unwelcoming', although a similar number considered it 'not religious enough'.[10]

Expounding on these findings, Sacks has written:

Sadly, there are those who see it as a *weakness* of the United Synagogue that it includes among its members those who do not yet keep every one of the 613 commandments, and that according to the Kalms

Report [named after its chairman, Stanley Kalms], 90 per cent of its membership are only 'traditional' or non-observant. I use the word 'sadly' advisedly, because those who take this view have no understanding of what Torah and the sages meant by 'the congregation of Israel' [*Knesset Yisrael*, the United Synagogue's Hebrew name] ... The time has come for the United Synagogue to stop being apologetic for what is in fact its greatest strength and its most authentic Torah value: that it embraces all Jews from the most to the least observant, and that it forges from this range of commitments a deep sense of community. For that is what 'the congregation of Israel' has represented from the day our ancestors stood at Sinai to today.[11]

Faith Against Reason seeks to test the fidelity of these arguments against the interaction of the United Synagogue components and the Progressive movements across five Chief Rabbinates, and to probe their complex psyches as discord and divisiveness continue to dominate the polarising community. Nor should it be overlooked that since the appearance of *A Time For Change*, despite its radical recommendations for revival and regeneration, affiliation to mainstream Orthodoxy within Anglo-Jewry has dropped rapidly, losing 31.1 per cent of its support between 1990 and 2005/06. The greatest beneficiary has been Masorti, up 63.3 per cent in the same period, and 43.2 per cent in the last five years. Membership of the Union of Orthodox Hebrew Congregations rose by 51.4 per cent, while both Reform (-3.5 per cent) and Liberal (-5.5 per cent) showed increasing losses, and the Sephardim (+3.5 per cent) a latter-day gain.

Overall, the share of mainstream Orthodoxy in synagogue membership fell during those fifteen years from 66 to 55 per cent, with increases for the Union (up from 6 per cent to 10.5 per cent), Reform (17 per cent to 20 per cent), Liberal (7 per cent to 8 per cent), and Masorti (1 per cent to 2.5 per cent). In Greater London alone, mainstream Orthodoxy now accounts for less than half of membership (49.5 per cent), with Reform attracting 19.9 per cent, Union 12.4 per cent, Liberal 9.9 per cent, and Sephardim and Masorti (combined because of the small number of synagogues) 8.4 per cent.[12] The continued slump in male membership of centrist Orthodox congregations[13] – as embodied in the United Synagogue which the Chief Rabbi was elected (in the words of 'A Friend of Truth') to teach, guide and direct – questions the efficacy of Sacks' exhortation that closes this book.

\* \* \*   \* \* \*   \* \* \*

One hundred and twenty years – the traditional Jewish lifespan symbolised by that of the Lawgiver Moses – separated the Reform secession from the second such cataclysm in British Jewry. At their heart lay that very Law entrusted to Moses, and in their wake stood two Chief Rabbis, Nathan Marcus Adler (1803–1890) and Immanuel Jakobovits (1921–1999), who were to suffer their schismatic consequences over long and often trying decades. The *modi operandi* of these rabbis, and of those who served in the intervening years – Hermann Adler (1839–1911), Nathan's fifth child and second son; Joseph Herman Hertz (1872–1946); and Israel Brodie (1895–1979) – reveal much about their backgrounds, personalities, authority and effectiveness, and helped to shape the verdict of history on their ecclesiastical leadership. Each of these elements will be explored in the following chapters in relation to the progressive sectarianism that gathered pace at crucial, and contrasting, stages in the onward march of Anglo-Jewry.

Both Adler and Jakobovits entered office as the effects of reform began to take hold in their increasingly fractious – and fractured – community, Adler during a period of rapid expansion in its size, strength and structure, and Jakobovits during its post-Second World War decline. Both were born in Germany to illustrious rabbinical families; both were deeply immersed in the dual disciplines of academia and *Talmud Torah*; and both subscribed to the *Torah im derech eretz*[14] philosophy popularised by the German theologian, Samson Raphael Hirsch (1808–1888), who himself competed against Adler for the British Chief Rabbinate. How much each was responsible for the diminution or perpetuation of internecine strife, and how far each was able to rein in expressions of dissent and dissatisfaction – both within and outside his immediate domain – strongly influenced the reputation and reliability of his exalted position.

Surveying the story of the British rabbinate, Jakobovits described himself as 'probably closest to Chief Rabbi Nathan Marcus Adler in background and outlook, or at least closer to him than to any other' British Chief Rabbi.[15] As 'an upholder, indeed an exemplar, of Victorian values', Jakobovits had, too, 'a spiritual quality which, with the possible exception of Nathan Adler, was not shared by any of his predecessors'.[16] The comparisons are apt, and they account for many of the similarities in attitude and approach, if not in outcome, which moulded the policies of the two men in their respective, and very different, centuries.

Each of the Chief Rabbis, in the 150 years spanned by this book, was called upon to confront reform during periods of exceptional upheaval within British Jewry, and each did so in different ways. But tempers and temperaments, colleagues and combatants, even whims and wiles – not to mention opportunistic wheeler-dealing – all featured in the formation and dissemination of responses and policies, with results that not infrequently played into the hands of opposing forces.

The chroniclers of Anglo-Jewry have not always been kind to Britain's Chief Rabbis. In truth, the verdicts have been mixed, and sometimes muted, but, with communal censure and strife continuing unabated, they have become increasingly forthright as the centuries have turned. In the pages that follow, some of these verdicts will be subjected to scrutiny; others will emerge and, with them, a clearer picture of the Chief Rabbinical record on religious pluralism as it has developed into our day.

\* \* \*    \* \* \*    \* \* \*

In October 1960, as a departing cheder teacher in search of greener pastures, I received a farewell gift from the minister of London's Kenton Synagogue, 'C.K. Harris (Rev.)', as he signed himself – later South African Chief Rabbi Cyril Harris, of blessed memory – inscribed with best wishes for my future success. The gift was a relatively unknown and unheralded book, *We Have Reason to Believe*,[17] by the equally unheralded and only slightly better known Louis Jacobs, and though I barely skimmed through it then, I remember reading the blurb on the jacket. It asked – among other questions – 'What is meant when it is said that the Bible is the word of God?' and it assured me that: 'You may disagree violently with some of the author's contentions. You may find yourself in accord with everything he says. But agreeing or disagreeing, you are bound to find it exhilarating to accompany him on his journey towards a faith that transcends, but is firmly grounded in, reason.'

Perhaps more than most other eventual readers of that book – for at the time no one, least of all C.K. Harris (Rev.) and, so it seems, Israel Brodie (Chief Rabbi Dr), had paid much attention to it – I took the suggestion literally. For the next four decades, I found myself accompanying Louis Jacobs – and scores of other communal personalities in the drama that became known as the 'Jacobs Affair' – on his (and their) journey through the mazes and minefields of Anglo-Jewry. Six months after receiving the book, I joined the staff of the *Jewish Chronicle* and, as a cub reporter, accepted as my first assignment the tracking of Jacobs' every word and every move as he and *We Have Reason to Believe* became household names. Forty years later, many of those personalities having intrigued as cohorts or commanders in the communal jungle, I withdrew, disillusioned, to advance some of the interests which my

Preface

involvement in Anglo-Jewry had nurtured along the way.

One of those interests – not altogether surprisingly, given my penchant as a child for sitting at my mother's feet and lapping up accounts of her life – was the history of our community, in which both my parents played a significant role. My immersion in the politics and pugilistics of Anglo-Jewry had strengthened that attraction, and towards the end of my JC (and Jacobs) journey, I wrote a dissertation entitled *Conflict and Conciliation*, under the amiable guidance of the late and much beloved Rabbi Dr Sydney Leperer, that helped earn me a master's degree at the very Jews' College so prominently featured in this volume. Thus were born the bones of *Faith Against Reason*, which developed as a doctoral thesis before I decided to open it up to a larger audience, in the recognition that British Jewry – and the wider world – had much to learn from this recurring tale of (to adapt Jakobovits' Churchillian allusion in his 1967 installation address) blood, toil, tears and sweat.

In a valedictory piece on my retirement from the paper, I drew attention to a book by my friend (and fellow news-gatherer) Doreen Berger[18] projecting, as I put it, 'an evocative, 600-page genealogical compilation of the achievements, misdemeanours, triumphs, tragedies, family milestones and communal associations of hundreds of British Jews', and I quoted Georg Wilhelm Friedrich Hegel's aphorism, as true now as when he penned it two centuries ago: 'What experience and history teach is this – that people and governments never have learned anything from history, or acted on principles deduced from it.' I wrote that one of my more fascinating (if less onerous) tasks during my years on the JC was to compile the kaleidoscope known as 'Back Issues', offering 'revealing glimpses into the lives of our forebears, who grew up in tumultuous, energising and often frightening times for the Jewish people in both Britain and abroad'. From Berger's equally fascinating collection, I drew example after example of splits and dissension in communal ranks, of disputes, discontent and denial, and of attempts at reconciliation that sometimes were successful but more frequently were spurned. I concluded with these words in the footsteps of Hegel:

> Sadly, all of these incidents – and many others besides – have found echoes in our day. They betoken a community bent on following the example of Chief Rabbi Joseph Herman Hertz, of whom it has been written: 'He enjoyed a fight almost for its own sake. In any conflict, it was said, he would resort to peaceful means if all else failed.' … This was a decade of vibrancy and experimentation, presaging a period of unparalleled growth in Jewish numbers and activity, yet

highlighting a community uncertain of its direction, and jealous of its traditions. Today, 130 years on, we are again unclear as to our direction, often at odds with one another, and facing an unprecedented decline in numbers, if not in activity. For each hesitant Jew coaxed into affiliation, there are many more who will fall by the wayside. For each couple getting married, another is approaching separation or divorce. With every three births that bring joy come four deaths that bring sorrow. Steadily, inexorably, our community is contracting. Less than two generations ago, we totalled some 435,000 souls. Today, Anglo-Jewry – many of whom seem fired more by the soccer pitch than by the synagogue pulpit – would fit comfortably into three Wembley stadiums. Imagine the value of being one Jew in only 280,000; imagine the enormity of even a single loss. We are a troubled and, at times, troublesome people. We patch up our differences, but the cracks reappear and threaten to consume us. We tinker with ideas, offering short-term panaceas, but rarely have the confidence to confront crises head-on. We must promote strong, honest and courageous leadership, on all fronts and on all issues. We must put communal priorities before personal ambitions and personal agendas, striving to teach by example, and with tolerance, integrity and trust. Only if we follow this path will our resolution of the crucial issues of today – the Back Issues of tomorrow – redound to the credit of the Jewish Elizabethan.[19]

To those sentiments, then Mizrachi president Arieh Handler – who knows a thing or two about Anglo-Jewish politics – subsequently added the following comment: 'What is needed is the readiness of communal leaders to meet the wider Jewish public, the haves and the have-nots, to encourage their participation, to listen – even to the disrespectful – and to answer their questions ... The present leaders of our community and their officials seem to know everything about everything, but seldom listen to the wider public, not even to an elected body like the Board of Deputies. Let us learn from history.'[20]

\* \* \*    \* \* \*    \* \* \*

In our desire to learn from history, and to meet the wider Jewish (and general) public, I offer this volume as an extensive excursus into the frailty and fragility of communal relationships. Others have touched on the topic subjectively, politically or theologically. *Faith Against Reason* examines the 'how' as well as the 'why', allowing the key protagonists to speak for themselves and benefiting from the incisive introduction by Todd M. Endelman, William Haber Professor of Modern Jewish History at the University of Michigan and the foremost scholar on Anglo-Jewry among the growing ranks of communal historians. I am delighted to acknowledge my gratitude for his contribution to this book, and for his help, advice and friendship over many years.

I am also indebted to Professor Geoffrey Alderman, Naomi Bar-Yosef, Rabbi Dr Sidney Brichto (Brichto Papers, London), Myrna Carlebach, Rabbi Elliot Cosgrove, Dr Benjamin Elton, Judge Israel Finestein, Rabbi Dr Irving Jacobs, Ivor Jacobs (Jacobs Papers, London), Lady (Amélie) Jakobovits (Jakobovits Papers, London), Dr Lionel Kopelowitz, Rabbi Dr Abraham Levy, Elkan Levy, Rabbi Dr Harvey Meirovich, Professor Aubrey Newman, Menachem Persoff, Professor Stefan Reif, Rabbi Dr Jonathan Romain, Rabbi Dr Julian Shindler and Rabbi Geoffrey Shisler – as well as to my cousin, the late Menachem Ezra Abramsky – for their invaluable assistance and co-operation, and to the librarians, archivists and staff of the following institutions, at many of which I spent inspiring and fruitful hours: Assembly of Masorti Synagogues; Bar-Ilan University; Board of Deputies of British Jews; British Library Hebrew Collections; Cambridge University Library; Dorot Jewish Division, New York Public Library; Federation of Synagogues; Hartley Library, University of Southampton;[21] Hebrew and National Library, Hebrew University of Jerusalem; Jewish Chronicle; Jewish Historical Society of England; Jewish Memorial Council; Law Society Library; Leo Baeck College; Liberal Judaism (Union of Liberal and Progressive Synagogues); London Beth Din; London Metropolitan Archives (LMA);[22] London School of Jewish Studies (Jews' College); Mendel Gottesman Library of Hebraica and Judaica, Yeshiva University; Mocatta Library, University College London;[23] Office of the Chief Rabbi; Reform Synagogues of Great Britain; Schechter Institute of Jewish Studies; Schocken Institute and Library; Spanish and Portuguese Jews' Congregation; Special Collection Reading Room, Library of the Jewish Theological Seminary of America[24] (and its Joseph and Miriam Ratner Center for the Study of Conservative Judaism); Sternberg Centre for Judaism; S. Zalman and Ayala Abramov Library, Hebrew Union College – Jewish Institute of Religion (Jerusalem campus); United Synagogue; Western Charitable Foundation; West London Synagogue of British Jews.

The publisher and author acknowledge the assistance of the Jewish Chronicle in the provision of the illustrations.

\* \* \*    \* \* \*    \* \* \*

Frank Cass, the chairman and managing director of Vallentine Mitchell, who welcomed this study and followed its development with interest, passed away the very week it was delivered to his office. A man of extraordinary insight, vision, wit and wisdom, he devoted his working life to the written word and printed book, through a vast array of academic, political, military, religious and historical titles. His contribution to Anglo-Jewry was wide-ranging, unstinting and boundless, and his literary legacy will serve as an unparalleled testament to his love of, and dedication to, every aspect of communal endeavour. In recognition of Frank's life-long commitment to the underlying theme of *Faith Against Reason* – the pursuit of unity without uniformity – I am honoured to associate his name with it *in memoriam*.

MEIR PERSOFF<br>
Jerusalem<br>
May 2008, Iyar 5768

# Introduction

The decorous tone of Jewish worship in Britain's mainstream Orthodox congregations from the onset of the Victorian age to the immediate post-Second World War years is deceptive. It misleadingly suggests that the Anglo-Jewish religious scene was a sea of calm gentility, its surface rarely disturbed by embarrassing squabbles and schisms. Meir Persoff's richly documented book shows how mythical this view is.

From its emergence, with the arrival of Nathan Marcus Adler from Hanover in 1845, the Chief Rabbinate was embroiled in a welter of conflicts and quarrels. Chief Rabbis from Adler to Jakobovits variously battled with their own clergy and lay leaders, as well as with the religious leadership of congregations both to their left (Reform and Liberal) and to their right (immigrant and sectarian Orthodox). Some of these conflicts were of their own making, initiated by them to suppress the spread of ideas that challenged fundamental tenets of traditional Judaism. Others were thrust upon them, usually by less acculturated, yeshivah-trained rabbis who challenged their halachic authority.

Meir Persoff's is the first comprehensive account of the battles that Britain's Chief Rabbis fought against those, both within and without the United Synagogue, whose approach to Judaism was more flexible than their own. It begins in the early 1840s with the well-known episode of the founding of the West London Synagogue of British Jews and the *cherem* that followed.

As Persoff shows, even though the innovations in question were relatively moderate, Nathan Adler and his lay ally at the Board of Deputies, Moses Montefiore, persisted for decades in their effort to marginalise and delegitimise the Reform congregation. In 1883, for example, the ailing Adler, in semi-retirement in Brighton, intervened to prevent its minister, D.W. Marks, from delivering a sermon at the Western Synagogue in London. The following decade, Adler's son and successor, Hermann, faced challenges for liberalisation from within the Orthodox fold, especially from the newly established Hampstead Synagogue and the Jewish Religious Union, the forerunner of Liberal Judaism in Britain.

Incumbents of the post in the twentieth century – Joseph Herman Hertz, Israel Brodie and Immanuel Jakobovits – continued to oppose moderate reformers within the United Synagogue, as well as secessionists who made no pretence of accepting their authority. Hertz pressured Joseph Hockman to resign from the pulpit of the New West End Synagogue in 1915, declared all-out war on Liberal Judaism in the 1920s, and skirmished throughout the interwar years with the decidedly heterodox head of the nominally Orthodox United Synagogue, Robert Waley Cohen. Brodie launched the most widely publicised Anglo-Jewish brouhaha of the century – the 'Jacobs Affair' – when he blocked the appointment of Louis Jacobs as principal of Jews' College in 1961, and then refused to sanction his reappointment as minister of the New West End Synagogue in 1964.

Persoff allows the Chief Rabbis, their supporters and their opponents to speak for themselves, incorporating into his narrative generous excerpts from their correspondence, sermons, broadsides and disputations. The central place he assigns to this material, much of which is reproduced here for the first time, invites us to meet the controversialists face-to-face, on their own terms, without the interpretive baggage of today's religious divisions.

This invitation to return to the sources acts as a cautionary reminder that the past has an integrity of its own and that neither Orthodoxy nor Reform is a monolithic, unchanging phenomenon, immune to the influence of time and place. Commitments and understandings shift over time, as do the meanings and values that different generations assign even to the same terms and phrases. The Orthodoxy of the late-Victorian United Synagogue is not the same as the Orthodoxy of the United Synagogue in the early twenty-first century.

That said, continuity is not absent from this story. The failure of the conflict between the Chief Rabbinate and the representatives of more liberal forms of Judaism to moderate or fade away between the 1840s and the present is striking, as is its passionate, often intemperate, tone. Even seasoned historians of British Jewry will be struck by the persistence and vehemence of the debate.

This, in turn, raises the question of whether intra-communal religious strife was more common in Britain than elsewhere, consuming time, energy and resources in unparalleled ways decade after decade. This is difficult to answer. Jews are a fractious people. The story about the Jewish shipwreck survivor whose rescuers are puzzled by the existence of two synagogues on the otherwise desolate island where he is found testifies to this. (One is the synagogue in which he prays; the other is the synagogue in which he would not be caught dead.)

Religious conflicts, tensions, squabbles and breakaways were common in other Western Jewish communities, especially in Germany, Hungary and the United States. Moreover, comparing peaks and troughs of quarrelsomeness is no easy task. An alternative, more fruitful approach, is to ask, instead, whether the institution of the Chief Rabbinate (not its incumbents or its ideology but its very existence and structure) in some way facilitated or encouraged religious strife.

To begin, it is essential to note that Britain's Chief Rabbinate was unique: no similar institution, with similar claims to authority, emerged in other Western Jewish communities in the modern period. In the United States, the organisational basis of religious life for both Jews and Christians was entrepreneurial, laissez-faire and voluntaristic. Congregations were local bodies that hired and fired their rabbis at will. Members who objected to the state of divine worship (be it too liberal or too conservative) decamped to create new synagogues that better reflected their sentiments.

In Germany, Austria and Hungary, Jewish religious life was almost as decentralised, but membership in the community was not voluntary, as in Britain and the United States. (Even when it became possible, in the late nineteenth century, for Jews to renounce Judaism and withdraw from the community – without converting to Christianity – few availed themselves of the opportunity.) However, because the community (*Gemeinde*), a State-authorised body, encompassed all the Jews of a locale – liberals and traditionalists, along with the indifferent and the unobservant – it tended to be inclusive rather than exclusive in its outlook, maintaining both Orthodox and Reform synagogues. In any case, by the end of the nineteenth century, religious strife was no longer the explosive issue it had been earlier in the century, when the Reform movement first emerged.

French Jewry was far more centralised and hierarchical than any other Western community, thanks to the consistorial system that Napoleon imposed in 1807. At the head of both the national *consistoire* and each of the regional *consistoires* was a *grand rabbin*. But, unlike Britain's Chief Rabbis, they were weak figures, very much servants of the secular-minded notables who managed communal affairs. The French Jewish bourgeoisie as a whole, moreover, evinced far less interest in religious matters than its British counterpart and rarely noticed what took place in the synagogue or what its rabbis preached.

In Britain, from the Cromwellian resettlement to this day, membership in the Jewish community has been voluntary, a matter of self-identification, as in the United States, rather than a matter of civil status, as in Imperial and Weimar Germany and the Habsburg Empire and its successor states. Congregations, schools and charities emerged as a result of Jewish initiatives. When the lay leaders of London's largest congregations formally created the Chief Rabbinate following the death of Solomon Hirschell in 1842, they, not the State, bestowed on Nathan Adler 'the general religious direction and superintendence of each of the uniting congregations'.[1]

In 1847, in his *Laws and Regulations for all the Synagogues in the British Empire*, Adler consolidated the control of the Chief Rabbinate over the administration and direction of synagogue life and expanded the reach of its authority (apparently without consultation) to all synagogues, not just in Britain but in its overseas empire as well. When leading figures in the same London congregations established the United Synagogue in 1870, they reaffirmed the Chief Rabbinate's claim of primacy. However, the parliamentary legislation establishing the United Synagogue (legislation was required because various trust funds and charities were involved) pointedly declined to award this power to the Chief Rabbi. The Government was then engaged in disestablishing the Anglican Church of Ireland and felt that it would be inconsistent to award Jews what it was taking away from Anglicans in Ireland.

Thus, from very early in its history, there was a gap between the claims of the Chief Rabbinate and its ability to enforce those claims. As long as most Jews voluntarily accepted its authority, the system worked well. However, as Persoff shows, there were always practising Jews who were unwilling to acknowledge the Chief Rabbi as their Chief Rabbi, believing he was either insufficiently rigorous or insufficiently flexible.

Because the Chief Rabbinate lacked legal backing for its claim to primacy, those who questioned its authority were able to establish congregations and other religious institutions without hindrance. At the very most, Chief Rabbis were able to delay (but not ultimately block) the certification of marriage secretaries at breakaway synagogues. This gap between the ideology or myth of the Chief Rabbinate and the power it enjoyed to supervise synagogal life throughout Britain invited conflict and contention. Successive Chief Rabbis, firm in the belief of their own primacy, championed their understanding of Judaism and battled against those whom they opposed.

Because the lay leaders of the United Synagogue entrusted them with the supervision of its member synagogues, they were able to impose their will on its ministers and rabbis. But that was as far as they could go. They could not inhibit the spread of Reform, Liberal, Masorti and sectarian Orthodox Judaism. The intensity of their attacks on the first three movements reveals, in fact, the weakness of their position: there was little they could do actually to prevent the growth of synagogues that rejected their authority. Their claim outstripped their clout.

At the time the Chief Rabbinate came into being, most British Jews were willing to acknowledge its primacy. The Reform movement in Britain was weak, attracting few families relative to the size of the community. The same can be said of Liberal Judaism at its emergence early in the twentieth century. By this time, however, East End Jews outnumbered West End Jews. For many of them, the decorous, upper-middle-class Judaism of the United Synagogue, with its begowned Chief Rabbi, was alien.

While many of their descendants, having prospered and moved to the suburbs, in time joined congregations that acknowledged the Chief Rabbinate, some remained critical of what they saw as its willingness to compromise with modernity and Englishness. Their quarrel with the Chief Rabbinate was not theological – no Chief Rabbi ever denied the notion of *Torah min hashamayim* or the eternally binding character of the Written and Oral Law – but, rather, what might be called strategic. Acculturation and integration mattered less to them, as did the whole notion of *minhag anglia*.

In the second half of the twentieth century, this kind of strict, sectarian Orthodoxy grew by leaps and bounds. At the same time, for different reasons, liberal forms of Judaism began to expand. For many descendants of East European immigrants, the ethos and discipline of Orthodoxy, even in its mainstream English incarnation, were out of touch with the demands of living in the modern world.

The growth of Reform and Liberal Judaism, on the left of the religious spectrum, and strict Orthodoxy, on the right, has slowly shrunk the segment of Anglo-Jewry that recognises the Chief Rabbinate. As Persoff notes, mainstream Orthodoxy now embraces less than half (49.5 per cent) of synagogue membership in Greater London. Reform congregations account for 19.9 per cent, and Liberal for 9.9 per cent, while, on the right, the Union of Orthodox Hebrew Congregations accounts for 12.4 per cent. Sephardi and Masorti congregations make up the remaining 8.4 per cent. None of these groups accepts the authority of the Chief Rabbi.

While the ability of the Chief Rabbinate to guide the religious life of British Jewry as a whole is weaker today than it was in the Victorian period, its influence on centrist Orthodoxy may be stronger – largely because there is now less distance, in terms of religious practice, between the lay leadership of the Orthodox mainstream and the Chief Rabbinate. Before the Second World War, the management of the United Synagogue and its constituent synagogues was in the hands of wealthy Jewish families with deep roots in Britain. While they were far more observant than Jewish notables elsewhere in the West, in most cases they were not strictly observant Orthodox Jews. They valued the idea of a Jewish religious establishment and the notion of time-honoured religious traditions, but their observance of the law was far from scrupulous.

At times, this led to conflicts between them and the occupant of the Chief Rabbinate, the most notable being the pitched battles between Robert Waley Cohen and J.H. Hertz. But most of the time, both parties tolerated the tension between the public Orthodoxy of Britain's mainstream congregations and the less-than-traditional behaviour of their members, including many of their leaders.

In practice, the Judaism of the United Synagogue membership was latitudinarian and undemanding, concerned more with unity, respectability and civility than with distinctions between 'authentic' and 'inauthentic' forms of Judaism. As the eminent geneticist and veteran communal worker, Redcliffe Nathan Salaman, told the Jewish Historical Society of England in 1953: 'In the community at large, there was [before the First World War], if not religious peace, at least an atmosphere of kindly make-believe and gentlemanly behaviour which for long had been no inadequate substitute. That it covered much indifference and more ignorance distressed neither leaders nor led. A sense of brotherhood and the acceptance of collective responsibility was then, as now, a firmer bond than religion in our time is ever likely to be.'[2]

In the second half of the twentieth century, the gap between theory and practice in the United Synagogue narrowed. The old communal élite faded from the scene, leaving control of the United Synagogue and other institutions in the hands of self-made men of East European background whose level of observance and commitment to tradition outstripped theirs.

At the same time, as in the United States, there was a shift towards tradition at the congregational level, not only within the United Synagogue but more broadly as well. The less observant slowly transferred their allegiance from centrist Orthodoxy to Liberal, Reform and Masorti Judaism (or drifted from Jewish practice altogether), while those who remained behind accepted new levels of observance as the norm. As a result, the outlook and practice of the United Synagogue's lay leadership and membership now more closely match those of the Chief Rabbi than at any time in the past. Fewer British Jews recognise his authority, but those who do so are much more likely to follow his lead in practice as well as in theory.

Despite this convergence, religious strife remains a hallmark of the Anglo-Jewish community, as even casual readers of the *Jewish Chronicle* are aware. Critics of the Chief Rabbi and the targets of his wrath, however, are today less likely to come from the ranks of his own ministers or lay leaders, as was often the case in the past. His strongest critics are those to the left of the United Synagogue, who claim that the old minhag anglia is dead and that its central institutions – the Chief Rabbinate, the Beth Din and the United Synagogue – support an increasingly fundamentalist version of Judaism resembling, in some respects, that of strict, sectarian Orthodoxy.

Meir Persoff's book is a treasure trove of primary sources illuminating how British Jewry arrived at this point. It sheds light on episodes both well-known and obscure, elucidating what was at stake in each. It strives for objectivity, forswearing both hagiography and polemic, wisely leaving the reader to reach his or her own judgment.

TODD M. ENDELMAN<br>
William Haber Professor of Modern Jewish History,<br>
University of Michigan

Prologue

# The Great Secession

Born a British subject on 13 January 1803, in Hanover – significantly, then an appanage of Great Britain under George III – Nathan Marcus Adler was the third of eight children of a respected rabbinical family, of priestly stock, that traced its origins back to Rabbi Shimon Hadarshan ('The Preacher'). A resident of Frankfurt-on-Main in the thirteenth century, Shimon was the author of *Yalkut Shimoni*, verse-by-verse homilies to the Bible culled from the *midrashim* and the Talmud.[1]

Centuries later, Nathan Adler's son, Marcus Nathan, was to describe how, after a succession of anti-Semitic riots that led to their expulsion, the Jews of Frankfurt were in 1616 'brought back in triumph amid the sound of drums and trumpets. At the head of the band, according to family tradition, marched our ancestor,[2] carrying the imperial standard with the *Reichsadler*, the black eagle emblazoned thereon. This incident, it is said, led to our family assuming the name of Adler ["Eagle"].'[3]

Among the greatest of Adler's subsequent forebears was Nathan Hacohen Adler (1741–1800), Chief Rabbi of Boskowitz, Moravia, a pupil of, among others, David Tevele Schiff, Chief Rabbi of London from 1765 to 1792 and himself a grand-uncle of the future Chief Rabbi. Bolstered by this glowing lineage, Nathan Marcus received his early religious and secular education under his father, Mordechai (Marcus Baer) Adler, the unofficial Chief Rabbi of Hanoverian Jewry.[4] 'A good foundation it must have been', wrote Nathan's contemporary, Michael Friedländer,[5] 'for it had to support a high and wide building', including his brothers Gabriel, a future rabbi at Mühringen and Oberdorf, and Baer, destined to become a dayan in Frankfurt.

But Mordechai's educational ambitions for his sons – particularly Nathan, whom he had singled out as the most promising (if precocious)[6] – transcended the purely spiritual. The legacy of the early *maskilim*,[7] notably Moses Mendelssohn and Naphtali Hartwig Wessely, found a place in the Adler household, so that, to many, a university backdrop became a natural corollary of Torah and talmudical learning.

After graduating from the Royal Würzburg University, where he learned to express his theological and philosophical thoughts in Latin even as he deepened his knowledge of Semitic languages, Adler went on to earn his master's degree at the University of Erlangen. In June 1828, having submitted a dissertation described by his examiners as 'a thoughtful thesis on the concept of deity and divine providence', he gained his doctorate in philosophy at the age of 25.

Three months earlier, he had received his *semichah* (rabbinical ordination) from the Chief Rabbi of Würzburg, Abraham Bing (1752–1841), a disciple of Nathan Hacohen Adler and a teacher of, among others, the emerging luminaries Isaac Bernays, Jacob Ettlinger, Yitzchak Dov Bamberger and Samson Raphael Hirsch. In conferring the honour, Bing had commended young Adler's knowledge of rabbinical literature as well as 'the zeal and earnestness with which he applied himself to the understanding of the Talmud and to the solution of the most difficult problems in the science of halachah'.[8]

In 1828, in anticipation of these rabbinical and academic achievements, Adler's name was put forward for a post of some significance. By a decree of the Grand Duchy of Oldenburg, Lower Saxony, the 700 Jews of the city and its surrounding communities had been instructed to appoint a *Landesrabbiner* (Chief Rabbi), whose election would be confirmed by the Grand Duke, Peter Fredrick.[9] The edict had arisen out of the elderly Duke's concern to keep his Jewish subjects loyal to the government by insulating them from the radical influences and subversive trends then rife in the country.[10] Though in favour of reform, he sought to unify the opposing forces of tradition and modernity. The community's elders were similarly anxious to find a spiritual leader capable of modernising and strengthening their rank and file.[11]

Support for Adler came in a letter to Oldenburg from J.J. Gumprecht, of Frankfurt, who, as chairman of the Jewish community, had recognised the young rabbi's centrist proclivities and described him as fluent in Hebrew, German, Latin and Greek and 'of excellent oratorical skills'.[12] Adler had moved to Frankfurt soon after his graduation and had met and married the well-heeled Henrietta Worms, a niece of Nathan Mayer Rothschild and sister of Baron Solomon Benedict de Worms. His scholastic skills were noted by the Frankfurt Senate in the citizenship papers granted him in April 1829 on his marriage, which had 'connected him to the Jewish élite and buttressed his ambitions'.[13] Oldenburg's elders were clearly impressed by the reports they received, and the post became his.

His stay in Oldenburg was brief, however – lasting barely a year – yet time enough to set out the stall from which he continued to draw inspiration at every stage of his sixty-year rabbinate. He lost little time in tackling the question of synagogue decorum, a topic that was to loom large years later on his arrival in London, where it had featured robustly on the road to Reform. Adler's sojourn in Oldenburg was foreshortened by a decision of the Hanoverian government to appoint a Chief Rabbi in the 'modern' mould, one who (unlike his father, whom it did not recognise) combined rabbinical training with an academic education. The son was seen as the 'obvious choice' and, pressed by the authorities, the kingdom's Jewish congregations promptly elected him as 'the man fittest for this important post',[14] which encompassed, among others, the cities of Hanover, Kalenberg, Göttingen and Lüneburg.

An early and important factor in Adler's growing success and popularity in Hanover, and in his later election as British Chief Rabbi, was his close relationship with the viceroy, Prince Adolphus Frederick, Duke of Cambridge and seventh son of George III. His appointment had received the backing of the viceroy and the government, and the compliment was speedily reciprocated. Adler was 27 when he became Chief Rabbi of Hanover, whose Jewish population nearly doubled during his incumbency to around 11,600[15] by the time of his departure. Modelling his leadership on the liberalism and 'air of moderate reform' introduced by the Duke,[16] he attracted praise for the 'conscientious and praiseworthy performance of his official duties'[17] by furthering the policies he had launched in Oldenburg – among them the reorganisation of Jewish schools, the encouragement of sermons in German, greater order and decorum at services, and the development of choirs, all designed to make the synagogue a place of devotion and centre of communal dedication.

Underlying Adler's ministry during this period, though little evident on the surface of his native Hanover, was the onrush of radical reform in much of Germany, inaugurated by the establishment of the consistorial synagogue in Seesen in 1810 and the Hamburg temple eight years later. The early reforms were confined to the liturgy and the conduct of the synagogue service, yet they reflected a profound internal shift in the perception of Judaism itself; the efforts to delete any mention of the Messiah and the rebuilding of the Temple, for example, were concerned not only with outward forms but with many of the fundamentals of faith.[18]

Adler was conscious of these developments and in touch with his rabbinical colleagues across the country and beyond. Acting in unison, they circulated a manifesto, eventually signed by more than 100 German and Hungarian rabbis, signalling the growing strength of the Orthodox opposition. Ninety years later, Elkan Nathan Adler was to write of his father's participation: 'A representative "hard-shell" Orthodox *Rav* of the good old school, he nailed his colours to the mast when he signed the petition against the Reform programme promulgated at the Brunswick conference of rabbis.'[19]

In 1845, on his election as British Chief Rabbi, Adler left Hanover for London with the praises of the local communities and of the government ringing in his ears. A testimonial to the departing *Landesrabbiner* from the Council of the Jewish Community described him as a 'trustworthy judge in religious questions, pillar of Jewish faith, true guide and excellent preacher, speaking to the heart as well as to the intellect'.[20] The *Jewish Chronicle* observed:

> The parting on both sides was not without genuine sorrow. The many strong ties of affection which formed a threefold cord by which he had become attached to the community of Hanover were not easily sundered. While rejoicing at his promotion, his flock expressed in no uncertain voice their deep regret at their parting with him, and he on his part did not regard their separation with a light heart. During the fourteen years of his rabbinate, Dr Adler had ruled with conspicuous success over the hundred synagogues which acknowledged his spiritual sway.[21]

\* \* \*   \* \* \*   \* \* \*

It was their convergence of outlook and background that persuaded Adler to recommend Samson Raphael Hirsch for the Chief Rabbinate of Oldenburg in 1830, during the latter's two semesters at the University of Bonn. Seventeen years later, Hirsch left Oldenburg to become Chief Rabbi of Moravia, with its 40,000 Jews in some fifty communities. But, despite the prestigious nature of the appointment – the largest such rabbinate in Europe[22] – he held the post for only four years, dissatisfied with the pace of progress in implementing his proposals for communal improvements. His transfer to Frankfurt, to head the secessionist *Israelitische Religionsgesellschaft* (IRG, or Jewish Religious Society, known in Hebrew as *Adath Yisroel*) – with Baron Mayer Amschel Rothschild as its leading member – was to have a profound impact on the development of Orthodoxy in Germany and beyond.

Within a decade of Hirsch's death, on the last day of 1888, his IRG community had expanded from an initial eight members to over 1,000 families, and his religious philosophy[23] had filtered through Europe. Britain's established Jews, wrote one of his disciples seventy years later, were, however, less receptive to his separatist policies: 'Although it was already clear in those days that the influence of Hirsch was bound to reach far beyond the frontiers of his native country and far beyond his own generation, the Anglo-Jewish spirit and the climate of the placid Victorian era were not favourable, either to the non-compromising attitude of Samson Raphael Hirsch in matters of halachah or to the philosophical depths of his *Torah-Weltanschauung*.'[24]

While a handful of the faithful found their way to Britain, it was not until the arrival of Victor Schonfeld in 1909 that 'a new chapter in the influence of Hirschian conceptions on Anglo-Jewry was started'.[25] Born in Hungary in 1880, Schonfeld was, 'in his whole training and outlook, a typical disciple of Hirsch's conception of Orthodox Judaism'.[26] Following his secondary education, he attended the Pressburg (Bratislava) yeshivah of Rabbi Simcha Bunim Schreiber, from whom he received semichah. He also studied philosophy and pedagogics, first at Budapest and later in Vienna, where he gained his doctorate of philosophy with a thesis on 'The Ethics of Shaftesbury'. In Britain, he became rabbi of the North London Beth Hamidrash, which he expanded into the renamed *Adath Yisroel* as part of his newly formed Union of Orthodox Hebrew Congregations. Following a three-year stay in Palestine as a schools inspector, in which post he was sharply critical both of political intrigues and of the religious position of Mizrachi schools, he returned to London. There, in 1929, he launched a secondary school, the forerunner of an educational network which his son, Solomon, was to build up after his sudden death only a few months later. The influx of Hirsch's followers into Britain between 1933 and 1938 provided ready-made subscribers to these synagogues and schools.

As executive director of the Religious Emergency Council founded by his Chief Rabbinical father-in-law, Joseph Herman Hertz, Solomon Schonfeld was responsible for rescuing hundreds of Jews – adults and children – from the horrors of Nazism. One such youth was Immanuel Jakobovits, born in Königsberg, East Prussia, in 1921 and the eldest of the seven children of Julius (Joel) Jakobovits, who in 1928 had settled in Berlin on his appointment as a dayan.

Julius had been born, in 1886, in the Austro-Hungarian village of Lackenbach, the eldest of nine children of a family steeped in rabbinic tradition. As a child, he had spent a period at the talmudical school in Deutschkreutz, before reaching (like Victor Schonfeld) the famed yeshivah of Pressburg and gaining the first of his two rabbinical diplomas. From there he proceeded to Adler's alma mater, the University of Würzburg, where his studies, including philosophy, led to a doctoral dissertation on 'The Lie in the Judgment of the Latest German Ethicists'. Then followed a spell at Berlin's seminary for the training of Orthodox rabbis, from which, in 1913, his second ordination ensued; rabbinical posts in Randegg (south-west Baden) and Königsberg; and, finally, the move to Berlin, culminating in the position of communal rabbi in 1933, and of chairman of the Beth Din in 1937.

The influence of Julius Jakobovits (and, by association, of Hirsch) bore weightily on his son. In a career retrospective, Immanuel was to write: 'From my earliest years, working with communal and religious leaders who were not necessarily Orthodox in thought or practice was perfectly natural – a philosophy that was to leave a permanent mark on my attitudes and convictions in later communal life. In this, as in so many other respects, my father's impact on me was dominant from my childhood to the present day.'[27]

Like his mentors before him, Immanuel Jakobovits adopted Hirsch's synthesis of academic and Torah studies almost from the moment he landed in Britain. He soon began attending the Etz Chaim yeshivah in London and later enrolled at Jews' College and University College, where his studies included Greek, Latin and Syriac. Following temporary engagements at two London congregations, during which he graduated and received his rabbinical ordination, Jakobovits in 1947 became minister of the Great Synagogue, Duke's Place – by then, following its bombing six years earlier, a shadow of its former self. But his ministry there was of short duration: within fifteen months he accepted an approach from the representative council of the Jewish communities in Eire to become Chief Rabbi, a position left vacant in 1934 by the departure of Isaac Herzog as Chief Rabbi of Palestine.

Jakobovits' decade in the Irish community, which numbered some 4,000 Jews, was relatively uneventful, but it provided him with his first brush with non-Orthodox elements. Perturbed by the encroachment of Reform into the community, yet anxious to emulate his father's enlightened example, he used the opportunity of the 1957 Conference of European Rabbis, in Amsterdam, to address the issue and the prevention of a 'lasting rift' in the Jewish world. Asking 'What ails Orthodoxy? Why have we lost our hold on the masses?' he declared:

> The Reform movement, it seems to me, is not our chief problem. It is merely a symptom, not the cause, of the general malaise. Reform has not drawn its ranks from the Orthodox camp, but from those already lost to us. The State of Israel has virtually no organised Reform, yet the religious problems there are much the same as they are here.
>
> Our main enemy, I submit therefore, is not Reform but the secularisation of Jewish life. The real challenge before us is not the low proportion of strictly observant Jews – for which there are ample

precedents in our history – but the widespread refusal to recognise our spiritual leaders as the true custodians of our national destiny, for which there are only few precedents ...

Perhaps more imagination is required in our public enlightenment drives ... I can see no reason why we should not follow the example of the prophets and personally enter the Reform strongholds to preach our message on their own platform. There are surely also ample precedents for rabbinical disputations with the sectarians of earlier generations; why should we shy away from such direct contests between truth and falsehood? And, after all, the Torah was not given for Orthodox Jews only. We cannot win the battle of the minds unless we are prepared to fight it ...

I believe we have to decide whether to write off the Reform movement and its followers as a dead loss, and try to insulate it completely from the adherents of Orthodoxy, or go all out to retrieve what can be salvaged even at the cost of some formal compromise with them. In the havoc wrought by these dissenters, we must distinguish between irreparable damage, which will leave sores festering on the body of our people for generations to come, and purely temporary infractions of the sanctities of Jewish life, causing wounds which can be healed by individual acts of repentance.

Into the former category belong, notably, the Reform's arbitrary incursions into the spheres of marriage and proselytisation in complete disregard of Jewish law, leading to untold personal tragedies and, above all, to an increase in the number of persons who cannot be recognised either as legitimate or as Jewish by the law-abiding majority of our people. To eliminate this appalling evil, gnawing at the very roots of Jewish existence, must be our foremost aim.

It might be worthwhile to explore the possibility of offering the Reformers, as an earnest of our anxiety for the preservation of Jewish unity, some kind of truce based on their acceptance of our exclusive jurisdiction in all matters affecting marriage and conversion, even if this means closing our eyes to their forms of synagogue services and religious education for the time being. Their agreement to this suggestion would, to my mind, constitute an invaluable gain and possibly pave the way to their eventual return to our fold.

On the other hand, if they rejected the offer, we would at least win a substantial moral victory. Their refusal would publicly reveal more clearly than ever before who are the real disruptive influences in Jewish life today. The true causes for disunity and strife would be exposed for all to see.

> I still maintain that our chief enemy today is the secularisation of our national and even communal life. By our rift with the Reform, we are dissipating our vital energies and deflecting our attention from the most crucial struggle ahead of us.[28]

Jakobovits was to return to the rift when it confronted him, head on, during his British Chief Rabbinate. In Eire, meanwhile, he gained his doctorate of philosophy from London University, for a pioneering thesis on Jewish medical ethics, and prepared to assume the pulpit of the newly established Fifth Avenue Synagogue in New York City.

\* \* \*     \* \* \*     \* \* \*

As a formal institution, the British Chief Rabbinate evolved rather than appeared, although historians are divided over the duration of its development. The title of 'Chief Rabbi' during the Georgian period was held by the rabbis of the Great Synagogue – where Jakobovits ministered briefly 150 years later – but their authority was not recognised by the State, and their power within the Jewish community extended only over congregations and individuals who voluntarily looked to them for guidance in matters of Jewish law.[29]

In fact, in 1801, when the Ashkenazi synagogues of London were discussing the appointment of a new 'Chief Rabbi' after a nine-year interregnum, following the death of David Tevele Schiff,[30] those members of the Hambro' Synagogue entitled to vote decided by a ballot of twenty to thirteen that it was 'unnecessary' to have a Chief Rabbi at all.[31] In the event, Solomon Hirschell was appointed. The overwhelming body of opinion suggests that the formal institution of the Chief Rabbinate came into being only in 1842[32] and that 'it was under the aegis of Hirschell's successor, Nathan Marcus Adler, that the office of Chief Rabbi took on substance as well as form ... At bottom, Adler was "Chief Rabbi" because that was how he was treated by the non-Jewish world – by Government departments, by Parliament, and by the general press'.[33]

On Hirschell's death, steps were taken to create an officially recognised Chief Rabbi,[34] although 'the rabbi of the Great Synagogue had already come to be recognised in the London and provincial Ashkenazic community as the chief religious authority in the country when Nathan Marcus Adler took office in 1845'.[35] On that recognition, however, there is a divergence of view:

> The verdict of history on Solomon Hirschell has not been particularly favourable, and it is difficult to believe that he consciously turned the Rabbinate of the Great Synagogue, which he had assumed in 1802,

into the virtual Chief Rabbinate which existed at his death, forty years later. He had, in fact, been carried along by developments, some of which perhaps he hardly understood and may even have disliked. Had the other leading London congregations possessed the financial resources of the Great Synagogue, it is quite possible that the Rabbinate of London might have developed differently. One of the other synagogues might have assumed the leadership, or the Rabbinate might have become supra-synagogal.[36]

Indeed,

the evolutionary process by which the Rabbi of the Great Synagogue became the 'Chief Rabbi' was by no means inevitable. The position of British Jewry vis-à-vis the State differed fundamentally from that which regulated the legal status of Jewish communities in mainland Europe. There were in eighteenth-century Britain no 'Court Jews' or '*Landesrabbinat*', the members of which might, under the official auspices of the Government, pose as the authorised spokesmen of the community. Nor were there any yeshivot whose rabbinical heads might have emerged as natural communal leaders.

Thus, during all those years, 'there was no one undisputed Ashkenazi "Chief Rabbi" in London'.[37]

By the last decades of the eighteenth century, however, David Tevele Schiff was, in practice, Chief Rabbi, and the authority of his successor at Duke's Place, Solomon Hirschell, was 'never in doubt'.[38] This was demonstrated most forcibly by Hirschell's 'Caution' (in effect, *cherem*, or excommunication), drawn up in concert with the dayanim of the Sephardi Beth Din, against the initiators of Britain's first Reform congregation and prayer book, which he ordered to be promulgated in all Orthodox synagogues on 22 January 1842. Of far-reaching consequence, it signalled what has been termed the Great Secession,[39] the revolt of eighteen Sephardim (including nine Mocattas and three Montefiores) and six Ashkenazim (among them three Goldsmids) – members of Bevis Marks and the Great Synagogue – against the 'evils' they perceived in the traditional Orthodox service.

At a meeting in Central London some two years earlier, on 15 April 1840, they had drawn up the following declaration:

We the Undersigned, regarding Public Worship as highly conducive to the interests of Religion, consider it a matter of deep regret that it is not more frequently attended by the Members of our Religious

Persuasion. We are perfectly sure that this circumstance is not owing to any want of a general conviction of the fundamental Truths of our Religion, but we ascribe it *to the distance of the existing synagogues from the place of our residence; to the length and imperfections of the Order of Service; to the inconvenient hours at which it is appointed; to the unimpressive manner in which it is performed; and to the absence of religious Instruction in our Synagogues*. To these evils we think that a remedy may be applied by the establishment of a *Synagogue in the Western part of the Metropolis*, where a revised Service may be performed at *hours more suited to our habits, and in a manner more calculated to inspire feelings of devotion*, where *Religious instruction may be afforded by competent persons*, and where, to effect these purposes, Jews generally may form an *United Congregation* under the denomination of *British Jews*. Anxious for the accomplishment of these objects, it is our wish that a meeting may be called for the purpose of considering the best means of carrying them into effect.[40]

The upshot of their protest was the consecration, on 27 January 1842, of the West London Synagogue of British Jews – known also, at its inception, as the Burton Street Place of Worship – and the introduction into the community of Reform Judaism.

\* \* \*   \* \* \*   \* \* \*

The establishment of the West London Synagogue, formidable in its own right, comprised only one-third of the Reform agenda. Of equal weight were the secessionists' rejection of the Oral Law – or at least of its divinity – and their institution of a prayer book and ritual ('proscribed by authority') which included the abolition of the second day of the festivals. The prayer book, edited by the congregation's first minister, London-born David Woolf Marks, was published in August 1841 and forthrightly set out the founders' aims and motivations:

> It being ... evident that time has exerted influence on [our] prayers, it is but meet that the exigencies of the time should again be consulted, when we have arrived at the conviction that the house of prayer does not exercise that salutary influence over the minds and hearts of the congregants which it is intended and capable to exert. History bears us out in the assumption that it becomes a congregation of Israelites to adapt the ritual to the wants of its members; and it must be universally admitted that the present mode of worship fails to call forth the devotion so essential to the religious improvement of the people.

> Two indispensable requisites of a petition with which man may approach his God are, first – that the prayer should be perfectly intelligible to the mind of the humble supplicant; and, secondly, that the sentiments which it expresses should be of a pure and elevating character. In our collection we have, with all solicitude, retained only those portions of the common rituals in which these essentials are to be found. We have removed those parts of the service which are deficient in devotional tendency; and have expunged the few expressions which are known to be the offspring of feelings produced by oppression, and are universally admitted to be foreign to the heart of every true Israelite of our day.

Discussing the differences formerly existing between the Sephardi and Ashkenazi (or, as the editor termed them, the Portuguese and German Jewish) congregations, 'which caused them to consider each other as half aliens in religious matters', Marks commented:

> [Such differences] have happily, by the progress of liberal tendencies, been removed, in as far as they obstructed that brotherly feeling which the unity of our religious system requires; and the efforts of our newly established Congregation have been directed, we hope successfully, to the obliteration of every vestige of that useless and hurtful separation ...
>
> And if, by promulgating this improved form of the Jewish ritual, we contribute to the glorious end of endearing our holy institutions, and the pure fountain from which they flow, to the heart of every member of Israel; if, by the measures we have adopted after mature deliberation and with all the seriousness befitting our great cause, we become instrumental in attaching our rising generation to a mode of worship as impressive in its form as it is holy in its essence, we shall have ample cause for unbounded gratitude to our Heavenly Guide, for the glorification of whose name this work is wrought, and by whose omnipotent hand we humbly hope that it will be made to prosper for the peace, happiness and salvation of Israel.[41]

The peace and happiness (let alone the salvation) of Israel, as exemplified in the congregations of London, were scarcely advanced, however, by this outpouring of emotion. Nor were they helped by what a contemporary historian, a convert to Christianity,[42] described as the 'bold step' initiated by the Sephardi rebels, on 24 August 1841, with the publication of a defiant letter to 'the Gentleman Elders of the Spanish and Portuguese Synagogue'. Having outlined the principles by which their new congregation was to be guided – including 'proper decorum during the performance of divine worship', services at 'convenient' hours and of 'moderate length', a 'careful revision' of the daily and Sabbath prayer book, sermons to be given in English, and the abolition of *aliyot* and offerings, except on the 'three great festivals' – the secessionists declared:

> Such are the views we have endeavoured to carry into effect, and we earnestly assure you they have not been suggested by any desire of schism, or separation – as seems to be implied in some resolutions passed at a late meeting of *Yehidim* [members of the congregation] – but through a sincere conviction that substantial improvements in the public worship are essential to the weal of our sacred religion, and that they will be the means of handing down to our children, and to our children's children, our holy faith in all its purity and integrity.
>
> Indeed, we are firmly convinced that their tendency will be to arrest and prevent *secession from Judaism – an overwhelming evil*, which has at various times so widely spread among many of the most respectable families of our communities.
>
> Most fervently do we cherish the hope that the effect of these improvements will be to inspire a deeper interest in, and a stronger feeling towards, our holy religion, and that their influence on the minds of the youth of either sex will be calculated to restrain them from traversing their faith, or contemplating for a moment the fearful step of forsaking their religion, so that henceforth no 'Israelite born' may cease to exclaim, 'Hear, O! Israel, the Lord our God, the Lord is one!'

Anticipating the reactions to their move, the rebels added:

> In thus establishing a new Synagogue, on the principles hitherto not recognised or approved by your body, we may possibly encounter a considerable difference of opinion, and a strong prejudice against our proceedings; but, having been actuated solely by a conscientious sense of duty, we venture to hope that on further consideration, our intentions and our motives will be duly appreciated, and that those kindly feelings which ought to exist between every community of Jews will be maintained in all force between the respective congregations which you represent, and the small body whose views we have herein endeavoured to explain.[43]

It was not to be. Angered by this mutinous show of strength, which over a period of years had threatened to tear apart the fabric of London Jewry, a meeting of communal leaders was held on 9 September, at which an edict of excommunication was drawn up by Hirschell and his ecclesiastical colleagues – held in abeyance, however, in the hope that the 'refractory reformers' would relent and return to the fold. From a second meeting, on 24 October, emerged a denunciation of the 'iniquitous' prayer book and its errant editor:

> To all who bear the name of Israel. From the Chief Rabbi, and the Beth Din of the several congregations of Great Britain.
> Our brethren, the children of Israel, who pursue justice, and seek the Lord! Incline your ears to the words of righteousness; hearken that your souls may live!
> It is known throughout the dispersions of Israel that the prayers and blessings which we address to the Creator of the world (blessed be His holy name) have been arranged and appointed by our sages of the great convocation, among whom were some of our Prophets, and that these forms have been adhered to by the whole house of Israel, from generation to generation, for more than two thousand years.
> But now behold, we have seen innovations newly springing up, and a new book of prayer, called Forms of Prayer, used in the West London Synagogue of British Jews, edited by D.W. Marks, printed by J. Wertheimer and Co., A.M. 5601, in which it is evident to the eyes of all that the manner and order of our prayers and blessings have been curtailed and altered, and otherwise arranged, not in accordance with the Oral Law by which we have so long been guided in the performance of the precepts of the Lord, and of which it is acknowledged that 'whoso rejecteth the authority of the Oral Law opposeth thereby the holy law handed down to us on Mount Sinai by Moses the servant of the Lord'; and without which it is also admitted that we should have no knowledge of the Written Law.
> Seeing this evil, we have risen and strengthened ourselves for the service of God, in order to remove and set aside the stumbling-block from the path of our brethren the sons of Israel, and hereby we admonish every person professing the faith of Israel, and having the fear of God in his heart, that he do not use, or in any manner recognise, the said book of prayer, because it is not in accordance with our holy law; and whoever shall use it for the purpose of prayer will be accounted sinful, for the wisest of men hath said, 'That he who turneth away his ear from hearing the law, even his prayer shall be an abomination'; but he who regardeth his soul will avoid the iniquitous course thereby attempted, and pursue the righteous faith so long trodden by our ancestors. And we supplicate the Lord God of our

fathers, to incline and unite our hearts that we may all serve Him with one accord, and that He may bring peace and brotherly love among us, and that the Redeemer may speedily come to Zion. These are the words of truth and justice!

S. HIRSCHELL, Chief Rabbi; DAVID MELDOLA; A. HALIVA; J. LEVY; A. LEVY; A.L. BARNETT.

Undeterred, the secessionists addressed to their mother synagogue a further letter, dated 13 January 1842, 'on the eve of consecrating our new house of prayer', expressing regret at the threat of excommunication (as promulgated in the congregation's *Ascamot* [laws], drawn up in 1663), which had

> forced upon us the necessity of taking the only course which, consistent with honour and principle, we can pursue: to withdraw at once our names from the list of the *Yatridim* [members] of the congregation. Thus have you, Gentlemen, by the threat of adopting certain measures which, we venture to affirm, are alike inefficient and injudicious, driven us from the last hope to which we had fondly clung – that of being able to introduce ameliorations into our religious worship, under the sanction or in connection with the parent synagogue.
>
> In having taken this step, which, we must again reiterate, you have forced upon us, we beg to assure you that we do not entertain the least ill-will or unkindly feelings towards any individual member of the congregation. We freely give you credit, Gentlemen, for being influenced by conscientious motives, however we may deplore the conclusion you have arrived at. All we ask of you in return is to do justice to the views by which we are actuated.
>
> If you consider the sacrifice of time, labour and means we have made (to say nothing of the greater sacrifice of quitting a synagogue with which we and our fathers have been for so long a period connected) to establish a house of prayer where we may worship our Creator agreeably to the dictates of our conscience; and you will not, you cannot believe that we are swayed by any desire for innovation or schism, or for promoting ill-will between one son of Israel and another, neither will you believe we are so lost to a sense of philanthropy as to shut out the poor from that relief which they are entitled to claim at our hands. Indeed, it must be evident to all (however they may dissent from our views) that we can only be influenced by a pure love for that law which the Holy One of Israel has commanded to be written for our unerring guidance, and which it is our

ardent wish to transmit to our descendants in perpetuity.

This final display of defiance prompted Hirschell to act swiftly in enforcing the *cherem*, implemented through a series of letters circulated by Sir Moses Montefiore, president of the Board of Deputies, to the wardens of every Jewish congregation in the country:

> Grosvenor-gate, Park-lane, London, 10 Shevat, 5602 [1842].
> Gentlemen, – I have the honour to convey to you the copy of a letter which I received yesterday from the Rev. Dr Hirschell.
>
> In compliance with the request contained therein, and also agreeably to the accompanying copy of the resolutions unanimously adopted at a meeting held on 9 September last, I likewise forward to you a copy of the declaration referred to in such letters and resolutions.
>
> Most deeply do I deplore the necessity of having to request that you will, without delay, give all the publicity in your power to the declaration in question.
>
> I have the honour to remain,
> Your obedient servant,
>   MOSES MONTEFIORE.

Copy of the communication addressed by the Rev. Dr Hirschell to Sir Moses Montefiore:

Bury Court, 9 Shevat, 5602.
Dear Sir, – With grief I have ascertained that a body of persons calling themselves 'British Jews' are about to open a place of worship. I deem it my duty to request you to communicate to the different synagogues the declaration made by me on 24 Ellul, and further, that you will circulate the said document in any manner that will give it the greatest publicity.

I have the honour to remain,
My dear Sir, yours most truly,
  S. HIRSCHELL, Chief Rabbi.

Copy of resolutions unanimously adopted at a meeting of the wardens and honorary officers of the several metropolitan synagogues, and of the members of the London Committee of Deputies of the British Jews and others, held at the residence of the Chief Rabbi, the Rev. Solomon Hirschell, 23 Bury-street, St Mary Axe, on Thursday evening, 24 Ellul, 5601 – 9 September, 1841; Sir Moses Montefiore, FRS, in the chair.

The following resolutions were unanimously adopted:

'That the declaration signed by the Rev. Solomon Hirschell and the members of the Beth Din be received and adopted by this meeting.'

'That the Chairman be requested to forward a copy of the Chief Rabbi's declaration, and the accompanying certificate of the Beth Din, to the wardens of the several synagogues in the United Kingdom and the colonies, at such a time as he may deem expedient.'

DECLARATION
23, Bury-street, 24 Ellul, 5601.
Information having reached me, from which it appears that certain persons calling themselves British Jews, publicly and in their published book of prayer, reject the Oral Law, I deem it my duty to declare that, according to the laws and statutes held sacred by the whole House of Israel, any person or persons publicly declaring that he or they reject and do not believe in the authority of the Oral Law cannot be permitted to have any communion with us Israelites in any religious rites or sacred act. I therefore earnestly entreat and exhort all God-fearing Jews, especially parents, to caution and instruct all persons belonging to our faith that they be careful to attend to this declaration, and that they be not induced to depart from our holy laws.

S. HIRSCHELL, Chief Rabbi.

We, the undersigned, fully concurring in the foregoing doctrines, as set forth by the Reverend Solomon Hirschell, certify such our concurrence under our hand this 24 Ellul, 5601, A. M.

DAVID MELDOLA; A. LEVY; J. LEVY. A.S. BARNETT; A. HALIVA.

The promulgation of the above declaration has been delayed in the hope that there would have been no necessity to give it publicity: circumstances, however, now require that it should be no longer withheld from the community.

9 Shevat, 5602.

With the exception of three congregations – the Western in London, and those at Liverpool and Manchester – the declaration was proclaimed by 'the secretaries of the principal Metropolitan Synagogues ... from their respective reading desks'[44] on Saturday, 22 January 1842. The Western's leaders, never averse to communal dissidence, asserted that 'it would be impossible to follow out the spirit of the declaration without producing a schism in the congregation and disunion among the members, many of whom were entirely opposed to displaying any feelings of intolerance towards their brethren in faith; deeming it advisable to conciliate rather than by hostile measures to irritate them and thus prevent the possibility of restoring union, peace and brotherly love in Israel'.

The Western was quick to add, however, that its decision was taken 'not out of opposition nor in rebellion against the authority of our venerable Chief Rabbi, for whom we entertain the most profound respect and reverence', but through 'a firm and sincere conviction that irreparable mischief would inevitably result to the whole of the Jewish nation by following a contrary one'.[45]

*Ascama* I of the Spanish and Portuguese Jews' Congregation of London stipulated, inter alia:

> we in unanimity and harmony forbid that there be any other Congregations in this City of London, its districts and environs, for reading prayers with minyan, and that ten persons meet for this purpose in any private house, except it be in the house of bridegrooms and *avelim* [mourners], without separating themselves from this Congregation, [under] pain of *cherem* ... unless in future times to come, through circumstances that may happen, it may be needful to divide ourselves as may be found fitting, whereof the disposition remains reserved for the *mahamad* [governing body] which shall be in office at the time, being united and harmonious and under a government as we are at present.[46]

The force behind the law was explained in the printed editions of the *Ascamot* of 1785 and 1831:

> Duly considering how important is our Union, to keep us from giving offence to the inhabitants of this city, against which we have been cautioned by his Majesty, King Charles II, of glorious memory, all the *Yehidim* of the *Kaal Kadosh* [holy congregation] have, with an unanimous accord, agreed that there be not allowed in this City of London and its suburbs (that is, within six miles distance of our Synagogue) any other than this our Synagogue of Shaar Ashamaim ... And every Spanish or Portuguese Jew now residing, or shall hereafter reside, within this city, or in the limits above described, failing to observe this injunction, shall incur the penalty of *cherem* as is above described.[47]

The Sephardim were not alone in suffering such restrictions. Much to the chagrin of the more affluent members of the Ashkenazi congregations, Hirschell, too, had refused to sanction new synagogues outside the City limits, seeing them as a threat to the revenue available for the relief of the

East End poor. As early as 1829, residents of Bayswater and Maida Vale had petitioned him, unsuccessfully, to allow branch synagogues in their localities.[48]

For several years, the *cherem* dominated the affairs of the community, influencing the debate on the Chief Rabbinical election and the role of the eventual winner.[49] Within days of its imposition, the *Voice of Jacob* reported that the seceders had applied to Montefiore, as president of the Board and under the powers granted him by the Act of Registration, to certify 'the minister of the seceders' as 'the secretary of a synagogue in England of persons professing the Jewish religion'. Montefiore had refused to do so – 'and, with the declaration of the ecclesiastical authorities before him', said the paper, 'we cannot see how he could do otherwise. God forbid that the sanction of a legal marriage should be withheld from any class. The seceders have their remedy, but they must not bring misrule into "the convocation of Israel". And what else but misrule is it, *flagrantly to disregard the law, as it is written; and to contemn it, as it is explained?*'[50]

# 1

## Omens of Peace

We have agreed as one man to present to your Reverence the Rabbinical Chair in our several communities, 'the government shall be on your shoulder', and the staff of pleasantness in your hands, for such a leader have the congregation of the Lord desired, to heal the wounds, to remove every stumbling-block, 'to stand as a breakwater', and to maintain the cause of His people at all times ... You are our leader, our preceptor. May our desire be speedily fulfilled by your superintendence as our Chief Rabbi! May the study of the Holy Law of God be encouraged and increased; and may the splendour of your light shine on us and on our children! 'For the priest's lips should keep knowledge, and they should seek the law at his mouth, for he is the messenger of the Lord of Hosts.'[1]

Replete with biblical imagery, this offer from Samuel Helbert Ellis,[2] in London, to Nathan Marcus Adler, in Hanover, came days after the Chief Rabbinical election on 1 December 1844, in which Adler had polled 121 votes against a combined total of 15 for his three opponents – Hirsch Hirschfeld, Chief Rabbi of Wollstein (13); Samson Raphael Hirsch, Chief Rabbi of Emden (2); and Benjamin Auerbach, Chief Rabbi of Darmstadt (nil).[3] Ellis' letter elicited an equally scriptural response as high-flown as it was humble:

Estimable friends, synod of councillors, who love truth and delight in equity, men of worth, the guardians of the Congregation and leaders of the community, who are appointed by the United Congregations in London assembled. May the Lord grant to you His blessing individually and collectively, and life and peace for everlasting.

GENTLEMEN,

Your worthy and estimable writings, breathing the spirit of kindness and affection, have inspired me with confidence, and demand my most grateful and heartfelt acknowledgments.

Thereby have you crowned me with honour and eminence, in conveying to me the intelligence that the Lord has enlarged His grace unto me, and planted my lot in a pleasant place, – in the seat of the house of DAVID, and on the throne of SOLOMON.

You have called me from the herds, to be to Israel a father and a priest; you have placed the government on my shoulder, to guard, with the staff of gentleness and the rule of honour, the holy flock of the people chosen of the Lord.

Verily! my soul trembleth with hope and fear, when I reflect, How can I aspire to soar on high, to govern various precious Congregations in distant localities? or how find strength of heart to remove the ashes, and to inspire with the light of truth and faith the thousands that encompass me round about? how sustain each spirit, give delight to each soul, and pleasure to each mind, – to youth as to the aged, to the exalted as to the lowly, to the poor as to the rich, – to content all equally?

But my trust is in the Lord, the God of the spirits of all flesh, as the son confideth on the love of his father. To his word do I hearken, which speaketh in the recesses of my heart: 'Gird thy loins and strengthen thyself; droop not, for I am with thee!'

His light and His truth will lead me to cast aside the stumbling-block from the highway, to put away the thorns from the pastures of my people, to restore the fainting soul from the shadow of death to the protection of the Almighty. He will strengthen and sustain me; but deeds not words will I place before you; those will testify my righteousness on the future day, for it is not the spirit of arrogance that has caused me to aspire to this eminence, nor has vanity of pride called me to this guardianship, but solely the desire to exalt the horn of the Law, and to guard the way of the tree of life.

To you, worthy and excellent Gentlemen, with whom dwelleth the spirit of wisdom and understanding, and whose main object is peace, for it is your glory, to you I humbly supplicate, that each of you may, according to his power and means, sustain and assist me in my endeavours to lead your offspring in the path of righteousness and good conduct, to enlighten them in the way of everlasting truth, that the youth of Israel may thirst after the waters of the well of life, which princes have dug with their staves.

On you, the heads of the Assembly of Israel, I depend for aid, that I may guide our youth, like unto the eagle, which at times swiftly darts to its young, but at other periods gently indicates its presence, though invariably it so shapes its course that the arrow pierce not its offspring.

May the good Providence shield both fathers and children, and grant you every blessing, and that good fruit may be your reward, which at maturity will be to you a sustenance and protection, until the throne of His glory, that was from the beginning, be established!

The words of your friend, who is now of your number, whose heart is with you, and whose soul longeth to dwell in your courts.

With profound esteem and desire to serve you,

NATHAN MARCUS ADLER.[4]

Adler arrived in Britain on Monday afternoon, 7 July 1845, thirty-three months after the death of his predecessor, Solomon Hirschell. The Chief Rabbi-elect was welcomed at Dover by a delegation of representative Jews headed by Sir Moses Montefiore as sheriff of the county and president of the Board of Deputies.[5] Sir Moses 'had resolved on paying this graceful compliment to one called on to fill so sacred and responsible an office among the Jews of this Empire'.[6]

On the day preceding his installation, another delegation – this time of deputies alone and again headed by Montefiore – called upon Adler to present a testimonial, inscribed on vellum, 'congratulating him on his entry upon the sacred duties of his vocation'. Delivered on behalf of 'nearly the whole of the Jewish community in this country' – an allusion to the schism that had so recently rocked London Jewry – the document declared: 'Your talents, piety, experience and high position warrant us in anticipating the highest results from your ministry, and we feel that it is our duty, the performance of which affords us the sincerest gratification, to avail ourselves of the earliest opportunity to offer you our fervent wishes for your welfare, and that of your lady and family.'

Clearly moved by this display of solidarity, Adler replied:

> I feel highly honoured by the very gratifying manner in which you have been pleased to express your very kind sentiments and wishes on my arrival in this country, and on my entrance upon the duties of my sacred office. The more extensive, influential and important is the body which you represent, and the greater your own merits – not only towards our brethren in this country but throughout the world – the more highly must I esteem and value these marks of your kindness towards me. I already feel the full weight of the high and important office which has been confided to me, but I hope that, through the assistance of God, my earnest efforts will be attended with those beneficial consequences which we all have so devoutly at heart. That your great endeavours on behalf of all our congregations may be continued by the divine blessing will be my constant prayer.[7]

Such sentiments were undoubtedly boosted by a visit the Chief Rabbi had made the previous day, by appointment, to his patron, the Duke of Cambridge, who had expressed a desire to see Adler – 'favourably known to HRH during his viceroyalty at Hanover'[8] – at the ducal mansion, Cambridge House. The substance of their conversation was not revealed, but their mutual admiration must have shone through their every utterance.

Adler's reference in his acceptance statement to 'removing the ashes', to 'casting aside the stumbling-block from the highway', to 'thorns' and 'fainting souls', was the closest he had then advanced to the boundaries of Burton Street, but he had made it clear that 'deeds not words will I place before you'. His detailed agenda was destined to await his induction in London, held two days after his arrival. Nor was he to disappoint his listeners – or at least those of more traditional inclination who understood the German in which it was delivered.[9]

'Allow me to explain', he told his august congregation at the Great Synagogue, 'with what purposes, and with what hopes, a minister enters on the duties of his sacred office.' Quoting from the prophet Zechariah, he proceeded to summarise his fivefold task: 'To walk in the ways of God; truly to maintain His Law; to superintend the institutions for education; to watch over the places of worship; and lastly, with a deep hope that I shall make my way into your hearts.' Enlarging on the first of these aims, he asked:

> How shall the pastor succeed in his efforts if his own life be not an example – if he point out a path which he does not follow? Can it be more than a mere false appearance if his sermons, his knowledge, his labours, are opposed to his actions, or if his deeds and his words stand in opposition to each other? Can he recommend and procure mutual love and peace if his own conduct be not that of love and charity – if he do not, like a true follower of Aaron, strive to promote peace? How shall he gain followers to the duties of religion if it is needful that he himself be reminded of them? ... No; he must himself tread in the desired pathway of the Lord ... It is only where warmth of feeling exists that such warmth can be communicated – only where the spirit of life pervades that it can be excited, or burst forth in others.

'In a word', said the new Chief Rabbi, 'investigation and activity, word and deed, conviction and conduct, must go hand in hand; and then, surely and silently, they will do their work.'[10]

Of the second aim – 'truly to maintain God's Law' – Adler reminded his flock of the

> true priestly calling: he should be, he must be, the watchman, the

guardian, the preserver of the holy Law. It is indeed arduous, very arduous, to take good care of it in a time when some rest their hopes on rapid innovation, and others on steadfast adherence to whatever time has sanctified, even though it should be contrary to the Law.

It is indeed difficult, very difficult, to take good care of it while urged on by some to constant advance, and implored by others to remain immovable. It is indeed difficult, in such circumstances, to find the golden mean. But if he be seriously resolved to do his duty to God and to his holy Law, then will he place himself in the watchtower, preserve the sacred inheritance undimmed and uninjured, secure it from all injury, and defend it from every attack …

He will judge according to his fullest knowledge, and direct conscientiously. He will distinguish the false from the true, the bad from the good, the wrong from the right, the dark from the light – he will stand between the living and the dead, and bid the religious pestilence to cease.

Yes, my beloved brethren, I also do purpose to become a guardian of the Law, to protect, promote and advocate it. This may seem to you grandiloquent boasting: yea, it must seem so, if I did not add that even should much escape me, should I lack power to bring my purpose to its complete fulfilment, one thing I cannot want – one thing which man has, above all other gifts, at all times within his reach – and this is a holy will. The will to become a pious guardian in the true spirit fills me, rushes and throbs through all my veins; and therefore my God will vouchsafe to me the fulfilment of the prescribed task.[11]

Similarly, pledged the Chief Rabbi, he would direct his energies towards education in the home and the school, in the synagogue and the 'forecourts of the Lord', so that – at all times and in all places – he would win his way to the hearts of his flock. 'Heart to heart must be the watchword. And this, my beloved brethren, this is my hope.'[12] To that end – and in his clearest and most uncompromising reference to cleansing 'the forecourts' of alien influences – he added:

It is the duty of the pastor to watch well the forecourts, to have a care that they accomplish their holy purposes, that everything be banished from God's holy house which might prevent holy respect and decorum, which might diminish holiness and devotion; and also, that nothing be permitted to enter there which is contrary to the holy Law … And I too have the purpose to watch over your forecourts, to take charge of your synagogues, to have a care – above all – that all honour and respect due to holy places will be not diminished.

> It is also my purpose, fearlessly and without hesitation, to lay before you the word of the Law, unclouded and pure even as the wise have transmitted it to us, as our ancestors have taught it to us, as the noblest minds have presented it to us. It is therefore my purpose to explain it in the different houses of the Lord, now here, now there, so that none shall be void of instruction; and so to strive that it may be more studied, be better known, and more easily brought into actual use in the affairs of life; so to strive that our love for our fellow-man may flourish, prosper and increase, and prejudices disappear.[13]

\* \* \*   \* \* \*   \* \* \*

'Rapid innovation', 'religious pestilence', 'steadfast adherence', 'constant advance': while there could be no mistaking Adler's intentions in this litany of contrasts, there was yet a possibility of change if 'the golden mean' were to be contained within the ambit of the Law. Nor was this, in essence, far removed from the demands of the reformers, most of whom had been content to remain within Orthodoxy before Hirschell's *cherem* had swept them away. Such motives, indeed, had been summed up by their newly installed minister, David Woolf Marks, at the consecration of the West London Synagogue some three years earlier: 'love for the religion in which we have been born, and veneration for the laws in which we have been reared'.[14]

> But [Marks had argued] we must not confound the form with the substance; we must not regard an infinity of ceremonials as the final aim of religion – viewing as secondary all that is moral, all that is spiritual, all that embraces the eternal salvation of man. For, while we owe to our God love, veneration and gratitude, we must not think that we have acquitted ourselves towards Him if to the few but most salutary acts of devotion which He has enjoined we superadd many unwholesome, because unmeaning, ceremonies ...
>
> Now since, in the progress of time, it has been the misfortune of our people to fall into this peculiar error, we, who purpose to rectify the evil, as far as it relates to religious worship, consider it a duty we owe to ourselves, and to our brethren at large, to declare, at the very outset of our career, that it is not a desire for innovation, not a want of respect for those institutions which our more immediate ancestors obeyed, but a paramount obligation, a deep sense of right which nothing can weaken; a conviction, resulting from a long, cool and serious reflection, that impels us to those measures which, in our inmost hearts, we consider

the only means of arousing our brethren from that indifference to spiritual matters into which they have unhappily sunk; and of preserving our sacred religion from the blight of infidelity, to say nothing of apostasy, which is making inroads among us.[15]

Referring to the authority and validity of the Oral Law – specifically, the Mishnah and the Talmud, which 'we recognise as a valuable aid for the elucidation of many passages in Scripture' – Marks had added, however:

> We must, as our conviction urges us, solemnly deny that a belief in the divinity of the traditions contained in the Mishnah, and the Jerusalem and Babylonian Talmuds, is of equal obligation to the Israelite with the faith in the divinity of the Law of Moses. We know that these books are human compositions; and though we are content to accept with reverence from our post-biblical ancestors advice and instruction, we cannot unconditionally accept their laws. For Israelites, there is but one immutable Law – the sacred volume of the Scriptures, commanded by God to be written down for the unerring guidance of His people until the end of time.[16]

Every effort made for the regeneration of their synagogue, Marks had said:

> we have striven to confine strictly to the spirit of the immutable Law of God ... Let it not be supposed that this house is intended as a synagogue of ease or convenience; that it has been established as a formal place of meeting for those who set at nought the declared will of God.
>
> No, my friends, such men need not labour for improvement, they need no sacrifice of time, ease, and means, to effect ameliorations in our religious worship, since any system will please that affords them a formal connection with a nominally religious community. But for those who cherish a sincere love for their religion, who consider their well-being in this life and their immortal hopes hereafter to be indissolubly bound up in a rigid practical observance of the Mosaic Law, this synagogue has been reared.[17]

Responding, in due course, to this view of the Law, Adler told a Great Synagogue congregation:[18]

> There are some who think that the Oral Law has altered and disfigured the Written Law, so that it is no longer the same. How erroneous, how false, is such an opinion. Nothing but superficial reflection could have engendered it.
>
> You are aware it is an article of our belief that the law given

through Moses – the greatest of prophets, who excelled all the sages that either preceded or succeeded him – has not been changed, nor ever will be changed. Consequently, the Oral Law is not, and cannot be, a different code; but both the Written and the Oral Law emanated from the same shepherd, the same legislator.

'God hath spoken one, but I have heard two.'[19] For if even the text of a human law requires interpretation, and often admits of different constructions, how much more needful is interpretation to the profound word of God, which is like a fire, and a hammer that breaketh the rock in pieces, so that the sparks fly about.

No, my brethren, though Moses and the prophets, inspired by the holy spirit, declared, explained and unfolded the statutes, and handed them down to us, though our teachers derived decisions from the Written Law according to the exegetical canon, though our sages made ordinances and institutions to preserve the law, and established fences around it, so that the holy mountain might not be touched; yet they never deviated from or counteracted the Written Law. On the contrary, they strove and laboured to explain every word, every letter, nay, every dot, to keep it as a sanctuary, as the greatest treasure of life.[20]

In reality, despite Marks' denial, many of the changes sought by the reformers were more socially than doctrinally motivated. Later and shorter services, English sermons, the abolition of offerings, the establishment of branch synagogues – these had little relevance to the Oral Law or the immutability of the Torah, and much in common with congregational convenience. The removal of the second day of the festivals was the one radical reform, and even this had been demanded less by the seceders, who eschewed it in their original declaration, than by their bibliocentric minister, architect of the ritual and liturgical platform of the new congregation.[21]

Departing noticeably from the Central European and American models, British Reform was a lukewarm affair. Hebrew remained the language of prayer; liturgical references to the messianic redemption, the return to Zion and the chosenness of the Jews were retained; organ music was delayed for two decades; and mixed seating was to await the twentieth century. As time progressed, it became clear that the modifications introduced at Burton Street differed little from those eventually sanctioned by Adler himself.[22]

Weeks before the Chief Rabbi's installation, a letter from Benjamin Elkin, one of the staunchest advocates of ritual reform – who had, however, retained his membership of the Great Synagogue – appeared as a five-page advertisement in the *Jewish Chronicle*. Tracing the years-long campaign to effect change within the system, it repeated the reformers' consistent assertion that this threat of *cherem* produced the secession. The very intensity of our attachment to our holy blessed religion, and desire of its perpetuity, have caused the dissolution of union. Many of the founders of our synagogue – men far advanced in the autumn of life, and of staid religious habits – these and others of our congregation wished to see something done calculated to inspire a well-grounded hope that our children would continue steadfast in their parents' creed ... We have not been actuated by any abstract love of reform – we have done nothing but what we thought essential to improve our public worship – we have given strength to the weak in faith, and caused the discontinuance of the desecration of the Sabbath ... Since our synagogue has been established, we have not made a single alteration; nor does there exist the remotest intention of making any. Our reform, therefore, speaking humanly, may be said to be final.[23]

The significance of Elkin's letter – indeed, of Elkin himself – lies in events that occurred some three years later when, after a protracted illness, the wealthy merchant died, aged 65. A pious Jew to the end of his days, he had been born at Portsea, in 1783, into a family of modest means. At the age of 21, he moved on to practise the increasingly prosperous trade of watchmaker in Barbados, where he was befriended and mentored by the island's Jewish minister, the Rev. Carvalho.

In 1810, Elkin returned briefly to Portsea, married 17-year-old Sarah Levi – 'a lady of gentle disposition, sweet and engaging manners, deep and lasting affections, cultivated mind, sterling good sense, and of the most sincere piety, free from every particle of superstition and sectarian prejudice' – and took his bride to Barbados. As his situation flourished, he found time – now a synagogue warden – to advance the affairs of the congregation, for which 'he had the satisfaction of receiving the thanks of the late Drs Hirschell and Meldola, of London, for the public spirit, the zeal and ability, which he had displayed with such marked success'.

No one, the *Jewish Chronicle* was later to recall,

> could have undertaken this important task with better grace than Mr Elkin. He was one of the most exemplary Jews of the island, a rigid observer of the Sabbath day and of those festivals enjoined by God in the Pentateuch, and most conscientious in the fulfilment of the several requirements of his faith.
>
> Nor was his Judaism confined merely to the synagogue; his domestic hearth was also a sanctuary at which his wife and his children assembled for family prayer. Here the Bible was read, here the word of God was practically illustrated, here the father and the mother

united their pious efforts to each by their example, no less than by their precepts, that man's first duty is to God, and his chief care is the salvation of his soul; and here the good parents first sowed in the hearts of their infant children the seeds of religion, with which they have respectively grown into manhood and womanhood.[4]

Returning to Britain in 1830, Elkin joined the Great Synagogue, though he seldom attended its services. These, he believed, were performed 'without fervour, without unction, indeed without respect or propriety, and took no hold upon the feelings'. So the family united as a household for their Sabbath and festival prayers until, in 1840, Sarah Elkin succumbed to an 'excruciating malady' and was buried in the Great Synagogue cemetery, where her husband bought an adjoining plot.

When the Reform congregation was founded the following summer, Elkin 'joined heart and soul' in the movement and became one of its most vocal advocates. Despite this display of support, he remained a member of the Great, which not only did not expel him – as the Sephardi rebels had suffered at Bevis Marks – but continued until the day of his death to accept his contributions. He 'rejoiced to think that his claim on the Old Synagogue was still recognised, and that the wish which he had so much at heart, of being laid after death near the remains of his beloved wife, would be realised'.

A victim for many years of a painful disease, Elkin did not recover from an operation performed in the closing days of 1847. Anticipating his end, he drew his family to his bedside and declared: 'I have made my peace with God, and with man my peace has long been made: see now how a Jew can die. There is a heaven, my friends, there is a reward for a good life; I feel it, I see it. Strive, then, to merit it, and to obtain it by your actions on earth.'

As dusk beckoned, Elkin asked for his position to be changed, so that he might see – for one final time – the precise spot where his wife had breathed her last. That wish accomplished, 'he yielded up his spirit into the hands of the Great Giver of it'.[25]

The subsequent events dismayed large sections of the community, not least among the Orthodox. Having purchased his burial plot beside that of his wife, Elkin had secured his right to it – so he believed – by paying ten guineas a year to the Great Synagogue, fully expecting the authorities not to take his money unless they were prepared to honour its purpose.

On his deathbed, he had reaffirmed this desire to his children, but added: 'If the bigoted party who excommunicated us should impose any obstacles, or should refuse to grant my remains any of those rights to which I am entitled as a member of the Great Synagogue, on the plea of my being connected with Burton Street, then I desire that I may be buried in the cemetery of the West London Synagogue.'

Upon his death, one of Elkin's executors applied for his remains to be interred in the reserved grave. The Great's president, Sir Anthony de Rothschild,[26] and the wardens voiced no objection, but Adler – invoking the support of the Ashkenazi and Sephardi dayanim – ruled that the service could not be conducted, as was customary, by the funeral officiant, the Rev. Benjamin Henry Ascher, but only by Hendricks the sexton. For two days, well beyond the halachic deadline for burial, Elkin's children remonstrated, while Rothschild and his colleagues implored Adler to desist from implementing 'a decree unsuitable to an enlightened age'. A family friend noted that 'the only modification they could obtain from the pertinacious ecclesiastical chief was that Mr Pyke [the clerk] should officiate instead of Hendricks. This proposition Mr Elkin's family rejected with indignation, and mindful of their parents' oft-repeated words, the remains of Benjamin Elkin were consigned to the [Reform] burial ground at Ball's Pond, Islington', where Marks and Löwy officiated and where 'a goodly number of gentlemen belonging to the Orthodox synagogue' mingled with the Burton Street mourners.

Commenting on this outcome, the *Jewish Chronicle* remarked:

> We learn that Dr Adler's proceeding was generally canvassed and met everywhere with merited disapprobation, even by a great number of the Orthodox party, his adherents. We are exceedingly pained at this step of Dr Adler's, as we had hoped that he would seize the opportunity with avidity to establish peace and union among the distracted body of the Jews of the metropolis, and not to widen the breach, which his harsh proceeding cannot fail to do.[27]

Of the burial service, the paper declared: 'A feeling of deep and sad emotion, enhanced by the injury inflicted on the truly pious deceased by the hand of superstition and intolerance, pervaded the whole mournful assembly.'[28]

As in death, so in marriage did Adler's actions provoke widespread unrest. The marriage dispute had festered since Montefiore's refusal, in 1842, to certify Marks as 'the secretary of a synagogue in England of persons professing the Jewish religion'. The 1835 Marriage Act had recognised the legality of Jewish marriages, in order that 'persons professing the Jewish religion may continue to contract and solemnise marriage according to the usages of the said persons', and the 1836 Registration Act had stipulated that 'the proceedings in relation thereto [must] have been conformable to the usages of the persons professing the Jewish religion'.

The controversy centred on the definition of 'usages' and their application to the Reform congregation. As the *Voice of Jacob* put it:

> The usages of the British Jews, in respect to marriage, form a system, nicely balanced between the laws of the country, as declared by Act of Parliament, and the requirements of the Jewish religion and polity, as defined, in need, by our own ecclesiastical authorities (judicial decisions have established this). Hence it is that we have no marriages now among us without ecclesiastical sanction ... no irregularities in these hallowed contracts, whether religious, moral or legal; and it was confidence in our scrupulousness as to these essentials which obtained the special privileges granted us by the legislature. Can it then be expedient to concede powers which, if not to be held irresponsibly, must at least be exercised where no control would be recognised?[29]

The matter came to a head soon after Adler's arrival, with suggestions in the *Jewish Chronicle* of 'tyrannous conduct':

> We were just going to press when we learned with deep regret that, owing to a certain line of conduct which Dr Adler has intimated his intention to pursue to the Burton Street Synagogue, a severe blow will be inflicted on the peace of the Jewish community. It is said that the members of the new congregation, feeling the Chief Rabbi's proceedings to be unjustifiably harsh and rigorously persecuting, have summoned a general meeting of their body, prior to publishing to the world at large the tyrannous conduct which they charge Dr Adler of having displayed towards them ... We confess that we had confidently indulged the hope, in common with the Jews at large, that the elevation of Dr Adler to the rabbinical chair would prove the precursor of reunion and peace; and most bitter will be the disappointment of the community if the cup of expectation is dashed from their lips.[30]

Disputing this account, which it described as 'evidently calculated to create mischief',[31] the *Voice of Jacob* published its own version of events. Prior to the marriage between a member of the Western Synagogue and the daughter of a Burton Street 'dependant', it reported, the Chief Rabbi's authorisation had been sought for one of the Western's officiants to solemnise the union. Alerted to the conditions of the *cherem*, Adler 'felt himself unable to allow an officer of one of the recognised synagogues to perform the ceremony, unless both parties disavowed the imputations of heterodox adhesion'.

When, therefore, the couple presented themselves before him,

> they at once, after an explanation of these circumstances and without

the employment of any persuasion, consented to sign, and did sign, a paper to that effect – that they henceforward undertook to abide by the laws as prescribed by constituted authority. But, in order to afford the parties an opportunity for reconsideration, and of consultation with their relatives and friends, the Rev. Dr Adler appointed them finally to attach their signatures on the following day, in the beth hamidrash – which, without any objection or hesitation, they did.[32]

The bridegroom was Morrice Hyman, and his bride Jane Angel, whose father, Daniel, was keeper of the Reform burial ground. The circumstances surrounding their intended marriage were described by the West London Synagogue in the appendix to an eight-page 'Appeal' in the *Jewish Chronicle*, largely an account of the congregation's evolution:

> A Mr Hyman applied to the authorities of the Westminster [Western] Synagogue (of which he is a member) to procure from Dr Adler a licence of marriage with Jane Angel, daughter of a servant of the Burton Street Congregation. Mr John Salmon, acting as warden of the Westminster Synagogue, brought this application in due course before Dr Adler and related to him all the particulars connected with the intended marriage. Dr Adler gave his unconditional assent, stating that he could see no objection to the marriage taking place.
>
> Three days afterwards, Mr Salmon, having been requested to call upon Dr Adler, was informed by him that he had reconsidered the matter and that, since the bride-elect was a member of the Burton Street Synagogue, he had determined to summon before him both contracting parties. This much has been learned from the statement of Mr Salmon.
>
> A written declaration from Jane Angel, bearing her signature, which has been furnished to the authorities of the Burton Street Synagogue, adds the following particulars: that she attended at the house of the Chief Rabbi, agreeably to his order, accompanied by Hyman; that Dr Adler reprimanded Hyman for engaging himself to a member of a synagogue placed under the ban of excommunication, and declared that he could allow the marriage to be solemnised by the minister of the Westminster Congregation only upon the condition of Jane Angel's signing a declaration, *there and then*, renouncing the synagogue at Burton Street, and all its usages.
>
> Dr Adler [said Salmon] retired to an adjoining room to procure the formal declaration, which appeared to have been prepared, and Hyman, having in the meantime represented to her that it was evident Dr Adler would not allow them to be married unless she signed

the paper, she was induced to affix her signature. Dr Adler said not a word about affording her time for consulting her friends (a pure invention of the Editor of the *Voice of Jacob*), but merely requested her to attend before the Beth Din on the following day.

A copy of Jane Angel's statement was forwarded to the Chief Rabbi by the authorities of the Burton Street Synagogue, accompanied by a respectful letter, requesting to know if it were true, and if not, in what parts incorrect – and also entreating that they might be furnished with a copy of the document of abjuration which the young woman had been required to sign. Dr Adler declined giving any written reply on the subject, and refused to furnish a copy of the declaration or test which he had imposed.[33]

Addressing a meeting of the West London Synagogue some six weeks before the 'Appeal' was published, Sir Isaac Lyon Goldsmid – an early proponent of reform – expressed a desire 'to make every sacrifice consistent with principle and honour to prevent the evils that must result from the appearance of strife and persecution between one portion of the Jewish body and the other'. But, he said, since Adler had 'completely shut the door against all further correspondence on the subject, no course was left open to the meeting but respectfully to inform the Chief Rabbi that, in the absence of his written reply, the Burton Street Congregation would be compelled to conclude that Jane Angel's statement was correct, and that they would be obliged to act on that conclusion in any steps they might be induced to take for their own vindication.'[34]

Despite the contentious nature of the 'Appeal' in relation to the marriage, the *Voice of Jacob* found, in other aspects of

> this new authoritative publication, much occasion to rejoice ... While in the opening sermon of the Rev. D.W. Marks, the rejection of the Oral Law is openly asserted, the present publication represents the whole difference to consist in deviation from the received liturgical forms! The Seceders then, while silently dropping that most dangerous and injudicious assertion, have narrowed the breach by half and have, in our opinion, rendered it possible to an officious friend to help them over that unfortunate moat which they themselves have dug, separating them from the community of Israel.[35]

The paper's comments, though reflecting a conciliatory tone hitherto absent from its pronouncements, were quickly dismissed by the West London wardens. In a robust rebuttal, they declared that

> the Appeal having vindicated the prayer-book of the West London

> Synagogue, but not having restated or justified the views respecting the Tradition, or "Oral Law", as set forth by the Rev. Mr Marks in the discourse delivered by him on the opening of the Synagogue, it seems to have been inferred that the congregation intend to depart from those views.
>
> Nothing can be further from the fact. The simple reason why the congregation have justified their prayer-book, and not justified Mr Marks' opening discourse, is that the former, and not the latter, was condemned by the Rev. Dr Hirschell in the 'Caution', which has formed the basis of Dr Adler's late proceedings; and most assuredly, not that the slightest idea is entertained by the congregation of abandoning the opinions respecting the Tradition, or Oral Law, or any other of the views expressed by their minister, in the consecration sermon.[36]

Despite this journalistic jockeying, some movement had been made, on both sides, towards repairing the rift. Six months later, under the heading 'Omen of Peace', the *Jewish Chronicle* editorialised that Adler 'deserves the grateful acknowledgements of all who delight in the removal of dissensions from within our community by a recent act of *practical* abrogation, or non-recognition of the much-talked-of *bull of excommunication*'.

This recent act was the marriage, solemnised by Adler himself at the home of D.Q. Henriques, a Burton Street member, between Henriques' sister and Walter Josephs, of the Great Synagogue,

> without the previous imposition of any religious tests whatever on the lady, who, as well as her relatives, has long attended, and does now attend, worship at the West London Synagogue.
>
> Did the Chief Rabbi recognise the existence and the efficacy of a *cherem* against the reformed synagogue [commented the paper], he could not thus commune with its members and congregants, as an inspection of the rabbinical laws on the subject, collected in the Shulchan Aruch (Chapter 334, Section 2), will sufficiently show. We sincerely congratulate the Chief Rabbi on having availed himself of this favourable opportunity utterly to destroy the supposition (favoured by a late act of severity) of his connivance at the machinations of designing zealots, who abuse his name and authority for keeping up a dangerous ferment, where there should be nought but peace and good will.
>
> By sanctioning, without the prescription of odious tests, a marriage between a member of the West London Synagogue and a gentleman of a City congregation; by officiating in his sacerdotal

capacity on the occasion, at the house of a prominent member of the reformed congregation; by allowing the name of that very member of the Burton Street Synagogue to be connected with a solemn blessing (*misheberach*) at the *bimah* (reader's desk) of the Great Synagogue in Duke's Place – the Rev. Dr Adler has taken a decisive step in the right direction towards effecting that reconciliation with the West London Synagogue which all friends to the Anglo-Jewish community have so much at heart.

We trust that this virtual abandonment of the shadowy *cherem* will be speedily followed up by a formal and public revocation of the edict itself, which, as long as it even nominally exists, may become a means of molestation, as (we are sorry to have to make the allusion) is proved by Jane Angel's vexatious case. The dignity of the British rabbinate claims the unequivocal suppression of an edict which might else appear inoperative, indeed, in the case of the rich, but ever ready to be called into action against the poor.[37]

Barely a month later, 'More Omens of Peace' were reported, this time at the Burton Street burial ground, where Marks and Löwy, clad in canonicals and in the presence of 'several highly respectable members of the Duke's Place and New Synagogues', officiated at the funeral of Jonas Levy, a member of the West London congregation. Boosting the Orthodox presence during the week of shivah was the rabbi of the Hambro' Synagogue, whose discourses 'appeared to pour the balm of spiritual consolation into the distressed minds of the mourning family'. Thus 'a more liberal and rational feeling began to manifest itself among the members of the City congregations towards their brethren of the West London Synagogue'.[38]

Elkin's interment, at the same burial ground some eighteen months later – although also attended by an Orthodox contingent – put back the clock, but the campaign for reconciliation was set in motion, and the days of the *cherem* appeared to be numbered.

\* \* \*   \* \* \*   \* \* \*

In social and religious terms, the edict had had a profound effect on both sides of the communal divide: 'brothers and near relations ceased to visit one another, the closest families were broken, and much hardship and bitterness ensued'.[39] Early in the dispute, the Bevis Marks wardens had expressed their 'anxious and earnest hope that either here or in a meeting of the *Yehidim*, or in concert with the authorities of the other congregations, some course may be marked out, some measures determined upon, likely to conciliate discordant feelings and prevailing opinions; and that by a temperate and full consideration of any just cause of complaint or dissatisfaction and of every well-digested plan of improvement, and, above all, by a cordial and sincere approximation of all parties in so good a cause, the peace and union of the Congregation may yet be restored and permanently re-established'.[40]

Within weeks of Adler's installation (the timing appears coincidental), the Sephardi Beth Din 'manifested a disposition to relax that stringency of the exclusion enforced against the Seceders, *individually*, which is still maintained towards them in a corporate capacity, and towards their synagogue as a non-conformist one'. As an act of compassion, the dayanim 'formally sanctioned the attendance at a funeral of several Seceders as chief mourners, and tacitly recognised their claim to participate in all the melancholy offices usual on such occasions, except the recital of the kaddish'.[41]

In their further desire to conciliate feelings and opinions, the authorities revised the penalties imposed on those violating or incurring the *cherem*. While maintaining the ban on religious services within six miles of Bevis Marks, *Ascama* I was amended to allow attendance at 'established places' other than Burton Street; fines of varying severity were to be levied in lieu of ostracism; and conditions imposed on the burial places of those deemed 'contumacious'. While few risked breaking the ban, 'the more moderate portion of the Sephardi Congregation' – not to say of those of the Ashkenazi camp – regarded it, even in its amended form, as 'opposed to the enlightenment of the age and to the spirit of true religion. The fact that some of their former friends and relatives might be labouring under *cherem*, or religious disabilities, was disquieting to the majority of right-thinking members of Bevis Marks.'[42]

The tentative relaxation by the Sephardi Beth Din precipitated the launch of an uphill battle by two of the congregation's leaders, Hananel de Castro and Haim Guedalla – supported by, among others, Elias Haim Lindo and David Brandon – for a total repeal of the *cherem*. The dayanim, however, were divided over the issue. David Meldola and Abraham Haliva ruled that it was for the mahamad to rescind the *cherem*, 'provided that those under excommunication are anxious for the abolition and are prepared to return to the body from which they seceded'. Abraham Belais stated that 'a majority of three to two of the Board of Elders is sufficient to repeal the *cherem* without even the concurrence of the Beth Din'. Faced with this divergence of view, the mahamad – at a meeting in April 1847 attended by Montefiore – voted in support of Meldola and Haliva, declaring that they were the 'official dayanim' and were, in any event, 'a majority of two to one'.[43]

The abolitionist campaign was bolstered later that year by the ruling of 'a learned rabbi of Leghorn – a most respected and profound talmudist, of strictly Orthodox principles' – who sided with Belais in declaring, unequivocally, that

> I altogether deny the present ecclesiastical courts the power of issuing a *cherem*. Since no *cherem* can be *enforced* nowadays, would it not have been more advisable, more expedient, nay more just and upright, to act according to the maxim of our sage, 'To push away with the left hand and draw near with the right hand' – to reprove them [the seceders] rather than estrange them from the house of Israel? Would it not have been better to point out to them the injury they inflicted on the unity of Israel, by separation from the body, than to use means for perpetuating that separation? Has not the gate of repentance in return been violently shut against them?[44]

Extolling the 'beautiful letter by the Rabbi of Leghorn', a *Jewish Chronicle* reader – signing himself 'An Orthodox' – lent speedy support:

> Having ascertained the illegality of the *Ascama* by the Sephardim, and the joined declaration by the Sephardi and German authorities, I do 'rest in hope'[45] that if these Boards do not now meet the question upon *legal* grounds, a stir will be made to *enforce* the abolition of the obnoxious law ... If those of my brethren who are affected by the *cherem*, and who are now put in possession of talmudical authorities showing the illegality of that cruel law, do not follow it up by a proper representation to the Beth Din, and to the mahamad, they have *themselves* to blame for its continuance.[46]

'M' ('I inclose my name in full') followed this up a week later with an invocation of Adler:

> The *cherem*, having been issued solely with respect to the prayer-book, must of necessity – according to the [Leghorn] decision – be totally illegal and consequently of none effect; and, on such ground, can with the very best grace be expunged from the minute books of the various Synagogues and of the Ecclesiastical Court, by and with the sanction of the Rev. the Chief Rabbi, Dr Adler, who had no hand in its promulgation ...
>
> Let me solicit all parties calmly and dispassionately to consider the causes which gave rise to the formation of the Burton Street Synagogue, and perhaps ask themselves the question whether it was not, in the first instance, the fault of the ultra-Orthodox party, who denied them even the most innocent alterations of our outward

synagogue observances, so as to bring our ceremonials within the enlightenment and the acquirements of the age; and whether they were not met with clamour, contumely and scorn, such as no gentlemen could brook ...

Let, therefore, all parties who may be desirous of peace acknowledge that they have been in the wrong and, by mutual concessions, restore peace, love and unity in Israel.[47]

The reference to Adler may well have spurred the Spanish and Portuguese congregation to meet, on 11 January 1848, with a view to debating the following resolution:

Having maturely and seriously considered the resolutions of the Elders regarding the seceders, and having had reference to the speech of the *mahamad* on that occasion, wherein it is expressly declared that those resolutions (prepared and submitted by them) 'applied solely to the civil offence to the congregation, and that as far as regarded the religious offence, it had already engaged the spiritual cognisance of the ecclesiastical authorities of the United Congregations', this meeting is decidedly of opinion, and does hereby declare its conviction, *that the penalty of cherem was never contemplated or intended*, and that in as far as regards the breach of the old Ascama of *Kaal* No. 1, *it has never been inflicted on the parties* by any act of the Elders. But as doubts exist in the minds of some of the *Yehidim*, whether religiously such penalty is not implied, this meeting, *actuated by an anxious desire to restore that unanimity so desirable in our congregation*, do hereby resolve that an appeal be made to the Rev. Dr Adler, the Chief Rabbi of the German Congregations, for his advice and decision on the case, and appreciating the high character, piety and learning of that rev. gentleman, this meeting will consider his decision as a final settlement of the question.

The introduction to the resolution, the *Jewish Chronicle* asserted,[48] contained 'facts which could not be controverted'; and the reference to Adler 'was adopted by the mover [Solomon Almosnino] and seconder [Haim Guedalla] with an anxious desire to restore unanimity in the congregation. But strange to say, although a large majority was expected, yet it was carried by only two votes' (nineteen to seventeen). At a further meeting, at which 'a very warm and angry' discussion took place, a letter from the Sephardi Beth Din was discussed, but 'its meaning was not very intelligible and it was certainly not favourable to the resolution before the room'. As a result, the decision was overturned, by twenty-seven votes to seventeen. 'Thus', declared the paper, 'has intolerance gained a triumph. This question, from the increasing and powerful minority, threatens much mischief. Both parties are determined, and further secessions will no doubt arise from this schism.'[49]

How much longer, the *Jewish Chronicle* asked the following month, 'are the few antiquated gentlemen, the main supporters and upholders of "anathema", to confer upon us *all* the stigma of intolerance?'[50] The answer, it seemed, was 'Not long'. Another page of the same issue[51] carried the text of a resolution – formulated by de Castro and reported to have produced 'much sensation' – that 'every person who may have incurred the penalty of *cherem*, by an infraction of the old *Ascama* I (now repealed), shall no longer be considered under that penalty, but subject only to the pains and disqualifications as are in force against the members of the Burton Street place of worship, under the Declaration of the Ecclesiastical Authorities of the United Congregations.'[52]

At a meeting called to settle the issue, the resolution was carried by sixteen votes to fifteen, with three abstentions. 'We hope', the report concluded, 'that the true friends of religious liberty will muster their forces on the occasion and, by an overwhelming majority, blot out that disgraceful *Ascama*, the abolition of which must lead, sooner or later, to the repeal of the odious "Declaration" by the Ecclesiastical Court.' Repeal, however, came later rather than sooner, for de Castro's resolution limped but slowly towards peace. The subsequent meeting failed to secure confirmation, and a year was to pass before rescission was achieved.

Eventually, on 21 January 1849, following the mahamad's delayed acceptance of the vote, de Castro and Guedalla were successful in persuading Meldola, as acting ecclesiastical head, to remove the *cherem* – by then largely nominal. Thereafter, events moved speedily. The Elders ruled that if Moses Mocatta and his fellow reformers admitted to having transgressed *Ascama* I 'by establishing and attending services in an unauthorised place of worship', they would be relieved of the *cherem* and shorn of its penalties. This they did, and the path was cleared for the final act of reconciliation.

Six weeks later, 'the ecclesiastical authorities performed the ceremony requisite to purge the reformers of *cherem* ... This act enabled families that had long ceased holding mutual communication to resume friendly intercourse; and one of the leaders of the Reformers paid at once a visit to one of the chiefs of the Orthodox party, between whom family ties had not prevented the birth of a bitter religious feud.'[53]

As for the Ashkenazi Chief Rabbinate, it never formally revoked the 'shadowy *cherem*'.[54]

# 2

# Under the Canopy

Hananel de Castro's act of reconciliation was his last major contribution to communal affairs: a fortnight later, on 23 March 1849, he died suddenly, aged 54, some six hours after suffering an apoplectic fit. Among the large gathering at the funeral were 'the leading men of the Jewish community of all congregations, Orthodox as well as reformers, the Rev. Dr Adler and the other members of the ecclesiastical courts (Portuguese and German)'. Active in both the Sephardi and wider communities, de Castro was described by David Meldola, in his funeral oration, as 'one of the disciples of Aaron, who loved peace and pursued peace ... He not only loved peace, but followed hard after it. The repetition manifests the real love of peace in those who make it their daily object of anxious pursuit.'

In its front-page obituary, the *Jewish Chronicle* declared:

> Alas! That he died before he could celebrate the final triumph of his peaceful efforts; alas! That he did not live longer to witness what we hope will soon take place – a complete union in the Jewish community. But he rejoiced at the success of the first step, for which he fought for several years; and his dying lips uttered his great satisfaction at having accomplished so much towards peace.[1]

That 'complete union in the Jewish community' was never to be, and as the years wore on, the forces opposing it became increasingly strident. Writing at the turn of the decade, the apostate Margoliouth – no friend of Orthodoxy – laid the blame squarely at Adler's feet:

> Great hopes were expressed respecting the new Rabbi's liberal spirit, so that the progress of reform would be expedited by his assuming the important office. In fact, Dr Adler gave the Anglo-Hebrews to understand that such would be his policy.
>
> The day of installation – 9 July, 1845 – at length arrived. Dr Adler still intimated his readiness to espouse improvement, and all was congratulation and complacency. But before many months elapsed, Dr Adler – 'Adler' means 'Eagle' – treated his flock like a vulture. He ratified the excommunication against the British Jews, which it was

fondly hoped died away with the death of the fulminator.

Dr Adler began to carry out the Bull in every iota, and actually prohibited matrimonial alliances between members of the respective congregations. The consequence was such a general dissatisfaction as was never before experienced among the Anglo-Hebrews heretofore ...

[Dr Adler] is now endeavouring to redeem his pledge and his character. He is consenting to reform in the liturgy, and the next vestry meeting is to decide the affair. Of course, it does not come with so good a grace as it would have done at the beginning of his ministry. But Anglo-Hebrews admit the force of the adage, 'Better late than never', and they already congratulate themselves that the British synagogues will date a new era from the year 1850.[2]

The *Jewish Chronicle* was more generous – and more open-minded – in determining the root of the rift. In the first of two leading articles, it again drew attention to

yet another obnoxious declaration in existence, emanating from the joint ecclesiastical courts of the Sephardim and Germans (Ashkenazim) which awkwardly stands in the way of perfect reconciliation. And though that declaration was originally fulminated in consequence of the alteration of the Prayer-Book, yet we are led to hope, from the improvement in the tone which now prevails, that the 'bitterness of spirit is gone', and that the alleged innovation in the ritual will not prevent the recall of that sad declaration, if nothing else interferes with the religious scruples of the Ecclesiastics.

But another factor did interfere with religious scruples. The abolition of the second day of the festivals, the paper wrote, would be 'the rock on which the most courageous champions of peace, and the most zealous advocates of union, will founder. We fear that as long as that important innovation is persisted in by our Burton Street brethren, the ecclesiastics of the City synagogues will never relax the rigour of their anathema.'

Would not the congregation's leading members therefore consider 'modifying the innovation by opening the synagogues on the second holidays and having a service performed, leaving the attendance to the option of the individual members?' The hand of peace, recalled the *Jewish Chronicle*, had been held out and had been accepted. 'Let it be followed up by the heart, and there is at present every chance in favour of a complete reconciliation and union.'[3]

Four weeks later, on the eve of their move to larger premises in Margaret Street (off Cavendish Square), the paper urged the 'British Jews' of Burton Street no longer to alienate themselves from other British Jews. So long as they are separated from the majority of their brethren, who are also British Jews, whether Sephardim or Ashkenazim, they cannot claim that title as a distinction. Let them, true to the British character, sacrifice private notions to the public good; let them, in the genuine sense of British Jews, jealously watch the public interests of their community, and heal the breach which mars the progress of the common weal.[4]

\* \* \*     \* \* \*     \* \* \*

Ritual and liturgical reform, along with synagogue decorum and congregational devotion, were not the exclusive preserve of the Burton Street campaigners. From the outset, Adler proposed a similar agenda, if in dissimilar terms, 'to inspire my brethren and sisters, who have been confided to my spiritual charge, with love for our most holy religion, such as it has been transmitted to us by our fathers, and taught by our sages'. This aim, contained in the Chief Rabbi's first pastoral letter – dated 13 August 5605 (1845) and conveyed to 'the Presidents and Wardens of the Jewish Congregations in the British Empire' – was to be attained by

> the raising and perfecting of those institutions which enjoy the countenance and support of my Congregations and which, from their nature, are calculated visibly and clearly to demonstrate what hold religious sentiments have acquired on the minds, and to what degree they are entwined with the lives and conduct, of the members composing those Congregations.[5]

Referring to the synagogue, which he acknowledged to be below educational establishments in his scale of priorities, Adler stressed the need for 'quiet and decorum, dignity and solemnity during divine worship, so that it may awaken the fear of the Lord, foster feelings of devotion, and promote brotherly union' – hopes not far removed from Marks' ambitions. In translating those ideals into action, the Chief Rabbi initiated a census to provide the names and numbers of seat-holders and functionaries, and of teachers and pupils, hours of public and private instruction, the sale of mitzvot, and the provision of mikvehs, charities, burial grounds and books.

The *Laws and Regulations*[6] emerging from the survey[7] were designed both to enhance the function and spirit of divine worship – ends sought not only in the 1840s but by disgruntled congregants, Ashkenazi and Sephardi, three decades earlier[8] – and to consolidate Adler's control over the administration and direction of congregational life. Laid out over five sections, they covered all aspects of synagogue administration, liturgy and ritual, from 'outward decorum' and prayers, to the reading of the Law and 'casual solemnities'. But the most forceful was the opening section, headed 'Superintendence', in which the primacy of the Chief Rabbi was repeatedly proclaimed and which, with far-reaching ramifications, was to underpin the United Synagogue's Deed of Foundation and Trust when that organisation was established, under Adler's prompting, in the summer of 1870:

> The duty of superintending the Synagogue, as far as religious observances are concerned, devolves on the Chief Rabbi, when present; in his absence, on the Dayan; in the absence of the Dayan, on the Minister; in the absence of the Minister, on the Reader, provided these latter officers be authorised for that purpose by the Chief Rabbi and their respective Congregations ...
>
> Should anyone think himself aggrieved, he shall apply for redress, if in religious matters, to the Chief Rabbi ... The erection of a new Synagogue must have the sanction of the Chief Rabbi; and the formation of a new Congregation must have the sanction of the Chief Rabbi, besides that of the Board of Deputies ...[9]
>
> The sale of *mitzvot* within the Synagogue is prohibited. The order of *aliyot* (unless already legislated for) is left to the Honorary Officers. In the event of the Congregation not being able to agree on this subject, the matter to be referred to the Chief Rabbi ...[10]
>
> Without the consent of the Honorary Officers and of the Chief Rabbi, no one shall be permitted to deliver a religious discourse in the Synagogue ...[11] Every alteration of these Regulations must have the written sanction of the Chief Rabbi.[12]

Even before releasing his *Laws and Regulations*, Adler had introduced changes into the Sabbath-eve liturgy, covering the repetition of prayers and the manner of their recitation – 'insignificant in themselves but important in their consequences', wrote the *Jewish Chronicle*:

> It is enough for us that *he* has authorised them, and our duty is to obey. The Chief Rabbi should be invested with the authority due to his high office, with all the confidence due to his commanding position. No committee of surveillance should be tolerated. He is our judge, and by his decision we must abide; he is our teacher, and his instructions we must adopt; he is our spiritual guide, and we must follow him.[13]

Adler was urged, however, to widen the application of the changes, initially restricted to the Great Synagogue:

> Why should one congregation be deprived of the decorous regulations introduced into another? By abolishing those petty differences which at present divide the metropolitan and provincial synagogues, an *entente cordiale* will be established which will give fresh vigour to the united efforts of the British Congregations of Jews who, we are sure, have one common object – the welfare of Israel.
>
> When we consider how painful is the effect of secession to the feelings, and how injurious to the interests, of both parties, our principal aim and our chief purpose ought to be directed to unite the dissenting, and to join the separate, 'to proclaim peace to him that is distant as well as to him that is near'.[14]

Anticipating the opposition of his more traditional critics, Adler sought to allay the fears of those who, he suggested, were being

> more talmudical than the Talmud. Do not be alarmed for fear that I shall introduce any regulations in our synagogue worship which are against the Law. Rely on me that whatever I shall ordain will be in accordance with the Law.
>
> By bringing divine worship in the synagogue to as much perfection as lies in our power, by securing the fervency of devotion which is as indispensably necessary to prayer as the soul is to the body, and by maintaining that decorum in which we should present our petition to the Almighty, this house of God will become a pattern and a guiding star to the other places of worship, and its example will be readily followed.[15]

Thus, a year later, for the first time in Britain's Orthodox synagogues, laws governing dress, decorum, children's attendance, the timing and length of services, the mode of prayer, and the solemnisation of marriages and *milah* became a regular feature of congregational life. When finally published, they were greeted, despite earlier misgivings, with cautious acclaim. 'Although far from comprehending the correction of all the abuses which have crept into our synagogue worship, yet they contain much that must lead to improvement. We rejoice that they have now been adopted by the vestry of the Great Synagogue, and we trust that the executive will see them carried into effect.'[16]

\* \* \*   \* \* \*   \* \* \*

Although tackling the reformers' demands on their own ground, Adler left unaddressed a major plank of the secessionist platform – the abolition of the second festival day. Marks, however, had reverted to the subject, couching his references in circumlocutory terms. In a Shavuot sermon some months before Adler's edicts, he justified the observance of a single day as ordained in the Law:

> We cannot be said to be true disciples of Moses, and faithful followers of our ancestors at Sinai, unless we hold firmly and inviolably that no article of the Sinaic covenant can ever be altered or superseded, and that no dogma which is not there set forth in its plain and obvious sense can ever be entitled to our religious belief. When the Jew speaks of the divine revelation, he of course understands by that term the whole Mosaic Law ...
>
> The Omniscient One grasps in His intelligence all time, the future as well as the present, and He knows what will be as certainly as He knows what is: and as it is impossible that God should at any future time be wiser or holier, more benevolent to His children, or more desirous to promote their happiness, than He was on the day when He revealed Himself to our fathers at Sinai, so it is impossible that He should ever change His perfect Law for any other.[17]

At the consecration of the Manchester Congregation of British Jews, eleven years later, Marks returned to the theme, invoking the biblical verse, 'Remember ye the Law of Moses My servant':[18]

> For *Torat Moshe*, our fathers have borne and suffered much ... I know full well, and I speak it with sorrow, that the fervour which warmed the breasts of our ancestors for the code of which the text speaks is far less felt by us.
>
> But it must also, in fairness, be admitted that many superstitions and abuses which our fathers were wont to confound with the pure principles of Sinai, as if the former had been the growth of the age of Moses, have made themselves felt at the present day as most intolerable evils, and as obstacles which, unless removed, must deprive Judaism, in its outward worship, of a genuine devotional character, and fail to impress the communicants of the synagogue with those spiritual sentiments of religion to which the prophet evidently alludes, when he admonishes us in the words of the text.
>
> The inference which it is reasonable to suppose that the world will draw from the labours and the sacrifices you have imposed on yourselves, my friends, in erecting this temple of prayer, is that you feel it

a conscientious obligation to remove those abuses, to sift the wheat from the chaff, and to consecrate your synagogue and your practices to the observance of the Mosaic code in its pure spirit, and not to confound its inspired doctrines with human ordinances and human institutions ...

Here, let every Jewish rite be practised that commends itself to rational piety, and let every traditional observance be maintained that gives no countenance to superstition, and is not in open conflict with the letter and the spirit of the Law.[19]

A decade was to pass before Adler delivered his response to these charges of 'superstitions and abuses', of 'evils and obstacles', and Marks' call to 'sift the wheat from the chaff' in synagogue worship. But when it finally came, it was cogently argued and carefully sourced.[20] Guided by the biblical texts, he said, he would proceed to demonstrate that the celebration of the second days of the festivals was 'intimately connected with the whole system of our chronology'; that it served 'as the bond of our nationality'; and that 'it is in full accordance and entire consistency with our holy law'.[21] On the first score, having expatiated on the workings of the Hebrew calendar, he continued:

> At the time when the members of the Great Sanhedrin were sitting in Jerusalem, the ocular observation of the new moon was indispensable, but the results of this were always checked by astronomical computations. Although the New Year was fixed for the date that had been arrived at by astronomical calculation, its actual solemnisation did not commence until after the new moon had been actually observed. This observation had to be reported to the Great Sanhedrin, who thereupon proclaimed the festival.
>
> When such observation had not been reported by the thirtieth day of Ellul, the following day was also observed as a festival in Jerusalem, but two days were invariably kept in all other places, those situated both in and out of the Holy Land. At the present day, when there is no Sanhedrin, and ocular observation cannot be verified by authority, this doubt as to which is the proper day extends to all the other festivals, and in our anxiety to observe the proper day, we keep two days.
>
> Now, it may be asked, such a procedure may have been perfectly correct at a time when astronomical science was in its infancy, but now that it has attained such perfection, there surely can be no doubt as to which is the right day.
>
> The answer to the argument is this: If at the present moment the

Temple would be restored and the Sanhedrin re-established, the very same course as of old would be the only one that could be pursued, owing to the circumstance that the fixing of the calendar depended entirely upon ocular observation of the new moon, and that calculation was only employed with a view to check and control that observation. Should, therefore, the new moon not be observed on the thirtieth of Ellul at all, or at so late a period of the day that the fact could not be reported to the Sanhedrin in time, two days of New Year would have to be solemnised everywhere.[22]

Progressing to the question of 'bonding', that the second day of the festival had been instituted 'on the basis of our nationality', Adler cited the biblical declaration that the observance of the festivals 'is a statute forever throughout your generations, in all your dwellings'.[23] All Israel, he said, dwelling as they did in every quarter of the habitable globe, were to solemnise the festivals 'at one and the same time'. There were, however, time variations across the globe of up to twenty-four hours, depending on geographical location, and therefore, 'by allowing a full forty-eight hours for the observance of the festival, all Israel in all their dwelling-places are enabled to observe one complete day of twenty-four hours simultaneously. In the days of old, when the nation was assembled at Jerusalem on the three great festivals, one day of twenty-four hours naturally sufficed'.[24]

Turning, finally, to his third point – that the second day was consistent with the Law and obeyed the injunction 'neither to add to nor to diminish from the commandments of the Lord'[25] – Adler stated:

> Can we imagine that the sages, whose sole anxiety it was that every word of the Law should be conscientiously carried out, who sacrificed their lives in order not to transgress one of its behests – is it credible that these men would have dared to act contrarily to one of its precepts?
>
> I affirm that those who adduce this argument do not know the import, do not understand the meaning, of that prohibition ... Can we be charged with adding to the divine command if – labouring, as we are, in doubt, whether the first or the second be the proper day – we consider ourselves religiously bound to keep both days holy?'[26]

Imploring his flock 'to withhold from violating an institution that has been kept sacred by our forefathers, an institution that has been unanimously sanctioned by great and holy men from very remote times', Adler added:

> Bear in mind that, with respect to institutions of far less importance,

the rule holds good that no court of law, no Sanhedrin, can abrogate or rescind an institution that has been established by another court, unless it be superior in wisdom and in numbers.

And can this present age, in which the study of the law is so sadly neglected, produce men superior in learning and authority to those of ages gone by, when the teachers of Israel devoted their days and their nights, their talents and abilities, to the study of the law?[27]

\* \* \*   \* \* \*   \* \* \*

More worldly matters, in which the reformers and their camp were resolutely involved, meanwhile occupied Adler's attention. That they also preoccupied Montefiore, as president of the Board, bore heavily on the minds of the Reform campaigners. As briefly noted, following his involvement in the declaration and imposition of the *cherem*,[28] Montefiore had become embroiled in the battle to register marriages at the West London Synagogue. Six days after its consecration, a delegation headed by Francis Goldsmid, Moses Mocatta and John Simon had notified him of the establishment of 'a synagogue of persons professing the Jewish religion' and requested him to certify Marks as its secretary, in order to validate marriages solemnised by him under the terms of the Act.

Montefiore had brought their request 'before our ecclesiastical authorities' and, though reluctant to issue a certificate in view of Marks' declared views, had told Hirschell that it was 'the duty of the president of the London Committee of the Board of Deputies of British Jews to give such a certificate' and that, if the Chief Rabbi sanctioned the request, he should 'give me such in writing'. Following Hirschell's refusal to do so, Montefiore had told Goldsmid: 'It is my duty to state that I cannot certify Mr Marks to the Registrar General as being the Secretary of a Synagogue' – reaffirming, in a note the following day 'to prevent the possibility of your misconceiving my letter, I think it right to add that I do not consider the place of worship in Burton Street, referred to by you, to be a Synagogue'. His reasoning was recorded by his secretary, Louis Loewe, in an entry in his edited *Diaries*:

> Sir Moses ... apprehended great agitation in the community, and felt much anxiety as to the result. He entertained the most liberal principles in matters of religion; although himself a staunch supporter of the time-honoured usages of his religion, he did not interfere with the opinions or acts of those who differed from him unless compelled to do so by actual duty. But when, as President of the Board of Deputies, or of any other institution, he had to give his opinion on

religious matters, he invariably referred to the Spiritual Head of the community for guidance; he regarded a word from him as decisive, and obeyed its injunctions at whatever cost to himself.[29]

While retorting that it was 'impossible to show that the persons constituting the congregation in question do *not profess* the Jewish religion', and despite Montefiore's reluctance 'to give any reason for the view upon which he based his refusal to certify', Goldsmid told him: 'The new congregation abstains from the course still open to them – that of compelling, by mandamus of the High Court of Justice, the fulfilment of the Act of Parliament – on the ground that it will not be well for legal proceedings to be instituted at the very moment when the Jewish community is struggling for the removal of religious disabilities.' That course, however, was 'within the power of the new congregation. Counsel's opinion has been taken upon it, and Sir Roundell Palmer, QC, gave it as his opinion that a mandamus could have been obtained.'[30]

For several years, Adler delayed action on the matter. In the absence of progress, 'the Reform Congregation submitted to celebrate their marriages in a civil way, the parties attending at the local registrar's office in the morning, the religious ceremony being afterwards performed by their minister. The first marriage in the congregation was that of Mr John Simon[31] and was conducted in that manner. Later on, the difficulty was partially met by obtaining the presence of the ordinary registrar at the marriage ceremony. That arrangement saved the bridal couples the inconvenience of the double function.'[32]

As a face-saving exercise, Burton Street's leaders drew up their own marriage certificate, declaring that 'We, the undersigned wardens of this Synagogue, authorise you, or one of you, to perform the ceremony of marriage, according to the usages of persons professing the Jewish religion ... provided that, before so doing, a Certificate be delivered to you of the marriage of the same parties on the morning of the same day, at the Office of the Superintendent Registrar.'[33]

The registrar, in turn, sanctioned the procedure with the publication of an official notice to the effect that

> The West London Synagogue of British Jews, situated in Burton Street, Burton Crescent, in the parish and district of St Pancras in the county of Middlesex, being a building certified, according to law, as a place of religious worship, was on the fourth day of December 1846 duly registered for solemnising marriages therein, pursuant to the Act ... Witness my hand and seal this fifth day of December, 1846.
> – Joseph Ivimey, Superintendent Registrar.[34]

A decade later, the Registrar General took steps to regularise the West London's position through the insertion of a clause in the Dissenters' Marriage Bill. Having been considered by the Board of Deputies' law and parliamentary committee, the matter came before a plenary session on 2 July 1855. Montefiore was away and his presidential chair was occupied by Isaac Foligno, one of the six Sephardi representatives. Under discussion was the West London clause 'modified in accordance with a suggestion made by the Rev. the Chief Rabbi'.

The original clause read: 'That upon a requisition signed by twenty householders, being members of the West London Synagogue of British Jews in Margaret Street, Cavendish Square, in the City of Middlesex, stating the name of their Secretary, the Registrar General shall furnish to him books, etc., as provided by the Act for registering Births, Marriages, and Deaths, and that the furnishing such books, etc., shall impose on such Secretary the same duties and have the same effect as is prescribed by the aforesaid Act of Parliament.' Adler told the Board that while he was 'not opposed to the essence of the newly proposed clause, the locality of the parties ought to be more defined'.

Henry Harris, of Maiden Lane Synagogue, and B.S. (Benjamin) Phillips, of the Great, moved to adopt the proposal, but were challenged by Jonas Levy, of the Hambro'. Expressing surprise 'that the Rev. Dr Adler could give his assent to such a clause', Levy told the meeting he was there 'for the very purpose of opposing any assistance that might be given to the seceders for the accomplishment of their object'.

It was 'most unfair', he argued, that in Sir Moses' absence, 'it should be endeavoured by a side-wind to smuggle into a Bill intended for Christians a clause so materially affecting the prerogative of the president'. For this, he said, he blamed not the dissenters but the Board, 'for not acting up to its constitution, a principal article of which is that the Board should oppose any infringement of the rights of the Jews. Whoever has heard of Jewish Dissenters? They are quite an anomaly in Judaism. And yet, Mr Harris – the zealous champion for Orthodoxy – has come forward to move the adoption of the report.'

Louis Cohen,[35] of the Great, asserted that the Board had 'steered a middle course, framing a clause which, while it excepted the Jewish body from the operation of the clause, satisfied that functionary, and did not meet with any opposition on the part of the Chief Rabbi'. His view was echoed by several deputies, and the Board eventually voted to adopt the resolution as moved by Harris.[36]

The matter, however, was not quite settled. Behind Adler's recommendation – that 'the locality of the parties ought to be more defined' – was a shrewd directive, aimed at restricting the authorisation of marriages to the West London and its minister. This led to a spirited exchange between Montefiore and Marks at the Downing Street residence of the Prime Minister, Lord Palmerston:

> The [Marriage] Bill passed the second reading, but in Committee the seconder of the clause tried to get it expunged at the instance of Sir Moses Montefiore. Mr Marks, however, succeeded in prevailing upon Bishop Wilberforce and the Earl of Harrowby to reintroduce the expunged clause in the House of Lords. Before this, Sir Moses Montefiore asked Lord Palmerston to resist the reintroduction. On the suggestion of Lord Harrowby, Lord Palmerston invited Mr Marks to meet Sir Moses with his lordship at Downing Street.
>
> The meeting took place and Lord Palmerston asked Sir Moses why he objected to certify this new congregation. Sir Moses replied that 'it is not Orthodox', upon which Lord Palmerston observed, with a smile, 'Sir Moses! We can't maintain orthodoxy in the Church, why should you expect to do so in the Synagogue? The measure was intended for the Jews at large, and we should consider it persecution of conscience to exclude the West London Synagogue.'
>
> Mr Sampson Samuel, the solicitor and secretary of the Board of Deputies, who was also present, asked Mr Marks to retire for a moment, as he had a communication to make to him. It was this. He was authorised by Sir Moses to say that if he would agree to the withdrawal of the clause, Sir Moses would at once certify the secretary of the West London Synagogue.
>
> But at that time a similar congregation was about to be formed in Manchester, and Mr Marks asked Mr Samuel what course Sir Moses would pursue in that case, or in any other one which might thereafter arise. Mr Sampson Samuel replied that he was not authorised to make any promise, upon which Mr Marks refused to agree to the withdrawal of the clause.[37]

On 29 July 1856, 'an Act to amend the Provisions of the Marriage and Registration Acts' received royal assent, authorising the Registrar General 'to furnish marriage register books and forms to each certified secretary of the West London Synagogue of British Jews', and of 'some other Synagogue ... being in connexion with the West London Synagogue and having been established for not less than one year ... Every marriage solemnised under any of the said recited Acts or of this Act shall be good and cognisable in like manner as marriages before the passing of the first-recited Act according to the rites of the Church of England.'[38]

The significance of these clauses was discussed in a leading article in the Jewish Chronicle:

> The tendency of every new enactment is to obliterate the narrow boundaries drawn in former times by sectarian hatred and prejudice, and to widen the dominion, until it shall hold on the same ground all Her Majesty's subjects. We may, therefore, confidently expect that Acts of Parliament, in future, will only mention Jews in cases where the religion of the latter shall require some exemption from, or modification of, some general measure, or when some old disability is repealed.
>
> Of such a nature is Clause 23 in the Marriage and Registration Acts Amendment, just passed. This clause permits Jewish marriages to be solemnised by licence. One of the privileges formerly withheld from the Jews is thus accorded to them. Inconsiderable in itself as it is, it yet evinces the spirit which pervades the legislature. The same Act also brings to an issue a point which has long and greatly agitated the community, and has caused more bitter feeling than any other on which opinion differed.
>
> Clause 22 enables the members of the Margaret Street Synagogue to have their place of worship registered. The dissent in the community is thus acknowledged by the Government. The legislature takes cognisance of the 'British Jews', in contradistinction from the Jews in general, the secretaries of whose congregations are certified by the president of the Board of Deputies.
>
> This is an important epoch in the history of the English Jews. From it dates the legal status of Jewish non-conformity. It will now be known through the whole length and breadth of the land that there is a division in the Jewish body, a majority and a minority – which, though differing in their religious views, are yet, by Parliament, equally considered as Jews, and endowed with the same rights.
>
> We rejoice at the termination of a difference which, by granting to all like privileges, may deprive controversy of its acrimony, and rub off the asperities which might have proved painful in future collisions. Divested of all practical bearings, while yet retaining its former vital interest, the questions at issue may now be coolly analysed and examined by dissenters and conformists, and conscientious opinions formed on their importance.
>
> The Margaret Street Congregation will no longer have occasion to demand a concession from the Board of Deputies, which this, as long as the constitution obliges it to require, in religious matters, ecclesiastical

sanction, could not legally accord; and the Board of Deputies will no longer appear in the hateful light of bigotry by not granting what it was not in its power to concede.

The bone of contention is thus removed from the community. Let us hope that peace and concord will now dwell among us, that if we cannot consent to agree, we can at least agree to differ; and that if uniformity be disturbed, we may yet preserve unity.[39]

This was, indeed, a defining moment, both in 'the history of the English Jews' and in Adler's Chief Rabbinate. A year earlier, Jonas Levy had expressed surprise at Adler's consent to 'such a clause'. What, then, had prompted him to give it? A clue lies in the 'Omens of Peace' discerned early in Adler's ministry: opposition to the reformers at one moment, social and communal fraternisation at others.

In 1849, another such 'omen' had presented itself 'in the Jewish communities of London'. In circumstances not unlike the Henriques wedding, Adler had officiated at the marriage of Horatio Micholls, of the New Synagogue, to the daughter of Horatio Montefiore, a West London member. The ceremony was again held at the home of the bride, but, unlike the Angel affair, 'no pledge, declaration or signature was required by the Rev. Dr Adler in the case in question'. In the interests of peace, wrote the *Jewish Chronicle*,

> we do not now inquire into the analogy of the case with that of Jane Angel, nor into the reasons why the Rev. Dr deemed it proper to take a different course than he did then. It is enough for us that the Rev. the Chief Rabbi has acted in the spirit of toleration, and thus virtually abandoned the odious excommunication.
>
> It appears, moreover, that the Rev. Dr expressed his wish to the bridegroom that he would, after the marriage, induce his wife to refrain from attending the Reform Synagogue; but upon being told by Mr Micholls that he would make no promise to that effect, and that he would submit to no dictation or condition, the Rev. Dr consented to perform the ceremony as usual.[40]

\* \* \*     \* \* \*    \* \* \*

Little evidence of that 'spirit of toleration' emerged, however, when the final act in the Reform marriage drama was played out in relation to the Royal Commission on the Laws of Marriage. In June 1865, its chairman, Lord Chelmsford, addressed a letter to 'all the Bishops, a selection of the Clergy of the United Kingdom, Protestant and Catholic', and 'certain

Ecclesiastical Officers and other individuals' likely to assist in the inquiry. Among those invited to submit 'information as to the practical operation of the present law in those places with which you are best acquainted' were the Chief Rabbi and Sir David Salomons, MP,[41] who, although Orthodox, was a staunch advocate of Reform rights. Their evidence highlighted the divergence of opinion among the Orthodox, and the reception of their views by the Law Lords and others on the commission panel.[42]

In his pre-examination submission, Salomons traced the passage of the Marriage and Registration Acts as they affected Jews, under both William IV and Victoria, and sought to explain why, in his view, they required 'some alteration'. By their operation, he wrote,

> the registration of the secretaries of synagogues is encumbered with unnecessary formalities, and the element of thorough religious liberty, granted to all other dissenting bodies, is in the case of the Jews but imperfectly secured ... This manifest violation of the true spirit of these Acts for the purpose of enforcing religious conformity, and of establishing ecclesiastical conformity over Jewish congregations, by the assumed authority of Parliament, has been productive of great bitterness, which, after years of contention, is hardly yet allayed. A somewhat awkward attempt at a remedy has been since made in the 19 & 20 Vict. c. 119 [the 1856 Marriage and Registration Acts Amendment Act], but it neither sets free Jewish congregations, nor does it relieve the State from being a party in their religious disputes.

When, Salomons stated, the secretary of a synagogue was presented by a congregation of persons professing the Jewish religion to be certified as such, 'the question mooted is not, "Is he the secretary?" but "Are they a conforming congregation? Are they an Orthodox synagogue?"' Registration in this manner had been raised into 'an element of religious discipline and of sustaining Jewish ecclesiastical authority by the assumed power and action of Parliament; and according as a congregation of worshippers have conformed strictly to the Rabbinical rule, or deviated therefrom, so have secretaries of synagogues been accepted or repudiated'.

Salomons argued that the attempted 'modification of this extraordinary position' in the 1856 Act 'has not relieved the Legislature from the inconsistency of interfering in these internal dissensions that concern only the Jews themselves. Nor has it given complete and thorough independence to the several synagogues of the United Kingdom.' He therefore ventured to propose a remedy which, he suggested, 'ought to be readily welcomed by Jewish congregations':

Jews' synagogues are generally registered like other places of religious worship. Each one so registered should have the right of having the secretary of the congregation appointed registrar of marriages for that synagogue on the signature of the warden or wardens, or of five or ten of the regular worshippers, declared to that effect before a justice of the peace. This would give a simple and direct mode of registering the secretary of a synagogue.

It would afford to congregations the independent position they ought to hold as between the State and themselves. It would avoid the question of religion, whether founded on difference of doctrine or discipline, a matter in which the public could have no concern. It would free the State from the singular position it is now made to hold on the appointment of a registrar, whether presented by Orthodox or by dissenting Jewish congregations. It would afford to synagogues a suitable and unobjectionable remedy for that which hitherto has fostered strife, contention, and heart-burning, without one single countervailing advantage.

By the proposed change, the Jews would have the secretaries of their synagogues registered by the unfettered action of the congregations. By it, the Jews would secure whatever convenience they now enjoy in the celebration of their marriages, together with the thorough independence accorded by Parliament to all other denominations.[43]

In his formal examination, eight months later, Salomons referred to the role of the president of the Board of Deputies in authorising synagogue secretaries to register marriages. Describing the Deputies as 'a standing committee very much like that of Grievances of the Society of Friends, which observed all matters between the Jewish body and the State', he told the commissioners:

> They have at their head a gentleman [Montefiore] whom I am sure everybody respects for his high character and most exalted behaviour on all occasions. He has been president of the Board of Deputies for a great many years.
>
> It is under his signature, or that of a gentleman similarly placed at its head – who is chosen by the voice of the Board as president – that any secretary of a synagogue is made a registrar of Jewish marriages. Hence, though the power is given to one individual who may be a gentleman of high character, very enlightened and very Orthodox, you might on the contrary have it given to a man quite as Orthodox but much less enlightened.
>
> The whole power is now centred on one individual to determine

whether secretaries of synagogues shall be registered or not. Here the State lends itself, as it were, to giving authority to an individual beyond what should be possessed by any person in such a case as this.

Outlining the changes that had enabled the 'synagogue of British Jews' to register marriages, Salomons cast doubt on the efficacy of the system. 'There are', he said,

> really two Jewish powers now, I will not say independent of the State, but in accord with the State, that can certify secretaries of Jewish synagogues. That seems to me both undesirable and inexpedient.
>
> In the first place, it promotes discord in a small body by one party being enabled to assume power over the other, which is always undesirable. The next thing is that it puts the State in a very anomalous position in having to appear as a party to these religious disputes, which I believe to be very inexpedient. I have suggested a mode by which these difficulties may be entirely got rid of, giving perfect liberty to the synagogues without compromising any of their customs or convenience.

Asked by Chelmsford to describe 'the particular evil of which you complain', Salomons replied:

> If you look at it theoretically, it may be difficult at once to see where is the grievance; but if you look at it as I have seen it practised, you will see what a very great hardship it is. I will give you an instance which occurred in my own family.
>
> While these disputes were going on, a niece of mine was to marry one who belonged to the 'British' Jews' congregation. The synagogue of the British Jews' congregation was registered as a building for celebration of marriages, and there would have been no difficulty whatever in her marrying within the walls of the British synagogue. But the British Jews' synagogue having no certified secretary, the marriage could not lawfully be celebrated at home; the civil marriage was therefore first performed at the register office at Marylebone Court House by the registrar, and then afterwards the religious marriage at their own house.
>
> Even now, when reverting to the subject, it renews to my mind a most disagreeable scene of needless and painful indignity. I do not see why, as regards Jews or any other religious society, there should be a power stepping in between the State and independent congregations, which should control them in the name of the State merely on religious grounds.

Professor Travers Twiss asked Salomons: 'Are the usages of British Jews different from those of the Orthodox Jews?' 'No', he replied. 'They differ in some trifling matters, but what I understand as usages are those which have been the custom for ages. Among those congregations I have been speaking of – the Orthodox Portuguese and German Jews – even in their marriages they are not precisely the same in all their forms. Their usages are traditional. They have come down for very many years, but they are not alike.'

Twiss asked whether the Board of Deputies was an ecclesiastical authority, to which Salomons replied: 'No, but they assume to be in the interest of Orthodox ecclesiastical authority.' After further questioning, he added: 'I was a member of the Board of Deputies when this dispute first broke out and I left on record a notice of motion as a protest against their not certifying the secretary of the British Jews' synagogue. I considered that it was an attempt to promote Jewish Orthodoxy by the authority of Parliament, and nothing could be further from the object of the Marriage Act.'

Twiss: 'Does the synagogue elect its own minister, its own rabbi?' Salomons: 'Everything is elective among the Jews. It is the most complete model of a republic you can well imagine.' Chelmsford: 'How is their Chief Rabbi elected?' Salomons: 'In the same way.' Sir W. Page Wood: 'By the members of all the synagogues?' Salomons: 'Yes. The whole machinery is purely republican, and that is another reason why I object to the State creating this governing power.'[44]

\* \* \*   \* \* \*   \* \* \*

Adler's evidence was delivered in the names of the Rev. Dr Nathaniel M. Adler, Chief Rabbi, and the president of the Board of Deputies. 'I may at once state', he wrote, 'as the result of my experience, that this Act has worked well; and, after careful consideration, it seems to me that no alteration is desirable.' Referring to the modifications in the 1856 Act relating to the West London Synagogue, he submitted that

> it appears to me to be neither expedient nor judicious to extend these provisions ... Any alteration would be contrary to the wishes of the great majority of Jews in the kingdom. There are, besides, arguments involving questions of order, discipline and the constitution of the marriage contract which, in my humble opinion, militate against the extension of exceptional legislation to the general body of Jews:
>
> I. – Order.
>   1. The Board of Deputies naturally possesses better opportunities

for becoming acquainted with the personal character, attainments and diligence of the secretary of each synagogue. As it requires annual returns from each of the synagogues, it exercises a due supervision over the registry, and prevents any irregularity occurring in the same.

2. There are some provincial synagogues which have not a trustee; others in which there are not twenty or ten Jewish householders. Although there would be a sufficient number to form a synagogue (ten male adults), they would still be prevented from having a certified secretary. In other congregations, there would be the required number of (say, ten) Jewish householders, but these would consist of members of the same family, to whom it would surely be impolitic to entrust powers relating to questions of legality of marriage and legitimacy of children.

II. – *Discipline.*

1. The provisions of the Act require a synagogue of persons professing the Jewish religion, which signifies a place appropriated to, and set apart for, the public worship of the Jews, and provided with a reader or minister. Hitherto, the Board has been made acquainted by the Chief Rabbi whether a congregation possessed such a real Jewish synagogue or not.

2. Experience has taught me that petty dissensions, altogether unconnected with religious matters, have sometimes arisen in the smaller provincial congregations. But the intimate connection subsisting between those congregations and myself or the Board of Deputies has enabled me or the Board to bring about a speedy reconciliation between the disputants.

III. – *Constitution of the Marriage Contract.*

The Act provides that every secretary shall satisfy himself that the proceedings in relation to a marriage solemnised between two persons professing the Jewish religion, of whom the husband belongs to his synagogue, have been conformable to the usages of the Jewish religion. Now, according to the Jewish religion, the marriage is not merely a civil contract, but bears an essentially religious character. From Genesis 2:18, where it is declared that God institutes matrimony, down to Malachi 2:14, where we read that 'God is witness between man and the wife of his youth', the idea runs throughout Scriptures that wedlock is based upon religion. Now, in order to render the marriage normal and valid according to Jewish laws, the following is required:

1. That it be fully ascertained that the persons between whom the

marriage is to be contracted do not stand within the degrees of consanguinity or affinity prohibited by the Jewish laws and the law of the land.

2. *Evidence is needed that both the parties are Jews.*

3. In the case of a widow or a widower, who are about to be married, convincing proof of the death of the former husband or wife is required.

4. Two fit and proper witnesses must be present during the solemnisation of the marriage and attest the same.

5. The religious ceremony consists of

(a) the putting of the ring on the finger of the bride by the bridegroom, while pronouncing the words, 'Thou art wedded unto me, according to the law of Moses and Israel';

(b) the pronouncing of the benediction by the minister before and after the marriage vow (alluded to in Genesis 24:60, and Ruth 4:11–12);

(c) the publication of the marriage contract (alluded to in Tobit 7:13–14).[45]

Hitherto, all these conditions (involving the necessary investigations and observances), which are indispensable for the marriage being conformable to the usages of the Jewish religion, have been duly fulfilled, as the secretary of the synagogue has stood directly under the control of the authorities. Should this control be withdrawn, there will be no guarantee that the marriage takes place in conformity to the usages of the Jewish religion, as required by the Act of Parliament.

Adler concluded his evidence with an expression of hope 'that the Acts at present in force, which are applicable to the entire body of Jews, will remain unaltered'.[46]

\* \* \*  \* \* \*  \* \* \*

When the Commission issued its recommendations, that hope seemed dashed. Siding with Salomons in most respects, it declared:

It has been strongly represented to us by Alderman Salomons that the manner in which the secretaries of Jewish synagogues are now required by law to be certified is objectionable, as giving to the president of the London Deputies of British Jews a virtual control over the liberty of marriage in all synagogues (other than those in connection with the West London Synagogue), which he may deem not to be properly constituted, according to his own views of Orthodox Jewish doctrine or discipline.

The circumstances which led to the exception, by a special Act of Parliament, of the West London Synagogue, and other synagogues in connection with it, from this control, and the exceedingly anomalous character of that legislation, would alone be sufficient to satisfy us of the soundness of this opinion: and we think it will be proper (as Alderman Salomons suggests) to give to all synagogues of persons professing the Jewish religion in the United Kingdom (whether separatists from other Jewish synagogues, or not) the same means of obtaining State recognition for their secretaries (as official witnesses of marriage) which are given to other congregations of Nonconformists desirous of having their places of worship registered for the solemnisation of marriage.

We should, therefore, propose that the secretary of every registered Jewish synagogue should be entitled to act as registrar of marriages for that synagogue, upon the certificate of the warden or wardens, or of ten householders, declaring before a justice of the peace that they been regular worshippers in such synagogue for not less than one year next preceding.

Whatever may be the ceremonies or usages of Jews, appropriate to the due solemnisation of marriage, we are of opinion that the State ought not in any case to take notice of or enforce compliance with such ceremonies or usages, as necessary to the validity of any marriage, in other respects duly solemnised. Marriage ought, in all such cases, to be held well constituted by words of mutual consent to be husband and wife (or of mutual declaration that they are husband and wife), solemnly interchanged between the parties, in the presence of any authorised celebrant or official witness.

On the other hand, we do not propose that any deviation should be required by law from the internal regulations, usages, or discipline of any church or religious body, with respect to the solemnisation of marriage, or with respect to the obligation of ministers to solemnise marriage on compliance with the legal requisites. Marriages cannot lawfully be contracted in England or Ireland according to the usages of Jews, unless both parties are Jews.

It has, however, been suggested to us, by witnesses from different parts of the United Kingdom, that power ought to be given to some proper authority to dispense, in proper cases, with the ordinary length of notice and period of residence.

If such a power is entrusted, not to all those who are authorised to give the ordinary certificate, but only to to superior authority, when such an authority is provided by the organisation of the particular religious communion, and (in the absence of such a superior authority) to the superintendent or district registrar, and if its exercise is strictly limited to cases in which both the parties to be married are certified to be of the same religious profession by the officiating ministers (or by the official witnesses, if they are Quakers or Jews), of the places of worship, or synagogues, which they usually attend, we think it may safely, and even advantageously, be granted.[47]

In the event, Adler's view on the significance of a 'real Jewish synagogue' prevailed. The commissioners' recommendations, based on Salomons' evidence, were disregarded, and the prerogatives of Reform contained. To this day, the West London, in its role as 'parent synagogue' and in consultation with the president of the Board of Deputies, is alone responsible for authorising the marriage secretaries of all newly established Reform congregations in the United Kingdom.[48] Compared, however, to the Orthodox camp's earlier victory in what has been termed 'the Anglo-Jewish revolt of 1853'[49] – the exclusion of four newly elected Reform representatives from the Board – this success by Adler was but a minor achievement.

# 3

# Censure and Silence

In fact, the Board of Deputies' controversy of 1853 – in which Montefiore again played a crucial role, with Adler acting as a silent bystander – was less a revolt than a rout. As evenly divided as were the deputies over the issue – Reform representation on the Board – its outcome was dictated, through the organisation's constitution, by its ecclesiastical authorities, and by their ruling that any congregation on Reform lines was deemed not to be 'a synagogue of persons professing the Jewish religion'. That this ruling was hotly disputed and widely discarded, given the mood of the times, was well-nigh inevitable, leading to simmering dissension long after the altercation had faded away.

The 1836 constitution had laid down the conditions of synagogue membership under which deputies could be formally elected, adding, in 1841, the hitherto unwritten remit of the ecclesiastical authorities as the community's (and the Board's) spiritual guides. A year later – following Hirschell's refusal to certify Burton Street as a synagogue, and Montefiore's veto on Marks as its marriage secretary – the president reported that he had taken 'eminent counsel's opinion on the subject, which confirmed that he had exercised a sound discretion and that, as he had acted on the advice of the Chief Rabbi and Beth Din, the courts would not compel him to grant a certificate'. Goldsmid had invited Montefiore to rule that 'the new place of worship is "a synagogue of persons professing the Jewish religion – although you may not consider ours to be the *right kind of Judaism*" – but apparently he found himself unable to comply with this suggestion'.[1]

Montefiore's sensibilities, however, were more real than 'apparent', leading to a decade 'of mounting agitation against the Board's self-perpetuating conservatism, undemocratic system of governance, anachronistic structure and communal torpor'.[2] His successes as overseas emissary had 'greatly reinforced the self-confidence and influence of the oligarchic regime which dominated the community and of which he was the centrepiece. At the Board, he occupied an apparently unassailable position. He combined great personal courtesy with a stubborn disdain for opposition and a reluctance, of varying depths, to depart from office.'[3]

Salomons and his fellow emancipationist, Lionel de Rothschild, questioned what they regarded as 'archaic'[4] attitudes towards the secessionists and their exclusion from the Board. New men among 'the better-off Jewish middle classes' were also striving to be heard, as were those Jews anxious to buttress provincial representation over and above the existing deputies for Manchester and Liverpool (themselves London residents), an indication of their 'increasing self-consciousness and confidence, especially in the newer and growing urban centres'.[5] Thus, when Board elections were held in the spring of 1853, designed to address some of these concerns, the scene was set for what its secretary was to describe, some sixty years later, as 'a complete fiasco'.[6]

The central figures in the dispute were four West London members – three from the metropolis, the fourth a Sunderland colliery owner – who presented themselves as candidates for provincial congregations. David Jonassohn, a member of the Israelite Congregation of Sunderland, had joined the West London Synagogue after the death of Benjamin Elkin ('whose name I never heard mentioned before that day') in protest against what he perceived as the 'religious persecution adopted by the Chief Rabbi and other authorities'.[7] The three Londoners were Elias Davis (standing for Norwich), Jacob Levi Elkin, Benjamin's son (for Portsea/Portsmouth), and Samuel Ellis (for Chatham).

Elkin, a Moorgate merchant, was president of the West London, and Ellis had been a member since its foundation, having briefly represented the Western Synagogue before resigning in 1838. Davis, a clothier and common councillor of the City of London, was a member of both the Great and the West London. In the Chief Rabbinical election, he had voted for Hirschfield as 'a challenge to the largely self-perpetuating committee which ruled the Great Synagogue', regarding it as wielding disproportionate power within the community.[8]

The Board elections were held on the first Sunday in Iyar,[9] within months of the Commons vote (subsequently overruled by the Lords) for the removal of Jewish disabilities. All four Reform candidates were successful and, as a result, 'the members of the Reform congregation, recognising the parallel between their exclusion from the Board of Deputies and the exclusion of Jews from Parliament, seized the opportunity to test their rights by employing in Bevis Marks the same methods that Baron Rothschild and Mr Salomons had employed at St Stephen's'.[10] Notice of their success reached the Board at its scheduled meeting on 18 August 1853, attended by fifteen deputies, under Montefiore's chairmanship, in the vestry room of Bevis Marks.[11]

\* \* \*   \* \* \*   \* \* \*

The 'test' had begun. First on his feet was Montefiore's nephew, Louis Cohen, of the Great Synagogue, seeking to move a resolution that 'any member or seat-holder of a place of worship which does not conform in religious matters to the ecclesiastical authorities as heretofore, and agreeably to laws one and two of the constitution, is not qualified to fill the office of deputy at this Board'. The motion was seconded by Nathan Defries, of the Maiden Lane Synagogue, with the support of Henry Harris, president of Maiden Lane, and Judah Aloof, of Bevis Marks. They were vigorously opposed by, among others, the two Rothschilds – Baron Lionel and Sir Anthony – and Salomons, whose 'stout resistance'[12] during the four-hour debate was largely responsible for the resolution's withdrawal.

Crucially, the Board followed its usual custom of allowing the newly elected members to take their seats at the next meeting. Since these deputies included the West London members, the tinder-box was primed for an explosive session. On 31 August, during proceedings later described as 'extraordinary',[13] the thirty-two deputies prepared to argue the issue. No sooner had Cohen sought to resubmit his resolution than David Hesse (Manchester) drew Montefiore's attention to letters which, he said, 'should be placed before the Board as the first business of the evening'. After consultations between the president and the secretary, Montefiore ruled that the letters were inadmissible. Published the following week,[14] they were from Ellis, Elkin and Davis protesting against 'the proposed resolution for creating a new qualification for the office of a deputy being put to the vote, and against any exclusion of members of this Board which may be founded on such resolution, if carried'.

At this point, the three men (Jonassohn was away) entered the vestry and took their seats in the chamber. Declaring that he 'espied strangers in the room', Montefiore asked them to leave and warned that, if they failed to comply, he would send for the police and have them forcibly removed. The three, however, remained in their seats. After a lapse of a several minutes, in total silence, Montefiore appealed to his fellow deputies for support, threatening to walk out if it were not forthcoming:

> A scene of the most indescribable uproar then ensued, one party contending for, another against, the right of the three members to take their seats.
>
> The uproar was so great that no one could be distinctly understood. A precipitate member procured a police constable; but, by the judicious orders of the wardens of the Great Synagogue, Sir Anthony de Rothschild and Mr Lewis Jacobs, the officer was not permitted to enter the building.

The chairman then vacated the chair. Baron de Rothschild, Sir A. de Rothschild, Mr B.S. Phillips, and other members, attempted to address the meeting, but failed, so intense was the clamour liberal members met with whenever they essayed to procure a hearing. Mr Alderman Salomons, in the difficult position in which the meeting was placed, was requested to take the chair, so that business might be proceeded with; but, under the circumstances, he declined doing so. At this stage of the meeting, the president and the secretary retired from the room, the latter carrying away with him the books and papers. All idea of business then vanished. The members formed themselves into groups, discussing what the majority considered the very extraordinary proceedings of the meeting.[15]

Dispersing in disarray, the deputies were summoned to reassemble the following Thursday.

\* \* \*   \* \* \*   \* \* \*

Several weeks into the affair, Adler's silence had begun to be noticed. The anger over Benjamin Elkin's funeral had largely evaporated, but the perceived disparity between the Chief Rabbi's aspirations and his actions remained dissonant and divisive. Addressing itself directly to Adler, the *Jewish Chronicle* declared:

> You need not be told by us – it might be deemed presumptuous were we to do so – that the first duty of a minister of religion is to promote peace and good will among the flock committed to his pious charge. To this desirable end he should devote every energy of his mind and every effort of his will; and never were those exertions more imperatively demanded than at the present hour.
>
> Dr Adler, as Chief Rabbi of the Jews of this mighty Empire, you occupy a station, and possess an influence, equalled by no other Jewish ecclesiastic. You preside over congregations who are disposed to pay the utmost deference to your influence, to your advice, and to your exhortations.
>
> The community of Israel in this land of liberty and enlightenment is divided – O how unhappily divided – into hostile camps. There is no one who comes forth to save God's heritage from the chaos into which it is falling. Come forth, we beseech you, in the might of your moral power. Instil the desire for peace and brotherly love into the hearts, minds and souls of those who thus wage internecine war.
>
> Call these discordant elements together; compel them, by the force

of your prerogative, to reunite in the bond of holy brotherhood. Counsel the promoters of an ill-omened resolution to withdraw it ere the fatal words be pronounced – 'It is too late'.[16]

Montefiore, for his part, was urged to 'withdraw the support of your name and influence, used for the purpose of carrying out a resolution which, if successful, would destroy among your brethren every vestige of religious liberty'. As for the 'liberal deputies, both metropolitan and provincial', their task was vital, 'in the name of every liberal principle – in the cause of the acquisition of our civil and religious liberties from without, which are placed in jeopardy': to

> set the final seal of your disapprobation to the attempt to fetter the consciences and religious privileges of your brethren and constituents ...
>
> A single vote may decide at this momentous crisis, and it will hereafter be some consolation for you to reflect that, if even unsuccessful, you did your duty in the hour of danger and that, come what will, you at least had no share in the responsibility.

On the appointed day, with Montefiore again presiding, the deputies gathered at Bevis Marks to face 'this momentous crisis'. It soon became clear, with suggestions of reconciliation continually surfacing, that Adler's authority was central to a solution.

Responding to a motion to admit Jonassohn, for forty years a member of an Orthodox synagogue, Harris said that, while wishing 'the olive-branch' to have emanated first from the West London, 'in the interests of peace in the community' he desired that 'extreme opinions be avoided and some middle course devised'. He therefore proposed an amendment that 'consideration of the returns of the deputies from Portsea, Sunderland, Chatham and Norwich be postponed for two months and that a committee of five members of the Board be appointed to confer with an equal number of members of the Margaret Street congregation, with a view to effecting a reconciliation between the said congregation and the ecclesiastical authorities'.

Seconding the proposal, David Barnett (Birmingham Old Congregation) argued that 'we shall not be doing justice to our community if we do not strain every nerve to bring peace into it. If the wound be not soon healed, the unfortunate breach, already too wide, will widen and widen.' Judah Hart (Dover) urged his colleagues to 'know no difference, but let him who is in error, whether Orthodox or Reformer, give way. Let us not strive for victory, for the triumph of one man or one party over another. Our mission is peace and reconciliation.'

Speaking, he said, for the Orthodox who 'disclaim in toto those sentiments of bigotry and intolerance imputed to us', Abraham Joseph (Plymouth) remarked of Adler:

> Our religious rights and ceremonies are in the keeping of a gentleman who, as an enlightened ecclesiastic, would be only too happy to see peace restored to his flock, so that it could be brought about without a sacrifice of any of the fundamental laws of our holy faith. Our worthy ecclesiastical chief has suggested a mode of reconciliation; and I am certain that the day on which peace shall be attained will be prized by him as the happiest day of his life. The amendment offers preliminaries of peace on the part of the Orthodox, and it now remains to be seen if other parties are willing to meet on equal ground.

While declaring himself 'opposed to the admission of these gentlemen', Joseph Aloof told the meeting that he was 'willing to aid in restoring peace to our community', since he 'regretted to see the disunion at present existing in many families. Let all matters be referred to the Chief Rabbi, and no doubt he will try to effect a reconciliation. But a stand must be made against our splitting into sects, for it will not redound to our credit for Christians to be able to say that we, the Jews, are split into sects.'

Once again, the most vigorous opponents were Salomons and Lionel de Rothschild. While applauding the 'conciliatory spirit' in which the amendment had been tabled, Salomons condemned its assuming 'a right to inquire into the religious principles of gentlemen who have been returned as deputies'.

He would allow no man to judge of his Orthodoxy, he said; he was there as one who had a right to form his own Orthodoxy. He denied the right of any man to question him

> whether I am an Orthodox or a reforming Jew. I am here as an Englishman, and on that I take my stand. Let us remember how much we have suffered from religious inquisitions and persecutions, and let us not act thus among ourselves.
>
> By the course to be adopted, might you not seriously injure the community at large? You are running the risk of losing the heads of your schools, the patrons of your benevolent institutions, and the supporters of your charities, for many of such honourable positions are held by members of the Margaret Street Synagogue. It is rather late in the day to dive into men's religious opinions, for to do so you will have to go with a lantern to examine the texts and Orthodox principles of the religious opinions held by parties appointed and fit for office.

Similarly declaring himself 'most decidedly' opposed to the amendment, Lionel de Rothschild said that the question referred 'not to the Margaret Street congregation, or to Orthodox or Reform synagogues, but to whether a gentleman, duly qualified, is entitled to sit on the Board. It matters not to what synagogue he belongs, but having been elected, he is entitled to his seat.' Yielding to none, he declared, in his desire for peace, he believed it was for the Board, the representatives of more than 30,000 Jews,

> to use every exertion to restore peace and union among the community. It is not that we should go over to their [the reformers'] opinions. Nor is it by telling them that we are right and they are wrong, but by acting generously, and by admitting them, that we will gain them over to our opinions.
>
> We are not compelled or called on to give up our opinions, but we might be enabled, by a judicious course of proceeding, to induce them to change or modify theirs. Let us set an example that might confer incalculable good on our community, that might be the means of establishing peace among friends and relations who have unhappily been too long separated.

Put to the vote, the amendment to establish a conciliation committee was carried by nineteen votes to eighteen. Four members were absent from the division, and the returns of five – the representatives of Chatham, Norwich, Portsea, Sunderland and Sheerness – 'awaited decision'. It was agreed to forward a copy of the resolution to the ecclesiastical authorities, to the Margaret Street congregation, and to Elkin, Davis, Jonassohn and Ellis.

Harris then rose to propose the members of his committee. On mention of Montefiore's name, Salomons objected, stating that it was 'unfair to place the president in a position where he could not be impartial'. Montefiore thereupon declined to serve, and Salomons followed suit. The committee, he said, would be 'of an inquisitorial nature', having to inquire into 'the religious opinions entertained by gentlemen claiming seats on the Board', and he 'could not entertain any such interference with a man's honest religious convictions'. With others similarly declining to serve, the committee remained unformed by the close of the meeting.

Five hours into the deliberations, the four Reform members, who had been waiting in an anteroom, were summoned to the vestry and told of the decision. After addressing the Board, Ellis submitted a written appeal on behalf of himself, Elkin and Davis, protesting against any resolution being passed, or proceedings being taken, at the meeting held this evening, by reason of our having been illegally excluded therefrom when desirous of being present and thus prevented from offering our opinions upon any subjects which might be brought forward. We shall therefore consider and treat any such resolutions or proceedings as wholly illegal and void. This our protest is without prejudice to our remedies for our exclusion from the meeting of the deputies.

As the three left the room, Jonassohn remained in his seat, asserting that he had a duty to his constituents and that he would be failing in that duty were he to retire from the meeting, 'unless on the application of physical force'. On Montefiore's orders, the secretary ordered Jonassohn to leave, 'such order entitling the gentleman to consider that physical force has been applied'.[17]

* * *   * * *   * * *

On the morning after the meeting, Montefiore sent a copy of the resolutions to 'J.L. Elkin, Warden-President, Margaret Street Congregation', in the 'fervent hope that they may be effectual in producing that concord and unanimity which are so essential to the welfare of the whole Jewish community'. Acknowledging the letter, Elkin wrote: 'I have to inform you that I am not warden of the Margaret Street congregation, nor do I know of any establishment existing under that denomination. I am one of the wardens of the West London Synagogue of British Jews, and any communication addressed to me or my colleagues will receive every attention.'

Montefiore responded that 'if you will be so good as to refer to the resolution which accompanied my letter, you will observe that the congregational body therein referred to is designated "The Margaret Street Congregation". It must be obvious, therefore, that it was my duty to adopt the words of the resolution.' Elkin retorted: 'I am not unmindful of the wording of the resolution to which you refer and I venture to think that you, on reflection, will perceive that I cannot recognise such title, the "congregational body" over which I preside being the West London Synagogue of British Jews.' He assured Montefiore that he had 'no intention of creating difficulties' and that 'any communication I may receive in my official capacity shall meet with my best attention'.[18] These letters were laid before a meeting of the Board on 22 September, during which the conciliation committee was eventually formed. With Henry Harris as chairman, it also comprised Jonas Levy, Moses Haim Picciotto (Bevis Marks), Judah Hart and David Hyam (Ipswich).

A fortnight later, Harris wrote again to Elkin, addressing him as 'Warden-President' and pointing out that the committee 'have no doubt that the body described in the resolution as the Margaret Street Congregation is the same as the body designated by you in your letters as the West London Synagogue of British Jews. We trust, therefore, that you will consider the preliminary objection before referred to is now obviated and that, in the spirit of peace and conciliation, the joint committees will, without delay, enter upon their important duties.'

After further fruitless exchanges spanning almost a month, Elkin again wrote that he was prevented from considering as official 'any document which is not addressed to me as warden of the West London Synagogue of British Jews' and that, 'if you persist in designating me by a title which I cannot acknowledge, I must suggest that, in such case, our correspondence should now cease, as it can lead to no practical result'.

Anxious to advance the affair without conceding the principle, Harris agreed as a 'technicality', for the purpose of enabling Elkin to place the resolution before his council, to describe him as warden of the West London Synagogue, 'in the sincere hope that this may be the precursor to a peaceful and satisfactory settlement of the questions at issue'. One object, he wrote, had pervaded the minds of his committee throughout – 'the extreme desirability of effecting, if possible, a reconciliation between your congregation and the authorities, thus reuniting in the bonds of brotherhood all classes of the Jews in England'.

On 6 November, the matter was considered at a meeting of the West London council. Its findings, contained in a letter from the congregation's chairman, Daniel Mocatta, to Harris, drew the bitter and long-running duel to an unhappy conclusion:

> 1. That this Council approve of Mr Elkin's having refused to receive, as official, letters not addressed to him under his official designation; but are of opinion that a similar objection applies to their founding any proceeding, such as the appointment of a Committee, on Mr Harris' last letter, which, although addressed to Mr Elkin, as a warden of this synagogue, couples that designation with reservations and stipulations of a highly objectionable character.
>
> 2. That it appears, however, to this Council that it will prevent future misunderstanding at once to state that if Mr Harris' communications had been addressed in the ordinary and proper way to Mr Elkin, in his official capacity, this Council would still have considered themselves as wholly precluded from appointing a Committee to confer with the Committee of which Mr Harris states himself to be

the chairman, and which is alleged to have been appointed by the Board of Deputies of British Jews.

3. That this Synagogue has taken no part in, and is in no way connected with, the election of certain members of other synagogues, who are also members of this congregation, to represent such other synagogues at the Board of Deputies; and that those gentlemen have acted in the matter in their individual capacities, or on behalf of the congregations which they represent, but certainly not under any authority from the 'West London Synagogue'.

4. That this Council would, therefore, have been desirous not to express any opinion on the proceedings arising out of those elections; but find themselves compelled to do so in order to explain the reasons which must have prevented this congregation from entering into communication with the Committee just referred to.

5. That it appears, from statements contained in public prints, and to which no contradiction has been given, that the appointment of the Committee in question took place at a meeting of certain members of the Board of Deputies, from which other members of that Board were excluded; and that the Committee would not have been appointed, except by means of such exclusion.

6. That it further appears that that Committee was appointed for a purpose wholly beyond the functions of even a duly constituted meeting of the Board of Deputies; to which Board the congregations electing it have entrusted the duty of guarding, on their behalf, against legislative and municipal enactments infringing the rights of the Jews, but not that of interfering in religious questions among the Jews themselves.

7. That this Council would, therefore, in any case, have felt it to be impossible for this synagogue, desirous as its members are of cultivating friendly feelings with all their coreligionists, to communicate or to appoint a Committee of their number to communicate with a Committee whose appointment is affected by the irregularities above described.

Harris replied:

I have to acknowledge the receipt of a document purporting to be a copy of resolutions alleged to have been passed at a meeting of the Council of your Congregation, holden on the sixth inst., and appearing to bear your signature as chairman, and forwarded to me as chairman of a committee appointed by the Board of Deputies of the British Jews on the eighth of September last. I have submitted such document to the committee, and they entirely dissent from the sentiments expressed therein.

The committee deeply deplore that your Council would, under any circumstances, have declined to appoint a committee to confer with any committee appointed by the Board of Deputies for the purposes mentioned in their resolution of the eighth of September last.

The committee also desire to state that, in their opinion, your Council, in their sixth resolution, have not correctly stated the extent of the duties and functions of the Board of Deputies of the British Jews, which are not only to guard against legislative and municipal enactments, etc., but also 'to use such means as they may deem requisite in order that no infraction from the religious rites, customs and privileges of the Jewish community may ensue therefrom'.

Moreover, it must be obvious that the Board of Deputies, appointed as it is to watch over, act for and seek the general welfare of the Jewish community at large, was justly anxious and fully justified in taking such steps as they believed to be conducive to the settlement of those unhappy differences which all right-minded persons must regret, and to seek the establishment of peace and concord among the British Jews.

The committee, in now closing the correspondence, lament to observe that it has not led to a more happy result; and request me to intimate to you that, in making their report to the Board of Deputies, they will not fail to lay before them a copy of the document directed to be forwarded to me as their chairman.[19]

Reporting on the failure of his mission to a meeting of deputies nine days later, Harris expressed regret that their efforts, and the wishes of the Board, had been unavailing in seeking to restore harmony throughout the community, 'by reason of the Margaret Street congregation having refused to appoint a committee to confer on the subject, upon alleged grounds equally applicable (if at all) at all times, and to any committee your Board might appoint for the same purpose'.

Following consideration of the report, Benjamin Phillips gave notice of a motion to be debated at the next meeting of the Board – that Jonassohn, Ellis, Elkin and Davis, having been elected deputies, 'be requested to take their seats' – in the light of a challenge issued by the four. 'We have become indirectly aware', they had written,

> that the Board is to meet tomorrow [23 November], and although we shall not present ourselves at that meeting, wishing for the sake of peace to give every reasonable time for calm deliberation, yet we remind you that such a period has now elapsed, and that if we are not

summoned to the next following meeting [7 December], we shall consider our admission as permanently opposed and feel bound to act accordingly.

One further document had been placed before the November meeting – a response received that week from the Chief Rabbi to the Board's resolution, passed nearly three months earlier, seeking a reconciliation between the Margaret Street congregation and the ecclesiastical authorities. Brief and blunt, Adler reaffirmed his determination 'to protect the sacred ordinances of our holy religion' and expressed his 'great anxiety to see peace restored to the community'. No remedy was advanced, however, and no other statement had emanated from his office since the controversy erupted after the Iyar elections.

\* \* \*     \* \* \*     \* \* \*

The penultimate act in the drama, before a much-delayed finale, took place under Montefiore's chairmanship on 7 December 1853.[20] After expressing gratitude to the Harris committee for the 'judicious and able fulfilment of the trust confided to their care', the deputies set about debating, along familiar lines, the admission of the four Reform members. Before them was Phillips' resolution of the previous meeting – that the four, 'having been duly elected, do take their seats' – and a speedily appended amendment, tabled by Joseph and citing the constitution's seventeenth clause, seeking to disqualify the men and to nullify their election.

Following heated argument on both sides, Louis Cohen – who, four months earlier, had launched the battle to reject as a deputy 'any member or seat-holder of a place of worship which does not conform in religious matters to the ecclesiastical authorities' – rose to reaffirm his position. 'I am ready', he conceded,

> to admit that there is no excommunication in existence. The Chief Rabbi possesses no such power. Maimonides has said that, even if a Chief Rabbi and a whole congregation were to issue an excommunication, if would be of no effect.
>
> There is, in this case, no excommunication; there is only a caution. But in the responsa of Maimonides, it is distinctly stated that we dare not hold *religious* intercourse with them [the seceders], nor join with them in forming a minyan. I am ready to eat, drink and trade with these gentlemen, and with the members of their congregation. But I will not join with them in any *religious* act; and therefore, considering them disqualified, I cannot vote for their admission.

While supporting Cohen on the question of admission, Israel Barned, of Liverpool, disputed his view of the caution. 'I know very little about *cherems*', he admitted, 'but one stands in the way of these gentlemen. We cannot abolish this excommunication: the gentlemen of the Margaret Street congregation must make an application to the ecclesiastical authorities. Nor are they asked to go down on their knees, but if *they* yield nothing, why should *we* yield everything?'

The ecclesiastical authorities, conversely, troubled Lionel de Rothschild. 'I have every respect for them', he declared, 'but I am not going to be led by them as by a Catholic priest. They might be – and no doubt are – very learned, but they have no right to inquire of me whether I keep one day or two days of the festivals ... Have we a right to go into a neighbour's house and ask him what he is doing? We all talk of peace, but the only mode of preserving it is to admit the four gentlemen to those seats to which they have been legally and duly elected.'

Salomons took issue with Cohen – 'a high authority in this room' – who had spoken of 'no excommunication, only a caution'. Any such caution, he said,

> does not operate against these gentlemen taking their seats. In 1840, we knew not how far this Reform movement would go, but now we know its extent. Besides, intermarriages have taken place between the two parties: a nephew of the president is married to the daughter of a founder of the Reform movement. Not only did Baron de Goldsmid and Sir Moses attend the wedding ceremony, but they later acted as godfathers. Where, then, is the disqualification?

As midnight passed, the deputies divided and cast their votes. Three months earlier, the *Jewish Chronicle* had predicted that 'a single vote may decide at this momentous crisis'. And so it transpired: twenty-three for the amendment to disqualify, twenty-three against.[21] Montefiore thereupon cast his vote, supporting the amendment and sealing the exclusion of Reform representatives on the Board for the next thirty years. Later that day, he defended his decision:

> I deem it to be a duty which I owe to the London Committee of Deputies of the British Jews, over which I have the honour to preside, as well as to my coreligionists generally, that I should avail myself of an opportunity which was not afforded me at the meeting of the Board held last evening, briefly to state the reasons which influenced me in giving my casting vote in favour of the amendment on the motion of Mr B.S. Phillips.

> My vote was based on religious grounds and the declaration of the ecclesiastical authorities, and it was also supported by the fact that I had obtained the legal opinion of two eminent counsel as to the powers of the Board, who advised that 'the Board of Deputies is not only fully entitled, but that it is its duty, to ascertain whether the persons nominated by the respective synagogues possess the qualifications prescribed'...[22]
>
> I think it proper to add that a sense of impartiality, and a desire not to influence the Board in its own view of the momentous subject submitted to its consideration, alone prevented me from causing the case and opinion to be read previously to the division taking place.

Montefiore's handling of the debate angered Salomons, who, in an exchange of letters over subsequent days, berated the president on questions of procedure.[23] And in a message to the congregation he represented – the New – Salomons submitted his resignation from the Board, asking them bluntly, 'Why have we not peace?'

> I will fearlessly tell you why. It is in consequence of the false pride and high notions of ecclesiastical prerogative which prevail in one of the London 'congregations', and that one, the synagogue from which the Margaret Street Synagogue has mainly sprung. If we wish to know why we are yet in collision, we must look to Bevis Marks for a reply. A minority is there overruling the great majority of the Jewish community; and you must therefore prepare yourselves to be emancipated from the control of that minority.
>
> Show yourselves resolved to do it, and you will effect it without much trouble ... The fact can no longer be concealed that the Margaret Street Synagogue has been long and unjustly deprived of rights which Parliament enacted for it as well as for us – for the minority as well as for the majority of persons professing the Jewish religion. Their rights are based, as are ours, on the authority of the legislature; and no ecclesiastical caution can avail on this point, either in reason or in law, if justice and fair dealing prevail.
>
> Let such a course be adopted, and peace will be restored to the community; and even those who now so obstinately maintain an opposite policy will be among the foremost to rejoice at the re-establishment of harmony and of that brotherly love which is characteristic of the Jewish people throughout the world.[24]

Salomons' resignation was strongly opposed by the New and, a fortnight later, he agreed to withdraw it, torn between his disgust at the 'retrograde proceedings' of the Board and the trust shown in him by his congregation, 'who have in so marked a manner sanctioned my conduct there'. But, again, he reverted to the question of ecclesiastical authority:

> Parliament, in the year 1836, enacted a general registration for marriages, requiring all marriages, those of Jews as well as others, to be registered by a civil authority. The legislature enacted that the secretary of every synagogue of persons professing the Jewish religion should be the registering officer of every Jewish marriage, and these marriages were to be according to the usages of the Jews. The president of the Board of Deputies has to certify who is the secretary of a synagogue of persons professing the Jewish religion.
>
> In all this, not one word arises about ecclesiastical authority, the object of the legislature being to allow every person to marry according to his own religious forms, and not to give religious power or authority to any individual whatever. Yet this great privilege, conceded by Parliament to every synagogue of persons professing the Jewish religion, has been withheld from the Margaret Street congregation, on the hollow pretence that it is not a synagogue, and that it cannot be, without the consent of the ecclesiastical authorities.
>
> Moreover, that synagogue is under the ban of a 'caution', or excommunication, pronounced against it by the ecclesiastical authorities, which is still unrepealed. Not satisfied with denying this privilege to that synagogue, the Board of Deputies even refuses to acknowledge the election of any person chosen to represent an Orthodox synagogue who is at the same time a member of the Margaret Street congregation, and would declare such an election to be null and void. It desires to bolster up this monstrous doctrine by a show of legal opinions, which fail in the main point submitted.
>
> It is unfortunate for ecclesiastical authority to be engaged in such a contest, for it is our duty to pay it all due respect. But it becomes us also to take care that it is kept within proper bounds, and that it shall not be used by any persons whatever to the prejudice of any public or social right.
>
> There is no class of Her Majesty's subjects more interested than the Jews in the great principle that the complete enjoyment of public rights ought to be perfectly independent of religious conformity. Our own dire sufferings in all ages and in all countries attest the evil consequences resulting from the violation of this great principle.
>
> We have wisely stipulated with our superior ecclesiastical authority that no excommunication should be pronounced. Yet shall we

now sit quietly by and permit the Board of Deputies, on the miserable pretence of giving effect to a 'caution' or excommunication pronounced by ecclesiastical authority, to cancel the privileges of duly qualified members of congregations, and deprive other members of the Jewish family of public rights, given by Parliament to all synagogues of persons professing the Jewish religion, simply because they do not adhere in all religious matters to ecclesiastical authority?[25]

The efficacy of Adler's authority became, for the time being, the last word on the subject. Was there or was there not, inquired the *Jewish Chronicle*, an excommunication in existence? If the latter, did a 'mere caution' carry the same, 'or a portion of the same', consequences? 'Who shall decide? To whose opinion are we to look in this emergency? To whom but to him who is our spiritual adviser – the Chief Rabbi. He can no longer remain silent.'[26]

'Will Dr Adler respond to this call?' asked the paper a week later. 'And how can he make known his opinion, whether there be or be not an excommunication? Or will the Chief Rabbi continue to remain silent when he sees that his flock are being torn asunder by internecine contentions and feuds?'[27]

\* \* \*   \* \* \*   \* \* \*

After a period of silence that had taxed the patience of even his closest supporters, Adler's response to Reform – as he put it, 'to the struggle of Judaism within' – came within days of this appeal, in a Chanukkah sermon entitled 'Solomon's Judgment',[28] which provoked widespread reaction throughout the community and again gave rise to questions about Montefiore's role in ecclesiastical affairs. Taking as his text the scriptural passage describing the mothers' tussle over their respective children – one dead, the other alive – Adler compared 'the struggle within' to the bitterness and strife that had confronted King Solomon:[29]

> You know our holy faith has two elements, the Written and the Oral Law, both of which are divine – each requires the other, they supply each other, and are 'like two young roes that are twins'. Without the Oral Law, the written word of the Bible could not be rightly read, because the whole mode of punctuation and accentuation is handed down by tradition; every doctrine, every ordinance and every law would be a sealed book, a riddle without solution, for the word of God is exceedingly deep, deep as the sea.
> And although not all is divine which is found in the writings of

our sages – and a large portion is avowedly of human origin, and only our adversaries confound and confuse both together, to serve their own purpose – yet the existence of an Oral Law cannot be denied. Nevertheless, there have been, and there are still, some within our own pale who will believe in the divinity of the Written Law and who yet deny the divinity of the Oral Law; and, like the Sadducees with the Pharisees of ancient times, and the Karaites with the Rabbanites of the Middle Ages, they contend with each other for precedence.[30]

Reverting to his analogy of the Solomonic judgment, Adler continued:

> While these say, 'Ours is the living, and yours the dead one', those contradict, saying, 'The dead is yours, the living one ours.' But, in truth, the struggle can be but in words, for when it comes to the judgment – when the sword should be used to divide the living child in two, to give half to the one and half to the other – or, in other words, without metaphor, when they would attempt to divide Judaism as it is in its present totality, in its organism – which is the natural growth of a long history, of a moral and religious constitution – if they would attempt to cut it, and separate from it all which is traditional, would they not extinguish its vitality, its every spark of life, so that what is now in full pulsation would become a dead body, a lifeless corpse; and, like the false mother, its destroyers would have the malicious pleasure of saying, 'It shall be neither thine nor mine; divide it?'[31]

Then followed an olive branch to the Reformers, the closest the Chief Rabbi would come to bridging the chasm his predecessor had opened:

> Like the true mother, we must not allow the child to be divided; not allow the remnant of Israel to be engaged in perpetual warfare. It is the duty of every Israelite to heal the breach which unfortunately exists between brethren and brethren; to try and exercise all his influence, all his personal and mental power, to make our people *one*, our Law *one*, as our God is *one*; to try that those who have gone too far and have, intentionally or not, made organic changes, may be brought back to the bosom of our established religion.
>
> But if such be impossible – if all efforts, all sacrifices, for such a happy result are exhausted and fruitless – then let us agree to differ, and let us have peace in our own camp ... Is it not better, we ask you, to devote your leisure and influence, your talent and energy, to the improvement of your educational establishments, which confer on

you so much credit; to the amelioration of your charities, and of the condition of your poor, who need so much at this inclement season, than to lavish them in an unprofitable difference?

Let us put away all anger and all ill-feeling; let us flee all clamour and strife; let us, like the true mother, avoid and hate any injurious division; let us subdue all unfriendly feeling, and let us be kindly affected to one another; and we shall, by the assistance of God, go on prospering and rejoicing, in all worldly and spiritual blessings, and shall continue to be a pattern for imitation and example to other communities in Israel: and we shall reap, both here and hereafter, the fruit and happy produce of that union and harmony; for heaven is the region as well as the recompense of peace, and those who desire and promote it, who love, seek and follow it, are best qualified for heaven.[32]

But even as he was preparing to extend this olive branch, Adler had commented uncompromisingly on the perpetuation of the *cherem*. In a letter dated 23 December 5614 (1853), responding to a Manchester congregation then proposing to disregard the ban, he stated: 'The ecclesiastical authorities have the power to remove, annul or dissolve the caution or excommunication, provided that the parties referred to therein alter the religious position in which they were at the time when the same was issued.' Asked to clarify his answer, he wrote: 'The ecclesiastical authorities have no power to annul the decree in question until the parties therein referred to will yield in certain religious points, the nature of which is more a matter of detail.'[33]

Adler's wish to 'make our people *one*' was never to be fulfilled – either in his Chief Rabbinate or in those of his successors – although his agreement 'to differ' was in itself a significant advance. Equally unattained was his desire to 'put away all anger and ill-feeling', to 'avoid any injurious division' and to 'have peace in our own camp', protestations that led to charges of duplicity, and of outside influences, in the execution of his endeavours.[34]

# 4

# Bonds of Brotherhood

'I am ready to eat, drink and trade with these gentlemen, and with the members of their congregation. But I will not join with them in any *religious* act.' Thus asserted Louis Cohen, Montefiore's nephew, in his condemnation of the Reform movement and its adherents. And this, in essence, was the approach adopted by Adler, Montefiore's ecclesiastical chief, in his relationship with the rebels. Benjamin Phillips, in his closing address to the Board's final debate on admission, had said as much when he declared:

> Mr Cohen, in unmistakable language, has delivered it as his opinion that an excommunication does not exist. And if an excommunication does not exist, how can these four men be disqualified? The worthy president will forgive me if I draw any individual name into the question. The daughter of the founder of the Margaret Street Synagogue is married to Sir Moses' nephew – with his consent; and thus the *cherem* has, by him, been set at defiance.
>
> Does Mr Cohen not know that at a religious ceremony at Chatham, the Chief Rabbi and the minister of the Margaret Street Synagogue met and held friendly converse? Was not this setting the excommunication at defiance by the Chief Rabbi? And I myself was returned as a deputy by eighty-three votes of the Great Synagogue, despite the fact that the electors knew my own daughter is married to a member of the Margaret Street Synagogue.[1]

Throughout his battle against the reformers, which had decades further to run, Adler had demonstrated ambivalence in his public and private stance, consorting with them on one level, avoiding them on another. Salomons had been quick to observe, in the same closing debate, that 'the gentlemen of the Margaret Street Synagogue are the presidents and vice-presidents of our charities – they regulate them. Mr Francis Goldsmid has acted as president of the Jews' Hospital and of the Jews' Free School, and some of them are now on the committee'.[2]

Indeed, early in office, Adler had shown a reluctance to shun the philanthropic congregants of the West London Synagogue, upon whose wealth were dependant some of the community's most vulnerable institutions. Isolating them would have imposed on the Orthodox a financial burden which even the richest would have found it onerous to bear. It was not unusual, therefore, to see the Chief Rabbi in close proximity to Reform leaders, as when he appeared publicly as Goldsmid's guest – and travelled in his carriage – during a visit to the Jews' Infant School in 1845.[3] Despite attempts by Bevis Marks to ban the seceders from charitable bodies,[4] Goldsmid had fought a spirited campaign to win the presidency of the school by thirty-eight votes to thirteen, setting a precedent for the continuing election of West London members to high office in the community's leading charities, where Adler perforce had duties to perform.

That he adopted an ambiguous and, arguably, self-seeking approach (as his critics alleged) was not without foundation: assertions of 'one rule for the rich and another for the poor' had a credible ring. That there was a mutual dependence between the religious and lay chiefs was equally manifest: one needed the other to bolster his authority. As forceful as each wished to appear in the public eye, there was an element of uncertainty in even the mightiest of men.[5] Adler's experiences in Oldenburg and Hanover had taught him to avoid confrontation, and to seek unity and fraternity, wherever and whenever conflict threatened to pursue him.[6] In Britain, his social leadership was seen to be 'weak ... he was careful not to widen the breach but he did nothing to bridge it. Material help could be gained only from the wealthy Jews of the City.'[7] Authoritative and zealous as he may have been, he was also benign and benevolent,[8] and his attitudes and moods often changed with the wind. Apprehensive about defections to Reform, he was 'compelled to walk a tightrope, lest the wealthy openly renounce Orthodoxy and undo the good that remains. He does not want to fight with sinners who show themselves as friends.'[9]

The Deputies dispute, meanwhile, hovered in abeyance, and its resolution, in 1885, turned out to be a muted affair. Thirteen years earlier, the Board had mandated Alfred Henriques, the member for Portsmouth, to establish a committee aimed at 'providing for the admission of the representatives of a synagogue or synagogues which had hitherto been excluded from representation'. Within six months, coinciding with Montefiore's retirement as president,[10] it had adopted constitutional changes in favour of the West London Synagogue, designed 'to promote concord in the general community and to prevent any disturbance of the peace which now prevails'.[11]

The West London council, however, was divided over the changes and left the final decision to the members.[12] Their vote was to set back representation for several more years. 'In conclave assembled', reported the *Jewish*

Chronicle, 'the congregation made a mistake in rejecting to avail themselves of the new constitution of the Board of Deputies, and it is best for their sake that we should have the courage to tell them so. The grounds on which a refusal to accept the arrangements of the new constitution is based are of a nature calculated to widen a breach which the ancient congregations have long been desirous to close.'[13]

Taking issue with the constitutional amendments, Julian Goldsmid, MP, explained his congregation's decision:

> Alfred Henriques proposed that the invitation to send deputies should be accepted and to this I moved an amendment, which was carried by a majority of twenty-eight to six and which runs as follows: 'That this Congregation much regret that they are unable to accept the proposal contained in the amended constitution of the Board of Deputies that this Synagogue should send representatives to the Board, as rules one, six and twenty-four are inconsistent with the principles upon which this Synagogue was founded.'
>
> I pointed out that if the Synagogue agreed to send delegates to the Board, it would, of course, be agreeing to the rules of the Board, just as a gentleman on entering a club undertakes to be bound by its rules. Now some of the rules, which Mr Henriques had in vain endeavoured to modify, are directly opposed to the principles upon which the congregation was founded.
>
> Rule six clearly lays down the authority of the heads of the Sephardim Congregation and the United Congregations – an authority which from the very establishment of the West London Synagogue has never been acknowledged by it; but to them, if we had sent deputies, we should have agreed, *pro tanto*, that 'all matters involving questions affecting the religious customs and usages of the Jews should be referred'. That would have been admitting that the principle upon which the members of our congregation originally seceded was wrong – which I, for one at least, totally deny.
>
> Section One of the constitution of the Board specifies the congregations who may send deputies either as certified under the old Acts of Parliament, or as being one of an appended list of metropolitan congregations. The Berkeley Street Synagogue is named in that list, but I must point out that the recognition of its existence as a synagogue does not depend upon the certificate of the president of the Board of Deputies (which was formerly the only method of obtaining certification of the secretary of any synagogue, and which has never been given to it), but was granted by an Act of the 19 and 20

Vict. [the 1856 Act to Amend the Provisions of the Marriage and Registration Acts], passed notwithstanding the opposition of the Board of Deputies; and not only enabling the seat-holders of the West London Synagogue to certify their own secretary, but also empowering him to certify the secretary of other synagogues.

It is under this Act that the Manchester [Reform] Synagogue was certified, and that any other synagogue might be hereafter certified. But of this Act no mention is made. Could we then only accept admittance to the Board of Deputies by ourselves, and that only by a sidewind, when it was denied to those who owe their origin to us?

Moreover, in order that there might be no mistake with regard to the intention of the majority of the Board of Deputies, a rule (number twenty-four) has been added which did not formerly exist at all, but which was placed among the bye-laws a few years back and which really goes entirely beyond the Act of Parliament, which gives the authority to the president of the Board to certify a secretary.

That rule says that 'hereafter, every synagogue desiring to be certified must send in an application accompanied by a certificate from the Ecclesiastical Authorities referred to in clause six, testifying that the applicants do constitute a Jewish synagogue', which is obviously intended to prevent any synagogue certified by us from sending deputies to the Board.

If, said Goldsmid, the Board were to modify their 'exclusive constitution' and

confine themselves to watching over the secular interests of their coreligionists, we shall be ready to meet them in the most friendly manner. But we cannot sacrifice the principles of our existence in order to obtain a hollow and unreal outward uniformity.

I am told that the effort was made in the interests of peace. All I can say is that, until these ill-advised steps were taken, I was not aware that there was not peace; and certainly the Board of Deputies did not show their anxiety to promote it, since they made their exclusive rules yet more exclusive when they revised the constitution of the Board.[14]

Thus collapsed another 'honest and spirited effort to bring nearer together the links of a chain which had been relaxed, if not broken'.[15] But while the West London remained unrepresented, one effect of the constitutional changes was to enable Reform members, on an individual basis, to stand as deputies for provincial congregations, 'with no objection raised to their taking their seats'.[16] So it was that Goldsmid himself, bowing to an appeal to 'see at the Board men whose names belong to the aristocracy not of birth or wealth or ability only, but to the aristocracy of tried service',[17] made his debut as the member for Merthyr Tydfil, which had been established as an Orthodox community in 1848 and received synagogue status five years later.[18]

Meanwhile, even as he pleaded to be allowed 'peacefully to continue in the course of improvement which we have initiated and which has, we have seen with pleasure, to a considerable extent been imitated by other synagogues',[19] other elements fought on for West London's representation both on the Board and in the wider community. During the ensuing decade, across the educational and charitable spectrum, Reform leaders steadily extended their activities and influence and, by 1883, had breached even the inner sanctums of the Orthodox community. In recognition of their bearing the cost of pauper funerals, the West Londoners had received a place on the United Synagogue burial committee, rendering it 'manifestly absurd for the Board of Deputies to retain any scruples against the admission of delegates of the Reform synagogue to its councils on their own terms'.[20]

The Board's triennial poll that year resulted in the election of forty-five deputies for the fourteen metropolitan and eighteen provincial synagogues represented. Anxious to effect a rapprochement with Reform, deputies again made overtures to the West London but were told that, despite further constitutional amendments, the previous objections remained in force. However, meeting at Bevis Marks under the presidency of Arthur Cohen, MP, the new Board was apprised of correspondence between the parties over the previous decade and was asked to consider a conciliatory resolution proposed by Goldsmid, the congregation's president.

Sir Julian, as he now was – having succeeded to the baronetcy five years earlier – voiced his certainty that 'a feeling prevails among all the members of the Board that, if possible, the Jews should be united. Without giving any pledge', he said, 'or forgoing any principles which the Board has at heart, it would be a matter of courtesy to the West London Synagogue to consider its correspondence and to see whether, before the next revision of the constitution comes round, a form of words might be devised which would meet its wishes and yet not run counter to the scruples entertained by the Board.'[21] Although not sanguine of success, he added, he believed that, by appointing a committee, the Board would at least have shown its willingness to consider his submission.

Some thirty months later, the first signs of success emerged – significantly, within weeks of Montefiore's death.[22] Meeting at Bevis Marks in

October 1885, the Board was told of a resolution by the committee 'to recommend such alterations in its constitution as would enable the Berkeley Street Synagogue to avail itself of its right to be represented'. The principal modification was an addition to the controversial sixth clause which, it was proposed, would read as follows (the addition appearing here in italics):

> That the guidance of the Board on religious matters (inclusive of all matters relating to marriages) shall remain as heretofore, with the following authorities, viz., the Ecclesiastical Authorities for the time being of the United Congregations of the British Empire, and the Ecclesiastical Authorities for the time being of the Sephardim Congregation of London, to whom all matters involving questions affecting the religious customs and usages of the Jews shall be referred; *but nothing in this clause shall abridge or affect the individual rights or action in regard to its own internal affairs of any congregation, certified under the provisions of the Act 19 and 20 Vic., Cap. 119* [the 1856 Act].[23]

Asked to comment on the West London's likely response, Joseph Sebag-Montefiore, who had presided over the July meeting at which the amendment was formulated,[24] offered Goldsmid's opinion. Sir Julian, he said, had declared that 'he perfectly approved of the intended alterations in the constitution, and although he had no mandate to speak on behalf of the Berkeley Street Synagogue, the alterations were in accord with the wishes and feelings of the council of that synagogue. He had no doubt that when the matter came officially before that body, the arrangement would be found acceptable to them.' Two other deputies, Henry Harris and Samuel Montagu, took the view that the Board's constitution would be 'practically unaltered' by the proposed modification, since it was not intended that the ecclesiastical authorities would in any way interfere with the religious affairs of the Berkeley Street Synagogue.

On the motion of the president, the recommendation was unanimously adopted, and seven months later, following the 1886 elections, Goldsmid's name appeared twice in the list of deputies, as the member both for the West London Synagogue (with Philip Magnus) and for the congregation of Merthyr Tydfil.[25] Jubilant deputies described this as 'a gratifying circumstance',[26] while the *Jewish Chronicle* declared the new Board to be 'of a more representative character than any of its predecessors.

> For the first time since the memorable secession which led to the establishment of the West London Synagogue of British Jews, that synagogue will be represented on the Board of Deputies. The entire community may be congratulated on this happy reconciliation, for at

no time was it more necessary than at present that minor dissensions should give way to harmony and union.

The Berkeley Street Synagogue could not find better representatives than Sir Julian Goldsmid, MP, and Mr Philip Magnus, the two gentlemen who have been nominated as its deputies. The selection of Sir Julian Goldsmid is especially fitting, as it was he who, in his capacity as member for the Merthyr Tydfil congregation at the old Board, obtained the appointment of a committee to consider the relations between the Board and the Berkeley Street Synagogue.

The outcome of the proceedings of this committee was the adoption of such judicious alterations in the constitution of the Board as will render it practicable for the West London Synagogue, without losing one iota of its independence, to join Orthodox congregations in sending representatives to that body.[27]

\* \* \*   \* \* \*   \* \* \*

Half a century after Reform rumblings first reached Chief Rabbinical ears, religious pluralism seemed a small step closer. But it was, as yet, a fragile affair. Although Adler had distanced himself from the Deputies controversy, there had been other brushes with Reform and its leaders. Manchester in the 1850s had been the scene of one challenge to his authority, when Solomon Schiller-Szinessy – described variously as dynamic, enigmatic, idiosyncratic and bizarre[28] – had sought to establish himself as an independent rabbi on the European model. A political refugee from Hungary, he had called himself 'Local Rabbi' and, to win support among the apathetic and uncommitted, had begun preaching reform of the synagogue service.

While not contemplating any major halachic changes, he wrote to Marks supporting his views on the Oral Law. 'There is a vast difference', he declared, 'between appreciating the merit of the talmudical writings and believing in the inspiration of their contents.'[29] His plan foundered, however, on an increasing reliance on Reform support. The traditionalists became alarmed, and their anxiety was heightened when Schiller-Szinessy announced his intention to determine, without reference to Adler, whether marriages might or might not be performed within the community.

Unwilling to incur the opprobrium such unilateral action might incur, the leaders of Manchester Jewry forced him to resign and, with nowhere else to go, he became rabbi of a small Reform congregation established soon afterwards. He was determined, however, to observe the second days of the festivals, although, as he told Marks, 'such observance can in no manner contravene the principle already admitted – not as Mosaic or biblical ordinance but purely and professedly as ancient institutions on which many of our members look with a feeling of reverence'.[30]

At the price of permitting a new congregation to emerge, Adler had successfully defended the authority of his office.[31] But this was more easily preached than achieved. Whereas, in terms of numbers, London had once exercised overwhelming ascendancy over the provincial communities, those centres were now claiming lives of their own, drawing on sources independent of the Chief Rabbinate and the London oligarchs. Claiming greater spiritual validity for their own practices, they began to ferment a growing rivalry between London and the provinces. While some of the immigrants pouring into Britain from Eastern Europe had joined existing congregations, becoming 'heirs to their original series of arguments and disagreements',[32] far more had established their own religious institutions and gone their own ways. These ways, however, were not always in strict conformity with the law of the land and they thus frequently found themselves in conflict with the Anglo-Jewish establishment and, not least, with the Chief Rabbinate itself.

Nor was opposition confined to the East Europeans. Adler's attitude to Reform had 'hardened with age, and as the gospel of Reform, transmitted by German-Jewish merchants, was spread more widely within England'.[33] A Reform congregation had been founded in this way in Bradford in 1873, and Adler's resolve to make no concessions remained intact and without qualification. There was to be no accommodation with them, nor any compromise that might afford them even a modest status in the communal hierarchy.

For all that, there had been unexpected fraternity some five years earlier, when the question of licensing kosher butchers had come before the courts. Moses Schott, a Dutch Jew, had opened a butcher shop in London and, holding a licence from the Chief Rabbi of Emden, had considered himself authorised to sell kosher meat. Adler, however, refused to endorse it and issued a warning to the public that Schott's meat was not kosher. The butcher sued Adler for libel and leading counsel were briefed – Lord Halsbury, the future Lord Chancellor, for the plaintiff, Sir Charles Pollock for the defendant.

Schott maintained that certificates of competence for a shochet were internationally valid; Adler argued that they applied only to their country of origin. Alarm was raised in Orthodox circles when Schott called Marks as an expert witness, but, in the event, the West London minister 'proved a veritable Daniel come to judgment'.[34] His evidence staunchly supported Adler's contention, and the court found in the Chief Rabbi's favour. Marks' support, however, went unrewarded when, in 1870, the West London moved to Berkeley Street. Adler declined an invitation to attend the opening ceremony unless the congregation reinstated the second days of the festivals as an acknowledgement of the divinity of the Oral Law. 'Despite improved relations in the community, this issue still rankled.'[35]

Nor was this Adler's final snub. In 1883, the Western Synagogue announced a series of Sabbath sermons to which six ministers, including Marks, had been invited to preach. The move was hailed as 'wise, courageous and helpful, a potential contribution towards closing the gulf that still divides Orthodox Jewry from its nonconformist brethren'. Hopes were expressed that it might even lead to 'a complete reconciliation'.[36] But the plan was frustrated. Adler sent a message expressing 'keen regret' and 'painful surprise' at the invitation to Marks. 'I do not feel justified', he wrote, 'in giving my sanction to the reverend gentleman delivering a sermon in your place of worship.'[37] The matter was thrashed out in the columns of the press, with the Western challenging the Chief Rabbi's right to 'interfere', especially since Marks had been associated with the congregation for some fifty years.

Nevertheless, after an extraordinary meeting of the honorary officers, the synagogue announced that the sermons had been 'withdrawn'. In fact, while 'influential counsels' had urged the committee to drop Marks as a speaker, they had manifested their feelings by cancelling the series.

\* \* \*   \* \* \*   \* \* \*

In 1892, preaching at the West London's golden jubilee service, Marks dismissed predictions by 'some of its sturdy but no doubt honest-minded opponents' some fifty years earlier that Reform would become 'a harbinger of infidelity'. Since its founding, he said, 'our brethren of other synagogues have also moved on the lines of progress. Their services are now conducted with decorum and reverence; the pulpit has become with them a permanent institution; and their sacred offices are performed by a cultured and superior clergy.' Of his own synagogue's changes, he declared:

> Our modifications may be considered as final, in so far as the term 'finality' can be reasonably applied to any work undertaken by fallible and short-sighted mortals. For who can be so rash as to contend that conditions may never arise that will compel changes to meet their exigencies? We are all children of our time and of our environment, and the influence of these factors cannot fail to colour the several petitions that we offer up at the Throne of Grace.

> Now, after fifty years have passed over our congregation, we feel that we may not unreasonably appeal to our brethren at large, whether its action has tended to retard or to advance spiritual Judaism? Has it violated any of the sacred barriers of Mosaism, or has it shaken the pillars of revelation?
>
> Before God and before Israel, I maintain that our pious founders have done essential service to the community by letting light into the synagogue and by making it more venerated within, and more respected without. Judaism has nothing to fear from the adaptation of its external helps to the necessities of the times, for it rests on a deeper and a more durable foundation than that of stereotyped form.
>
> A religion which, marvellous to relate, has survived its nationality, a religion that has had to face more than fourteen centuries of proscription, exposed to the fiercest fanaticism and to a systematic persecution to which no parallel is to be found in the wide range of history ... can incur no danger from moulding its forms to the requirements of the age.
>
> Over the contention that disturbed the infancy of our congregation, the curtain has happily fallen, and it is cheering to know that, notwithstanding the minor ritual difference between our synagogue and our sister institutions, we are all knit together in the bonds of amity and brotherhood, and that a common sentiment animates us all to work with hand and heart in support of every effort for the promotion of the well-being of the community at large.[38]

Alluding to Marks' reference to the 'brethren of other synagogues', the *Jewish Chronicle* noted that 'in order to give point to the excellent relations now maintained between the "Reform" and the "Orthodox" communities', invitations had been sent to the 'foremost men in the London community who are not connected with Berkeley Street'.[39] Both Hermann Adler, who had recently become Chief Rabbi on the death of his father, and the Sephardi Haham, Moses Gaster, declined to attend the service, but the United Synagogue was officially represented.

Most of its ministers and honorary officers were present, led by their president, Lord Rothschild, who sat alongside Sir Julian Goldsmid. The absence of the ecclesiastical heads led the *Jewish Chronicle* to comment that 'even if the two Chief Rabbis had been present, and by their presence given the one final touch needed to make the ceremony a source of unalloyed satisfaction, they would have heard nothing from the pulpit that could have caused them discomfort, and much to which they might have yielded a hearty assent'.[40]

Six weeks later, Adler, Gaster and Marks joined company for the foundation-stone laying of the Hampstead Synagogue, a congregation with reformist tendencies, born of frustration and (as a later minister put it) 'religious restlessness'[41] over ritual and liturgy.

* * *   * * *   * * *

After a decade of failing health, spent in reclusion at Hove, Nathan Marcus Adler died on 21 January 1890, aged 87. He had regarded himself, eulogised the *Jewish Chronicle*, as 'a veritable Sentinel of the Law. He had received the Torah from the faithful guardians who had preceded him; to him was committed the charge of guarding "the fence", and no defender could have been more faithful and stout-hearted.'[42]

Even a member of the West London Synagogue was moved to remark that,

> however differently some of us may have been trained in our views of Judaism from the conceptions which the Chief Rabbi represented, all of us who are attached to our religion and our race feel that in him has passed away one of the purest and one of the most cultured exemplars of them which the present century has produced.
>
> Higher Judaism – that is, the most spiritual view of religion – was brightly illustrated both by his life and his teaching. And in this age of widespread apathy, by no means confined to one branch of the community, such lessons are invaluable. We do well to ponder over them.
>
> The writer of these lines can recollect some of the most impassioned eloquence in behalf of the spiritual truths from the lips of the departed rabbi. Some of his sermons in the Great Synagogue and elsewhere will never fade from the memory of those who heard them. But the lessons which he taught were not confined to the pulpit. A vast deal was gathered from personal conversation. As a man as well as an Israelite and a rabbi, the personality of Dr Nathan Marcus Adler reflected those finer emotions of the ancient faith which are sadly becoming more and more rare.[43]

Such views were for long widely held. By the time of Adler's death, wrote one chronicler, the Chief Rabbinate 'commanded a wider authority than it had done when he was first appointed'.[44] His period of office, wrote another, was 'of tremendous importance in the history of Anglo-Jewry, which was converted from a roughly organised pre-Emancipation *kehillah* into a community similar in essentials to that of today. No religious innovations or reforms were permitted to invade the congregations over which he presided, though he certainly exerted himself unstintingly to bring about an improvement in congregational decorum and discipline.'[45]

The keynote to his life 'was to be found in his unflinching Orthodoxy. His sincerity was everywhere admitted, and his love for Judaism and his loyalty to its Orthodox presentation were acknowledged to be genuine and real. Great zeal for the cause of education, a benevolent disposition and a union of talmudic scholarship and genuine culture, unusual among the rabbis of his generation, were his most prominent characteristics.'[46]

For almost half a century, wrote his son Elkan Nathan, Adler had

> officiated as chief of the British rabbis and lived to witness, under his leadership, the phenomenal growth of his community in political, social and ethical importance. It was his life's work to smooth the way, to heal internal dissensions, and to remove his community's external disabilities. Instead of widening the breach, he bridged it. For some time, he strove for a formal reconciliation. This he failed to accomplish, but himself he endeared to both parties, and it is generally admitted that to his wise influence is due the conservatism of London Jewry.[47]

Commenting on Adler's stance in the aftermath of the secession, the *Jewish Chronicle* asserted that

> Bravery was characteristic of the man. In his earliest years, it showed itself in the courage and the energy with which he attacked the exacting duties of his position. And that his difficulties were immense, even those who innocently created them were the first to admit.
>
> His rabbinate extended over the most momentous period that has yet been recorded in the history of English Judaism. His accession to office was almost exactly coincident with the establishment of the 'Reform' synagogue in London. That event was at once the witness and the impulse to a discontent with the special interpretation of Judaism which Dr Adler was chosen to uphold.
>
> There can be no question that the religious opinions of English Jews have undergone slow but considerable changes during the past forty years; and it is almost equally certain that the 'Reform' movement has largely helped to produce them. Still more potent has been the influence of the social and intellectual progress which has marked the annals of the community during the last few decades.
>
> Dr Adler was installed in 1845 and, in the long interval that separates that era from the present time, how vast are the strides that

English Jews have made in point of culture and in social power! One by one, the disabilities, both legal and prescriptive, under which they laboured half a century ago have been removed. They are now the peers of their fellow countrymen, not only in the eyes of the law, but in the eyes of that equally potent authority – public opinion.

It was inevitable that so mighty a revolution in their lot would be accompanied by important changes in their religious ideas. The English Jew could not possibly have taken the place in the wide world which was his by right without feeling the impact of the world's thought. He could not avoid being swept on by the great wave of inquiry which has so powerfully influenced the recent history of every religious communion.

Turning to the altered condition of Anglo-Jewry, and to Adler's role at its helm, the paper declared:

The English Jew of today is no more like his predecessor was forty years ago in his views of Judaism than the end of our century is, in its general conditions, like the middle of it. Almost everything has changed since that time, and English Judaism not the least.

That the changes it has undergone have been so gradual and comparatively so small is an eloquent testimony to the success with which Dr Adler exercised his moderating power. Had a man of smaller ability and with a less commanding personality occupied the rabbinical chair, it is probable that the wholesale reforms, and the undesirable extravagances which characterise American Judaism, would have found their way into our community. But so consummate was Dr Adler's tact, so profound was the respect with which his opinions were received, so powerful was the effect upon other minds of his own leanings to conservatism, that the forces making for drastic changes were neutralised, or diverted into safe channels.

The difficulties he had thus to encounter must nevertheless have been at times prodigious. Nor were they diminished by the existence of a reactionary section which strenuously opposed even harmless modifications of established ritual practice. This source of difficulty, far from decreasing, has grown with the progress of time, and the final years of Dr Adler's rabbinate were clouded by perplexities arising out of the rapid growth of the East End Jewish population, with its pronounced Orthodox tendencies.

Called to the Rabbinate of the British Empire in order to expound Judaism in accordance with the view prevailing forty years ago, he faithfully discharged the trust confided to him, though he was willing to sanction changes demanded by communal opinion, as long as they did not absolutely conflict with Orthodoxy. One of his last official acts was to concede certain slight modifications of the synagogue service at the request of the Hampstead Jews; and even those who deplored his inability to make greater concessions recognised that the grounds of his refusal were strictly logical.

And his sincerity was as universally admitted as his consistency. Everyone perceived that his love for Judaism and his loyalty to the Orthodox presentment of it were genuine and real – the fruit of his convictions – a part of his very self. It was thus that the veneration he inspired was so great and so general. His look and his bearing joined with his qualities of mind and soul to pronounce him a veritable Chief Rabbi – one worthy to be the religious head of the great Anglo-Jewish community.[48]

That in the hands of 'a man of smaller ability and with a less commanding personality' Reform would have made greater strides is, however, open to question, as are references to Adler's 'tact', to the 'respect' with which his opinions were received, and to the 'powerful effect of his own leanings to conservatism'. Several factors confute these contentions, not least the evidence questioning his 'bravery' and 'courage' in the face of the sustained assaults on his modus operandi.

Adler's close ties to Montefiore had long provoked debate and dissension. Even at the end of his life, well after Montefiore's death, their relationship remained a source of two-edged comment. Referring to Adler's last official public engagement – at the Montefiore centennial service in Brighton, for which he composed and recited a commemorative prayer – the *Jewish Chronicle* noted that there had been 'personal reasons for his thus emerging from his enforced retirement.

> From the moment Dr Adler set foot in England to the day of the death of Sir Moses, there was an unbroken bond of personal affection between these two leaders of the community.
>
> Dr Adler invariably attended the services held on the eve of the departure of Sir Moses on his several philanthropic missions, and the venerable baronet never failed on his journeys to visit Frau Rebecca Adler (mother of the Rav) at Hanover to receive her benediction.[49] And Sir Moses kept up with Dr Adler an intimate and cordial correspondence, never omitting to be among the first to offer his good wishes on the New Year and on occasions of family rejoicings.
>
> Dr Adler had the pleasure of not only repeatedly tendering to Sir

Moses his felicitations on the happy termination of his several missions, but had the satisfaction of offering his congratulations to all the distinguished Jews who have during the last half-century – the most important period of Anglo-Jewish history – been the heroes of the Jewish emancipation struggle and the representatives of Jewish talent and perseverance.[50]

For all the congratulations, not least among those 'heroes' and 'representatives of Jewish talent and perseverance' had been some of the most outspoken champions of Reform and the most vigorous opponents of Montefiore's, and Adler's, leadership. Pragmatism and expediency had vied with courage and bravery in pursuance of both men's communal ambitions, while family ties and personal friendships had played a significant role in ensuring that they and Reform remained on closer terms than the Chief Rabbi's utterances and actions had sometimes suggested.

What power Adler wielded had reflected 'both the need for a central jurisdiction to preserve the framework of Jewish life, and the unique position of the secular plutocracy in London from which his powers emanated. The Chief Rabbinate was as much the ecclesiastical arm of the plutocracy as the president of the Board of Deputies was its secular representative.'[51]

Nor had it escaped his critics that Adler kept one eye on his plutocratic patrons – Montefiore in particular – even as he focused the other on the followers of Reform. In fact, the organisational separation of the Reform synagogue from the established community had 'owed, in part, to the strong opposition of Montefiore and the Sephardi immigrants from North Africa'.[52] Far more effective than the Chief Rabbi's opposition to the seceders had been that of Montefiore, 'their sworn enemy. From the beginning, he did his best to stifle the infant Reform congregation, even though his younger brother was prominent among the founders. When that failed, he simply made every effort to ensure that the schismatics would remain outside the umbrella of institutional legitimacy.'[53]

From the outset, it was Montefiore who had orchestrated the anti-Reform campaign, 'resisting every attempt to accommodate or come to terms, and anxious to find a new Chief Rabbi of sufficient authority and capacity to save British Jewry for Orthodoxy. Centralising authority and imposing discipline upon a scattered and diffuse community was a point upon which the lay élite and the Adlers could work in common purpose. Each, as the nineteenth century went on, found the enhanced power of the other useful for its own purposes.' And yet, at the end of the day, 'saving British Jewry for Orthodoxy meant little more than seeing Orthodox Jews … make increased use of English and witnessing United Synagogue

Orthodoxy stress decorum in the same way as the Reform leaders did'.[54]

Indeed, the secessionists, many of whom maintained close links with Orthodox congregations, had had no wish to secede and would have preferred their reforms (limited as they were) to be made within the established communal framework. Some, driven in part by their desire to halt the march of indifferentism,[55] had used their influence to restrain the West London from radicalism, resisting efforts to widen the distance from Orthodoxy.[56] Notable among these had been the Sabbath-observant Abraham Mocatta, ever reluctant to cut his ties with Bevis Marks, and Sir Francis Goldsmid, whose obituarist had lauded his 'strict adherence to all Mosaic rites and ceremonies'.

Many of the innovations – the introduction of sermons and choirs, the abolition of auctioned mitzvot, the revision of ritual and liturgical practices, the establishment of branch synagogues – had been permitted by Adler himself, as a result of pressure from the wealthy Jews who dominated communal affairs. They had

> believed that religious change, by which they meant essentially alterations in public worship, could be obtained if sanctioned by the established ecclesiastical authority – that is, the Chief Rabbi – for in their eyes he had the power to make reforms by virtue of his position alone, regardless of the halachic status of the changes. They thus invested him with power that no traditional rabbinic scholar would have claimed. They did so because they saw the Chief Rabbi as a Jewish archbishop of sorts rather than as an halachic authority.[57]

And, in so doing, they had taken much of the ground away from the new congregation, helping to account for the fact that, in Britain, an institutionally distinct Reform Judaism was a 'feeble affair'.[58] British Reform had thus involved no radical doctrinal reformulation of Judaism, nor any wholesale repudiation of traditional practice. By comparison with its German counterpart, it was 'rather tepid', its appeal 'very limited', and the differences between the Reform and Orthodox services (at least in London) 'slight'.[59]

Those who did join Reform, at least initially, had done little more than strive 'to make their service more decorous rather than more rational, more genteel rather than more theologically correct. Not surprisingly, rabbis and scholars, who were few and far between in England before the late nineteenth century, played a negligible role in shaping the course of reform.'[60] Even in Manchester, where Reform was more Germanically inspired, the initiators had sought, above all, 'freedom from central control and flexibility in shaping a service that had become, in their judgment, unseemly and undignified'.[61]

By adopting this line, the West London Synagogue had itself been partly responsible for its early failure to gain support. 'In attempting to disarm critics, it became apologetic, stressing that the changes instituted at the beginning were final, that it would go no further.'[62] In this regard, the British reformers did indeed differ from their German contemporaries. Absent from their intellectual world were the idea of religious evolution, so central to the ideology of continental Reform, and its supporting discipline of *Wissenschaft des Judentums*. Moreover, the fixed commitment to scripturalism proved a practical liability as historical criticism undermined the revelatory status not only of Talmud but also of Torah.'[63]

The founding of an independent Reform congregation might have been long delayed were it not for the demographic trends that had brought increasing numbers of affluent and established Jewish families to London's West End, separating them by a considerable distance from the synagogues in which they had been raised.[64] The dominance of these families (notably the Mocattas, Goldsmids and Henriques) in the leadership of the movement had served to have a 'stultifying effect' on its radicalism and reforming tendencies, eschewing any appeal to the working classes and devoid of a 'driving zeal to recapture the pristine glory of the past and retain a vision of a great future'. By the end of the century, the West London was still headed by these families, its leaders characterised by their 'sheer inertia and lack of drive' and their absence of 'theological backbone'.[65]

In contrast to the moneyed classes' drift towards reform, it is estimated that by the 1870s 'a moderate Orthodoxy was still overwhelmingly dominant in Britain', although a large proportion of middle-class Jewish families were 'very lukewarm' in the practice of their faith. The relative poverty of British congregations, their dependence on voluntary contributions, and the burden of providing for large numbers of poor Jews had combined to provide strong financial incentives to remain within the Orthodox fold and to avoid the costs of establishing parallel networks of Jewish institutions.[66]

The decline in religious observance, among all strata of the Jewish community, had begun a century earlier, evidenced by 'a growing sense among many English Jews that religion *per se* was no longer a necessary ingredient in their lives. Many became apathetic or careless about the performance of ritual and attendance at synagogue because the world seemed to them to have become a less sacred place. If they still believed that God existed, His existence did not impinge on them in any immediate way, affecting them instead in only a very remote manner.'[67]

To them, by the time Reform had begun to take hold, the issues raised by the secessionists were of minor concern. Halachah meant nothing, and neither Orthodoxy nor Reform addressed their predominantly secular interests.[68]

The nineteenth-century journalist Henry Mayhew[69] wrote that the street Jews he had interviewed knew little about Yiddishkeit and possessed the haziest notions of their religion; whether trefa or kosher meat was consumed was to them immaterial. Nor were they interested in prayer, for the interior of the synagogue was alien, if not hostile, territory. Less than one tenth of London's Jews were members of a congregation,[70] the rest precluded by lack of means or, as likely, lack of faith. Even those who found a spot in the pews were made to feel unwelcome. As 'One of the Humbler Classes' wrote in a letter to the *Jewish Chronicle*, commenting on non-attendance at Sabbath services:

> Our poverty is thrown in our face at the synagogue. We are pushed and shoved about as soon as we go beyond the aristocratic bar, and more especially so when the Chief Rabbi delivers his monthly lectures. We are all heaped together in a cluster at the bottom of the synagogue in a corner, while at the top the benches are empty and present a most dismal appearance. There is, in fact, too much distinction between the rich and poor in all the metropolitan synagogues, except in the Reform one at Margaret Street; and this is the cause of many poor Jews absenting themselves from the place of worship.[71]

But even the poor Jews at Margaret Street were few in number. Most, wrote Mayhew, were more likely to be seen at one or other of the East End theatres – if, that is, they could afford even the cheapest of seats – or in pubs, clubs and establishments of low repute. According to the 1851 religious census, only 16 per cent of Anglo-Jewry – as against 40 per cent of the Christian population – attended services on their respective Sabbaths.[72]

At the upper end of the scale, among the 16 per cent who attended synagogue, other factors were at play.

> Their continued attachment to Orthodoxy owed more to religiosity than to religion, to what was prescribed by 'Society' than commanded by the Almighty. Sabbath observance, for example, remained *de rigueur* in the best social circles throughout the Queen's reign and beyond. No one who was anyone worked on the Sabbath, and few upper-class Jews did so. Public worship and family prayers were the 'done thing', and Jews were determined to do them. Conformity in religion, as in speech or dress, defined that gentility to which they aspired. In short, religion was respectable, and for that reason alone, it was worth the upkeep.[73]

Such Jews showed little enthusiasm for Reform and were content to retain their Orthodox affiliation, despite the absence of doctrinal or ritual rigour in their Judaism:

> The Anglo-Jewish notables were not traditional Jews outside the synagogue. While content to incorporate some aspects of traditional practice into their lives, they were hardly inclined to observe the full regimen of Orthodoxy.
>
> At the same time, however, they felt no compelling need to alter the face of Judaism – that is, its theology and worship service. The political pressures that induced the Jews of Germany to make Judaism acceptable to the Christian majority were absent in England. There was no widespread clamour that Jews renounce their particularistic ways in order to receive the rights of citizenship (which, in fact, English Jews already enjoyed in the eighteenth century). Thus, unlike their counterparts in Berlin, London Jews did not feel that their religion itself was on trial or that they had to prove their own loyalty to the State by abandoning their ethnic solidarity.[74]

It was this acceptance of Orthodoxy and the lack of desire for Reform by the most acculturated and modernised class in the community that set London apart as a unique example of Jewish life in the nineteenth century. 'Even the London reformers had little in common with their German counterparts, remaining far more moderate and closer to Orthodoxy than were they.'[75]

Another factor contributing to the relative moderation of the movement was the neo-Karaite structure of British Reform, which accepted the divinity of the Written Law while denying that of the Oral. Both in its ceremonial and its internal structure, it continued largely to conform to Orthodox practice, strongly limiting the gulf between the two strands. By adopting this approach, 'Reform reflected the impact of the non-Jewish environment ... [Protestantism] not only supplied the sources of Victorian neo-Karaism; it also determined the prospects for reform within the minority religion. The moderating influence of the Church of England upon progressive opinion within the Anglo-Jewish élite in no small part accounts for the arrested development of Reform Judaism in Britain.'[76]

There, as everywhere, wrote an early historian of the movement, 'the Jews are affected by their surroundings, and the doctrine of conformity to an established church which represents the prevailing religious attitude in England reacted, and reacts, without a doubt upon the Jews. For that reason, it proved so difficult for Reform to gain a foothold in Anglo-Judaism.'[77]

Clearly, then, factors other than Adler's conservatism or courage had served to retard Reform's growth in Britain, not least the conservatism of the reformers themselves. As Marks had put it, their modifications were to be considered, for the duration at least, as 'final'. The congregation had 'reached the haven of peace after years of trial and struggle. Since then, it has continued along the lines first laid down, but has not made much further headway in this direction. In fact, it has become quite as wedded to its traditions as are the Orthodox congregations to theirs.'[78]

But the 'haven of peace' was to be short-lived. The Hampstead Synagogue, which had seen Marks, Adler and Gaster congregate together in incongruous circumstances, was soon to become the breeding ground of far greater infidelity than any of them could, or would, have imagined.

# 5

# Joseph's Coat

For thirty-five years, Dr [Nathan Marcus] Adler has served the Jewish community ably, zealously and unremittingly as their revered Spiritual Chief. During this long period, the congregations of London, under his pastoral charge, have grown in number and in importance. While the circumstances of the different synagogues have undergone a change probably greater than in any previous similar period, their attachment to their sacred faith has remained unimpaired and has been cemented under his wise and enlightened supervision, and feelings of unity and mutual affection have been developed and matured.

The [United Synagogue] council cannot but regret that the state of Dr Adler's health prevents his affording the same continuous attention as heretofore to the incessant duties of his high office; but they feel that his long and indefatigable labours well entitle him to command that assistance which he states he is reluctantly compelled to seek, and they congratulate themselves that his wise counsels and advice will still be available to the whole community in any matters of weighty importance.

In considering the best means of reconciling the exigencies of the public service with the comfort and convenience of Dr Adler, the council have fortunately not had a difficult task. If Dr Hermann Adler were entirely unconnected with the Chief Rabbi by the near ties of relationship, his great learning and high abilities, his conciliatory disposition and the manner in which he has succeeded in gaining the affection of a large and important congregation would designate him as eminently fitted for the discharge of the responsible duties from which Dr Adler is compelled to seek relief.

But in addition to these advantages, Dr Hermann Adler, as the son of the Chief Rabbi, must have already acquired a large amount of experience of the Chief Rabbi's important sphere of duty and will possess facilities for assisting his father which no other gentleman could enjoy. The council, therefore, assuring the Chief Rabbi of their entire confidence in the learning, judgment and abilities of his son,

Dr Hermann Adler, recommend that he appoint him as his delegate, to attend at his office on his behalf, to issue authorisations of marriage, and to represent him at the Court of the Beth Hamidrash and at the meetings of the Board of Shechitah ...[1]

Thus, in the opening weeks of 1880, twelve years before he was elected in his own right, Hermann Adler assumed the duties and responsibilities of Delegate Chief Rabbi, together with the pressures and pitfalls they inevitably attracted. Nor was he blind to their consequences. As he was later to write to the officers of the Bayswater Synagogue, on his subsequent election:

You will believe me, my dear Sirs, when I tell you that my official connection with your congregation has been to me a source of unqualified satisfaction. It has proved to me a wellspring of spiritual joy and mental comfort, more especially during the last twelve years when the anxieties caused by the discharge of the duties of the Rabbinate began to press upon me.[2]

Born in Hanover in 1839, Hermann was six years old when he witnessed from 'yonder gallery, nestling close to my dear mother, gazing with childish wonder on the strange ceremonial that was being enacted below – the installation of a new Chief Rabbi'.[3] Forty-six years were to pass before he found himself similarly installed. During that period, he was to study at University College School and then (at least for the first part of his bachelor's examinations)[4] at the College itself, where one of his contemporaries was Julian Goldmid,[5] later to become his, and his predecessor's, adversary as president of the West London Synagogue.

Hermann's 'first and last teacher was his late lamented father: he began to teach his son the Decalogue when he was four years old, and studied Talmud with him practically to the very last day of his life'.[6] His other teachers included Barnett Abrahams,[7] a dayan of the Spanish and Portuguese Congregation, Marcus Kalisch, the Chief Rabbi's secretary,[8] and David Asher,[9] of Leipzig, as well as Rabbis Salomon Loeb Rapoport and Samuel Freund, from whom he received semichah after two years at the Prague yeshivah (1860–1862).[10] During this latter period, he also gained his doctorate from the University of Leipzig.

For much of the next thirty years, Adler combined his ministry at Bayswater with duties as tutor (and later as president) at Jews' College, and with honorary positions in the wider community.[11] Defeating Birmingham-based Abraham Pereira Mendes, scion of a distinguished Sephardi family, for the Bayswater post, he (or at least his supporters) regarded the contest as a 'referendum' on his father's Chief Rabbinate: 'The synagogue was both large and influential. Hermann's gift for preaching and homiletics suited his congregation. The new generation was prepared to step into the place of the old.'[12]

This gift for preaching, and the sense of continuity – and contiguity – displayed in his sermons, marked out young Adler as the natural heir to his father's throne. It was thus no surprise that 'two generations of Adlers'[13] should have spent many years together treading the path which Nathan Marcus had mapped out in his first encounter with British Reform, describing his role as 'the watchman, the guardian, the preserver of the Holy Law'. It had been, as he predicted, 'difficult, very difficult, to take good care of it, whilst urged on by some to constant advance, and implored by others to remain immovable – difficult, in such circumstances, to find the golden mean'.

* * *   * * *   * * *

The 'golden mean', never attained during the father's Chief Rabbinate, was even more elusive during that of his son. Liturgical and ritual reform, sought – and obtained, after a fashion – both within and outside Orthodoxy, was proving increasingly contentious as the century wound down. The Adlers had confronted it in the opening months of Hermann's delegacy, after the heads of the nine metropolitan synagogues had met in an attempt to reverse declining attendances.[14] But their reforms had proved unavailing, leading the *Jewish Chronicle* to remark: 'The recent slight modifications have not had all the effect anticipated by sanguine folk. Many chazanim take advantage of the omissions sanctioned by authority to indulge themselves more than ever in wearisome lengthening of the services by the idiosyncrasies of *chazanos*.'[15]

Such liturgical tinkering carried little weight among the reforming elements in the Orthodox camp, unmoved by the pace and paucity of the Chief Rabbi's directives. As a result, a movement gathered steam in Hampstead to create a place of worship which would be 'not quite of the United Synagogue type but an institution *sui generis*'.[16] With the aid of Morris Joseph, a Jews' College alumnus who had shown early promise as an Orthodox minister, it was to play a prominent, if unwitting, role in the Reform advance and, indirectly, in the emergence of its Liberal offshoot.

The plan drew in residents from the surrounding areas, members of Orthodox and Reform congregations anxious to establish a synagogue that would appeal to both groups. A petition was submitted to Nathan Adler, but his opposition to a number of key issues was to split the organising committee and to pitch the Chief Rabbinate against the more radical members.

The emergent congregation had sought later services, recitation of the Ten Commandments, the dropping of *duchaning* (the priestly blessing) and the omission of other prayers, modifications long since introduced at Berkeley Street. But Adler was to sanction few of them, and in a letter to the secretary, Ernest Löwy, he wrote of his findings:

> I should greatly prefer your adoption of the plan which at present obtains, of reading the *shacharit* and *musaf* services consecutively, with a brief pause being introduced, as is done in some of the places of worship, so as to enable the congregants to enter without disturbing the worshippers present at the earlier part of the service. But I will not withhold my sanction from your reading the *shacharit* service at eight-thirty and holding the second service at eleven.
>
> I permit the omission of a special *mi-sheberach* for each individual called to the Law and shall prepare a form to be recited at the conclusion of the reading of the Law, referring collectively to all the *kero'im* [those called up]. It gratifies me to learn that you intend abrogating the announcement of offerings during the reading of the Law, as I am persuaded that such abrogation will greatly contribute to the maintenance of decorum.
>
> I am not at liberty to sanction the reading of the priestly blessing by the minister in lieu of the Cohanim who are present in the synagogue, as such a procedure would be contrary to divine law. There is a ritual objection[17] to the Decalogue being read as part of the regular Sabbath service. I sanction the public reading of portions of the Holy Scriptures in the vernacular, provided that it be fully understood, and clearly indicated, that this public reading does not constitute a part of the regular and authorised liturgy. The prayer for the Queen and the Royal Family may be recited in English.
>
> A special religious service may be held for pupils of the proposed classes who have concluded their course of instruction and satisfactorily passed their examination in Hebrew and religion. This service must, however, not be termed a Confirmation, such act being foreign to the synagogue.

'I hope', Adler added, pointedly, 'that you will be enabled to obtain the services of a minister who will recite the prayers and the portions of the Scriptures with befitting reverence and dignity, and who by his pulpit utterances will imbue the worshippers with sentiments of piety and devotion. And in these efforts I hope he will be zealously seconded by all the members of your congregation.'[18]

The Chief Rabbi's wishes, however, were to be denied. Three months later, having expressed his desire 'gladly to receive this place of worship, when established, under my pastoral care', he died, leaving his son to face the aftermath of his final prohibitions.

* * *  * * *  * * *

Born in 1848 into an Orthodox family – his father, David, was chazan of the Maiden Lane Synagogue – Morris Joseph was a protégé of Nathan Adler's at Jews' College and was briefly to teach there some forty years later.[19] His first appointment was as minister-secretary to the newly established North London Synagogue, where he served until 1874, moving to Liverpool's Old Hebrew Congregation until ill health cut short his ministry there after seven years. Between then and his involvement in the Hampstead movement, his theological stance shifted, as he put it, 'midway between the Orthodoxy which regards the Shulchan Aruch, or at least the Talmud, as the final authority in Judaism, and the extreme liberalism which, setting little store by the historic sentiment as a factor of the Jewish consciousness, would lightly cut the religion loose from the bonds of Tradition.'[20]

> The Bible [he wrote] never commands us to believe, though it commends belief. Such a command would be useless. Belief cannot be coerced ... [it] is a matter of mental persuasion. We believe in a statement only because our minds are satisfied as to its truth. Real belief is an intellectual condition. Reason is its ultimate foundation.
>
> We say real belief, because to accept a statement as true in spite of the protests of reason, to believe in a doctrine, as someone said he did, because it is impossible, is not belief but credulity. Judaism asks us not for credulity, but for true faith – faith based on reason.
>
> The Bible never commands us to believe. It commands us to know, to get that intellectual persuasion in which belief, to be worth anything, must be rooted. 'Know therefore this day, and consider in thy heart, that the Lord He is God in the heavens above and upon the earth beneath: there is none else.'[21]
>
> But though the Bible never commands us to believe, it expects belief, and supplies us with the means of attaining it ... From time to time, great teachers have attempted to frame a more or less elaborate scheme of necessary Jewish belief. Maimonides,[22] Chasdai Crescas,[23] Simon Duran,[24] Joseph Albo[25] are instances.
>
> But all such schemes, differing as they did from each other, were put forth on the individual responsibility of their respective authors, never in the name of the Jewish Church. And there is reason to believe[26]

that their varying form was largely determined by the passing religious needs of the various ages in which they appeared.[27]

Despite the heterodoxy of such views from a Jews' College standpoint, not everyone in Orthodox circles saw it that way. Adler's successor at Bayswater, Hermann Gollancz – a fellow student of Joseph's – was to remark of the College:

> It is inevitable that varying schools of thought must proceed from Jews' College, and the community should not be shocked or alarmed when such conditions assume practical shape. It is the only honest way, and the only rational process. Jews' College is a training school, an intellectual centre; it is not a forcing-house. The plants therein trained have to develop naturally; the students are, or should be, encouraged to be thinking subjects, not moulded in a cast-iron form.
>
> Whatever views they may imbibe at the College, or may have imbibed before they even entered the College, these views may change, either in the course of training, when experience becomes riper and knowledge wider, or when the methods of congregational life come home to the minister when in office, as he comes face to face in later life with the reality of things, with apparent abuses or real hypocrisy in the name of religion, unfortunately so frequently inseparable from all religious denominations.
>
> In such cases, there dare be no oppression, no persecution, no hardship; it matters not whether a would-be minister finds, after years of study, that he cannot start upon the work he and others had for years marked out for him, or whether a full-blown minister, in office for years, finds for one reason or another that he cannot continue in the same trend of thought upon which he started his official career. There can be no bonds, no price, for the failure to comply; no penalty to be exacted for the change of religious views.[28]

The two Hermanns were to differ sharply in their approach to the advocates of reform. Meanwhile, as the ramifications of Nathan Adler's rulings became increasingly divisive, and the agitators for change ever more vocal, the seeds were being sown, under Joseph's leadership, for the launch of Sabbath afternoon prayers – or 'revised services', as they came to be known – in Hampstead.

They were so framed 'as to meet the wants of those who are not *en rapport* with the present form of public worship. The reason for initiating a service as distinct from a synagogue, and for holding it on Sabbath afternoons, is to avoid competition with any synagogue or with any movement for establishing one. The fact that only a minimum of change is needed in order to make the ancient afternoon prayer a means of arousing devout feelings is an additional consideration which has led to its selection in preference to the morning service.'[29]

Its features were to include a mixed choir with organ accompaniment; psalms, prayers, scriptural readings and sermons delivered in English; and a modified traditional service in Hebrew. One notable change involved substituting in the new prayer book the Hebrew word *v'shirei* ('and the songs of') for *v'ishei* ('and the fire-offerings of') in the supplication for the restoration of the Temple.[30] 'This apparently simple, yet highly important, change', Joseph wrote, 'has not been made without mature deliberation. It is the result of the conviction that no one who has faith in human progress can really believe in the future revival of the sacrificial rite; and what is impossible to believe in, it would be a mockery to pray for.'[31]

At the inaugural gathering, on 22 February 1890, Joseph outlined the aims of his innovative service. 'If the truth is to be made clear', he told the 200 worshippers, 'that Judaism can in sooth be reconciled with modern ideas and made to minister to modern needs, that it still has a message and a mission even for the most advanced minds, provided they have not lost their faith in God nor their reverence for duty – if this truth is to be made clear, it must be preached, and preached amid the solemn associations of public worship.'[32]

Nor was it without significance, the *Jewish Chronicle* observed, 'that the Rev. Morris Joseph and Mr Israel Abrahams, who conduct the services, are on the teaching staff of Jews' College, an institution founded and maintained on strictly "Orthodox" lines'.[33] Their leadership had been noticed in the College itself. At a meeting of the council, within weeks of the inaugural service, Samuel Oppenheim voiced regret that 'two of the teachers have not been acting up to the principle for which the College was established. They are not fit to remain teachers, and more care should be taken that all the teachers are good Jews.'[34]

Adler, conducting the meeting as president of the College, responded that 'it would be best to speak plainly on this matter'. Oppenheim's observations, he said, could not apply to Abrahams, since 'he teaches English and mathematics and it is not for the council to inquire into the religious principles of a gentleman who gives instruction in these subjects'. But with regard to Joseph, the situation was different. The question did arise in respect of a teacher in homiletics and it had exercised the council's attention for some time. They had 'unanimously resolved to inform Mr Joseph that he was called upon to teach his subject in accordance with the principles and rules of traditional Judaism, and they had received from him an answer that he would conform to their directions'.

* * *   * * *   * * *

Joseph's 'revised services' lasted three years and drew approval and criticism in equal measure. At a conference of seat-holders and 'others interested' soon after the launch, Abrahams claimed that Orthodox ministers had 'applauded our efforts' in the belief that the community would achieve 'some, if not all, of the changes we have introduced'.[35] His comment followed remarks in the press by 'A Minister of the United Synagogue' that 'anyone present on Sabbath last at the first of the services inaugurated by the Rev. Morris Joseph must have realised the truth how, with a little judicious treatment of the materials in hand, we may obtain a form of prayers that will appeal to our reason and our feelings and satisfy the yearnings of the human soul'.[36]

This view, wrote a second minister,

> accurately expresses the feeling of the majority of the metropolitan clergy on the ritual question. The clergy are as desirous of seeing some material alterations in our liturgy as are the majority of their congregants. There is no synagogue in London where the services are conducted with greater decorum and solemnity than the Bayswater Synagogue [where Hermann Adler still officiated]. And yet is it not a fact that the greater number of the so-called worshippers at this synagogue are attracted thereto by the discourses of the Delegate Chief Rabbi and not by the service proper, their disregard for this being plainly marked by their absence on any Sabbath when it is known the pulpit will be unoccupied.[37]

Declaring his own congregation to be 'neither more nor less pious than those of the other constituent synagogues', another minister added: 'But this I know well – that of the compact band of regular attendants at the local service and observant Jews in their homes, an overwhelming majority feel that the present liturgy needs very considerable modification before it can adequately interpret their religious sentiments.'[38]

Responding to these comments, Joseph said that it was his wish 'to spread words of hope and encouragement such as are especially needed in these times by the many who feel their Judaism melting away under the solvent of modern criticism, and by the many more who are losing their hold on faith and duty in the presence of life's grim problems'.[39] Most of his sermons had 'little to do with those minor religious questions which divide and sub-divide our community, and more to do with the larger and infinitely more momentous difficulties which vex the conscience and disquiet the soul'.

One such 'difficulty' involved liturgical references to the sacrificial rite, sanctioned by 'the God of a far-off age'. The conservative Jew, declared Joseph in one of his Sabbath afternoon sermons,

> declines to regard the institution as dead. For him, its vitality has not departed: it is merely dormant. In common with many other ordinances of the Law, the sacrificial rite is in a state of suspended animation. The Messiah will come one day and summon it back to active life.
>
> The pious Jew of today who looks forward into the future and sees the old Temple service restored in every detail, who beholds the victim stretched on the altar of sacrifice and its smoke ascending to Heaven as a sweet savour, is doubtless within his right. He gives the rein to his imagination, and his imagination is but the reflection of his spiritual state. He still worships the God of primitive Israel, still thinks that the Supreme can take pleasure in 'the blood of lambs' or 'the fat of fed beasts'.
>
> It would be useless – perhaps it would be wrong – to forbid him. But others, and we among them, are differently constituted. Our conception of God will not permit us to think that He, who is infinitely higher than the most exalted ideas that we can form of Him, can find delight in the burning sacrifice, that He who lovingly provides for the wants of the meanest creature that breathes – He whom our conscience reveals to us as having willed that men should hold all life in veneration as one of the holiest of His mysteries – can desire the slaughter of sheep and oxen for His greater glory.
>
> We cannot think so, for our souls revolt at the thought. The God who loves sacrifice is not He whom we worship, but the God of a far-off age – an age darkened by the shadows of idolatry. He is not, and never can be, our God. For it is impossible to believe that a rite which today seems too gross to be made a means of approaching the Almighty can ever lose its repulsiveness, ever become a fitting mode of doing honour to the Highest.
>
> And so it is in regard not only to sacrifice but to religious institutions generally. The observance which yesterday was living, because it drew its life's blood from union with the soul, may be already dead today, since there is no longer any contact with our spiritual needs to nourish it.
>
> Tomorrow some of today's symbols, too, will have perished and given place to more faithful exponents of our religious ideas. Those only are the true friends of Judaism who recognise this truth, who see that Judaism lives at this present moment only because it has ever yielded a

willing obedience to the law of change, and suffered its merely outward shape to be determined by the shifting needs of successive ages.

Citing the talmudical reference to the brazen serpent, which Moses made and Hezekiah destroyed because it had become 'an object of idolatry',[40] Joseph declared:

> The brazen serpent stands for every religious institution that has lost its old spiritual usefulness and becomes a mere fetish. The sooner such outworn, misused elements are eliminated from religion, the better it will be for religion; and those who sweep them away, instead of being stoned as heretics, ought to be crowned as faithful and far-sighted leaders.
>
> 'There are times', says the Talmud, 'when to break the Law is to establish it more firmly than ever.'[41] And the Talmud itself has set many an example of this pious disobedience. Why not? For what is the object of religion but to make the higher life possible, to lead men nearer to God. And if, owing to the revolution that time has wrought in man himself, the ritual law no longer ministers to the spirit, but fetters it and chains it down, the breaking of the bonds becomes a duty.[42]

Alongside Joseph's Sabbath afternoon services, the Hampstead Synagogue proposal assumed form and formalisation: on Purim 1892, in the presence of Adler, Gaster and Marks, the foundation stone was laid by Benjamin L. Cohen, vice-president of the United Synagogue. Only two months before, the Chief Rabbi and the Haham had turned down invitations to attend the golden jubilee service of Marks' congregation.[43] Now, the West London minister drew loud applause for his comments on congregational unity:

> It is pleasing to note that, side by side with the desire to bring the sanctuary within reasonable distance of the homes of the faithful, there is growing up the idea, which is daily ripening into a conviction, that Judaism – or the synagogue which represents it – is broad enough to receive within its embrace all its disciples who bend in reverence before the covenant of Sinai, what minor differences soever may obtain among them touching the mere form through which their devotion to it is expressed.
>
> The past may be said to have accomplished in a great measure its preceptive mission when it proves a storehouse of memory for the guidance of the future. And if the past shall have rooted in our minds the conviction that congregational union may be maintained and consolidated apart from a rigid conformity in every minutiæ of outward

practice and in every syllable of a given ritual, then we may be disposed to look upon the contention of bygone days as a mere phase of development that has wrought prospective good out of evil.

Describing Marks' attendance as 'historic', Herbert Bentwich, vice-chairman of the Hampstead committee, noted the Chief Rabbi's 'cordial approval of the view that all sections of the community be invited, through their chiefs, to take part in the ceremony ... It is to Professor Marks that we are especially indebted.' Frank Lyons, the chairman, asserted that 'the bringing together of the different religious heads of the community on the same platform after a lapse of fifty years is in itself a justification of the building of a synagogue. Its promoters have at least commanded unity if they could not obtain uniformity.'[44]

That spring, the committee were ready to appoint a minister, though less ready to heed the late Chief Rabbi's caution to appoint one who 'by his pulpit utterances will imbue the worshippers with sentiments of piety and devotion'. Joseph was their choice and had signified his readiness to serve under Chief Rabbinical jurisdiction, subject to being granted freedom of speech. All that remained was to secure Hermann Adler's approval, 'a condition precedent to the election of a minister of the United Synagogue'.[45] But this the Chief Rabbi declined to give and, in a letter to Lyons, he explained why:

> I had a long interview with the Rev. Morris Joseph yesterday. You will remember having admitted to me at our recent interview that your committee would not be justified in appointing a minister who, in the event of being called upon to read any service or part of a service, felt himself compelled to decline undertaking such duty. Mr Joseph, when questioned by me on this point, stated that he could not conscientiously read any of the prayers in which supplication is offered up for the restoration of the sacrificial rite.
>
> I also deemed it advisable to afford him the opportunity of explaining the religious views which he has embodied in various sermons which have been published in the *Jewish Chronicle*. The explanations that he offered proved that I had been correct in my surmise that his opinions are not in accord with the teachings of traditional Judaism. These opinions, Mr Joseph proceeded to state, he would have felt it his bounden duty to expound and to advocate, if appointed minister of the Hampstead Synagogue.
>
> I have, therefore, to my keen regret, no alternative but to adhere to the determination which I communicated to your honorary secretary and to withhold my sanction of the appointment of Mr Joseph as minister of the Hampstead Synagogue.[46]

In a public riposte through the columns of the *Jewish Chronicle*,[47] Joseph described his reaction to the dissolution of his 'dream':

> In your impression of 20 May, you announced my acceptance of the call to the ministry of the Hampstead Synagogue, which had been sent to me in compliance with the unanimous desire of the committee. By this time, it is pretty widely known that the Chief Rabbi, in the exercise of his undoubted right, has definitively declined to sanction my appointment. He has set forth, in a letter to the committee, his reasons for adopting this course; and it is necessary, not only in justice to myself, but as a matter of deep communal interest, that those reasons should be made public.
>
> It is obviously of the highest importance to the community to know what, in the judgment of its chief religious guide, constitutes heresy. For the Chief Rabbi would certainly not have taken the extreme step of deliberately placing a veto upon a congregation's choice of a pastor, and so of preventing it from giving effect to its religious aspirations, on account of any, save heretical, opinions held by the minister thus chosen.
>
> The Chief Rabbi declares me unfit for the ministry of one of his synagogues, first, because I have sanctioned the use of instrumental music at my Sabbath afternoon services; secondly, because I have publicly expressed a disbelief in the future revival of sacrifices, such disbelief being, in the judgment of the Chief Rabbi, opposed to the teachings of Scripture; and thirdly, because in several sermons reported in the Jewish newspapers I have published views 'at variance with traditional Judaism'. This is the head and front of my offending.
>
> Comment from me would be superfluous and unbecoming. I would merely state that the *Jewish Chronicle* is the only newspaper that has reported any of my sermons for some years past, and that those who are anxious to know what my religious position is will find it set forth fully, though necessarily in general terms, in a sermon which you were good enough to print *in extenso* on the fourth of last March.[48]
>
> At the risk of fatiguing your readers with a personal explanation, I am constrained to add some further facts, so as to supply the necessary data for those who wish to arrive at a fair judgment on this important matter in its various aspects.
>
> The invitation I received from the committee of the Hampstead Synagogue was entirely unsought by me. I can go even further than this and say that I deprecated the idea of sending it. When, some eighteen months ago, the chairman of the committee first spoke to

me on the subject and asked me to promise that I would favourably consider such an invitation, I at once pointed out the difficulty that stood in the way of the committee's wishes being realised and suggested their abandonment.

The chairman's overtures, however, were renewed on subsequent occasions and were always met by me in the same way. It was only a few weeks ago, after a long interval, during which I imagined that the affair was at an end, that these unofficial negotiations were once more resumed. This very persistence, so flattering to myself, proved the earnestness of the committee's desire to appoint me, and the request for a favourable reply was made in such urgent terms that I felt bound to give it the most serious consideration.

By far the easier course would have been to decline the proposed invitation. I could not ignore the fact that in taking service with an 'Orthodox' congregation, I should expose myself to misconstruction. On the other hand, a call from an important congregation was one which it seemed to be a duty to accept even at the risk of personal misrepresentation.

The religious tendencies of that congregation, so far as they can be ascertained at this early stage of its existence, are known to be of an advanced character, and in inviting me to its ministry the committee, it appeared to me, were simply giving effect to a local desire to have those tendencies reflected in the pulpit. Thus it was only after great searchings of heart, and after consultation with friends upon whose disinterested advice I could rely, that I yielded at last to the solicitations that had been so often addressed to me.

I could not thrust aside the opportunity of continuing, in a wider sphere, those labours for the cause of spiritual Judaism which I have been carrying on in Hampstead for the past two years and a half. But I spared no effort to make it plain to the honorary officers and the committee that, in accepting the call, I must be considered as reserving my right to preach my opinions in their synagogue.

I told those gentlemen, and I told the Chief Rabbi himself last week, that it was my intention to teach progressive Judaism; and the opportunity of teaching it, and of bringing its influences to bear upon the religious life, in the case of a larger congregation than I am able at present to reach, was my sole motive in accepting once more the ministry of a synagogue under the Rabbinate.

I confess that, against my judgment, I had caught the optimism of the Hampstead committee and, hoping against hope, indulged the belief that at last the 'Orthodox' pulpit was, under authority, to be made broad enough to admit the enunciation of the liberal doctrine. I suppose the wish was father to the thought. I have no taste for controversy as such, nor a weak predilection for sensationalism, but I entertain the deliberate conviction that if there is to be a real, a living Judaism in this country in the coming days, it is only an enlightened teaching that will ensure it.

Well, my pleasant dream has been rudely dispelled. My only wonder is that I ever allowed myself to dream it. I have long felt – and the episode I have been describing has only deepened the conviction – that progress, with its attendant salvation for English Judaism, is impossible within the confines of the synagogue as by Rabbinical law established.

I place the conviction on record in sorrow only, and not with the slightest scintilla of anger. My inhibition has not caused me any feeling that approaches vexation in the smallest degree. On the contrary, it is with a sense of relief that I find myself free from ties which, in my anxiety to preach what my conscience should declare to be true and right, might easily have proved to be galling shackles.

Moreover, I cannot be angry at being denied a position in which I must almost inevitably have challenged ungenerous criticism. Nevertheless, I cannot deny that I deeply regret the loss of an opportunity of doing something, however little, towards securing for Judaism some of its wavering adherents, and especially of attaching to it the minds and hearts of our younger coreligionists, and of helping them to lay the foundations of a truly religious life.

Nor would I have anyone cast a stone at the kind and learned man who has passed upon me this sentence of minor excommunication. The Chief Rabbi is but the administrator of a system, and so long as the community acquiesces in the existence of that system, it is only the community that is really responsible for procedure whose logical effect would be to exclude from the pulpits of English synagogues some of the most gifted and renowned of Continental rabbis – men who have a world-wide reputation as authorities on Judaism.

And lest it be thought that I am appealing to the supreme tribunal of public opinion on the mere personal issue, I hasten to add that by this post I inform the Hampstead committee that I unreservedly withdraw my acceptance of the call which they have been good enough to send me. With a grateful sense of their uniform courtesy and consideration, I take the initiative in bringing my relations with them to an end.

The community, then, is free to deal with this episode from the widest standpoint. All that has to be considered is whether the religious needs of a progressist congregation are to be ignored, and its spiritual life starved, in obedience to a rigid system, or whether the time has not come for identifying the synagogue with that catholic spirit and policy which, while duly respecting the opinions of conservative minds, will give full satisfaction to liberal aspirations.

I cannot profess to be very sanguine as to the result of this appeal. Despite its progressist sympathies, the Anglo-Jewish community is not easily roused. But if it prefers the *laisser faire* policy, it shall not be for want of having the true issue put broadly and clearly. It is mainly with this purpose in view that I have written this letter.

To return to myself once more, let me say that the incident has left me a little wiser and a little sadder; but it has not infused one drop of bitterness into my mind. If I can be of use to my 'Orthodox' brethren in any sphere outside the synagogue, they have but to command me. I shall not discontinue my work for the visitation committee of the United Synagogue, whose minister I am not deemed worthy to be, nor shall I relax my philanthropic efforts for a community in whose spiritual instruction I am not allowed to take part.

I have dreamt dreams; but having discovered them to be but dreams, I shall not be so foolish as to reject the reality, Work, with all its consolations.[49]

A year later, Joseph was elected senior minister at the West London Synagogue, in succession to Marks.[50] He served in the post for thirty-two years and, in 1911, was present at the Great Synagogue service in memory of Hermann Adler, sitting alongside Dayan Moses Hyamson (who delivered the eulogy), Dayan Asher Feldman, and Rabbi Moshe Avigdor Chaikin, chief minister of the Federation of Synagogues.[51] The gesture was reciprocated in 1930 when, in the 'progressive-conservatism' of the post-Adlerian era, Chief Rabbi Joseph Herman Hertz, Gaster and three of the dayanim gathered at the Reform cemetery in Golders Green as Morris Joseph's cremated remains were laid to rest. Hertz and the dayanim were also present at the West London memorial service later that day.[52]

\* \* \*    \* \* \*    \* \* \*

Israel Abrahams' prescience was bearing fruit. The Sabbath afternoon services had indeed spurred movement within the United Synagogue and, in an 1891 report on the rabbinate, the US council called for 'the question of synagogue ritual and practice to be solved to the benefit and advancement of the religious well-being of the entire community and consistently with the maintenance of the traditional observances of our faith'.

In one of his first acts as Chief Rabbi, Adler responded by convening a conference of 'preachers of the metropolitan and provincial congregations under my pastoral charge' to consider, with him, modifications in the synagogue ritual. The three-day conference met in May 1892, when 'assiduous attention was given to every proposition of practical value'. The delegates, Adler wrote later, were 'fully penetrated by a sense of the momentousness of the subject that engaged their deliberations'.[53] Publishing his findings, confined mainly to the *kaddish*, the repetition of the *amidah*, the recitation of certain psalms, the penitential prayers (*selichot*), the priestly blessing, and the High Holy-day liturgy, Adler stressed that he had given his sanction to 'those alterations which do not violate any statute (*din*) of traditional Judaism and which do not affect our statutory liturgy'.

In response to a request from the Central Synagogue, he conceded – 'with great reluctance' – that the Sabbath morning service could commence

> at the late hour of 9.45. I only do so in the hope that this arrangement may induce a larger number of worshippers than heretofore to attend at the commencement, and with the understanding that, as proposed, the three sections of the Shema be read at the first recital. The regulation of the precise hour at which each portion of the service is to be read, and when [it] is to terminate, must be left to the boards of management, with the one stipulation that no part may be hurried or slurred over.[54]

In a plea to the chazanim and choirmasters, reflecting the *Jewish Chronicle*'s comment on the earlier reforms, Adler urged them

> always to recite the prayers and portions of Scripture correctly, impressively and devoutly, avoiding all singing of an elaborate character. Earnestly and affectionately I beseech the preachers to rouse in the hearts of their congregants a renewed love and reverence for our venerable liturgy, around which there cluster so many holy associations. And I entreat the worshippers not to imagine that divine service can be performed vicariously for them, but to offer up the prayers with concentrated attention and fervour and to join with heartiness in the responses, psalms and hymns. In order to enable the congregants to do this, I would ask the choirmasters to use the simplest harmonies and to eschew all melodies of an ornate and florid character.[55]

Yet again, however, the Chief Rabbi's modifications lacked universal appeal. Putting momentum before momentousness, the most radical of the disaffected, roused by the Hampstead reformers, began to sow the seeds of a movement that, in due course, would give rise to the 'new religion' of Liberal Judaism. And yet again, in an uncanny sequence of events, the kinsfolk of two of the staunchest opponents of reform – a Montefiore and a Montagu – were to turn faith on its head.

# 6

## Singer's Song

In July 1890, just six months after the death of Nathan Adler but with 'the stamp of his sanction and authorisation', there appeared in London the first edition of what was to become universally known as the 'Singer's Prayer Book'. Missing from the unsigned preface, in its reference to the 'entirely new' translation, was the name of the individual responsible for the biblical passages, described merely as 'an accomplished scholar'.[1]

A year later, with Chief Rabbinical control briefly suspended, the preface to the second ('carefully revised') edition – signed by Simeon Singer himself – rectified the omission. 'It should be noted', he wrote, 'that in the translation of the various biblical passages, the Revised Version (text or margin) has throughout been adopted as a basis. Several changes have, however, been made, chiefly in the direction of greater literalness. These are mainly the work of Mr Claude G. Montefiore. For this service, as well as for much other help, I am greatly indebted to him.'[2] The amended preface was to grace all subsequent editions until, during the Chief Rabbinate of Israel Brodie, conservatism overpowered progressivism in the hearts and minds of the centrist establishment and restored the 'accomplished scholar' to his unsung place in Orthodox liturgical history.

Singer, trained at Jews' College, destined to become a household name in United Synagogue circles, a close colleague of Chief Rabbis and a traditionalist of repute, was also a friend of the 'accomplished scholar' and the childhood tutor of Lily Montagu, Montefiore's partner in the creation of the Jewish Religious Union that welcomed Liberal Judaism to Britain.[3] Their shared dismay at the rise in religious indifference, declining attendances at synagogue – both Orthodox and Reform – and the absence of godliness in the lives of so many resulted in a convergence of approaches that, albeit briefly and controversially, was to make bedfellows of rabbis and laymen from across the communal divide.

Claude Joseph Goldsmid Montefiore,[4] with impeccable Orthodox and Reform antecedents as the paternal grandnephew of Sir Moses Montefiore and maternal grandson of Sir Isaac Lyon Goldsmid, imbibed his liberal, ethical and universalistic theologies at the feet of his Oxford mentor,

Benjamin Jowett, translating them – in Jewish terms – into 'a Judaism which shall be broad enough and humble enough to believe that its own truths, its own treasures, can be enriched and added to from the truths and treasures that may have been vouchsafed to other than Jewish teachers'.[5]

His associate, Lily (Lilian Helen) Montagu,[6] was the youngest of the three daughters (and the sixth child) of Samuel Montagu, first Baron Swaythling, the unswervingly Orthodox founder (1887) of the Federation of Synagogues.[7] Of her father, whom she greatly admired but, doctrinally, vigorously opposed, she was to write:

> He would not admit the necessity of adapting religious belief and practice, and consequently never recognised that such adaptation could be the expression of honest conviction, the result of intellectual training. It was in his view merely a pandering to selfish convenience and self-indulgence. He was born too soon to recognise the inwardness of Liberal Judaism, and to see that it is the logical outcome of principles as clear as his own, and often held with the same intensity and reflecting the same power of self-sacrifice.
>
> He could never believe that it is conviction, and not cowardice, which discards certain observances which require for their justification a weakening of the God-Idea of Truth. He could never see that it is conviction, and not obduracy, which causes a man to find divinity in biblical lessons rather than in the Bible as a whole.
>
> He could never understand that Liberal Judaism owes its existence to a different authority – to the God Within, as interpreted by the trained conscience – while Orthodox Judaism owes its authority to the Bible as interpreted by tradition; but that the first authority – like the second – is powerful and exacting, and demands an equally stern and sometimes painful discipline.[8]

In 1899, the paths of the inspirational philosopher and the dedicated pragmatist were to cross through the appearance of Lily Montagu's first major foray into literary endeavour. 'We are required', she wrote in Montefiore's journal,

> to use in God's service all the gifts of mind and heart which He has granted to us, since it is a form of blasphemy to conceal or to pervert truth, in order to render our service of God acceptable to Him. We, who are conscious of our great needs, must organise ourselves into an association to rediscover our Judaism, encouraging one another to reformulate our ideal. We shall be able to rally round us the discontented and weary, and together we may hope to lift Judaism from its desolate position and absorb it into our lives.[9]

Montagu's 'association' took three years to emerge, during which time she garnered the support of, among others, three United Synagogue ministers – Simeon Singer, of the New West End; Aaron Asher Green, of Hampstead; and Joseph F. Stern, of East London – as well as Albert H. Jessel, a vice-president of the US; Felix A. Davis, its treasurer; Hermann Adler's brother-in-law, Nathan S. Joseph; and Isidore Spielmann, Lily Montagu's cousin and a former warden of the New West End.

At a meeting in February 1902, Montefiore was elected president, Montagu, Singer and Jessel vice-presidents, and the association – at the suggestion of Morris Joseph and Green – was named the Jewish Religious Union. The stage was set 'to provide means for deepening the religious spirit among those members of the Jewish community who are not in sympathy with the present synagogue services, or who are unable to attend them'.[10] The first of the weekly Sabbath afternoon services, it was announced, would be on 18 October 1902; worshippers would 'sit together, without distinction of sex'; prayers would be mainly in English, 'conducted by ministers and laymen belonging to various sections of the community'; and 'the musical portion (with instrumental accompaniment) will, it is hoped, be led by a voluntary choir'.[11]

\* \* \*   \* \* \*   \* \* \*

St John's Wood Synagogue – sixty years later to feature prominently in another case of sectarian brinkmanship – played an unsupporting role in the launch of the Jewish Religious Union, contrary to the organisers' original aspirations. Determined to locate their Sabbath afternoon services within the sanctum of an established synagogue, they had 'waited upon'[12] the Chief Rabbi in order to learn whether any such building under his jurisdiction might be available for their purposes.

Despite the camaraderie of the meeting, held between long-standing friends and acquaintances over a cup of tea, Adler unsurprisingly declined to give the project his blessing, citing the United Synagogue's Deed of Foundation and Trust as the basis for his refusal, and urged the organisers to moderate their proposals by holding a customary, if choral, minchah service, with a Bible reading and a prayer in English.[13] Stung by this unsympathetic response, the committee turned instead to the Wharncliffe Rooms of Marylebone's Great Central Hotel.

Adler's rebuff, however, was but a foretaste of the oncoming storm. Pressure began to build on the Orthodox members of the committee, and one by one they faded away – though none without vocal (and in some cases organisational) support. Singer, who was the last to go, had been among the first to join and was, with Green and other liturgists, responsible for the original and subsequently enlarged edition of the Union's prayer book.[14] Of the expanded version, its compilers observed:

> The present edition of the *Selection of Prayers, Psalms and Hymns* is, like its predecessor, of a provisional character. It is, however, considerably larger and will, it is hoped, be found more adequate for the needs of worshippers at the services of the Jewish Religious Union.
>
> For a number of metrical versions or paraphrases of psalms, the committee are indebted to Mrs Henry Lucas,[15] who has also permitted them to make further selections from her *Jewish Year*. Both in the prose and metrical portions of the book, considerable use has been made of the liturgical poems of Jehuda ha-Levi.[16] Most of the prayers now added are derived or adapted from the traditional Jewish liturgy, but a few have been specially written for the services of the Union.[17]

Before the prayer book was put to use, however, Green had left the committee, though he continued to evince sympathy with its motives and aims. Even as his former associates were preparing to enter the Great Central precincts for their inaugural service, he explained his volte-face in a pulpit statement to his Hampstead congregants. Acknowledging that 'many reforms are necessary', that he had 'always advocated them and will continue to do so', he had never swerved, he said, from his contention that 'what is needed is conference, so that advance can be made all along the line'. He wanted 'a mile of reform'. But he would rather 'the whole community moved unitedly one inch than that a section should advance alone one hundred miles'.

He had wanted the movement kept within the synagogue, and he had now left it because it had 'gone outside the synagogue without trying what could be done inside it, and broken existing laws instead of trying to alter them'. When the committee had determined to carry forward its programme of service and had refused to consider its position, it was, he felt, 'driving the extreme Orthodox party on to their firmest defences and setting back, instead of helping forward, the desire that so many have to help advance along easily and with security, without disruption on the one hand or increase of bigotry on the other'.[18]

Green's departure did not deter Montefiore, Montagu, Singer and their colleagues from pursuing their goal, and the Jewish Religious Union launched its inaugural service later that day. The *Jewish Chronicle*'s correspondent was not impressed:

When the Rev. S. Singer, who conducted the service, ascended the pulpit to give out a few preliminary instructions, a mixed congregation of some three or four hundred ladies and gentlemen must have faced him. A stranger entering the stately apartment where the service was held might have been excused if he failed to recognise that he was in the midst of a Jewish congregation, for the characteristic of the gathering was its divorce from almost all that we have become accustomed to associate with the Synagogue. The synagogal trappings were, of course, absent. The Hebrew tongue had receded into a place of minor importance. Chazanut, with all the medieval and latter-day Judaism that is intertwined with it, was banished from the scene. Even the Sefer Torah was conspicuous by its absence. A service without an Ark, without a cantor, almost without Hebrew! It was hard to believe that, as Mr Montefiore claimed, it was still a Jewish service.[19]

Explaining, 'very simply and briefly', why the responsibility of establishing a new kind of service had been incurred, Montefiore told his flock:

We believe that there are many Jews and Jewesses in England who seldom or never attend a place of worship, and more especially a Jewish place of worship. This fact we regard as deplorable. What are its causes?

Now the causes are many and various, and some of them are beyond our power to lessen or remove. But among them we believe one cause to be that many Jews and Jewesses do not like the only kind of service which is open to them to attend. For various reasons, the ordinary and regular Jewish services do not appeal to them; these ordinary and regular Jewish services have become distant, unsatisfying and, in the literal sense of the word, unattractive.

This cause is only one cause out of many, and it may well be that the other causes are so strong and effective that, even if this one cause were removed, the result would not be different. But we believe that this one cause is not purely isolated. It helps the other causes. Remove it, and others will also become weaker and fewer ...

It would have been far easier to sit still and do nothing; but, as no more authoritative and better organised attempt was in view, we thought it our duty not to let things go, as the saying is, from bad to worse, without making a small attempt, at any rate, to interpose a tiny barrier against the evil stream.[20]

Hermann Adler begged to differ. Six weeks later, he used the St John's Wood Synagogue as the venue for an attack on the Union rather than, as

# Singer's Song

they had hoped of him, a sanctuary for the Unionists. Responding to an 'earnest appeal' from members of the community who had asked for his views on the Union's services – 'and charged, as I am, with a large measure of responsibility for the religious well-being of Anglo-Jewry – I dare not shrink from this task, however painful it may prove'.

Adler conceded that the purpose which the new movement had set itself was 'laudable' and 'a worthy endeavour', in seeking to deepen the religious spirit of those 'who, at present, hold aloof from the services of the synagogue'. But, he questioned, was their method acceptable?

> It is contended that members of the community are out of sympathy with the ritual, because it is couched in an unknown tongue. There would be some justification for this plea if the worshipper, by his ignorance of Hebrew, were altogether debarred from joining in the devotions and from understanding the Torah and the Prophets read during service.
>
> But is this plea just, seeing that in the *Authorised Daily Prayer Book* we possess a translation which reproduces the liturgy with admirable fidelity and in terse English – a book which, by the wise generosity of a worthy sister in Israel,[21] has been placed within the reach of the poorest? And versions of the Bible, happily, are not less accessible.
>
> But it is argued that there are prayers and aspirations which jar upon the feelings of men and women who are deeply imbued with the culture of the present age. We may ask: Does then Judaism, so sublime in its purity and so pure in its sublimity, teach dogmas that are repugnant to our common sense? Granted that there are a few isolated supplications which an individual cannot conscientiously offer, does that justify absenteeism?
>
> Yet another cause is said to promote abstention: that a husband is compelled, at the threshold of the synagogue, to part from his wife, and a father from his daughter – an argument which I must be permitted to describe as grotesque. This lamentable separation has never for a moment kept the merchant from his counting-house, nor debarred an Englishman from delighting in his club. But, in sooth, is the pious husband parted from his faithful helpmate in God's house? Even as Isaac entreated the Lord for (literally, over against) Rebecca, so the devout prayers of man and wife still mingle before the Heavenly Throne of Mercy.
>
> And to meet these grave objections, some well-meaning men and women have departed from the old paths, and have devised a service which has banished itself from the synagogue on account of certain

> 'novel features', or rather drastic innovations, that involve a departure from historic Judaism.
>
> I have given most careful consideration to the *Selection of Prayers, Psalms and Hymns* which has been prepared for use at these gatherings. And I am constrained to say that a service which almost entirely dispenses with the use of the sacred language, a ritual for the Sabbath Day which practically ignores the Sabbath and the Sabbath ritual, which repudiates the predictions of our Prophets, which maims some of our finest psalms, and borrows from the hymnary of the Church – such service cannot, I maintain, be considered a Jewish service ...

Anticipating disapproval of the 'negativism' of his remarks, Adler admitted that

> there can be no possible objection to the institution of Sabbath afternoon services, with special addresses. Such services have been held in the Great Synagogue for many years and have attracted crowded congregations.
>
> As soon as the aim and object of the Union were brought before me, I readily approved the holding of similar services in the West. But I asked that the prescribed *minchah* prayers should be offered up – prayers that quiver with love and throb with gratitude for the glory and greatness of the Day of Rest. Readings from the Bible, prayers and psalms in the vernacular might then be readily added.
>
> But the principal feature of the service should be the discourse, in which the preacher should plead with all earnestness, all the enthusiasm at his command, for the keeping of the Sabbath. He should seek to combat the evils we deplore – religious decadence, with its accompanying materialism and abstention from divine worship. He should strive to rouse his hearers to a more loyal Jewish life, with the spirituality and the aspiration of the human soul Godward, which it enforces.
>
> These efforts should be seconded by direct personal influence. And if enthusiastic ministers and earnest laymen would come into touch with the Jewish residents in their respective districts, impressing upon those who were systematic absentees the duty and the privilege of public worship, they would not labour for nought, nor spend their strength in vain.

Adler told the congregation that he would

> gladly welcome services established on these lines in connection with one or more of the existing synagogues. For the [Union] service, as at present arranged, does not spell Reform, but Revolt. It makes not

for Union, but Disunion. It has within itself the germs of division, discord and severance. And assuredly, at a time like the present, when our communal life is beset by dangers and difficulties on every side, we need union of hearts and efforts, but not a movement calculated to cause bitterness and estrangement in Anglo-Judaism.[22]

Adler's sermon attracted a robust response from Israel Abrahams, a committee member of the Jewish Religious Union (and Singer's son-in-law). 'Your interesting sermon', he told the Chief Rabbi in an 'Open Letter',

> certainly demanded close attention, and with much that you say I fully sympathise. Some features of the service of the Jewish Religious Union are, as you urge, not wholly unobjectionable; but the committee have all along felt this. They never regarded their brief pamphlet as a complete expression of their Judaism, nor did they put it forth as a final form of their service.
>
> But taking the pamphlet as it stands, I venture to submit some considerations which may convince you that the compilers of the pamphlet were not animated by a 'non-Jewish' spirit ... The Jewish liturgy has always made the freest possible use of the Bible; it has modified texts, has selected odd verses, has quoted consecutive verses in the opposite order to that in which they occur in the Bible. I need not delay to cite illustrations from the *Authorised Daily Prayer Book* of all these facts.
>
> You object to the omission made by the Union on a specific ground, and on this very ground, historic Judaism supports the right to omit. You ask: 'Is it consonant with the teachings of historic Judaism to ignore the punitive justice of the God of Mercy?' I fully agree that if the Union did this, it would deserve to be stigmatised as 'non-Jewish'. But can this be fairly urged of a service which includes the Second Commandment?
>
> The Ten Commandments have been read (in Hebrew) on three out of the four occasions on which I have attended the Union service. But it does not imply any theological principle if a few verses are omitted because they seem to break the serene, lyric beauty of the psalm for the holy day of peace and rest ...
>
> I will recall your attention to some points in the service which, though you do not mention them all, are of great importance. The Union has included the *Shema*, the *Ahavah*, and also *Adon Olam*. Could any but a thoroughly Jewish service include these passages? Do they not of themselves constitute a Jewish worship? Of these three passages, the first and third are week by week said in Hebrew ...

Besides the Jewish prayers referred to, the prayers and selections contain the following ideas: again and again the choice of Israel is insisted on; God is invoked as the 'God of our Fathers', thus asserting Jewish tradition; Israel is 'God's people'; the departure from Egypt is several times alluded to; the service speaks of the 'House of Israel', scattered over the face of the globe, thus acclaiming the religious community of all Jews; it lays stress on the 'joy of living' – a peculiarly Jewish attitude towards life; it repeatedly cites messianic passages, and many prophecies as to Israel's mission; it uses the strikingly Jewish formula 'as it is written in the Law', and appeals for obedience to the commandments of God; it quotes verse on verse insisting on the covenant between God and Israel, 'God's peculiar treasure'; quotes pointedly a passage in which the Jewish doctrine of atonement, 'Turn yourselves and live', is enforced; God's omnipresence, the value of righteousness, the imperative appeal of the moral law – all these Jewish doctrines are illustrated by carefully chosen texts ...

In the firm conviction that our service is fully Jewish, and that it is adapted to its particular end, we trust to promote the cause of Judaism, and to win back to enthusiastic allegiance those who at present are half-hearted or worse.[23]

\* \* \*   \* \* \*   \* \* \*

A second United Synagogue minister quit the Union committee, under Chief Rabbinical pressure,[24] days after Adler delivered his sermon. In what must have been one of the shortest reports in its history (though under a headline considerably more prominent), the *Jewish Chronicle* tersely announced: 'We understand that the Rev. J.F. Stern has severed his connection with the Jewish Religious Union.'[25]

\* \* \*   \* \* \*   \* \* \*

Singer's role – as, to a lesser extent, that of others – in the activities of the Union, and in wider areas of the reformist movement, provoked strong reaction within the Orthodox community. But he was no stranger to controversy and had drawn notice for his participation in Reform services a decade before his fraternisation with Montefiore and Montagu. Addressing his New West End congregation on Chanukkah 1891, on the theme of defence and construction, he had drawn attention to an upcoming 'notable event in Anglo-Jewish history – the jubilee of a sister synagogue'. Few present that day, he said, were old enough to remember the establishment of the West London Synagogue and the causes that had led to 'the memorable schism'; but the impartial inquirer would have 'no slight difficulty in deciding, I will not say with which party the fault lay, but with which the greater fault lay'.

Fifty years on, was it not time

> to bury the past and to cease to keep each, so far as religious fellowship is concerned, at arm's length? ... Am I uttering an unreasonable or an unseasonable wish, am I uttering a wish in which any Israelite – of whatever school – need hesitate to join, when I express the hope that the jubilee of the West London Synagogue of British Jews may be distinguished by a closer approximation of all sections of the Anglo-Jewish community; that fifty years of separation may be followed by countless years of generous reunion, during which the ancient quarrels of brethren shall be forgotten in the re-integration of the spirit of Jewish brotherhood?[26]

Singer, for one – despite his deference to Chief Rabbinical authority[27] – was ready to facilitate that 'generous reunion'. Two years later, he occupied the Sabbath morning pulpit at the Manchester Congregation of British Jews – the premier Reform synagogue outside the metropolis – and announced unequivocally:

> Standing in this place, it is possible to feel that Judaism has more, and more important, matters that unite us than those it is worth while to quarrel about, and that our distinctions, whatever else they are, are not vital.
>
> It is possible for me, a minister of a synagogue under a different ecclesiastical régime from yours, to come into this House of God and to deliver my message, and to do this without apology either to you or to the congregation to which it is my privilege and happiness to be attached. I almost owe you an apology for suggesting, though it be only to brush it aside, the thought of an apology. Thanks be above all to Him who is true to his twofold promise to give strength to His people and to bless His people with peace![28]

Singer's first, and only, sermon to the Jewish Religious Union was delivered a week after its inauguration – which event, he noted,

> as might have been anticipated, attracted a certain amount of attention in our community. Whatever criticism it may evoke, one consolation is ours: we have set out with no selfish object in view. It is the

highest of all our common interests that is at stake. We are helping to perfect one another's lives through the medium of the faith of Israel.

It is all a question of methods. Methods other than those which the Jewish Religious Union has after due deliberation adopted happily succeed elsewhere, and with others. To be associated with the older methods is, to many of us, and to myself especially, a privilege and a joy. If there had been any likelihood of their proving serviceable to those for whom the Union has been formed, how gladly, how eagerly they would have been embraced!

But it seemed right that some effort should be made to win and keep for Judaism those brothers and sisters of ours who were drifting from it, and to do this by means, legitimate in themselves, by which they would be likely to be attracted and secured. If you want to do any good to people – to people of mature age and judgment – you must do it in the way they are prepared to accept it ...

We are full of hope in the ultimate success of our undertaking. If we can point to fifty, to ten, to a single one of our brethren whom we have kept and strengthened in the faith and hope of Israel, we shall have justified our existence. 'He who saves a single soul in Israel is as though he had saved a whole world', says the Talmud, for in that soul a whole spiritual world is potentially contained. And if we fail, we shall have the consciousness of having failed in a noble cause.

Others will follow, will learn from our errors, and will succeed. In God's name may they do so. We only know, 'It is time to work for the Lord' ...

But, Singer warned,

> they err greatly who imagine that all that is required to constitute a Jew is to give an intellectual assent to some abstract proposition, such as the existence or the unity of God. Judaism is more than a creed; it is a discipline. Frankly, my friends, it is useless to expect that Judaism can ever become an easy religion. Let no one who joins this Union be under any misapprehension on that point.
>
> You may to a certain extent modify the outward form and ritual of your faith; you may correct your historical perspective by a deeper study of the past; you may plead for a due adjustment of the relations between morals and ceremonial – you can never reduce Judaism to a religion of mere convenience, offering a maximum of reward for a minimum of obligation and effort.[29]

In 1903, over his participation in the Union, Singer may still have believed – as he had in Manchester ten years earlier – that an apology was inappropriate, but his resignation became unavoidable after yet another outspoken sermon, this time to his own congregation, which aroused the discomfort of his foremost patron, Lily Montagu's father, Sir Samuel. Taking as his text, on the first day of Pesach, the biblical exhortation 'Art thou for us or for our adversaries?'[30] Singer had declaimed:

> Great care is needed that we do not unwisely and uncharitably contract the notion of who shall be reckoned on our side, and widen out the notion of who shall be accounted on the side of our enemies. It would be nothing short of a calamity if we arrogated to ourselves the right, for instance, of branding as on the side of our adversaries everyone who could not find room on the particular theological shelf – a very narrow one it may be – which we happen to occupy.
>
> Terms like 'un-Jewish' are flung about rather wildly nowadays and in a spirit which, to say the least, is anything but Jewish. The Talmud has taught us better things. There you may read, 'Whosoever denies and repudiates idolatry is as though he had confessed the whole Torah.' 'Whosoever denies and repudiates idolatry is called a Jew.'
>
> Of course, we must not press such noble utterances as these too hard. We must not make it appear as if Judaism were simply a negative creed, or a bundle of negations. What sensible people do is to strive to grasp the spirit of a broad-minded and tolerant principle like this.
>
> The question as between us and many of our fellow Jews is: Are you with us in the great essentials of Judaism? Is that which unites us not more and of more importance than that which separates us? When the angel is asked by Joshua, 'Art thou for us, or for our adversaries?' he gives more than a formal reply. 'Nay, but as Captain of the host of the Lord am I come.' That is: Assuredly not for your adversaries am I. I am on God's side; how then can I be otherwise than on your side also, if you are on God's side? I am a servant of the Lord; if you, too, are a servant of His, then am I your natural ally.[31]

These remarks brought a rapid response from Samuel Montagu. In a letter from his Kensington home, he told Singer that he had listened 'with much interest' to his 'eloquent address', and added:

> Rest assured that it would be impossible for those who have known your devoted work to doubt the sincerity of your wish to serve the highest interests of the community, even though many, like myself, are not prepared to alter the basis of our time-honoured service in order to attract worshippers.

Personally, however, I fully sympathise with your wish to keep all the members of our race within the community; and I would welcome the organisation of Sabbath afternoon services with additions which would satisfy the less Orthodox.

But, apart from my personal views, I think you should recognise that your connection with the Religious Union is causing much unrest among the members of your congregation, and that this unrest may in time be subversive of your influence.

I would ask you seriously to consider whether you should not now withdraw your connection with the Union. Indeed, I feel sure that you will be ready to make this sacrifice, if, as I believe, the continued welfare of our synagogue depends upon it.[32]

Singer's reply was as swift and sincere: 'I am much obliged to you', he told Montagu,

for your kind letter. You have, during recent occurrences, acted so completely in the spirit of a true gentleman and a sincere Jew, and your personal relations with me for the last quarter of a century have been so constantly those of a genuine friend, that your views and wishes are entitled to have especial weight with me.

Now, it is certain that the Jewish Religious Union has been, and is engaged in doing, and successfully doing, a great and sacred work among numbers of Jews on whose behalf hitherto no one has stirred a finger, and whose drifting from Judaism and sometimes from religion altogether no serious attempt has been made to arrest. I had hoped that the privilege and the happiness might be mine of aiding in some slight measure in the realisation of the ideals of the Union.

If, however, as under present circumstances seems to be the case, that privilege and that happiness can only be mine at the cost of the peace of the congregation I have for the major portion of my active life striven to the best of my powers to build up, then I acknowledge that the price is too high for me to pay. So much have I felt this that for some time past I have not taken part in the Union services. At the next meeting of the committee, I shall send in my resignation.

It is with intense regret that I take the step of severing my connection with the Jewish Religious Union. I do so solely under the belief, which your letter confirms, that the peace and welfare of the synagogue I love and have so long served demand this great sacrifice from me.

In a postscript, Singer added:

I will not now enter into the other matter touched upon in your letter – the alternative of the 'Statutory' Sabbath Afternoon Service with additions, &c., except to say that that alternative was carefully considered and that it was felt that such a service would not appeal to those for whom the Union caters. There is, however, no reason why it should not appeal to others.[33]

Three years later, Singer – lauded by Hermann Adler as 'my gifted pupil and colleague'[34] – died in London, aged 59. His last sermon,[35] preached on Shavuot 1906 in the almost certain knowledge of his impending mortality, was a backwards (if oblique) glance at the heady days of sectarian discord. Taking as his text the verse in Habbakuk (2:4), 'The just shall live by his faith', he observed:

> To many of us in this age, accustomed to let faith lie dormant, or to suspect it, or even despise it, it may seem strange to note the place here assigned to it.
>
> Faith, we are apt to think, is the mark of an age long past and never to be recalled. Faith is a toy of childhood, which we cast aside in maturer years, and exchange for manlier reason. Yet here the prophet, with evidently no thought of giving it merely a temporary application, declares that it is – along with right conduct, of course – at once the test and promise of true life.

Citing examples of 'how large a portion of our daily life is based upon faith', Singer added:

> In what has been said, no one, I trust, will hear a plea for mere blind unreasoning and unquestioning faith, or sheer credulity ... The faith that is needed in our intercourse with our fellow men – the faith that makes the whole wealth of past experience our own – is the same as that we need in religion, only enlarged, purified, exalted in accordance with the higher object at which it aims.
>
> I will say it frankly and risk the consequences of the avowal, that while faith and reason are blended in the religion of Israel as perhaps in no other, it is not the second place that must be assigned to faith. A child believes in the love of father and mother, and responds to it without reasoning as to the cause or the justification of that wondrous love. And, before God, what are the greatest, the wisest, the most gifted among mortals, but feeble, faltering, helpless babes? ...
>
> Am I wrong in suggesting that we need in our age above all a stronger flow of faith? Am I wrong in asserting that gradually, but perceptibly, the current that once refreshed every Jewish heart is

withdrawing and leaving behind it large spaces, bare, arid, sterile?

Many causes contribute to the regrettable result. Some people say: O our faith is shaken. Can it be otherwise when the Bible tells us one thing, and science another? Why will not people understand that the Bible was not sent into the world to teach us science. Its function is not to tell us how the world was created and life produced, but how we are to make a right use of life and the world ...

Then again, people say: Our faith is undermined. The Bible contradicts itself. One messenger speaks in one strain, another in another. Some of them, too, are by no means free from faults themselves. But can we not see that it is not in their faults that we are to follow them, but in their virtues? Can we not understand that God, using human agents for His purposes, they must necessarily have the defects of their humanity?

When the spirit of God is poured into a human soul, it will manifest itself according to the nature and disposition of the human receptacle. If you pour water into a vessel, it will accommodate itself to the shape of the vessel, be it round or square or oblong.

Not otherwise is it with that which flows from the Source of all inspiration into the hearts of His prophets. In form, in style, in contents they may differ; but the spirit within them has been fed from the same Heavenly fount.

Once more it is urged: Of course our faith is tottering. Consider our distraction. All creeds claim to be true, to be divine. Which are we to believe? Which to follow? Well, the answer to that question ought not to be very difficult.

Unless you have the learning and the talent, the leisure and the opportunity, to examine carefully and impartially, to weigh the claims of every creed under the sun – and there are few, I take it, here or elsewhere, so favourably situated – there is but one course loyal and honourable to follow: cling to the faith of your fathers ...

And in words that could have been crafted for a Jewish Religious Union pulpit, Singer rounded off his message:

The spirit of our age is a critical, searching, analysing spirit. Let us not dread it or condemn it altogether. Be sure it answers a good purpose in God's plan for the education of man. But let us not forget that without faith, religion is meaningless – and more, that we cannot sacrifice it without doing some fatal injury to our moral constitution.[36]

*  *  *   *  *  *   *  *  *

The lay resignations from the Jewish Religious Union were far longer in coming, although an early attempt was made to implement their execution. In a debate that struck at the heart of Chief Rabbinical jurisdiction, and of the place and fidelity of Orthodoxy within the United Synagogue, the US council was urged – shortly after Adler's 'Old Paths' sermon – to condemn the actions of its honorary officers and ministers who had supported or participated in the affairs and services of the Union.[37] Leading the attack was Leopold J. Greenberg, later to become owner and controlling editor of the community's most influential mouthpiece, the *Jewish Chronicle*.[38]

The meeting – at which United Synagogue vice-president, Albert H. Jessel,[39] one of those facing condemnation, occupied the chair[40] – opened with a letter from the Chief Rabbi to Jessel's colleague, Henry Lucas: 'In the report of the last meeting of the council', Adler had written,

> you are stated to have said, in your capacity as chairman, that the honorary officers had no cognisance of the fact that the services of the Jewish Religious Union were conducted in defiance of Jewish Law.
>
> I therefore deem it my duty to hand you herewith a copy of the sermon I preached on Sabbath last, in which I have set forth some of the reasons why I am constrained, regretfully, to say that the services in question are not in conformity with Jewish Law, and I must beg you to bring this fact to the knowledge of the members of the council.[41]

Moving his censure motion against the honorary officers, Greenberg told the council that if a person did not wish to see Jewish religious worship carried on by the authorised ritual; if he felt that there was the necessity for some other, and that the synagogue and its ritual were insufficient; if in deference to that he supported actively some other form of worship – 'then obviously he might be an excellent Jew, but his right place is not in the United Synagogue, and his remaining within the United Synagogue must be to that extent a weakening influence'.

So obvious was all this that the framers of the Act of Parliament upon which the United Synagogue was founded, and its Deed of Trust and byelaws, had never felt it necessary to formulate any rule upon the point:

> They took it for granted that, as the United Synagogue was founded for only a certain class of persons, no others would wish to become or to remain members, and they never imagined that the council would require the authority of a rule or law to maintain its rightful position so far as its membership was concerned.
>
> Were the objects for which the Jewish Religious Union had been

founded, and were its practices – its ritual – inconsistent with the objects and practices for which the United Synagogue had been established? There ought not to be much question about that, for the Chief Rabbi had declared in unequivocal language, as a definite considered judgment, that the services of the Jewish Religious Union were Gentile services.

It surely was inconceivable that the council charged with the administration of the United Synagogue, formed for the purposes he [Greenberg] had described, would wish to retain within its body those who actively engaged in supporting, founding and carrying on Gentile services. How was it possible for men thus to serve two masters? How was it possible for men at one and the same time to further interests so diametrically opposed?

And how was it possible for the council, without flinging to the four winds of heaven every vestige of the trust reposed in it, to refuse to ask those of its members whom they found engaged in thus promoting and actively supporting Gentile services to recollect the position in the synagogue they occupied, and to desist?

Above all else, Greenberg contended, one issue was paramount. How far was the United Synagogue going to retain or to win the confidence and respect of the Jews of the East End – 'even of those Jews there who, though they are unobservant mainly by circumstances they are often unable to control or are free in thought in matters of religion, are at least loyal to the great underlying principles of their faith' – how were they going to regard the council, if that body countenanced and tacitly approved 'the insidious attempt to undermine the foundations of that fabric upon which loving hands have lavished the choicest they could devise?'

Herbert Marsden, seconding the resolution, declared that since the United Synagogue council had been one of the organisations which had appointed the Chief Rabbi, it was 'most unfortunate' that some of its honorary officers should have joined the Union – 'one of their first duties being to uphold the authority of the Chief Rabbi and the dignity of his office'. By their action, he said, they were prevented from fulfilling a most important duty, and by reflection they had 'discredited every member of the council' and provided 'an incentive to some of the ministers to do the same'.

Rising to explain why he and Davis had 'decided actively to participate in the management of the Jewish Religious Union', Jessel asserted that it was the duty of all persons placed in positions of responsibility within the United Synagogue 'to investigate the cause of religious apathy and to see whether we cannot find some means partially to cure it'. It was with that object in mind that he and Davis had helped in the formation of the Union.

> He very much regretted indeed [said Jessel] – he could not tell them how much he regretted – having to be even for a moment in conflict with the Chief Rabbi. He had the greatest possible respect for Dr Adler and for his office. Dr Adler was one of his oldest friends, and he had great pleasure in listening to his sermons.
>
> But when all was said and done, he was constrained, with the greatest respect and deference, to protest against the notion that any one man was to dictate to the conscience of each individual member of the Jewish community. They were not children; they had the right to think for themselves; and although he was placed in a position of responsibility, he protested against that new cult, that sort of papalism, which some people desired to introduce, and which for want of a better word he termed 'Chief Rabbinism'.
>
> He appreciated the fact that in the United Synagogue, under the terms of the Act coupled with the terms of the Deed of Foundation and Trust, the religious worship was under the control of the Chief Rabbi. The synagogue ritual was under his control for the ordinary service. That was a defect which the promoters of the Jewish Religious Union had felt immediately the idea was conceived.
>
> Every one of the founders desired the services to be held in synagogue, and the suggestion that the members of the Jewish Religious Union wished to sever themselves from the synagogue was totally contrary to the true facts of the case. In fact, the founders of the Union had approached the Chief Rabbi with a view to getting the services held in one of the synagogues of the United Synagogue. It was recognised that his consent was necessary, but the Chief Rabbi did not see his way to grant it.

Jessel urged the council to remember for whom the Jewish Religious Union catered. Its services, he stressed, were for those discontented with the ritual of the ordinary Sabbath morning service. The founders of the Jewish Religious Union had taken steps to ascertain as well as they could the reason why so many English Jews did not attend synagogue, and they were made acquainted with several objections which were felt to the ordinary ritual as provided by the Jewish prayer book in the synagogue.

The desire had been expressed for a service with some modification. 'I do not see anything very shocking about that. It is a question only of degree, and I object to the application of the expression "Gentile" or "non-Jewish" to persons who desire, and whose every wish, is to call themselves Jews.'

To loud cheers, Jessel ended his appeal on a strident note. The council was wrong, he said, if it supposed they were desirous of doing anything to injure the community at large. The United Synagogue was unhappily 'somewhat narrow' in its sphere, and he protested against the view that nothing should be done outside the scheme of the United Synagogue Act. There was already 'the best evidence' that the Jewish Religious Union would stimulate the community.

> I have the greatest sympathy for those who are content to walk in the 'Old Paths'; but I do say that to walk along with your head down in meditation, congratulating yourselves that you are as others are, and remaining deaf to the cry of those who are wandering on the hillside or in the marsh while struggling to reach the goal to which you are walking – I say that that is not Judaism and is not the course which should be expected of honourable men.

\* \* \*   \* \* \*   \* \* \*

United Synagogue treasurer Felix Davis was quick to rise on his own behalf. Greenberg, he said, 'might choose to twist and turn my intentions as he likes, but every member of the council will agree that, practically, the motion before the meeting is a vote of censure on the honorary officers. It is in that sense that Mr Jessel and I desire to meet him.' But first he wished to state the reasons that had caused him to join the Jewish Religious Union and that still led him to believe in its utility, 'despite the unfortunate remarks of the Chief Rabbi'.

> It was his earnest endeavour [said Davis] not to say a word which could possibly lead to ill-feeling in the council of the United Synagogue or out of it; and in fact he hoped to do nothing that would intensify the passions that had been roused by the motion before the meeting.
>
> He was one of the financial officers of the United Synagogue and had worked hard in its interests for very many years. During that time, he had been brought into close contact with many members of the United Synagogue, had observed somewhat narrowly the sphere of activity of the United Synagogue, and had had opportunities of judging of the success it had attained.
>
> At that point it was not, perhaps, out of place to draw attention to the fact that the objects of the United Synagogue were not solely confined to maintaining places of worship. That was undoubtedly its main object, but there were subsidiary objects of no less importance.

His experience had taught him that, in many respects, the United Synagogue had done splendid work, but it had failed in one great respect. It had proved itself unable to attract worshippers to the splendid synagogues it had helped to build.

That unpleasant fact had been strongly impressed upon him during the years he had been one of the honorary officers. Believing, as he did, that public worship was necessary in order to maintain the continuity of Judaism, he deplored the lack of facilities that were to be noticed in connection with the United Synagogue; and knowing, as he did, that it was quite impossible for the United Synagogue to enlarge its scope for religious services, he had felt he was well within his right in helping the formation of services elsewhere, which might be attractive to those to whom the services of the United Synagogue did not appeal.

In that action, he did not consider that he was disloyal to the United Synagogue. Within the scope of the United Synagogue, Jessel and he acknowledged that the Chief Rabbi was supreme. They did not desire, for one moment, to question his supremacy.

His [Davis'] personal opinion was that the Jewish community and the United Synagogue had made a mistake when it subjected itself to the spiritual supremacy of one man; but so long as it lasted, all members of the United Synagogue were bound to obey the Chief Rabbi, and all the services in the synagogues of the union must be those of which the Chief Rabbi had approved.

But he did not admit the authority of the Chief Rabbi outside the confines of the United Synagogue, and, in fact, he considered that the Chief Rabbi had somewhat complicated the issue in the letter he had addressed to the vice-presidents. The duties of the Chief Rabbi were clearly detailed in the Deed of Foundation and Trust, in which it was stated that all matters connected with the religious administration of the United Synagogue should be under the supervision and control of the Chief Rabbi.

The sole duty, therefore, of the Chief Rabbi was to state whether the [Union] services were or were not in accordance with the German and Polish ritual, and if the Chief Rabbi had confined himself to a pronouncement on that subject, no one could possibly have objected; but he had gone beyond that, and charged it with being non-Jewish. And Greenberg, desiring to rub in the salt a little more, had styled it a Christian service.

He [Davis] recognised that it would be impertinent on his part to enter into a discussion on a religious question with the Chief Rabbi, but he did claim to have a Jewish heart and a Jewish spirit, and if an honorary officer of the United Synagogue actuated by those motives desired to give to those whom the United Synagogue could not cater for an opportunity of participating in divine service, if under such circumstances a censure was deserved, then it was merited by Jessel and himself.

The one section of the work of the United Synagogue with which an honorary officer had nothing to do was its spiritual side. There was work of every kind to do in connection with the sub-committees of the United Synagogue, but in advancing the spiritual activity of the United Synagogue, the honorary officers were powerless.

'The vote which the council is being called upon to consider is a serious one', Davis concluded, 'and I hope it will hesitate before passing it. The council should look back fifty years and remember how schisms were then made; and it should think twice before it condemns those whose actions it does not consider wise.'

Hesitate and remember it did, and by thirty-eight votes to four[42] it threw out the resolution and, on the insistence of Greenberg – who remarked that 'it seems to me that a certain section of the governing body of the United Synagogue, and not the ministers, deserves condemnation' – withdrew a second motion that had sought to censure Singer and Stern.

# 7

# A New Religion

For several years, the Jewish Religious Union continued to hold services in Marylebone, with an East London branch operating intermittently between 1903 and 1907. Membership in both areas fluctuated, and preachers were often difficult to secure. As a result, it was Claude Montefiore who was the most frequent, most prominent and most controversial of the speakers, and as the Union moved on, his message became louder and bolder – and his aim ever more certain: the creation of a separate branch of Judaism, with its own forms of worship, its own theology and, above all, its own synagogue. This view he spelled out in one of his most outspoken sermons, the strongest blow he had aimed thus far at his former West London colleagues.

> I differ from those who think that this Union can be a Union only for worship, that it cannot be a special home, a special bond, for those who form a distinct religious group or circle among themselves. I fully admit that the shades of religious differences, the nuances and varieties of religious opinion, are almost infinite; but nevertheless I do not think that within the one larger Jewish community there need be nothing but the extremist individualism ...
>
> There is room in Judaism, there actually exists in Judaism (for all who have eyes to see), two main tendencies, two main parties. We may call them the conservatives and the liberals; or if we prefer the terms, the traditionalists and the progressists. These two sets of distinguishing words seem to me better and truer than the old catchwords of Orthodox and Reformers.
>
> Now these two parties can each respect the other, each can recognise the measure of agreement which unites them, in spite of differences, within the larger circle of Judaism; but yet each party can also recognise the measure of difference as well as the measure of agreement; and above all – and on this I lay most earnest stress – each can rejoice in the special truths and views wherein they severally differ, as well as in the common truths and views wherein they agree.
>
> The liberals, or progressists, are united by their common belief in the principles of religious development and of religious liberty. They

are united by a common belief in the validity and justification of the application of these principles in the field of Bible interpretation and criticism, in public worship, in outward ceremonial.

Aiming his arrow at the followers of Reform, Montefiore declared:

> There are those who attempt to mediate between the two, as they call them, extreme positions, who seek to combine a little of the liberty of the progressists, upon the one hand, with a little of the bondage of the traditionalists, upon the other. These mediators may be honest, but they will infallibly fall between two stools.[1] The advancing tide of thought, with a fuller clearness of vision, will sweep them away.
>
> But we, my friends, shall not be swept away. We have principles to cleave to, and through them we shall be strong. To halt between two opinions will avail men little. Let them clearly sing the old song or clearly sing the new. And just as I asked you to recognise your agreements, so I ask you to recognise your differences ...
>
> The smaller the unions, the more definite their obligations, the more insistent the duties which those who form them must discharge. To our common Judaism we have obligations and duties, but I ask those who think with me to acknowledge not only these, but also the special obligations and duties towards our liberal hope, our liberal purpose, our large and liberal faith.[2]

* * *   * * *   * * *

Seventeen years after rejecting Morris Joseph for the Hampstead pulpit, Hermann Adler found himself – for the second time as Chief Rabbi – listening to Joseph preach at a Berkeley Street gathering. The occasion marked the death of David Woolf Marks, at whose funeral and memorial services Adler and his dayanim were prominent mourners. Four years earlier, Adler had made history by attending the West London memorial service for Frederic David Mocatta, philanthropist, bibliophile and son of one of the congregation's founders – an ecumenical event that sent waves through the Orthodox fraternity. The *maariv* service was conducted by the junior minister, Isidore Harris,[3] accompanied by a mixed choir.[4]

Of those present that evening, the *Jewish Chronicle* had declared:

> One name may be singled out – that of the Chief Rabbi – for though Dr Adler attended in a personal capacity as an intimate friend of the late Mr Mocatta, and particularly as no service was held at the house of mourning, the presence for the first time of a Chief Rabbi in the

'Reform Synagogue' is not without significance. Dr Adler was accommodated with a seat near the wardens' seats.[5]

Nor was the significance lost on the wider community when, in May 1909, Adler – together with Haham Moses Gaster and members of the Beth Din – was present at Balls Pond Reform cemetery for Marks' funeral, and at West London Synagogue for the memorial service, again seated alongside the wardens' box. Although they had been on friendly terms – yet nothing as close as his relationship with Mocatta – the Chief Rabbi attended for the first (and only) time in his official capacity, and a few days later gave public expression of his admiration for the departed leader of British Reform. The passing of 'this veteran', he wrote,

> vividly recalls the events of seventy years ago. These memories are fraught with keen regret, but, happily, they are free from acrimony.
> 
> Who cannot but grieve that a secession took place which undoubtedly weakened Anglo-Jewry, and which might have been averted had counsels of forbearance prevailed on both sides? But it must be gladly acknowledged that the wound is in process of healing, for it is recognised more and more that it is the mission of religion not to sunder and embitter, but to unite and reconcile.
> 
> Professor Marks, no doubt, greatly contributed to this desirable end by his tact and moderation, and by putting forth his influence that the reforms he had initiated, though, unfortunately, constituting a breach with traditional Judaism, should not be radical and subversive, but primarily promote the dignified ordering of divine service and prevent desertion from the fold. These views the gifted minister enforced by extraordinary powers of oratory, by a remarkable combination of thought, language and delivery, which charmed his hearers and riveted their attention ...
> 
> Though compelled during the last few years to live in retirement, he continued to evince a deep interest in passing events. The writer had the privilege of receiving from him, only a few days ago, a letter marked by the characteristics above indicated, and couched in words which proved that age had not withered his native gift of eloquence.[6]

That letter, congratulating the Chief Rabbi on his seventieth birthday, had been couched in similar terms. Written three weeks before Marks' death, it assured Adler of

> my great respect for your high personal character and of my admiration of the dignity you have imparted to the sacred office of Chief Rabbi,

and of the distinguished ability with which you have discharged its important functions.

I bear willing and grateful testimony to the cordial and courteous relations which have existed between yourself and the congregation of which I am the representative. It has evidently been your purpose to maintain peace and harmony with all sections of the community and to unite them for the advancement of its highest interests.[7]

From his pulpit at Bayswater, Hermann Gollancz added a second Orthodox voice to the paeans offered up to Marks, 'one who was epoch-making in the annals of Anglo-Jewish history'. It was but meet, he said,

> that now, after years have passed since an unhappy feud set up a barrier between two sister communities, this congregation should, in the hour of sorrow, evidence its devout sympathy with the congregation bereaved of its chief pastor, who was bound up indissolubly with its fortunes, with its origin, rise and development.
>
> As a minister of religion, he was not content to follow slavishly in the path marked out for him, but stamped the impress of his individuality on his surroundings. He assumed the right of initiative in the work of guiding a body of his earnest and devout brethren, who discerned the blemishes which obtained in the then existing systems and methods, who saw that some change and progress were necessary, and who were determined to try and effect some improvement, with a view to evoking greater enthusiasm for Jewish services among the sons and daughters of Israel, and inducing greater respect and admiration for Judaism itself from those outside our communion.
>
> Whether he succeeded in his ideal will always, in a community like ours with its variety of judgment, be a matter of debate; but his memory will be held in esteem for the manner in which he acted up to his convictions.
>
> It is, after all, sorrowful to reflect that, with all the experience gained by the Jew since the disruption of his polity and the dispersion of his people owing to internal feuds at the time of the destruction of the Temple nigh two thousand years ago, a secession was allowed to culminate here over half a century ago, and that wiser counsels did not prevail to prevent a division of forces, and a weakening of strength, at the very time when it was imperative that the few Jews should stand shoulder to shoulder in the attempt to gain their rights and privileges as English citizens. How true that frequently the broader and larger interests are sacrificed in the desire to magnify the smaller differences that exist!

Let me not be misunderstood. The demands which, in the first instance, were made with regard to an improved service and other details were not such as to have made a modus vivendi impossible, had the spirit of conciliation and that of toleration (which we are continually, even to this day, expecting and demanding for our brethren from without) been brought into play in dealing with a serious and momentous communal problem. What has been lost to Anglo-Jewry as a consequence of the failure at compromise or peace in those days will never be known.[8]

\* \* \*   \* \* \*   \* \* \*

Despite the vicissitudes in the fortunes of the Jewish Religious Union, a committee was established late in 1908 to consider 'the advisability and practicability' of establishing a congregation on Liberal Jewish lines, a proposal subsequently structured by Montefiore into what became known as 'the Union's manifesto'.[9] A meeting the following June mandated the committee to set up 'a fully organised congregation by every means in its power', and within four months the *Jewish Chronicle* was able to announce: 'We understand that arrangements are in progress for the establishment of a synagogue in the West End of London in conjunction with the Jewish Religious Union, and that, *inter alia*, Sunday services will be held at the new place of worship.'[10]

The report aroused the wrath of the Union and, more pointedly, that of the Chief Rabbi. In the next week's issue, the paper was compelled to publish both a qualification and an addendum, announcing, under the headline 'The Jewish Religious Union. Important Resignations':

> We are requested by the Hon. Secretary of the Union to state that the announcement in our last issue was made without the authority of the Union; and that the interpretation placed upon it in various quarters that the Union intends transferring the Sabbath services from Saturday to Sunday in its proposed Synagogue is entirely inaccurate. [It is obvious that the statement referred to is not in the least impugned by the above. – Editor, *Jewish Chronicle*.]

It added: 'In consequence of the course decided upon as announced in our last issue, Sir Isidore Spielmann, CMG, Mr Albert H. Jessel, KC, and Mr Felix A. Davis have withdrawn from the Union. Mr Michael A. Green and Dr A. Wolf, MA, have consented to fill vacancies on the committee caused by these resignations'.

Dedicated officers of the United Synagogue, Jessel and Davis could no longer – as they had done six years earlier – countenance an opposing congregational body, now bent on building its own house of worship; and, as Jessel told the Union, while he approved of mixed seating, a modified liturgy, and prayers in the vernacular, he preferred to see these achieved within the United Synagogue orbit.[11]

Adler's reaction to the initial report was swift – though, in the light of the Union's clarification, precipitate. In a sermon at Bayswater Synagogue on the first day of Sukkot, he described the proposed Sunday services as

> the most disquieting element in the movement, for it is in direct opposition to the Word of God as contained in the Torah and the prophetic writings, and a menace to Judaism, being calculated to sap and to undermine the most sacred institution of our faith ... What right have we to make the first day of the week, which is neither a Sabbath nor a festival appointed by the Lord, a day of convocation?
>
> And now it is proposed to build a synagogue to signalise this assault upon the inner citadel of Judaism! I am informed that the promoters have been led to this decision by the fact that there are large numbers of Jews who hold aloof from the synagogue and have joined ethical societies. I would ask the leaders seriously to consider whether this is a sufficient reason for establishing a new congregation – a fact which spells schism and disruption.
>
> If these nominal Jews have not been attracted by the Sabbath afternoon services held heretofore, will bricks and mortar exercise a magnetic attraction? Our community has had to deplore a secession seventy years ago, from the effects of which it is still suffering today. Shall we witness a second at a time when a union of hand and heart is so imperatively needed? Is it meet that a body styling itself the Jewish Religious Union should promote *un-Jewish, irreligious disunion*?
>
> Instead of attracting those who have hitherto kept away from divine service, may not the new place of worship wean members from existing synagogues? ... There is undoubted peril in the projected action – peril to the religious life of the community, peril to your children, peril lest the ties that bind them to our ancestral faith become more and more weakened ... Have the promoters realised to themselves whither this will lead?[12]

The Chief Rabbi's strictures left the *Jewish Chronicle* 'profoundly unsatisfied'. What, it asked, was Dr Adler's remedy?

> He is as cognisant as Mr Montefiore of the life-blood that is flowing away through the wound. He cannot declare, like some time-serving

politician, that he has not been called in to prescribe. He *is* 'in', and it is his business to administer something more effectual than denunciation.

What, we repeat, is his remedy for the evil that is eating at the vitals of the community and which threatens to leave it wasting away to death in anaemic helplessness? The disregard of the claims of the Sabbath which is forced upon Jews today by conditions over which they have no control is the real menace to Judaism. It is not a local menace; it is well-nigh universal. East and West – there is little real difference.

It would be absurd to suppose that Dr Adler is indifferent to our religious condition, or to our real religious needs; but what the community demands of him is not merely condemnation. They look for a constructive policy at his hands adequate to the circumstances and, it goes without saying, consistent with Jewish spirit and Jewish tradition. In this all-important respect, Dr Adler's sermon is a blank.[13]

Adler's comments were as nothing, however, compared to his condemnation of the movement following the paper's publication, in full, of what it termed 'Mr Claude G. Montefiore's Apologia', heralding 'A New Religion in Anglo-Jewry'. As an aid to its readers, the *Jewish Chronicle* quoted in bold type the fundamental principles of the manifesto:

- There are Orthodox Jews, and there are Liberal Jews, and there are endless shades of each. There are Karaite Jews, and Rabbinic Jews; there are Berkeley Street Jews, and United Synagogue Jews, and Federation Jews. Judaism, the big common mother, enfolds and acknowledges them all.
- We have no creed, and we will have none. We have no narrowing cut-and-dry series of dogmas; no articles, whether Thirteen or Thirty-Nine. We do not say, Believe this and that, and you are a Unionist; deny it, and you are not.
- We are most anxious to show to those who, from one religious reason or another, are drifting away from Judaism that they are wrong, that their drifting is unnecessary, and that they can rightly and truthfully call themselves Jews.
- If we are to keep or bring back the drifters, must it not be by some definite teaching, by giving them something to cherish and believe in, something which both they and we may regard as supremely true and good, and which may enable both us and them to hold and cohere together in the bond of a religious

Union? And this something, what else can and should it be than our conception of Judaism? What other Judaism can we offer, for what other do we regard as true?
- Our 'dogmas' or principles are not, and will not be, formulated once for all. They will need, and will doubtless receive, readjustment and development.
- We stand first and foremost for those great theistic affirmations in which we are at one with all our fellow Jews — and, indeed, with so many thousands outside Israel.
- We want to make our drifters feel not merely that it is better for themselves to remain Jews, and to attend a Jewish worship, but that they ought to remain Jews, and that, given certain fundamental agreements, it is their duty to identify themselves with the religion and religious cause of Israel.
- We recognise no binding outside authority between us and God, whether in a man or in a book, whether in a church or in a code, whether in a tradition or in a ritual.
- Even if the whole Pentateuch were unquestionably the work of Moses, we should still declare that no book, be its human author who it may, can be for us an unquestioned and binding authority. To free ourselves from the heavy bondage of the Rabbinical law and of the Shulchan Aruch may be, and indeed is, desirable and necessary. But the bondage of the written law of the Pentateuch, or the view that 'the Bible, and the Bible alone', is the religion of Judaism may be even heavier, or at all events more fossilising, than the Bible plus the interpretations and additions of Tradition.
- We stand for a fresh and changed attitude towards authority, and especially towards that particular type of authority which is of central importance in Orthodox Judaism — the authority of the Book and the Code. We need accept nothing which does not seem to us good. The authority of the Book, so far as it goes, is its worth, and so far as that worth reaches, so far reaches the authority. The book is not good because it is from God; it is from God so far as it is good. The book is not true because it is from God; it is from God so far as it is true.
- The main festivals of the Pentateuch must remain our main festivals today and tomorrow. We may charge them with new meaning, following in this the method of our predecessors, but the festivals themselves must continue. Passover, Pentecost, Day of Memorial, Day of Atonement, Tabernacles — these must still be the main festivals or holy days for us. And the Sabbath? We recognise

- the immense difficulties which the observance of the Saturday Sabbath presents to the Jews of Europe and America; but though we do not preclude, and rule out of court, *ab initio*, the possibility of extra services on Sunday, we still stand for the historical Sabbath.
- I hope and believe that we should all 'stand for' the view that Judaism is essentially a universal religion. By this I mean that its doctrines are not suited to one race, but might be the common belief of all races. And I also mean by it that no taint of partiality or national limitations adheres to our conception of God or of His relation to man, or of His relation to 'Israel'. We do not interpret the doctrine of the 'mission of Israel' in any partial, national or non-religious sense.
- We want a synagogue which is frankly and definitely built upon our own lines, which is founded to teach Judaism as we conceive it, which in doctrine and embodiment, in teaching and ceremonial, is the general expression of our principles, as I have already described and enumerated them.
- Now the traditional conception of Judaism, both in theory and in practice, is, we think, doomed. It mixes up so much error with truth, so much of the obsolete with the living, that the erroneous and the obsolete clog and ruin the living and the true. The ivy is killing the tree.

'If', wrote Montefiore, 'the Union is dependent upon the truth of its principles, and would desire their wider acceptance and diffusion, then the logical course for it to pursue is, should other conditions and circumstances permit, to establish a separate and independent synagogue, and not merely to hold occasional and supplementary services over and above the services now held in the existing synagogues of London.'[14]

* * *   * * *   * * *

With the 'praiseworthy intention to heal irreligion and to check apostasy', Adler retorted in a New West End address a fortnight later,

> an attempt is being made to make void God's law ... This manifesto proclaims a new "Judaism" with many essentials of Judaism left out, or whittled down almost to vanishing point... With the stroke of a pen, the divine authority of the Pentateuch and of the prophets, the authority of every teacher in Israel, is denied ...
> What do we witness now? Members of the house of Israel, who

have hitherto gloried in being the People of the Book, rise up and declare that the view of the Bible as containing the religion of Judaism is fossilising – out of harmony with the ideas and progress of our days. This is the new view to be entertained about the Bible – the Bible that has been our stay and comfort throughout the ages, that has kept us from being merged and absorbed among the nations of the earth, for which our fathers joyfully shed their life's blood.

The members of the Union protest: 'We readily accept the moral law of the Bible, not because it is in the book, but because it is good, because our reason and conscience approve it.' This argument involves, I submit, a grave fallacy. How is it that reason and conscience teach us that the moral law has to be kept? Because the Torah has so guided our reason and so educated our conscience throughout the ages that we recognise the moral code as true, and willingly obey it.

But to argue that, because reason and conscience tell us that the moral code is good, we are free to reject the authority of the book and the code is almost as grotesque as the saying of the boor, who remarked that we ought to be grateful to the moon which gives us light on dark nights, but that we owe nothing to the sun which only shines by day, when there is plenty of light ...

The members of the Union, said Adler, were standing 'at the parting of the way, at the head of two ways'. Reverting to an earlier theme, he appealed to them, 'earnestly and affectionately':

> Pause, ere you go further on this precipitous descent. Ask for the old paths and inquire whether in them you cannot find rest for your souls.
>
> We have learned by bitter experience the unwisdom of excommunication. Why will you cut yourselves off from communion with your brethren by seeking to form a new sect or section? Why will ye forsake places of worship that must have established a profound claim upon your filial piety and reverence? Ought we not to fight in unison against the common enemy, materialism, love of Mammon, the reluctance to make sacrifices?[15]

Dismissing Adler's arguments the following week, in a lengthy letter to the *Jewish Chronicle*, Montefiore concluded with a confident assertion:

> It is only we, and such as we, who can keep those Jews who are infected with the modernist spirit within the religion of Judaism. Of that we are assured. And even as Liberal Judaism has been the salvation of Judaism for thousands in America – and is rapidly becoming again

the hope and salvation of many in Germany – so do we believe that it may become the salvation of hundreds of Jews and Jewesses in England. At all events, we mean to have a try. Have our Orthodox brethren of the House of Israel no word of Godspeed for us?[16]

* * *   * * *   * * *

There were, needless to say, few words of Godspeed from the Orthodox community. But expressions of discontent continued to flow, both within and outside the traditional fold, both in favour of further reform and, among Reform circles no less, against going too far. Even as – in response to the Liberal onslaught – Berkeley Street was urging more radical measures to help stem its decline, a contra-reformation seemed to be brewing in its ranks. The creation of Montefiore's movement was to draw Chief Rabbinate and Reform closer, spiritually and physically, than at any time in the seventy-year history of the Great Secession.

Not the least vocal in the Orthodox clamour for more decisive action had been Gollancz – one of Adler's closest colleagues and his successor at Bayswater – who felt repeatedly called on to air his misgivings over what he termed the 'religious neglect' of congregational absentees, including the 'too large a proportion of members who, observing the Sabbath and abstaining from the ordinary pursuits of the week, do not put in an appearance at synagogue (certainly not regularly) on the holy Sabbath'.

Several attempts had been made, he acknowledged, to render the service 'more in harmony with modern requirements. But these attempts, we must confess, have singularly failed in their object. There has been too much tinkering with the matter, but the evil has not been grappled with. Far better to have left matters alone than to have introduced half-measures.'

It was on that account, said Gollancz,

> and seeing the trend which the modern Jew's action or inaction is taking, that I personally have no hesitation in adopting this attitude on the subject of our public worship; and I take my stand, as a minister of religion, upon the broad principle enunciated by our rabbis ages ago: 'When it is a case of serving God and, by timely intervention, safeguarding and protecting important ceremonials of our religion, it is permissible even to abrogate something of the Torah of old.'
>
> How much more so, then, is it lawful – nay, imperative – to deal with the synagogue service and the prayer-book, if the matter

involved be the life and vitality of the religion itself, the very preservation of Judaism and the Jewish people.[17]

Gollancz's stark solution – advanced from the very pulpit that Adler had vacated, and advocating, in effect, the suspension of age-old tradition in the cause of public prayer – was to rally the opposing forces into unprecedented action. Within weeks of Montefiore's manifesto, the first Conference of Anglo-Jewish Ministers was held at Jews' College, attended by clergy from across the spectrum, though without the support of the Sephardim, whose absence (noted the *Jewish Chronicle*) 'was the subject of much adverse comment'.[18]

The Chief Rabbi was quick to latch on to the confluence of forces. Addressing his dayanim and 'reverends' – as well as the ousted Morris Joseph and his Reform colleagues from Manchester and Bradford – Adler remarked that

> this is certainly the first time that the ministers and officials of well-nigh all congregations in the United Kingdom have met together.
>
> This gathering is not intended as a counterblast to a manifesto recently issued. It had been arranged some considerable time before that unfortunate secession was announced ... [But] never have loyalty and steadfastness been more urgently needed than now, when assaults are projected upon the inner citadel of our faith – attacks the more perilous because they are led by men actuated by good intentions, but who have failed to realise the effect of their acts.
>
> It is, alas, not the first time in our history that we have been 'wounded in the house of our friends'. May our Heavenly Father bless our deliberations, so that they may help to build, to safeguard and to strengthen, to stir vigour and enthusiasm in minds numbed by languor and half-heartedness. May no stumbling-block be cast on our hands. May we not fall into error on a matter of religious duty. May we not declare permitted that which is forbidden, nor pronounce pure that which is impure.[19]

Preaching at the New West End Synagogue on the eve of the deliberations, the conference chairman, George Joseph Emanuel, of Birmingham, noted the modifications to the synagogue ritual effected by the ministers' conference eighteen years earlier, and added:

> We shall be meeting animated by higher purposes. Our objective is the strengthening and deepening of the spiritual life of the community.
>
> We recognise the imperative need of reform. Be not alarmed at the

ominous word. The reform we think to be urgently needed, the reform for which we strive, is not the reform of our religion, not the reform of its doctrines or observances, but the reform of ourselves. Not the different prayers that make up our worship, nor the hours and days of our worship, will at the coming meetings occupy our attention, but the needs of the worshippers, or of those who should be worshippers, in God's houses. We recognise that it is not well with Anglo-Jewry. Its soul is sick – sick unto death.[20]

\* \* \*    \* \* \*    \* \* \*

On the Reform side, similar views were being expressed, although not always to the gratification of their intended audiences. The West London Synagogue entered the fray with proposals – long sought but hitherto resisted – to amend the ritual and to shorten the service, in a bid to boost ever-diminishing attendances. The recommendations included curtailing the Sabbath morning prayers; reading portions of the liturgy on alternate weeks instead of every week; and reciting certain portions in English – some every Sabbath, others alternating with Hebrew. These alterations and excisions, said the revision committee, 'enable us to recommend that the ordinary Sabbath service should begin at 11 a.m.'[21]

The proposals, however, aroused 'strenuous opposition' among a segment of the congregation (and the committee) and led to the circulation of an appeal in advance on a meeting scheduled to consider them. Signed by seven leading figures on the council – Sir Philip Magnus and Cecil Q. Henriques, members of the revision committee; B. Elkin Mocatta and Henry S.Q. Henriques, treasurers; and J.M. Ansell, Harry B. Lewis-Barned and Laurie Magnus, past wardens – their letter described the changes as being

> in direct conflict with the traditional Jewish ritual. They must, if adopted, have the effect of widening the breach that divides the Berkeley Street congregation from other Jewish synagogues – the breach which, during seventy years, has been growing less and less and, in the near future, might have been expected to be completely bridged.
>
> The effect of the proposed changes would be to bring our synagogue into close relation with the synagogue of the Religious Union, which is about to be opened. The establishment of this new Union congregation provides a strong reason for postponing the adoption of such changes as the committee suggest, even were they approved,

until the opportunity shall have been afforded of ascertaining if the new form of service is found to result in increased and more regular attendance on the Sabbath and in a closer observance of the essential principles of Judaism ...

What we wish to avoid is any action which, at this critical period of transition, would cut us off irrevocably from the general body of British Jews and leave us stranded, as an isolated synagogue, or drive us into the fold of the Religious Union. These considerations of wider policy should, we venture to think, give us pause and induce us at least to wait and watch developments in the near future.

In the spirit of true toleration, therefore, so dear to Jews, we earnestly appeal to those even who feel the need – the very present need – of some form of service more akin to that of the Religious Union not to force their views upon those who differ from them and who may be a minority, but rather to recognise that in religious matters the convictions of a minority claim respect.[22]

Despite these exhortations, the West Londoners proceeded apace with their ritual changes. Introducing the proposals at the first of a series of meetings, Magnus said that if particular recommendations of the committee – on which he had been prevented from sitting because he found himself 'so entirely out of sympathy with their methods of revision' – were passed, not only would he have to resign his chairmanship, but the service would be so distasteful to him that he would have to retire from the synagogue altogether.[23]

As a result of his strictures, the recommendations were referred back to the council, which was mandated to consider 'a modified scheme' of changes to the service.[24]

Six weeks later, Magnus conceded a recognition by the committee that

a substantial majority of the seat-holders of this synagogue are in favour of the introduction of a considerable portion of English into the Sabbath morning service, and we feel it will be difficult altogether to resist the views of so large a section ...

The council propose that the English should be at the beginning and end of the service, as far as possible, and that the middle of the service should be in Hebrew. They further suggest that the parts sung by the choir should be in Hebrew and that, in accordance with the vote of the seat-holders, the service should be shortened by something like a quarter of an hour.

Magnus, however, was clearly unhappy. 'I need scarcely add', he said, that if these changes are adopted, it will be very difficult to revert to the former order of service, and I am very much afraid that the attendance at synagogue will not be increased by their introduction into the service.

But I repeat what I said at the beginning. It is difficult to resist the change which I believe is desired by a large section of the congregation, and I therefore place before you the recommendations of the council of the synagogue and, as chairman of that council, move the reception of the report.

On its adoption, he hastened to pray: 'May the changes result in a better observance of our ancient faith.'[25]

\* \* \*    \* \* \*    \* \* \*

Three days after the proposals were sealed, Hermann Adler sat alone in his study, writing a letter that was to be opened, he instructed his family, 'immediately after my death'. In mid-July, some five months later, that eventuality occurred. The *Jewish Chronicle* announced:

It is with profound regret – which will be shared by all Jewry throughout the world – that we have to record the death, in his seventy-third year, of Dr Hermann Adler, the Chief Rabbi. Dr Adler's health for some time past had been a matter of anxiety, but the illness that has terminated fatally may be said to have begun last Shavuot, when his attendance and ministration at the Great Synagogue seem to have proved a considerable strain ... It was not, however, until late last week that the doctors who attended him regarded his condition as critical.

On Thursday, when we went to press, he was progressing favourably. On Saturday evening, a vast change for the worse set in; he was seized with violent rigor, and the end was thought to be near. From this seizure he rallied, only to suffer a severe relapse on Sunday; but he again rallied, and on Monday morning he was well enough to read *The Times* after reciting the morning prayers.

It had been contemplated that, as soon as he was well enough, he should proceed to North Wales for recuperation, and it was in reference to this that on Monday, when the doctor visited him, he, with a merry twinkle in his eye and a cheery laugh, greeted him with the query: 'Well, doctor, which is it to be – North Wales or Willesden?[26] Both are N. W.'[27]

Willesden it was – paving the way for the opening of Adler's farewell letter.

* * *   * * *   * * *

Hermann Adler had opened his Chief Rabbinate with a fervent plea for communal unity, imploring in his installation address:

> Give me your confidence, I ask of the various sections of the community, with their many divergent opinions. That such diversities exist it would be but foolish and ostrich-like to deny. But I would entreat them to deal with a forbearing spirit toward each other, devoid of suspicion, devoid of distrust.
>
> To my brethren in the West [of London] I say: Do not stigmatise the denizens of the East as bigoted fanatics, lost in the slough of medieval superstition. Granted that some of them may be inferior in refinement and culture to their wealthier brethren, they certainly teach many a precious lesson of staunch, manly religious allegiance, and of glad willingness to make heavy sacrifices for the sake of their faith.[28]
>
> To my brethren in the East, I say (though, happily, the East cannot claim a monopoly in the possession of strictly observant Israelites): Do not look upon those who are not in entire agreement with you as though they were outside the pale of Judaism. Give them credit for being as solicitous as you are yourselves for the welfare of our common faith.[29] And to both East and West I appeal: Let not your divergence of opinion lead to schisms and divisions, to discord and disruption. May the union of hearts continue and strengthen.[30]

Twenty years later, as instructed by the Chief Rabbi, Adler's family opened his sealed letter immediately upon his death. 'I have tried', they read,

> to do my duty, to act in conformity with *Torah ha'ketuvah veha'mesorah* [the written Torah and the traditional interpretation of the text].
>
> I am strongly convinced that, to ensure the welfare of Judaism in this country, it is essential that a successor in the Rabbinate should be appointed with the least possible delay after my demise. He must be a strong personality, strong in piety and learning, one who will be equally acceptable to the East and the West, the native and the immigrant.
>
> And realising the grave difficulty of meeting with such a personality, I pray with all my heart: 'May the Lord God of the spirits of all flesh set a man over the congregation, who may go out before them,

and who may go in before them, and who may lead them out and bring them in,[31] that the Congregation of the Lord be not as sheep which have no shepherd.'[32]

The unity of metropolitan Jewry, and the Chief Rabbi's attempts to draw harmony out of heat, were themes discussed by Albert Jessel, as United Synagogue vice-president, in a memorial tribute at the council, days after Adler's passing. 'To this institution', said Jessel, who a decade earlier had put Union before union,

> his death is a very great and profound loss. Questions of difficulty must continually spring up in every organisation, in this among others, yet it was to him as the ultimate tribunal that we always could appeal, not only for our internal difficulties, but also for those difficulties which, from time to time, arose in connection with other bodies.
>
> He did not always have an easy task, because there are in our community many men of profound convictions and determined opinions, and many men who possibly in a heated moment give expression to views which make subsequent negotiation and settlement difficult. But by that persuasiveness to which I have alluded, and that extraordinary influence which sprang from a sense of devotion to duty, he was always able to assuage hostility and reconcile opposing elements.

This led Jessel to 'the question in the minds of every one of us: the succession to this high office'. It was, he said, not an easy question. No person stood 'conspicuously forth in the community' as when the late Chief Rabbi had been appointed.

> It is, as I say, not an easy question. There are many persons whose views are entitled to be consulted. It is not a question we can hurry. I expect none of you can have read that passage from Dr Adler's will,[33] which has appeared in the press, without echoing the hope that a man would be found able to reconcile conflicting interests. The late Chief Rabbi was such a man.
>
> What I think we will all agree on is that we must bear ourselves patiently. It is not a thing to be hurried, and, above all, not a thing to be discussed in any spirit of acrimony, either because we stand for a particular set of principles, or because this community or that individual thinks that one candidate or one possible candidate would best fill the office.
>
> We shall be paying a poor compliment to the memory of him whom we mourn if we allow any feeling of strife on this occasion.

And I do hope – in this council such an expression may be unnecessary, but my words may reach beyond this room – I do hope that we shall see in the community a reflection of that desire for peace which was one of the great characteristics of Dr Adler.[34]

The question of the Chief Rabbi's authority, and of his success – or failure – in wielding it over the wider community, was clearly as crucial as Jessel had suggested. It lay, in fact, at the heart of Adler's incumbency, and – despite the fulsomeness of the praise – he had left the community more dissentious than before he held office. Liberal Judaism had followed Reform; discontent over United Synagogue Orthodoxy had spawned first the Federation of Synagogues and then, in 1891, the Machzike Hadath (Upholders of the Faith),[35] with 'the East' regarding English Jews as 'reformers' and Adler himself as 'the Chief Reformer'.[36] The question of finding 'a man able to reconcile conflicting interests' assumed paramount – and urgent – importance.

* * *   * * *   * * *

Across the communal divide, Adler's passing drew equally deep, and heartfelt, emotions. His death, wrote Morris Joseph, was

> a severe personal loss to me. I had the privilege of his friendship and was the recipient of more thoughtful acts of kindness at his hands than I can recount ...
>
> I hold him to have been the greatest of our English Chief Rabbis, because, owing to the rapid growth of the Anglo-Jewish community in recent years, he had many serious problems to grapple with which were unknown to his predecessors, and he grappled with them in a remarkably statesmanlike manner.

Turning to the uncertain future, Joseph declared:

> It is impossible at the present moment to measure adequately the loss which his death has occasioned or to estimate the gap which is created in our communal life. By a strange coincidence, our communal organisation – like the constitution of this country – is now in the crucible. What will come out of it no men can foresee, but we can only pray that the issue may enure to the true well-being and stability of Anglo-Jewry.
>
> The situation which now confronts us will need all our best statesmanship. But this may be said: To whomsoever the reins of office are deputed, he will not surpass the distinguished man whom we are now mourning in ability, in conscientiousness, and in profound love for his religion and his people.[37]

Montefiore, in turn, remarked that it was

> not out of place to strike just for once a more personal note and to say that, although in the exercise of what I conceived to be my duty I often said and did things of which the Chief Rabbi did not approve – and which sometimes, I fear, even gave him pain – our relations with each other always remained most friendly and cordial. He was, indeed, wonderfully kind and considerate to me, and it is a mournful pleasure to take this opportunity of saying so.
>
> In talking and working with him, one felt one was in the presence of a man of distinction and dignity, a man of wisdom and experience, but also a man of kindness, a man of honour. The last word escaped me almost unconsciously. But it is what we all feel.
>
> Dr Adler's death is a true bereavement to our community, and for one reason or another there is hardly a man among us, I suspect, who does not think it so. At a time when old ideals are being challenged, it is pleasant for one who, like myself, was reared in the traditions and ideals of the emancipation period, to recall how thoroughly Dr Adler shared them.[38]

\* \* \*     \* \* \*     \* \* \*

In the formative years of the Jewish Religious Union, Montefiore had launched a withering attack on his colleagues in Reform. 'These mediators may be honest', he had declared, 'but they will infallibly fall between two stools. The advancing tide of thought, with a fuller clearness of vision, will sweep them away.' His forecast was misplaced, but his calculations were not without foundation.

Largely as a result of their common front against Liberal Judaism, the new century had begun to witness a narrowing of the differences between Orthodox and Reform, though also a 'climate of indifference [among the latter]: the enthusiasm that had accompanied the birth of Reform was drifting away'.[39] Efforts were made 'to galvanise the petrifying body of Jewry into life', but the West London Synagogue – in the eyes of a contemporary observer – 'has not gone forward, has lived upon its past, and has ceased to be an energising liberal force'.[40]

Political rather than religious issues were sapping the energy of its leaders, and the Liberal Synagogue was reaping the rewards, having leased premises in Hill Street, Marylebone, and appointed an American minister, Dr Israel Mattuck.[41] Montefiore recognised the dividends, and he made the most of them in his published works.

'Since 1911', he was to tell his followers, and those who had chosen to reject him,

> Liberal Judaism in England has become more definitely organised and, I hope, a more powerful religious force. There is, it is true, only one Liberal Jewish synagogue, but that one maintains the cause of Liberal Judaism with emphasis and ardour.
>
> There is in London one other synagogue – it is large, wealthy and important – which, though not avowedly Liberal, is yet 'Reform'. It may, however, be questioned whether there is really room in Judaism for more than two main directions or types, one distinctly 'Orthodox', 'Traditional' or 'Conservative' (whichever word is preferred), one distinctly Liberal.
>
> No synagogue can, in the long run, maintain a strong and vigorous life which does not teach, depend upon and cherish certain *doctrines*, and these doctrines must form an harmonious and homogeneous whole. There are two such 'wholes' which are available and possible: one is Orthodox Judaism, and one is Liberal Judaism. I hardly think that (for England, at any rate) there is a third.
>
> If Reform means only a few externalities, it can scarcely expect a future of much significance. Still less can it expect such a future if it seeks to take its stand upon Pentateuch and Bible as against Talmud and Rabbinism.
>
> The days of a supposed 'Mosaism' are over. It is possible that the Reform synagogue might prosper more if it were more closely allied with the main Orthodox body and with Orthodox Judaism, but it is even more probable that it would flourish more if it were more closely allied with Liberal Judaism, and if, without changing one of its beloved externalities, it became – like the synagogue of which Rabbi Mattuck is the honoured spokesman and chief – an avowed and articulate representative and champion of the Liberal Jewish cause.[42]

\* \* \*   \* \* \*   \* \* \*

In April 1911, weeks after Adler had written his farewell letter, and as Mattuck was preparing to deliver a trial sermon at Hill Street, a South African-based rabbi passed through London on his way home from the United States. Highly successful in his home city of Johannesburg, where he had ministered to the Witwatersrand Old Hebrew Congregation for some eleven years, he had been offered the pulpit of New York's prestigious Congregation Orach Chayim to fill the position left vacant by the death of Professor Joseph Asher.

In London, he was interviewed briefly by the *Jewish Chronicle* and admitted to being 'quite undecided' about the New York post. 'What will finally determine me', he said, 'will be where I can do best work. All else I shall put aside – that and that only will decide me in acceding to the call, or in yielding to the call back.'

Questioned on his attitude to Reform, he was asked: 'I know you would not reckon that as a "regenerative force" in religion, though religious?' 'I am more than ever convinced', he replied, 'of the total and absolute unsoundness of the entire Reform movement in Judaism.' 'Rather a sweeping statement?' the interviewer remarked. The rabbi responded:

> Perhaps so, to such as are unacquainted with the history of German-American Reform. To anyone, however, who judges it by its fruits, no other view is possible.
>
> Take a simple test – the lives of Reform rabbis, for example. Surely it is passing strange that in one generation they have furnished more apostates than in all the preceding three thousand years. I am not referring to riff-raff reverends, but to such 'rabbis' as were the immediate pupils of Abraham Geiger[43] and Isaac M. Wise.[44] Of the four pupils of Geiger in America, Dr Felix Adler publicly renounced Judaism. And to deal fully with the apostasies among I.M. Wise's friends and pupils would require a monograph. I will mention only Rabbi J. Moses, who apostasised, and Rabbi G. Wertheimer, who joined the Christian Scientists.[45]

These comments provoked a correspondence in the paper which led to further remarks from the travelling rabbi. Writing from the European continent before his departure for Johannesburg,[46] he added:

> in America there are no defections from Judaism, except among Reform rabbis. Their ratio of apostasy is as high as, perhaps higher than, among laymen of the worst country of Europe.
>
> There is, of course, nothing surprising in this. Reform Judaism is schismatic. It is a violent breaking away from tradition, a deliberate self-estrangement from the collective consciousness of Israel. Those of its spokesmen today who leave Judaism merely follow in the footsteps of other antinomian Jewish schismatics. Shabbetai Zevi became Mohammedan. The leader of the Frankists (Jacob Frank) turned Catholic. The founder of 'New Israel' (Joseph Rabbinowich, of Kishinev), who anticipated Mr C.G. Montefiore by enrolling the New Testament among the Jewish Scriptures, became a Lutheran missionary.[47]

A second test, wrote the rabbi, demonstrating the 'crowning proof of the unsoundness of Reform Judaism', was suicide.

> Suicide, unless the direct outcome of insanity, means the bankruptcy of a man's faith in God and humanity, and is always a pitiable exhibition of cowardice, pessimism and infidelity. If this is true of laymen, how much more so of teachers of religion ...
>
> Reform rabbis in the course of one generation have furnished such an alarming number of suicides as to cause the most callous to blush for the honour of his people. Geiger's Berlin seminary has furnished at least two suicides. A shocking case of double suicide in I.M. Wise's seminary at Cincinnati filled columns of the American daily press some years ago. The rabbi of a leading Reform congregation in the South, a man of nearly seventy, shot himself; while a Pennsylvania rabbi, a co-worker of I.M. Wise in the Pittsburg Conference[48] – the Sinaitic Revelation of true Reform – took his life and left behind him an 'ethical note', in which he curses the man who would utter any word of religion at his interment ...

The rabbi signed himself, quite simply, 'Yours obediently, J.H. Hertz'.

# 8

# Holy War

Joseph Herman Hertz was approaching his fortieth year when he passed through London, his fury unleashed against the followers of Reform. Those who knew him would have evinced no surprise at the strength of his censure: fifteen years in the front line – first in Syracuse, New York, and then in Johannesburg – had girded him for the battles that would lie ahead in any pulpit he chose to occupy.[1]

Born in Pebrin, Hungary, into a family reared on the modern and open-minded Orthodoxy of Ezriel Hildesheimer,[2] Hertz had celebrated his barmitzvah as the family were settling in the United States, where his father Simon – a one-time Hebrew poet – made ends meet as a *melamed* on Manhattan's Lower East Side. Tutored in Jewish studies mainly by Simon, this second of three sons was in due course enrolled at the newly established Jewish Theological Seminary, an institute of learning opened in 1887 'in obedience to the demands of an enlightened Orthodoxy'.[3]

In 1894, young Hertz became the seminary's first ordinand, and in his graduation address proclaimed his life's mission as encompassed in that of his alma mater. 'During the past two generations', he declared,

> our religious life has experienced fundamental changes – external as well as internal. Our ancestors even in the near past not only loved the religion that they were taught in their youth; they lived it.
>
> The greater part of their lives was consecrated to the perusal of its sacred literature, and to the scrupulous observance of the precepts commanded therein. But today, the formula which so strikingly expressed their religious life – 'to dwell within the four cubits of the halachah' – requires a long commentary for many modern ears. In brief, their whole spiritual being is in the present day well-nigh unintelligible.
>
> It is the mission of the Jewish Theological Seminary to train men who are to bridge this chasm between the past and the present: who will bring back to contemporary Israel a knowledge of the ideals proclaimed by our religion, and spiritualise the life, the everyday life, of the present by loyal and intelligent observance of the duties

demanded by our sacred faith. These aims and ends beckoning the Jewish religious guide of today are not to be realised in the correcting of eternal verities by the fleeting, illusive will-o'-the-wisps of the moment ...

We shall be accused of clogging the wheels of progress, of stemming the tides of advance, of aiming to hurl our brethren back into the exclusiveness of the ghetto. And, what is worse, we may be rejected by the very men we are serving; mocked and heartily abused. But the prophets loved Jerusalem, though she slew them.

Ours is a resolute band. We are actuated neither by the glory to be won on the field, nor by its vain trumpet-show. We are fighting in a holy war. In spite of contumely, in spite of misrepresentation, we will follow the Elijah who is now calling us to be zealous for Israel's Law, because we love Israel, because we love its Law.[4]

His first post, at Syracuse's Adath Yeshurun, did not bode well for Hertz's ambitions. As his reference to the Pittsburg Conference – 'the Sinaitic Revelation of true Reform'[5] – made clear, he had early imbibed an antipathy to the perpetrators of classical Reform (describing it as 'that German-American mutation of Judaism'[6]), and he was soon to encounter examples of its 'will-o'-the-wisps'.

Mixed seating had been introduced at his newly adopted synagogue, and other enticements were being considered in the face of competition from the local Reform. 'Syracuse', wrote a friend of Hertz's, 'was no fertile field for Orthodox Judaism'.[7] Little wonder, then, that a mere four years later he was struck by an advertisement in *The American Hebrew*[8] for 'a Jewish minister for the Witwatersrand Old Hebrew Congregation: rabbinical diploma, university training and degree, speak English, good appearance, under forty-five years of age, fluent preacher, irreproachable character, be competent to lead in all humanitarian projects, and command the respect of all'.[9] When – as if with a candidate in mind – it added the rider, 'short American experience preferable', it amazed no one that 'he packed his bags quickly'.[10]

\* \* \*   \* \* \*   \* \* \*

Attending a *minchah* service at Witwatersrand in September 1898, few could have been unaware that Hertz had incurred the displeasure of his local Reform colleagues even before making their acquaintance. At his installation ceremony – at which 'every pew in the worshipping-house was filled', from the British vice-consul and the chief of prisons to representatives of the chevrah kadishah and the Hollandsche Kerk – the clergy of two neighbouring synagogues, the Johannesburg New Hebrew and Modern Hebrew Congregations, 'were conspicuous by their absence'.[11]

The force of Hertz's inaugural sermon – as 'a true exponent of the Rabbinical traditions' (to quote the council's welcoming encomium)[12] – may have indicated why. Consecrating himself once more 'to the service of Judaism, to the task of saturating Jewish men and Jewish women to the beliefs, teachings and duties of the religion of Moses, the prophets and the sages of Israel', he told the gathering:

> Let the day never dawn when I shall have to speak before armed critics and not to sympathetic worshippers. Somebody has finely said: 'The preacher ought to be a man of light and leading.' In the severe strife of battle against *darkness* and *misleading*, my hands, like those of Moses of old, may become heavy and weary. I hope that you will ever be the friends who shall support my hands and steady them in my holy war against the Amaleks of materialism, irreligion, crime and vice ...
>
> I shall aim to destroy, wherever I find it, that smug self-contentment which is the enemy of all spiritual life. I shall foster within all of us a noble discontent with our present mode of life, a divine longing for the realisation of all the angelic powers that God has planted within our spirit's core.
>
> A minister of religion must be the determined enemy of all irreverent sneering at divine things – the sin of modern Jewish life. And, as ignorance is the swamp where all the uncanny shapes that haunt our religious life lurk and hover, the exponent of Judaism must aim to deserve his title of *Rabbi*, Teacher. He must teach us to love our faith, to be proud of our literature. He must bring home to us Israel's history, her glories, her triumphs.
>
> He must bring back to the congregation of Jacob those spiritual possessions to which they, blinded by error, befogged by prejudice, have so long been indifferent, which they have openly repudiated. He must help all of us to regain possession of our Bible, our own Bible, which has passed, so to speak, into the hands of strangers, which has become a *terra incognita*, a fable, a myth, to many of the sons and daughters of our people; regain that Judaic fervour, that Hebraic zeal for truth, for justice, for the 'knowledge of God', which has overthrown empires, annihilated idols, turned the course of history, and changed the face of the globe ...

I shall preach to you the Judaism not of my making, not of your liking, no easy Judaism, no fashionable Judaism; but the Judaism which demands of every child of Israel unconditional obedience to that Law which Moses gave as an eternal inheritance to the congregation of Israel. I shall therefore plead for the retention of all those ceremonies which sweeten the life of the Jew, of those customs which link generation to generation in filial piety, of those observances which, as nothing else can, unify the dispersed atoms of the House of Israel.

Our motto shall be: The Torah, and the *whole* Torah. We shall not imitate those of our brethren who 'choose their path' and, as a consequence, even in prayer separate themselves from the community, and thus divide the House of Israel against itself.[13]

Not to Judaism alone had Hertz dedicated his future, but to 'that Judaic fervour for truth, for justice', and – as he declared elsewhere in his sermon – to 'solidarity with the poor and persecuted of whatsoever creed, responsibility for the low and ignorant of whatsoever class: in a word, the Fatherhood of God and the Brotherhood of Man'.[14] In the early days of his ministry, however, such zeal was to lead to a temporary setback. Barely a year after his arrival, he was expelled by the Boers for his fiery oratory against Jewish and Catholic disabilities,[15] but returned to South Africa in 1901[16] for ten years under – and in an advisory capacity to – its new British rulers. While conditions were less settled within his post-war congregation, this alliance of pulpit and politicians – and the many doors it opened[17] – was to serve him well in the furtherance of his rabbinical aspirations.

By the turn of the decade – having lost out, midway, to the Rev. Dr Joseph Hochman (of whom more later) in a bid to secure the New West End Synagogue following Singer's death – Hertz felt ready to move on once again. The Congregation Orach Chayim was beckoning him, but, he had told the *Jewish Chronicle*, he was 'quite undecided' about whether to go. 'Standing as you do, as a guardian of Torah and Orthodoxy' – the paper had persisted – 'South African Jewry will, I can well understand, be poorer without you. On the other hand, equipped as you are as a missioner of those ideals, American Jewry sadly needs you'.

Hertz replied: 'Well, be that as it may, I shall consider the matter quite impersonally, and if I finally decide to go across the Atlantic, it will not be because I shall have light-heartedly put aside the call – perhaps I should say, the call back – of South Africa. Only if I feel that I can better serve the Jewish cause, can better serve Judaism, in New York than in Johannesburg shall I relinquish the position I prize in South Africa for the prize that has been held out to me in America.'[18]

And so it was. Deciding, after all, that he could 'better serve the Jewish cause, can better serve Judaism, in New York than in Johannesburg', he prepared to set sail – with a stopover in London – towards an uncertain future, with unforeseen results.

\* \* \*   \* \* \*   \* \* \*

Weeks after Hertz's comments to the London paper, Hermann Adler had succumbed to his lingering illness. Almost overnight, the situation changed, and the Chief Rabbinate lay ready and waiting. By then, however, Hertz had pledged his troth to Orach Chayim, and a date had been set for his third installation. British Jewry, meanwhile, was abuzz with speculation, and with preparations for the election of Adler's successor. Contrasting scenes were being played out on both sides of the Atlantic; the key player in both was Joseph Herman Hertz.

Founded in 1880 by German Jews along strictly traditional lines, Congregation Orach Chayim was well suited to Hertz's temperament and inclinations. Following the philosophies of Hildersheimer and Hirsch, it harmonised with his Orthodox-academic bent and modernist approach, points he was quick to underscore in his inaugural sermon. Calling for a partnership between himself and his congregants, Hertz told them:

> In these my endeavours to deepen the spiritual life of this community, to bring back those who have strayed from the olden paths and rescue those who have never even trod them, I shall demand two things of you. One of these is loyalty [and the other is charity]. You must help me fulfil that service to Judaism I have it in me to render.
>
> I will be no hesitating or stammering witness to the Truth. You realise what this means. For over sixty years, Orthodox Judaism has in America been subjected to a running fire of ridicule, blasphemy and merciless warfare by the leaders of the liberalising, the revolutionary, wing of our faith. And these children of progress deny us the right to defend ourselves! I shall look to you for loyal help in my conflict with illiberal liberalism.[19]

His congregation's response to this plea is difficult to gauge, however, for no sooner was it voiced than Hertz began to cast his eyes – and thoughts – elsewhere. In fact, he had cast them even earlier, for his stopover in London had proven to be, as Hertz himself told the press, a pivotal event.[20] During his ten days in Britain, he was approached by 'some of my old friends in London who urged me to apply for the vacant position'. He was 'brought into touch' with Lords Rothschild and Swaythling – respective presidents of the United Synagogue and the Federation of Synagogues, and prime movers in the Chief Rabbinical appointment – 'and, as a result of the conversations I had at the time', received an official invitation to visit England.

'Personally, I have so far been to them [the presidents] not more than a name. They have known nothing about my personality, and it is only right that they should have gathered as much information [as possible] from various sources about me.' Hertz said that, as far as he understood, the leaders wanted

> an active man, a man of energy, capable of instilling new life in the community. The English Jews are beginning to perceive that the 'years of plenty' are over, that the happy times when the Jews in England sat safely 'under their vines and fig trees' have gone.
>
> There already exists a permanent immigration question, and internal new lines that affect the Jews who are already settled there. The future Chief Rabbi must concentrate in great part the energy and activity of the whole community. He must constantly be on his guard.

Of himself, Hertz conceded – after some modest hesitation – that his career as a rabbi offered proof that he was 'the possessor of enthusiasm and energy'. His years in South Africa testified to his being 'of an active disposition. Under such congenial circumstances as can be found in England, I could achieve a great deal.' Without elaborating, Hertz ended the interview by hinting 'of a certain scheme I am contemplating for the advancement of Judaism in England in the event of my being elected Chief Rabbi'. Clearly, then, he was 'more than a name'.

\* \* \*   \* \* \*   \* \* \*

The invitation to visit London had reached Hertz in February 1912, only days after his New York installation, and by April he was back in Britain for a three-month stay, 'with a view to becoming a candidate for the office of Chief Rabbi in this country'.[21] For that purpose, the Orach Chayim board had accorded him the necessary leave of absence and had intimated that, 'if he should not undertake the high office of Chief Rabbi, means will be found on his return to New York for much enlarging the field of his work, to which will be attached even better conditions than those at present prevailing'.

It was further announced in London that 'Dr Hertz – whose religious attitude may, perhaps, be best described in the words applied to his own master, Dr Sabato Morais, as cultured Orthodoxy' – would give a series of sermons at the Great, Bayswater, Philpot Street, Hampstead and Dalston synagogues, as well as to other metropolitan and out-of-town congregations. A 'forceful and eloquent preacher', he had met a number of provincial delegates to the Chief Rabbinate Conference – the electoral body – who had gathered in London as he reached Britain's shores.

In his opening sermon, entitled '*Kiddush Hashem* and *Chillul Hashem*',[22] Hertz remarked that '[while] we have succeeded in making non-Jews respect Judaism, our problem today is nothing less than to make Jews respect Judaism. We are witnessing an alarming loss of faith of Israel in Israel. We stand appalled at the mass of unbaptised apostasy in English-speaking countries'. With his second address, at the Bayswater Synagogue a week later – in the presence of its resident preacher, Hermann Gollancz – views were beginning to form about the quality and substance of his oratorical style, 'a good means for any man to prove if there is anything "in him" for the purpose of an office in which the pulpit must of necessity play a large part'.[23] Based on the biblical text, 'You shall hallow the fiftieth year and proclaim liberty throughout the land',[24] the discourse was hailed as 'a powerful homily on the value of Jewish self-respect, calling on the "emancipated" Jew not to despise his heritage but to honour it and obey the responsibilities it involves'.[25]

By the time of the formal election, in February 1913, this 'possessor of enthusiasm and energy' had garnered enough support to see off the – admittedly weak and dispirited – opposition. The two candidates were Hertz and Dayan Moses Hyamson, the latter campaigning despite widespread unpopularity among both 'East' and 'West'.[26] The confluence of factors in Hertz's favour made the outcome a foregone conclusion, and the winning margin – 298 votes to 39 – was greatly to underpin his authority in the Battle of Traditional Judaism that lay ahead.[27]

The armoury for that battle was bared as soon as the vote was announced. 'Prayerfully', he told his future flock,

> I answer *hineini* – 'here I am' – to the summons extended to me, under the guidance of Providence, by the Electoral College of British Congregations. I am deeply conscious of the vast and sacred responsibility which the office of Chief Rabbi imposes upon its incumbent, and equally so of the immense difficulty of any attempt worthily to succeed Hermann Adler.
>
> From my heart of hearts, I pray that the God of our fathers sustain

and guide me. With His help, and the help of my spiritual and lay co-workers, whose willing aid I now invoke in the communities throughout the Empire, my life and my strength shall be consecrated to upholding and maintaining the sway of Torah over our lives and the sanctification of the Divine Name, both within and without the ranks of Anglo-Jewry.[28]

If Hertz's dedication to 'upholding and maintaining the sway of Torah over our lives' instilled force or fear into progressive ranks, such were clearly out of sight (and of mind) as news of his victory filtered through the corridors of power. A warm, if qualified, welcome greeted him from the pulpit of the West London Synagogue, where Morris Joseph offered 'hearty greeting and felicitation to the accomplished gentleman upon whom the communal choice has fallen', but warned of no 'sacrifice of [our] distinctive doctrines or practices in the interests of communal unity'.

The members of the West London Synagogue, said Joseph, would do all they could to hearten and uphold the new Chief Rabbi. But their respect for his office, and their recognition of him as the chief religious representative of English Jewry, were 'necessarily conditioned by faithfulness to the great principles which our synagogue was established to affirm almost exactly seventy-one years ago'. Any weakening of their attachment to those principles would be 'singularly inopportune today, when the religious views of the average English Jew have become virtually identical with those of which our congregation is the exponent. Any sacrifice of our distinctive doctrines or practices in the interests of communal unity will not only be disloyal, but superfluous.' As long as official Orthodoxy meant what it did, they could not serve under its banner without self-contradiction. They, at any rate, would be consistent.

The West London, he added, hailed the new Chief Rabbi and prayed for the success of his labours on behalf of the ancestral religion which, in common with him, they venerated and loved. But they were going to keep to their own view of that religion, believing that both Orthodoxy and Reform, 'in the memorable phrase of the Talmud', were the word of the living God. Each was true and divine, seeing that each might uplift the soul that responded to its message and its appeal.

Isidore Harris, Joseph's colleague at Berkeley Street, offered a more pragmatic view. Addressing the Jewish Religious Education Board (the only Reform representative at the meeting) on the morrow of the election, he described his synagogue as 'occupying the position of intermediary between the Orthodox wing and the extreme radical wing – and its policy is to maintain the most cordial relations with both'. It was thus 'in the unique position to preserve not merely the semblance but the reality in communal harmony, and to help the Jews of England stand before the world as a united religious brotherhood'.

West London's relations with Hermann Adler, said Harris, had been 'of a most cordial character, notwithstanding that my congregation has not sacrificed one iota of its theological independence'. It had extended to Adler 'the deference due to the religious head of the community, and co-operated with him on every single occasion. We shall be no less generous to his successor, to whom we extend our support in the formidable task that confronts him.'[29]

No less generous were the greetings of the Liberal Jewish Synagogue, which, by yet another coincidence, had held its first annual meeting on the evening of Hertz's triumph – a day, said Claude Montefiore,

> that is bound to be eventful in the annals of the Jewish community in England.
>
> Although our congregation stands outside the rule of the Chief Rabbi as not being one under his jurisdiction, still the election cannot be without interest to anybody in this room. I am sure we all hope that the new Chief Rabbi will prove of advantage to the community in general and that he will become, as it were, an ornament to the Chief Rabbinate and will follow worthily in the footsteps of the dearly lamented Dr Adler.
>
> Our best wishes go out to Dr Hertz. No matter what differences of opinion on the subject of Orthodoxy or Reform might exist, I earnestly hope our relations with him, and with every branch of the community, will be comfortable, pleasant and auspicious.

Mattuck, too, wished 'the new incumbent of the Chief Rabbinate every success in his new sphere. I heartily welcome any new force, personality or institution which has close at heart the interests of Jews and Judaism, and I trust that Dr Hertz – in the task he has set himself of enthusing new life and hope, and of strengthening the old love for the ancient faith that has been handed down to us – will meet all the success he deserves.'[30]

Eight weeks on, 'practically the whole of the ministry' (reported the *Jewish Chronicle*[31]) was present at the Great Synagogue for Hertz's induction – 'severely simple', due to the recent loss of his father.

> At their head, in his robes of office, was the learned Haham, whose dignified presence added no little to the general dignity of the proceedings. With him near the Ark were Dayan [Moshe Avigdor]

Chaikin and Dayan [Asher] Feldman, and the Rev. Morris Joseph, who thus represented the Reform Synagogue. The Rev. Israel Mattuck was there, while Rabbi Dr [Joseph] Strauss, of Bradford, represented, with him, the extreme left wing of Anglo-Jewry.

Looking at the serried ranks of ministers who, most of them in their canonicals, crowded the almemar and a considerable section of the seating in the body of the synagogue, it would have been a difficult task to name any minister at all well known in the community who was absent.

The mark of universal loyalty on the part of the ministry must have been gratifying to the Chief Rabbi, and, bearing in mind all that has gone by, it was a splendid manifestation of loyalty of the community, as well as of a high-minded sense of duty to their calling and to their cause, on the part of the spiritual workers in our midst.

Addressing the 'serried ranks' but embracing the totality of the community, from the 'extreme left wing' to the 'foreigners' on the right, the newly installed Chief Rabbi of the United Hebrew Congregations of the British Empire was characteristically forthright in his message:

> Ours is an age of doubt and disillusionment. Times are out of joint. Theological foundations are rocking. Dreams of humanity, that but yesterday seemed within grasp of realisation, are dissolving into thin air in the face of the malicious race-hatred that is being fanatically preached, and the purposeless human slaughter cynically practised, in the opening decades of the twentieth century.
>
> Within the House of Israel also, old sanctions are weakening, home influence waning, and there is an alarming subsidence of the sense of worship. The generations are separated as by an abyss; hosts of our men and women of tomorrow are losing belief in Israel's future, and drifting into unbaptised apostasy ...
>
> The Jew very often can see only one thing at a time. He is intensive in his loyalties and antipathies, in his differences and indifferences. Pre-eminently does he need constant reminders that infinitely more important than all the issues that divide us are the things that should bind us, unite us; that it is as noble a striving for brother to rediscover brother as to preserve an unbroken connection with Israel's past.
>
> And to all parties alike comes this warning for moderation in judgment. The revolutionaries need it. Theirs is the cry of 'New lamps for old.' But there is no inherent, sacramental virtue in change as change. The new is not always the true. 'The seal of the Almighty

is Truth', say the rabbis. But He has no Keeper of the Seal; and even the latest theory of the youngest revolutionary thinker may be mistaken.

And, ye men of older years and views, be moderate in judgment. 'New occasions teach new duties', and new conditions require new methods. In classical phrase, 'the methods of the quiet past are inadequate for the stormy present. The occasion is piled high with difficulties, and we must rise with the occasion. As our case is new, so we must think anew, act anew.'

Let us, therefore, whether we be traditionalists or revolutionaries, first of all disenthral ourselves, on the one hand, from masterly inactivity or from methods obsolete even in Russia; and, on the other, from the spell of new remedies which have proved pathetically futile, and worse than futile, in Germany and America – and we shall save our young for the future. For our children's sake, therefore, be ye deliberate, moderate, charitable in judgment.

It is essential that a united Jewry be ever ready loyally to support my hands and steady them. Once more I beg for sympathetic understanding and co-operation. Vast are the potentialities of British Jewry, with its hegemony in contemporary Israel, with this community the axis round which so many of Israel's endeavours revolve. The eyes of our brethren throughout the world are upon us – their hopes and prayers are all with us.

Who shall live up to the great trust? Who dare fail to try? In the words of Hermann Adler, I ask you all – young and old, men and women, laymen and scholars, ministers and rabbis – 'what can be grander or more glorious than to become fellow workers with God in securing the immortality of Judaism?'[32]

\* \* \*   \* \* \*   \* \* \*

Among the 'well-known ministers' absent from the installation service was Moses Hyamson, Hertz's defeated opponent, who with his fellow dayan, Asher Feldman, had overseen Chief Rabbinical affairs following Adler's death. Despite vocal support from his ministerial colleagues, and votes of confidence from his United Synagogue heads, Hyamson had bid farewell to Britain and sailed for New York to occupy Hertz's former pulpit at Orach Chayim, 'finding sanctuary there' – in the words of a prominent activist who came to know him – 'for thirty eccentric years'.[33]

But if one, unsuccessful, minister was missing, another, more forthright, was very much in evidence – and one, no less, who had pipped

Hertz at the post some six years earlier.[34] The New West End's Joseph Simon Hochman, a graduate of Jews' College and Heidelberg University, had himself earned an eccentric – and controversial – reputation during his brief ministry in London and, in the highly charged atmosphere over progressive Judaism, was to cross swords with Chief Rabbis on a number of occasions before resigning his pulpit and being called to the Bar.[35]

# 9

## Strangled Spirit

The *Jews' College Jubilee Volume*, which contained Hermann Adler's exhortation quoted at the end of Hertz's sermon, records the award of three scholarships to Joseph Hochman between 1902 and 1905, the largest number to a single student up to that time.[1] Born in London in 1883, Joseph was one of eight children of the Rev. Aaron Hochman (1860–1939) by his first wife. The father came from Skaden, West Russia, and served as a minister and shochet in Halberstadt, Germany, before assuming similar duties with the Nottingham Hebrew Congregation. He subsequently worked on the London Board for Shechita for more than fifty years, settling on his retirement in Westcliff-on-Sea.[2]

The most prestigious of Joseph Hochman's awards, the Sir Moses Montefiore Studentship, enabled the young graduate to complete his studies at other institutions – and it was to Germany, the hotbed of classical Reform, that he chose to travel. There he came into contact with some of the foremost scholars in the Jewish world – Steinschneider, Ellbogen, Barth, Hoffman and Wohlgemuth in Berlin, Becker, Bezold and Windelbaud in Heidelberg – before emerging with a doctorate of philosophy and the plaudits of his native-born colleagues ringing in his ears.[3]

Why the inexperienced Hochman was selected, and Hertz rejected, at the New West End is none too clear,[4] though the future Chief Rabbi was not the only South African aspirant to be turned down for the post: the Rev. Professor Alfred P. Bender, minister of the Cape Town Hebrew Congregation – who visited London in 1907 and preached at the New West End on the first day of Shavuot – was likewise unsuccessful.[5] But with credentials such as his, Hochman – a full two decades Bender's junior, and eleven years younger than Hertz – was patently seen as a promising star in the Anglo-Jewish firmament.

That the appointment was initially of a temporary nature might have indicated some anxiety – justified, as it turned out – on the part of his paymasters.[6] In 1909, however, the post was regularised (if not yet cemented), and when Hochman had had time to consolidate his position and, as he thought, test the mood of his flock, he primed his fuse. In a series of sermons over the ensuing twelve months, he castigated those within the United Synagogue who called for uniformity before unity, and vented his frustration at its 'strangling of the spirit'.

'It is now three years', he told his congregants in April 1910,

> since first I entered this pulpit. You will excuse the personal note if I add that I have never entered it with a heavier heart than I do today, when I come to you with a failure to my record. I begin to fear there was truth in the warning which some friends in the Anglo-Jewish ministry gave me more than once when they remarked that to enter the service of the United Synagogue was to say goodbye to one's ideals.
>
> Short as my experience of the United Synagogue has been, even the buoyancy of youth hardly saves me from the fear that we are all in the grip of an organisation the success of which strangles the spirit. It seems to be an institution whose power prevents great issues, and its strength seems used to secure the smallness of its ends.[7]

But even while finding fault within his own union, and preparing to cloak himself in Reformist garb, Hochman was scathing in his condemnation of the Liberal advance. Writing the same month in the first issue of his much-heralded literary magazine, the *Jewish Review*,[8] he asserted that

> the Jewish Religious Union ... is being reorganised as the Jewish Religious Union for the Advancement of Liberal Judaism, in order that it may be brought into line with the similar unions in France and Germany. It no longer stands as a half-way house to win the indifferent for the synagogue, but seeks to call them – and others – to a synagogue of its own, in which universalist doctrines are to be emphasised and separatist ceremonials suppressed ...
>
> When the leaders of the Jewish Religious Union demand a separate synagogue, in which the universalist doctrines of Judaism and the 'Mission of Israel' shall be emphasised, and the national elements of which these doctrines are born eliminated, they proclaim a conception of religion which is anti-Jewish, and betray that assimilation in thought which must herald assimilation in life. Once make creed the basis of religious organisation, and the religious society that results is unstable. Every varying shade of opinion will justify desertion and lead on to the promotion of new sects or absorption into existing churches.
>
> Of Jewish reform it is true that *plus ça change plus c'est la même chose*. Whether its alleged motive is a desire to purify Judaism of supposed superstitious excrescences, or to denationalise it, or to accommodate it

> to the teachings of (Christian) Higher Criticism, always and everywhere its true inwardness is the impulse towards assimilation, towards the breaking down of the separateness of the Jewish people ...
>
> Possibly the programme of the Union may hold its immediate members in some kind of tie with the Jewish community; but does any honest man doubt that it will fail to hold their offspring? Religion and nationality have been woven together in traditional Judaism for nearly three thousand years as warp and woof in cloth. They cannot be severed without destroying the fabric.
>
> In England, indeed, the attempt to denationalise Judaism and to liberate it from the law is the more dangerous because here the assimilation of the Jew has not to encounter the opposition of the non-Jew. The social bar erected against anti-Semitism is the last bulwark which the most Liberal Judaism abroad has not yet contrived to storm.
>
> There, the Liberalism is all on one side; in England, the road which leads to absorption and the Church is easier to traverse. The leaders of the Jewish Religious Union, by their rejection of law and nationality, are leading away a stream from the living fountain of Judaism to lose itself in the arid plains of universalism.[9]

Hochman's powder-keg at the New West End exploded later that year, during the penitential period, when the pews were full and the congregation poised. The catalyst for the eventual conflagration was his series of sermons on Orthodox observance, the first noted more for its obscurity than for its reputed 'outspokenness':

> Liberal tendencies when organised create the danger of needless opposition to them. Rejection of tradition on the one side brings it about that loyalty to tradition is regarded on the other side as involving purposeless observance ... I say with great deliberateness that the God of those whom we look back to as our fathers may be for us the shame of our youth ...
>
> The authors of the Babylonian Talmud involved themselves in so bewildering a confusion of minutiæ that the teachers of Palestine applied to them the verse in Lamentations, 'He hath made me to dwell in dark places as those that have been long dead.' The cultured rabbis of Spain spoke with even greater disdain of the like tendencies of the rabbis of France.
>
> Today there is evident everywhere in Jewish circles, in greater or less degree, a revolt against the domination of the minutiæ of Rabbinical laws. If we were more truly Jewish, we should all of us honestly proclaim in words the thoughts that our deeds proclaim,

and honestly try to let our worship proclaim that we seek not the God of our fathers, but Him who is our God and the God of our fathers.

The danger is great, I know, that if we seek our God, we shall forget He is the God of our fathers; but the danger is no less than in worshipping the God of our fathers we forget that he is our God. The danger is great that if we, for ourselves, do seek each his God, we shall find no more than the God of our age; but the danger is far greater that if we seek the God of our fathers, we shall find no relation between Him and our age.[10]

Perplexity and puzzlement followed these words, both within the congregation and in the wider community. 'One of the Old School' spoke for many when he commented:

> I tried hard to penetrate the mist which enshrouded Dr Hochman's 'outspoken' sermon on Orthodoxy. I read it again and again but have not yet mastered its object ...
>
> The idea of abandoning the God of 'those whom we look back to as our fathers' for a new God, a God of our own, is admittedly novel, quite unique; nay, quite contrary to the most essential teaching of Judaism ... I have not the time at present to enter into a discussion with Dr Hochman concerning 'the bewildering confusion of the minutiæ of Rabbinical Law'. There is a very easy and available remedy to rid oneself of this confusion, and nowadays it does not require any great heroism to have recourse to it.
>
> I feel, however, bound to declare that this young 'outspoken' minister does not seem to understand the rabbis whose words he is supposed to quote. The application of the verse in Lamentations, cited by Dr Hochman from the Palestine Talmud, is not made, as he erroneously thinks, against the *laws* in the Babylonian Talmud, which as a matter of fact are the laws embodied in the Mishnah, expounded and compiled in Palestine, but merely concerning the obscure and confused style of argument.
>
> This, indeed, may also be applied to Dr Hochman's style of exposition. We live in an age of 'outspokenness'. It is now in fashion to be frank and fearless. Frank and outspoken words are not, however, always wise and correct.[11]

Be that as it may, fearlessness won out, and Hochman proceeded to demonstrate it in force on the first day of Rosh Hashanah 5671,[12] when he declared, in a reference whose source was for years to mystify the community:

'We must take our bearings anew' is what was recently said to me by one of the religiously most observant members of this congregation.[13] Well then, let us try to do it.

Let us face the problem as it affects ourselves. Some of you are still quite Orthodox. That is to say, you still believe that the Bible is literally and verbally the word of God; that it is equally valid in every part; that its commandments are, all of them, binding for all time; that even those which by force of circumstances are suspended will one day be restored at the advent of the personal Messiah.

For you, Judaism is a system of laws and duties clearly defined and authoritatively binding on every Jew. You need the lawyer to interpret the laws. You do not need the preacher. You listen to him with condescension, if not with positive impatience. You are perhaps more observant of religious ceremonial than I am, though I am not aware that any member of this congregation scrupulously obeys all the details of the law. In matters of religious observance, however, you are not of those who would look to me for guidance. I would not want you to.

But let us be frank, and frankly you must admit that you are very few. The great majority in this congregation do not agree with you. They are less observant by far than I am, and the Bible is not for them and me what it is for you. However much the conservative tendencies in modern Bible criticism and the corroborations of archaeological science may strengthen faith in the student, the Bible cannot be what Jewish Orthodoxy would make it.

Now, is it not obvious that unless we find our consciousness of religious individuality somehow, apart from the formulation of creed of an individual authority in the past — that is, apart from the Orthodoxy which we will not, because we cannot, make our own — is it not true that unless we find that consciousness elsewhere, we or our children or our children's children must be lost to Judaism and, with them, the forces that make for the victory of Jewish ideals in life? ...

It is true that blood sacrifices are no more, but does not official Orthodoxy regard our present worship as a temporary substitution for them? Are not many of our Orthodox observances bound up with the ideas that were associated with them? And is it not, in any case, equally true of the Orthodoxy of our day that it regards the disintegration that threatens the Judaism of our day as avertable only by a rigorous fulfilment of the requirements of our national religious forms and ceremonies? And do not Orthodox preachers generally preach as if religion's task were to promote a self-satisfaction and self-righteousness and secure the rest of soul which indifference to religion can equally secure?

No, Orthodoxy has no place in the religion of the modern world, but personality. And we have all along been proclaiming against our persecutors that Orthodoxy has no place in religion at all. *A Jew cannot be Jewish and Orthodox* [Hochman's emphasis] ... It is as true in our day as it was in Jeremiah's day that the survival of the Jew is independent of our Orthodoxy, and with the Jew the survival of Judaism is secure.[14]

The sermons provoked immediate and profound dismay. 'We are informed', reported the *Jewish Chronicle*, 'that considerable feeling has been aroused among the congregants of the New West End Synagogue in consequence of certain recent pulpit utterances on the part of the minister, Dr J. Hochman. We understand that the matter has been under consideration by the Chief Rabbi [Hermann Adler] and the board of management, and that a satisfactory arrangement has been come to.'[15]

The strength of that satisfaction is, however, open to doubt. On the eve of the following Sabbath, with barely two hours to spare, Adler sent a hurried message to Leonard Schlesinger, one of the wardens: 'Deeply regret cannot permit minister [to] preach tomorrow. Am willing to occupy pulpit tomorrow. Confer with you after service. C.R'.[16] On the Sabbath itself, Adler met with Hochman, and a day later addressed these words to the recalcitrant preacher:

> At our interview yesterday afternoon, I communicated to you the result of my conference with Mr Schlesinger. I pointed out to you the passages in your New Year sermon which were interrupted by several of your congregants and which I hold to be a diatribe against the practice and the ordinances of Judaism.
>
> I decided that, as a condition of your being allowed to preach on Yom Kippur, you were in the sermon on that day to explain that it had not been your intention to impugn traditional Judaism and the practice of its observances. I asked you to submit the sermon to me for my approval and, moreover, to give me an undertaking that you will, in future, be careful in your sermons to refrain from stating anything which might be interpreted as being antagonistic to the ordinances of Judaism.
>
> I now ask you to be good enough to write to me that you accept these conditions and that you will let me have your Yom Kippur sermon not later than Wednesday next at ten o'clock. I will return it to you with the least possible delay.[17]

While Hochman concurred with regard to Yom Kippur, later describing the Chief Rabbi's request as an 'inhibition',[18] it took him little time thereafter to breach his undertaking. By the end of October, the offending sermon had been 'Printed by Request' and appeared in pamphlet form for general circulation. An irate Adler wrote yet again:

> A copy of the sermon preached by you on the first day New Year has been handed to me. I was greatly surprised to see the sermon in print, as I asked you to abstain from publishing a discourse for the delivery of which both your board of management and I had been compelled to censure you. I understood from you that you agreed to that course, and it is a source of deep regret to me that your present action is at variance with the advice which I tendered you and which I had confidently anticipated you would follow.
>
> I see that you propose preaching on Sabbath next on 'Religious Observances'. I herewith ask you to bring me your manuscript on Friday next at ten o'clock to submit it to me for my approval. I hope that this sermon will not contain anything at variance with the principle for the maintenance of which the U[nited] S[ynagogue] has been established.
>
> Should, however, the discourse contain any statement to which I am forced to take exception, and should you, unhappily, refuse to make such correction as I may deem necessary, it will be my painful duty to prohibit you from preaching this discourse. Should so unfortunate a contingency arise, your wardens have asked me to occupy the pulpit that day, and I have no alternative but to comply with their request.[19]

Adler's attention to the planned sermon had been drawn by Hochman's introductory paragraph in the printed pamphlet:

> This sermon is the third of a series of four sermons, the first of which was published in the Jewish Chronicle on the 23rd Sept., under the heading 'Orthodoxy and the Knowledge of God'. The second, on 'The Knowledge of God', was delivered on Oct. 1st, when the announcement was made that the third sermon, on 'Orthodoxy and Religious Observance', would be preached on New Year, and that the fourth of the series would treat of 'Religious Observances'. It is obvious that the terms 'orthodoxy' and 'observance' were not used indiscriminately, even could any authority be found for the identification. The sermon is nothing but a concentration of the preacher's teaching from the pulpit of the New West End Synagogue during the whole period of his ministry there. This New Year's sermon is a criticism of 'Orthodoxy' in the usual acceptation and common meaning of the

term; that is to say, it is a criticism of the attitude of mind which unquestioningly accepts a formulated creed as the basis of religious practice, both creed and practice being accepted entirely, as received from an external human authority, whatever sanction that authority may claim. On the other hand, it is a plea for faith in the Election of Israel as a basis of Jewish Religious Observance – that faith which seeks God's voice rather in the purpose than in the origin of His commandments. I hope to deliver the sermon on 'Religious Observances' on Sabbath *parashat Noach*, Nov. 5th.[20]

The ensuing sermon – and ensuing months – passed peacefully enough, and Adler soon after passed peacefully away, but a year later Hochman's position remained unresolved. He had accepted the renewal of his contract for a further two years, 'on the assumption that the announcement is made within that period of his permanent appointment'.[21]

Seeking to explain these terms, the senior warden, Neville D. Cohen, told the congregation's annual meeting: 'Not that we are dissatisfied in any way, but as he [Hochman] is still a young man, it would be advantageous to see how he gets on during that period. If he gives as much satisfaction as he has given in the past, no doubt he will then be elected permanently.'[22] Despite a subsequent announcement to the latter effect,[23] Cohen's enigmatic statement hid a host of concerns, the revelation of which would ultimately expose Hochman as perhaps the most maverick of ministers in the United Synagogue's history.

\* \* \*   \* \* \*   \* \* \*

One of those concerns encompassed the question of ritual reform. With Swaythling and Adler dispatched to their eternal rest, Hochman had encouraged the notion among his less pious congregants of progressive modification in the Sabbath service. Among his recommendations were an English prayer, read by him from the pulpit; a psalm, selected by him, to be recited in English; and the reading of the Ten Commandments, in Hebrew or English, every fourth week.

Although approved by the members, the proposals were by no means universally popular – the objection being, however, of a practical rather than a theological nature. Many thought that the service, already lengthy, would be prolonged still further, and within a year the changes were dropped. Piqued at this setback to his proposed reforms, Hochman had reflected his mood in a eulogy to the departed Chief Rabbi. 'The Anglo-Jewish ministry as it is today', he declared, is a product of the Chief Rabbinate. Jews' College was called into being by the father and predecessor of him to whom we owe so much, and to whom Jews' College was a cherished object of concern.

If the Chief Rabbinate, as interpreted by father and son, deprived the Jewish minister of a great measure of influence and authority and responsibility in his congregation, it also delivered him in the same degree from dependence on those to whom he owed his position as a teacher of the synagogue, but who, nonetheless, cannot claim to be qualified judges of his teaching.[24]

Hochman then came up with a second, and more far-reaching, proposal – for the triennial reading of the Torah, in place of its customary cycle over the course of a year. In the spring of 1912, with no Chief Rabbi to scotch the idea, a meeting of New West End seat-holders agreed upon the formation of a committee 'to consider the possibility and desirability of introducing the Reading of the Scriptures in the Synagogue in a Triennial Cycle, and to report thereon'.[25]

The scholars they consulted, 'chosen for their special knowledge only, and not on account of any bias'[26] – from Hyamson on the right to Joseph on the left, and with Hochman (and others) in the centre[27] – were asked to review the practicality of the proposal and whether or not it conformed to halachah and (perhaps, to some, of greater significance) to the constitution of the United Synagogue. In the committee's unanimous opinion, reached after numerous meetings and months of consultations,

> in theory and in principle we approve of the introduction of the Triennial Cycle and we regard it as a desirable reform ... Nevertheless, we find an insuperable difficulty in the way of recommending the change owing to the cast-iron constitution of the United Synagogue.
>
> We are bound to admit that the new system of reading the Law would not be in accordance with the German or Polish ritual, nor would it receive the consent of the ecclesiastical authorities if the matter were submitted to them as one of din. The Act affords no scope for freedom of usage and no elasticity to meet the needs of congregations of varying outlooks and modes of thought.
>
> To break in any respect from the established ritual is to break with the United Synagogue and, indeed, from Orthodoxy. In this instance, the introduction of a desirable reform is rendered impossible by the fetters at present imposed by the provisions of the United Synagogue Act and the veto possessed by the ecclesiastical authorities.

> We are, therefore, of opinion that the seat-holders should earnestly consider whether the time has not arrived to take steps to modify the inelasticity caused by these barriers, so as to admit of a degree of local option under which certain modifications of the ritual would be permissible. We recommend that this Report be circulated amongst other synagogues with the object of eliciting their views thereon.[28]

Commenting on the recommendations and on the ultimate decision not to implement the proposal, Hochman's successor, Ephraim Levine, remarked years later: 'Perhaps it was as well. Any such innovation would have struck at the root of the whole system of metropolitan worship and prepared the way for more subversive reform.'[29]

Hochman himself, as he was in due course to make clear, had his own views on the matter – as he had, indeed, on Adler's successor. Referring in a sermon to Hertz's election, 'the *fait accompli* in which, rightly or wrongly, fortunately or unfortunately, the pulpit was not involved', he asserted that 'great mistakes have been made', but that the ministry would 'certainly endeavour to save the community the consequences of any mistake. Its loyalty is to a cause and not to any man.'[30]

The 'mistakes' to which he referred were constant irritants to the young minister. In frequent editorials in the *Jewish Review*, he had questioned the functions – indeed, the very existence – of the Chief Rabbinate, and as the election drew near and then passed into history, he had sharpened his pen against the individuals involved. In the selection procedure, he thundered on one occasion, 'the Anglo-Jewish ministry has been unjustifiably ignored, as if the Chief Rabbi of the community were not to be, primarily, the chief of its ministry. No rabbi of commanding importance has been presented to the community' – (this at a time when Hertz was the clear front-runner) – 'and nowhere is there a rabbi who exercises the authority which Anglo-Jewry would entrust to its Chief Rabbi'. Moreover, the prestige of the community 'has not suffered through the absence of a Chief Rabbi'.[31]

Two months later, with Hertz's position secured, Hochman thundered afresh:

> The electoral body proved as powerless as we prophesied. The delegates summoned to elect the Chief Rabbi were 'tied hand and foot' – to quote Mr Jessel's confession – by the decisions of the previous Rabbinate conference. The protest of the clergy was ignored. The protest of the laity was ignored. The fear of losing financial support, in the event of the defeat of the lay leaders of the community, outweighed the fear of losing the support of those who can but render personal service in the interests of the community. And rightly so; for

it may be assumed that all who have the interests of the community at heart will accept the situation.

Communal workers, however, should note that a continuance of this attitude on the part of the lay leaders will be utterly destructive of democratic spirit, and prevent recruiting among the rising generation for the ranks of our communal workers. The community must learn to resist financial pressure if it would escape spiritual stagnation.

Dr Hertz has our sympathy in the difficulties which face him. He has to lead three sections of the community between which there is, at present, little in common – the lay leaders to whose influence he owes his appointment; the ministry which opposed his nomination; and the unorganised masses of the community whose feelings were expressed in an effective protest. It is to be hoped that, with statesmanlike foresight, he will emancipate his office from the control of the few, secure for it the broad basis of popular approval, lengthen the cords to strengthen the stakes, and find opportunities of service for all who are willing to serve.[32]

That Hochman and Hertz were bound to clash personally was, in these circumstances, only a matter of time. Theological issues apart, the minister's horse-riding habits rankled with his chief – and with his wardens – leading to public spats (in more than one sense) on several occasions. Members of his congregation related how he would ride to synagogue by horse from Rotten Row, tie the animal to the railings and, still in his breeches, enter the sanctuary for morning prayers. They also told of an instance when, in open defiance of a request by Hertz for ministerial beards, Hochman proceeded – with much ado – to shave his off.[33]

Of greater moment, however, were Hochman's continued calls for synagogue reform, for a diminution of authority within the Chief Rabbinate, and for greater responsibilities on the part of the ministry, all placing him increasingly – and openly – beyond the pale. One final outburst, after several others both written and verbal, paved the way to ministerial ruination:

> The welfare of a community [he wrote] is too intimately bound up with the status of its ministry to justify the apparent disregard with which the problem, as it affects the Anglo-Jewish ministry, has been treated since the election of the Chief Rabbi.
>
> It speaks much for Dr Hertz that, since his election, little has been heard of him on this subject; for, undoubtedly, there was need of great restraint on his part in order that there might be a relaxation in the strain which was placed upon communal good will by the

struggle which raged around his election, and the manner in which that struggle was ended. We need recall, however, that the election of a Chief Rabbi was declared to be necessary for the consideration of the problem, and was not to prelude the shelving of it ...

The Chief Rabbi is associated most closely with the United Synagogue, in which the spirit of self-sacrifice has almost sacrificed the spirit. The United Synagogues Act places upon the Chief Rabbi the onus of responsibility for the ritual and teaching in the constituent synagogues, and conformity is secured by the Deed of Foundation and Trust.

Congregants, in order to retain the right of worshipping in the synagogues in which they, or their fathers, helped to found, sacrifice their opinions and convictions to submit to the authority of the Chief Rabbinate; and the hands of the Chief Rabbi are tied by the legal requirements of the United Synagogue. The Chief Rabbi can hardly find pleasure in such sacrifice of religious enthusiasms as results in the retention of the right, and the surrender of the practice, of effectively using synagogues for their primary purpose. He should be relieved of personal responsibility for the ritual of synagogues.

The United Synagogues Act should be amended to relieve the strain involved in the sacrifice of religious enthusiasm by which uniformity is secured, and to render possible the closer co-operation of all synagogues which, by contributing to the Chief Rabbi's Fund, declare their willingness to acknowledge his moral authority.

So long as the members of any Jewish congregation do not forfeit their right to Jewish burial, so long have we no right to question their claim to be considered Jewish in life, however much we may be dissatisfied with the degree of their Jewishness. Increased local autonomy and responsibility would stay the sacrifice of religious enthusiasms, and the close co-operation of all Jewish congregations would deepen Jewish consciousness. It were better to put our trust in that spiritual factor than to rely on an Act of Parliament for the solution of our religious problems.

If, instead of striving after uniformity, the community would direct itself to securing unity, constituent synagogues soon would realise the public advantage which would result from their surrender of the right to have, each for itself, a fully qualified and partially paid minister, dependent on the voluntary offerings of its congregants as a supplement to his salary. Meanwhile, we can move in this direction.

One of the ministers in each district should be appointed as chairman of a committee, consisting of the clergy working in the district, so that the local needs may receive fuller consideration and more effective care than individual action can secure. And it should not be impossible to secure some measure of local autonomy by freeing the Chief Rabbi's hands, to some extent, and placing upon these chairmen, as a body, the right of veto now exercised by the Chief Rabbi on his sole responsibility. Such organisation in London would serve as a basis for future developments, and a model for provincial organisation.[34]

This two-pronged attack, by an insider counting himself (in his own words) among 'those who do not claim that we are orthodox, nor claim ourselves liberal, but would regard ourselves as conservative Jews',[35] was as much as his masters would bear. Yet Hochman – or Hockman, as he had now taken to calling himself[36] – was to have one last taste of communal recognition. In May 1915, the council of Jews' College, which had bestowed great honours upon him a decade earlier, elected him to its staff – proposed by none other than Hertz himself (inexplicably, and paradoxically, in the light of events). Following meetings with the dayanim and other dignitaries, it had been decided to appoint a lecturer in the formal aspects of homiletics, the techniques of sermon preparation, and by a margin of eight to one he was voted into office.

But it was a post he never assumed. Matters came to a head – bluntly and abruptly – later that summer with a statement that Hockman had tended his resignation as minister of the New West End 'as he feels himself "unable to bring his views into harmony with the standpoint of the synagogue"'.[37] Reflecting the consternation behind the scenes, the synagogue took a month to publish its response: 'At a special meeting of the board of management, held on Tuesday, 31 August [1915], it was resolved to accept with regret the Rev. Dr Hockman's resignation as minister, and that it should take effect forthwith.'[38] Joshua Abelson, principal of Aria theological college, had agreed to preach in his stead during the upcoming holy-days.[39]

In contrast to this low-key statement, Hockman's own response – which forestalled it – exemplified the 'outspokenness' that had launched him on his path to reform in his early sermons. Headed 'Why I Resigned', it came in the form of a lengthy interview in the *Jewish Chronicle*, which began: 'A strange and unwonted thing has happened in the community. A minister of the United Synagogue, the Rev. Dr Hockman, has resigned his pulpit. To have yielded it up was an act of courage, not minimised by the age at which this minister has arrived – thirty-two.'[40] The report revealed, moreover, the source of the mystery quotation that had so baffled his congregants during the Rosh Hashanah service five years earlier.

'We may agree or disagree with his reasons [for resigning]', the paper told its readers. 'But we shall not grudge him the tribute of admiration which is the meed of honesty, and perhaps it may profit us somewhat to inquire into the motives of his sacrifice. The why and the wherefore of Dr Hockman's action it will be better to let the minister of the New West End Synagogue explain in his own words.'

> You ask me why I resigned. I did so because I found the synagogue out of touch with the spirit and purpose of true Rabbinic teaching. To put the matter in a sentence, the so-called conservative Jew at the present time is hampered, and his religious practice reduced to a sham, because he professes in public, though often not in private, a conformity to a set of ecclesiastical ordinances framed for totally different circumstances, a totally different generation, and an entirely different civilisation.
>
> My standpoint, from the time I entered the ministry, was that the variation of the circumstances in which we lived demanded the proper adaptation of those ordinances to the changing times, and that there is nothing inconsistent with the spirit and purpose of traditional Judaism in such an adaptation. On the contrary, traditional Judaism required it.
>
> In a sermon on 'Orthodoxy and Religious Observance', which I delivered on New Year 5671, I used these words: '"We must take our bearings anew" is what was recently said to me by one of the religiously most observant members of this congregation.' That member, I may perhaps now state, was none other than the late Lord Swaythling.
>
> *Your standpoint is that the Jews of London have chained themselves to an outworn series of ordinances in the mistaken belief that in so doing they remain traditional Jews?*
>
> Yes. For instance, you have, in order to meet the difficulties presented by the great distances in London, created a large number of scattered synagogues, which impose a heavy burden on the community, while by dissipating energies it makes it almost impossible to secure effective religious leadership.
>
> On the other hand, you find that the Conservative rabbis of France, faced with a similar situation to that which exists here, have boldly declared it to be in harmony with the traditional Jewish spirit of Sabbath observance to avail oneself of the public mechanical means of transit within the city. The rule of the Sabbath-day journey, intended, no doubt, to preserve home life on the Sabbath, is by no means violated by this concession. It preserves the spirit of the Sabbath by adapting the Rabbinical Sabbath law to modern exigencies.
>
> Take, again, the attitude of the synagogue towards women. We feel

very much that the future of Judaism must depend very largely on the influence exercised by mothers over children. Nonetheless, we are under the impression that it is a demand of the Rabbinic law that women should be excluded from participation in public religious life.

Turn up the Shulchan Aruch itself and you find it there stated quite clearly that women have the right to lead in public worship. But, we are told, a change was introduced in this regard out of respect for the feelings of the congregation. This change evidently dates from the same time, and originates in the same circumstances, as the Christian requirement that women should keep silence in the churches.

They are the circumstances of Hellenistic civilisation, when no woman of moral character could take part in public life. The exclusion of women from religious life was a concession on the part of the Rabbinic law to the spirit of that age. The same rabbis would, surely, more readily make the concession required today of going back to the original standpoint, which gave women an equal position with men in the religious life and activity of the community. The rabbis of France, in this matter also, have acted accordingly – they have said, for instance, that women may be counted for a *minyan*.

Consider the language of prayer. Rabbinic teaching allows that public worship may be held in any language, though private prayer should be in Hebrew. The seemingly superstitious reasons given in a later Rabbinic age are really popular statements of common sense. A congregation safeguards its Jewish spirit in its very assembling, though an isolated individual must secure the inspiration of that spirit from its language.

Contrast the obstinate Rabbinism of our own day, which comfortably maintains the ignorant Orthodoxy that supports it. Or take again the 'second days' of festivals. The synagogue is open and practically empty, thus proclaiming that its members are invited to ignore what it upholds, if only they pay their rentals and so secure their burial. In fact, the United Synagogue stands on its cemetery.

*How would you apply your adaptation theory to the synagogue service?*
Well, it is generally felt that the service in the synagogue is very much over-burdened, and, indeed, that it lacks refinement. This result comes down to us from the time when the Jews were cut off from the life of the world, and the synagogue was, indeed, as much a place of recreation as of prayer or instruction.

That time has entirely passed away; yet we cling to the service that has come down from those generations instead of returning to the service as it was when, and where, the Jews were free. The separation of the sexes in the synagogue is not a Jewish requirement, but has imposed itself upon the synagogue under Hellenistic and, to a still greater extent, Mohammedan influences.

*You contend that such things as the synagogue ritual, the place of women in the synagogue, and the laws of Sabbath observance could all be modified and adapted to present circumstances, without in the least departing from the spirit of Rabbinic law and teaching?*
I do.

*A man can ride to synagogue on the Sabbath, and still be a good Sabbath-keeping Jew?*
By all means.

*What has been the practical result of what you regard as the stereotyping of the old ordinances, and the refusal to adapt them to modern conditions?*
The synagogue has become petrified. The United Synagogue is content to be merely a house of prayer – spiritually a church, however different externally, however different in ceremonial and ritual. The members find a certain consciousness of religious satisfaction in philanthropic activities. But the synagogue is not what it primarily should be – a place of instruction and a centre of leading, from which Jews should take up their attitude towards the large problems affecting Jewish life.

It is a house of prayer, and not a centre of activity. It is, spiritually, an unconscious instrument of assimilation and not the centre of a conscious mission. The synagogue is the one basis of organisation which the Jews in the diaspora have. Yet, as a result of the insincerity which pervades it, it is, practically, entirely without influence, and stands self-confessed in its futility, at a time such as this when we are confronted with a tragedy which in some respects is greater than that of the year 70, because then it was *churban beth hamikdash*, whereas today we are threatened with a *churban Beth Yisroel*.

The insincere atmosphere of the synagogue is repellent to the sensitive minds of the young. I base that remark only on what they themselves have said to me. The congregation outwardly pretend to conform to the old ordinances, but in actual fact they do not. The result is a painful dissonance between profession and practice.

The synagogue becomes a place where men pretend. The home is the place where they practise – what they believe. And each is completely out of sympathy with the other. Imagine the difficulty of instructing the children of the members of such congregations. Almost every lesson you give involves a contradiction of the Fifth Commandment.

You tell the children they must not ride on Saturday, or eat butter after meat, that they must only partake of meat ritually prepared; and they say: 'But we don't keep these things at home.' And all the time one feels that Judaism would become a religion of joy which one could teach with love, if only one were willing to be sincere by allowing life to do its work, and the practice of Judaism to follow the line of historic development.

*What, in your view, are the consequences of the dissonance to which you refer?*

That the children come to the synagogue while their parents bring them; that the parents attend while they have children to bring; that hardly anyone cares for the synagogue for its own sake or his own personal good; and that the young people, when they reach years of discretion, gradually and almost inevitably fall away from the synagogue and, in very considerable numbers, from Jewish life – witness the increase of extermarriage.

*Your standpoint is really that of the old Reform movement?*

That is so. But it is the obvious that is always being ignored.

*You would say that, owing to the circumstances to which you refer, the influence of the synagogue is dead?*

Yes. If you want an illustration you will find it in the fact that the movement for the Jewish restoration to Palestine – an object which we daily pray for – has practically been ignored by the synagogue, so that the movement has, in its turn, ignored the synagogue – and by the synagogue, all the time, I must be understood as meaning the United Synagogue.

*What have you done in your own synagogue to correct these evils?*

I asked, in the first instance, that I should be allowed to attend the meetings of the board of management and the various committees, so that I might bring whatever influence I had to bear when the opportunity occurred. But I was told definitely that it was better to give up trying to secure this – which, in effect, meant that I must remember I was a paid servant and had no right to take the initiative.

I tried to accept the situation and make the best of things. I secured at one time Sabbath afternoon choral services, with sermon, in order that a better opportunity might be given for those who could not, or would not, avail themselves of our one weekly opportunity of effective public worship. The effort was destroyed by internal opposition, and I said at the time, in a sermon which was published in the *Jewish Chronicle*, that the conditions were taking my heart out of my work. I have been trying to secure the enfranchisement of women seat-holders. Our own seat-holders were unanimously in favour of the change. But the United Synagogue prevented its accomplishment.

I tried to secure the introduction of the triennial cycle of the reading of the Law, as to the influence of which for preserving a knowledge of Hebrew and of the Torah I may remind you that Professor Graetz[41] has said that we pursue a sisyphean task unless we return to the old practice of reading small portions of the Law, with each person 'called' to the Law reading his own portion of about three verses. A committee was appointed to investigate the question, and it reported unanimously in favour of the change.

But, of course, we were up against the United Synagogue; and I have come to the conclusion that the United Synagogue is far too satisfied with itself to leave room for any hope of vitality within it. As Dr Israel Abrahams has written to me, since my resignation, 'the United Synagogue is liable to become detrimental to a sincere Judaism'.

*Do you agree with that view?*

Yes, as the United Synagogue is, because not only has it the power to strangle all development in the synagogue, but by its legal constitution it is compelled to do so, the United Synagogue being legally obliged to keep to the German-Polish *minhag*. Even the Chief Rabbi himself is powerless, being also tied by the same legal instrument.

*What do you regard as a possible remedy for the present state of things?*

What we need, I think, is a reform of the legal constitution of the United Synagogue; but that can be brought about only by a very strong opinion, which cannot be obtained within the United Synagogue at the present time. You have to overcome the influence of the asphyxiating gas which pours from the United Synagogue, and that can only be done by the great effort of those who are willing to consecrate themselves to the purpose.

Those who feel that a sincere Judaism is worth while should, I think, combine for the establishment of a Free Conservative Synagogue in London. For my own part, I feel that religious work should be, among Jews, the work of laymen and not of a professional class. I believe in the validity of those sayings in the Ethics of the Fathers that a man should not make of the Torah an axe to grind with, and that one should not be as a servant who serves his master for reward. If, as a lay member of such a body, I could be of voluntary assistance, I should be glad to do so, with what leisure my work for a living will leave me.

Of course, it would have been easier for me to go on living an acquiescent – or quiescent – life, reading two services a day, preaching two sermons a week, conducting a children's service, teaching half-truths, visiting a few patients in hospital, and drawing a comfortable emolument. But I should have continued to be thoroughly unhappy – not, assuredly, because of my congregants, whose great considerateness and kindness to me I want warmly to acknowledge and with whom, indeed, I feel myself in agreement, but because the surrounding conditions, imposed by external influences, made my pulpit a spiritual prison, in which I could find no peace. 'Man does not live by bread alone.'

People say I was unwise to take this step. But I had rather be honest than a wise hypocrite to the end of my days.[42]

Despite the Jews' College appointment, Hockman's fate had perhaps been sealed even before the offer was made. Alluding to his wayward minister in a eulogy to United Synagogue president Nathan Meyer Rothschild, who had died in April, Hertz remarked:

Never will I forget the spontaneous words Lord Rothschild addressed to me before this very Ark two years ago, at my induction into the Chief Rabbinate: 'I give the Torah into your keeping to bring up the congregations of Israel in your charge in conformity with *Din Torah*' ...

He was impatient of the individualism that would rend in twain the unity of Israel, and distrustful of all revolution in religion. He agreed with the rabbis, 'If the young, in contradiction to their elders, tell thee, "Come with us and we will rebuild the Temple", follow them not; for often the destruction of the elders is construction, and the construction of the young is destruction.'[43]

\* \* \*   \* \* \*   \* \* \*

Fifty years later, the New West End and the Chief Rabbinate reverberated to a second such affair, with ramifications of far greater consequence to the wider community. As for Hockman, he was to make one final appearance on the communal stage before embarking on his career at the Bar and as legal adviser to the King of Siam.[44]

# 10

# Traditional Judaism

The central years of the decade engaged the combatants in fields other than the purely religious. Anti-Semitism, alien agitation, Zionism and, of course, the trenches sucked up the energies – and the lives – of many in the vanguard of ritual reform, and as a result the theological debate subsided within Anglo-Jewry. One of its last public manifestations before the Great War was a sermon by Hertz, delivered as the ministry of the transatlantic import, Israel Mattuck, began to fire the enthusiasm of his Liberal followers and reach out to 'those whom others had failed to interest'.[1] On the theme of religious schism, the Chief Rabbi warned of the American

> individualists [who] laboured, and not altogether in vain, to hasten the return of what to them seemed the Golden Age: no king in Israel, and every man doing that which is right in his own eyes.
>
> Each 'rabbi' – for some mysterious reason, men who have definitely broken with Rabbinic teaching and the Rabbinic scheme of Jewish life insist on assuming this title – each 'rabbi' a law unto himself, at will abolishing the Sefer Torah from his synagogue, abolishing Sabbath and festival, and hailing even the most blasphemous vagaries of that form of Higher anti-Semitism called Bible Criticism as final and definitive truth.
>
> Outwardly, and at a distance, the pomp and brilliance of American Reform Judaism may be dazzling. At a nearer view, its light is seen to be but a phosphorescent sheen, the accompaniment of disintegration and decay. Divine fire warms, cheers, is a Sinaitic bush of everlasting life and light. 'Strange fire' devours, cremates the soul, even when the body remains intact. The loyal son of the Torah should not be blinded by a passing phenomenon of today, nor disheartened by defections from the historic form of the faith.[2]

A more conciliatory approach to schism was suggested by Hermann Gollancz midway through the war, when – as he admitted – 'other thoughts' tended to engage his attention. 'It is a thousand pities', he told his congregation, that seventy years ago a direct schism was brought about in the communal life of the metropolis, which has certainly not redounded to the strength and vitality of London Jewry. As I have in effect often remarked, Judaism is elastic enough to admit of various forms of thought, without driving anyone from its fold, or anyone excluding himself or herself from its all-embracing fold.

It is to be hoped that old dreary feuds in the domain of religion will, when the day of peace has dawned, give way to a broader and more humane appreciation of each other's beliefs and principles, and that, having borne each other's burdens in wartime, the lesson of toleration will not be lost in the times of peace.

A cold and callous indifference in religious matters, standing still and not moving, leaving the life of the community in a stagnant and fossilised condition – this attitude on the part of those who should be active is equally culpable, for it is responsible for the decline of the community in consequence of religious anaemia.

We Jews have to decide whether in our communities we are to have more religious cohesion for the uplifting of the general mass of the community, or whether we shall become weaker through our neglect of matters that should engage our consideration in all seriousness, urgent problems that should draw our young men and young women nearer to the service of the synagogue and the observances of our religion.[3]

Thereafter the clerical canons fell largely silent, but a ceasefire on the military front saw hostilities resumed in communal ranks, with the synagogue ringing out to the notes of religious disarray. The 'passing phenomenon' was adopting a permanency, and a potency, that troubled the Torah loyalists, and Hertz was once again impelled to sound the great trumpet. 'A Temple of the Lord', he told them,

cannot be where there is discord, violence or revolt. Its ramparts must arise without noise of axe or hammer.

A timely truth this, and especially timely at this moment when temple-builders are abroad in the land, and the watchword 'Reconstruction' is the order of the day. Hardly a week passes but our press devotes a letter or article to it; quacks whose stock-in-trade is the phrase 'social service', as well as busy communal leaders, speak of it with unctuous wisdom. But the very word 'reconstruction' is a prolific source of confusion and fallacy. It means that everything hitherto constructed in Anglo-Jewry is so bad that it has to be done all over again.

> And such, in effect, was the message of those theologians from the trenches who, three years ago, first raised this cry. Young men of much enthusiasm but less discretion, and very little knowledge of Judaism, came back from the front and gave it as their expert opinion that 'when the boys come home', the old forms and old faith would vanish for ever more. It is pleasant to note that these prophecies of woe are no longer taken seriously.
>
> Much the same judgment must be passed on the wild schemes of religious reconstruction advocated by the small group of radicals who derive their inspiration from German-American sources. To them, the individual is the ultimate seat of authority in religion – not the Torah, not Tradition, not the Synagogue ...
>
> Too often Liberal houses of worship resound with abuse of 'the Judaism of the Synagogue' and re-echo with the noise of hammer and axe wielded against ideals and institutions vital to Judaism – and all in the name of spirituality and faith, for the sake of 'possessing God', and the rebuilding of the crumbling Tabernacle of David.
>
> Far more numerous and worthy of attention is the Conservative wing of those who clamour 'Reconstruction'. They do not desire a complete break with the past – far from it. They, however, believe that the door to a better future for Anglo-Jewry is the complete independence and absolute autonomy of each and every congregation.
>
> Synagogues would then be free to introduce any changes and reforms deemed necessary by their worshippers. In the way of this consummation so devoutly to be wished for, they tell us, stands the Rabbinate. Despite their sincerity, however, these critics can never be the architects of our future.[4]

And it was around the 'architecture of our future' that communal passions were to be set ablaze. The structure in question was 'Traditional Judaism', and the bricks and mortar employed to build its foundations. Were they to be cemented to the old forms and faith – or to the changes and reform? Hertz had no doubts, but his growing band of opponents had their own ideas.

The demand for a definition of Traditional Judaism arose with the launch, in the summer of 1919, of the Jewish War Memorial Scheme. Among its primary objectives was the creation of a 'British School of Jewish Learning' to redress the acute post-war shortage of teachers and ministers, then regarded as 'the most urgent problem facing the community'. Jews'

College was seen as a crucial component of the scheme, with its possible relocation from Bloomsbury to Oxford or Cambridge.

Proposing the scheme at a meeting of the College council, Robert Waley Cohen[5] – vice-president (and later president) of the United Synagogue, and soon to become a constant thorn in Hertz's side – noted that the community had 'depended for the maintenance of traditional Judaism on the steady influx from abroad of men imbued with the knowledge and enthusiasm of traditional Judaism'. That influx was likely to be 'very greatly diminished for a long time, and if Judaism is to have a future in this country, we should find some way of developing in those who are brought up here something of the same enthusiasm for Jewish traditions'.

In a letter soliciting Rothschild support in launching the project, Waley Cohen and his co-sponsors – the second Lord Swaythling[6] and Major Frederick C. Stern[7] – had written:

> To create as the British War Memorial a great organisation of traditional Judaism should, in our view, be the answer to this irresistible call. The false idea that the religion of our ancestors conflicts with modern ideals must be wiped out.
>
> The British community must be so organised that the 'trumpet of Sinai', which still sounds in every Jewish ear, may find its echo in a community whose teachers, having studied our literature in an atmosphere of British freedom, will interpret it to the generations of Jewish citizens inspired by those British ideals for which the present generation has fought and died, expound the true faith of our ancestors, and make it illuminate the secular ideals of progress and freedom ...
>
> We believe such ministers can be created only by a college of traditional Judaism, situated in an atmosphere of British learning, such as Oxford or Cambridge, where Jewish scholars may devote their lives in the study of theology and rabbinic literature, and where university students who aspire to qualify for the ministry may take up their learning as a postgraduate course.

An element of potential conflict was injected with a suggestion from Stern that 'the College, the ministry and the religious education of British Jews should be put on a firm footing *and modern basis*'. Many differed in their religious opinions, he said; there were many shades of belief. 'Is it not a sign of health that these differences exist? A man's belief is his own private property. Can we not agree to differ? Are we not all Jews? Have we not all the same traditions, the same Book, the same literature, the same hopes, the same wish to help men to be good Jews and faithful citizens?'

In England, Stern added, 'we want our own rabbis, men of the world, full of sympathy and understanding, men not only scholarly in rabbinics and leading good lives, but also men with knowledge of the world, of broad outlook, intellectual in the science and philosophy of the world, tolerant of all forms of thought. Can we produce such men in the narrow confines of Bloomsbury?'

While supporting the scheme, Hertz affirmed that the constitution of Jews' College was to remain as it was, as were its 'platform' and 'seat of authority', and that conditions had to be attached to the transfer proposal: that 'the teaching of the College shall continue to be in accordance with the principles of traditional Judaism, and that a sufficient endowment be raised ... as part of a large memorial scheme for the strengthening of Judaism in the British Empire'.[8]

Conflict deepened with the formal launch of the scheme, held at Central Hall, Westminster, under the chairmanship of Lionel de Rothschild and attended by representatives from across the community. Reiterating his stance on traditional Judaism, Hertz rejected

> the fears entertained by many in regard to the alleged un-Jewish milieu of university towns. In the new Jews' College, as in the old, there will be no destroying of the letter and ignoring the spirit of Judaism. There will be no ambition to educate neutrals in religion. The religious principles of the institution will remain as they have always been – to teach the positive, historical Judaism we have inherited from our fathers, and so train men with deep Jewish convictions and broadest sympathy with the aspirations and ideals recorded in our sacred literature.

Adding his support, Morris Joseph was, however, far less sanguine. It needed more than a change of external atmosphere, he asserted, 'to make Jews' College the power it ought to be. It requires a change of atmosphere inside'. He could not blind himself to the 'unsatisfactory position' which the College had hitherto occupied. Why had it not possessed the wholehearted support of the community? 'Because the system is not right.'

One speaker, said Joseph, had remarked that the students should not be taught by clerics. 'I go a step further and say that they should not be taught by theologians, and that the theological atmosphere should be very considerably diluted.' He had in mind 'a seminary like that of Breslau, where students come in free, and go out free. Students should be able to study what we are wont to call Jewish service without being inculcated with a theological bias.'[9]

When murmurings intensified, shortly after, over the meaning of 'traditional Judaism', Hertz was quick to intervene. 'May the New Year bring with it', he declared in his Rosh Hashanah message,

> on the one hand, the realisation that no movement can have a future within Judaism that sets its face against Jewish tradition and Jewish religious solidarity; and, on the other, an ever clearer and more unshakeable *will to be, and to remain, Jews*.
>
> We are face to face with grave dangers to our religious future. Unless we bestir ourselves, community after community will wither away, will eventually perish, through lack of religious teaching and guidance. A unique opportunity is now ours for constructive, creative work, by worthily supporting the War Memorial Scheme before the Jewish public'.[10]

His warning against any movement 'that sets its face against Jewish tradition' was, however, to unleash a theological storm every bit as fierce as the gales that had begun to lash across autumnal Britain. At the close of the festive season, on Shabbat Bereishit, Hertz strengthened his Rosh Hashanah plea with a fervent call for traditional values:

> A demand has been voiced for a preliminary definition of Traditional Judaism, for a precise statement of the lines for maintaining Traditional Judaism which the promoters of this scheme proposed to adopt ...
>
> This is quite a novel criticism. The usual complaint has always been that there is too much definition about Traditional Judaism; that the *do's* and *don'ts* of Orthodox Judaism were too rigid, too well-defined. The demand, of course, cannot be for ultimate definitions. The task would then be endless ...
>
> There is not the slightest doubt in our mind in regard to the connotation of 'Traditional Judaism'. The words mean what they say – the teachings and practices which have come down to the House of Israel through the ages: the positive, Jewish beliefs concerning God, the Torah and Israel; the sacred festivals; the traditional service; the holy resolve to maintain Israel's identity; and the life consecrated by historic Jewish observance – all of these in indissoluble union with the best thought and culture of the age, and with utmost loyalty to King and Country.

This, declared Hertz, 'is a working description of Traditional Judaism, the Judaism of a Saadiah, a Maimonides, a Manasseh ben Israel, a Moses

Montefiore, or a Nathan Marcus Adler. What is more, it may fairly be called the Anglo-Jewish position in theology, as even those who three generations ago separated from the Orthodox body have in the main zealously stood for these principles and practices.'

Adding fuel to the furnace he was determined to stoke, Hertz challenged his opponents:

> If a man is a follower of the reformers of Germany and America, if *religiously* he is a German-American Jew – this would be a far more correct designation than the self-righteous and question-begging name 'Liberal Jew' – he need not, of course, support this Jewish War Memorial.
>
> Far otherwise must be our attitude *if our ideals are Anglo-Jewish ideals – the ideals of the fathers of Anglo-Jewry*, the ideals of a Manasseh ben Israel, a Moses Montefiore, or the founders of this synagogue [the New West End]. We shall then help 'according as we are able, according to the blessing wherewith God has blessed us'. And we shall do so because we realise that on its success largely depends the entire future of Judaism in England and the Empire at large.[11]

\* \* \*   \* \* \*   \* \* \*

The Liberal response was immediate – and vociferous. In a letter to Lionel de Rothschild, declining an invitation to send delegates to the council of the Jewish War Memorial Scheme, Montefiore declared that

> representatives of a specifically Liberal organisation have no fit place upon the council of an Orthodox institution for the maintenance of Orthodox Judaism, or upon the council of a scheme for the improvement of an 'Orthodox' college, or for the better remuneration of 'Orthodox' ministers.
>
> Their presence would be, from every point of view, inconsistent, undesirable and meaningless. It would also be a waste of energy and time ... And we conceive that, if the position were reversed – if the large majority of the Jews and the ministers and the synagogues in this country were Liberal, and the small minority were Orthodox – the council of the United Synagogue would also refuse (and rightly so) to send representatives for the improvement and upkeep of a Liberal college, and for the better payment of Liberal ministers.[12]

The progressives' stance on 'The Great Communal Scheme', as it came to be known, was strengthened some weeks later by divergent sermons from the pulpits of the Liberal and West London Synagogues. In the former, Mattuck asserted that 'mere honesty' prevented the participation of his organisation.

> There are many things in which Liberal Judaism agrees with Orthodox Judaism, but there are some fundamental differences in principles. We have never concealed that fact, we have always called attention to it; we have urged Liberal Jews, and invited others, to think about these differences.
>
> We of this synagogue are distinguished from the Orthodox Jewish congregations not only by a different service – that is a comparatively minor matter – but by different teachings reaching down to the very roots of spiritual life. And where principles are concerned, honesty is at stake. To comply with the wishes of others, or to compromise with them, at the expense of loyalty to a fundamental principle, is dishonest. We do not believe in Orthodox Judaism; we can honestly have no share in furthering it.
>
> The value of a minority lies in its independence and in its loyalty to its own principles. If, for any reason, it sacrifices principle – yes, even for the sake of peace and unity, adopting an attitude of compromising conformity – then its value to the community is gone; and if it allows itself to be lured by pleasant words, or driven by fears, or bullied by threats into compliance with the wishes of the majority, despite its principle, it is guilty of dishonesty, and guilty, too, of treason to a trust of service for the community.

Anxious to put a positive gloss on the call for a War Memorial, Mattuck concluded by noting that,

> in conjunction with the older Berkeley Street Congregation, we have established one in the East End wherein the modern spirit of religion is embodied – the spirit of progress and social service. I hope, too, that in the not distant future we shall have a new synagogue to stand both as a memorial and a force, a memorial to enshrine the spirit which values truth and righteousness above all things, and a force to make for constant devotion to them in the life of Jewry. And as for conformity, we know only one kind that is worth while – the conformity of practice with faith, of conduct with principle. That is honesty; any other kind is dishonesty.[13]

In contrast to this Liberal approach, the themes of unity and tradition underscored the words of Isidore Harris at Upper Berkeley Street. Like Mattuck, he raised the question of their justification, as a Reform congregation, in helping a measure whose purpose it is to strengthen the hold of traditional Judaism on the community of English Jews. It may seem, at first sight, inconsistent. But deeper reflection will, I think, approve the attitude we have taken up.

For what is the traditional Judaism which the scheme has in view? It is a tradition permeated by a spirit of progress and development; it is not a perpetuation of old-fashioned Orthodoxy. The very intention to re-establish Jews' College in such a centre of liberal thought as Oxford or Cambridge indicates the conception of traditionalism which is in the minds of the founders ...

We have done well to associate ourselves with the communal leaders in the great effort they are making to lay deep the foundations of the religious life of English Jews, and to rear thereon a structure which future generations may bring to a glorious completion. We may not see eye to eye with all those with whom we are called upon to co-operate; we may be inclined to be impatient with those who insist upon lagging behind in the march of thought ...

[But] no community is composed of people who think alike. Different minds travel at different rates of progress. Hence it is a mistake to force the pace and to expect all the hosts of Israel to march abreast in perfect unison. We must have consideration for the stragglers,[14] and recognise that we might easily kill the religious life of many if we deprive them of the simple faith in which they have been nurtured.

This congregation is fully alive to such considerations. It has set an admirable example of toleration in the broad-minded attitude it has taken up towards this and other communal movements having for their object the advancement of the educational and religious interests of our fellow-Jews. Its policy is dictated by the old rabbinical adage, 'Separate not thyself from the community'.

Let us not, then, magnify minor differences into major differences, but let us rather think of the larger matters upon which we are all agreed ... The call today is for unity. We need to be banded together, all sections of Anglo-Jewry, the representatives of every school of religious thought, in order to repel the attacks of our implacable foes. And to this end, no more suitable work could unite us than the scheme of communal reconstruction whose aim is to broaden and deepen the foundations of our spiritual, religious and educational life.[15]

While the two progressive ministers differed sharply on their approach to the scheme, there was clearly a convergence of views – on a lay if not ministerial level – over their sharing of pulpits. A month after Harris' sermon, Mattuck occupied the pulpit of the West London Synagogue at the invitation of its honorary officers, though there was 'reason to believe'[16] that this was extended behind the backs of the Berkeley Street ministers. The affair raised questions reaching to the core of unity and uniformity in Anglo-Jewry, questions, said the *Jewish Chronicle*, 'much weightier than that of procedure'.

> Some two years ago, the same gentleman occupied the same pulpit, not without strong protest from congregants of Upper Berkeley Street. But since then, and only recently, we have seen Rabbi Mattuck affirming that the differences between his congregation and those of the rest of the community were fundamental; while a prominent member of the congregation,[17] adopting the doctrine of one of its chief founders (Mr Claude Montefiore), has declared that the Bible has no binding authority upon the 'Liberal' Jew.
>
> Now the Berkeley Street Synagogue is a synagogue definitely attached to Traditional Judaism. This it has always passionately maintained, and a declaration to that effect is made in the course of a foreword to its prayer-book. It follows that it is to Traditional Judaism that the synagogue pulpit is dedicated, as its regular occupants – and not least the present respected senior minister, the Rev. Morris Joseph – have always insistently declared.
>
> It is surely, then, a glaring inconsistency for the synagogue to invite a minister of the 'Liberal' Synagogue to teach Judaism according to the lights of the congregation of which he is the spiritual head, and which he himself has shown to be so palpably opposed to the faith for which Berkeley Street stands ...
>
> To the plain man, the invitation to Rabbi Mattuck reads, and can only read, like an intimation that notwithstanding all that has been proclaimed as the attitude of 'Liberal' Judaism, no 'fundamental' differences subsist between the real opinions of Berkeley Street and the teachings of the 'Liberal' congregation.
>
> Since the very gravest differences do in fact exist, nobody who cares an iota for the sheer decencies, not to say the mere honesty, of religious belief can regard that as other than a serious matter. There is no question here of broadmindedness or toleration; it is a matter of clear understanding and of knowing just where we stand in these vital matters.
>
> If there are 'fundamental differences' between the 'Liberal' congregation and the remainder of the community, then it is useless, and

worse, to pretend that they are not fundamental, and represent merely shades of the same religious colour ... Much of the weakness of our community in the past has been the habit of make-believe and of self-confusion on religious matters, which has tended to tarnish the clarity of its outlook in regard to so much with which it is concerned.

Unless the issues are cleared, there can be no hope of amendment or progress – or, indeed, of true unity – in a community in which religion must necessarily be so vital an element. And the disservice towards, and the hindering of, communal unity is not one of the least sins involved, when a traditional synagogue like Berkeley Street gives up its pulpit to the exponent of a religious faith in fundamental difference from its own.[18]

The issues were further clouded when, despite Harris' passionate appeal and his synagogue's representation on the War Memorial council, a meeting of West London members equivocated the following month over support for the scheme. Moving a resolution in favour, Osmond D'Avigdor-Goldsmid declared that 'the Memorial must appeal to all educated Jews to whom religious education is real'. They should consider not merely what special benefits they would receive, but the interests of the community as a whole. Sir Edward Stern seconded the motion, which, he said, was 'designed to put an end to the community being broken up into small sections'.

But a majority of members were less convinced. Philip Waley moved an amendment – carried by thirty-five votes to twenty-nine – which, while approving the objects of the Jewish War Memorial, withheld organised support until the congregation had 'examined and approved the detailed proposals for carrying these objects into effect'.

'We should see', said Waley, 'that facilities are given for the teaching of the essential truths of our faith, together with the study of the Scriptures involved, without this necessitating the inculcation of a hard and fast Traditionalism, with its outworn creeds and ceremonials.' His seconder, Arthur Stiebel, concurred, fearing that 'the Traditionalism referred to in the scheme means Orthodoxy'.[19]

Responding elsewhere from a United Synagogue standpoint, Waley Cohen sought to allay the fears of the Reform congregation. 'The promoters of the Jewish War Memorial', he told them,

> are determined to keep a free and unfettered hand for the council to settle, from time to time, how this memorial to the Jewish heroes of this generation can best serve the religious life of future generations of Jews in the British Empire.

> We are determined that the council shall not be tied to support the views of any sect or section; that the funds shall be devoted to assist all those who are contributing earnestly and genuinely to the Jewish life of the community according to their own ideals of Judaism.
>
> Different sections of the community have expressed disappointment at our determination to adhere to this fixed intention, but, in the long run, we believe that every section of the community will rejoice at this decision, realising that the Jewish War Memorial can be worthy of those whom it is designed to commemorate only if it represents the sentiment of all those Jews and Jewesses in the British Empire who have the right to share in the great inheritance of Judaism.
>
> If, as we hope, the memorial erects a great college of Jewish learning in this country, we are determined that the college shall be open to every scholar who seeks genuinely to study Jewish literature and learning. Similarly, every competent body engaged upon Jewish religious education, so long as they be teaching effectively and efficiently the great traditions and the great ideals of Judaism, will be entitled to the support of the Jewish War Memorial Fund.[20]

Unwittingly, and by his dogged pursuance of this inclusivist policy, Waley Cohen had opened the floodgates of dissent – not least from within the Chief Rabbinate – and paved the way for the eventual demise of the 'great college' dream.

* * *   * * *   * * *

The opening gambit in the campaign to establish 'a great college of Jewish learning in this country', one that would represent the exponents of Reform and Liberal as well as 'Traditional' Judaism, came from an unexpected – though not unlikely – source, one who had, in his own words, 'resisted hitherto the impulse to intervene in communal controversies'. The player was plain Joseph Hockman, of 'Pelham', Croham Road, South Croydon, who attributed his recent restraint

> partly [to] the knowledge that many who do me the honour still to shrink from me have not yet recovered from the hard blows I had to deal a few years ago, and that I myself am not yet free from black and blue.
>
> I am irresistibly impelled, however, to utter a word of thanksgiving that at Berkeley Street the efforts were checked which of late have been made to submerge, under a flood of platitudes on unity, the isolated strongholds of religious sincerity within our community.

> I am in favour of what is declared to be the principle involved in what seems to be the nobly conceived Jewish Memorial Scheme; but until details are revealed, I think it necessary to plead that support (beyond contributions for preliminary working expenses) should be withheld, and that Anglo-Jewry once again owes a debt of gratitude to the congregation at Berkeley Street, this time for refusing blindly to pledge its support to the scheme which, while advocating unity, promises to fortify the already strongly entrenched United Synagogue Act and Chief Rabbinate ...
>
> The whole of Anglo-Jewry owes a debt of gratitude to the Reform congregation for refusing to hinder those who are struggling to secure for themselves the congregational liberty which the Reform congregation has won for itself. The Reform congregation would have dipped its banner very low if it had pledged its support to the Jewish War Memorial Scheme before the evils of the United Synagogue Act and the Chief Rabbinate system are remedied – before congregationalism is secured.
>
> Those who support the scheme now may find – too late – that they have riveted more firmly the fetters which the United Synagogue already is able to impose on congregations which accept the considerable financial assistance it is able to offer, even without the Jewish War Memorial's endowments.

If, wrote Hockman, the Memorial aimed solely to endow Jews' College,

> that object is sufficiently worthy without the elements of danger involved in United Synagogue extensions. If the aim is simply to endow the Provincial Ministers' Fund, I think it is agreed that that does not justify the title 'Jewish War Memorial'.
>
> If the object is to create a Union of Anglo-Jewish Congregations, that requires the release of Jews' College from all ecclesiastical control; the rabbinical diploma as the leaving certificate at Jews' College; the agreement of every congregation – Orthodox, Reform or Liberal – not to appoint as its religious head anyone who has not a rabbinical diploma; the revision of the 'United Synagogue Act' and the Chief Rabbinate system in order to establish congregationalism; a Synod of Rabbis under the 'Chief Rabbi of the United Hebrew Congregations of the British Empire', in future not necessarily the Chief Rabbi of the United Synagogue; and a lay council of the United Hebrew Congregations of the British Empire.
>
> Something of this kind is what I thought the Jewish War Memorial was to create. If so, it should not be difficult to make its

object clear, nor to explain the plans and lines on which it is to be achieved. Pending specifications, contributions already have been excessive.[21]

The wide-ranging nature of Hockman's vision was lost on the scheme's organisers, but the reasoning behind it found sympathy with many, and not merely those in the Reform camp. Waley Cohen, for one, began to broaden his notion of the College's role and used the opportunity of Hertz's departure from Britain later that year to further his aims.

Two months after the publication of Hockman's views, the Chief Rabbi received a letter from United Synagogue president Lionel de Rothschild notifying him that its council had passed a resolution inviting him to visit the overseas dominions and dependencies – 'of the utmost value in helping to bind together the Jewish communities of the Empire, and in stimulating their religious activities'. The tour was to last from 8 October 1920 (Hertz reached South Africa on the *Llanstephan Castle* nineteen days later) until 30 August 1921, when the Chief Rabbi sailed into Southampton from New York on the *Aquitania*.

Faced with the potential defection of Berkeley Street from his War Memorial scheme, Waley Cohen conceived of a plan during Hertz's eleven-month absence for the establishment of a Reform 'Academy of Jewish Learning' to operate in conjunction with Jews' College (described as the 'Jewish Theological College'), the two to be run by a common council. The parameters of the proposal were thrashed out by the memorial committee during the Chief Rabbi's trip and were presented to him on his return.

A long and often acrimonious correspondence, punctuated by fiery meetings, ensued between Hertz and Waley Cohen over the proximity of the institutions and their shared governance. Waley Cohen wrote on one occasion:

> I recognise – I think everyone recognises – the disadvantage attaching to the plan of combining in the same building with the reorganised Jews' College another department in which Berkeley Street – and also other congregations which, whilst claiming the flag of Traditional Judaism, do not subscribe to your and our presentation of it – may supplement the full training of Jews' College by instruction of their own colour to their own future ministers.
>
> It would, of course, be better in some ways to have two institutions, but experience has – I think we must all admit – proved quite conclusively that the Anglo-Jewish community cannot and will not sustain them.

I am absolutely satisfied that what is sought is not to supplant any shadow of a part of the education which in your conception of a Jews' College it ought to give. That must be complete and as good as it can be made. But in addition to it, there is this demand for some supplementary teaching which shall describe in a truly academic spirit the views of those who believe themselves not to be entirely satisfied with the current interpretation of Traditional Judaism.

I do beg you to believe that this demand is not confined to Berkeley Street, but is endorsed and much strengthened by a very considerable section of the members of almost every congregation in England. As you know, I do not much sympathise with it, but I feel that if we allow this line of controversy to be opened and debated in the War Memorial council, the lead given by Berkeley Street in making their demand will be followed and immensely strengthened by representatives of those who, quite outside Berkeley Street, entertain these views and have expressed them at all the committee meetings, and even at the council meetings, during this year ...

I think perhaps you feel that the extreme Orthodox section of the community may criticise your silent acquiescence in the formula. I do not think that you need entertain that apprehension. I have had long discussions with many of the ultra-Orthodox men in the community during the last year, and I think they almost all feel some uneasiness arising from their inability to instil into their own children their own understanding of and respect for Jewish tradition, and that they are consequently much more tolerant than they used to be.

But if you think I am wrong, and if you think they would be driven by a too-narrow view of the issues to take up a hostile attitude, would it not be possible to meet the case by your sending to the president of the council a written statement which could be read out to the council, and which could be somewhat as follows: That, whilst you feel that the amendments suggested in the constitution of the College do possess some elements of danger which you would have been glad to remove, you have felt that they could not be removed without subjecting the community to a controversy which would do infinite harm to the great religious cause for which you stand; that, on the other hand, the reorganised College and the whole War Memorial scheme is fraught, in your view, with such immense possibilities for the future religious life of the Anglo-Jewish community that you advise the council to accept as they stand the recommendations of the executive committee and trust to the loyalty and wisdom of the Anglo-Jewish community to protect the future of its College.[22]

Hertz, however, strongly rejected this argument, suggested further changes to the draft resolutions, and expressed fears over the eventual outcome, leading Waley Cohen to condemn, in a subsequent letter,

> the disastrous nature of the policy you have lately been pursuing ... You cannot expect – and ought not, I think, to ask – that all [our] labour should be thrown to the winds to meet every point of detail on which you would like something differently worded. Not one iota has been sacrificed of the great religious principles and ideals which you so warmly approved, and which lie at the root of – and give its force to – the War Memorial movement.
>
> There have been concessions of form and method, but no shadow of concession on principles. Your views on ecclesiastical and religious matters have been given – and rightly given – overwhelming weight, but on other matters you must surely give some weight to your colleagues ...
>
> If a great principle were in jeopardy, you would be justified in wrecking the scheme to save it, but no such principle nor anything approaching it is at stake at present, and if you wreck the scheme for the sake of anything less you will, I am sure, be doing a grave wrong to yourself and you will never cease to regret it.

Waley Cohen pointed to meetings discussing the proposed recommendations at which

> You told me that if I could get either the word 'separate' or the word 'distinct' applied to distinguish the 'Academy' from the Theological College, you would be satisfied and you would accept the whole thing in the form in which you and I settled it. I immediately set to work on the not very easy task of securing the acceptance of your final wishes, and the acceptance was secured from all concerned. By that settlement we must, in my view, either stand or fall.

Imploring Hertz 'not to be swayed by personal considerations in coming to your decision [on the final wording]', Waley Cohen concluded: 'If it be favourable, I shall be more than happy. If it be not, I shall cease all connection with the movement, and I fear we shall witness the break-up of the Jewish War Memorial scheme, and of more that you and – if I may say so – I, too, value in our community.'[23]

Thus it was that, on 18 and 19 January 1920, the council of Jews' College met to consider nine resolutions, the primary one – Clause 2(b) of the proposed constitution – seeking to establish 'an Academy of Jewish Learning, distinct from the above [the Jewish Theological College], in which all presentations of the Jewish religion as taught in synagogues represented on the council of the Jewish War Memorial may be freely expounded'. The council, with the one Reform exception – Frederick Stern – was almost equally divided between the staunchly Orthodox and the more latitudinarian members. Some opposed the academy outright; others argued passionately in favour; a few, though unhappy, were prepared to accept it with stringent conditions.

Moving to reject the resolution, Augustus Kahn contended that the governors would be landed with 'all sorts of inconsistencies'. The future of the academy, he said, would be determined by the governing body, but the governing body would be influenced by the association of the academy with the theological college. 'If we have a governing body, some members of which are Jews' College members and others are academy members, the council will be rent in twain and there will be religious strife. If the academy members are predominant, there is nothing to prevent them from sending Jews' College to the kitchen while the academy occupies the drawing-room.' Similar views were voiced by Dayan Harris Lazarus, Herbert Bentwich, and the College principal, Adolph Büchler.

Describing himself as 'a party to the compromise – an unwilling party but still a party' – Hertz pleaded that 'this bifurcation of the institutions was not my work'. On his return to Britain, he said, he had found the scheme in an even worse state, with the organisers determined on 'one institution absolutely'. He had made it clear that that was 'totally out of the question'. They could not have an institution in which certain principles were taught in one room, and opposing principles in another. No Jewish father would send his son to such an institution, where his soul and convictions could be tampered with and played with; he himself would reprobate it. Therefore, instead of having two departments in one institution, he had declared that the academy must be 'absolutely distinct and independent' from the college.

'I fought hard for the introduction of the words "distinct from the above". Thank God I succeeded'. If the members accepted the compromise, said Hertz, he urged them to make it clear to the War Memorial council that they stressed those words and that they expected a different management of the academy from that of the college – 'because I will have nothing to do with the academy so long as it is a possible training-ground for Reform and Liberal Judaism'.[24]

After further, frequently contentious, discussion, the council approved the academy proposal by ten votes to seven, with similar sanction for the other resolutions, covering a range of issues from candidates for admission and departmental curricula to scholarships and grants, and future relations with the War Memorial committee.[25] But the disputes and dissension were far from over. As Hertz had anticipated, he soon came under fire from his right-wing critics and found himself fending off allegations of 'outrages against Traditional Judaism on the part of communal leaders'. Such charges were levelled at an East End conference arranged by the recently formed Organisation of Observant Traditional Jews of Great Britain[26] and attended by no fewer than five of the dayanim and by Isaac Herzog,[27] who had become Chief Rabbi of the Irish Free State the previous year.

In line with Hermann Adler's death-bed plea to close the gap between 'the East and the West, the native and the immigrant', the organisation's launch had coincided with the 'new spirit which the Great Communal Scheme has introduced into Anglo-Jewry'. Described as 'a movement which has no precedent in communal annals', it was designed to deal with 'all matters in which the interests of Orthodox Jews are affected'.

> So far as the War Memorial is concerned, it is by no means intended to approach the scheme in any spirit of opposition, as it is felt that the scheme may ultimately be of great service; but it is desired to formulate the demands of Orthodox Jews so that the promoters may be aware of the aspirations of this section of the community.[28]
>
> It is felt that it will probably be more advantageous for the promoters of the scheme to deal with an organised body of opinion than to have to face haphazard criticism or studied indifference. The new organisation may do much to bring together the 'foreign' and 'English' Jews and to break down a spirit of suspicion and misunderstanding that has too often existed.[29]

Addressing delegates at the Aldgate conference, Rabbi Isaac Bloch said that they had 'many serious and vital questions affecting Orthodox Judaism to deliberate upon'. Manchester's Rabbi Jacob Shachter expressed his 'delight at the opportunity afforded us to combat the growing tide of Reform making its way into Anglo-Jewry'. This view was reflected in Rabbi Hirsh Hurwitz's attack 'against the recent actions of the Chief Rabbi in connection with matters vitally affecting Judaism'. The position, said Hurwitz, was 'full of peril, and the community must be warned. It is monstrous for synagogues to espouse a new system of teaching Judaism.'

In Hertz's defence, Dayan Feldman – lampooned by one delegate as 'the SOS of the Chief Rabbi' – asserted that, on his return to Britain, Hertz had been 'astounded to find the state of affairs prevailing'. Dismissing Feldman's plea, the conference passed a resolution 'strongly protesting against the decision to establish an academy for the teaching of aspects of Judaism contrary to Traditional Judaism, and deeply deploring the Chief Rabbi's compromise on this matter vitally affecting Orthodox Judaism'.

Rising to move a second resolution, Herzog noted that, 'inasmuch as Jews' College has failed to satisfy the requirements of Orthodox Jewry, this conference is of the opinion that it is imperative to establish an independent institution for the training of rabbis, teachers and shochetim in the spirit of true Judaism'. There was, said the Irish Chief Rabbi, no need to condemn the Reform academy: it stood self-condemned. The question was, had they made provision for the future? He could not speak of the teaching imparted within the walls of Jews' College, but he could judge the tree by its fruits, and by this test it had failed and been found wanting:

> The ministers from Jews' College have not upheld Traditional Judaism. Instead of inspiring, radiating, energising, they have cooled enthusiasm. Samson Raphael Hirsch founded an institution to impart Torah, reverence and knowledge, so that its talmidim could address the public in their language with as much ease as the Reformers. Such an institution here would save Judaism from the deluge that threatens it.

Hertz himself, though not present at the conference – 'it would certainly not be dignified to invite the Chief Rabbi to a public arraignment', one delegate had declared – was alive to the vilification heaped upon him. In a letter to Lionel de Rothschild, he wrote:

> It is a matter of vital importance both to me and to the community that the question of the absolute distinctness of these two institutions be definitely disposed of. There can be no peace without it.
>
> This is no threat – nothing but sheer ethical necessity. I would never have consented to plead for a college of which an academy of Reform Judaism was part and parcel. I am prepared to do a great deal in order to avert disgrace and disaster to the cause we both have at heart, but I am not prepared to sacrifice the honour and the spiritual welfare of those entrusted to my care.[30]

Threat or not, the *Jewish Chronicle*'s 'Mentor'[31] perceived it as such and, some weeks later, penned what proved to be the last words on the subject:

> What has become of the War Memorial council's proposals in respect to the future of Jews' College? The gist or gravamen of those proposals is in the establishment of a kind of bifurcated institution to consist of an Orthodox traditional Jews' College and an Academy

of Jewish Learning for the propagation and teaching of all sorts and kinds, shapes and makes of dissentient Judaism – from Upper Berkeley Street in London to Carnegie Hall in New York, and from Berlin, the home of the first springs of Reform Judaism, away to the unknown wilds of every esoteric form which our faith has assumed.

I understand that the Chief Rabbi is standing like a rock against this onrushing tide of go-as-you-please Judaism. Dr Hertz refuses to budge upon a definite separation being made between Jews' College as a Traditional Jewish seminary and any other adjunct that it is being sought to attach to it. He contends, and it seems to me rightly, that the idea of teaching Traditional Judaism and that of imparting all other cults and conceptions of Judaism must be separate and distinct, carried on in separate establishments by separate staffs with separate controlling bodies.

Against Dr Hertz, I hear, there is a strong force of those who are ordinarily recognised as, and called, the leaders of our community. Chief among them is Sir Robert Waley Cohen, who indulges, and so frequently tries to give expression to, cloudy notions which would make black white, or rather both of them indistinguishable pigments in pursuance of the very crazy idea that the unity of the community is to be achieved by substituting for either Traditional Judaism or definite Reform a colourless anaemic sort of creed which Sir Robert has deluded himself into believing is really Traditional Judaism.

For my part, I hope that the Chief Rabbi will continue to stand firm because, if he does, so long as he is Chief Rabbi the crazy plan cannot be carried through. It is only fair to Dr Hertz to add that it is currently reported that he has told the powers-that-be that sooner than give way on a compromise College and assent either actively or passively to the War Memorial scheme, he would prefer to be relieved of the high office which he holds.

Whether this is a fact or not, the currency of the statement is some evidence of the very stern, unbending attitude which the Chief Rabbi is now taking upon the matter, and which is in contrast – it must be admitted – to the earlier position upon it which he assumed.

It occurs to me that Dr Hertz is really doing as much service to Reform Judaism as he is to Traditional Judaism in the course he is taking. I can imagine nothing more likely to set back true Reform than its hocus-pocus admixture, it being merged (to use a City expression) into the teaching of Traditional Judaism. Just as Traditionalism would suffer if it became permeated with the canker of dry rot by its being merged with Reform in the manner contemplated by the War Memorial committee.

The upshot of this deadlock is being watched with keen interest – and not without serious anxiety.[32]

In the event, the 'crazy plan' never materialised, remaining 'a hope to be realised perhaps one day when means are available',[33] and the transfer to Oxford or Cambridge was speedily abandoned. One million pounds had been asked of the community – a sum never achieved – and Jews' College had to be content, over the first few years, with a £500 grant from the War Memorial council to wipe out half its deficit.[34] The College did, however, move in 1932 – to Woburn House, at the corner of Tavistock Square and Upper Woburn Place, as part of a Jewish community centre built on Waley Cohen's initiative.[35]

As for Hertz's 'threat' to quit, the Chief Rabbi lived to see another day – and far more than just another communal row.

# 11

# The New Paths

Writing to an associate during the last quarter of the decade, Hertz confessed to an all-consuming battle 'in defence of Traditional Judaism against the Liberal onslaught' that had precluded much else from his communal agenda for that period of time. 'This duty', he stated, 'took up all my energy, and took precedence over all other tasks'.[1] He had launched it, he wrote elsewhere, 'in view of the religious unrest of the age, aggravated in the Jewish community by misunderstanding from without and within', leading to the need for a presentation of Judaism that endeavoured 'to bring out the truth and eternal timeliness of Israel's historic beliefs and institutions'.[2]

Using as his model the Hasmonean struggle against the Hellenisation of the Jews, two thousand years ago, Hertz chose to launch his campaign on the first day of Chanukkah 5686. It was, he said,

> not difficult to see that we, too, are witnesses of a fundamentally similar spiritual conflict in Anglo-Jewry today.
>
> This clash between the forces that cherish our Jewish heritage, and those that would break away into religious adventures recalling the aberrations in Maccabean times, is an undoubted fact. This fact must be openly faced. And, as ever, the first defensive step against this new Hellenism is neither to mock nor to denounce nor even to lament it, but to *understand* it; that is, to consider it in the light of history, and fully realise its fatal consequences to Jewry and Judaism.

At the heart of the conflict remained the conception of Traditional Judaism – 'the Judaism of the overwhelming majority of the Jews of Great and Greater Britain' – which, Hertz recalled, he had defined six years earlier as

> the teachings and practices which have come down to the House of Israel through the ages; the positive Jewish beliefs concerning God, the Torah, and Israel; the sacred festivals; the holy resolve to maintain Israel's identity; and the life consecrated by Jewish observances.
>
> Today, it is my sorrowful duty to speak to you of a Jewish school of thought whose position on many of the fundamentals just

enumerated is diametrically opposed to the Judaism of our fathers. This school of thought originated nearly a hundred years ago in Germany and is generally known in this country as Liberal Judaism ...

In England, a small group of London religious Liberals has long been struggling to transplant this German-American mutation of Judaism to these shores. After many years of effort, they have erected a stately house of worship. So loud is their rejoicing thereat that earnest men and women are perplexed by the claims of this movement. They are dazzled by its ephemeral successes, and bewildered by the new shibboleths of its spokesman.

They turn their eyes to the Rabbinate for guidance. I dare not shrink from the painful duty confronting me and shall begin today a brief examination of Liberal Judaism's attitude towards institutions and beliefs that are essential to Israel's existence, in order to unveil its true nature and show whither Liberal Judaism is leading.

We will begin with the institutions and take a primal commandment like the Abrahamic Covenant [brit milah] ... In striking contrast with the unbounded devotion of Universal Israel to this vital institution, the apostles of Liberal Judaism have everywhere worked for its total abolition.

Abraham Geiger, the founder of the whole movement, denounced milah as far back as 1845. His disciple, Emil G. Hirsch, of Chicago, who in his day was probably the most influential Jewish preacher in the world, boasted that a growing number of his followers resisted their Zipporahs[3] and omitted to make their children sons of the Covenant.

Nearly all the guides of this new Judaism today are in agreement with these views of Geiger and Hirsch. They dispense with the Abrahamic rite in the case of proselytes; but they find it advisable to retain it in the case of infants 'for an indefinite period of transition', as the principal founder of the London group carefully and officially phrased it in 1909.

This distinction between proselytes and infants seems also to have obtained in the early Christian Church; but after milah was once set aside in the case of proselytes, it was not long 'retained' even for infants. With open eyes, Liberal Judaism is repeating the experience of early Christianity.

Turning to the sacred days of the Jewish year, Hertz observed:

Sabbath and holy convocation, fast and festival, fare ill at the hands of these moderns. One prominent religious guide advocated that Passover be struck off the Jewish calendar and proposed that, instead,

Christian and Jew should together celebrate Easter under the name of 'Martyrs' Day', whatever that may mean; another sneered that Tabernacles was a dying festival, a withered branch that should be cut off from the Tree of Judaism; while still another has arranged in his synagogue that these two festivals be celebrated only on the Sunday of the week in which they occur.

Many of these 'rabbis' declare that fasting on the Day of Atonement is a superstition; and they practise what they preach. One of them has gone further. He has started an agitation to do away with Yom Kippur itself.

The Ninth of Av is the day on which Jerusalem and the Temple were twice taken and destroyed by the enemy, and commemorates what has well been called the crucifixion of the Jewish nation by the Romans. The eve of Tisha b'Av, the hour when in sorrow and anguish the House of Israel has for eighteen hundred years and longer read the Lamentations of Jeremiah, is not infrequently selected for dances and balls by American Liberal congregations.

And what of the Sabbath Day, the Sabbath of the Decalogue, that veritable pillar of fire in the soul-life of the Jew? It is now eighty years since Holdheim's *Reform-Gemeinde* at Berlin started with services both on Saturdays and Sundays. It soon abandoned the Saturday services altogether and adopted the Christian day of rest as its own. Several American ministers have succeeded in inducing their congregations to follow the Berlin example and to discontinue religious service on the Jewish Sabbath.

The latter ideal – that is, to make Sunday the Sabbath of the Jew – is the real objective of most Liberal leaders. In communities where there is still strong Jewish feeling, and considerable opposition would be shown to an open transfer of the Sabbath to the Christian day of rest, the Sunday service is at first represented as *supplementary*, and as intended only for those Jews who will not, or cannot, attend on Saturdays.

History tells us that the Jewish Christians likewise observed both Saturday and Sunday. But, as in every revolution, whether political or religious, it was the radical party, which desired a complete break with Judaism, that proved victorious in the Church. Not only was Sunday declared to be the Christian Sabbath, but in time there was direct condemnation of those who, besides Sunday, still kept the Jewish day.

When, in addition to this historical warning, we reflect that no modern religious community can possibly expect its adherents to observe two Sabbaths in one week, it is easy to see whither Liberal Jews are being piloted.[4]

In the second of his sermons, Hertz turned to the wider issues of faith and belief, declaring that

> this uprooting of sacred immemorial institutions that are interwoven with the very existence of Israel is part of a system. It is the logical outcome of the rejection by these Jewish teachers of the binding character of the Torah and of the sacredness of the Scriptures.
> ... The action of the late Dr Emil Hirsch in banishing the Sefer Torah from his synagogue is symbolical of the attitude of the whole movement towards the Torah. All these religious radicals, whether they follow Dr Hirsch's example or whether they still find place for an Ark and a Sefer Torah in their synagogue, proclaim that the Torah is no longer their guide of life and boast of having emancipated themselves from what the vice-president of the London Liberals calls 'the bondage to the Bible' ...
> Expressions of cynical unbelief can be paralleled by warm affirmations in the realm of personal religion and the spiritual life. However, in a revolutionary movement like Liberal Judaism, the expressions of unbelief on the part of its spokesmen are at least as characteristic as the affirmations, and can on no account be passed over in silence. Especially so as these denials are infinitely graver than, for example, the issues that were under discussion in London eighty years ago at the time of the Reform schism.
> Then, the English Reformers, apart from their negative attitude towards the Oral Law, lopped off a few branches from the Tree of Judaism; they abolished the second days, shortened the prayers, and introduced the triennial cycle in the synagogue reading of the Law. Now, German-American Liberals lay the axe at the very roots of the Tree itself: it is the existence of God, His revelation to Israel, and the immortality of the soul that are being doubted ...
> In its attitude to the Torah, to the Sabbath, to *milah*, to the Holy Land, no less than in its feminism, its not over-scrupulous missionary methods, and its 'summons to Christian fellowship', the Liberal Synagogue reproduces with alarming accuracy the attitude of mind which prevailed eighteen centuries ago in the Jewish-Christian Church.
> To all competent observers, Liberal Judaism is a moving staircase carrying those who have taken their stand on it out of Judaism. In the long run, there will be no other Judaism but Traditional Judaism. Cut flowers wither; the tree alone, with its roots deep in the soil, survives. Those who sever themselves from the Tree of Historical Judaism doom themselves to speedy disappearance and death.[5]

\* \* \*   \* \* \*   \* \* \*

The 'London Liberals' lost no time in rebutting these observations. In a statement circulated throughout the community, the Jewish Religious Union again made clear 'What We Stand For':

> Since some of the things that the Chief Rabbi of the United Hebrew Congregations of the British Empire said in recent addresses give a wrong impression of some of the teachings and practices of Liberal Judaism, we think that we owe it to the community to state clearly, though it must be briefly, what the attitude of the Jewish Religious Union is in these matters. In doing this, we are just stating facts, not expressing opinions or controverting opinions. Dr Hertz said: 'The preachers of the new doctrine are hostile towards the Abrahamic Covenant, the Jewish Sabbath, and several of the festivals; and are labouring for their abolition.' This is not the fact.
>
> THE SABBATH AND HOLY DAYS. – An official statement issued in 1913 by the Liberal Jewish Synagogue says: 'Liberal Judaism maintains the need for observing, in home and synagogue, the holy days of our faith – the Sabbath, the Day of Atonement, the Day of Memorial, the feasts of Passover, Pentecost and Tabernacles, and the minor feast of Dedication.' In the Liberal Jewish prayer-book, there is a special Seder service. In the new synagogue, there is a succah which, on the last Feast of Tabernacles, was visited by nearly one thousand members and their children.
>
> It is our view that, in each case, the observance must be such as will bring out the religious meaning and influence of the holy days for our generation. The Jewish Religious Union has from the beginning, without question and without hesitation, upheld the Saturday Sabbath. And whatever may be the views of a few isolated individuals, this is also the position of the Central Conference of American Rabbis, which includes nearly all, if not all, the Liberal Jewish ministers of America ...
>
> It is, therefore, not the fact that 'to make Sunday the Sabbath of the Jew is the real objective of most Liberal leaders'. But we will not shut our eyes to the fact that a large number of Jews must work on Saturday; the Liberal Jewish Synagogue, consequently, has inaugurated a service on Sunday morning for such as cannot attend the service on Saturday.
>
> This Sunday service is, however, a *weekday* service, not a Sabbath service. This is also the case in America, where the Sunday service, established fifty years ago, has remained a weekday service; even in the very few congregations – probably not more than half a dozen

out of *several hundred* – where the Sunday service is the only service. So we repeat: *Saturday remains the Sabbath for Liberal Jews*.

THE 'ABRAHAMIC COVENANT'. – It is true that we ask for circumcision only in the case of infants, but not in the case of grown-up proselytes. Though we do not value it so highly as a religious rite as Orthodox Judaism does, it is not true that we are working for its abolition. There is in our prayer-book a special service for this rite.

OUR ATTITUDE TO THE BIBLE. – It is true that we do not recognise the binding character of the Pentateuchal code as a whole, but it is not true that Liberal Judaism stands for 'the repudiation of Israel's Law' if by 'Israel's Law' is meant the Bible. Liberal Judaism not only venerates the Bible, but, in the words of its official statement, 'It recognises the value of the Bible as containing the fundamental truths of a progressive divine revelation'.

Our attitude to the Bible is briefly as follows. We fully recognise its divine inspiration in many parts, but we do not recognise it in every part. We do not accept the literal truth of all the stories, and especially of the miraculous stories, contained in the Bible. For example, we do not believe in the literal truth of the story in Exodus 19, but yet we do believe in the binding or divine authority of the Ten Commandments.

Again, we do not recognise binding force in the commandment, 'Thou shalt not suffer a sorceress to live', but we do recognise the binding authority of the commandment, 'Holy shall ye be'. We do not recognise divine authority in the laws concerning animal sacrifices, but we do recognise divine inspiration in Micah's pronouncement: 'He has shown thee, O man, what is good, and what does the Lord require of thee but to do justly, to love mercy, and to walk humbly with thy God'. And we believe that Judaism stands for truth; as the rabbis said, 'Truth is God's seal'.

OUR ATTITUDE TO CHRISTIANITY. – With Dr Hertz's opinions (as distinguished from his statements) about Liberal Judaism, we are not here concerned; except that we feel it our duty to point out that when he says that Liberal Judaism leads to Christianity, he is merely giving a personal opinion unsupported by any evidence drawn from the facts in the history of Liberal Judaism during the century of its existence.

He implies that a number of Liberal rabbis have gone over to Christianity, and he accuses the London Liberals of an unmistakable move in that direction because they took a leading part in a recent conference of Jews and Christians. The relevant facts are as follows: The Hebrew Union College, which is the American training college for Liberal Jewish ministers, has, in the course of its existence, sent out more than two hundred and fifty Liberal rabbis. We are doubtful about two cases; but except for these, not one of them has 'gone over to Christianity' ...

IN GENERAL. – In regard to the general assertion about Liberal Judaism that 'it is the existence of God, His revelation to Israel, and the immortality of the soul that is being doubted', here is the statement of the Liberal Jewish Synagogue: 'It (Liberal Judaism) emphasises faith in God, His unity and goodness, and faith in the immediate relation subsisting between God and man. It teaches the duty of man to serve God by righteousness, love and holiness; and seeks to inspire the hope of immortality. It adheres to the conviction that the Jewish brotherhood has a religious work to perform in diffusing the knowledge of the essentials of Judaism.'[6]

\* \* \*   \* \* \*   \* \* \*

'"Cry aloud, spare not; lift up thy voice like a trumpet, and declare unto My people their *rebellion*"', quoted Hertz from the prophets at the start of his final 'New Paths' sermon:

'Rebellion': that one word expresses the inmost nature of the movement in Jewry which I examined in two pulpit addresses some weeks ago. It is a revolt against the Jewish Law, the Jewish life, and the whole historic Jewish outlook.

This is a serious indictment; and no one appreciates its seriousness, and my responsibility in framing it, more than I do; but it is the only interpretation that the facts of Liberal Judaism and its history permit. The prophets of that new doctrine tell us that they look forward to a 'Judaism' in many respects different from any Judaism which the world has hitherto known.

And with the rejection of the Torah, the virtual abolition of the Abrahamic Covenant and the Sabbath, the repudiation of Zion and the Restoration, and the transvaluation of all Jewish values – their 'Judaism' is already different from any Judaism the world has ever known. Some of them add that when that New Judaism has been fully evolved, its expounders will not quarrel over the name – whether it should be Judaism or Christianity or some new neutral term – by which it is to be known.

It is pronouncements like these that enable us to estimate at its true value the protest issued against the two preceding sermons by the council of the Jewish Religious Union for the Advancement of Liberal Judaism. That document furnishes an excellent illustration of the Liberal attitude to the Torah, and the ethical consequences of such an attitude.

Its authors accept, of course, the results of the barbarous vivisection of the Torah by the Higher Critics. They tell us, 'We do not believe in the literal truth of the story in Exodus, chapter 19, but yet we do believe in the binding or divine authority of the Ten Commandments.' In other words, the Giving of the Law at Mount Sinai and Israel's divine consecration as a priest-people are a myth, according to the spokesmen of the Jewish Religious Union.

The next chapter they do approve of, and they accept the Ten Commandments as binding. Why? Because that chapter appeals to them. But suppose someone comes and declares that he does not approve of this or that among the Ten Commandments, what then?

Liberal Judaism is dry rationalism – irreverent and disintegrating. Above all else, it is devoid of faith, of fructifying belief. And therefore spiritual sterility is its portion, as it has been of all other schismatic sects in our history. None of them – Samaritans, Sadducees, or even the greatest of them, the Karaites – have created anything of permanent worth in the realm of Israel's endeavour.

'The Karaites', says Rabbi Abraham ben David, five centuries ago, 'have never helped the cause of Israel. No great book for the advancement of the Law, or the spread of Wisdom, is theirs; not even a great song, strengthening or consoling.'

Similarly, Liberal Judaism, as it is not the outcome of Jewish knowledge, has not proved a fountain of Jewish knowledge. During the hundred years of its existence, Liberal Judaism has not even produced one notable hymn. And no wonder. When Israel has faith in God and in the Divine Law of Moses, Israel sings. But where there is faith neither in the God of Israel nor in the Torah of Moses, there cannot be song or lasting scholarly achievement.

Strong resentment is felt by the authors of the protest over the statement that the New Paths not infrequently lead to Christianity. But surely it is fatuous for Liberals to fight history, their own history at that. 'Israel is a spiritual nation; it *exists only through its Torah*', is the memorable saying of Saadia Gaon, a thousand years ago.

Whenever or wherever any portion of Israel forsakes the Torah, that portion disappears from the ranks of Israel. All antinomian parties in Judaism, all schismatic movements that reject the binding authority of the Torah, sooner or later abandon Judaism and Israel altogether. It was so in the case of Paul, in the case of Shabbetai Zevi and the Frankists, and it will be so in the case of our latter-day Paulinians.[7]

* * *   * * *   * * *

Despite the 'masterly effort' and 'unerring force' expended by Hertz in his denunciation of the Liberals and their 'parodying of true Judaism',[8] even his closest sympathisers were less than satisfied. Lambasting as they did those Religious Union leaders who entered 'into public conference with perverts from Judaism or with those whose life-work is devoted to the snatching of Jewish souls', they nonetheless cautioned Hertz that his task was 'by no means completed'.

> He knows quite well – no one better – that there are thousands upon thousands of Jews in this country for whose spiritual welfare he is directly responsible; who, adherents to congregations that profess and call themselves Orthodox, yet have no true affinity to them, do not believe in the doctrines preached in them, and abide not by their nominal teachings.
>
> Will Dr Hertz have no word for all of these, and will he not teach them also whither they should go? Has he nothing for them but to stand firm and still in the Old Paths, and bid them do likewise? In which case, will he say why he speaks of 'paths', which are designed for progress?[9]

Alert to this admonition, Hertz told his congregants at the end of his third sermon:

> It is in obedience to an irresistible call that I have spoken of the New Paths. In the light of forty years' study and personal observation of the movement in both the New and the Old World, I presented Liberal Judaism to the community not in vague generalisations, but by an array of historical facts which show all too clearly whither it invariably – nay, inevitably – leads.
>
> But my task is only half done: Traditional Judaism is more than the negation of a negation. It is that vivid, vitalising realisation of God which found expression at the Red Sea: 'The Lord is my strength and my song, and He is become my salvation; this is my God, and I will glorify Him; my father's God, and I will exalt Him.'[10]
>
> Alas that, to many, this living religion of Orthodox Judaism is but a matter of hearsay. I therefore hope to supplement the series of addresses

which I conclude today with another series on the foundations and affirmations of Traditional Judaism, on the problems and duties that the present hour brings to the loyal sons and daughters of Israel.

Within weeks of this assurance, 'Affirmations' was launched, comprising seven detailed and, to unscholarly ears, complex sermons on the oneness of God, the revelation at Sinai, the books of the Torah, Jewish life, the holiness of the home, the brotherhood of Israel, and the imitation of God, plus two addresses on Jewish religious education.[11] From the very first, in his spirited appraisal of the Unity of God,[12] Hertz let loose his formidable armoury against the 'enemies from without and within', permitting

> no toying with polytheism, be its disguise ever so ethereal; no departure, even by a hair's breadth, from absolute monotheism ...
>
> The long and arduous warfare begun by the prophets and continued by the rabbis is not yet ended. The Unity of God has its antagonists in the present age, even as it had in former ages; and today it is the sacred duty and privilege of the teachers of Traditional Judaism to stand guard in its defence.

Turning, in his second sermon, to latter-day attacks on the revelation at Sinai, Hertz declared:

> A new ethic has arisen, as subversive as it is godless, which bids each man, woman or child do that which seems right in his or her own eyes. It teaches that all moral laws are man-made, and that all can therefore be unmade by man. There is, in consequence, on all sides a questioning of the sacredness of human life, a scoffing at the holiness of purity, an angry repudiation of the idea of property.
>
> In some lands, this has led to social upheavals, resulting in immemorial human institutions being torn up by the roots. Even in English-speaking countries, there is today an impatience with moral authority; and things are tolerated, extenuated, nay, encouraged – in fiction, on the stage, in everyday life – that only a generation ago would have been the subject of unqualified condemnation. Ethically, people seem to be groping as in a thick fog; and they ask, 'Why should I?' – a question often accompanied by a subtler 'Why shouldn't I?'
>
> Amid this spiritual confusion, Traditional Judaism stands clear-eyed and unmoved. It proclaims the divine origin of the Moral Law; that there is an everlasting distinction between right and wrong, an absolute 'Thou shalt' and 'Thou shalt not' in human life, a categorical imperative in religion – high above the promptings of passion, the peradventure of inclination, or the fashion of the hour.

> God is not only our Father. He is also our Lawgiver; and in the Covenant at Sinai He has made known to the children of men the foundations on which alone human welfare can be built. These eternal laws cannot be broken with impunity, whether by the individual or by a nation.[13]

From his defence of the Torah to his upholding of the rituals and observance of Jewish life, Hertz was scathing in his attacks on 'those who have lost or abandoned' them:

> 'But', I will be told, 'all these commands and repressions of the old Judaism concerning Sabbath, ritual, food are not in line with modern thought. We are waiting for a re-interpretation of Jewish tradition "in accordance with the times"; a Judaism clinging merely to the religious idea behind the ceremonies, and, for the rest, trusting the Jewish spirit.'
> Our answer is that mankind does not live in a world of ideas only. Men and women as we know them cannot dispense with symbols that give tangibility to ideas – at least the Jew cannot. He either says his morning prayers in *tefillin* or he does not say them at all. The war against forms and symbols which is preached with such crusading zeal in Liberal Jewish circles in the name of the Jewish spirit is itself a revolt against that Jewish spirit.

'Whoever separates himself from the community, refusing to share in the sorrows of his fellow Jews, as if he were not one of them, that man has no portion in the world to come.' With this saying of Maimonides[14] – 'as profound as it is true' – Hertz encapsulated his concept of the Brotherhood of Israel in his penultimate 'Affirmations' sermon.

> That way lies one of the cardinal sins of Liberal Judaism. It pursues a policy of definite estrangement from the collective consciousness of the Jewish People and the Jewish past. In the sensational newspaper articles and interviews by which the local leaders advertise and magnify their movement, they never fail to emphasise that their form of Judaism cuts straight at the root of customs and laws more than two thousand years old; that, among other things, they permit work on the Sabbath and do not deem fasting essential on the Day of Atonement; and that, rather than recede from the position they have taken up, they would separate themselves from Jewry altogether ...
> But we who believe in the God of Israel and in the Torah of Israel; we who believe in the People of Israel, in its perpetuity, unity and spiritual power; how are we to plant Jewish Brotherhood within the souls of our children so that nothing Jewish be alien unto them; that

to them Israel be like a harp-string which, wherever it is struck, vibrates throughout? How can we prevent different Jewries from drifting apart, disintegrating, disappearing?

The answer that first comes to our lips is, 'By means of Jewish religious education.' Now, no one will dispute that religious education is the indispensable basis for our survival. But it is only the basis of Jewish life; it is not the whole edifice. Knowledge alone cannot, and will not, ensure the true Jewishness of our children. 'Not learning but doing is the principal thing.'[15]

True loyalty is more than a loyalty of mere knowledge and words; it is a loyalty of life and deeds. And such real loyalty to God and to Israel manifests itself in at least three activities: in religious observance, synagogue affiliation, and participation in the rebuilding of the Holy Land.[16]

\* \* \*   \* \* \*   \* \* \*

Like the 'New Paths' before them, 'Affirmations' created a storm across the community. It was inevitable that the Chief Rabbi's assaults would provoke violent counter-attacks from non-Orthodox circles, but they attracted criticism even from the honorary officers of the United Synagogue. Of his assertion that Traditional Judaism was 'more than the negation of a negation', and of their consequent hope that he would give a vindication of it 'as a practical religion for Jewish men and women growing up in this country', Waley Cohen wrote to Hertz on behalf of his colleagues:

> Many of us had felt that the destructive criticism of Liberal Judaism [in *The New Paths*] would not serve to strengthen genuine doubting waverers in their allegiance to Traditional Judaism. We respected your feeling that the task of criticising Liberal Judaism was necessary, but we understood that you were satisfied for that to be carried out in your first series of three sermons.
>
> If the press reports are correct, you have in your second series done little more than to continue your criticism of the views of Liberal Jews, some of which apparently they do not even admit to be theirs.
>
> This continuance of polemical criticism is very disappointing to those who are still looking to you to show to the large numbers of men and women who are moving away from Traditional Judaism that it is fully capable of providing truly and completely the religious basis of their lives of which they feel the need.
>
> In looking for such a thing, men and women of today are deterred by a polemical atmosphere, and I very much hope that you may be

able to preach some sermons which will fill this very urgent need and stem the tide of disaffection which, I think we all agree, is undoubtedly flowing in this country.[17]

Waley Cohen had, in fact, sought to redraft the sermons – 'in terms that were less offensive'[18] – but had been rebuffed by Hertz. Of one such text, the Chief Rabbi responded: 'I have carefully considered the redraft suggested by you and regret that, apart from deleting another adjective ("crass" before "materialism") in addition to "frightful" and "hypocritical", no further changes are feasible. The words as redrafted by you sound apologetic. This would, of course, misrepresent my attitude.'[19]

Elsewhere, Hertz cited the commendation of a prominent American Liberal rabbi, Alexander Lyons, to repel suggestions of 'destructive criticism' in his sermons. 'You may be surprised to hear', Lyons had written, in appreciation of a copy of *The New Paths* sent by Hertz, 'that after a careful perusal, I find myself in fundamental agreement with your criticisms of Liberal Judaism.'

> I am by conviction and conduct a Liberal Jew. I have been identified with the movement long enough to be entitled to a judgment. I find that many of the objections of Orthodoxy to it are valid. Mainly, it is without an appealing background of authority and gives too much scope for individual action, converting Liberalism into licence.
>
> Liberal Judaism shows also decided failure to promote Jewish cultural values, with resulting loss of respect for the Torah as in a vital sense divine in origin and purpose. It lacks loving study of, and devotion to, the subject. The Liberal Jew handles religious education in a superficial way that promises little good. In consequence, he has to be attracted and held by things of transient appeal and interest.[20]

* * *   * * *   * * *

For a full ninety months – from the launch of the Jewish War Memorial in 1919 to the conclusion of 'Affirmations' in 1927 – Hertz had conducted his campaign against the Liberal 'onslaught'. Yet his vigorous efforts were to little avail. With each passing year, the movement announced increasingly concrete progress in its appeal to the masses, with growing attendances, communal recognition and international support. In 1921, a Liberal congregation was launched in Stamford Hill, with its own permanent synagogue six years later. In 1922, following an approach from the Board of Deputies and a change in its constitution giving women the franchise, Hill Street voted for representation on the Board.

By 1925, 'Progressive' services initiated jointly by the Liberals and Reformers at St George's Settlement in Whitechapel, the heartland of East End Orthodoxy, were attracting up to 1,000 worshippers on Sabbaths and festivals;[21] and in the same year, an impressive sanctuary seating 1,400 – the largest in London – was consecrated by the Liberal Jewish Synagogue in St John's Wood. Crowning these achievements was the founding, a year later, of the World Union for Progressive Judaism, the brainchild of its first honorary secretary, Lily Montagu.

In the face of this seemingly unstoppable Liberal bandwagon, Hertz's protagonists looked on in dismay. None of his addresses, bemoaned the *Jewish Chronicle*,

> deals in any sense with the particular problems and duties thrown up by the present hour ... Merely to recite the beauty and grandeur of Orthodoxy built up for the purposes of another hour, or even admiringly to parade the ingenuity of its exponents, to employ a colloquialism, cuts no ice.
>
> And it is from the ice-bound lethargy, the cold and frigid *laissez fair*, the frozen stagnated life-blood of modern Jewry, that it is supremely the duty of those who stand for Orthodox Judaism to endeavour to release their brothers and sisters. For the vast majority of these are anxious, above all things, to be loyal; but they are faced with problems arising from the duties of the hour which, let us put it quite plainly, are in so many instances irreconcilable with not perhaps the principles, but certainly the practices, of Orthodoxy.
>
> The task is not one for a man, however learned, however gifted in point of eloquence, whose spirit is otherwise than big and lofty. Its accomplishment, or even an essay towards its accomplishment, would bring honour and glory even to a great man; and it is a task urgent beyond measure.
>
> The more we realise the truth of all that Dr Hertz has told us about 'Liberal' Judaism on the one hand and the affirmations of Judaism on the other, the more clearly we must come to understand how important and vital it is that our rabbis and leaders should, in the words of Dr Hertz, 'deal with the problems and duties that the present hour brings to the loyal sons and daughters of Israel', so as to 'help them to make their Judaism a matter of living experience'.[22]

1. Nathan Marcus Adler

2. Moses Montefiore

3. David Woolf Marks

4. Moses Gaster

5. Hermann Adler

6. Samuel Montagu

7. Claude Montefiore

8. Lily Montagu

9. Hermann Gollancz

10. Simeon Singer

11. Morris Joseph

12. Israel Abrahams

13. Joseph Hochman

14. Joseph Herman Hertz

15. Israel Mattuck

16. Victor Schonfeld

17. Yechezkel Abramsky

18. Robert Waley Cohen

19. Isaac Herzog

20. Solomon Schonfeld

21. Isidor Grunfeld

22. Harold Reinhart

23. Israel Brodie

24. Ewen Montagu

25. Louis Jacobs

26. Isaac Wolfson

27. Yaacov Herzog

28. Immanuel Jakobovits

29. Morris Swift

30. John Rayner

31. Sidney Brichto

32. Tony Bayfield

# 12

## Call and Recall

While the Liberals continued to make spectacular gains across the board, the Reform advance – though far more modest – proceeded apace. The retirement of Isidore Harris as acting senior minister at Berkeley Street was followed, in 1926, by the appointment of Joel Blau, of New York, a follower of the conservative school of American Reform who, on his arrival in London, had asked of his colleagues: 'Am I coming to a synagogue or a movement?' It was, replied the chairman, Philip Waley, 'by the members of the congregation – who, through their faith in the vitality and the future of Reform Judaism, and their willingness to serve its cause if the call should come – that the answer Rabbi Blau looks for can alone be given'.[1]

But the answer was not so readily forthcoming, for, despite Blau's conservatism, the congregation itself was torn between its hold on tradition and its desire to further co-operation with the Liberals. Blau's standpoint was that of 'moderate' Judaism, which, while accepting the need to bring it into accord with the conditions of modern life, eschewed any antithesis between 'true Reform' and traditionalism. He was 'far removed from the vagaries of "Liberalism" and deeply resented the "de-Judaising" of our faith, characteristic of the extremists in America and elsewhere'.

This summary of his position, pronounced on his premature death only a year after his appointment,[2] characterised the dichotomy between him and his flock and led to claims, which Waley acknowledged (and disputed), that the West Londoners were 'dallying with Liberal Judaism'. They wanted, said Waley, to keep the synagogue independent as a religious institution. They had neither the wish nor the intention to adopt the forms of Liberal Judaism, but they had close ties with the Liberal congregation, 'ties that should unite all Jewish congregations'. He continued:

> We desire to work with them for the uplifting of the community. We have very deep sympathy with the Liberal Jews, because we know they are earnest, believing and high-minded Jews, and we feel that an attempt is being made to proscribe them after the method of the somewhat stupid ban which was incurred by our own synagogue in 1842 ...

While our hands are stretched out in fellowship to the Liberal Jews, they are equally open to our Orthodox brethren, although we have had many rebuffs. With them we would like to work harmoniously for the good of the community.

If there were some who preferred Reform, said Waley, their synagogue was open to them; if there was any body desiring to start a second Reform synagogue, then, although they could not offer financial support, they would offer all the moral support in their power.[3]

This reference to a second synagogue bespoke Blau's desire to create a movement, much as the Liberals had succeeding in doing. A revival in services, progress in ritual revision – which, while retaining a framework that was 'absolutely traditional', would gain in 'warmth and freshness' – and the involvement of younger members in congregational affairs all suggested, said Waley, that there was stirring in the community a move towards Reform, and that 'no cold-shouldering of our congregation will stand in its way'.

Talk of a Reform movement sent alarm bells ringing in Orthodox ears. Isaac Herzog, who only weeks earlier had lent weight to the fury heaped upon his Chief Rabbinical counterpart, now rushed in with praise for Hertz's 'powerful and stirring sermons in which, with consummate skill and masterly eloquence, he has laid bare the unmistakable *shmad*-drift [apostatising] of "Liberal" Judaism'. Calling for a campaign against the followers of the new paths, and for 'a mission of Israel to the Jews', Herzog declared:

> We have organisations for the relief of starving Jews in the physical sense. Why not have an organisation for the relief of those who suffer from a famine in the land, not a famine of bread, nor a thirst for water, but of hearing the word of the Eternal?
>
> An organisation that would agitate by means of the spoken and the printed word, as well as by other methods and devices, for the strengthening and uplifting of traditional, of true, Judaism in our midst would prove a great force, an immense power of incalculable good.[4]

Herzog's appeal found a ready and willing advocate, one who likewise paid tribute to Hertz's 'very fine and telling pronouncements, which I know have had a great effect',[5] and who, alongside another personality of even wider influence, was to signal a seismic shift in the highest councils – and counsels – of Orthodox Jewry.

* * *   * * *   * * *

Victor Schonfeld was the first of these figures. His Adath Yisroel congregation in Stamford Hill,[6] reflecting the religious outlook of Samson Raphael Hirsch, had begun to assert itself as a considerable force, particularly among the young, in the fields of Jewish education and cultural recreation. Conditions were ripe, he believed, to 'assist by weight of numbers in the struggle the community is waging against the "Liberal" inroads'.[7] His solution was the establishment, under Adath auspices, of 'a new union of London synagogues, of a definitely Orthodox type, which not only profess but also practise traditional Judaism.

> It is, in a sense, a reply to the challenge of the 'Liberal' Jewish movement. We feel that no mere theoretical discussions and refutations of 'Liberal' Judaism are sufficient to stay the inroads which the movement is making. I would compare 'Liberal' Judaism to a fungous growth which only flourishes on decay. We believe that the decay can be arrested only by uniting the forces of traditional Judaism, not in a spirit of make-believe but on a basis of practical sincerity.

Asked whether the new organisation would be under the Chief Rabbi's jurisdiction, Schonfeld replied:

> Our attitude towards the Chief Rabbi will be such that we shall not seek to interfere with the representative character of his office.
>
> We realise, however, that the Chief Rabbinate is largely under the control of the United Synagogue, which stands for a concession-making type of Judaism to which we cannot subscribe, so that internally we cannot very well be subject to its authority. So far as marriages are concerned, our congregation enjoys complete independence.
>
> I should like to emphasise that it will be the aim of the new organisation to be a constructive and not a disruptive force in the community. While we shall stand for a very pronounced type of Orthodox Judaism, there will be no 'test' for membership, though it will be a requirement that the governing bodies of constituent congregations shall be practising traditional Jews.

Schonfeld's dismissal of 'a concession-making type of Judaism' lay at the heart of the United Synagogue's woes. It lay also, in different terms, at the core of Hertz's unhappy relationship with his lay leaders, notably Waley Cohen, in whose company the temperature, and tempers, continued to rise as the years rolled by.

'Especially in our own camp', the Chief Rabbi bewailed at this time, 'leadership has almost everywhere today been wrested from the Jewish minister by the lay element, who desire the clergy to surrender their independence and perform the functions delegated to them as the controlled servants of the lay element, and as the paid interpreters of the aspirations or prejudices of that lay element'.[8]

Waley Cohen's response to such complaints – and there were many, on both sides – surfaced some months later when, during one particularly bitter exchange, the United Synagogue vice-president implored his ecclesiastical chief 'to consider carefully before resuming your continued attacks upon first one and then another of those who are working for Anglo-Jewry ... It is a source of continual grief to the rest of us that you should always find it necessary to hinder when you might do so much to help.'

In response, Hertz invoked a clause in the United Synagogue's Deed of Foundation and Trust that 'all matters connected with the religious administration of the United Synagogue and of its subsidiary charities shall be under the supervision and control of the Chief Rabbi'. Calling on Waley Cohen to 'give up slandering me' and 'pay me the respect that an English gentleman should show the Chief Rabbi', Hertz urged him to 'understand that the Chief Rabbi is the moral teacher and guide of the community, and not the bondman of any one individual of the community'. Threats and invective were 'of no avail to divert me from any course of action which I deem is dictated to me by conscience, self-respect, or considerations for the welfare of Judaism and the Jewish people'.

To this, Waley Cohen replied:

> I do not think you will ever find the Anglo-Jewish community willing to submit to the unquestioned authority of anyone in any matter other than on questions of pure *din*. I certainly am not.
>
> I count it as a great blessing that it has always been the practice in our community for the leaders, lay and clerical, to take counsel together and to reach a common agreement and work together in the interests of the community, and we should all be only too delighted if you would do that with us. I do not think pontifical authority could be justified and I should very much regret it if you finally decided that it is essential to your self-respect.[9]

The ends to which Hertz's 'self-respect' was to be employed – on his own behalf, as Waley Cohen implied, or for the welfare of Judaism, as the Chief Rabbi contended – lay behind Schonfeld's swipe at the 'concession-making' instincts of their synagogal body. Nor was the charge without foundation. As early as 1915, Berkeley Street's chief minister had been an honoured participant at the consecration of the New Synagogue, Stamford Hill; indeed, 'the significance of the occasion was enhanced by his presence'.[10] Hertz had headed a procession of twenty-five scroll-bearers, followed by the Haham, three dayanim – and Morris Joseph.

Two years later, the Chief Rabbi had preached a Sabbath-morning eulogy at the Central Synagogue for Waley Cohen's mother, Julia, a life-long member of Berkeley Street who had been buried under its auspices. 'Everywhere', Hertz had declared before a congregation of Orthodox and Reform, 'she looked for the unity underlying the diversity in our religious life and refused to admit that the various movements at present agitating Jewry were irreconcilable.'[11] And on Blau's death, despite his cremation contrary to halachic principles, Hertz and Dayan Lazarus had joined Mattuck and Joseph for the Berkeley Street service conducted by Simmonds.[12]

In 1925, the Chief Rabbi's delivery of a lecture in the Goldsmid memorial hall of the West London Synagogue was hailed – somewhat optimistically – by its chairman, H.S.Q. Henriques, as 'a sign that the old bitterness which existed in the past is now buried for ever',[13] and by its minister as 'a red-letter day in the history of our synagogue'.[14] With Hertz, Joseph had added, he had 'always been on the friendliest possible terms', a relationship similarly acknowledged by Henriques, who spoke of 'the great esteem in which the Chief Rabbi is held on account of his great learning and brilliant abilities'.

Isidore Harris had noted that the gathering included 'one of the leading members of the United Synagogue, Albert M. Woolf' (the senior vice-president), who had come 'in the hope of hearing Dr Hertz speak in the synagogue itself'. That had not been not possible, said Harris, because their lectures were always delivered in the hall, 'but I hope the time is not far distant when the Chief Rabbi will make his way into the synagogue itself and we will have the pleasure and advantage of hearing him speak from the pulpit'.[15]

That 'pleasure and advantage' were, however, to be 'far distant', for nine years were to pass before Hertz found himself at the West London on what the *Jewish Chronicle* described, without hyperbole, as a unique communal occasion,[16] 'the first time in our congregation's history', said Philip Waley, 'that we have with us on one platform the religious leaders of our three great sister Jewish communities' – the Chief Rabbi, Bueno de Mesquita, and Mattuck. The service of dedication, conducted by the senior minister, Harold Reinhart,[17] marked the opening of the synagogue's educational centre, heralding, in the words of Sir Samuel Instone, 'a great future for Judaism, or at least Reform Judaism'.

Understandably defensive in a Reform setting, Hertz told the congregation that, while he was 'the last person in the world to minimise the significance of religious difference in Jewry', he had nevertheless decided to attend 'because of my conviction that far more calamitous than religious difference in Jewry is religious indifference'. He continued:

> The erection and dedication of a building such as this, intended primarily for school purposes, means a determination on the part of the West London Synagogue of British Jews to provide the only adequate safeguard against religious indifference – a more intensive and extensive system of Jewish religious education that will bring all the children and adolescents within the sphere of your influence to the living fountains of Jewish inspiration and faith.
>
> For some time, we have hailed with enthusiasm every effort that has for its aim the rescuing for our faith of the religiously neglected children of the poor. It is heartening to find that, in many directions, there is today an equally laudable endeavour to rescue the religiously neglected children of the rich.
>
> Your co-operation is especially necessary at the present day, when there is a need for emphasising the religious nature of Anglo-Jewry in the face of the exaggerated racialism proclaimed by some Jews. For you are of those who maintain that Anglo-Jewry is far more than a racial group with certain social and civic interests; and that Israel is first of all a spiritual community, to whom the God of our fathers in the days of old entrusted a Law of Truth and thereby planted everlasting life within us.

Conciliation and congregational unity were also themes permeating the leader columns of the *Jewish Chronicle*,[18] which acclaimed the 'far-reaching significance' of an event wherein 'the lion lay down with the lamb – or, at any rate, the Chief Rabbi foregathered with Dr Mattuck ...

> We shall better preserve our Judaism if we cultivate a broad tolerance, and as much co-operation as may be possible, than if we indulge in disputations which embitter and divide. And may there not gradually evolve a central body of Jewish thought united on the broad essentials of our faith, as adjusted, with prudence, to the needs of our day?
>
> We believe that that vision will be realised, however distant it may seem, given mutual sympathy and right thinking. We hope that it will, for without it the future of our creed and our people in this country seems obscure and dubious indeed.

* * *   * * *   * * *

But not all in the community saw it that way. Schonfeld's Union of Orthodox

Hebrew Congregations was quick to lash out at Hertz and the United Synagogue for their 'wavering ambiguity' and 'lukewarm colourlessness':

> Orthodox Jews, irrespective of the particular community to which they belong, have been undoubtedly shocked by the report that the Chief Rabbi of the United Synagogue, together with his most active lay leader, Sir Robert Waley Cohen, participated in the inaugural celebration of the Reform Synagogue last Sunday fortnight, thereby strengthening a movement which has always stood, and still stands, profoundly antagonistic to the Orthodox camp.
>
> It is all the more surprising, therefore, that no single voice of objection has been raised by any of the more Orthodox elements of the United Synagogue. This move towards the left by the United Synagogue, which claims to be the official Orthodox community of the metropolis, is fraught with the gravest danger for the future of Judaism in this country, and [the Union] executive feels compelled to utter its protest in the strongest manner possible at the action of Dr Hertz.
>
> The existence of the Union of Orthodox Hebrew Congregations is in itself a protest against the lack of Orthodoxy in the established community, but this wavering ambiguity on the part of one who is also the permanent chairman of the Rabbinical Commission for the Licensing of Shochetim, upon which our [Adath] community is represented, demands our most emphatic declaration of dissent.
>
> The argument that is employed in defence of this action is the plea for a united Jewish front at this serious juncture in Jewish history.[19] But to bring our spiritual standards to such a level of lukewarm colourlessness is surely the absolute denial of the validity of faith, dogma and creed.[20]

In the face of this attack, the Chief Rabbi remained silent, but Samuel Daiches, Brondesbury's minister, took up the cudgels on his behalf. Referring to the Union's 'surprising' complaint that Hertz had participated in the event, Daiches contended that he had 'merely attended the formal opening of the new classrooms and communal hall ... The few words he spoke after the ceremony had been directed against religious indifference and neglect of Jewish education.' No one, wrote Daiches, could cavil at such cooperation with the Reform Synagogue,

> least of all the spokesmen of the Union of Orthodox Hebrew Congregations. They have themselves co-operated even with the Liberal Synagogue – and that in the matter of shechitah.
>
> In the fight concerning the licensing of shochetim,[21] the leader of

the Union sought and obtained a 'rabbinical opinion' in shechitah affairs from Dr Mattuck! Men who stand for strictest Orthodoxy should be scrupulously fair, especially towards one who, like the Chief Rabbi, has repeatedly shown himself to be their friend.[22]

Further altercations were soon to follow. In his press interview some years earlier, Schonfeld had noted his movement's 'complete independence' in the matter of marriages, an arrangement secured from Hertz in 1919 after the Adath had threatened legal action. Reform's leaders had likewise fought – and eventually won – a lengthy battle, and by the 1930s the Liberals were bent on a similar course. But they, too, found the path strewn with rocks.

Each of their synagogues (as the West London a century before) was registered as a place of worship, with a civil registrar present at all weddings. Now they sought a marriage secretary of their own and to that end approached Neville Laski, the president of the Board of Deputies. He, in turn – as required by law – asked Hertz for a ruling that the Liberal congregation was 'a synagogue of persons professing the Jewish religion', thus inevitably engaging Waley Cohen in the process.

Hertz's predictable rejection provoked the United Synagogue leader into another fierce exchange. 'Nothing you do or do not do', he told the Chief Rabbi,

> will have any influence on the situation of the Liberal Synagogue with regard to the violation of Jewish laws of marriage and divorce. Whether, therefore, you make this declaration or not does not really have any sort of connection with that question.
>
> The statement of the fact that the Liberal Synagogue is a synagogue of Jews – a fact which you and all of us have rightly and abundantly recognised in a hundred-and-one directions – does not, of course, affect the fact that you do not sanction their religious practices, and that they do not recognise the Chief Rabbi's religious authority.
>
> I suggest, therefore, that the making of that statement can have nothing to do with the resolutions which you require from the synagogues whose religious practices you do recognise and who do recognise your authority.
>
> Apart from that, I think we must recognise that the resolutions have had to be modified on more than one occasion, and that every lawyer of authority has told us that they would be immediately disallowed in a court of law by anyone who chose to raise the question.
>
> I suggest to you, therefore, that the making of this statement in regard to the Liberal Synagogue can also have no influence upon the question of the resolutions which you endeavour to enforce – and I

think wisely so – on the synagogues of Orthodox Judaism before you give a certificate in regard to them.

Countering recommendations Hertz had proposed to resolve the matter, Waley Cohen added:

> I consider that it would be in the highest degree impolitic to encourage the Liberal Synagogue to urge either that the [Board's] president should utilise his original powers derived from Section 30 of the 1836 Act without any previous certificate from a religious authority, or that the Board of Deputies should start a new precedent of recognising a multiplicity of 'ecclesiastical authorities'.
>
> I am most anxious that you should reconsider your view, because I feel that a decision along those lines would create far-reaching damage to the cause of traditional Judaism in this country and ultimately would altogether destroy the position of the Chief Rabbinate as we have known it.[23]

Hertz's first response was to write, in the margin of this letter (in bright red ink), 'I have no *locus standi* and will be laughed at'. On reflection, however, he met with Waley Cohen and agreed that, although he would not at the Liberals' request grant them a certificate, he would, at the request of the Board's president, certify that the Liberal Synagogue was 'a synagogue of persons professing the Jewish religion'.

Waley Cohen was mandated to ask Laski to proceed and to draft the Chief Rabbi's reply to such a request. But on receipt of the text, Hertz retracted, telling Waley Cohen that

> your draft of the reply that I was to send to Mr Laski was, I regret, one I could not possibly sign. It was essential that my position be made absolutely clear, and for that purpose I enclose a revision of the draft, such as at one time I thought I might be able to sign.
>
> I am, however, convinced that the effect of even such a letter – in which I carefully avoid calling them a 'synagogue' – would be disastrous to the cause I have at heart. Jewish public opinion throughout the world would interpret it in one way: that the Chief Rabbi has issued a *hechsher* on the Liberal Synagogue, in order to enable it to obtain a marriage secretary.
>
> The evil results would, I am convinced, immeasurably outweigh any benefits that might accrue from the contemplated action.[24]

Waley Cohen was equally inflexible. Having 'set aside some hours' for further discussion, he told Hertz,

> I gave myself the trouble necessary to prepare a carefully thought out draft and sent it to you on 25 June. I heard nothing further from you until 4 July, when I received your letter completely reversing the arrangements reached between us after so much labour and thought.
>
> In the circumstances, I feel sure you will wish to examine the matter again, and I would ask you most earnestly to do so. I would particularly ask you to read again my letter to you of 18 June, which explained why, in my opinion and I think also in your own, the course which you now propose would be permanently and finally disastrous to the position of the Chief Rabbinate in this country and to the causes to which you and I have devoted our lives.
>
> I venture to suggest to you that no motive can be more dangerous for the refusal to do what is right than a fear that ill-disposed people may wholly misinterpret your action. Your certificate, to fulfil its purpose, must copy the words of the Act of Parliament, which are 'a synagogue of persons professing the Jewish religion'. As you explained to me before, there is no Jewish significance whatever in the word 'synagogue', and to avoid using it would be to fail to fulfil the requirement of the Act.
>
> We have been more than a month considering this matter and I very much fear that, unless we give some reasonable answer to the approaches which were made to us, the position will be lost, and that will involve very serious consequences which I shall be glad to explain to you if you would like to discuss the matter further with me with a view to finality.[25]

The seriousness of the consequences was not spelled out – at least for public dissection – and the matter proceeded even more slowly, behind closed doors. A further six months were to elapse before Hertz dispatched his ruling to Laski:

> Although I strongly disapprove of the religious practices and principles of the Liberal Synagogue, I am not justified in declaring that its members have left the ranks of Jewry, and do not profess Judaism. If that had been the case, they could not have been given representation on the Board of Deputies.
>
> Moreover, if the recognition requisite for the appointment of a marriage secretary is now denied them, they will, as Berkeley Street have done years ago, seek relief by Act of Parliament. Such a course would in all probability bring with it a discussion in Parliament of minor religious differences. I feel that such a discussion would be especially undesirable at the present moment.

In the circumstances, I am prepared to agree to the formality of certifying that the body in question is an organisation for purposes of worship and kindred activities on the part of Liberal Jews, and therefore constitutes for the purposes of the Act of Parliament a synagogue of persons professing the Jewish religion.

However, it must be clearly understood that, by this formal act of certification, the Chief Rabbinate can take no responsibility for the legality or otherwise in Jewish law of any ritual act performed by the ministers of that Congregation.[26]

\* \* \*   \* \* \*   \* \* \*

The paths to other issues were similarly blocked, though not – occasionally – without points of entry. In May 1937, a communal service at the Great Synagogue to mark George VI's coronation was conducted jointly by Hertz, Mattuck, Simmonds and Beuno de Mesquita as representatives of all four movements, 'for the first time in the history of Anglo-Jewry',[27] and with their lay leaders seated together in the wardens' box.

To mark the occasion, Mattuck wrote to Hertz two months earlier acknowledging the offer of tickets for the coronation procession and 'the spirit it shows', and adding:

> There arises in my mind the question whether it would not be possible to use the Coronation as an occasion for further evidence of the unity of the Jewish community. I do not know whether it would be possible for us all to use the same service, but could we not, at least, agree in advance about a special Coronation Prayer? It would be issued by you, and the sections of the community not under your jurisdiction could announce that they would use it. We could prepare the way for such a course by previous consultation, which would make it certain that the prayer would suit the diversity of views among us. If it could be made to cover the whole service, so much the better.[28]

The idea, however, did not appeal to Hertz. Nor did Mattuck's subsequent request to 'use in the Coronation service which is being printed for our use here a portion of your special prayer. Naturally, I should print an acknowledgement, which would show that it is from the prayer you issued.'[29] But the Liberal minister's participation in the Great Synagogue service clearly served as a welcome second best.

Less successful were Liberal approaches to the British Broadcasting Corporation for the use of air time involving Mattuck's participation. In 1929, a BBC director had written to Hertz following a suggestion from the Hon. Mrs Franklin[30] that we should broadcast a service on the evening of the Day of Atonement from the Liberal Jewish Synagogue, with an address by Rabbi Mattuck, or alternatively a service on Saturday morning. Before proceeding further with the suggestion, I shall be glad to know whether such a course would be acceptable and not in any case offensive to Orthodox Jews.[31]

Hertz had replied:

The suggestion of the Hon. Mrs Franklin would be most unacceptable to Orthodox Jews, who form the overwhelming majority of the Jewish population in this country. Furthermore, as 'no address or service given under your auspices should be open to the charge of propagandist intentions', the suggested service with address could not be given under the auspices of your Corporation. The Liberal Jewish Synagogue represents a new subversive movement in the Anglo-Jewish community and has always been propagandist.[32]

Ten years on, a further BBC approach to Hertz referred to

some correspondence we had recently with Rabbi Mattuck, of the Liberal Jewish Synagogue, in which he asked for a broadcast. I told him of our meeting with you and that the only Jewish broadcast we had promised would be that arranged and taken by you.

You will excuse my ignorance about the Liberal Jewish Synagogue and perhaps be kind enough to tell me whether the movement it represents is one of which you would approve if a broadcast by Rabbi Mattuck were even considered. We are anxious not to do anything without first securing your advice.[33]

In response to Hertz's negative reaction, the BBC indicated that 'if he [Mattuck] represents such a very small section of the Jewish community, it is unlikely that we shall wish to broadcast from the Liberal Jewish Synagogue'.[34]

The coronation service marked the end of Hertz's honeymoon with the forces of 'traditional' reform. A number of factors had come into play, not least the growing harmony between Berkeley Street and the Liberals, nurtured by Reinhart and Mattuck and cemented by their movements' joint membership of the World Union for Progressive Judaism. Avenues were opened with a view to linking them through an association of Liberal and Reform synagogues, the implementation of which was, however, delayed until after the war. Such fraternisation worried Hertz – and worried even more those on his right who had begun to exert influence over him, foremost among whom was a recently arrived rabbi of Lithuanian stock.

* * *   * * *   * * *

Born in the village of Dashkovchi, near Mush in the province of Vilna, Yechezkel Alter Abramsky – 'destined for greatness from early childhood'[35] – received semichah at the age of 17 from Yechiel Michal Epstein, the sage of Novaradok and one of the leading halachic authorities of his day.[36] After studying at the yeshivot of Telz, Ramailis and Brisk, and serving the communities of Smolian, Smolevitch and Slutzk, Abramsky was invited in 1929 to succeed Yisrael Abba Citron as rabbi of Petach Tikva, but was refused permission to leave the Soviet Union.

Ten months in hiding were followed by charges of slandering the State, and a sentence of five years' hard labour in the wastelands of Siberia. On the eve of Yom Kippur 5692 (1931), through the intervention of the German Chancellor and by means of a prisoner exchange, Abramsky was granted permission to emigrate and, some months later, arrived in Britain to become rabbi of the Machzike Hadath. Within four years he was appointed senior dayan at the London Beth Din.[37]

His selection, on the recommendation of the United Synagogue's executive after consultations with Hertz, received strong support from Waley Cohen, despite his earlier denial of Abramsky's candidacy. The committee, said the United Synagogue's vice-president, had noted the rabbi's 'outstanding qualities, which include the advantage of having already acquired a wide knowledge of the organisation and special problems of the Jewish community of London and its neighbourhood'.[38]

What they desired, and was 'obviously necessary', said Waley Cohen, was a dayan who would 'carry weight throughout the whole of Jewry. With the assistance of the Chief Rabbi, we have sought Jewry throughout the world and have left no stone unturned. The executive regards it as a cardinal principle in the appointment of a dayan that he should feel he is serving the whole community and not feel that he is connected in any way with any section of it.'

The appointment, lauded by Waley Cohen for having won the backing of the Federation of Synagogues, was received with reservations by Schonfeld's Adath, which asserted that 'a new dayan to the Beth Din of the United Synagogue does not in itself solve the problems raised by the Union. The various features of the existing Beth Din to which the Union has taken exception, and for the removal of which the Union has been striving, remain unaltered.'

That Abramsky had been the spiritual head of the Machzike Hadath – 'a congregation which has never been able to identify itself with the religious standard of the general community' – was, declared the Union, 'an admission on the part of the United Synagogue that it was incumbent upon them to do fuller justice to Orthodoxy. It is to be hoped that the new dayan, whose appointment was doubtlessly due in no small measure to the representations made by so-called "militant Orthodoxy", will do his utmost to bridge the gap that still exists.'[39]

Reflecting, on the other hand, the viewpoint of many East Enders who had sought the selection of 'a resident English-speaking dayan', a correspondent to the *Jewish Chronicle* described Abramsky's appointment as

> a blunder ... considered from its narrow aspect and not from the larger and more important communal aspect. What was good enough for East London twenty or thirty years ago is not good enough now. Yiddish *deroshas* [discourses] are no longer wanted; a new generation has arisen that knows not Yiddish ...
>
> The appointment will not heal any existing religious breach in the community. It is a source of profound disappointment to many in the East End, particularly to those who have been patient in their demands but who now realise how futile and utterly hopeless any further efforts for communal betterment must be.[40]

Represented by the *Jewish Chronicle* as 'the champion of Orthodoxy', Abramsky told its Yiddish-speaking reporter that he looked forward 'to working with the other members of the Beth Din in all the work appertaining to the welfare of Jewry in this country ...

'My aim is to strengthen Yiddishkeit, in both the practice and knowledge of Judaism. I hope in the course of time, as my English improves, to be able to devote myself more to the Jewish youth of this country. I shall be very happy to do so.'

Pressed to say how he proposed to bring Judaism 'more into conformity with modern needs', he declared that 'a strong Orthodox Judaism is the best way of making a really good Jew. This is my strong belief, and it will be my object to implant as much as I possibly can of this belief into the hearts and minds of the young generation and to bring them closely into contact with the living fountains of our faith – the Torah.'[41]

From the outset of his sixteen-year tenure as dayan, Abramsky – in the words of his biographer –

> excelled as a fighter in the wars of Hashem. With rare and great courage and persistence of spirit, he conducted a fierce campaign against Judaism's internal enemies who emerged from the Liberal and Reform ranks, in the spirit of Isaiah the son of Amoz: 'Your builders outdo your destroyers, and those who laid you waste go away from

you.'[42] In the persistent battle he waged against Liberal Jews, he was not prepared to make even the slightest concession. He fought and struggled strenuously for the principle that the Liberals did not represent the Jewish religion.[43]

The full force of Abramsky's influence over the Chief Rabbinate, as 'a fighter in the wars of Hashem', was to be felt only gradually. But the onset of the Second World War brought a new dimension, and direction, to Anglo-Jewish Orthodoxy as the dayan and his Beth Din grappled with the crises that ensued, and as Solomon Schonfeld – Hertz's son-in-law[44] – was perceived to tighten his grip over an increasingly isolated Chief Rabbi, who came to regard him as his 'right-hand man in everything'.[45] Such was their relationship that, on one occasion, Schonfeld – executive director of Hertz's Religious Emergency Council – was mistakenly described by a government official as 'Deputy Chief Rabbi', following a visit the two made to the Home Office over the case of a refugee rabbi.

Innuendos in a United Synagogue letter to the Home Office, disclaiming the post, were condemned as 'grossly improper' by Hertz, who wrote irately:

> Those words 'Deputy Chief Rabbi' rather startled both Dr Schonfeld and me. Only two years ago, I recorded to the [United Synagogue] honorary officers in writing my refusal to consider the creation of a Deputy Chief Rabbi.
>
> As to Dr Schonfeld, he has at no time encouraged anyone in the belief that there was such an office as 'Deputy Chief Rabbi', let alone that he was the holder of it. Any suggestion to the contrary, or that I – as his father-in-law – did so is an abominable untruth.[46]

Despite the Chief Rabbi's rejection of backdoor influences, the belief was growing – not least in the minds of Waley Cohen and many of his lay and ministerial colleagues – that Hertz was being swayed by those to the right of the United Synagogue involved more with religious organisations 'far removed from the sort of tradition'[47] in which it had been moulded.

Orthodox ministers previously close to Reform began to feel intimidated by the change in direction. Birmingham's Abraham Cohen, who had preached at the West London Synagogue, wrote to Reinhart that 'I am arguing a few points with the London Beth Din and have a feeling that my appearance in Berkeley Street may prejudice the chances of a successful outcome for those people whose affairs I have taken up'. Another earlier guest preacher in the West London pulpit, Bueno de Mesquita, told his Reform counterpart that 'a goodly number of my congregation would be deeply disturbed if I preached at Berkeley Street – and peace within the congregation is of paramount importance'.[48]

In 1943, following the retirement of Dayan Mark Gollop as senior chaplain to the forces, Waley Cohen – in his capacity as chairman of the Jewish War Services Committee – secured the services of a Liberal minister, Leslie Edgar,[49] to fill the post. Hertz intervened with Bernard Homa, the Machzike Hadath's representative on the committee, to help block the appointment, telling him later that 'I could have done nothing without your co-operation'.[50] After some delay, during which Edgar acted as chaplain, Israel Brodie[51] was selected instead.

Right-wing pressure was also blamed for the loss to the United Synagogue of many refugee rabbis who, it was claimed, might have remained within the Orthodox fold had Hertz implemented a scheme of Friday-night services designed to attract them, and who eventually helped to swell the ranks of the Reform ministry.[52] Difficulties existed, too, in the Emergency Committee for the Religious Education of Jewish Refugee Children, established by the Board of Deputies with Hertz's co-operation and with Berkeley Street's Owen Mocatta among its members.

Earlier educational enterprises, initiated by the West London, had attracted the support of the United Synagogue, the Sephardim and the Liberals, who had drawn up a joint religious-studies curriculum. By 1939, however, the climate had changed and Reform leaders alleged discriminatory practices in the allocation of homes to refugee children, with the breakdown of an agreement to refer those from Reform backgrounds to like-minded congregations. Such was the sense of injustice perceived, with Reform children 'being denied education along Reform principles',[53] that all hope of communal progress 'was dashed to the ground when the ultimatum of the Orthodox ecclesiastical authorities – to the effect that all teachers and all courses of study had to be subject to the approval of the Chief Rabbi – was accepted'.[54]

As a result, Reform congregations across Britain convened, in 1942, to create an independent educational structure and, subsequently, a national federation. It was, they later declared, a momentous decision, marking

> the transition of Reform Judaism from being a common feature of disparate synagogues to becoming the ideological thrust of an active association.
>
> What had started as a protest meeting against the Chief Rabbi's ruling on matters pedagogic ended as the foundation of a new movement in British Jewry. There was an ironic parallel with the establishment of the first Reform synagogue.

Just as West London had not been a deliberate breakaway premeditated from the outset, but had been pushed into existence by the refusal of the Bevis Marks authorities to countenance a branch congregation, so the Reform movement came into existence accidentally in reaction to moves by the Chief Rabbinate limiting the scope of Jewish education.[55]

\* \* \*   \* \* \*   \* \* \*

Alarmed by defections from their own congregations and by the growing strength of the Liberals and Reform, United Synagogue leaders sought in 1940 to close ranks as wartime exigencies exacted their toll. Differences existed, however, over the formulation of the crisis strategy. 'The United Synagogue, and with it many of the institutions on which Jewish religious life in this country depend', Waley Cohen told a council meeting, 'stand at a very critical crossroad: the whole of our future depends on the community showing itself as ready as our forebears to rally to the cause of Judaism.' One positive move, he said, was that 'every minister has pledged his time and energy to the work of recalling the community to the synagogue'.[56]

'Recall to the Synagogue' thus became the slogan of a spirited movement towards that goal. But if Waley Cohen and Hertz were ever at odds over means to an end, they were seldom more highlighted than in the new endeavour. Launched at a conference attended by representatives of some fifty congregations, the campaign was, said United Synagogue president Lionel de Rothschild,

> a striking testimony to the part we play in the religious life and welfare of the community. The war has brought innumerable difficulties in its train and at no time in the United Synagogue's history have we been faced with more critical problems than at the present time.
>
> Evacuation has resulted in a large number of our members leaving the metropolis; many no longer worship in their synagogues; very large numbers of children are being deprived of normal facilities for religious education. It is vitally important to maintain the connection between the individual member and the synagogue: if that connection is weakened, the basis of their religious life is in danger.[57]

From the outset, Hertz sought to assert his own authority within the Orthodox community. 'The architects of the United Synagogue, Sir Anthony de Rothschild and Lionel Louis Cohen', he told the delegates,

> provided it with a constitution that permits no ecclesiastical interfer-

ence in matters of finance; and, at the same time, these great-hearted Jewish gentlemen had a horror of lay interference in religious law. They therefore placed the entire religious administration and educational supervision under the control of the Chief Rabbi; and, of course, his remained the religious leadership and public representation of the community.

On such foundations there arose an institution that stands for the Golden Mean in Judaism – for religious advance without loss of traditional Jewish values, and without estrangement from Zion or from *Klal Yisrael*, the House of Israel, the world over ... The whole *raison d'être* of a Jewish community is the advancement of Judaism. And by Judaism we mean, first of all, the web of fast and festival, precept, symbol and ceremony that is the foundation of the Jewish way of life.

That way of life has come down to us from our fathers of old. It is rooted in the Hebrew Scriptures, and the inheritance of Israel as the depository and guardian of the truths held by it for mankind. It has been nurtured by the instruction of God-enlightened prophets and seers, sages and saints; and upheld by the teachings of self-denying generations.

In a word, it is the fruit and outward expression of a religious civilisation aglow with the passion for righteousness, a religious civilisation in which are enshrined world-old, original, spiritual forces which to this day have lost none of their effectiveness.

Given such a conception of Judaism, we at once see that the financial side of synagogue administration is not all-important; and that we can have nothing but contempt for those zealots of business efficiency in religion who would tear down the two Tables of the Law from the front of our houses of worship and replace them by the balance-sheet. Besides, deification of business management, coupled as it so often is with colour-blindness to Jewish spiritual and cultural values, is unwise even from the purely business point of view.

As long as a born Jew is still possessed of some reverence for things Jewish, as long as there is still a spark of Jewish feeling in him, so long may there be in him loyalty to his people and generosity in the support of its institutions. But when his heart is void of every religious memory, there is refusal to support even Jewish philanthropic institutions, which are then dismissed by him as 'sectarian' charities.

In brief, immeasurably more important than even a communal consciousness is the reawakening of a communal conscience that shall ask every one: 'Are you pulling your full weight in your community *as a Jew*?

'Has your community become more Jewish, more spiritual, more self-sacrificing, through your presence in its midst? What is it doing to fan the flame of Judaism in the hearts of the men and woman of today? What is being done to plant our sacred faith in the hearts and souls of the men and women of the coming generation?'[58]

A month later, at the Hampstead Synagogue, Hertz returned to his theme of 'Recall':

Anglo-Jewry, with its exemplary progressive conservatism in things of the spirit, holds the key position in the world of Judaism. If it can rouse itself to a full realisation of its duty and destiny at the present hour – not only as political champions of our outlawed brethren on the Continent, but as Guardian of Jewish Learning and as Defender of our religious Tradition – it will do infinitely more than merely save itself.

It will not only keep the Light of Judaism burning with a clear-shining flame within its own borders, but it will, with the help of God, help to rekindle the Lamp of the Torah wherever it has been extinguished by the insolent and godless destroyer, when that godless destroyer vanishes like smoke from under the heavens of the Lord.

The 'Recall to the Synagogue' movement has thus a significance undreamed of by those who first sponsored it – provided always that it seriously translates into action its resolve 'to make the utmost efforts to strengthen the synagogue and the religious forces of the community'.

And here I wish you to note that this is not 'A Recall to Religion', but 'A Recall to the Synagogue'. The difference is profound. There is no such thing as religion in the abstract; religion exists only insofar as it is embodied in any one of the religions of the world.

And just as you cannot teach a child language in the abstract, but only *a* language, his mother tongue, in the same way, if religion is to be moral force in a man's life, it must be by means of *a* religion, the religion into which he was born. In brief, religion must have a label, a history, a brotherhood, an outward form.

Therefore, our Recall is not to some nebulous something, allegedly spiritual, that opposes itself to nothing in particular; nor is it to some modernist religious vagary from overseas; it is a 'Recall to the Synagogue' – to the positive, historical Judaism of our fathers, with its sanctification of everyday existence through symbol and immemorial rite; with its 'Thou shalts' and 'Thou shalt nots', and its absolute demand of justice, pity, and purity in life; with its priest-people consecrated to the humanisation of man through the teachings of righteousness and holiness proclaimed by our faith.

One further thing I should wish you to note. I shall not dwell further on the financial aspect of the movement, as I have done so sufficiently at the inaugural meeting. Today I shall be the spokesman of those who see little evidence of the United Synagogue crumbling financially but who sense a slow but real crumbling of the community religiously.

Two facts spell danger to the present and future of the Anglo-Jewish community. The first of these is the revolt against religious authority. The men who reorganised our *kehillah* seventy years ago dreaded any return to the days of the judges, when there was no king in Israel, and each man did that which seemed right in his eyes. And their spiritual attitude on that fundamental question was shared by men of light and leading outside the Jewish camp ...

In Judaism, authority in matters of religion is not mute; and there is a word of command. Refusal to heed that word of command on the part of the lay administrators of an Orthodox community means religious anarchy. Listen to the words of that beloved leader in Israel, the late Dr Cyrus Adler: 'Obedience to the Divine Teaching and law is the cornerstone of our life as Jews. I firmly believe that the maintenance of Judaism rests upon the recognition of authority'.[59]

Understanding of this elementary fact would restrain lay administrators from the ambition to *pasken*, to pronounce religious decisions even in wartime! In certain quarters, 'wartime' is the all-sufficient justification for suspending religious law. This attitude is quite untenable and, I may add, un-English.

In times of war, Englishmen put forward not less but greater efforts to remain true to their ideals; and they recoil from no sacrifice when it is a question of maintaining their historic institutions, whether civic and religious. So much for the vital need of religious authority in Jewish life.

The 'second danger' to which Hertz drew attention was 'the absence of vision, and of so-called long-term spiritual investment, in Anglo-Jewry. What are we doing to ensure a community of loyal Jews fifty, and a hundred, years hence? ... Our neglect hitherto of all agencies for the strengthening of Jewish conviction among the rank and file of our community is astounding. There must', he concluded, 'be an end to all this blindness'.[60]

It was a plea that went unheeded to his dying day.

# 13

## Omens of War

Months after the 'Recall' sermons, with their robust emphasis on ecclesiastical authority, Hertz was embroiled in further conflict with his lay leaders. As the war continued to ravage the fabric of communal life, accusations abounded in Orthodox circles that the honorary officers of the United Synagogue were sabotaging the Chief Rabbi's efforts to induce a religious revival and were seeking instead 'to eliminate all distinctions between Orthodox, Reform and Liberal Jews'.[1]

Hertz had discovered that, behind his back, Waley Cohen and his colleagues were involved in meetings with Liberal leaders, including Lily Montagu, to establish a committee on Jewish education that, allegedly, would be under non-Orthodox control. The honorary officers rejected the charge, claiming that it was their alarm at the 'growing alienation of many Jews from their faith' that had resulted in the campaign for a return to Judaism.

Despite their denial, Hertz sought to redress the situation. In a letter circulated privately to a number of leading personalities, he expressed his 'deepest concern' at the state of Jewish religious education in Britain and the problems that would confront it after the war. 'What makes the situation especially grave', he wrote, 'is the serious danger of Jewish religious education being deprived of its Jewish and religious character'.

Warning against the elimination of religious supervision of teaching, and deploring 'the lack of support by the present leaders of Jewish education' for efforts to provide kosher and Passover food for evacuated children, Hertz described as 'the most sinister sign of all' the inauguration – 'by one with very great influence in all educational matters' – of a new movement, in concert with the heads of the Liberal Synagogue, that would give Liberals and Reformers 'a prepondering vote' in all religious questions.

> It is clearly my duty as Chief Rabbi to open the eyes of the Jews of Great Britain to the deadly peril threatening our traditional Jewish life; to rescue our educational machinery from the hands of men who are inimical to Traditional Judaism and its fundamental institutions, like *milah*, Sabbath, Passover and *kashrut*; to reawaken all sections of the

community to the vital importance of greater sacrifice and effort on behalf of the religious future of our children; as well as to make full use of any new possibilities in the educational field.

One of these possibilities is Government support of religious education in State schools. The leaders of the new movement referred to above are already at work to frame, and eventually to impose, a curriculum of Jewish religious education in State schools on Liberal Jewish lines, though Liberals have less than one per cent of the child population of Anglo-Jewry. Unless we are to acquiesce in such an outrage, a properly representative body must exist to safeguard the religious rights of the overwhelming majority of Jews in Great Britain.

In view of what I have adduced, I have decided to call together communal leaders to form a National Council of Jewish Religious Education. At the first meeting, I shall give a full survey both of the dangers of the situation and of the measures necessary to meet those dangers, and especially of the new ways and means that must be devised if we are to put Jewish religious education throughout Great Britain on a satisfactory basis.[2]

Responding to Hertz's charge of Liberal domination, Norman Bentwich – the 'one with very great influence in all educational matters' – asserted that the Chief Rabbi was 'under a most unfortunate misapprehension'. He [Bentwich] was one of three people who had invited 'a few men and women concerned about Jewish religious education and Judaism' to meet and discuss Jewish teaching

> in relation to the problems of our time. There was, and is, no question of any revolution in the teaching, and no suggestion that the Reform and Liberal wings should have a preponderance. On the contrary, it was recognised that the Orthodox centre must be the principal element in any group. It is unfortunate that several of the Orthodox rabbis invited were unwilling to take part in the preliminary meeting. It would be more than unfortunate if the community were now to be split on the question of religious education, and if the leaders of the Orthodox majority should refuse to meet together with those of other sections to consider problems which are common to all Anglo-Jewry.[3]

But refuse they did, and each side went its own way. Hertz convened a meeting at his home 'to defend the religious standards of Traditional Judaism in Jewish education' and to announce the establishment of his National Council, with the participation of the Beth Din and other rabbinical organisations, the United Synagogue, Federation of Synagogues, Sephardim, Union of Orthodox Hebrew Congregations, provincial communities, and Zionist bodies.[4]

For their part, the Reformers and Liberals, who were initially prepared to work with one another, fell out over 'major differences ... which reflected the tensions that had nullified earlier attempts at closer union'. As a result, they decided not to frame a joint syllabus but 'to work independently in harmony', a proposal that itself was left to languish, having been described by Reinhart as 'an association in which the parties concerned agree only in this: that they won't agree to anything'.[5]

Underlying Hertz's action, and implicit in his inclusion of the London Beth Din on his educational council, was the dayanim's growing involvement in communal affairs. Hitherto subordinate to the Chief Rabbi and his lay leaders, they now assumed a proactive role within the United Synagogue, a development noted with some degree of alarm by its secretary, Philip Goldberg, in a note to the honorary officers: 'Since Dayan Abramsky's appointment, there has been abundant evidence of the endeavours of the Beth Din to take over administrative functions, which were by long tradition done by the so-called laymen.'[6]

Their involvement was vividly demonstrated in 1944 following a dispute that had erupted three years earlier between the chazan and a warden of the Finchley Synagogue. The dayanim backed Hertz in an attempt to summon the honorary officers of the synagogue[7] – from which the warden claimed indemnification over a slander suit he had lost to the chazan – to appear before them, a move strongly opposed by Waley Cohen and his colleagues. After a year's deadlock, and a letter from the United Synagogue officers to Hertz accusing him of 'capriciousness' and of seeking 'to assume dictatorship and to rule the community by coercion',[8] the Beth Din's patience wore thin. Castigating the United Synagogue leaders for failing to support Hertz, the dayanim protested at

> this flouting of the Chief Rabbi's ecclesiastical court, which undermines the authority of the Chief Rabbinate and the Beth Din and thus endangers the future of Orthodox Judaism in this country ...
>
> Your unheard-of suggestion that the Beth Din 'withdraw its decision to intervene' would be the first step in religious chaos and communal ruin in Anglo-Jewry. It would be tantamount that 'there is neither religious law nor judge in Israel', and would be a virtual secession from Orthodox Judaism.[9]

At a meeting of the United Synagogue council in June 1945, a motion submitted by Aaron Wright declared that 'it is the duty of the honorary officers of the Finchley District Synagogue to obey the summons which has been issued to them by the Beth Din at the suit of the complainant, and accordingly the council asks the honorary officers of the United Synagogue to advise the honorary officers of the Finchley District Synagogue to obey the summons'. Wright reported that the United Synagogue officers had declined to support the Beth Din and had 'preferred to fight the issue to the bitter end'.

An addendum to the motion, proposed by Frank Samuel, noted that 'the complainant's suit comes within the constitutional provision entrusting to the Chief Rabbinate the "supervision and control" of "the form of worship and all religious observances" in the Synagogue, and its "religious administration", and provides that the Chief Rabbi entrusts it to the Beth Din for examination on his behalf'.[10]

A month after the council meeting, which ended inconclusively, Waley Cohen reversed his year-long opposition and recommended the adoption of Wright's motion, adding that the Finchley officers had agreed to appear before the dayanim.[11] Stung by this display of disloyalty on the part of his lay lieutenants, Hertz vented his pent-up frustration in a *cri de coeur* to Waley Cohen and his team:

> Having disposed of those portions of your letter which deal, or evade dealing, with the Finchley Synagogue case, I must not neglect answering the other charges you level against me.
>
> You stigmatise my letter as 'the culminating effort to exercise a dictatorship in disregard of the constitution of the United Synagogue'. This is odd. It attributes to me the bearing and manner of 'dictatorship', which is notoriously characteristic of one of your own body.
>
> You wisely give no details; but, as it is a libellous charge, I must request you to furnish me with a list of those dictatorial efforts. And I assume you will accompany each item in that list with concrete details, and some evidence for the allegations made.
>
> In the meantime, you assure me that the authority of the Chief Rabbi 'has always been recognised and maintained by the honorary officers'. This assurance that you give me sounds like mockery. In confirmation, I need but bring a few memories which will clearly point out on which side real, and not imaginary, dictatorship is to be found.
>
> (a) You may still remember the abortive attempt made to destroy Jews' College by the introduction of an un-Orthodox 'Academy'. I fought that proposal with all my might because I deemed it fatal to Judaism; and the overwhelming majority of British Jews, whether

within or outside the United Synagogue, fervently applauded my stand. Not so the honorary officers of the United Synagogue. In that historic conflict, all the then honorary officers publicly voted against me!

(b) But to come to more recent cases of 'dictatorship':

1. In October 1943, Sir Robert appointed, without my knowledge, a minister of the Liberal Synagogue as temporary senior chaplain in circumstances that made it probable that he would become the permanent head of the Jewish chaplaincy department, at any rate 'to the end of the war'. As my protest was disregarded, I appealed to the Army Council, with the result that Rabbi Brodie is now the occupant of that responsible office.

2. When, three years ago, the Hampstead Synagogue printed a sermon of mine in which I urged the duties of kashrut and obedience to authority in Judaism, Sir Robert ordered the destruction of the whole edition of that printed sermon. I have never found out how it was destroyed, whether by fire or otherwise. 'Please don't press me', piteously pleaded the *parnas* [warden] when I asked him for details. At any rate, never before has a British Chief Rabbi's sermon been suppressed by the lay administrators of the community.

3. In 1939, Sir Robert would not consent to my giving a Passover address to thousands of German refugees at Richborough Camp. I placed the matter before the Marquess of Reading, the chairman of the Central Council. Sir Robert was *ordered* to invite me to give the address. This is further evidence of the loyalty to the Rabbinate on the part of the president of the United Synagogue!

4. Even stranger is the following act of *all* the honorary officers. When, as a result of the dispersion from the blitzed metropolis, United Synagogue groups sprang up in central and southern England, I asked to be furnished with a list of those associate synagogues, for the purpose of pastoral visitation. I received an official *refusal*. This was an astounding reply to have sent, and I called attention to it at the next meeting with you, in vain. So I went to Mr Lionel de Rothschild [the since-deceased president of the United Synagogue] and asked him point-blank whether he really wished me to take legal action. The list duly arrived.

5. This ardent desire to shut the doors of United Synagogue houses of worship in the face of the Chief Rabbi was accompanied by an attempt to eliminate me from the executive of the educational organisations. This was undertaken by several of the honorary officers, who decided against requiring the approval of the Chief Rabbi for syllabuses of instruction, and also against his certification of teachers. As

I could not consent to such monstrous proposals, the whole matter had to be placed before the public, and the president of the Board of Deputies had to intervene before you came to see that Jewish religious education was one of those 'subsidiary charities' of the United Synagogue which are 'under the supervision and control of the Chief Rabbi' (Deed of Foundation, 1871).

All the above instances – and they could be multiplied tenfold – show but too plainly how little the eight signatories of the last letter to me respect the rights and office of the Chief Rabbi. It seems that when you complain of the Chief Rabbi's 'dictatorship', you are adopting the all-too-human device of ascribing *our* failings to those whom we desire to discredit.

(c) You never tire of reiterating that 'the authority over financial and secular matters is vested solely in the council'. Everyone agrees; but you are not satisfied with this. You maintain, in effect, that whenever in any human situation a financial factor enters – and where does it not enter? – there the religious guidance by the Chief Rabbi is 'impertinent interference'.

Thus, in September 1938, I ruled that a male proselyte who had not undergone *milah* could not become a member of the United Synagogue. I am informed on high authority that when Sir Robert heard of this ruling, he fairly fumed over 'priestly dictatorship'.

I soon received a curt communication from him, telling me that admission to synagogue membership was a 'financial matter' and was no concern of the Chief Rabbi; and that the secretary of the synagogue in question had been instructed to disregard the interference of the Chief Rabbi, and to proceed with the membership admission. Though eventually, after I had met you, Sir Robert retreated from the untenable position taken up, there were the usual table-bangings.

This *milah* incident left an unpleasant memory behind it – namely, the readiness on the part of the honorary officers to abolish even the Abrahamic Covenant for a membership fee. Such definition of the financial came as a complete surprise to me, and fully justified me in my lament that there are leaders in Anglo-Jewry who, so to speak, are ready to tear down the Tables of the Law from the portals of our synagogues and replace them by the balance-sheet.

Your personal hostility to me leads you to defame me even to Government departments. I need not recall your Home Office denunciation. Though you proudly refer to it even in yours of 14 March, it was something distinctly damaging to the Jewish name, and against all ethical teaching. 'Thou shalt not bear false witness against thy neighbour.'

But enough. There is little more that I could say to induce you to give up your quixotic fight against the windmill of 'priestly dictatorship'. It is pure hallucination.[12]

\* \* \*   \* \* \*   \* \* \*

All this came to a bitter and lonely end on the morning of 14 January 1946, when Hertz, aged 73, died at home in his sleep – 'his strength sorely taxed by the many anxieties that beset his office'.[13] His wife and confidante, the former Rose Freed of New York, had predeceased him in 1930, 'cut off in the midst of her years',[14] leaving a fraught and increasingly fractious Chief Rabbi to face the effects on his divided community of the catastrophe unfolding in Nazi-occupied Europe. It was under these circumstances that the perception gained ground of Hertz's domination by the extreme right wing, feelings accentuated during the war.[15]

Despite this view, the *Jewish Chronicle* remarked in the week of his passing:

> It can be recorded without dispute that while – as with the general population in these islands – there was no great religious revival during his years in office, and while there was even a continuation of the weakening of religious ties which he could not arrest, he did succeed, as perhaps few others might have succeeded, not only in maintaining but in enhancing the supremacy and leadership of the British Chief Rabbinate.
>
> Many people in these islands, and still more abroad, realise what an invaluable asset to Jewish prestige and to the strength of British Jewry the Chief Rabbinate provides, and the years of office of Dr Hertz have very forcefully brought this fact to light.[16]

Describing Hertz as 'a spiritual warrior' conducting the 'staunch defence of Orthodoxy against the insidious attacks on the old paths made by Liberal Judaism', the New Synagogue's minister, Simon Lehrman, a close friend and trusted adviser, wrote:

> Dr Hertz was a dynamic and overtowering personality; small in stature, he was every inch alive.
>
> Glancing back at his stormy and eventful career, one can only admire his boundless energy, militant spirit, and the possession of the qualifications of spiritual and administrative leadership which are as welcome as they are rare.
>
> He was no mere 'yes man', securely ensconced in the Chief Rabbi's office, at all times cowered into submission by the monetary whims

and undigested views of the powerful lay leaders of Anglo-Jewry. He was more than a match even for them; for he was, at no time, an insignificant political puppet content to mouth platitudinous or conventional phrases of unctuous piety, aloof from the vital problems besetting the community.[17]

* * *  * * *  * * *

With Hertz's departure, Abramsky and his fellow dayanim came into their own. One of their number, Harris Lazarus, temporarily assumed the ecclesiastical mantle as Deputy for the Chief Rabbi, 'setting his face absolutely against appeasement'[18] in the wake of an ever-more strident Liberal advance. Abramsky had joined the Beth Din some months after Hertz's reluctant agreement to recognise the Liberal Synagogue as 'an organisation for purposes of worship' and had thus been precluded from influencing that decision. But he had published at the time a forthright denunciation, written in Yiddish and 'sent in his own name to all the rabbis of the British Empire',[19] branding the ruling as 'a mistake' and the Board of Deputies' position as usurping the authority of the Beth Din,

> the only body with the right to register marriages, as grounded in law. The true danger that emerges from this mistake [Abramsky had written] can be assessed only after clarifying a number of questions:
> 1. Will the Liberal Synagogue desist from conducting *chuppah* and *kiddushin* [religious marriage] when the woman's previous marriage was annulled only by civil divorce – when, that is, she did not receive a *get peturin* [Jewish bill of divorce] according to the law of Moses and Israel?
> 2. Can those who were 'converted' by the Liberal Synagogue be considered true proselytes when the [process of] their acceptance into the community of Israel does not include circumcision and ritual immersion, and is based solely on the convert's declaration of commitment to the laws of Israel?
> 3. Does the Liberal Synagogue refrain from performing *chuppah* and *kiddushin* between a Cohen and a divorced woman who, according to the Torah, may not marry each other?
> 4. Does the Liberal Synagogue have any interest in *chalitzah*,[20] and is it prepared to forgo registering a woman for marriage who should carry out this ceremony?
> 5. How does the Liberal Synagogue relate to the marriages of relatives who are forbidden by the law of Moses and Israel to enter them? Will it take note of the halachic requirements?

> 6. Does the Liberal Synagogue conduct *chuppah* and *kiddushin* according to all the details required by Jewish law, especially in respect of employing unqualified individuals, as our sages have warned us (Talmud, tractate Kiddushin, 13a): 'Anyone who does not know the peculiar nature of divorce and betrothal should have no business with them', since every detail is crucial, and even the slightest deviation from the demands of halachah could decisively result, heaven forbid, in sins of immorality and the disqualification of the halachic status of the family.
>
> All these questions unequivocally indicate the critical nature of this declaration. In warning our people, and protecting them against this painful error of granting a permit to the Liberals, I am supported by the Chief Rabbi and given his sanction to publicise the matter and to attract the attention of the wider community, so that every single Jew should know for himself and teach his children, that they, too, shall know and understand.[21]

Ten years after circulating his decree, and with a weakened Hertz only months from death, Abramsky was better able to stamp his authority. On his initiative, though with the Chief Rabbi's name heading the list of signatories,[22] a letter went out 'to all the communities of Israel in Great Britain' warning of the heightened dangers of intermarriage under wartime conditions. 'This abomination that has descended upon us in such abundance', they wrote, 'has destroyed all the "barriers" which the sages imposed, to the point where there are even community leaders married to Gentile women.'

After detailing the halachic status of such marriages, of the individuals involved, and of their offspring, the dayanim ruled – 'in order to preserve the continuity of our religion and of family pedigree' (*yichusin*) – that

> 1. The children of every Jewish male who marries a Gentile woman are considered Gentiles in every respect ... No mohel may circumcise them, lest he should cause the public to think that the child is now subject to the laws concerning a Jewish child.
> 2. A [Jewish] man married to a Gentile woman who has not been converted according to Jewish law is not prevented from praying in a synagogue or bet midrash; he is also deserving of [burial in] a Jewish cemetery. However, on the death of his wife or offspring, one should not involve oneself in their burials.
> 3. A Jew who marries a Gentile woman not converted according to Jewish law may no longer be counted as part of the Jewish community: there is no place for his philosophical outlook or his opinions.

Nor is he to be counted in any forum concerned with the Jewish religion, even if he was considered to be a member of the community before the publication of this announcement.[23]

By the time of Lazarus' incumbency, the stage was thus set for a showdown with the Liberals which, hitherto, Waley Cohen had been able to thwart. Now, as president of the United Synagogue but with Abramsky de facto at the helm, Hertz's nemesis began to find his wings clipped, as did the Board of Deputies in its parallel endeavours.

At the end of 1946, three more Liberal synagogues – North London, South London and Brighton – applied to the Board for the certification of marriage secretaries. They had chosen the interregnum as a convenient period to avoid recourse to a Chief Rabbi whom they did not recognise and who, for his part, was bound to repudiate responsibility for their practices. Their application was sanctioned by the Board's law and parliamentary committee, which supported the majority recommendation of a sub-committee that Clause 45 of the constitution, making certification dependent on ecclesiastical approval, be amended to include the words 'or, in the case of a Liberal synagogue, by a certificate from the president of the Liberal Synagogue, St John's Wood, London', following the reference to the ecclesiastical authorities.

Bernard Homa, who had come to Hertz's aid over the chaplaincy issue, was the dissenting voice on the three-man sub-committee. Moving to refer back the 'absolutely unconstitutional' amendment, he told his fellow deputies that it was their duty to defend the authority of the Chief Rabbi. 'No one can deny that Liberal Jews are Jews', he said, 'but that is different from a recognition that they are a religious section of the community.'

Godfrey Cherns, of Stoke Newington Synagogue, described Hertz's 1935 decision to issue a certificate to the St John's Wood Liberals as 'a major blunder' and asked, 'What have we to fear if they go to Parliament and ask for a special Act?' Opposing this view, George Webber, who had framed the amendment as a member of the sub-committee, described Homa's attitude as 'misguided', since the Board, he said, was 'composed of all sections of the Jews in the British Empire'. He was sure that in an English court of law, Liberal Jews would be regarded as professing the Jewish religion. 'Surely we do not want the Liberal Jews to go to Parliament as the Reform Jews did a hundred years ago.'

As the dispute deepened, the committee chairman, Reuben Lieberman, allowed the reference back. The debate, he warned, was 'developing into an argument over Orthodoxy and Liberalism' and there was a need to reach an understanding. The Liberals' president, Louis Gluckstein, responded that his synagogue would apply for redress to the president of the Board and that, if no progress were reached, they would 'take action ... A challenge has been thrown out and I accept it. We are not going to lie down under a stigma.'[24]

Others, too, accepted the challenge. Following the debate, the Chief Rabbi's office published the text of a *psak din* (religious ruling) by the dayanim which, it said, had been 'considered and defied' by the law and parliamentary committee. On the question of whether the Board – 'which comprises an overwhelming majority of representatives of Orthodox communities' – could authorise Liberal synagogues to solemnise marriages, the Beth Din had ruled that it was prohibited by Jewish law from doing so.

> To grant such authority would mean that the Board of Deputies gives in the name of the larger Orthodox community the consent to marriage by Liberal Jews, who ignore the marriage laws of the Divine Lawgiver as contained in the Torah, with the result that many of these marriages are invalid in Jewish law and the offspring of such marriages are *mamzerim* ...
>
> The responsibility of the members of the Board of Deputies is a very grave one indeed. The majority of these members are Orthodox Jews. They are now asked to give tacit consent to a marriage procedure which undermines the very foundation of our family life. The Orthodox members of the Board can never justify such an action before God and the history of our people.
>
> In the face of such a position, political considerations or striving after a false peace cannot count. If the Liberal Jews, after having been refused a certificate of marriage licence by the Board of Deputies, should decide to go Parliament and seek there to get what loyal Jews could never agree to give, the responsibility for what might result must lie with the Liberal Jews and not with the Board of Deputies.[25]

In a covering letter, sent with the *psak din* to every member of the Board, the dayanim wrote:

> The law and parliamentary committee of the Board of Deputies, in defiance of the decision of the Deputy for the Chief Rabbi and the Beth Din, have decided to recommend that the certification of marriage secretaries for Liberal synagogues be now permitted without reference to the ecclesiastical authorities and, for this purpose, are recommending a change of the constitution.
>
> We have, therefore, no alternative but to declare that it is the sacred duty of every Orthodox Jew who is a member of the Board of Deputies to vote against this recommendation. Any Jew who votes for

this recommendation or abstains from voting against it has on his conscience the terrible guilt of being *marbeh mamzerim b'Yisroel* [responsible for increasing the number of *mamzerim* in Israel].[26]

A resolution in support of the *psak din* was unanimously carried at an assembly of rabbis representing the United Synagogue, the Spanish and Portuguese Congregation, the Federation of Synagogues and the provincial congregations. In it, they described the Board's recommendation as 'amounting to official recognition of Liberal Jews as a body of persons professing the Jewish religion, although they deny the binding force of the Torah. As there is no Jewish religion without the Torah, such recognition can never be given.'[27]

Following an approach from Gluckstein, Mattuck issued a vigorous response to the Beth Din's ruling:

> The statement of the Beth Din cannot be allowed to stand unchallenged. The attitude which it adopts towards Liberal Jewish synagogues can be treated as simply another manifestation of religious intolerance.
>
> According to the relevant Act of Parliament, the president of the Board of Deputies is required to certify for marriages any congregation of Jews. In urging the Board to refuse this certification to a Liberal synagogue, the Beth Din would have the Board rule that a Liberal synagogue is not a congregation of Jews. Only intolerance could explain such a judgment.
>
> But the attitude of the Beth Din goes further, and with grave moral implications. It condemns all Jewish women who have received a divorce in a court of law, and have remarried without receiving a *get*, as adulteresses, and their children as *mamzerim*.
>
> There are such cases all over the world. In the United States, outside a very small section of Jewry, the *get* is completely ignored. It is truly a grave responsibility which the Beth Din assumes in stigmatising these women with the guilt of adultery.
>
> Can it be said of them with the slightest justification, as the Beth Din says, that they are living an immoral life and that their children are the offspring of immorality? They have divorced their former husbands, are no longer married to them. That is a legal fact, a social fact, and a moral fact.
>
> The law of the land has given them a divorce; and by the principle of *dina d'malchuta dina* [the law of the land is the law], even the Orthodox Jewish authorities must recognise the fact that where a court of law has pronounced a divorce, the marriage relation has ceased to exist – the woman is no longer the man's wife.[28]

Mattuck's rebuttal launched the sides into further confrontation, on both the theological and practical levels. Describing his statement as having 'at least one merit [in that] it shows clearly the true face of so-called Liberal Judaism', the dayanim declared:

> This clear position is of great value to Anglo-Jewry at the present juncture in its history ...
>
> Dr Mattuck, to whom the Talmud apparently means nothing, has the audacity to give the Beth Din guidance in talmudical law. 'By the principle of *dina d'malchuta dina*', he writes, 'even the Orthodox Jewish authorities must recognise the fact that where a court of law has pronounced a divorce, the marriage relation has ceased to exist.'
>
> Now even a schoolboy who is able to read the Talmud in its original and does not get his Jewish knowledge from textbooks on Liberal 'Judaism' knows that the talmudical dictum *dina d'malchuta dina* refers only to *dina mamanot* – laws relating to money matters – and not to Jewish marriage laws ...
>
> Dr Mattuck himself ... naively admits that those deserters from the Torah who come to him do so not for an idealistic urge but because they get from the Liberals what loyal Jews cannot grant them – their own heart's desire, against the demands of Jewish law. [He] omits, however, to enumerate among his recruits another category of people apart from those who want to be remarried by him without a divorce in Jewish law.
>
> We may as well mention this category here too. For often do we hear at the Beth Din, when we refuse, according to Jewish law, to allow co-respondents to marry their partners in adultery: 'If you do not allow us to marry in an Orthodox synagogue, we shall go to the Liberal Synagogue.' Such are the recruits the Liberal Synagogue gets from the ranks of deserters from Orthodoxy.[29]

In a continuing pendulum of invective and pilpulism, Mattuck denied saying or implying that the dictum of *dina d'malchuta dina* applied to the Jewish marriage laws. 'What I did say was that since the principle that "the law of the country is law" has been given a place in talmudic law, the Beth Din should not so far ignore an act of a civil court as to call women who remarry, after obtaining a civil divorce, adulteresses, and their children *mamzerim*.'

Of the dayanim's assertion that 'the guilty party to a divorce suit and the co-respondent need only apply to the Liberal synagogues to be married', he retorted: 'In my recollection, and according to the secretary's records, there have been just two such marriages at the Liberal Synagogue in

London in thirty-four years. And in each case the parties gave clear evidence that they had repented of their sin and had learned to appreciate the sanctity of marriage. And our interpretation of Judaism calls for forgiveness of sinners who repent.'

The opposition of the dayanim to Liberal Judaism, Mattuck concluded,

> cannot be news to the community, though the things they say about it must surprise anyone who has even an elementary knowledge of it, and an elementary sense of justice.
>
> Both the contents and tone of the virulent attack on Liberal Judaism only show that religious intolerance was the motive behind the Beth Din's attempt to stop the president of the Board of Deputies from giving marriage certification to Liberal synagogues. But the Beth Din supported its position by putting on thousands of Jewish women throughout the world who have remarried after obtaining a divorce in a civil court, and on their children, the stigma of adultery. That is the judgment I challenge.[30]

Threats of legal action by the Liberal authorities, and protracted negotiations with the Board of Deputies, led to deadlock between the parties. At one stage, the Board proposed arbitration, to which the Liberal Jewish Synagogue agreed on the understanding that the Beth Din would not be a party to it. Not unnaturally, the dayanim opposed this and, reluctant to proceed without their approval, the Board withdrew the proposal.

An abortive intervention by the Registrar General, following an approach from the South London Liberals – seeking confirmation that the congregation were 'professing the Jewish religion' – was sidestepped by the Board and a stalemate ensued. A further two years, and a Chief Rabbinical election, were to pass before the matter was raised again.

* * *   * * *   * * *

At the height of the controversy, the historian Cecil Roth spent some months abroad on a lecture tour. On his return to Britain, he wrote that he had found the communal scene

> radically changed. I do not think it an exaggeration to state that the Anglo-Jewish community which we knew, and in which most of us were brought up, has entirely collapsed.
>
> During the interregnum in the Chief Rabbinate, the Beth Din has issued a pronunciamiento not only that marriages conducted under the auspices of the Liberal Jewish congregations are invalid (which,

from their point of view, is obviously correct), but also that no 'Orthodox' Jews may do anything which even in the remotest fashion will suggest that they are [valid].

The obvious way out of the quandary thus presented was for the 'Orthodox' to absent themselves from the Board when this matter was being discussed (rabbinic ingenuity has got over worse difficulties before). But it seemed a heaven-sent opportunity for some of them to smite the Philistines, in association with others of the nationalist group whose Orthodox leanings are normally covert, to say the least.

They have been entirely successful. The Liberal Jewish communities are seeking redress by legal channels. But it will not be remarkable if, thus denied their title to the name of Jewish congregations, they cease to feel any sort of loyalty to the body which has hitherto been regarded as representative of the common interests of all British synagogues, of whatever religious viewpoint ...

The Liberal Jews ... were willing to acquiesce, however reluctantly, in the institution of the Chief Rabbinate as formally representing the community, so long as a certain degree of tolerance was maintained. But it is too much to expect them to maintain this attitude now that they have been declared by the Chief Rabbinate, *sede vacante*, to be entirely outside the bounds of Judaism. Thus, extremes are meeting; and it may be questioned whether a Chief Rabbinate so diminished will be a Chief Rabbinate at all.

The Jews of this country, and indeed of the Empire, enjoyed the benefits of this institution for the best part of a century and a half. Now, with all the good intentions in the world, it is being busily undermined from all sides, within and without; and unless a sense of responsibility triumphs at last, historians will look back on Joseph Herman Hertz as the last Chief Rabbi in the former sense.[31]

Anticipating such sentiments following Hertz's death, the *Jewish Chronicle* had written:

Dr Hertz's career did more than preserve a tradition: it exemplified, as never before, the vital functions of the Chief Rabbinate and its absolute indispensability to the welfare of Jewry in Great Britain and the Empire. It would be the crassest folly, therefore, to contemplate abolishing this precious office, or reducing its power, however difficult the task may prove once more to fill it.

For the community, as a whole, it represents the chief, if not the only, unifying power in British Jewry. To non-Jews, it is the symbol of that unity and the direction to which they more and more turn for the expression of Jewish views and wishes.

To eliminate or in any way reduce it, therefore, would be to invite disunity and confusion, to weaken the ties between the community and the State, to court the attentions of those who wish us ill, and to throw away an invaluable instrument of progress. Least of all in these critical and cloudy days can we afford to play fast and loose with an institution that has served us well and that holds within itself, as Dr Hertz has shown, infinite promise for future service ...

The community must be on its guard against any weakening of the powers of the Chief Rabbinate, a policy which would be sheer fatuity, robbing it of all its value and heading the community straight for chaos and disintegration.[32]

Of Hertz and his successor, the paper added: 'Let us pray that we may be so guided ... that the example he set may be carried on into the years to come, to the glory of God and the welfare of His people; for the memory of the righteous is blessed.' Such prayers were clearly in the minds of the selectors themselves, as United Synagogue secretary Philip Goldberg was later to note:

There is not, and cannot be, a Pope in Israel, nor can 'sanctions' – at any rate of an earthly character – be employed against the ordinary Jew or Jewess or Jewish organisation. The extent to which the Chief Rabbinate in this country and the Empire will be assured of loyal support and respect depends entirely on the hold which the individual whom the community shall choose is able to establish – by his high ideals, his exemplary character and life, his ability to promote co-operation and concord in the communities, and the maturity and wisdom of his judgment in dealing with the affairs of British Jewry on lines that are at once in conformity with the basic principles of our Traditional Judaism and the well-established order and procedure of Jewish congregational life in the 'free' countries of the diaspora.[33]

Names, policies and procedures were put forward, and debated, over a lengthy period, although Waley Cohen's preference was known all along to be Israel Brodie. Born in Newcastle in 1895, and educated at Jews' College, University College, London, and Balliol College, Oxford, Brodie had served twice as an army chaplain and, between times, as a minister in Newcastle, Hammersmith and (following semichah in 1923) Melbourne. As early as 1946, the United Synagogue president had regarded him, in relation to the post, as 'a determined individual, with personality ... a firm holder of

Orthodox opinion'.[34] That view prevailed when, in June 1948, the Chief Rabbinate Council made Brodie their unanimous choice.[35]

Unhappy about 'what seemed to be restrictions on his powers', he agreed to accept the invitation once 'given verbal assurances and written confirmation that his authority was unfettered',[36] adding that while he would 'willingly consult' on appropriate matters, he would nevertheless make his own decisions.[37] How 'unfettered' his authority turned out to be was, however, open to question. Indeed, almost from the outset, complaints were voiced that Brodie was 'too inclined to turn for guidance to his Beth Din, leaning on them perhaps to a greater extent than would have been expected',[38] and such suggestions were to be tested throughout his tenure.

The first such tests were not slow to arise – and, to judge from his initial apprehensions, not entirely unexpected. The true leader in Israel, he declared in his installation address,

> has to renew and strengthen our religious and moral preparedness to meet the challenge of the hour. Our lives have to be cleansed and sanctified. We need a spiritual purification to remove mean and sordid thinking, the battening sloth of smug selfishness, and the besetting sin of disunity.
>
> We have to strengthen those traditional defences which our sages tell us require constant support and firmer attachment – Torah, prayer, good deeds and worthy conduct. They must not be neglected or cheapened or become atrophied. Our tasks are very heavy indeed, but the end is glorious, and the enterprise worthy of all our endeavours.[39]

Even as the newly installed Chief Rabbi was defining these goals, the first steps were being taken to usurp his authority and that of his dayanim, to sow further in the community the 'besetting sin of disunity' he was at pains to disown. As the war had progressed, and the religious problems of marriage, divorce and conversion intensified, so did efforts gather pace within the Reform community to alleviate the ramifications highlighted by the Deputies controversy. Rates of intermarriage had soared, as became evident in the number of applications for conversion to the West London Synagogue, rising annually from around thirty before the war to more than 100 by its close.[40]

It was Reinhart's aim to establish a central Reform Beth Din in place of the *ad hoc* courts maintained by the individual congregations. The arrival of some thirty-five Reform rabbis as refugees from Nazi-occupied Europe facilitated the realisation of that hope, and the establishment, in 1942, of the Associated British Synagogues, following the Reform community's disillusionment over educational inequality, provided the platform for progress. By February 1948, the structure was in place and, despite a six-year delay in gaining recognition from the wider movement, the court was operational from its very inception.

Although independent of the Liberals' actions, the Reform Beth Din was in due course to occasion no less anxiety on the part of the Orthodox authorities. But for the time being, at least, it – and they – maintained a low profile. Not so, however, the Liberal agitators, who, within months of Brodie's accession, were once more on the march at the Deputies, renewing their case for marriage certification.

At a specially convened meeting of the Board, a resolution proposed by the Liberal Synagogue's Lady Hartog again sought to insert into Clause 45 of the constitution, after the reference to 'ecclesiastical authorities', the words 'or, in the case of a Liberal Jewish synagogue, by a certificate from the president of the Liberal Jewish Synagogue, St John's Wood Road, London'. Moving the amendment, Hartog said, she sought 'to remedy an injustice under which several of our congregations have been suffering for more than two years'. By accepting it, the Board would remove all cause for a repetition of the 'unfortunate controversy' that had followed the application by three of their synagogues.

> We recognise that it is wrong to place the Chief Rabbi and the Beth Din, the upholders of Orthodox Jewish law, in a position of any kind of responsibility in such a matter, or to ask them to do anything against their conscience. But we maintain that it is just as wrong to make any ceremony in a Liberal synagogue dependent on the sanction of a body that has no jurisdiction over it. Now the Board has the opportunity of ending an unjust, illogical and invidious situation without calling for any surrender of principle from any of the parties concerned.

Following Hartog's appeal, a ruling from Brodie was read to the deputies:

> Since my recent meeting with some of the honorary officers and three or four other members of the Board of Deputies at the offices of the Board, at which meeting my guidance was sought on certain religious matters, I have given particular consideration to the question then put to me concerning proposed changes in the clauses of the constitution dealing with the certification of secretaries for marriages.
>
> After long and serious deliberation, I have come to the conclusion that the effect of the proposed changes then put to me will involve the president of the Board of Deputies in committing himself and the

deputies (the great majority of whom represent Orthodox communities in the United Kingdom) to a wrongful and misleading impression that Liberal congregations, in the performance of marriages, conform to authoritative Jewish law.

I need not detail the wide social havoc that would consequently be created in Anglo-Jewry. An indication of the effect which marriages performed by Liberal congregations contrary to Jewish law is already having on the religious and social life of our community is evidenced in many of our communities, particularly the smaller ones.

I frequently receive letters from lay leaders and ministers of these communities in which they express their grave concern for the unity, integrity and future of their educational, religious and social institutions. Questions are submitted from them to the Beth Din on the religious rights and status of persons who have been married by Liberal synagogues and whose marriages cannot be recognised in Jewish law.

In almost all cases, the Beth Din finds itself confronted with difficulties and serious entanglements which are frequently incapable of resolution and bring domestic distress and communal disruption. I deem it my duty, therefore, definitely to advise that the proposed changes in the clauses of the constitution dealing with the certification of secretaries for marriages would be in their results contrary to Jewish law and would constitute a dangerous threat to the fabric of Judaism and Jewish life in this country. These changes should not be made.

A lengthy debate ensued, brought to an end by an assertion from the president, Selig Brodetsky, that 'there are only two ways to deal with the situation, one of which is to exercise toleration. A solution must be found that will not cause the break-up of the Board.' He appealed to his colleagues not to vote on the matter, but to settle it 'by means of some sort of discussion between the two sides – the Orthodox and the Liberals – so as to arrive at a solution that will satisfy the conscience of both without producing a break-up of the community'. He was supported by Barnett Janner, MP, who moved a resolution – carried unanimously – to adjourn the debate.[41]

After weeks of earnest discussion, Brodetsky announced his readiness to permit a revised amendment, adding to the original proposal the words 'testifying that the applicants do constitute a synagogue of persons professing the Jewish religion in the Liberal form'. However, when told that the Chief Rabbi had continued to oppose any constitutional changes, the Board rejected the revision by seventy-eight votes to sixty and, in consequence, the Liberal representatives walked out of the chamber.[42]

Following the vote, the Union of Liberal and Progressive Synagogues recommended its constituents not to elect deputies 'until the denial of rights by the Board to the Liberal Jewish congregations has been rectified'.[43] Moving a resolution to this effect at his synagogue's annual meeting, Gluckstein stated that 'we are now apparently described as "congregations of persons not professing the Jewish religion". What religion we are said to profess, if it is not the Jewish religion, I find it difficult to see.'

It was not their intention, he added, permanently to withdraw from the Board, but their self-respect, 'and the dignity of Liberal Judaism', demanded that they should no longer associate themselves with a Board that was capable of discriminating against their movement. 'As soon as the Board's constitution is amended to make it possible for the president to certify in accordance with the Act of Parliament, we shall certainly suggest that we should renew our membership.'[44] In solidarity, the North-Western Reform Synagogue passed a similar resolution, unanimously endorsed the following month, recommending its members to 'refrain from electing deputies until the Board's decision as to marriage secretaries be reversed, having regard to its implication that Liberal congregations are not congregations of persons professing the Jewish religion'.[45]

Away from the debating chambers, the halachic implications of the controversy were impacting heavily on Orthodox congregational life. At the Hampstead Synagogue, with its history of lax observance and reformist tendencies, Isaac Levy – later to feature prominently on the opposite side of the theological divide – felt it necessary to caution his flock on the dangers of flirting with Liberalism. He told them:

> A number of the members of this congregation have in the last few days expressed their anxiety, perturbed by the much-debated question of the marriage registration of the Liberal synagogues and the reflection which this problem seems to cast on the Orthodox community. Particular stress has been laid on the uncompromising attitude adopted by the leaders of the Orthodox community.
>
> It is because this thorny problem is so closely linked with the rabbinic interpretation of holiness that a word should be said on the subject, and efforts made to clear the atmosphere of misunderstanding. It is essentially the question of our approach to holiness and what that standard of conduct means to us. It is a question of morality and our conception of the sanctity of society.
>
> In recent years, the schismatic Liberal community has seen fit to discard the Jewish law governing Jewish marriage, divorce and marital morality, and they have replaced it by the acceptance of the secular law of the State, whatever that law may be and however frequently it

may change or vary at the discretion of the Government of the State. We are thus faced with an absurd situation.

There exists within the Jewish community an organised sect which contravenes all the accepted and basic practices of Traditional Judaism. They perform marriages which are considered utterly illegal by Jewish law. Men and women who, though separated by State legislation but who are yet bound by Jewish law, are married in the Liberal synagogues. Couples who are considered a forbidden union are nevertheless united in marriage ...

The Chief Rabbi has reached his decision, a difficult decision, after much heart-searching; and from my own intimate knowledge of the problem – for I was privileged to serve on the special communal sub-committee which investigated marriage guidance and its place within the Jewish community – I can affirm with assurance that intolerance in this connection is not the prerogative of one section of the Anglo-Jewish community.

We are facing a possible crisis in the community. We must take our stand fearlessly and not be terrorised by the threat of Liberal secession. For they will secede at their own peril just as other anti-traditional sects have done in the past. They may depart from the organised body of the community, but if they do, they spell their own doom. For they will be lost to Judaism, and within a generation no trace of them will exist.[46]

Three days after this sermon, a call for action issued forth from Brodie at the Conference of Anglo-Jewish Preachers in London, the first under his leadership.[47] Referring to the Liberal marriage controversy and to its implications world-wide, he told the assembled ministers:

We are living at a time when there is such lack of discipline that it becomes more than ever necessary to see authority properly established and enthroned. A Sanhedrin should be established, with close association to our communities; yet, while many will look to it for *heteirim* [dispensations], will they be prepared to accept its decision when it says that a thing is *assur* [forbidden]?

Unless we of the Orthodox wing stand together and are prepared to champion our Orthodoxy and interpret it as it should be, then far from my being accused of splitting the community because of the decision I gave, the Liberal or Progressive movement is going to destroy and disrupt the whole fabric of our Anglo-Jewish life.[48]

Later that year, undeterred by his drubbing at the hands of the dayanim,

Mattuck (by then emeritus minister of the Liberal Synagogue)[49] re-entered the fray, defending his movement's marriage ceremony as 'having a wholly religious character'. It was, he declared,

> based on four general principles: that, in marriage as in other matters, the spiritual and fundamental moral principles of Judaism must be applied in practice; that marriage is a religious — a spiritual and moral — relationship, not a contractual arrangement; that husband and wife have, according to the accepted principle of Western civilisation, equal status; and that the law of the land cannot be ignored where it applies. This implies a limited extension of the rabbinic principle that 'the law of the land is law'.[50]

On behalf of the Chief Rabbi and his fellow dayanim, Grunfeld responded to Mattuck's assertions with a withering tirade. Detailing the differences between their philosophies and application of Jewish law, and inveighing against 'the alien creed called "Liberal" Judaism which undermines the very foundations of Jewish life and creed', he wrote:

> Between those who deny the divine origin of the Torah and those for whom *Torah min hashamayim* is a reality, there is obviously no common basis for a discussion on Judaism.
>
> Experience at the Beth Din during the last few weeks has shown us that the misleading statements of the head of the Liberal Jewish movement have indeed misled a good many people, have interfered with the very foundations of their family life ...
>
> Once the binding authority of Divine Law is dethroned by our own people, and so-called 'progressive revelation' takes its place, it means a deification of the most dangerous enemies of all moral authority: subjectivity, individualism, and the spirit of the age.
>
> The Divine Law of the Torah has led us safely through all the vicissitudes of our history. If we put human individualism in place of the Divine Law, there can be only one result: 'There is a way that seemeth right unto a man, but the end thereof are the ways of death.'[51] Anglo-Jewry beware! Life and death have been put before you. Which will you choose?[52]

\* \* \*   \* \* \*   \* \* \*

Anglo-Jewry clearly experienced difficulties with this life-and-death dilemma. Despite an assurance by Brodie at the subsequent Preachers' Conference — that 'the arrival of Jews hailing originally from the great centres of Judaism in East and Central Europe will guarantee the further maintenance of Judaism in the lands of the British Commonwealth, strengthening Jewish consciousness expressed in terms of belief, learning and observance'[53] – the stability of Jewish family life in Britain was looking bleak indeed. By the time of the tenth Preachers' Conference, two years later, Grunfeld was reporting grim statistics, with a further prognostication of life versus death:

> As far as the Anglo-Jewish scene is concerned, we have a means of getting a rough idea of the number of intermarriages, by comparing the number of applications for proselytisation at the Beth Din with the number of applications for regular Jewish marriages at the Chief Rabbi's Office. As both proselytisation and marriages are centralised at the London Beth Din and the Chief Rabbi's Office respectively, the ratio of both gives a picture of the position of intermarriage in the whole of England.
>
> The average number of applications for marriage at the Office of the Chief Rabbi is two thousand per year; the average number of applications for proselytisation at the Beth Din is two hundred per annum. If one compares these figures, one comes to the most unpleasant conclusion that at least ten per cent, but probably 12.5 per cent, of the marriages of Jews in England are marriages out of the faith.
>
> This estimate is a conservative one, if one considers the following points. Those who apply for proselytisation are not all the candidates for intermarriage, as many of those who intend to marry a non-Jewish person simply do not care to have their intended partner in marriage accepted into the Jewish faith.
>
> In addition, there are those who apply for proselytisation to the Liberals or Reformers, where proselytisation is made much easier. Among those who apply to the Beth Din, about sixty per cent were previously married in the civil registry office. About ten per cent of the Beth Din applications come from such people who have been previously received into Judaism by the Liberals or Reformers but do not feel happy about it, and want to regularise their acceptance in the proper Orthodox way.[54]

\* \* \*   \* \* \*   \* \* \*

At this moment, there entered upon the communal stage Redcliffe Nathan Salaman, an eminent geneticist, Fellow of the Royal Society, and one-time member of Jews' College council.[55] As a former president of the Jewish Historical Society, he was appearing in the communal hall of the West

London Synagogue to deliver the annual Lucien Wolf lecture – in memory of the Society's founder – and had chosen to discuss the transformation of Anglo-Jewish life over the previous half-century and the shifts in religious behaviour to which he had borne witness. In the eighty-strong audience, despite its Reform setting, was Israel Brodie, who was scheduled to deliver a vote of thanks.

After analysing the growth of the two extremes, Salaman observed that

> during the last thirty years we have witnessed in all social relations, and not least in the realm of religion, a general atmosphere of liberalism and a wider tolerance between sects. Some might consider that religious leaders had gone some way to meet the lax and the indifferent, but that, I believe, would be a misreading of the facts, at least as far as Anglo-Jewry is concerned.
>
> Before the outbreak of the first war, the community was so well integrated, so conscious of its threefold task – the maintenance of its poor, the avoidance of any occasion for ill-feeling at home, and the assistance and protection of its brethren abroad – that neither religious nor lay leaders were unduly concerned with the attitude of the individual towards religious observance or belief. Nevertheless, a spirit of secularism and apathy was beginning to be evident in the Jewish, as it was in the Christian, world.
>
> In recent years, a limited reaction has set in: the conservative elements in both communities are demanding a return to the traditional religious discipline of an earlier generation ... Our [own] religious leaders appear to be more afraid of offending the ultra-Orthodox minority than of losing that rapport with the general Jewish public which was so notable a feature of Anglo-Jewry in the past.
>
> I do not know whether the Churches will succeed in their new policy, but I am confident that it will be found impracticable to persuade large sections of the Jewish community to accept rulings and decisions on matters of social and religious behaviour which are felt to be out of harmony with the spiritual aspirations of a cultured people.
>
> It is in this relation that one feels disturbed at the proposal of creating a *shaatnez*[56] bureau and the launching of a campaign for kosher clothing. More distressing are the policies which make the admission of converts all but impossible, the refusal to grant the privilege of registering marriage licences to the more recently created Liberal synagogues, and the continued denial to Jews of the right of cremation unless the ashes are interred in a coffin and masquerade as a corpse.
>
> Such matters as these would appear to be evidence of the direction

in which ecclesiastical policy is tending to advance – or, should we not rather say, retreat ...

The most alarming illustration of ecclesiastical policy occurred this year. A letter from the Chief Rabbi's Office appeared in the Jewish press addressed to all teachers, ministers and chairmen of local education committees, instructing them that those children whose mothers were technically not Jews must not be allowed to join, or remain in, religion classes under the authority of the United Synagogue.

In short, what we have been taught to believe was a priceless treasure of the spirit is to be denied to innocent children who do not happen to have secured to themselves mothers of unimpeachable Jewish birth. Surely this is endowing racialism with a value which today few of us are ready to give it.

No one will doubt the sincerity of the Chief Rabbi or his advisers, nor fail to sympathise with them in their difficult task of upholding tradition. But these considerations should not blind us, or them, to the fact that unless policy is attuned to the total environment, it will sooner or later fail.

The human environment transcends the summation of the material, spiritual, political, social and economic forces which impinge on man from birth to grave, for beyond them remains the controlling element, the maturing conscience of the individual. A policy which fails to take account of the progressive character of this element cannot hope to succeed in an era of intellectual freedom.[57]

Well before the lecture ended, Brodie was on his feet – 'pale and obviously angry'[58] – to register his protest. 'I find this most intolerable', he declared. 'We were invited to hear a Lucien Wolf memorial lecture, but all we have heard has been one sheer castigation of Orthodoxy – one which is painful to those of us who hold dear everything Jewish.' Salaman retorted: 'I must speak the truth as I find it' – and continued his address, ignoring several members of the audience who 'rose from their seats and noisily walked out of the meeting'. Before the interruption, it was noticeable that Brodie had viewed the sentiments expressed 'with considerable disapproval'.[59] He was seen to speak to the chairman – the Society's president, Bertram B. Benas – who had sought to restrain him from voicing his agitation.

Still clearly furious, Brodie again rose to his feet at the conclusion of the lecture and, in lieu of a vote of thanks, began to harangue Salaman for his 'most disappointing' address. While he was the first to concede, he said, that anyone who presented a case before the public should be 'animated with earnestness and sincerity', and should have his facts 'well marshalled' before making statements, so many forecasts of doom had been made that he could only conclude that the data available to the lecturer were 'most incomplete. Not only do we have to endure the criticisms and forebodings of those who are outside the community, but there are those in our own midst who pass judgment and rely on facts which are not full or complete.' In using 'a tone of irony with a tinge of mocking', the Chief Rabbi concluded, 'Dr Salaman has done a great disservice to the cause. I regret having to say this, but I have the same excuse as the lecturer – love of truth, and earnestness.'[60]

\* \* \*   \* \* \*   \* \* \*

Six years later, the issue of Liberal marriage secretaries was finally settled – and, as Hertz had predicted, through parliamentary means. On 17 February 1959, the Marriage (Secretaries of Synagogues) Bill passed through its committee and report stages; a day later, it was given its third and final reading; and on the following day, it received the royal assent. Originating in the Commons as a 'non-controversial measure' on the initiative of Sir Keith Joseph, and with the support in the Upper House of Lord Cohen of Walmer (both 'subscribers' to the Liberal Jewish Synagogue), the Act accorded to Liberal Jews the same right as the Reform had obtained in nominating marriage secretaries direct to the Registrar General without having to go through the Board of Deputies.

Making this point during the second reading – as the 'most satisfactory way out of the difficulty involving Liberal Jewish marriages' – Cohen had told his peers:

> When the new congregations of Liberal Jews were started, the Orthodox ecclesiastical authorities began to have doubts as to whether it was right to recognise them as congregations professing the Jewish faith.
>
> Your Lordships may think that I am perhaps suggesting that the ecclesiastical authorities are very tiresome people. But the exact meaning of 'Jewish faith' has been a matter of trouble not only to the Jewish ecclesiastical authorities but to your Lordships when sitting in a judicial capacity. It was not so long ago when your Lordships finally decided that the expression 'Jewish faith' was so uncertain that it had no meaning.[61]

The legislation, wrote a communal observer,

> lays to rest – for the time being – a bitter controversy which at one

time threatened a serious rift in the Anglo-Jewish community ...

The attitude of the Beth Din, which retained control of the situation on the religious side, made the idea that the president [of the Board of Deputies] certify the marriage secretaries of Liberal synagogues impossible. Ecclesiastical authority could not tolerate an olive branch in the shape of a declaration that Liberal synagogues were 'Jewish congregations', though it was later able to accept the formula that they were 'congregations of Jews'.

With this to satisfy honour, and a promise from the Board that it would not oppose legislation to rectify the situation if the Liberals were able to promote it, the breach was healed, or at least papered over.[62]

# 14

# Scraps of Paper

With the Liberal marriage settlement securely in place, the spotlight shifted back to the Reform arena. By 1954, the movement's Beth Din had received official recognition from its constituent bodies and, following further discussions over a two-year period, its Assembly of Ministers had set the standards required of Reform conversions:

> In accordance with Jewish tradition, we recognise the right of Gentiles, who are able to prove their fitness, to be accepted into the Jewish community, and we desire, in charity, to give such assistance as we can.
>
> A person who desires to be accepted into Judaism should, subsequent to a preliminary interview with the minister, be recommended by him for such instruction and observances as will give that person the opportunity to qualify as a Jew. The period of preparation must depend in each case on individual circumstances, but it is understood that, as a general rule, the length of tuition cannot be less than nine months to a year.
>
> The recommendation for such a person to present himself (or herself) before the Beth Din must come from a minister of the Association of Synagogues of Great Britain. The decision for acceptance into Judaism rests with the Beth Din.[1]

Over time, the 'Court of the Assembly of Ministers' had evolved into the 'Court of the Association of Synagogues of Great Britain' and subsequently into the 'Court of the Reform Synagogues of Great Britain', also styling itself *Beth Din Zedek* ('Court of Righteousness') to reflect 'its firm position and its confidence in its role'.[2] This last appellation aroused the wrath of the London Beth Din, with Dayan Morris Swift describing it as 'a departure from honesty'.[3] The Reform movement, he declared, 'has printed letters similar to those of the London Beth Din, on behalf of the *Beth Din Zedek*. That is a deception, as it is neither a Beth Din nor *Zedek*, and there can be righteousness only when it fits in with the *din*. There is nothing more righteous or just than the Torah, and when our Beth Din rejects an application, it is because of the iron wall of the *din*.'[4]

Gone were the days when relations between dayanim and Reform ministers on matters of conversion were 'mutually cordial, both on a personal level and institutionally'.[5] In 1930, Gollop, of the London Beth Din, had felt comfortable in writing to Simmons at West London, regarding a prospective convert engaged to a nominally observant Jew: 'The fact that the gentleman concerned is not a strictly Orthodox Jew would seem to point to her being more at home with you than with us. It would be almost absurd to train an applicant for strictly Orthodox Judaism when the man she proposes to marry does not observe the religion she is presumed to undertake. I see no reason why you should not deal with the case if he wishes to place it in your hands.'[6]

Similarly, observant applicants to Berkeley Street were occasionally referred to the London Beth Din. But by the late 1950s, when intermarriage was rife and proselytisation a thorny issue, the relationship had soured and the battle lines were drawn. Applicants rejected or left in abeyance by the Orthodox dayanim were accepted by the Reform Beth Din following tuition:[8] 'They came to us not as "rejects" on moral grounds, but because their Jewish partners could not comply with the ritual demands made on them by the Orthodox authorities.'[9]

The Reform rabbis were anxious to stress, however, that such traffic had never been their intention and for several years made no attempt to publicise their court. The London Beth Din, initially at least, ignored its existence, although the wider campaign against Reform soon gathered momentum. The opening salvo was fired by Brodie at the first Conference of European Rabbis, in Amsterdam, when he cited the biblical Abraham as

> the pattern of the complete Jew, to whom all aspects of Judaism are equally significant and mandatory.
> 
> The practical observance and the moral teachings and principles of faith constitute a whole Judaism. Our quarrel with some of our opponents is that they take one aspect of Judaism and ignore or belittle other aspects; they will emphasise the ethical side of Judaism, for example, and say it alone is to be preferred.
> 
> As far as the halachah is concerned, they almost throw it overboard, retaining only those features of it which can be useful to them, because of their realisation that you cannot have a characterless Judaism consisting merely of a few ethical principles and their application in conduct. There is nothing uniquely Jewish in this, because our neighbours of other denominations observe the Noahide Laws, which contain the fundamental ethical principles of Judaism.
> 
> Abraham represents the perfect example of the type of Jew whose

Judaism is comprehensive. We object to the caricatures which are presented of the Orthodox Jews — as those who devote themselves exclusively to the ritual aspects of Judaism.[10]

The declaration of war — for that was its cry — came three years later when, in the seaside town of Westcliff, the second Conference of European Rabbis took up arms against those who had 'separated themselves from the mainstream of Jewish life'.[11] Ber Rogosnitzky, the Communal Rav of Cardiff, set the tone with his defiant declaration: 'It is time we go out to war against the Reform and Liberal movements, this *chevrat mechalalei Shabbat* [association of Sabbath desecrators]. The *cherem* of the Chatam Sofer,[12] which decreed complete separation from Reform and Liberal Jews, must be upheld on every occasion.'

It was indeed time, the Chief Rabbi agreed, 'to go over to the offensive, for we have been on the defensive for too long and too much. We have to assert ourselves, not because we want any power, but to bring back into Jewish life the values without which Jewish life has no meaning.'

Responding to this call, in a resolution aimed directly against the Liberals and Reform, the 'custodians and teachers of Jewish law' (as the conference delegates styled themselves) called on the Jewish public 'not to be parties to marriages, divorces or conversions contrary to Jewish law, in order to prevent irreparable personal tragedies and to preserve the unity of the Jewish people'.

Swift, demanding a prohibition 'against mixing with Reform and Liberal Jews even on festive occasions', asserted that 'they falsify the Torah and present a greater danger than any previous schismatic group in Judaism because of their deception in parading as religious Jews'. He called for the establishment of a central record office of *mamzerim*, 'so that when a *mamzer* is born in London, it shall be known also in New York, Paris or Tel Aviv'.

Concurrent with this call, there appeared — in Hebrew — a pronouncement 'from the Court of the Chief Rabbi to all *batei din*, rabbis and ministers' which set the seal on their declaration of war. Headed 'To Remove A Stumbling-Block', it decreed:

> We wish to draw your attention to a serious and urgent matter. In this country, there exists an organisation known as 'Reform Synagogue' which calls itself 'Association of Synagogues in Great Britain'. Of late, they have ventured to issue documents in matters of marriage and divorce, proselytisation, etc., under the heading 'Court of the Association of Synagogues in Great Britain'.
>
> They deliberately mislead the public to believe that this is a real Beth Din and that their actions are according to the laws of the Torah

and the religion of Israel. In fact, they directly undermine all the foundations of the halachah and take no notice of the principles of the Shulchan Aruch, particularly in matters of marriage and divorce, proselytisation and family relationships, which have been sanctified for generations.

All their actions are in sharp contradiction to the laws and principles of the Torah, causing havoc in the personal and family life of our brethren in the diaspora. Of course, their actions have no validity and are completely worthless, while their documents are mere scraps of paper.

In view of the above, we consider it our sacred duty to call upon all *batei din* and other rabbinical authorities carefully to examine all certificates in religious matters which they may receive from this country, and to ensure that they do not emanate from the source indicated above. In all cases where there is the slightest doubt, the rabbinical authorities are requested to communicate direct with us.[13]

\* \* \* \* \* \* \* \* \*

Little note was taken at, or after, the Westcliff conference of another appeal by Brodie[14] which was to have far-reaching implications over the coming years. Defining the movements which, he said, 'threaten the integrity of Jewish life', he gave what he described as 'an emphatic warning' directed at the United Synagogue of America:

This body, which represents the Conservative elements in the United States and Canada, is now making an attempt to spread its wings and to have a world organisation. As far as Jewish communities in Europe are concerned which rally under the flag of the Torah, there can be no association with this movement. We shall discourage and resist these efforts by the Conservatives of America to infiltrate into Europe, even if they may speak to us in terms of traditional Judaism.

\* \* \* \* \* \* \* \* \*

The dayanim's 'stumbling-block' declaration was the first public manifestation of a new, sustained and ultimately counter-productive campaign by Brodie and his Beth Din – now dominated by Swift since Abramsky's retirement to Israel some years earlier – to combat the 'havoc in the personal and family life of our brethren in the diaspora' and the 'worthlessness' of the Beth Din Zedek's 'scraps of paper'.

The pronouncement attracted widespread comment in the press and the community and, ironically, provoked an ever-growing number of requests for Reform conversion and other family procedures, involving, in the main, applicants engaged or married to Jews from Orthodox backgrounds.[15] Other, more tangible, measures were introduced by the Chief Rabbi, including a ban on the use of United Synagogue premises by those whose weddings, barmitzvahs or other religious ceremonies were not solemnised in synagogues under his authority.[16]

The campaign intensified, in 1962, with the publication of a Beth Din booklet on Jewish marriage and divorce, written by Swift and with a foreword by Brodie. Opening with the talmudic quotation cited by Abramsky in his earlier decree – 'Anyone who does not know the peculiar nature of divorce and betrothal should have no business with them', – the Chief Rabbi wrote:

> This exhortation and warning, first uttered by the great *amoro* [interpreter] Samuel,[17] is directed against those who are ignorant of the laws, forms and procedures which alone give validity to deeds of divorce and marriage.
>
> The words of the sage go further, however. They are directed against those who, through ignorance or witting disregard, pay no heed to the divine sanctions of the marriage laws nor to the nature and purpose of the institution of marriage. Such heedlessness can have moral, social and psychological consequences affecting the lives of individuals, disrupting families and threatening the fabric of society.
>
> The present booklet, issued under the auspices of the London Beth Din and prepared by Dayan M. Swift, is an attempt to dispel some of the ignorance which prevails in the community concerning Jewish laws of marriage and divorce. It is written in the light of the many unfortunate cases that come before the Beth Din which often present insuperable difficulties and tragic human situations.
>
> When so much is being written on the decline of public and private morality in the modern world, and particularly in matters of sex, pre-marital chastity and marital fidelity, this booklet, with its simple and direct exposition of the Jewish approach to such problems, is indeed timely.[18]

Swift devoted the bulk of the publication to the laws of Jewish marriage, divorce and *chalitzah*, before concluding with a lengthy denunciation of the Reform developments. At no time in the past, he wrote, had the Beth Din been so profoundly concerned with the deterioration of Jewish family life in this country as today. The very foundation of this glory of Judaism is now in jeopardy because of the growing ignorance, among our young people in particular, of the divine laws that govern Jewish marriage and its dissolution ...

For the first time in the history of the Anglo-Jewish community, a 'Beth Din Zedek' under the auspices of the Association of Synagogues in Great Britain has made its appearance, with letterheads printed not unlike the letterheads of our own Beth Din. This is a presumption of the historic and acknowledged use of a title which, from time immemorial, has been applied to a body of rabbis who administer Jewish law according to the *din*.

'Beth Din' is an authoritative status given to a body of men who administer the *din*. Where there is no *din*, there is no beth din. Never before have so-called progressive elements claimed to possess such a body. This is now a direct invasion of religious territory which they have never hitherto claimed.

Anglo-Jewry must be guarded against the danger of their practices, particularly in cases of marriage, divorce and conversions. Their rulings are not recognised by any authentic rabbinic body in the world. In Jewish law, the *get* they issue is no *get*, and the conversions they perform have no validity ...

As a result of their widespread interference with our marriage laws, the term 'intermarriage', which hitherto applied to marriages 'out' of the Jewish fold, now applies equally to many marriages within the Jewish fold. Many of the marriages performed by them have no validity in Jewish law and have made a tragic impact on hundreds of Jewish families in this country; they have caused untold pain and suffering to the issue of these marriages which can never be repaired.[19]

In response to the publication, the Reform Assembly of Ministers issued a statement defending 'the sacred character' of its marriages and upholding the validity of its court; lay members of the movement threatened an action for libel against the London Beth Din; and the Chief Rabbi held a covert meeting with Werner Van der Zyl, the Assembly's chairman, and senior minister at Berkeley Street.[20]

In their statement, the Reform ministers emphasised that

respect for the sanctity of Jewish marriage and, what is equally as important, of the Jewish home which is subsequently established, is one of the cornerstones of Reform Jewish teaching.

The religious leaders of the Reform movement try as hard as they can to inculcate in the participants to the marriage the realisation that the ceremony beforehand must inaugurate a life and home built up on the strongest religious and moral foundations, and is even more vital in our modern day and age, when too much immorality and licence are practised and countenanced.

The solemnisation of the marriage, known in Jewish tradition as *kiddushin*, is therefore very much the core and essence of Reform Jewish practice and is the theme which pervades the whole ceremony. It is basically traditional and completely within the framework of Jewish halachic development.

There is nothing in the ceremony as at present performed in Reform synagogues which is contrary to halachic teaching. Far from it. The divine precept established in the Torah and later developed by rabbinic authorities, and summed up in the most important sentence in the marriage ceremony – 'Behold, thou art consecrated unto me with this ring according to the Law of Moses and of Israel' – is faithfully followed by Reform Jewish practice.

This, it must be stated, refers specifically to marriage between Jews whose religious status cannot be questioned by any Jewish authority in the country. There are a few instances where Orthodox Judaism may raise objections because they differ from their practices, as, for example, in the case of *chalitzah*, and marriage between a Cohen and a divorcee. But these form a very small part of the whole. They are the exception, not the rule.

Any doubts, therefore, about the legitimacy of the children of parents married at a Reform synagogue are not only completely baseless so far as Jewish teaching is concerned, but the expression of them is unwarranted. For it must surely be known to all aspiring to have Jewish knowledge in this matter that, where parents are both 'professing the Jewish faith', the marriage performed in a Reform synagogue is religiously *k'dat Moshe v'Israel* and legally 'according to the usages of the Jews'.

The allegation that the Beth Din of the Reform Synagogues of Great Britain is unhistoric is quite without foundation. Reform Judaism, like Judaism of all ages, has acknowledged development and progress and has tried to integrate into Jewish life all that is best in this progress and development.[21]

The libel threat was dropped, but not before Brodie was said to have given an assurance that copies of the booklet, having been exhausted, would not be reissued. In his meeting with Van der Zyl, held without the knowledge of the United Synagogue officers, the Chief Rabbi raised issues of marriage, divorce and conversion; hinted that if *tevilah* (ablution) were introduced, recognition of Reform proselytes might be granted; and confirmed that, 'as far as he was concerned, marriages in Reform synagogues between halachically acceptable Jews were valid'.[22]

When Van der Zyl suggested increased co-operation between the different sections of Anglo-Jewry, Brodie replied that he 'wished to settle the Beth Din questions first'. The meeting, however, led to no rapprochement, and the Reform Beth Din 'continued as an oft-used alternative to the Chief Rabbi's Court'.[23] In a statement, it justified its right

> to develop the Law and to adapt it to the changing conditions of the centuries, as was the aim of our great teachers in former times.
>
> Lack of courage, and rivalry among the religious leaders, have brought a factual standstill in the development of Jewish Law, which has resulted in a rigid legalism that bears no longer any relation to the needs of the Jewish community. That is why we have instituted our own Beth Din – not to abrogate the Law, but to develop it again. In all humbleness and in true Jewish spirit, we endeavour to make it again the living force that it has always meant to be.[24]

\* \* \*    \* \* \*    \* \* \*

While Brodie had, according to the West Londoners, indicated his willingness to 'validate' Reform marriages between halachically acceptable Jews, other 'subversive elements' were receiving shorter shrift. Some three years later, the Liberals' Sidney Brichto,[25] who was to assume a major role in the controversy over the coming years, had occasion to refer to

> rumours which can only cause greater dissension in our already regrettably divided community. It is being suggested in certain circles that the marriage ceremony of Liberal and Progressive synagogues is not recognised as religiously valid by Orthodox Jewish authorities.
>
> The Orthodox may refuse to accept as valid those few marriages in which they consider one or both parties to be ineligible – for example, a divorcee without an Orthodox *get*, a case involving *chalitzah*, an *agunah* ['chained wife'],[26] etc. However, where marriages are performed in Liberal and Progressive synagogues between two Jews whose eligibility for Jewish marriage is unquestionable, even according to their own rulings, I challenge any responsible spokesman of

Orthodox Judaism to state publicly and categorically that such marriages are invalid. As they cannot question the validity of these marriages, I would call upon all Orthodox rabbis to refrain from causing personal distress and communal friction, either by encouraging these false and malicious rumours or by allowing them to go unchecked.'[27]

Swift rose to the challenge. Addressing a London social gathering, he asserted that Reform and Liberal marriages could be considered valid, but 'no more so than those performed in a register office [which were not valid marriages in Jewish law]. They are merely contractual agreements between men and women and lack any sanctity.'[28] The London Beth Din's clerk, Marcus Carr, confirmed that 'this is a view that can be taken as the considered opinion of all the dayanim', while Dayan Isaac Golditch, of the Manchester Beth Din, said that such marriages 'are no different from cases where people cohabit. Participants in a Reform or Liberal synagogue marriage are being misled into thinking they are taking part in a valid ceremony.'[29]

Dayan Michael Fisher, chairman of the Federation of Synagogues' rabbinate, declared: 'My conscience cannot allow me to say that Reform or Liberal marriages are valid. They are not properly constituted.' Marriages, he stated, required two witnesses, and in the case of Reform or Liberal ceremonies, the witnesses – for example, the minister and the reader – were *posul* (invalid). 'They flout the laws of the Shulchan Aruch. The *ketubah* [marriage certificate] and the blessings are not properly made, and there are other reasons to invalidate the ceremonies. Participants in such marriages cannot live as man and wife: they are not wedded *k'dat Moshe v'Yisrael.*'[30]

On the other hand, Hampstead's Isaac Levy, who fifteen years earlier had waged war on 'the schismatic Liberal community' and their 'utterly illegal' marriages, now changed his tune. Preaching in the same pulpit, he said of the dayanim's remarks: 'While many of us are devoting our lives to the reconstruction of the shattered remnants of Jewry, it is utterly irresponsible for those who give expression to such views to attempt to break down the unity of the Jewish people.'[31]

Similar sentiments were expressed by Swift's brother, Harris Swift, at the traditionally untraditional Western Synagogue. Voicing 'surprise' that the dayan had 'made an issue of the matter', he commented: 'In my opinion, a marriage that takes place in a Reform synagogue is not invalid. A *get* presupposes marriage. Once it is admitted that a marriage at a Reform synagogue requires a *get*, then, *ipso facto*, that marriage must be valid. You cannot have "valid" for a *get* and "invalid" for a marriage.'[32]

Stronger and more authoritative condemnation of the dayanim came in a joint statement from the ministers' conference of the Union of Liberal and Progressive Synagogues and the ministers' assembly of the Reform Synagogues of Great Britain:

> We wish to make it abundantly clear that all marriages solemnised in our synagogues have complete validity under the law of the land and are recognised by the Registrar General as being in accordance with the usages of the Jews.
>
> We further reaffirm – and this has never before been officially challenged – that, where the eligibility of the partners to marry each other is unquestionable, even from the point of view of Orthodoxy, such marriages are unimpeachable on the basis of rabbinic law, for they satisfy all its essential requirements.
>
> It is significant that the reported remarks of Dayan Swift, Mr M. Carr and Dayan I. Golditch, concerning the validity of marriages solemnised in Reform and Liberal synagogues, are not in the form of an official statement from the London or Manchester Beth Din. It is surprising that a dayan should make a pronouncement on a matter of such seriousness, affecting the lives of countless fellow-Jews the world over, in the light-hearted atmosphere of a *melava malka*.[33]
>
> It is also to be noted that neither Dayan Swift nor Dayan Golditch has given any reasons in support of his statements. Therefore, it is not clear whether or not the Beth Din would endorse the alleged reasons put forward by the chairman of the Rabbinate of the Federation of Synagogues. His references to the *ketubah* and the wedding benedictions have no decisive bearing on the question of validity.
>
> As to the matter of witnesses, if their competence were to be judged not in terms of integrity and trustworthiness – which is, of course, what the spirit of Jewish law seeks to ensure – but in terms of ritual observance, the Beth Din would be compelled to declare invalid numerous marriages solemnised under the authority of the Chief Rabbi's Office and under Orthodox Jewish authorities all over the world.
>
> Such a policy would also involve a radical and deplorable departure from the attitude adopted by the late Chief Rabbi, Dr J.H. Hertz, who approved the authorisation of the Liberal Jewish Synagogue for marriage purposes under the aegis of the Board of Deputies.
>
> The emphasis on peripheral technicalities tends to obscure the true Jewish ideal of marriage as fundamentally a religious covenant expressed in the love and devotion between man and wife, in family harmony and in the establishment of a 'small sanctuary' dedicated to God and filled with the beauty of holiness.

Orthodox Jewry must be pained and embarrassed at the utterances of their leaders, for they show a spirit in which there is a total absence of *ahavat Yisrael* – Jewish brotherhood and love. Such statements, and the crude manner of their expression, can only be considered as mischievous attempts to stir up discord and strife in the community.

Unless the present Orthodox leaders are persuaded to refrain from abusing their ecclesiastical authority – whose basis should be Torah, of which it is said that all its paths are peace – through the sowing of dissension and the infliction of grief in the household of Israel, Anglo-Jewry will find itself the victim of self-imposed religious persecution and oppression, which must lead to the decline and disintegration of Jewish communal life.[34]

\* \* \*     \* \* \*     \* \* \*

Seeking to cool the atmosphere and to provide a structured and united Orthodox platform, the British Mizrachi Federation, advocate of the centrist religious Zionist philosophy, proposed a conference of batei din to discuss the marriage dispute and other aspects of Jewish family life. Its purpose, it said, would be 'to set out, in chapter and verse, where the Reform and Liberal bodies have abandoned vital principles of our faith' and to indicate to the community 'how they are inexorably leading their adherents towards total assimilation'.[35]

Swift, however, rejected the proposal, declaring that 'there can be no conferences on *dat Moshe v'Yisrael*'.[36] For its part, the United Synagogue Council of Ministers said that it had not considered the question of Reform and Liberal marriages and 'is unlikely to do so'.[37]

Of significance in the light of another controversy brewing within the community was a brief comment from the Jewish Theological Seminary of America, Hertz's alma mater and by then the foremost exponent of Conservative Judaism: 'It makes absolutely no difference where a marriage is performed', said its rector, Saul Lieberman, 'if it is done according to Jewish law.'[38]

# 15

## Jacobs' Ladder

'The challenge of Bible Criticism is acute. The confidence of many people in the Bible as the Word of God has been shaken by modern critical investigation, so that no work of Jewish apologetics, however limited in scope, can afford to fight shy of the problem.'[1] So wrote Anglo-Jewry's foremost theologian some thirty months before he was appointed moral tutor and lecturer in pastoral theology at Anglo-Jewry's foremost Orthodox seminary – whose president at the time was Chief Rabbi Israel Brodie. Discussing that challenge, he wrote further:

> From the talmudic view, it is clear beyond doubt that the doctrine of 'Torah from Heaven' – *Torah min hashamayim* – meant not alone that the Pentateuch is divinely inspired like the other biblical books, but that God dictated the whole of it (with the possible exception of the last eight verses) to Moses ...[2]
>
> There is undoubtedly a certain grandeur about the traditional view. It is exceedingly reassuring to know that we can rely for guidance in matters of religion and morals on a divine book complete in every respect, which we possess together with a divine guarantee that its text is free from error. But this view has been seriously assailed by critical and historical investigations, as most people are today aware ...[3]
>
> There is really nothing to deter the faithful Jew from accepting the principle of textual criticism ... The interpretation has now become as much part of the Torah ... as the text itself. But if to resort to textual criticism is not to offend against the doctrine of 'Torah from Heaven', we are on admittedly more dangerous ground when considering what is now known as the Higher Criticism, in which the traditional views concerning the authorship of the biblical books are seriously contested ...[4]
>
> Bible Criticism does not, of course, limit itself to the Pentateuch. It critically examines the traditional view concerning the authorship of the other biblical books. Thus, on linguistic, historical and literary grounds, the critics reject the Davidic authorship of Psalms, the Solomonic authorship of the Song of Songs, Proverbs and

Ecclesiastes, and the authorship by Isaiah of the second part of the book which bears his name. It must also here be pointed out that, in addition to literary analysis, modern criticism avails itself of archaeological discoveries ...[5]

The view of Maimonides, the dominant one until recent times – [... the eighth principle of the Jewish faith: 'That the Torah has been revealed from heaven. This implies our belief that the whole of the Torah found in our hands this day is the Torah that was handed down by Moses and that it is all of divine origin. By this I mean that the whole of the Torah came to him from before God in a manner which is metaphorically called "speaking"; but the real nature of that communication is unknown to everybody except to Moses (peace to him!) to whom it came'[6]] – is obviously at variance with critical theories, and those who accept it must perforce look upon the latter as negative and destructive of faith.

To talk about 'reconciling' the Maimonidean idea and the Documentary Hypothesis[7] (or, for that matter, any other view based on 'untraditional' methods of investigation) is futile, for you cannot reconcile two contradictory theories. But to say this is not to preclude the possibility of a *synthesis* between the old and new knowledge. There is a clear distinction between saying that two points of view are both correct and saying that they both *contain* truth ... The problem is this: are we compelled either to turn our backs on all criticism or dismiss over two thousand years of Jewish tradition and interpretation? Or can a synthesis be found? ...[8]

There is a view according to which a synthesis between the traditional and critical theories is possible and that, in any event, the attitude of respect, reverence and obedience vis-à-vis Jewish observance is not radically affected by an 'untraditional' outlook on questions of biblical authorship and composition ...[9] *The fundamental question [is] not whether this or that theory is correct, but whether the appeal to tradition is valid in matters to which the normal canons of historical and literary method apply, and whether the authority of Jewish Law is weakened as a result of scientific investigation.*[10]

The view holds that we can afford to be objective in examining the literary problems of the Bible and that it does not at all follow that because, as a result of more highly developed methods of investigation, including the use of archaeological evidence, we are compelled to adopt different views from the ancients, we must automatically give up the rich and spiritually satisfying tradition that has been built up with devotion and self-sacrifice by the wisest and best of Jews. This view is finding an increasing number of adherents ...[11]

It goes without saying that these or similar views which see no incompatibility between the idea of Scripture as the Word of God and the use of critical methods in its investigation can only be entertained if the doctrine of 'verbal' inspiration is rejected. It is true that in the vast range of Jewish teaching on revelation there are numerous passages in which 'verbal' inspiration is accepted or, at least, hinted at. But this is not the whole story. It can be demonstrated that long before the rise of modern criticism, some of the Jewish teachers had a conception of revelation which leaves room for the idea of human co-operation with the divine ...[12]

Allowing for the legendary nature of some of the passages, it must be obvious that many Jewish teachers conceived of revelation in more dynamic terms than the doctrine of 'verbal' inspiration would imply. For them, revelation is an encounter between the divine and the human, so that there is a human as well as a divine factor in revelation, God revealing His Will not alone to men but *through* men.

No doubt our new attitude to the biblical record, in which, as the result of historical, literary and archaeological investigations, the Bible is seen against the background of the times in which its various books were written, ascribes more to the human element than the ancients would have done, but this is a difference in degree, not in kind. The new knowledge need not in any way affect our reverence for the Bible and our loyalty to its teachings.

God's Power is not lessened because He preferred to co-operate with His creatures in producing the Book of Books ... We hear the authentic voice of God speaking to us through the pages of the Bible – we know that it is the voice of God because of the uniqueness of its message and the response it awakens in our higher nature – and its truth is in no way affected in that we can only hear that voice through the medium of human beings who, hearing it for the first time, endeavoured to record it for us ...[13]

The view ... that the Jew, if he is not to stifle his reason, must be free to investigate the classical sources of Judaism with as much objectivity as he can command, and should not look upon this as precluded by his religious faith, seems to me to be impregnable. Needless to say, this is not my discovery but is held by the vast majority of Jewish scholars of any academic repute.

The result of such investigation, involving the use of tried methods of research, a cautious weighing of the evidence and an unbiased approach to the texts, yields a picture of the Bible and the Talmud as works produced by human beings, bearing all the marks of human literary production, influenced in style, language and ideas by the cultural background of their day. Like other human productions, they contain error as well as truth.

For all that, and this is the most significant part of the discussion for faith, the believer can still see the Torah as divine revelation. The notion of divine dictation must, of course, be abandoned, once the human element is granted, and the Bible, for example, can no longer be seen as revelation itself. But it is the *record* of revelation. The whole is a tremendous account (and for this reason unique and not simply 'inspired' in the sense in which one speaks of Shakespeare or Beethoven being inspired) of the divine-human encounter in the history of our ancestors in which they reached out gropingly for God and He responded to their faltering quest.

This does not mean that we can naively mark (as I have been accused of trying to do) certain lofty passages as divine and others of a more primitive nature as human. In the new picture of the Bible, the divine and the human are seen as intertwined. Because humans had a hand in its composition, it is, from one point of view, all human. Because out of its totality God is revealed to us and speaks to us, it is, from another point of view, all divine.[14]

Louis Jacobs, the Orthodox author of these unorthodox thoughts, had resigned his six-year ministry at the New West End Synagogue in 1959 to take up the post at Jews' College, where 'the honorary officers (other than the Chief Rabbi) had indicated to him that, subject to the Chief Rabbi's approval of his candidature, they intended to recommend to the council his appointment as principal when that post became vacant'.[15]

His credentials for the post seemed impeccable. Born in 1920, the only child of Orthodox Mancunians from mixed Lithuanian and Latvian backgrounds, he had had a traditional elementary education at Reb Yonah Balkind's cheder in Manchester's Hightown district before enrolling in the after-school class at the local yeshivah, and becoming a full-time *bocher* at the age of 14.

Six years later, he was accepted as a student at the new Gateshead kolel, the post-yeshivah institution for the study of *Torah lishmah* – 'Torah for its own sake' – alongside graduates from the hallowed sanctums of Telz, Mir, Slobodka, Kamenitz, Baranowitz, Grodno and Radun. A visitor at the time was Norman Bentwich, who had crossed swords with Hertz over wartime religious education and who described the institution's regimen as 'semi-monastic'.[16] Jacobs' 'teacher *par excellence*' was the kolel's founder, Rabbi Eliyahu Eliezer Dessler,[17] who (he was later to write[18]) 'taught me, and so many others, to see Judaism in sophisticated terms'.

For all of Dessler's inspirational teaching, however, the kolel – and *musar* (ethical instruction) in particular – 'got under my skin',[19] and Jacobs returned to Manchester for his rabbinical ordination, his examiners being the rosh yeshivah, Rabbi Moshe Yitzhak Segal, and Rabbis Baruch Steinberg, Raphael Margolies and Isaac Lerner (the last-named a future London dayan).

With a second semichah from Rabbi Moshe Rivkin, of the Manchester Beth Din, he was well qualified for a spell at the Golders Green Beth Hamidrash as assistant rabbi to Dr Eliyahu Munk, 'who introduced me to the world of German-Jewish Orthodoxy, the world of Samson Raphael Hirsch and Frankfurt, where a valiant attempt was made to combine the riches of the Jewish tradition with Western life and culture – Torah and *derech eretz*'.[20]

While there, Jacobs studied at University College for a degree in Semitics, which he was awarded (with 'very disappointing' second-class honours) by, among others, Isidore Epstein, the Jews' College principal. His tutor was Siegfried Stein,

> who had managed to reconcile his totally observant life with a knowledge and acceptance of biblical and historical criticism. He warned me before the course[21] that I must expect to be disturbed by the facts we would be uncovering ...
>
> Here was I, teaching at the Golders Green Beth Hamidrash the wisdom of Torah, yet learning at University College that other wisdom of objective scholarship applied to the same texts. Could the two be reconciled? I had a sufficient sense of responsibility to refrain from even hinting at my uncertainties to the younger boys of the [Golders Green] yeshivah.[22]

At Segal's funeral service in 1947, held in Manchester's Central Synagogue, Jacobs was approached by the honorary officers to become its minister. Aged 27, he accepted the post, but before long began to receive 'intimations' that 'the Chief Rabbi [Brodie] wished me to come to London to serve as the minister of the Brondesbury Synagogue and as a dayan of the London Beth Din'. A meeting with Abramsky, and others with Brodie and Brondesbury, led, however, to the Chief Rabbi's retraction of the second offer and Jacobs' rejection of the first.[23]

The reasons for their change of heart became clear only many years later when, in 1962, at the height of the Jacobs controversy, Dayan Swift[24] sought Abramsky's aid (addressing him formally as 'the Rav'):

> Concerning the matter about which the Rav wrote to me recently, perhaps you can suggest the names of several people known to you.

> Just as we succeeded last time [over Brondesbury], perhaps we will succeed this time, with God's help.
>
> On various occasions over the past months, I have mentioned your name to my colleagues on the Beth Din and referred to your genuine words of prophecy in 1949. I recollect that when I was about to leave England, they recommended that same person [Jacobs] to serve in my place at Brondesbury, with the intention, in time, of his joining the Beth Din. The Rav said of him that he was a real *apikorus* [heretic].
>
> Only now, after twelve years, do I see the great wisdom in your prediction, for this [heresy] has been exposed in all his writings and speeches. I hope that Rabbi Brodie will stand firm in the face of all the pressure put upon him from different quarters on this matter. And if the Rav should happen to meet with him [the Chief Rabbi] and discuss the matter with him, this would be very important and productive, since it is known that Rabbi Brodie strongly respects your opinions.[25]

For his part, Jacobs was to write:

> With hindsight, I can see how disastrous it would have been to have become associated with the London Beth Din, a body with which I later engaged in battle several times. The views of the Beth Din on Judaism were not my views even then, and nothing could have so effectively killed off my theological quest as to have become a member of a body with no confidence at all in free inquiry.[26]

After the Brondesbury episode, five further years in Manchester were to elapse[27] before the pulpit of the New West End – Hockman's short-lived and unhappy home four decades earlier – became vacant, with the retirement of Ephraim Levine, and the post of minister-preacher dropped, most conveniently and welcomely, into Jacobs' lap.[28] Installed into office by 'our revered Chief Rabbi'[29] in February 1954, Jacobs was welcomed by him as 'an invaluable reinforcement to the rabbinate of this metropolis'.[30] Referring to the 'high traditions of the synagogue and the distinction of former incumbents', Brodie expressed his 'confidence that the new minister will enhance that proud record'.

In his induction sermon, Jacobs responded by outlining

> the two ideals that will form the basis of my plan to work as minister of this synagogue – the ideal of the effective implementation of Jewish tradition, and the ideal of unflinching courage in the attempt to transmit that tradition so that it becomes a vital force for Jewish living, with relevance to the spiritual needs and strivings of Jews in the world of today ...

It is necessary to love Judaism, with all that that implies in terms of exhilaration in contact, anguish in parting, perpetual effort to understand, ceaseless attempt to be worthy. In a very real sense, the Torah requires the dedication of the whole of our being to its service, of all our qualities of heart and mind and soul. In a very real sense, it demands our all, and, if we love it, we shall not be content to give less.

This is the ideal I have set before myself and which I now set before you – the ideal of personal commitment to and personal identification with the traditional Jewish way of life, unmarred by fanaticism, intolerance or narrow-mindedness of any kind. It is a difficult task to bring such an ideal to fruition, one which calls for determination, staying power and, above all, courage.

I do not delude myself that the going will always be smooth and easy and that there will be no difficulties. It requires great courage from both minister and congregation to further the Anglo-Jewish tradition: courage to tread the middle path and avoid the extremes of the right and the left; courage to be loyal to the old while welcoming the new; courage not to rest on our laurels but ever to strive to deepen our understanding and appreciation of Jewish life and thought and practice.

I hope that the Judaism I preach from this pulpit will be a courageous Judaism. To the best of my ability, I shall see to it that no shallow, spineless Judaism, one demanding no challenge and presenting no sacrifice, shall be preached here. But I hope that I shall also see to it that no harsh, unsympathetic, inhuman interpretation of Judaism is voiced here.

When the ancient Jewish legend speaks of the worm *shamir* which had the miraculous power of cutting through the thickest stone, and by means of which King Solomon built his Temple, it was but voicing the thought that a sanctuary cannot be built without resolute endeavour to see the thing through, without inflexible determination to arrive at the goal. But the legend tells us that the *shamir*, when not in use, was placed in cotton wool, in order to insulate it against destruction.

A Jewish minister, in his efforts to erect the temple of Jewish life, requires all the moral stamina and courage he can muster in order not to be deflected from his purpose. He must be gifted with the power of the *shamir* if he is to succeed. But it would be a sad day for him and for his congregation if his zeal ever allowed him to forget those basic human qualities of sympathy and understanding, without which a man soon becomes a soulless machine.

He must not fail to set before his congregants a vision of greatness, but he must ever be aware of their difficulties, their daily problems, and their sincere efforts to make the truth their own. He must at all times be ready to make their burdens more light, to strengthen them in their sorrows and to share in their joys. The modern congregation of Jews cannot be won by the critic with a big stick but only by the friend with a big heart.[31]

Several times in this inaugural address, Jacobs referred to 'courage', and his sermon's message of traditionalism 'unmarred by fanaticism, intolerance or narrow-mindedness', of loyalty 'to the old while welcoming the new', of challenge, sacrifice and moral stamina, permeated his every utterance – all preached in the presence of his 'revered Chief Rabbi'.[32]

And no sooner said than done. In desiring that he and his congregants 'write [our] own love letters' to and of the Torah, and 'to make the truth [our] own', he embarked on a series of study groups at the synagogue and, based on their outcome, 'tried to record my thoughts in my first controversial book, *We Have Reason to Believe*, published in 1957.[33] The book was fairly innocent, and no notice was taken of it until my acceptance in it of biblical criticism was brought to the attention of the Chief Rabbi [some four years later], in order to influence his decision to block my appointment as principal of Jews' College.'[34]

That Jacobs and Brodie were to end up at loggerheads was evident from the outset in their divergent aspirations to Jewish learning. At a service in 1955, marking the College's centenary, the Chief Rabbi spoke of its 'unique and responsible position' as

> one of the few surviving rabbinical seminaries in Europe dedicated to Jewish scholarship and enjoined to ensure a continuity of teachers of Judaism to spread the knowledge and importance of our heritage.
>
> Our institution, through its men equipped with the qualifications of zeal in a holy cause of education and learning, is especially called upon to inspire love and loyalty to Jewish values in the hearts of the waverers, to raise our spiritual and cultural sights, to overcome rampant ignorance, and to reassert the dominance of Law in our private and public lives ...
>
> The College was established as an institution of education and learning. A specific and permanent aim was, and is, to train men to be authentic exponents of the Judaism of tradition in the English-speaking congregations of the British Commonwealth.
>
> The exponents must be such as have amassed and garnered wide

Jewish and general knowledge under expert guidance. They must also be scholarly, with a humble but persistent desire to make their own contribution to the magnifying of the Torah.

The Judaism of tradition is the well of perennially living waters, which has to be rediscovered and claimed by every generation. It is rich spiritually; it throbs and is alive; it is relevant and constant in a world of unpredictable changes – social, political and cultural. It is 'the faith for our times', confirmed in those literary sources of Bible, Talmud, moral and philosophical texts, and the annals of Jewish history, to which the student at Jews' College is introduced by learned and devout scholars.[35]

Some years earlier, Brodie had warned against

the detractors in our own midst who say that Judaism can have no place in these times unless it is divested of its exclusive associations with the fate and destiny of the Jewish people, discards the dietary and family laws, modifies its beliefs concerning Revelation and authority, and confines itself to the enunciation of universal prophetic teachings of ethical monotheism, divorced from their natural context of implementation through Israel's redemption in the land of its fathers.[36]

Such 'detractors' were to host Jacobs when, as minister of the New West End and barely five months before his Jews' College appointment, he delivered a lecture at the West London Synagogue in a series on 'Movements in Judaism',[37] at which Claude Montefiore's son Leonard, vice-president of the Association of (Reform) Synagogues of Great Britain, was in the chair.

The visit, commented A.S. (Arthur) Diamond, the congregation's chairman, was an important occasion for their synagogue, many of whose members 'feel too isolated from their brethren in the Anglo-Jewish community, and desire that that state of isolation from one another should not continue. Rabbi Jacobs has said that he would be happy to come and lecture to us on a future occasion. I can assure him that our members would be very glad to welcome him again.'[38]

The lecture, on a Reform platform, provoked a vociferous, if veiled, response from Swift, who in turn chose the platform of Jacobs' own synagogue to berate its minister for his recent action. Speaking at the communal centre on 'The Challenge to Orthodox Judaism', the dayan declared:

We would have no quarrel with the Reform elements if only they would be honest and admit that what they preach is not Judaism but merely a vague humanism. But as they will not do so, it is our duty to go on exposing the lie.

> Much as I dislike sowing seeds of hate, I see no way out but for us to dissociate ourselves from them entirely, to impress upon our youth the dangers of fraternising with them, and to sit at square tables – not round ones – when the occasion demands association. Judaism requires obedience to the rabbinic law and the teachings of the Torah, and although we dislike discriminating between Jews, we must not surrender that standpoint.[39]

Jacobs was to delay replying to this attack until his 1962 Claude Montefiore lecture at the Liberal Jewish Synagogue, when he told the gathering:

> There have been and there are, thank God, Orthodox Jews – I use the term 'Orthodox' here in the sense of observant – who have been prepared to face the problems raised by critical investigation into the sources of Judaism and have not been prepared to accept the obscurantist position.
>
> On the other hand, in recent years, many Reform and Liberal Jews have discovered a new interest in the halachah and realise, as one of them put it, that religion does not appeal only to the intellect, to the mind, it has to appeal to the whole being of man and to satisfy psychologically as well as rationally.
>
> I doubt whether the leaders of Reform Judaism in the last century would have dreamed that in the mid-twentieth century there would be published Reform responsa. And so one senses there is a coming together of the two sections.
>
> It would be far too optimistic to imagine that there are no differences; it would be far too optimistic to imagine that in the foreseeable future those differences are going to be completely ironed out. But the debate continues – and perhaps it is as well that the debate continues ... seeking the truth in this world of error.[40]

* * *   * * *   * * *

In August 1959, the council of Jews' College announced its decision 'to offer to Rabbi Dr Louis Jacobs, subject to his release by the United Synagogue, the post of tutor and lecturer on the staff of the College. Rabbi Jacobs has accepted the invitation. Until his final release from his present duties, the appointment will be on a part-time basis.'[41] Five months later, the council's chairman, Alan Mocatta (later Sir Alan), confirmed that Jacobs 'has now taken up his full-time duties'.[42]

The appointment became publicly divisive in the closing days of 1961, a week after Victor Lucas – a future president of the United Synagogue and a leading figure in the Orthodox establishment – had introduced Jacobs to a meeting of the Anglo-Jewish Association (headed from 1926 to 1939 by the Reform movement's Leonard Montefiore): 'It is no secret that large numbers of Jews here and abroad are looking forward to Dr Jacobs' early appointment as principal of Jews' College ... We hope that under his leadership, it will once more make traditional Judaism a real and living force.' The tutor's position, said Lucas, had given Jacobs 'a unique opportunity to come into close contact with the students at the College and to influence them in the principle which seems to motivate all his work – that Judaism is not an outmoded set of observances but that, properly interpreted, it is relevant to all the problems of the present age'.[43]

A month before this declaration, however, Jacobs had tendered his resignation – 'with the deepest feelings of regret' – to Mocatta, bringing to a head an internal crisis that had grown steadily over several months. His letter to the council spelled out his concerns:

> You will recall that two and a half years ago, I was invited by you and your colleagues to come to the College as tutor. You pointed out at the time that it was the intention of the honorary officers that I should be appointed principal after the retirement of Dr Epstein, though there could be no definite promise on their part since the appointment depended, under the constitution, on the Chief Rabbi's approval.
>
> Since Dr Epstein's retirement last July, the Chief Rabbi has been asked to give his approval for the appointment, but has failed to do so on various grounds, the one recurring most often being that views I have expressed in writing render me unsuitable for the position.
>
> These views are contained in my books *We Have Reason to Believe* and *Jewish Values*. I remain firmly convinced that the approach to traditional Judaism I have sketched in these books is one that must commend itself to all who are aware of modern thought and scholarship.
>
> I have tried to show that intense loyalty to Jewish tradition and observance need not be synonymous with reaction and fundamentalism. Furthermore, I would claim that no reputable scholar in the world has an approach that is basically different from mine.
>
> What I had hoped to do at Jews' College was to help train men able to hold their own in the field of objective scholarship and, at the same time, imbued with the spirit of *yirat shamayim* [fear of Heaven]; men who would realise, in some measure, at least, the implications of the verse: 'For this is your wisdom and your understanding in the

sight of the peoples' (Deuteronomy 4:6).

In this task, intelligent Jews everywhere are engaged. It would be sad if Anglo-Jewry, with its traditional breadth of vision, were not to participate in such a presentation of Judaism.[44]

At a meeting of the council five weeks later, at which Jacobs' letter was discussed, a resolution by Mocatta was placed before its members 'respectfully requesting the Chief Rabbi to give his consent to Rabbi Dr Louis Jacobs being appointed principal of the College as from 1 October, 1962, with Dr H.J. Zimmels as director of studies'. Brodie asked that 'this item be not discussed by the council this evening', citing 'many reasons' for making the request but giving only one – 'I shall be away from the country for a while and consider that it would not be right to have this matter considered at present'.

Under pressure, he added later: 'I want to state it clearly that Dr Jacobs will not have my consent to becoming the principal of Jews' College. There are many matters in connection with this, but I will not mention them to avoid creating more divisiveness.' Pressed again after further discussion, he commented, 'I will now say this: I climb down. This letter of resignation, and even this motion, should be deferred until such time as I return. For the time being, I do not give my consent to the appointment of Dr Jacobs as principal.'

Following the meeting, a College delegation sought to persuade Jacobs to withdraw his resignation. His response was unequivocal:

> I have been asked to withhold my resignation until the return of the Chief Rabbi from Australia in April. The Chief Rabbi has been aware of my intention to resign on this issue for some weeks. But ever since I came to the College, two and a half years ago, the Chief Rabbi has had the opportunity of considering whether or not I would be a suitable principal.
>
> During the last few months particularly, the Chief Rabbi has had many and lengthy discussions with me and others on the subject. The facts of the matter are therefore all within his knowledge. The only answers the Chief Rabbi has given to requests that my appointment should be made have been that he would 'consider the matter' or that he hoped I would change my views.
>
> Latterly, and at last Monday's meeting, he said that he would consider the matter again in three months' time. This has introduced nothing new and still gives no indication when or, indeed, whether finality can be achieved. Nor does it commit the Chief Rabbi to anything that cannot be other than a delaying tactic which will lead to further delays.

> The appointment of a principal to such an institution as Jews' College cannot be made in this undignified fashion. Moreover, self-respect and my regard for the College prevent me from accepting an offer if it could only be made after elaborate deliberations as to my alleged suitability. I was therefore unable to withdraw my resignation.[45]

The next day, the London *Evening Standard* reported the resignations of Mocatta, the joint treasurers Lawrence Jacobs and Felix Levy, and the honorary secretary and lecturer in homiletics, Isaac Levy.[46] A day later, it added a comment from Jacobs: 'I am working out my notice. I leave at the end of the academic year. After that, I have no definite plans.' *The Times, Daily Express, Daily Telegraph* and *British Newsweekly* all carried the story that same weekend.

\* \* \*  \* \* \*  \* \* \*

With Brodie overseas, the dayanim lost no time in showing their hand. In an initial broadside the following week, they 'found it necessary to state that, considerations of special scholarship and other qualifications apart, some of the views expressed in recent years in publications and articles by the proposed candidate are in conflict with authentic Jewish belief and render him unacceptable'.[47]

This led to a riposte before the United Synagogue council from its president, Ewen S. Montagu, a staunch Jacobs supporter. 'From very early on in this problem', he declared,

> the Chief Rabbi made it clear that this was not a question of Orthodoxy. On more than one occasion, he stated quite categorically – to me and to others – that he had no complaint as to the Orthodoxy of Rabbi Dr Jacobs and that he regarded Rabbi Jacobs as a completely Orthodox man, or he would not have approved of his appointment to the most important office of tutor.
>
> The Chief Rabbi himself has never said that any decision he may make in this matter is a halachic ruling. His authority in this matter stems from a different power inherent in the Chief Rabbinate: no principal of Jews' College can be appointed without the approval of the Chief Rabbi, and – up to the present – he has not been willing to give his approval.
>
> Now, the authority of the Chief Rabbi in religious matters is something which is very precious to the community. The fact that we have one religious authority and not a multiplicity of voices has made this community the envy of all other Orthodox communities …
>
> It is most important that this authority should be maintained; and

if, eventually, the Chief Rabbi does finally veto Rabbi Jacobs' appointment to the principalship of Jews' College, we will have to accept that ruling loyally. But that is not the solution to the problem; indeed, in many ways it would be only the beginning.

No office, no authority, can exempt a man from criticism. Although authority is accepted, criticism is proper – if respectful. We obey, but if we are unconvinced, our enthusiasm can be impaired, and controversy and schism result.

The reason for my concern over these many months has been, to a large measure, the prestige and future of the Chief Rabbinate itself. In his daily tasks, the Chief Rabbi has been surrounded by many whose approach is not that of the modern educated student; by people who feel that Orthodox theological teaching must be based upon acceptance and not upon convincing the student as to the same eternal truths.

In addition, he has had immense pressure put on him by others who have never accepted his authority and who have been most critical of him in the past; who now, somewhat surprisingly, praise the value of his authority and who seek to deny, on this particular issue, even the right – the inalienable right – of criticism or discussion.

I am worried lest, if the Chief Rabbi should issue a final veto, the prestige of the Chief Rabbinate will suffer. My hope is that he will not exercise his veto. During his time abroad, he will be separated from the almost intolerable pressure that has been put on him day in, day out, by those who have had daily – or almost daily – access to him and who do not understand the intellectual approach to our verities ...

In one way, the Chief Rabbi's trip abroad at this juncture has been unfortunate, but in another most fortunate. It has given him the chance, free from the daily pressure, to think the matter over afresh before he makes a final ruling.

If, however, the veto should materialise I – and, I am sure, others as well – will do all in our power to try to ensure that Rabbi Jacobs can continue to exercise his great gifts for the benefit of this community of ours, an objective for which he has already made great personal sacrifices.[48]

Affronted by this undisguised attack on their authority, those 'whose approach is not that of the modern educated student' rose up as one in defence of themselves and their stand. In a statement unprecedented in content, direction and degree, the dayanim challenged Montagu – the lay leader of their parent organisation – on every aspect of his argument. The 'particular reason', they reiterated, for the Chief Rabbi's inability to support Jacobs' appointment – 'which Dr Brodie stressed again and again to the dayanim and others' – was his

> deep concern for the views expressed by the candidate in his writings and addresses, which the Chief Rabbi considered to be in conflict with the fundamental beliefs of traditional Judaism.
>
> The sentiments in this matter attributed to the Chief Rabbi by Mr Montagu are in striking contrast with the distress and expressed opinion of the Chief Rabbi on the attitude of Dr Jacobs to Jewish fundamentals and the religious concepts of traditional Judaism as propounded by the binding Jewish authorities ...
>
> Dr Jacobs but follows the critical hypotheses of predecessors and of scholars who ignore Orthodox tenets and traditional canons. His rejection of the doctrine of verbal inspiration, his acceptance of textual criticism of the Torah, and his compromising attitude to higher criticism which denies the divine origin and unity of the Torah, *Torah min hashamayim* – the truth of which is expressed in the familiar words which we repeat when the Scroll is held up after the Reading of the Law: 'And this is the Law which Moses set before the children of Israel, according to the commandment of the Lord by the hand of Moses' – do not fit in with any Orthodox school of thought ...
>
> An attitude to the Torah such as adopted by Dr Jacobs implies the tentative nature of the mitzvot and must, because of the absence of the sanction of the Sinaitic revelation as the ultimate basis of the observance of our mitzvot, finally lead to their abrogation.
>
> Mr Montagu has thought fit to cavil at those close to the Chief Rabbi for an approach that 'is not that of the modern educated student'. This is but another instance of his disrespectful and captious attitude to the rabbinates and the members of the Beth Din, which is calculated to undermine the foundations and authority of the Court of the Chief Rabbi. Mr Montagu is, of course, not unaware of the rabbinical qualifications, intellectual standards and academic attainments of the dayanim.

Rejecting 'the unsubstantiated accusations that pressure was exerted on the Chief Rabbi in this matter by the Orthodox rabbinate', the dayanim added:

> His mind was at one with ours. On the contrary, it would seem from his statement that Mr Montagu has exerted – and intends to exert – such pressure.
>
> We would appeal to all concerned not to proceed along 'the new paths' which have led in the past to disintegration and even apostasy,

and which would only lead to irreparable schism in our community; and we pray that all traditional Jews at this hour will exert every endeavour to protect and preserve the Orthodox character, unity and integrity of the United Synagogue and, indeed, of Anglo-Jewry.[49]

Determined to follow Waley Cohen's example, Montagu sprang back every bit as combative. It was 'most regrettable', he said,

> that the dayanim have seen fit to make such a pronouncement at this moment. My statement to the council of the United Synagogue was necessary, as that body is more deeply affected than any other by the future of Jews' College.
>
> Although the dayanim now say of the Chief Rabbi, 'his mind was at one with ours', I truthfully told the council that the Chief Rabbi had not yet made up his mind and had decided to postpone his decision until his return to this country. No one yet can truthfully say what that decision may be. And that is what makes the pronouncement deplorable.
>
> The Chief Rabbi alone has a veto on the appointment of the principal of Jews' College. The Chief Rabbi is the religious authority of the Orthodox community. In that enormous responsibility, he has the benefit of being able to ask for, and to consider, the advice of his Beth Din before he makes his decision.
>
> The slightest degree of loyalty to their Chief Rabbi – even the slightest decent feeling – would have told the dayanim, his advisers, that they of all people could not possibly publish their views on the point, especially when he has asked for time in which to make up his mind. 'Pressure!' It will need all the courage of a great man for the Chief Rabbi now to give his decision if, on reflection, it conflicts with that of the dayanim.[50]

\* \* \*   \* \* \*   \* \* \*

The first act in the drama – though decidedly not the last – concluded with the Chief Rabbi's return from Australia and his receipt of Abramsky's advice following Swift's appeal. Speaking at the annual meeting of the College's governors and subscribers,[51] Brodie asked that

> it be widely known that at no time did I directly or indirectly make any promises to Dr Jacobs when he was approved as tutor to the College.
>
> Nor am I aware that the honorary officers of the College had gone so far as to indicate to Dr Jacobs that he would be definitely appointed

principal, subject to my approval. The council minutes of 15 May, 1961, quoted the chairman [Mocatta] as stating that 'no undertaking has been given to the tutor that he will be appointed principal.'

When the question of filling the vacancy arose, I laid down certain essential qualifications required of a person who would be suitable for the post of principal. They are that he should be a talmudist of distinction, devout, and strictly Orthodox; an established Jewish scholar who had made original contributions to Jewish learning; a personality able to lead and inspire; and a man with some experience of academic administration.

If the College is to remain true to its aspirations and maintain its reputation as a centre of learning, education and research, then it is necessary to find a principal who is possessed of these qualifications, and who would head an able and erudite staff.

So far, we have not been successful in our search for a scholar of renown and high academic attainments willing to accept the principalship. There are many reasons for this unwillingness, one being the comparative inadequacy of the salary offered, and another the unpleasant press campaign which has stirred up prejudice against the College and made it the whipping-boy of squabble and controversy.

Apart from his published views, and having regard to the standards of outstanding scholarship and other qualifications required of a candidate for the office of principal – standards deemed essential in all Jewish institutions of higher learning – I found myself unable to accept the recommendation put forward that I approve Dr Jacobs to be principal of Jews' College in the coming academic year.

His resignation as tutor and lecturer, a position which he filled with great success, was tendered by Dr Jacobs of his own volition, despite the urgings of the council to withdraw it. His resignation has been regretfully accepted by the council and myself.[52]

As a postscript to the saga, Jacobs delivered a 'learned and spirited defence of his position' before a thousand-strong audience at his former synagogue, the New West End:

My thesis [he declared] is that many of the greatest Jews throughout the ages believed that reason should be our guide and should even be applied to revelation itself, even though there were, and are, others who argued differently and believed that it would be wrong to do so.

Up until now, the Jewish people found room within it for both points of view and I would claim it to be a serious departure from the grand and tolerant tradition in Jewish thinking when the protagonists of one point of view are hunted by the others as heretics, when, in fact, all of them are seekers after the truth ...

We can no longer accept the view that it is simply a question of direct, automatic and static transmission of our religious tradition. We must take into account all the influences which time and science have brought to bear upon this tradition ... Jews must come to grips with the question of Bible criticism as they have done with regard to the discovery that the earth is round, and in regard to the theory of evolution.

Apparently, I was spreading heresy because I suggested that there is a human element in the Bible. But how else can you understand the Bible, and how else is the word of God effected unless it is transmitted by human beings? And what is the word of God? One does not need to be a scholar to know that it means a thing of God, a situation and a record of the encounter between God and man ...

It is, of course, true that the Talmud contains a statement that a person who does not believe that every letter in the Bible was given by God to Moses is a heretic who forfeits his share in the world to come. It is also true that Maimonides repeats that statement. But people who argue that way forget that in the time of Maimonides everybody believed it, and that the aim of the statement was to stress the divine purpose of the Bible.

I do not believe that every single letter was dictated by the Almighty. But that does not affect the divine purpose of the Bible, or its spiritual value. The question is not what Maimonides said eight hundred years ago, but what he would have said had he lived today. I have no doubt that if he were alive today, he would have grappled with the perplexing questions of our time with the same courage and intellectual integrity with which he faced the problems of his own age.[53]

\* \* \*   \* \* \*   \* \* \*

Twenty-five years later, long after the second act had taken its toll and unaware of Abramsky's intervention in the spring of 1962, Jacobs revealed the identity of another *éminence grise* behind Brodie's veto:

Dayan Isidor Grunfeld, an author and lawyer, a man of culture and wide learning, and at that time a member of the London Beth Din, confessed to me that he had approached the Chief Rabbi and set the whole process in motion.

He explained that he had found it unthinkable to appoint a man who had expressed in his book doubts about the traditional doctrine 'the Torah is from Heaven'. However, Dr Grunfeld expressed his remorse for having done so, and on more than one occasion came close to directly apologising to me.

After the affair had begun and he had retired from the Beth Din, Dayan Grunfeld invited William Frankel [then editor of the *Jewish Chronicle* and a close friend and supporter of Jacobs][54] and me to his home for a discussion on the theological question.

He tried to convince us that the problems raised by biblical criticism could be solved on the basis of the Kantian distinction between the *phenomena* and the *noumena* – that is, that biblical criticism operated on the level of that which is perceived and could not, therefore, be applied to the Torah, which was not a human production but a divine communication.

I pointed out that if this distinction makes any sense when applied to the Torah, it would follow that no one has ever understood or can understand the Torah – hardly a position a devout Jew can hold.[55]

# 16

# 'This is the Law'

Left to his own devices, and with the help and comfort of his friends, Jacobs was installed as director of the Society for the Study of Jewish Theology, created for his benefit and with Mocatta as president.[1] Explaining its objectives in the light of Jacobs' 'learned and spirited defence' three months earlier, the chairman, Ellis Franklin, told the inaugural gathering, attended by more than 700 supporters:

> Some of us felt that these thoughts and this thinking should not just stop at this one address. We had to act quickly.
>
> If the matter was to be carried further, urgent steps had to be taken, as Rabbi Jacobs, then excluded because of his views from a post in which he could have done most for the community, was receiving offers of appointment in America, South Africa and Australia. We felt that the object of advancing this point of view could best be carried out by the formation of the Society.[2]

Its aims, as set out in the campaign literature, were fourfold: 'to further a philosophy of traditional Judaism based on sound scholarship; to encourage a more flexible attitude in the Anglo-Jewish community; to foster the study of the teachings of Judaism in their relevance to modern man's situation; and to strengthen and enrich Jewish observance'.[3] The Society operated for barely eighteen months, soon overtaken by events. But while it lasted, it did do, averred Jacobs, 'some useful work – and it brought much satisfaction to its members, who believed they were fighting the good fight'.[4]

Unexpectedly, the pulpit of the New West End once again fell vacant, with the departure to New York of Jacobs' successor, Chaim Pearl,[5] and the honorary officers – keen to secure their former minister – approached the Chief Rabbi for his required approval. Hardly surprisingly, Brodie declined to issue his certificate, whereupon the officers, going over his head, invited Jacobs to preach.[6] This he did, arising from the minister's seat and dressed in canonicals.

As a result, the United Synagogue leaders – headed by Sir Isaac Wolfson, who had succeeded Montagu as president after the Jews' College dispute –

called an extraordinary meeting to discharge the rebels and install their own men. The second act in the Jacobs drama had begun in earnest, presaging events almost as schismatic as the Great Secession 120 years earlier.

\* \* \*   \* \* \*   \* \* \*

Appealing to Wolfson for 'reason and moderation to prevail' in their attempt 'to proceed constitutionally with the appointment', the New West End officers invoked a prefatory passage in the United Synagogue bye-laws:

> The spirit which imbues the whole code of the bye-laws is that of Progressive Conservatism, which the United Synagogue itself exemplifies, rejecting on the one hand the clamour of those who, in the desire for constant change, would recklessly cast aside Tradition; and on the other, the invitation of those who regard all things as settled, deluding themselves with the pretence that time and environment and circumstances are factors of no account, as though our lives and our mutual relationships are not susceptible to change.

The New West End leaders asserted that Jacobs 'has served this congregation in the past with distinction and with success; his views then were known to be the same as they are now, and throughout his ministry he held the Chief Rabbi's certificate ... Rabbi Jacobs has intimated his readiness to accept the recall and to work under the jurisdiction, and accept the authority, of the Chief Rabbi'.[7]

In his reply, Wolfson challenged the last claim by submitting that

> the time has come when we ought to examine what these words mean when looked at calmly. I understand them to mean that, in whatever the Chief Rabbi would direct Rabbi Jacobs to do – and, more important, not to do – he would concur and respect; but we – you and I – know that Rabbi Jacobs has made it quite clear that he does not intend to change his ways at all.
>
> Having had pointed out to you how wrong your views are, my colleagues and I trust that you and the other signatories to the letter will now give tangible signs of your anxiety to maintain and enhance the authority of the Chief Rabbinate and the integrity of the United Synagogue, as expressed in your letter.[8]

Following frenetic exchanges behind the scenes, two major meetings brought the crisis to a head. At the first, before the United Synagogue council on 23 April 1964, Wolfson moved the resolution to 'discharge and depose' the New West End officers and to appoint 'managers' in their place.

After a lengthy review of the developments, he told the council:

> When I was elected your president, I thought I was reasonably acquainted with the position of the United Synagogue in Anglo-Jewry. What I did not appreciate then, but have now come to realise, especially from my recent travels, is the fact that the Chief Rabbinate, as well as the United Synagogue and its constitution and its traditions, are the subject of envy and admiration the world over. In my wildest dreams, however, I never thought it possible that we would ever reach the unhappy position facing us today.
>
> Our wise predecessors who were responsible for the constitution on which we now rest saw how important it was to repose in the Chief Rabbi the sole ecclesiastical authority over the religious affairs of the United Synagogue. Their wisdom has proved itself time and again over the years, and I am certain that on this occasion – as indeed always – we are right to uphold the decision of our revered and respected Chief Rabbi as the only path open if traditional Orthodoxy in the United Synagogue is to be sustained and carried forward as a heritage for the future.
>
> Our ecclesiastical authority is the United Synagogue's buttress against the attacks of those who would like to see some encroachment on our traditions. I want this council to show the Chief Rabbi in particular, and the community in general, in no uncertain manner that we, the council of the United Synagogue, are not going to allow anything to happen which will assist any erosion of our heritage.
>
> This council must show by its vote this evening that it believes in the unity of the United Synagogue and that the Chief Rabbi is the focal point of that unity, and by that vote expresses its confidence in the Chief Rabbi and what he stands for.[9]

Having secured its vote of confidence, Brodie delivered himself of a statement a fortnight later to a meeting of rabbis and ministers of the Anglo-Jewish community. He told them:

> At a meeting such as this it need hardly be stated that the Chief Rabbi, as the ecclesiastical head of the United Synagogue, has, by its Deed of Foundation and Trust, authority to decide all religious questions that arise. He regards himself bound, when making his decisions, by Jewish Law as laid down in the Shulchan Aruch (Code of Jewish Law binding on all Jews). His jurisdiction extends to the appointment of ministers, and particularly of those seeking to serve any congregation within the United Synagogue.

No one can be appointed unless the Chief Rabbi certifies as to his religious as well as his moral fitness. All the considerations which weigh with the Chief Rabbi when arriving at a decision whether to grant or withhold a certificate are not normally the subject of public discussion. Indeed, it would be repugnant to the whole status and dignity of the Chief Rabbinate were such decisions to be subject to public controversy, and normally it would not be in the interests of the candidate himself.

Nevertheless, in the case of Dr L. Jacobs, I did give a reason for my decision in my letter to the secretary of the United Synagogue. I indicated that it was with the deepest possible regret that I was compelled owing to the views of Dr Jacobs – expressed publicly both by written and spoken word – to state that I could not grant my certificate.

My decision, dated 23 January 1964, has sparked off a new controversy: a conflict which regrettably and irresponsibly certain elements have brought before the wider community through the press and the radio, no doubt in the belief that in this way pressure could be brought to bear on me and the honorary officers of the United Synagogue. In these circumstances, it is desirable to give a brief account and an explanation of recent events.

During the three months that have elapsed since my decision, it has been possible to assess its implications. Irrelevant arguments and facile theories have been propounded which have tended to conceal the real issues. With these issues I shall deal presently, but there is one point which I would like to clarify as it has been referred to by some members of the community.

They ask how it is that I allowed Dr Jacobs to hold the position of minister to the New West End Synagogue from 1954 to 1959, and also agreed to his appointment as tutor and lecturer at Jews' College, notwithstanding views he had expressed which were not in keeping with Orthodox belief.

A number of times during his ministry at the New West End Synagogue, I felt obliged to speak to Dr Jacobs regarding his views which he had expressed on particular occasions which were inappropriate for a rabbi. Nevertheless, I have described my support of Dr Jacobs during this earlier period as 'an act of faith'.

I considered, as many did at the time, that Dr Jacobs was possessed of ability and potentialities. I felt that here was a promising man passing through a phase of intellectual and spiritual struggle, and that it would be wrong to reject him before he had reached a fixed position, and his views had become crystallised.

That I did have misgivings in respect of the appointment of Dr Jacobs at Jews' College is shown by my decision not to allow him to lecture on Bible studies – the subject on which Dr Jacobs was going astray.

I wished to be helpful, and as I said in an interview in July 1962: '... I consented to his appointment as tutor, though I knew that some of his views were not completely acceptable; but bearing in mind his background and early training, I felt that an act of faith on my part would be justified, and that with the passage of time, and with further study of Jewish sources and continuing research, he would modify his views' (*South African Jewish Times*, 13 July 1962).

I deeply regret that my hopes for Dr Jacobs have not been realised. Subsequent utterances indeed have shown, particularly in his lecture, 'The Sanction for the Mitzvot', delivered in 1963 (and since published), that Dr Jacobs has travelled far from the accepted norms of Judaism. Moreover, it is now possible to obtain a clearer picture of the position and to see how basic and fundamental are the considerations which compelled me to make my decision.

The Torah, including the Written and the Oral Law, is the very basis of Jewish existence. Once undermined, as our historical experience has proved, Jewish life and tradition weaken and wither, and the way is open for the disappearance of the Jewish identity through mixed marriage and other forms of assimilation.

Those who are appointed rabbis and teachers of communities must by their very vocations, and by the terms of their ordination as rabbis, be the exponents of the Revelation of God's word embodied in the Torah, written and oral, with the sanction and authority attached thereto. That is what I would expect of Dr Jacobs, who has been ordained as a rabbi after the traditional manner, when ministering to a congregation under my jurisdiction.

But Dr Jacobs repeats the well-worn thesis that parts of the Torah are not divine but are man-made, and maintains that reason alone should be the final judge as to what portion of the Torah may be selected as divine.

His views on this subject were presented in a pamphlet published by the Society for the Study of Jewish Theology, entitled 'The Sanction for the Mitzvot', to which reference has already been made.

Dr Jacobs states that '... it is now seen that the Bible is not, as the medieval Jew thought it was, a book dictated by God, but a collection of books which grew gradually over the centuries, and that it contains a human as well as a divine element. This applies to the Pentateuch as well as to the rest of the Bible ... Those who are at all aware of what has been going on in the world of thought and scholarship know all this to be a commonplace ... Indeed, there would be no need to say it were it not that the Chief Rabbi and the London Beth Din are saying the opposite and trying to put the clock back.'

If this were all that Dr Jacobs teaches and preaches, it would be incongruous for him to occupy the pulpit of an Orthodox synagogue. Moreover, from his most recent written and verbal statements on Judaism, which in the main are a repetition of the arguments of earlier reformers, and especially leftist conservatives, it will readily be understood why I found myself unable to authorise his appointment as minister of the New West End Synagogue.

Even a cursory examination of these views reveals how incompatible they are with the most fundamental principles of Judaism and how they inevitably lead to a critical attitude to the observance of the mitzvot themselves, as evidenced by the claim of Dr Jacobs that ' ... In modern times, the Jew no longer asks, "Why did God tell us to keep certain mitzvot?" but "Did God tell us to keep certain mitzvot?"'

An attitude to the Torah such as this, which denies its divine source and unity (*Torah min hashamayim*), is directly opposed to Orthodox Jewish teaching, and no person holding such views can expect to obtain the approval of the Orthodox ecclesiastical authority.

It has been said that the decision I made was made under duress exerted by 'German' or 'Continental', certainly un-British, influences. These influences are said to be embodied in the persons of rabbis and others described as 'fanatical', 'obscurantist' and 'intolerant'. I think it most reprehensible to divide the Anglo-Jewish community into those with English and those with foreign attitudes to Judaism.

For the record, I think it is important to affirm that, apart from the unworthy implication that I have no mind of my own, nor sense of the responsibility attaching to my office, apart also from the disrespectful reference to men of deep learning and piety, there is absolutely no foundation for the assertion that I was subject to the pressures so luridly described. Rabbis and laymen, both in this country and overseas, have expressed their concern on the issues involved, and I have listened to them and consulted with them.

It is perhaps truer to say that pressures of one kind and another were ceaselessly exerted by the other side. For example, I was told by one pressure group that if I did not approve the appointment of Dr Jacobs, the Jewish press and the world press would be unleashed against me.

I was also urged to think of the verdict of the future historian of Anglo-Jewry who would describe me as the Chief Rabbi who split the community from top to bottom. To forestall such a verdict, I should change my decision.

I do not presume to dictate to any contemporary or later historian. I hope, however, he will give thought to the fact that the Chief Rabbi, after much prayer and deliberation, decided in accordance with his principles and that spiritual leaders and many laymen in this country and overseas sustained his stand.

There is one more point which deserves serious consideration. It has become apparent to me that there is much more involved in the present controversy than the pulpit of one synagogue. Regrettably, everything points to the fact that Dr Jacobs has been used as a central figure by a few resolute individuals who have openly declared their intention of trying to bring about a new orientation in our community.

As the spiritual leader of Anglo-Jewry, I know that the new trend is in conflict with basic Jewish belief and inimical to the spirit and sentiment in which our community has developed over the years. Clearly, in the face of this denial of traditional Jewish beliefs and the threat to the integrity of Anglo-Jewry, I have felt it my sacred duty to do everything in my power to strengthen the Jewish faith and to uphold and enhance our Anglo-Jewish tradition ...

Since preparing my statement, I have received letters as recently as this morning from members of the community deploring, and even condemning, the section of members of the New West End Synagogue and also Dr Jacobs for the flouting of the authority of the Chief Rabbinate and the constitution of the United Synagogue. Nevertheless, and in spite of this, I have been asked to reverse my decision and, for the sake of the unity of the community, to permit Dr Jacobs to be within the framework of the United Synagogue.

I sympathise very much with the motives of my correspondents. But a group has decided upon establishing an independent synagogue outside the jurisdiction of the Chief Rabbinate. It has appointed Dr Jacobs to be its spiritual leader. All this is a fact: it has been much advertised and should be accepted, however regrettably.

The United Synagogue accepts my spiritual jurisdiction. I made a decision with a heavy heart but in all conscience. Dr Jacobs was made aware of the actual conditions under which I was nevertheless prepared to withdraw my decision and to permit him to function as minister-preacher of the New West End Synagogue. He felt, however, he could not accept them. We pray that time and circumstances will bring healing and understanding, discipline and unity to our beloved community.

One last word. 'Everything has its fortune, even the Scroll of the

Law in the ark.' Yesterday afternoon, I was invited with others to view Scrolls of the Law once housed in synagogues in Czechoslovakia and now brought to this country under the custodianship of the Westminster congregation. Those of us who went round the rooms where the scrolls are arranged and laid out were shaken to our very souls at the sight of over fifteen hundred of them without mantles and appurtenances which we associate with a Scroll of the Law ...

Many of the scrolls will, we hope, be distributed to synagogues in Israel and elsewhere. Their use will be renewed and will witness Jews of today and tomorrow declaring of the Torah: 'This is the Law which Moses put before the children of Israel.'[10]

Following this address, Jacobs hastened to refute what he described as the Chief Rabbi's 'rhetoric over reason'. This was not the occasion, he declared in a statement,

to discuss in detail the theological differences between the Chief Rabbi and myself. It would, in any event, be difficult to do this, since he does not give us much indication of his own views on Revelation.[11]

He uses the vague term, 'the divine origin of the Torah'. As applied to the Torah, this term is meaningless, since as theists we both believe that the *whole universe* is of divine origin. What is to the point is whether the Chief Rabbi believes, with the London Beth Din, that the present text of the Pentateuch was *dictated* by God to Moses?

If he does, why does he not say so clearly and unambiguously? If he does, moreover, what did he mean when he said in a recent television interview that the Bible (and he did not exempt the Pentateuch) was written by 'inspired men'? Does not a book written by inspired men contain a 'human element'?

The Chief Rabbi's statement contains a number of factual inaccuracies which cannot go unchallenged. The statement declares: 'That I did have misgivings in respect of the appointment of Dr Jacobs at Jews' College is shown by my decision not to allow him to lecture on Bible studies – the subject on which Dr Jacobs was going astray.'

In fact, I did lecture on Bible studies – I conducted a class of biblical literary history – until my resignation from the College. The subject he would not allow me to teach, when Dr Epstein retired, was religious philosophy, on the grounds that he wished to encourage one of his ministers by inviting him to take this course.

The Chief Rabbi remarks that I have 'travelled far from the accepted norms of Judaism', and quotes from my lecture, published in pamphlet form, on 'The Sanction for the Mitzvot'. He implies in the whole of his observations that in this pamphlet (the only work of mine from which he quotes) I have expressed views far more to the left than those in my earlier works.

This is a complete travesty. I do not know whether the Chief Rabbi has read my books, but he cannot have read this pamphlet with any degree of care. Thus he quotes, in support of his contention that my approach leads 'to a critical attitude to the observance of the mitzvot themselves', the following passage, which he describes as my 'claim': 'In modern times, the Jew no longer asks, "Why did God tell us to keep certain mitzvot?" but "Did God tell us to keep certain mitzvot?"'

One would imagine from this that I question whether God commanded us to keep the mitzvot. In fact, the whole of the pamphlet is in the form of an affirmative reply to the question ...

The Chief Rabbi says: 'But Dr Jacobs repeats the well-worn thesis that parts of the Torah are not divine but are man-made, and maintains that reason alone should be the final judge as to what portion of the Torah may be selected as divine.'

This is a complete misrepresentation of my position. I have never claimed that reason is the sole arbiter in matters of faith, and I challenge Rabbi Brodie to substantiate this statement. My book is called *We Have Reason to Believe*, not *We Have Belief in Reason*.

The Chief Rabbi remarks further: 'There is one more point which deserves serious consideration. It has become apparent to me that there is much more involved in the present controversy than the pulpit of one synagogue. Regrettably, everything points to the fact that Dr Jacobs has been used as a central figure by a few resolute individuals who have openly declared their intention of trying to bring about a new orientation of our community.'

Rabbi Brodie resents suggestions that he has no mind of his own, but has no hesitation in casting this kind of slur on others. I deny categorically his imputation of sinister motives. Let the Chief Rabbi name these 'resolute individuals', and if 'they have declared their intention openly', state where and when they have done so.

The Chief Rabbi's reference to a 'new orientation' is a surprising comment from one under whose spiritual leadership the United Synagogue has moved more and more away from its traditional position and closer to the extreme right, and who is now acclaimed by Agudat Israel as a kindred spirit.

A trivial but telling example of the change is to be found in Dr Brodie's very statement, in which, contrary to his former practice, the English name of the Deity is spelled, in the copies circulated, with a hyphen between the 'G' and the 'd'. And would a minister holding views such as mine have been banned thirty years ago?

The Chief Rabbi declares that 'Dr Jacobs was made aware of the *actual* conditions under which I was nevertheless prepared to withdraw my decision and to permit him to function as minister-preacher of the New West End Synagogue. He felt, however, that he could not accept them.'

The *actual* conditions were contained in a letter brought to me by an intermediary from the Chief Rabbi for my signature in which I was to declare that my views were mistaken and that I would never express them. I was told that if I signed that letter, the Chief Rabbi *might* grant me a certificate.

The statement's preference for rhetoric over reason is seen nowhere more explicitly than in the frequent appeals it makes to upholding the honour of the Torah. The Chief Rabbi has no monopoly on love and respect for the Torah. It is not the Torah which those who think as I do attack, but, in the name of Torah honour, interpretations of it which fail to take account of the best scholarship. We weep over desecrated scrolls of the Torah as much as do Rabbi Brodie and his followers.

Dr Brodie says I am not 'Orthodox'. If by 'Orthodox' Dr Brodie means fundamentalist, then, indeed, I am not Orthodox. But since when has Orthodoxy in Anglo-Jewry been equated with fundamentalism? And how many ministers who have served Anglo-Jewry with distinction would qualify under Dr Brodie's definition? Certainly not Simeon Singer, the first minister of the New West End Synagogue. It is Dr Brodie who has deviated from the United Synagogue tradition, not I.[12]

Even as they were preparing to launch their 'independent congregation outside the jurisdiction of the Chief Rabbinate', Jacobs' supporters had persuaded him to make one final attempt at reconciliation – although he himself conceded that 'this seemed doomed from the start'.[13] Within days of Wolfson's statement, Jacobs had a meeting with the United Synagogue president and his son, Leonard, where they worked on a letter to Brodie

in which I [Jacobs] begged him to have second thoughts. He could now do this without loss of face, I said, since it was clear that in any event most of the regular worshippers at the New West End would have me as their rabbi in the new congregation and it was surely better all round for me to be under his jurisdiction at the New West End.

Sir Isaac took the letter to the Chief Rabbi the next day and importuned him to agree to my appointment, but to no avail. The Chief

Rabbi was in the position of a leader who had been accused of weakness and who therefore felt obliged to demonstrate his strength and courage even when wisdom dictated a more conciliatory attitude.[14]

* * *   * * *   * * *

Four years earlier, in Westcliff – when minds were on other issues – Brodie had given his 'emphatic warning' against the Conservative element in America 'now making an attempt to spread its wings. We shall discourage and resist these efforts to infiltrate into Europe, even if they may speak to us in terms of traditional Judaism.' His warning now – of 'an independent synagogue outside the jurisdiction of the Chief Rabbinate, with Dr Jacobs as its spiritual leader' – was clear evidence of failure, and of 'a schism in our old and all-embracing *kehillah*' of comparable weight and worry to that which had undermined his ecclesiastical forebears five generations earlier.

The new body, established in the former home of the St John's Wood (United) Synagogue,[15] was launched at a meeting of prospective members in May 1964, during which a motion was passed resolving to 'constitute an independent Orthodox congregation under the name of the New London Synagogue' (*Bayit Chadash*, 'New House' in Hebrew[16]). Addressing the gathering, Jacobs said:

> The question, friends, is not what the term 'Orthodox' means in other parts of the world – it has many different meanings – but what has Orthodoxy meant in the United Synagogue and in Anglo-Jewry.
>
> If by Orthodox you mean an attitude of mind which shows no hospitality to modern scholarship and modern thought and the inquiring mind, then I would say that we shall certainly not be Orthodox and we shall be proud not to be Orthodox. It was never the fashion of the New West End Synagogue to have the kind of Judaism taught and preached suitable only for know-alls, leading a congregation composed of docile sheep.
>
> However, if by 'Orthodoxy' you mean – and the words are not ours, but are taken from the preamble to the constitution of the United Synagogue – 'Progressive Conservatism', then we are as Orthodox as the next man. I hope that one of the things we will do in the new congregation will be to work out the implications of the term 'Progressive Conservatism'.[17]

At the New London, Jacobs was to later to record,

> the aim was to return in some way to the older Anglo-Jewish tradition,

albeit with certain reservations. There was no mixed seating, but we still have a mixed choir and we do not pray for the restoration of sacrifices.

A departure from tradition took place in the election of a woman as chairman of the congregation in the belief that, whatever the great sage Maimonides had said eight hundred years ago, it was a move in full accordance with the spirit of the times. In its constitution, the New London Synagogue is described as an Orthodox congregation, but we are all aware that the problem of when to go along with the Zeitgeist and when to reject it is acute, as it is in every Anglo-Jewish congregation which claims to be modern.[18]

Explaining 'What We Stand For' in his inaugural sermon on Rosh Hashanah 5725, the new minister turned again to the definition of 'Orthodox' since, he said, it was the term

> that has given rise to most misgivings. Are we justified in calling ourselves Orthodox?
>
> Where we differ from some congregations is in our refusal to equate Orthodoxy with the refusal to think and inquire. We stand firmly on the right to re-interpret our ancient traditions in the light of new knowledge and we believe, moreover, that this process of re-interpretation has always gone on in Judaism. It is completely untraditional to arrest Judaism's natural growth and development ...
>
> It is not because we are indifferent to our faith that we wish to see it unfettered by untenable ideas. It is because we love it and wish to live by it that we desire to utilise all that is permanent and worthwhile in modern scholarship.[19]

'This question of my "Orthodoxy"', Jacobs wrote later, 'was to be raised again and again during the following years. The one thing I did not want to do was to pull wool over people's eyes. I said repeatedly that if Orthodoxy denotes fundamentalism, I was not Orthodox and did not want to be Orthodox. But if Orthodoxy meant, as it had in Anglo-Jewry, an adherence to traditional practice, then I could claim to be Orthodox.'[20]

There were many religious Jews, he stated in another context, 'who see supreme value in the vocabulary of worship provided by traditional observances and who, for this reason, do not wish to embrace Reform Judaism. But these same Jews cannot bring themselves to compromise their intellectual integrity by accepting traditional theories which seem to them untenable.

> In the United States, they can join the Conservative movement. In Israel, they are searching desperately for a sense of identity. In this country, until recent events, they could have joined the United

Synagogue, an organisation which has always lacked a clear religious position but which, for that very reason, was an ideal spiritual home for those who wished to work out for themselves a new philosophy of Jewish observance. The fact that this is no longer possible led to the formation of the New London.[21]

But even as the controversy was raging in Britain, Jacobs had been flirting with 'Conservative elements' overseas. He undertook a lecture tour in America, where

> my thinking, for what it is worth, was very close to that of the thinkers of the Conservative movement.
>
> I was invited to address the students at the Jewish Theological Seminary, the college (far more influential than Jews' College) for the training of Conservative rabbis. In fact, the basic issue on which Conservatives differed from the Orthodox in the USA was precisely on the understanding of the doctrine, 'The Torah is from Heaven', the Conservatives refusing to interpret the doctrine in a fundamentalist manner'[22]

Discussing the New London's affiliations, long after its establishment, Jacobs admitted that

> over the years, my association with Conservative Judaism in the United States grew stronger. I became a member of the Rabbinical Assembly and a vice-president of the World Council of Synagogues, the Conservative body of lay leaders to which my synagogue also became affiliated soon after its foundation.
>
> For all that, I have never believed that the pattern of synagogal life prevailing in Conservative synagogues in the USA should or could be successfully transported to Anglo-Jewry. We have our own traditions, and what is suitable there can be very unsuitable over here ...[23]
>
> Most of us were, indeed, wary of throwing in our lot entirely with a movement, no matter how close we were to it in our thinking, that might compromise our ability to develop in our own way. We had not struggled for independence only to surrender it to toe even a more congenial party line.
>
> So we did host more than one convention of the World Council and were affiliated to that body ...[24] but we avoided using the actual name 'Conservative' for our synagogue because of its American connotations. When the Conservative movement in Israel used the Hebrew term 'Masorti', we were easier with this, but the subject remained a problematic one.[25]

While distancing itself from Reform philosophy through its 'independent Orthodox' approach, the New London nonetheless took an early stand on communal unity. Some months after Jacobs' inaugural sermon, at the height of the dispute over the Beth Din attack on Reform and Liberal marriages, its leaders entered the arena. They declared:

> While we differ from Reform and Liberal Judaism, we consider it outrageous to suggest that religious marriage ceremonies performed in a House of God between Jews eligible for Jewish marriages are invalid. This is an interpretation of traditional Judaism which equates it with fanaticism and bigotry and can only serve as a means of dividing Jewry.
>
> We are convinced that it is the duty of all who think as we do to protest against those who are creating dissension between Jews instead of strengthening the bonds which should unite all sections of Jewry.[26]

\* \* \*    \* \* \*    \* \* \*

Early in the Jews' College crisis, the *Jewish Chronicle* received a letter from a New York reader, writing as 'an alumnus of Jews' College and a rabbi formerly in the service of the Anglo-Jewish community'. The letter, heavily truncated, was published with others[27] and was the subject of extensive comment in the rival *Jewish Review*, organ of the Mizrachi Federation, where it appeared in full, with the deleted sections printed in italics:

> I find the account of the Jews' College controversy in your news, correspondence and editorial columns very painful reading indeed. Like many American friends of Anglo-Jewry to whom I have spoken, I am stunned with grief by the dissension, acrimony and ill-will evoked by the present crisis.
>
> What has happened, one wonders, to the vaunted graces of British Jewry – hitherto the world's example of communal discipline and decorum – that the Chief Rabbi can be publicly subjected to *such intemperate obloquy and to such brazen* defiance of his religious authority, for no other crime than displaying the courage of his sincere convictions in the conscientious exercise of his constitutional rights?
>
> *If, as you claim with evident relish, 'the religious issue in Anglo-Jewry has (now) been publicly joined', that issue should be dispassionately presented and openly discussed without rancour. But to understand the essence of the conflict – or rather rebellion – your bewildered readers are, I think, entitled to ask the following questions.*
>
> Dr Jacobs, in his (to my mind) *bombastic letter of resignation, betraying a lack of humility ill befitting a rabbinical leader,* asserts: 'No reputable scholar in the world has an approach that is basically different from mine.' Are men of the calibre of Dr

[Samuel] Belkin or Dr Epstein and numerous other Orthodox thinkers who do not share Dr Jacobs' views disreputable scholars?

Moreover, where and since when is a man's Jewish Orthodoxy adjudged by scholars other than rabbis who are themselves Orthodox? That the overwhelming majority of Orthodox rabbis the world over disagree with his views even Dr Jacobs would hardly deny. I can certainly testify to that fact from my European and American experience.

You, Sir, repeatedly berate the Chief Rabbi's opinions as opposed to those of 'thinking' Jews and of 'the majority of our community'. Are you, then, seriously suggesting that the many distinguished rabbis, scholars, scientists and enlightened laymen who uphold the Chief Rabbi's Orthodoxy in thought and practice are unthinking obscurantists? I, for one, resent this haughty insinuation as reprehensible and offensive.

As for the 'majority' whose sanction you seek, shall a man's rabbinical qualifications henceforth be determined by popular votes or Gallup polls? *Was the majority of our people required to endorse the religious views of Moses or the prophets after him? Are you urging us now, after having preserved our faith as a minority for thousands of years, to authenticate the teachings of Orthodox Judaism (or of science, or medicine, or philosophy) by subjecting them to the test of mass appeal and public confirmation?*

You deem it 'absurd' that the Chief Rabbi's (or any rabbi's) approval should be required to appoint a principal of Jews' College. *Would it be not even more absurd to demand the Chief Rabbi's consent for the appointment of any Anglo-Jewish minister (a requirement with which you have never quarrelled) and to ignore him when appointing the person in charge of training ministers?*

You charge the Chief Rabbi with 'lack of courage displayed ... in avoiding a decision...' by taking refuge in continual procrastination. Would it not be true to surmise that this 'continual procrastination' was in large measure due to the unbearable pressure (of which the *Jewish Chronicle lately gave ample evidence) which you and others have* brought to bear on the Chief Rabbi not to make a decision against Dr Jacobs' appointment? And had the Chief Rabbi some time ago announced his decision to object to the appointment (as he finally did at the last council meeting), would you then have applauded his courage, *as many do now?*

*Whether the Chief Rabbi's objections are justified, and Dr Jacobs' leanings really lie, as suspected, with the American brand of Conservative Judaism rather than with Orthodoxy, may soon become apparent. Meanwhile, all but the most credulous may be pardoned if they detect a lack of candour in those who, under the pretentious cloak of representing the 'thinking' Jews, are trying to subvert the authority of the Chief Rabbinate and to support, without saying so honestly, a religious system as alien to the traditions of Anglo-Jewry as to Orthodox Judaism, a system which will fragmentise Jewish communal life in England as it has done in America.*[28]

In a second letter, to *Congress Bi-Weekly* – which had carried a lengthy article[29] on the Jews' College controversy – the same writer concluded with the remark, 'the essence of the battle between the Chief Rabbi and his detractors goes far beyond a conflict of personalities. Its outcome will determine whether the religious leadership of Anglo-Jewry shall remain basically Orthodox, as it has always been, or be pushed into the camp of Conservative Judaism.'[30]

The signatory to both letters was Immanuel Jakobovits, then ministering to the Fifth Avenue Synagogue in New York City.

# Heart Talks to Heart

Immanuel Jakobovits and Yechezkel Abramsky joined forces at the Great Synagogue, Duke's Place, on Shemini Atseret 5708 (1947), when the young son of the dayan's late colleague, Julius Jakobovits, was installed into office. In his induction address, Abramsky paid tribute to the new incumbent as

> a worthy son of a distinguished father, and a worthy leader of an historic congregation. He is a man with the energy of youth: with learning and the will to add constantly to his knowledge; with ability inherited from his lamented father; and with a sincerity that is transparent and infectious. I believe that those are the qualities that a spiritual leader requires today more than ever: learning that leads to ability; energy that leads to activity; sincerity that leads to devoted service.
> 
> He will need all those qualities, because his task will not be an easy one. He is to lead an ancient congregation which for a long time has not had a minister of its own. He will have to revive the religious life of a vast area which has undergone great changes in our time, but which still contains one of the most important Jewish communities in these islands.
> 
> And he will have to attract young and old to our tradition at a time when many rival and often hostile distractions call them elsewhere. It will be a testing time for him, and I pray that God's blessing will always accompany him.[1]

Some twelve years later, after holding the Chief Rabbinate of Ireland, Jakobovits found himself in New York, where the newly opened Fifth Avenue Synagogue had secured his services and where, in many respects, 'we conformed more closely to Anglo-Jewish than to contemporary American practice'.[2] While immersed in congregational and communal duties, he managed nonetheless to maintain a deep interest in – and growing unease about – the schismatic events unfolding in London, hence his letters to the press on the Jacobs Affair. 'I had every sympathy with Chief

Rabbi Brodie', he was later to record,[3] 'but it was only the sentiments of a far-distant friend.'

As for Jacobs, wrote Jakobovits,

> by his increasing detachment from the Orthodox rabbinical world and his subsequent association with the Conservative (Masorti) movement, he showed that, whatever his scholarship and sincerity, he represented a trend that could not be accommodated within contemporary Orthodoxy.
>
> But communal gossip had it that Rabbi Brodie [who was recuperating on a cruise after the Jews' College crisis] no longer felt able to resist the pro-Jacobs clamour, would announce from abroad that he had withdrawn his opposition to Dr Jacobs' appointment as principal, and would follow this up with notification of his own resignation from office. Jacobs' progression to the Chief Rabbinate would thus be assured, since no other candidate of similar stature existed – as the community was being led to believe – or, in any event, would wish to become involved in such a poisoned atmosphere.[4]

To forestall this possibility, London associates of Jakobovits invited him to conduct a lecture tour of Britain, with a view to succeeding Brodie on his eventual retirement. 'The visit was successful', Jakobovits recalled,

> yet I could not really be certain that I wished to exchange the settled satisfaction of my life in New York for the hazards of the British Chief Rabbinate.
>
> The [position] was something to which I had no wish to aspire. Indeed, the feeling had been deepened by my knowledge of the ceaseless attacks launched on Rabbi Brodie over the preceding few years. Yet the office, if at times almost suffocating with protocol and responsibilities, also possessed an enormous and unrivalled prestige, and a vast potential to lead and to influence.
>
> Duke's Place, Ireland and Fifth Avenue had all been offered to me, and I had no reason to repine at the outcome. I would not fight or intrigue to become Chief Rabbi, but I was not sure that, under the right conditions, I would refuse an invitation.[5]

Brodie's retirement was announced within weeks of his New West End statement to the rabbis and ministers. In June 1964, Wolfson confirmed that the Chief Rabbi would step down on his seventieth birthday the following April, and the United Synagogue council took the first steps in 'the complex process of choosing a successor'[6] by convening a conference of bodies contributing to the Chief Rabbinate's maintenance. Over the hats in the ring, speculation was rife and names abounded. While Jakobovits equivocated, an early 'possible' was said to be Yaacov Herzog,[7] deputy director-general of Israel's Foreign Ministry and younger son of the country's late Chief Rabbi, who declared, however, that he had 'not been approached' and was 'unaware' of his candidacy.[8]

As further names emerged over the succeeding months, the list of 'suitably qualified rabbis'[9] on Wolfson's list grew to eleven, comprising, in addition to Herzog and Jakobovits, Bernard Casper (Johannesburg), Isaac Cohen (Dublin), Shear Yashuv Cohen (Jerusalem), Shalom Coleman (Sydney), Norman Lamm (New York), Israel Porush (Sydney), Louis Rabinowitz (Jerusalem), Emanuel Rackman (New York) and Joseph Soloveitchik (Boston).[10]

Herzog, whose family were close friends of Wolfson's and whose brother, Chaim, represented the tycoon's business interests in Israel, was the favourite, but his indecision in the very week of Brodie's retirement, when a formal invitation was extended to him, prompted the United Synagogue to announce that 'during the interregnum, the London Beth Din-in-Commission will act for the Chief Rabbinate'.[11]

A seven-man delegation to Herzog's Jerusalem home broke the impasse, however, and the diplomat-rabbi told his 'anxious'[12] visitors: 'I am deeply moved by the honour of this unanimous call. After deep contemplation and heart-searching, I have decided to respond. Providence has directed me from the course in life which I have pursued for many years and has guided me back to the world of religious thought, a world with which my innermost essence has always been linked.'[13]

Herzog's acceptance prompted widespread acclaim, and a revival of hope for communal unity. Expressing a desire to 'enjoy the full co-operation of all segments of the community', he had told the delegation: 'I need hardly say that I will not be dominated by any groups, institutions or individuals. I will be guided by my religious conscience, by the precepts of Judaism and by the concept of *Klal Yisrael*, ever aware of the inner meaning of the epoch of Jewish history now unfolding.'[14]

The *Jewish Chronicle* responded guardedly: 'The problems are many', it declared.

> The community is leaderless, torn and confused, and everything that makes up Jewish life – knowledge, observance, family cohesiveness, sense of continuity – is receding. He [Herzog] has become heir to a situation where his potentialities for leadership and diplomatic skill will be employed to their limit.
>
> Some may be apprehensive that his very lack of experience may

induce him to put too much trust in those who have had a great deal, and that he may in the course of time become the prisoner of one group or another. We believe this fear is unfounded ... [His] ready appreciation of the ideal of *Klal Yisrael*, of the unity of the Jewish people, raises the hope that we may be on the threshold of a new age in which Anglo-Jewish Orthodoxy will once again lay greater stress on what unites than on what divides.[15]

From the communal left-wing emerged similar sentiments. The Union of Liberal and Progressive Synagogues offered Herzog 'our full co-operation in all of your endeavours, which are motivated by your devotion to the concept of *Klal Yisrael*. We trust that the differences which exist between the various religious communities will not obscure the strong bonds which unite all Jews. May you succeed in your expressed determination to strengthen the spiritual ties between Jewish communities the world over.'[16]

Herzog replied: 'I am deeply grateful for your kind message and for your offer of co-operation in the cause of *Klal Yisrael*.'[17]

Enlarging on their hopes, the Liberals prepared a working paper on the realisation of harmony within the community, in which they declared:

> Anglo-Jewry today is divided and confused. It now clings to the hope that the new Chief Rabbi can end the existing strife and give the Jewish community a sense of clear purpose. But it is unrealistic to expect one man, no matter how talented in the arts of diplomacy and wise in the knowledge of the Jewish tradition, to solve the problems within Anglo-Jewry ...
>
> Only a religious reorganisation of Anglo-Jewry, patterned on the three distinct and differing approaches to Judaism – fundamentalist, conservative, and progressive – will lead our community out of the maze in which it finds itself. When this happens, an able peacemaker, hopefully Dr Herzog, will be able to bring leaders of all sections together with these words: 'Gentlemen, we know in what we differ. Let us discuss what we have in common, so that we can work for the benefit of *Klal Yisrael*' ...
>
> Having discovered where they differ, Jews may have the time to learn in what they are united and in which way they may labour for the religious flowering and happiness of the entire House of Israel. In this atmosphere, Dr Herzog would have the opportunity to utilise his office towards achieving such noble aims.[18]

Through the medium of one of its leading rabbis, the Reform community expressed its welcome in more cautious terms. While conveying congratulations on the movement's behalf, P. Selvin Goldberg, of Manchester,[19] placed Herzog's appointment in a wider context,

> having considered the implications involved in this new phase of Anglo-Jewish life. While we do not yet know Dr Herzog's attitude towards other religious bodies in the community, we do know that the period of office of the last Chief Rabbi was marked by definite lack of co-operation.
>
> At times, this even achieved the proportions of discourtesy, which was openly displayed by him, as well as by the members of his Beth Din, towards all those who were not part of the Orthodox establishment. The immediate result was to squeeze out any non-Orthodox body from participation in those occasions when all shades of opinion in the community should have been represented ...[20]
>
> I believe that the time is ripe for some positive action on the part of the Reform Synagogues of Great Britain and all 'free' synagogues – those not associated with the United Synagogue or other Orthodox bodies.
>
> We should convene a conference to appoint delegates to wait upon Sir Isaac Wolfson and the honorary officers of the United Synagogue, in order to express our dissatisfaction at the lack of co-operation and to seek assurances that this will not recur. If such assurances are not forthcoming, or they indicate that they are powerless to act, we should give notice of our intention to appoint our own representative on all State or civic occasions.
>
> While hitherto, through a sort of gentleman's agreement and in order to give the appearance of unanimity to the non-Jewish community, the non-Orthodox bodies have recognised the representative capacity of the Chief Rabbi, there is no law which states that this situation cannot be altered. Similarly, the time is right and opportune to change the constitution of the Board of Deputies so that non-Orthodox synagogues should no longer be placed in a position of jeopardy.[21]

Herzog's installation was set for November 1965, and preparations were well in hand for his induction service at the St John's Wood Synagogue.[22] But a fortnight after these plans were announced, he was compelled to withdraw 'owing to a serious deterioration of his health',[23] and the selection process began afresh. Thus it was that many hats returned to the ring, with further indecision from Jakobovits, the front-runner,[24] but, ultimately, with a not-unexpected result. He wrote:

> In the end, the decisive judgment came from my father-in-law, Rabbi

Elie Munk, of Paris. He asserted – perhaps ruled is the better word – that morally I was duty-bound to accept the challenge and had no right to refuse it, lest the office fall into the wrong hands.

I was swayed, moreover, by the feeling that I could never justify refusing to serve the community in a country that had saved my life. Gradually, there seemed to be an inevitability about it all, and it made my final acceptance inescapable.[25]

Although his acceptance may have been inescapable, doubts nonetheless continued to plague him. Telling Herzog that 'it may be my fate to step into your unused shoes',[26] Jakobovits wrote that his agreement was 'dependent, above all, on succeeding in bringing about a reconciliation and some *modus vivendi* with the JC-Jacobs faction as an indispensable condition to communal unity and, thus, to the discharge of my duties'. It was therefore his intention to undertake a 'peace mission' to London in the hope that 'I may render Anglo-Jewry a greater service before assuming office than I might ever have occasion to do later'.

Herzog questioned the wisdom of a 'peace mission', believing that

> if the various factions know that your acceptance may be dependent on the outcome of such a mission, they may put up obstacles in your way. I think the wisest course for you will be to accept without delay, while asking publicly for the co-operation of all sections of the community in the efforts you will make to restore peace.
>
> I believe that the basic sense of discipline and institutional attachment of Anglo-Jewry are in your favour. The spectre of schism is so great that you will have many avenues through which to work. I have the feeling that all sides will give you a year or so to chart your course. During this time, you will be able to assess the forces and find your way.[27]

Herzog added later: 'It is my general impression, though I cannot prove it, that the crisis in Anglo-Jewry has boiled over and that the community at large will resist any attempt in the future to revive it';[28] and, following Jakobovits' visit to Britain, 'I was pleased to read of your basically positive impressions of London and feel that you have started off very well'.[29]

Jakobovits' appointment was sealed, without dissent or discussion, at a meeting of the Chief Rabbinate Conference on 11 September 1966.[30] Presiding over the gathering, attended by around half of the two hundred and fifty delegates entitled to vote, Wolfson declared that he had been 'immensely heartened' by the fact that the selection committee's choice had been unanimous and that it had coincided with the views expressed both by the London Beth Din and by the representatives of the ministry. He praised Jakobovits' decision not to give an affirmative answer to the call extended to him until he had visited London and ascertained for himself the prospects of 'unifying the community under his leadership'.

In a subsequent message to the new Chief Rabbi,[31] Wolfson expressed his confidence that, 'with your appointment, Anglo-Jewry can now look forward to a new era, and one that will bring unity to the community, which has long been divided through lack of leadership'. As for the dayanim, whose views (as Wolfson put it) had 'coincided' with those of the committee, their sentiments were expressed to Jakobovits via the Beth Din-in-Commission. Its spokesman wrote:

> The dayanim believe that it is imperative that the Chief Rabbi should enjoy complete freedom of judgment and be unfettered in the conduct of his office.
>
> They feel sure that, when you are here, there will be frank discussions which will settle any differences of approach. They also know, and wish you to know, that the overwhelming majority of the Anglo-Jewish community are looking forward with eagerness to your arrival.[32]

To the retired Grunfeld, whom Jakobovits regarded as 'almost in loco parentis', the Chief Rabbi-elect confided:

> I have the impression that the prospects for a reconciliation may not be quite as distant as they generally appear. I imagine that both sides (the Beth Din no less than the JC-Jacobs groups) are by now sick of this purely destructive conflict and looking for an honourable way out.
>
> To find an acceptable formula will not be easy, but I believe that, while there will have to be some give-and-take on a few matters of substance, the main need is the creation of a new atmosphere of friendliness, trust and good will. I am prepared to go a very long way to achieve this, particularly since I continue to believe, as I did in my Amsterdam conference paper of 1957,[33] that our main challenge today is not Reform but secularism ...
>
> I am anxiously looking for some bridges to the other side. I have to disabuse their minds of their sedulously fostered image of me as a 'right-wing extremist' when, in fact, with my background and outlook – which I share with you – I am as critical of right-wing militancy as of left-wing extremism.
>
> In short, I have to create a climate of mutual confidence and amicability, of an 'agreement to disagree', so long as my right to submit

to halachic Judaism, and to interpret it as I, not they, understand it, is respected. In other words, the war against one another must be called off once and for all, and reasonable persuasion must take its place.[34]

Brodie, like Grunfeld, had meanwhile stepped down. His last sermon as Chief Rabbi had been preached at the Western Synagogue, where he spoke of the 'happy relationship' that existed between himself and the congregation.[35] Days later, he and his wife, Fanny, moved into a flat in London's Portland Place, gifted them through a fund set up by Wolfson.[36]

Reviewing Brodie's travails as Chief Rabbi, the *Jewish Chronicle* had been in a conciliatory mood: 'A man whose every instinct disposed him to tranquillity was at once thrown into a raging conflict which tore the community asunder and whose effects have not yet entirely abated. Yet he pursued his course with tenacity and resolution, at great cost in peace of mind, personal happiness and health. In all he undertook, Rabbi Brodie has been a dedicated servant of the community, of the Jewish people, and the interests of Judaism as he saw them.'[37]

* * *   * *   * * *

Watched by 5,000 people in London and (through closed-circuit television) the provinces, Jakobovits was installed into office – uniquely, at the time – by his careworn predecessor. 'I am content', declared Brodie,

> in the knowledge that a successor has been chosen who, like his predecessors, will uphold with steadfastness and constancy the authority, the validity, the relevance of the Torah, Written and Oral ...
>
> Certain and firm in conviction, mature in the gift of exposition, he is equipped to teach, to guide, to redirect and fortify those of our time who walk about as if in darkness, the doubting and the frustrated, the strayers and the discontented with the teachings and demands of our spiritual heritage. They will listen: many will respond when heart talks to heart.[38]

Describing his role as that of prophet and priest, guardian of 'the Judaism which was never in step with the times, which will never be in accord with the times until the times are in accord with Judaism', Jakobovits told his new-found flock:[39]

> It will be my priestly duty to offer you, as best I can, this Judaism, fragrant and refreshing like incense, to make it meaningful and attractive. But in my priestly charge, I must also insist on sacrifices. Do not ask me to make Judaism easier or cheaper, to devaluate its

worth to the soft currency of convenience. I can no more offer you a programme without toil and sacrifice than you can offer me a life of ease and leisure.

There is no instant Torah, prepared in one or three hours a week of study and practice, no Judaism without tears, just as there is no creation without travail and no triumph without hardship. Remember always, a religion which demands nothing is worth nothing, and a community which sacrifices nothing merits nothing.

Let me here make this quite clear: I am resolved to preserve the Orthodox traditions of my office and the predominantly traditional character of our community. To borrow from the memorable words uttered, in Britain's finest hour, by the man to whom we all owe our lives and our freedom: I have not become Anglo-Jewry's First Minister in order to preside over the liquidation of British Judaism.

I will do my best to serve and unite all sections of the community, but I am not prepared to replace the Torah by an umbrella, either open or closed, as the symbol of my office. In any event, I anticipate fair weather rather than rain or hail, and we should not require any umbrellas. For, in my priestly capacity, I also want to be among the disciples of Aaron in 'loving peace and pursuing peace'.

In my attitude to all my fellow-Jews, I will look to the example of the saintly Rabbi Kook's boundless 'love of Israel', and of my revered father's broad tolerance. In our free society, I cannot ensure that everyone will submit to my decisions, but I can aspire to earn respect for my convictions and for my right to make decisions as my conscience dictates. I cannot bend or compromise Jewish law which is not mine to make or unmake, but I can administer it with compassion and despatch.

To those whose faith in the divine origin of the whole Torah is weak and who do not accept the discipline of Judaism as entrusted to me, may I say this in all solemnity: Never forget the immense tragedy of our religious differences. Should your and our hearts not bleed with grief when we, your brothers and heirs to a common tradition, cannot worship in your synagogues, cannot eat in your homes, and sometimes cannot even marry your sons and daughters, because laws which we recognise as divine and sacred have become meaningless to you, because what has united us for thousands of years now estranges you? ...

Meanwhile, it will be my privilege and my duty to do all within my power and authority to close the gaps within our people, and I appeal to all segments of the community for help in this vital effort. To this end, I pledge all the skills and resources I command, for God will hold me to account for the failings of any Jew I can influence, as well as for my own many shortcomings.

Nevertheless, I recognise dissent as an inescapable fact of Jewish life today. I will seek to befriend those who dissent, and to work with them in Jewish and general causes unaffected by our religious differences. After the devastating losses we have suffered by slaughter, repression and assimilation, every Jew's contribution to the enrichment of Jewish life is now more precious than ever, and I will encourage all British Jews to give of their best to the common good.[40]

In the run-up to his installation, Jakobovits had laid out his terms for accepting the post. A memorandum to the Chief Rabbinate Committee had included a passage aimed at 'resolving the religious crisis', in the belief that

I can assume that all parties to the recent conflict are by now thoroughly tired of the costly strife, disenchanted with the sterile results achieved, saddened by the bitterness and disunity which have disrupted the once-solid structure of the community, and anxious to find an honourable solution.

I regard my ability to resolve the existing religious crisis in Anglo-Jewry as a crucial test of the community's confidence in my leadership, and my own confidence in measuring up to the skills needed in the discharge of my duties.

I cannot work in a climate of continuous tension, nor under the pressure of abuse, subversion and misrepresentation. Communal peace, good will and unity are indispensable prerequisites to my success in the office, and therefore to my acceptance.

The dignity of the Chief Rabbinate, too, cannot be upheld in a community rent by ill-will and destructive conflicts. I am not prepared, or able, to preside over a constant succession of quarrels and hostilities in which the community will be reduced to a shambles, my office to a partisan battle headquarters, and my health to a wreck ...

For my part, I am prepared to go a very long way in my quest for a lasting reconciliation, based on friendliness and mutual trust as well as on respect for our sacred traditions. Of course, I realise there will have to be some give-and-take on a few matters of substance, but primarily I think the situation calls for a new outlook and attitude on all sides, the creation of an atmosphere of good will, and an amicable 'agreement to disagree' within some well-defined limits.

Seeking 'an understanding [that] should not be beyond reach or reason', the incoming Chief Rabbi asked those on what he termed 'the left wing' to abide by four conditions:

> to respect the Chief Rabbinate as an institution which is and will remain Orthodox, reflecting the religious loyalties, if not necessarily the views, of the overwhelming majority of religious Jews; to leave the determination and interpretation of Jewish law to duly qualified experts, and to oppose any incitement against their rulings by pressure groups, newspapers or especially individuals who themselves neither acknowledge nor practise the dictates of the halachah; to refrain from subversion, abuse and denigration directed at any established communal institution or its leaders; and to make the maximum positive contribution to the enrichment and unity of Jewish life.[41]

In response to these terms, Goldberg had written to Jakobovits that 'I should like nothing more than to meet with you during your few days in London. As a senior minister in the Reform movement of this country, I am extremely concerned about communal unity, a problem which I know is also actuating your mind, and I feel sure that, as between colleagues, I could tell you a great deal.'[42]

That there was, indeed, a great deal to tell had become evident some months earlier when, on behalf of the Progressives, Goldberg and Brichto drew up terms of their own:

> While recognising that in matters of halachah there is little ground of agreement between the ecclesiastical authorities of the United Synagogue and other sections of Anglo-Jewry, it is nonetheless possible for the status quo in respect of the representative nature of the Office of Chief Rabbi to be continued if the Chief Rabbi recognises the existence of all religious elements in Anglo-Jewry other than those under the aegis of the United Synagogue and its affiliated bodies. In practice this means:
>
> 1. Rabbis under the aegis of the United Synagogue should not be barred from sharing platforms with religious leaders of different sections of Anglo-Jewry, nor from visiting non-Orthodox synagogues should they so desire.
>
> 2. On those occasions when religious services are held to commemorate or celebrate events of importance to the whole of Anglo-Jewry – for example, Israel Independence Day, occasions such as the Tercentenary, national anniversaries, and memorial days – such services should be sponsored by a representative body made up of all religious sections in the community.
>
> 3. On occasions where the individuals concerned wish it, religious

leaders of other sections should be invited to participate in ceremonial events.

4. As was usually the case in the days of the late Dr J.H. Hertz, the Chief Rabbi will be free to accept invitations to all synagogues and communal functions in the Anglo-Jewish community, and the terms of his appointment will encourage him to do so.

5. As it is obviously unfair to those congregations which are not under the aegis of the United Synagogue to be dependent on the Chief Rabbi as the ecclesiastical authority of the Board of Deputies for recognition as 'congregations of Jews professing the Jewish religion', the right is reserved to raise this matter at the Deputies with a view to change.

The acceptance of principles 1-4 would serve to make the Office of the Chief Rabbi a unifying rather than a dividing force in Anglo-Jewry; and while not leading to undesired uniformity, it would increase harmony between the different elements of Anglo-Jewry.

In order to further this aim, it is also hoped that a Conference of Rabbis might be formed in which religious leaders of all sections could work together towards the enhancement of Judaism in this country.[43]

Taking in these concerns, and anticipating the line he was to adopt in his installation address, Jakobovits concluded an open message to the community with words of hope:

> I will stretch out my hand in friendship to all who care to give me theirs, whether they share my beliefs or not; I will respect them even if I have to oppose their views.
>
> I have every faith in the yearning of most British Jews for turning a new leaf to inaugurate a fruitful era of reconciliation and religious reawakening. I hope you will sustain this faith by helping me to restore the solidarity of our people with its origin and its destiny as the proud bearers of our timeless heritage.[44]

The spiritual and lay leaders of the Progressive movements, in turn, were in generous mood: 'We assume', they responded,

> that this gesture is intended to include Reform and Liberal Jews and we gladly extend our hands in return.
>
> Indeed, in our case it will be but a renewal of handshaking, for when Rabbi Jakobovits came to London at the end of July, he was the recipient of warm good wishes sent to him by leading personalities in progressive Jewry, coupled with the earnest wish for a happy co-operation in communal matters. Moreover, two of the signatories of this letter met Rabbi Jakobovits, with whom they had a most friendly

discussion on various matters of common interest.

We think it is a very good augury for the future that the new Chief Rabbi of the United Synagogue not only appreciates that there are independent movements within Anglo-Jewry which exercise religious autonomy, but also respects them and is prepared to work with them.

We trust, indeed we regard it as essential, that this attitude should extend to a recognition of the fact that, as fellow Jews, we are entitled to express our own independent views and be represented on appropriate communal and national occasions. For, as Rabbi Jakobovits said in his letter, albeit in another context, 'We ought to be partners, not rivals or antagonists.'[45]

In a separate message to the Liberals, Jakobovits affirmed that his declaration reflected 'the letter and the spirit of our friendly discussions in London ... You will appreciate that the rapprochement we seek is bound to be a gradual process requiring patience as well as courage, and that any pressure or counter-pressure for sudden and drastic changes might seriously vitiate the chances for success from the beginning. We have to walk before we can run, so long as we move forward in the right direction towards a better understanding.'[46]

\* \* \*   \* \* \*   \* \* \*

A potential first step 'in the right direction' was an attempt, early in Jakobovits' incumbency, to clear the air over the validity of Reform and Liberal marriages, befogged by the Beth Din's attack two years earlier. In a statement, the Chief Rabbi's Office confirmed Brichto's assertion that 'no responsible Orthodox authority would ever deny that where a marriage took place in a Liberal synagogue which could just as well have taken place in an Orthodox synagogue,[47] the children of such a marriage could become members of, and indeed be married in, an Orthodox synagogue'.

It added, however, 'the view of Dr Jakobovits that the crucial issue between the communities is not that of marriages which could take place in an Orthodox synagogue, but those marriages "which contravene traditional Jewish law but are permitted by us [Liberals] – for example, cases of *chalitzah, agunah*, etc". He feels that the proviso "where a marriage ... could just as well have taken place in an Orthodox synagogue" should receive more emphasis than it did, since quite obviously the crucial point at issue – often leading to such tragic results – concerns the very marriages performed at Liberal synagogues which contravene traditional Jewish law.'

Welcoming the statement, the Liberals' president, Lord Cohen of

Walmer, said that their rabbis had agreed to 'co-operate fully in any attempt to alleviate the hardships caused by the differences between the two movements, and to further discussion with the authorities of the Orthodox community. I am sure that our Union will not spare any effort in working for the greater unity of our community which will result from the mutual respect and good will among all its religious sections.'[48]

Such confidence was, however, somewhat misplaced, since 'mutual respect and good will' appeared lacking among religious sections to the right of the Chief Rabbi, including those who accepted his authority. One such critic was Cardiff's Rogosnitzky, who years before had been Brodie's ally in the 'war on Reform'. Writing to Jakobovits, he warned:

> I know you feel that it should be possible to fraternise with the Reform and regard them as 'yidden', in the hope that proximity will help to 'convert' them back to Judaism. But this blinds itself to the harm it does to our youth, who, seeing such contact, will misinterpret it and consider the equal status in religion of the two groups ...
>
> I concur fully with your oft-repeated remarks regarding the need for communal support of our educational establishments, the provision of essential educational needs, and of talmidim for training and service as rabbis, teachers and communal leaders, to man our spiritual defences. When these ideals are brought to fruition, we will be able to reappraise the situation, perhaps on the lines you suggest.
>
> Until then, it is my earnest appeal that you withdraw from your present policy of rapprochement with the Reform, Liberals and so-called Progressive movements. I feel strongly that any closer association by you with them will serve only to alienate further the right-wing Orthodox.
>
> I know you expect little from the Reform. Why, then, do you harm yourself by diminishing the confidence of your most ardent supporters? Modern days and modern English Jewry require strong fences before proper bridges can be built.[49]

Despite this rap on the knuckles, and although aware of the pitfalls, Jakobovits was bent on pursuing his policy of dialogue and reconciliation, both before and after he took up office. On the eve of his arrival, he had written to Brichto:

> You must realise that the proposals I have made represent a most revolutionary departure from Orthodox attitudes in the past, proposals which have already encountered much bitter opposition from among some of my friends.

I cannot hope gradually to win widespread support for this new outlook unless a similar earnestness in the search for good will and understanding is manifested on your side without a dogmatic, take-it-or-leave-it attitude. What we want to initiate are historic developments leading to a gradual relaxation of the tensions produced by such challenges as 'you must attend my religious services'.

Altogether, I feel that the understanding we seek will be more readily forthcoming through private discussions and unobtrusive gestures rather than through public debates and widely advertised 'concessions'. Thus, I would like to feel that in time we can exchange speakers on each other's platforms without arousing public comment, inevitably leading to acrimonious arguments each time we do so.

In short, what is needed is a sincere, quiet quest for a fresh climate of 'live and let live', and not a noisy clamour for panaceas or *causes célèbres*. To achieve this *détente* and to open up such a new era of communal reconstruction I am committed, and I hope you will enthusiastically share this commitment with me.[50]

Perhaps mistaking the reference to 'each other's platforms' as a call for early action, Brichto wrote back asking whether 'it would be premature [for you] to accept an invitation to speak to a Liberal conference'.[51] Jakobovits replied that he 'looked forward to continuing our "dialogue" in person once I am settled in London', but added: 'At this early stage in our search for a *détente*, I am most anxious to avoid anything which may be construed as provocation by those who still have to be conditioned to the new climate we need.'[52]

\* \* \*   \* \* \*   \* \* \*

Among other partners in Jakobovits' sights was Louis Jacobs, who, unbeknown to him, was being courted – inconclusively, as it turned out – by both sides. During his pre-Chief Rabbinical visit to 'spy out the land',[53] the two met in London's Holland Park, 'secluded enough for no one to be likely to see us' (as Jacobs put it). In the course of their hour-long discussion,

Rabbi Jakobovits said that he would like us to be good friends if he came to England to be the Chief Rabbi. He did not think that differing views on the nature of Revelation (*Torah min hashamayim*) were a bar to co-operation, and he felt that I would have a role to play in the Orthodox community.

In his opinion, the unifying force was that of acceptance of the traditional halachah. He asked me if I had any criticisms of the manner in which the halachah was currently interpreted by the London Beth Din. I told him of the injustices that were being perpetrated in the Beth Din's refusal to accept the children of mixed marriages or adopted children brought up as Jews. He felt that a situation in which the rulings of more liberal-minded rabbis – such as the religious authorities in Israel – were adopted could possibly be arranged in this country.

He saw no reason why the enmity and bitterness in the community should not be gradually overcome, but for this to happen there would have to be 'give and take' on both sides.

Without Rabbi Jakobovits spelling this out, he seemed to be suggesting that I would be allowed to officiate at funerals, weddings, tombstone consecrations and the like even under the auspices of the United Synagogue, but in return the New London Synagogue would have to recognise the religious authority of the Chief Rabbi with regard to such questions as marriage, divorce and conversion.

He felt, however, that all this would have to come about gradually, and the beginning should be that a greater spirit of friendship and co-operation should be fostered.

My overall impression was that Rabbi Jakobovits was quite sincere in his quest for friendship and co-operation, but that the price he would demand would be complete acceptance of the Shulchan Aruch, at least in its more liberal interpretation.

On the personal level, I found him charming and considerate. But his general views on religion strike me as very reactionary, even though he poses as a 'modern'. For instance, he said that he was convinced that the future of Judaism was with the people in Stamford Hill and that, ultimately, his religious guides must be the *gedolei hador* – that is, the famous *heimische rabbanim*.

I found his attitude here frankly appalling. Our guides are to be Rabbi Moshe Feinstein, etc., and although one may have certain reservations about their attitudes, these must hardly ever be expressed because otherwise Judaism would vanish. He appears to hold that theological questions are not terribly important, but that 'acceptance of the supremacy of the halachah' is of supreme importance.

Moreover, there is not really much room for a liberal interpretation of the halachah since the authority of the *gedolei hador* must never, or hardly ever, be publicly questioned. If this means anything at all, it means that the ultimate religious authorities of Anglo-Jewry will be Rabbi Moshe Feinstein, Rabbi Soloveitchik and other famous rabbis of the old school in Israel and the United States.[54]

Probably, at first, there will be a semblance of liberalism in thought (quite sincere, I believe), but the fat will be in the fire as soon as practical questions of any significance arise.[55]

Describing their meeting as 'cloak-and-dagger stuff',[56] Jacobs was later to write: 'Neither of us had any clear idea about the expected outcome of the meeting. [Jakobovits] did make it clear, however, that he distanced himself from my views if not from my person. When he became Chief Rabbi, he did his best to be friendly, and I think I reciprocated.'[57]

At the same time, Brichto was 'doing his best to be friendly' and had approached the New London Synagogue for exploratory talks. 'Needless to say', Jacobs replied, 'I would like very much to meet you to discuss matters of mutual interest.'[58] They conferred at Jacobs' home and, as a result, Brichto concluded, 'I am very hopeful that all of us will have something very positive to contribute to the welfare of *Klal Yisrael*.'[59] But, as positive as they tried to be, these attempts at co-operation similarly evaporated.

Following their Holland Park encounter, Jakobovits and Jacobs were to square up again on the eve of the induction, when the New London minister examined 'Where the Chief Rabbi Stands' in a review of his *Journal of a Rabbi*. Commenting on a reference in the anthology to the controversies surrounding him, Jacobs wrote:

> Thoughtful readers will peruse the book in order to discover the Chief Rabbi's attitudes on Judaism and its relation to the particular problems of our day. It is to the author's credit that, on the whole, he states unambiguously where he stands, though whether this is where we would like to see him standing is another matter ...
>
> I do not wish at this stage to offer much comment on his remarks about me, except to say that it is clear that he sides with his predecessor in considering my views harmful to faith and that, consequently, his recent suggestion that if I were to accept his authority 'the path would be open to a reconciliation' is presumably an invitation to me to abandon my views.[60]

That suggestion had been made in an interview with the *Sunday Times*, in which Jakobovits had stated: 'If he [Jacobs] can see his way clear to accepting the jurisdiction of the Chief Rabbinate, the path to reconciliation would be wide open.'[61]

Responding, Jacobs had asserted that

> acceptance by the New London Synagogue of the authority of the Chief Rabbi ought to be seen clearly as irrelevant to the question of 'reconciliation'.
>
> I was brought up, by pious rabbis of the old school, to believe that

the Chief Rabbinate, of very recent origin, is an example of *hukkat ha-goy*, and further experience and study have convinced me that in this they were right.

It is not only that the idea of a superior rabbi is unknown in Judaism and involves the abdication by the subordinate rabbi of the responsibilities conferred on him by his *semichah*. The office of chief rabbi in Anglo-Jewry is modelled on that of bishop and archbishop in the Christian Church, which, in turn, is based on belief in the apostolic succession.

Thus, unlike the wearing of the clerical collar and canonicals, the institution has strong doctrinal overtones. It is not for us to cast stones at those who see fit to recognise the office, but for ourselves we prefer to abide by Jewish tradition.

What can 'reconciliation' mean in this context? If it means that our group will engage in friendly dialogue with other groups in Anglo-Jewry and work together with them for the many aims we all have in common, this is already happening; and where it is not, the remedy lies with Rabbi Jakobovits and his colleagues.[62]

'Many of his friends', retorted Rabbi Isaac Chait, of Sheffield, on reading this comment, 'were pained and puzzled by the letter which Dr Louis Jacobs wrote spurning the hand of friendship outstretched to him by the new Chief Rabbi, inviting him to come under his wing. It was an opportunity missed for closing the rift between himself and the community.'[63]

A disenchanted Jacobs begged to differ. 'I have not "spurned the hand of friendship"', he told his pained and puzzled friend,

because none has been offered. All that Rabbi Jakobovits has done is to communicate to our group (not directly but through an interview he gave to a Sunday newspaper) that if we were to recognise his authority, 'the path would be open to reconciliation'.

If we were to recognise the Chief Rabbi's authority, there would be no need for reconciliation, for then we would have no separate identity as a congregation holding its own views. Like the other congregations under the Chief Rabbi's jurisdiction, we would be obliged to accept his opinions even where these differ from ours.

We are anxious to be friends with Rabbi Jakobovits and the congregations he represents, but he must not ask as the price the surrender of all that we have built up and have stood for during the three years of our existence.[64]

Friendship of sorts manifested itself the following year when Jacobs and Jakobovits shared the platform at a Hampstead Synagogue meeting of B'nai B'rith, of which both were members. The Chief Rabbi was speaking on Jewish medical ethics, and Jacobs, who presided, remarked that 'anyone expecting the flashing of knives will be disappointed', for the gathering was to be in accord with the B'nai B'rith motto of 'benevolence, brotherly love and harmony'. But, he added, while he subscribed to the first two, he was 'not certain about the third'.

Jakobovits recalled the biblical story of two brothers who, after many arguments, had made a public reconciliation by shaking hands and kissing each other. The most important aspect, he said, was not the reconciliation but the fact that one of the brothers, Jacob, had successfully struggled on his own to overcome his ill feelings towards his opponent. The Chief Rabbi expressed the hope that 'everyone could go through such struggles with themselves when ideas assail them and become ultimately successful in carrying out the ideas behind the teachings of Judaism'.

Jacobs responded by asking if he should regard himself as the Esau of that biblical story, to which his guest replied that he had purposely mentioned only Jacob, whose name was incorporated in both of theirs. The verbal exchange took a more serious turn when a member of the audience suggested that their appearance on the same platform might 'signal a new phase in communal unity'. Jakobovits replied that the platform could be shared when the subject did not impinge on religious differences, 'otherwise we must go our separate ways'.[65]

That they were to go their separate ways had been demonstrated earlier that summer, when the New London Synagogue hosted the seventh international convention of the Conservatives' World Council of Synagogues, with the keynote address by its foremost rabbinical scholar, Louis Finkelstein, and with the participation of, among others, Danish Chief Rabbi Marcus Melchior – whose son and successor, Jews' College alumnus Bent Melchior, Jakobovits was to ban (as will shortly be seen) from preaching in a United Synagogue pulpit.

The New London's affiliation to the World Council occurred soon after the convention, at which the movement's director, Morris Laub, had declared: 'We do not proselytise or propagandise. Whether or not we start an affiliate here depends on whether there is any demand from Anglo-Jewry.

'We have room for diversity of opinion, and we are liberal in our interpretation. Our left is pretty progressive, and our right is pretty traditional. But we do insist that any synagogue joining us should be Sabbath- and kashrut-observing ... We feel that British Jewry, and the London community in particular, are as vibrant a branch of Jewry as one can find anywhere in the world today, and its intellectual quality is something that impresses us all.'[66]

Commenting on the convention, Jakobovits remarked in a New Year message to 'the leadership of Anglo-Jewry': 'Especially notable, in [the] context of unity, was the prudent restraint observed during the recent Conservative conference in London by protagonists, antagonists and other interested parties alike. The restraint on all sides undoubtedly prevented this conference from spawning a further tragic schism within Anglo-Jewry, as many had feared (without cause, as it turned out) and some had hoped (without effect).'[67]

That his optimism was misplaced was to become manifestly evident in the years ahead.

\* \* \*  \* \* \*  \* \* \*

Like the Reform and Liberals before them, the New London Synagogue faced the problem of marriage certification. 'We had to struggle at first to obtain a marriage secretary', Jacobs recalled,[68] 'and for the first two or three years [during Brodie's Chief Rabbinate], the local registrar of marriages had to be present at every one of our ceremonies. But when Chief Rabbi Jakobovits was elected, the problem was solved, and we had a marriage secretary without being compelled to recognise his authority.'

This was achieved within three months of Jakobovits' induction, in accordance with the constitution of the Board of Deputies. On 20 June 1967, responding to an application signed by the warden and five members of the New London Synagogue, the Chief Rabbi granted the congregation a certificate testifying that it constituted 'a synagogue of persons professing the Jewish religion'.[69] Two weeks later, on 2 July, the Board authorised its president, Solomon Teff, 'to certify the appointment of a first secretary (for marriages) for the New London Synagogue, which had obtained from the Chief Rabbi the appropriate certificate required under Clause 44 of the Board's constitution'.[70]

Seeking to allay later concerns on this score, Jakobovits told the Chief Rabbinate Council: 'Regarding the New London Synagogue, this is neither Reform nor Liberal and generally not in breach of our principles, as they recognise the guidelines of halachic law.' He added, however, that 'in the case of converts, they sometimes carry out marriages which our office would not accept'.[71]

Initially, marriages conducted at the New London between halachically Jewish partners were recorded (when requested) in the London Beth Din registry, but once New London conversions became a contentious issue, this practice was discontinued.[72] After what Jacobs described as 'a smear campaign'[73] by the Beth Din, raising 'a question-mark against every marriage performed under our aegis', he published a forthright statement on 'the question of personal status in Jewish law'.

> Since we do not perform any marriages where there is a legal impediment, the status of the children is unaffected in any event. The children of all our marriages are perfectly kosher. They can be married in the most Orthodox of synagogues.
>
> If any of our congregants, having been reassured about the kashrut of their children, are still worried about whether – having been married in our synagogue – their marriage is valid for the purpose of their living together as husband and wife, they need not have the slightest fear that it is all perfectly kosher.
>
> Whether, to introduce a personal note – which, unfortunately, I have to – I am *persona non grata* to some Orthodox rabbis is irrelevant. Couples married in the New London Synagogue are not married by me (the concept of a rabbi 'marrying' a couple has no meaning in Jewish law; the rabbi is not a Christian priest – indeed, he is not a priest at all). They are married by the fact that the marriage ceremonies (the delivery of the ring in the presence of witnesses, with the formal declaration) have been carried out in the proper manner ...

On conversion, Jacobs wrote:

> It has to be said clearly and distinctly that all the conversions which have been carried out under the aegis of the New London Synagogue are strictly in accordance with the *din* ... All our conversions are valid and there are no grounds on which they can be challenged. Of course, I cannot issue any guarantee that they will not be challenged, and always inform prospective converts of this.
>
> The procedures of the New London Synagogue in matters of personal status are in full accordance with traditional Jewish law. We cannot claim that we have an especially humane attitude because that would imply that the law is not in itself humane. Nor can we claim that we are 'modern' in our interpretation since the situation we have described is that which is inherent in the law itself.
>
> This defence of our procedures would not be required at all were it not that Orthodox officialdom is now determined to act in these matters in a manner far in excess of other Orthodox rabbis, and with an attitude beside which the Neturei Karta are a model of tolerance and sobriety.[74]

No sooner had this 'defence' appeared than the dayanim hit back with the challenge that Jacobs had predicted. 'The London Beth Din', its clerk announced, 'does not normally feel obliged to comment on unfounded generalisations, such as those from Dr Louis Jacobs. However, in view of the confusion that his statements may cause, I am instructed to inform the public that marriages performed by Dr Jacobs (the minister of the New London Synagogue), even in cases where both parties are eligible for marriage according to Jewish law, have no more halachic validity than marriages contracted in a register office in civil law. Conversions under the auspices of Dr Jacobs have no validity whatsoever in Jewish law.'[75]

Commenting on behalf of the Beth Din, Dayan Isaac Berger said that, on the marriage issue, the reason for their non-validity was that 'the halachic requirement of the status of the witnesses is not being complied with in all cases.

'As to the need for a *get* on the dissolution of such a marriage, as with civil marriages, each case must be submitted to the Beth Din to be decided in the light of its particular circumstances. In cases where the parties were eligible to marry in Jewish law, an invalid ceremony itself does not affect the status of the children.'[76]

During this very public dispute, which lasted several weeks, the voice of Jakobovits was nowhere to be heard. 'What has been very noticeable', declared one observer, 'has been the silence of the Chief Rabbi on the matter. The fact that he has been so silent can only be interpreted as meaning that he does *not* agree with the statement of the Beth Din.'[77] The New London, meanwhile, conducted its marriages and conversions as it had done before, and on this point the Chief Rabbi remained silent throughout his tenure in office.

\* \* \*   \* \* \*   \* \* \*

Jakobovits had not remained silent, however, when in 1972 an invitation was extended to Bent Melchior, who had succeeded to the Danish Chief Rabbinate following his father's death some thirty months earlier, to occupy the pulpit of London's Kenton Synagogue during its ministerial interregnum. The younger Melchior, then aged 43, was a graduate of Jews' College who, during his five years' rabbinical training, had preached at both Kenton and Kingsbury (where he lived), as well as to other congregations within the United Synagogue.

The Danish Chief Rabbi had been invited to attend the wedding in Kenton of a young man at whose barmitzvah he had officiated during his Jews' College studentship. Following his arrival in London, 'informal soundings' were made to ask him to preach in the synagogue, but – as warden Raymond Cannon later revealed – 'when I welcomed Rabbi Melchior in our midst, we could not extend to him a formal invitation to address us from the pulpit because the required consent from our own Chief Rabbi had not been forthcoming'.[78]

The Chief Rabbi's Office confirmed that although there had 'apparently been no objection to Rabbi Melchior personally', it was his continued association with the World Council of Synagogues, of which he was a vice-president, that prevented him preaching in any synagogue under the jurisdiction of Chief Rabbi Jakobovits. 'The pulpits under the Chief Rabbi's jurisdiction', said his spokesman, 'are open to rabbis who do not at the same time belong to any non-Orthodox religious body. It has been the invariable practice in all congregations under the Chief Rabbi's jurisdiction to extend the freedom of their pulpits only to men of unimpeachable Orthodoxy.'

Asked to comment, Melchior — who was described as the leader of 'a religiously unified community in the same spirit of traditional Judaism displayed by his late father' — recalled that he had addressed United Synagogue congregations not only in his college days but also later, when acting as rabbinical assistant to his father, and had been a member of the Conference of European Rabbis, of which Chief Rabbi Israel Brodie had been the founder and president.

'Yet all these years until my father died', said Melchior, 'he was at the same time a vice-president of the World Council of Synagogues, of which I too have been a member. It was only after my father's death, when I took over both the office of Danish Chief Rabbi and the vice-presidency of the World Council, that I found — to my astonishment — that I had become *persona non grata* with some of the Orthodox rabbis.

'I was no longer invited to their European conferences, and only when I inquired about the reason for my exclusion was I informed by the secretary, Rabbi A.M. Rose, who is also the executive director of the Chief Rabbi's Office in London, that it was due to my association with the World Council.'

Melchior added that when Jakobovits' consent to preach was withheld, 'I contacted the Chief Rabbi myself. On his suggestion that I sever my connection with the World Council, I told him frankly that such a step would contradict my entire approach to my fellow men and especially my fellow Jews, which abhors the isolation and segregation of sections of humanity or within the Jewish people.'[79]

Anxious to reinforce his position, Jakobovits circulated a letter to his ministerial colleagues — marked 'Not for Publication' — which appeared, in truncated form, in the *Jewish Chronicle*. It was not his intention, he wrote,

> to demean myself by entering into a public controversy on the sustained campaign waged against me by the JC. But since the purpose of these intemperate attacks is to subvert the integrity of Orthodox Jewry, the standing of my office, and my relationship with my col-

leagues, I want to share with you some information and reflections on what the JC has significantly chosen to term the 'Melchior Affair'.

Several months ago, informal soundings were made at my office to ascertain whether I would allow Rabbi Melchior, due to visit London in June, to occupy the Kenton pulpit. Normally, the question would have been resolved in consultation with the local minister. But Kenton had no minister.

I gave no definite answer, but simply said that I would take up the matter with Rabbi Melchior personally. I immediately wrote to him, inviting him to meet me together with the Haham, who had also been involved in the matter as a member of the standing committee of the Conference of European Rabbis.

The meeting duly took place on 7 June and lasted for over two hours. On behalf of the committee, we told him it was unanimously felt that his membership of the Conference (which has consistently resisted Conservative inroads into European communities) was incompatible with his association with the Conservative movement. We urged him to give the matter his most careful thought, since he could not owe two conflicting allegiances at the same time.

When he then raised the question of the Kenton pulpit, I explained that, once I would be asked to give a formal ruling on the matter, the answer would depend on his own decision. The so-far friendly discussion turned acid when he threatened that, failing my approval for his preaching, a highly unpleasant publicity campaign would be unleashed against me. I told him that I would never capitulate to threats, nor had I ever surrendered my conscience to the dictates of the press. I was confident I would prevail over such attacks, as I had survived others in the past.[80]

\* \* \*   \* \* \*   \* \* \*

In February 1979, fifteen years after his final immersion in communal controversy, Israel Brodie died. Describing him as 'my second father', Jakobovits said of his 'teacher and mentor':

> He was supremely courageous, inflexible in his defence of Jewish law and beliefs – and of the traditions of Anglo-Jewry – in the face of pressures that no other Chief Rabbi had ever encountered.
>
> Without his resolute steadfastness, Anglo-Jewry might have been very different today; the heart might have been torn out of the heartland of the traditional community. He truly merited the name Yisrael,

given to his first namesake for having 'wrestled with things divine and human, and prevailed'.[81]

Brodie's bête noire passed away a generation later, having months before been voted 'Britain's greatest Jew'[82] in the 350 years since the Cromwellian resettlement. On his death in 2006, the journal that bestowed the title declared of him:

> Rabbi Dr Louis Jacobs will inevitably be associated with the controversy that erupted more than forty years ago over his views on the origin of the Torah, leading to his banishment from the United Synagogue and almost certainly costing him the Chief Rabbinate.
> 
> But far more important than the historic conflicts are the achievements that made him such a seminal figure in this community and beyond. No one better embodied the spirit of *minhag anglia*, the broad-minded traditionalism that he believed to be the hallmark of British Jewry and which many now fear is receding in the face of religious polarisation ...
>
> Above all, he represented the idea of Judaism as a quest. For many, religion today is about certainty and knowing exactly where one stands in a stormy world. By contrast, Jacobs spoke – and through his books will continue to speak – to those who felt both the pull of ancestral faith and the challenge thrown up by advancing knowledge, recognising that the struggle to reconcile them might not be easy.[83]

Jacobs himself might have seen it differently. In his last word on the subject, written at the turn of the century, he asked:

> Was I not being naively trusting and optimistic in believing that I could be 'modernist' within the Orthodox camp?
>
> In the present climate of opinion, it would indeed be ridiculous for someone with my views to lay claim to Orthodoxy, which is why I do not now make any such claim. But at the time of the controversy, there had long been a tolerant, rather bemused acceptance of unconventional views within Anglo-Jewry.
>
> At that time, it was not completely hypocritical for me to label myself as Orthodox – meaning, at the time, simply kosher, in the sense of observant of the precepts – and yet wish to be the head of a traditional institution like Jews' College. This was not to be, however, and, though labels are often restrictive and misleading, honesty now compels me, in order to avoid confusion, to describe my position not as Orthodox but as Masorti.[84]

# 18

# Tokens of Disunity

Despite protestations of harmony and reconciliation, the new Chief Rabbi's relationship with the Reform and Liberal movements trod a mutually defiant and difficult path. The Progressives' positive reactions to his 'hand-of-friendship' gesture speedily dissipated as they perceived – in Goldberg's words[1] – that

> the *status quo ante* will continue, with the possible exception that, at some time he considers fit, he might deign to discuss with us 'our differences'.
>
> In my opinion, it is quite futile to hope that there will be any getting together at services of a communal nature, such as Israel Independence Day and days of national mourning or rejoicing, in view of Dr Jakobovits' statement[2] that 'we can participate together in communal and national events so long as they are not of a specifically religious character in form or locale, implying a mutual endorsement where there can be no mutual endorsement'.

For his part, the Liberals' chairman, Malcolm Slowe, advised caution, declaring that 'we ought to see how Dr Jakobovits behaves in practice and to give him an opportunity to hold out as promised his "hand in friendship". We also have to watch the situation in order to assure ourselves that Dr Jakobovits does not hold himself out as having any jurisdiction outside the community he serves, and this will take a little time.'[3]

Liberal Rabbi John D. Rayner[4] was similarly apprehensive. He wrote:

> On the one hand, we should co-operate with Dr Jakobovits in every possible way, as far as our religious principles permit (which is evidently somewhat farther than his religious principles would permit him to co-operate with *us*). And, within these limits, we should accord to him all the respect, tact, restraint and patience which he can legitimately expect.
>
> On the other hand, we must make it clear to him that he has no jurisdiction, authority or spokesman-status whatsoever vis-à-vis those sections of Anglo-Jewry, including ours, which had no share in

electing him, and that if he steps one inch outside these limits, he must expect from us polite but resolute opposition.[5]

That 'resolute opposition' – on both sides – was soon forthcoming. Within the year, Jakobovits forestalled an attempt to organise a 'unified' communal service, with the joint participation of the Orthodox and Progressives, to mark Israel's twentieth anniversary. In its place, two 'rival'[6] services were held on the same day, one at Marble Arch, sponsored by the United Synagogue, Federation of Synagogues, Sephardim, Zionist Federation and Mizrachi, and attended by the Israeli Ambassador; the other at Berkeley Street, under Reform and Liberal auspices.

The Progressives had suggested a unified service and, through the Reform Assembly of Ministers, had inquired of Jakobovits whether he intended 'to invite members of the Reform and Liberal movements in this country to take part in, and members of their congregations to attend, the service being arranged by the Orthodox'. Their approach followed a decision by the two movements to boycott any service unless their religious representatives were permitted to participate. Replying on Jakobovits' behalf, Maurice Rose stated: 'The Chief Rabbi will continue to encourage the spirit of unity within the Anglo-Jewish community in any sphere that does not impinge on religious differences. He therefore could not agree to combined religious services.'

Commenting on the response and on the Progressives' decision to hold a separate service, Brichto said that he 'much regretted both. We would have preferred one central communal service on such an occasion as Independence Day. We are arranging our own service not to create disunity, but simply to enable our own ministers and members to express their solidarity with Israel.'[7]

In a sermon at the Liberal Jewish Synagogue following the incident, Rayner delivered a scathing attack on Jakobovits' ruling:

> It is true that there never has been a united Anglo-Jewish service on Independence Day; consequently, Dr Jakobovits, as he has pointed out, did not disallow anything that his predecessor had allowed. But that is hardly the point. The point is that the new spirit of communal unity engendered by last year's crisis [the Six-Day War] created a fresh opportunity, and that that opportunity was, in this particular instance, thrown away.
>
> Nevertheless, it would have been no more than a regrettable incident if Dr Jakobovits had not felt obliged to justify his decision and, in so doing, to make remarks which threaten to undermine other attempts at co-operation also ...

> What is disturbing is his whole underlying attitude: his refusal to concede that there can be legitimate differences of opinion; his insistence that any view which differs from his own is not only mistaken but 'inauthentic'; his exaggeration of the differences to such an extent that he does not see the common ground; and his insensitivity which permits him to accuse of 'undermining' Judaism those who are, like himself, devoting their whole lives to its preservation and rejuvenation.
> My point is that such an attitude, certainly if overtly expressed, destroys the very atmosphere in which alone true co-operation can take place. Co-operation requires quite the contrary attitude of mind.
> It requires the kind of attitude which is now being manifested by some of the Christian denominations in their ecumenical dialogues with one another: a certain bigness of vision and generosity of spirit; an eagerness to search for common ground and joy in finding it; a realisation that most differences turn out, on investigation, to be less fundamental than they appear to be at first sight and that, where they persist, they must be handled with tact and delicacy; above all, a deep conviction that charitableness and brotherly love can work wonders.[8]

Following this sermon, Jakobovits and Rayner entered into a lengthy correspondence that became more heated with each passing letter. In his opening reply to Rayner, the Chief Rabbi delivered an uncompromising ultimatum:

> This lamentable lack of any substantive response to my overtures may now compel me to subject my policies of reconciliation to an agonising reappraisal.
> Your widely heralded decisions, at this stage in our efforts to achieve greater communal unity – first to appoint your own independent religious spokesman as a provocative new token of disunity, and then to hold your own Independence Day service for the first time in twenty years – together with your complete failure to acknowledge or match my gestures of good will, represent grave setbacks to the prospects of success.
> I fear that only some dramatic step on your part to narrow our differences can now save the situation from reverting to the breach in Orthodox-Progressive relations as it existed before my arrival on the local scene.[9]

Six weeks and as many exchanges later, Rayner rounded off the correspondence with

> one last attempt to state the position as I see it. The question, it seems

to me, is whether the Orthodox and Progressive sections of Anglo-Jewry, even while each remains as it is now, are willing to co-operate with one another in those areas where their respective consciences do not prevent such co-operation, and to respect reciprocally their differences while these remain.

The exploration of possible changes of policy on the part of one side or the other is indeed desirable, but is a separate issue, not dependent on the former. In my view, this describes the sort of relationship which we should try to establish, and the simple question to which I should still like to have a clear answer from you is whether you do or do not share that view.

In other words, do you or do you not believe in mutual co-operation irrespective of any changes of policy on our part? If not, you are really saying to us: 'I am willing to co-operate with you provided that you cease to be what you are at present.' If so, this is obviously not a basis on which we *could* co-operate and, what is more, this fact will be appreciated by the overwhelming majority of the community.

In that case, therefore, any discontinuation of such co-operation as exists between us at present will clearly be, and will be clearly seen to be, your responsibility. I am sorry if this way of putting the matter is unpalatable to you, but it seems to me to be the undeniable truth.[10]

Jakobovits used the opportunity of his 'New Year Message to the Leadership of Anglo-Jewry' to counter the points made by Rayner. Detailing his efforts 'to relax the tensions of the past', he declared:

Short of recognising, or appearing to recognise, non-Orthodox leaders as spokesmen or teachers of authentic Judaism in any sense – which, had I done so, would make a mockery of the sacrifices and discipline demanded by Orthodox teachings – I did all I could to open up lines of communication and to heal some of the wounds through friendliness and understanding.

In some respects, this spirit of friendliness has been reciprocated, and the quest for preserving unity where unity is possible has been mutual. The communal atmosphere today is certainly far more temperate than could have been anticipated only a short while ago, and this could not have been achieved without the contributions of good will from many quarters.

But I must now admit that my policies have not so far proved an unqualified success. While I was and remain convinced that the *détente* I was seeking would ultimately serve not only to promote communal harmony, but also to strengthen Orthodox interests – through improving the image of the traditional elements and their ability to concentrate on constructive endeavours – many of my Orthodox friends felt otherwise, some of them opposing my policies with great passion and bitterness.

Nor was this exposure to Orthodox suspicion and attack in any way rendered more worthwhile by any compensating response from the Left, or indeed by any recognition of the strides made from the rest of the community. In fact, I am still awaiting the first meaningful counter-gesture by the Progressives designed to relieve Orthodox anxieties and susceptibilities, as well as to help bridge the chasm of disunity created by their defection from traditional Judaism.

If the Liberals and Reformers, though a small and dissident minority in Anglo-Jewry, really expect equal rights within the wider community, they must be prepared to accept equal responsibilities, too. They cannot be rebels and partners at the same time.

This means, first, their recognition that reconciliation cannot be achieved through unilateral gestures on one side only, through taking without giving; and, secondly, their acknowledgement that there can be no beginning in reducing the painful rift between us so long as they continue to wreak havoc in Jewish life by their indiscriminate conversions, marriages and divorces, often in blatant defiance of biblical and rabbinic law, and with disastrous consequences which have already disrupted entire communities and not merely families.

Always sensitive to the charge of hypocrisy, they should not expect rabbis faithful to traditional Jewish teachings and observances to accept as equally or also authentic the denial or subversion of these teachings and observances. They should not preach unity and practise disunity by demonstratively announcing the appointment of their own 'independent' spokesman, as if they had not always been free to speak for themselves.

Nor should those who demand tolerance refuse to extend it to others. To belabour traditional Jews for insisting on the conduct of religious services by traditional Jews is surely an act of intolerance no less objectionable for turning unity into a fetish and principle into an expendable trifle.

In recent exchanges with Progressive leaders, I have therefore left them in no doubt that I could not persist in my efforts at reconciliation in the face of growing opposition and frustration unless there was to be soon some tangible evidence of reciprocity, particularly to show that the search for a rapprochement with traditional Judaism in matters of marriage and conversion would be translated from words, which were pledged to me at the very beginning of our encounter, into significant deeds.

I know that even larger Jewish communities than Anglo-Jewry, including important Orthodox as well as Conservative and Reform elements, anxiously and hopefully await our lead in what may prove to be one of the most momentous contributions to Jewish solidarity and unity the world over.[11]

Some months later, allowing time for tempers to cool, Brichto and Jakobovits met to clear the air in the Liberal-Orthodox relationship and to reach agreement on disputed issues of family status. As a result, the Chief Rabbi drew up a statement which, his office told Brichto, 'he thinks would sum up the tentative understanding reached with you following your recent discussions. [He] will be pleased to receive your observations as to the next stage in implementing this statement', which read as follows:

> In order to remove a major obstacle to communal harmony and, indeed, a growing threat to the unity of the Jewish people created by the rising marriage barriers between the Orthodox and non-Orthodox sections of the community, the Union of Liberal and Progressive Synagogues agrees:
> 1. Not to entertain or undertake any action in respect of the divorce of any members of an Orthodox congregation, nor to effect the conversion of any person contemplating marriage with a member of an Orthodox congregation, nor to effect the remarriage of any person who belongs or belonged to an Orthodox congregation, without ensuring that no impediment exists in Jewish law;
> 2. Not to deal with a divorce, remarriage or conversion of any person whose application is currently being dealt with by an Orthodox rabbinical authority or has previously been rejected by such an authority.[12]

Brichto's reaction, however, was distinctly cool. Describing the statement as 'some proposals for my private consideration ... as a basis for future discussion', and not a 'tentative understanding',[13] he told Jakobovits: 'As to the proposals themselves, I could not think of putting them before our Rabbinic Conference in their present form. They are too vague in general when they must be absolutely specific.'

In their place, following further discussions over a period of months, Brichto proposed guidelines of his own to which, he suggested,

> there is a possibility of my gaining agreement from the rabbis of the ULPS. While I am not in the position to promise any agreement without consulting the Rabbinic Conference, I am of the opinion that, for the

sake of communal harmony and in order to prevent personal hardship to future generations whenever this could be avoided without compromising our principles, it would agree to take the necessary steps.

I feel that the state of *gittin* presents such an opportunity for agreement between us. The Rabbinic Conference might agree to rule that couples who have married either religiously or civilly should not be remarried unless they have obtained a *get* from the Beth Din. Their agreement to do so, of course, would depend on the details being worked out in such a way that no inconvenience is caused to the parties who are members of our movement.

This might be accomplished by our Rabbinic Conference acting as agents for the parties, or by a Liberal rabbi accompanying the parties in their appearance before the Beth Din. However, in those cases where the Beth Din could not issue a *get*, the Rabbinic Conference would still have the liberty to remarry without such a *get* if, in their opinion, there are humanitarian and ethical grounds for doing so.

Were there to be such an agreement, the Rabbinic Conference of the ULPS would wish to make it known that while they, in principle, did not feel that a *get* should be necessary, it is taking this course of action for the sake of unity, and it does not feel that its new ruling imposes any hardship or any ethical compromise upon the parties involved.

I also believe that the Rabbinic Conference would agree that, once a candidate for conversion came before the Beth Din of either the Ashkenazi or Sephardi communities and began a course of instruction, and was fully aware of the nature of this instruction, it would not entertain an application from such a candidate if the candidate withdrew from the agreed course.[14]

As events will demonstrate, these proposals – and subsequent discussions over many years – led nowhere, but Jakobovits, meanwhile, acknowledged their receipt and agreed to forward a copy to the Sephardi authorities.[15]

\* \* \*    \* \* \*    \* \* \*

Having excluded the Progressives from the Independence Day service, Jakobovits proceeded to upbraid his own lay leaders for attending a service at the West London Synagogue. In keeping with past tradition, Berkeley Street marked the centenary of its opening with a thanksgiving celebration, at which the Lord Chancellor, Baron Hailsham of St Marylebone, headed a glittering congregation of one thousand guests. Lower down the list of notables were honorary officers of the United Synagogue, the Spanish and

Portuguese Synagogue, and the Orthodox president of the Board of Deputies, Alderman Michael Fidler, MP.

Men and women sat together at the service, part of which – the evening *amidah* – was led by Dulcie Halsted, chairman of the ladies' guild. United Synagogue vice-president Alfred Woolf, treasurers Frederick Landau, George Gee and Victor Lucas, and secretary Nathan Rubin joined with the other worshippers in reciting the prayers. The main officiants were Rabbis Werner Van der Zyl, Michael Goulston and Hugo Gryn,[16] the last of whom – West London's recently appointed senior minister – warned in his sermon (without elaborating) of 'a future fraught with spiritual uncertainties' facing the synagogue.[17]

After the event, a similarly fraught future seemed to face the United Synagogue leaders, with Jakobovits expressing 'strong objections' to their attendance at the service. The Chief Rabbi, said his office, was 'concerned about the action of some of the honorary officers of the United Synagogue whose attendance at the Reform service he considered to be a violation of Jewish law. Their attendance also damaged the best interests of the United Synagogue and has grieved many of their friends.

'As a result of a meeting between the honorary officers and the Chief Rabbi, which ended in a cordial manner, it was agreed that in the future the honorary officers could only act in an official capacity when invited to such functions and would consult with the Chief Rabbi before deciding whether they could attend.'[18]

Challenging these remarks, Rubin observed that the honorary officers were 'surprised to learn of the unilateral statement issued by the Chief Rabbi arising out of a private and confidential meeting between them on Sunday, 18 October, 1970. The honorary officers do not consider the statement to be an accurate record of what took place and they will be considering the matter further, possibly in consultation with the Chief Rabbi, before making any comment on this unilateral statement.'[19]

Asked whether they were invited 'officially, as representing the United Synagogue', one of the honorary officers told the press: 'We were invited as private individuals. The invitations came to our private addresses.' This, however, was disputed by a West London official, who said: 'I can confirm that the invitations were issued to the honorary officers of the United Synagogue in their official capacities, as in the case of the officers of the Union of Liberal and Progressive Synagogues and the Spanish and Portuguese Congregation.'[20]

Other statements by the Chief Rabbinate were also contested by the Progressive movements. Earlier that year, Judge Alan King-Hamilton, of the West London Synagogue, wrote to Jakobovits criticising his use of the term 'the spiritual leaders of Anglo-Jewry' – in relation to himself and the Haham – in a letter to *The Times*.[21] King-Hamilton was chairman of the Standing Committee on Relationships Within Anglo-Jewry, set up by the Reform and Liberals after Jakobovits' appointment to work towards 'better representation for non-Orthodoxy in both the Anglo-Jewish and national arenas and to look for areas of co-operation with the Orthodox establishment'.[22]

Of *The Times* letter, the judge wrote: 'I think it is a pity, if I may say so, that the opportunity was not taken to invite the chairman of the Council of Reform and Liberal Rabbis [Rayner] to join you in signing it, which he would gladly have done ... I hope you will agree that there are occasions when it is of the greatest importance for Anglo-Jewry to express a united opinion as a community on ethical and moral issues, as and when such occasions arise.'[23]

On Jakobovits' behalf, Rose replied that the Chief Rabbi 'does consult from time to time with the spiritual leaders of Reform and Liberal congregations on matters of common concern, particularly with regard to matters affecting Israel. However, he feels that he cannot compromise the traditional role of the Chief Rabbi and the Haham, who have always acted as religious spokesmen of the community, which, as you know, is predominantly traditional in character.'[24]

King-Hamilton retorted: 'It is not accurate for you and the Haham to describe yourselves in such a way as to convey the impression that you are the sole "Spiritual Leaders of Anglo-Jewry". I gather that the Haham shares my general views on this matter.

'From time to time, the Archbishop of Canterbury, the Cardinal at Westminster, the Moderator of the Free Church, etc., have joined in signing a letter to the national press without compromising their respective roles, or any loss of dignity. Isn't it about time that we Jews did the same and thus showed to the rest of the world that Anglo-Jewry can sometimes speak in harmony and unison?'[25]

By then, patience on both sides had reached breaking-point, leading the Reform chairman, Harold Langdon, to remark that 'the builder of bridges has proved to be a demolition expert',[26] and Jakobovits to comment: 'Adding irony to injury, the Reformers – having brought about the disunity which plagues modern Jewry and Judaism – now lambast Orthodoxy for "causing disunity" by not making common cause, and common services, with the dissidents.'[27]

These episodes, however, appeared trivial alongside a brewing storm that was to tear holes – though for different reasons – in the fabric of the Board of Deputies, and that remain unrepaired to the present day.

\* \* \*   \* \* \*   \* \* \*

The origins of the controversy went back six years to a meeting aimed at naming, in the Board's constitution, the Council of Reform and Liberal Rabbis as their movements' ecclesiastical authority. Prolonged discussion resulted in a decision to consult the new Chief Rabbi on the proposal, although (as Langdon wrote later) 'there was nothing in the amendment to the disadvantage of any religious group, and the matter was constitutional, not religious'.[28]

After further delays, the Board's law and parliamentary committee decided that, 'in the interests of communal harmony', it could not support the amendment. Offering an explanation, Jakobovits asserted that

> initially, there was broad agreement on granting the Progressive congregations their request to be consulted on religious matters concerning them. The Haham and I acknowledged the president's assurance that the proposed change, formalising an existing practice, would in no way affect the Board's ecclesiastical authorities.
>
> But when the Progressives subsequently revealed that what they really intended was communal recognition for their 'religious authorities' rather than mere consultative status, the Orthodox opposition hardened. It became evident that communal unity would be gained at one end of the spectrum only by sacrificing it at the other. We then decided not to support any amendment, unless it proved its purpose by commanding the agreement of all parties.
>
> The issue transcends the offices of the Haham and myself. By constitutionally acknowledging us as the Board's sole religious advisers, the Orthodox character of Anglo-Jewry is officially affirmed and maintained.[29]

The *Jewish Chronicle*, however, thought differently:

> The blame for a situation which should never have arisen must be divided between the Chief Rabbi for his ambition and lack of consistency; the right-wing Orthodox for their intransigence and intolerance towards their fellow Jews; and the officers of both the United Synagogue and the Board [of Deputies] for their pusillanimity ...
>
> It is a new manifestation of the Chief Rabbi's readiness to co-operate with the Progressives in all communal endeavours except those which have a religious connotation. It is an attitude impossible to sustain logically, at variance with the facts of Jewish life today and damaging to the best interests of the religious community.[30]

'Discontent and disillusion were by now rife among Reform and Liberal deputies and synagogues', Langdon related of the proceedings,[31] while Jakobovits, for his part, sought both to salvage the situation with a revised amendment and to placate his right-wing critics. In a letter to Bernard Homa, leader of the Board's self-styled Orthodox Group, he wrote:

> Let me first of all assure you that the Haham and I stand by our commitment not to give formal approval to any amendment which does not enjoy the agreement of all parties. But this obviously cannot prevent us from having personal opinions on what is best designed to break the present impasse, and for my part I gladly convey to you my views on the action now proposed by the Board's honorary officers.
>
> The Haham and I (who, while aware of the suggested formula, have refused to give it formal endorsement) have made it clear to the honorary officers that we are determined to maintain two fundamental principles: 1. The Board's constitution must not accord any religious recognition to Progressive Judaism and its spiritual leaders; and 2. The Board or its spokesmen shall not officially make any statements on behalf of the community which conflict with the norms of the halachah, even if such statements are represented as minority views.
>
> In my opinion (which, I believe, is shared by the Haham), these two principles are now safeguarded (1) by referring to consultations 'with those designated by such groups or congregations as their respective religious leaders'. and (2) by specifically stipulating that 'the Board *shall be guided* on religious matters ... by the Ecclesiastical Authorities to whom all such matters shall be referred'. This new formulation subjects the Board to our guidance on all religious matters quite unconditionally, and irrespective of any consultations which the Board may now be required to have with others.[32]

Disagreement over the amendment, in relation to the Progressives' ecclesiastical authority, had led to changes in the wording from 'religious authorities' to 'appropriate authorities' to 'religious leaders', and this latter compromise was finally accepted by the Reform and Liberals, with an ultimatum to the Board that they would withdraw their deputies by the end of the month 'unless in the meantime the constitution has been amended in the terms agreed with the officers of the Board'.

Thus it was, on 24 October 1971, by 228 votes to 7, that the Board amended Clause 43 of its constitution, requiring it henceforth 'to consult with those designated by such groups and congregations as their respective religious leaders on religious matters in any matter whatsoever concerning them'. As a result, the Federation of Synagogues and Union of Orthodox Hebrew Congregations quit the Board – the latter never to return, the former doing so after a two-year absence – and Homa resigned the chairmanship of its shechitah committee.

Seeking to defend their position, the Chief Rabbi and Haham pleaded:

> Having now concluded the long and divisive argument on how to amend Clause 43, we appeal to all Orthodox Jews to close ranks, to strengthen the Orthodox influence and representation on the Board, and thus to ensure the continued traditional character of the Anglo-Jewish community.
>
> Furthermore, realising that Jewish unity is meaningless unless it is founded on the unity of Judaism, we call upon all our fellow Jews to work unceasingly for this supreme ideal, whereby we will all subscribe to the same religious discipline, so that no Jew will be debarred from marrying into another's family or from eating in his home, from celebrating the same holy-days and worshipping at the same services. Let us now concentrate all our communal energies and resources on promoting this unity and inculcating the love and knowledge of it into our children.[33]

Reporting on the outcome of the dispute to a meeting of the Chief Rabbinate Council, Jakobovits stated:

> Once the Board's honorary officers were committed to a constitutional change granting the Progressives consultative status – a concession which even the 'Orthodox Group' has conceded was 'never in dispute' – we raised no objection to the change, provided we were assured that our guidance would be mandatory and that the Board would never act contrary to the halachah.
>
> Such assurance was given, and accepted by us. This was, and remains, our position. Since the avowed purpose of the exercise was to promote communal unity, we insisted that we could not formally endorse or support any amendment unless its wording commanded the agreement of all parties. This, too, remains our position.[34]

After the 'long, arduous struggle', Langdon pondered whether it had been worth the effort. 'I believe', he wrote,

> that it was a battle that had to be won if we were to remain on the Board of Deputies and play our full part in the mainstream of Jewish life.
>
> It shows that we are no longer second-class members of a secular organisation claiming to represent all Jews. We are no longer

'congregations of Jews' only for the purpose of communal activity; our synagogues are Jewish synagogues, and our rabbis are religious leaders ...

The Board has not changed overnight, but neither has it been bedevilled by religious sectarian differences. It is much more truly representative now, and perhaps, shorn of religious strife, it may attract more of that thirty-six per cent of Jews who, alas, have no synagogue affiliation.[35] It is, I believe – or at least I hope – inconceivable that the Board will in future select any broad delegation or representation without including a Reform or Liberal deputy.[36]

Both the belief and the hope were, however, soon to be dashed. Worried by this crack in the ecclesiastical armoury, Orthodox representatives on the Board – reflecting the rightward shift in the United Synagogue leadership – launched a campaign in 1984 to re-establish the Chief Rabbinate's hegemony in the corridors of power, both communal and national. Clause 43 – by then renumbered Clause 74 – had caused difficulties when the Board found itself unable to render a unanimous Jewish view on the Matrimonial and Family Proceedings Bill before Parliament, following conflicting advice from the Orthodox and Progressives.

As a result, and despite strenuous opposition from the latter, deputies voted – though by a narrow majority – to introduce a 'code of practice', making it mandatory for the Board 'to follow the guidance of its ecclesiastical authorities, and to support such guidance in all ways possible and with all due speed'.[37] They had earlier, similarly split, rejected a move by the Progressive wing to refer back the recommendation 'in the interests of communal unity'.

The new code, however, allowed for groups and organisations not under the jurisdiction of the ecclesiastical authorities 'to be notified in writing of any action the Board intends to take in accordance with the guidance of those authorities'. But the Progressives failed in committee to add the stipulation that, 'in the absence of a consensus, the Board must inform those seeking its advice or opinion that a minority view is held by some sections of the community'.

The decision, the *Jewish Chronicle* wrote, was 'in effect a victory for the United Synagogue, which had sought to strengthen the powers of the ecclesiastical authorities'. But the opposition put a different spin on the outcome, contending that 'a separate voice' had been granted it[38] and that 'a compromise was reached which will enable the Board to issue statements yet safeguard the Progressive position'.[39]

The Board's president, Greville Janner, MP, promised that 'we will do everything in our power to see that the code is operated in a way that is fair to all'. But that assurance did little to assuage Progressive concerns. Maurice Michaels, chairman of the Reform Synagogues of Great Britain, told the Board that 'we reserve the right to take whatever action we feel necessary in the light of consultations between the groups affected by the vote'. Aubrey Rose contended that 'the code is an attempt to alter the constitution by unconstitutional means. At best, it will produce a substantial disgruntled minority who might see it as the beginning of an assault on themselves and on their beliefs and institutions.' And Langdon asked: 'What is the use of consultations if the guidance of the ecclesiastical authorities is mandatory?'[40]

* * *   * * *   * *

In other areas, too, relations veered from strained to stifled, although occasional attempts were made to repair the rift. Following a tangle in 1974 at the Council of Christians and Jews, with Reform and Liberal rabbis unsuccessfully seeking to install a Progressive president alongside Jakobovits, the two sides agreed to establish a Consultative Committee on Jewish-Christian Relations, with the Chief Rabbi and the Haham, as well as Gryn, Brichto and Langdon, among its members.[41] At its inaugural meeting, Gryn welcomed the committee as 'a step in cordial relationships within the Jewish community itself'.[42]

Some years later, and under conditions of utmost secrecy, a sub-group, known initially as the Unterman Committee (after its chairman, Rabbi Maurice Unterman) and later as the Liaison Committee, was established to help diffuse difficult situations in the troubled partnership. Both groups, wrote a Liberal insider, 'enabled some collegiality and networking to be established between rabbis and lay leadership from the very diverse sections of Anglo-Jewry. A sincere attempt was made on all sides to listen and respect, if not to agree.'[43]

But even in the short term, efforts to reconcile Jews with Christians did little towards reconciling Jews with Jews, for the Chief Rabbi found cause yet again to vent his spleen.

> My argument with Reform [he said in an interview] is less that they allow individual liberties to their members than that they legitimise that which is illegitimate. I want members of a congregation, observant or not, to accept their rabbi as the custodian of absolute values without compromise.
>
> The majority of Anglo-Jewry recognise this. It is a tremendous

asset to our community that, though we all fall short of the ideal, at least we recognise both the ideal and the fact that we fall short of it. Leaving the car round the corner is a recognition of it. It is a virtue rather than a hypocrisy ...

In itself, the disunity implicit in Reform is not important. This obsession with unity is an Anglo-Jewish fetish. After all, for generations past, we have had different forms of prayer, slightly different forms of worship, different pronunciations. Nobody has ever suggested that unless we all pray together, we destroy the unity of our people.

This whole notion is based on false premises. I do not see that the holding of occasional joint services – to which I am totally opposed – has any bearing on unity. What we need is unity of purpose ... Where the Progressive element has chosen to dissent – we are not the dissenters – to reject something extremely sacred to us, we cannot work together because we have no common ideals to unite us ...

I cannot legitimise the teachings of Reform. It is not part of authentic Judaism. I do not see it as another form of Judaism. I see it as a challenge to Judaism. Reform will not prevail. It is self-liquidating.

Their birth-rate is so low, and their defection rate so high through assimilation and intermarriage, that in two or three generations there will be none left. The problem will solve itself through natural processes. Call it the survival of the fittest.

But I still regard Reform Jews as Jews. I do not deny their Jewish status, as long as they are Jews according to the halachah. But I do not regard their beliefs as authentically Jewish.[44]

The following year, in what appeared to be a major reversal, Jakobovits refused an approach from the Beth Din of the Union of Orthodox Hebrew Congregations to join its dayanim, as well as yeshivah heads and rabbis of independent Orthodox congregations, in a blanket denunciation of Reform and Liberal Jews. In a statement, he declared – despite his earlier dismissal of the 'Anglo-Jewish fetish' of unity – that

I cannot exclude non-observant Jews from my concern and co-operation. This would gravely damage Orthodox interests, as well as communal unity and the endeavours based on it, notably in the support of Jewish education. My experience convinces me that what drives waverers to Reform is Orthodox intolerance and divisive agitation, rather than any 'legitimacy' allegedly conferred by sharing secular platforms with its leaders.

All Jews are authentic Jews, but neither Judaism nor rabbis can be authentic, in the Orthodox view, unless they embrace the totality of

Jewish belief, law and tradition. Therefore, my own policies have consistently been guided by the principle I clearly spelled out in my installation address twelve years ago: 'I cannot join with Reformers in areas affected by dissent from our traditions, but I will work with them on matters on which we are united, such as Israel, Soviet Jewry, welfare and Jewish defence.'

In this, I follow the example set by my father, my predecessors and even such a distinguished pioneer of 'Independent Orthodoxy' as Rabbi Ezra Munk, of Berlin, who collaborated with Leo Baeck, the Reform leader of German Jewry. I believe that these policies are overwhelmingly understood and supported and have resulted in the intensified loyalty of our community to the values we cherish.[45]

In the wake of this policy of carrot and stick, the warring parties trod an uneasy path, prompting an anxious Jakobovits to assert, at a meeting of the Board of Deputies in 1984:

In the face of the likely trends of polarisation, followed by the renewed ascendancy of the most committed elements in the community, our communal statesmanship will have to be exercised to preserve the essential cohesion of Anglo-Jewry by preventing a form of confrontation in which a single section will make demands upon the rest of the community such as it cannot as a matter of conscience meet.

If the community is not to be riven by irreconcilable communal conflicts spilling over into areas at present at peace, we must uphold a form of tolerance which extends to recognising the fact of dissent, deems every Jew an infinitely precious brother whom we will always join in defending common Jewish interests, and encourages good will and solidarity, but which retains the right of traditional Jews refusing to accept, and rejecting, the claim that the beliefs of other segments are equally authentic.

To demand equal legitimacy for all in a predominantly traditional community would brand those making the demand as intolerant, and those ready to grant it as hypocritical – since fulfilment and non-fulfilment of religious conscience can never enjoy equal status.[46]

Recognising the risks involved in his policy of co-operating with the Progressives on 'common problems', in a bid 'to maintain the essential fabric of the cohesion of the community', Jakobovits told the Chief Rabbinate Council the following month:

It has been strongly argued that, by adopting this policy of working together with them in certain areas, I have helped in the process of the erosion of the Orthodox community. While such an argument is plausible, it needs careful investigation to see whether there is any substance to it; and, if true, it would greatly influence me in revising my guidelines and attitudes.

As far as I can see, however, that argument cannot be sustained. We have been remarkably successful in maintaining the strength of the mainstream Orthodox community.[47]

But, some weeks later, he did revise his guidelines, leading Reform and Liberal leaders to launch an unprecedented campaign against him. In a private memorandum to his ministers, the Chief Rabbi urged them 'not to allow their presence or their name to be used for promoting or sanctioning any activities which could be construed as according legitimacy to non-traditional Judaism'. Explaining the reasons for his change of heart, he declared:

> When I advised my colleagues not to engage in any activity that could be construed as conferring legitimacy on Reform Judaism, I did not tell them not to appear on a platform with Reform ministers. Indeed, I appear on such platforms, at Joint Israel Appeal meetings and on numerous other occasions.
>
> Because of certain events which had taken place,[48] what I did was intended to prevent their presence at, and participation in, Reform activities which might be interpreted by leaders of Reform as indicating that their activities enjoy the endorsement of the Orthodox community.
>
> The moment this abuse of an Orthodox presence takes place and is constructed as giving the event a *hechsher*, a formal stamp of approval, and the organisers go on to claim that they do not represent just Progressive Judaism but the totality of Judaism, then I have to tell my colleagues that they are being exploited, that their presence is being misrepresented and, therefore, 'be careful'. But I have never said they should not appear together on a platform where no such misconstruction can take place ...
>
> On Judaism, I am the spokesman not for the majority (even if I speak of Sabbath observance, I recognise that I do not speak for the majority), but I speak for authentic Judaism as I see it.
>
> It has always been understood that this would not compromise my ability to be a spokesman in the tradition of the Chief Rabbinate of this country. I think that if we were to continue with this mutual understanding, we should concentrate, as I have pleaded throughout my incumbency, on our constructive work, putting our own houses

in order, strengthening our education and our synagogues, without abusing one another, without throwing mud at one another.

But the community should know that if there is any threat of stirring up communal disunity beyond the truly internal religious confines, such a threat comes solely from the Progressives. They have recently published in the national press articles and letters grossly offensive to the Orthodox community; some of their leaders have called for breaking up such co-operation as has for years existed; and in utter disregard for the well-being and reputation of Anglo-Jewry, they now warn that they may carry the battle into the public arena and into areas on which we have been, and continue to be, united as Jews.

We have avoided a collision for nearly eighteen years. I don't say we have lived happily together. I was never happy about the divisions between us. But we have had a modus vivendi, a working relationship. We didn't abuse one another. I never went out of my way to denounce those who did not subscribe to my innermost beliefs.

If, occasionally, I have to tell my congregants or my colleagues that they should not do anything which will blur the distinctions, then I am only doing my duties as a rabbi, which means teacher. If the Progressives choose to disagree, then we have to agree to disagree, as we have done in the past. But if they are to take every assertion of Orthodox belief which conflicts with their teaching as a *casus belli*, then I am afraid there is bound to be friction leading to a great deal of communal heartbreak.[49]

Certainly, in Reform and Liberal eyes, the guidelines were a *casus belli*, and the resultant fallout was to lead to the most serious confrontation of the Jakobovits Chief Rabbinate.

# 19

# Broken Bridges

In his post-guidelines interview explaining his stand on Orthodox–Progressive relations, Jakobovits had included a mixed message: 'I care for a Reform Jew', he declared,

> and his safety and his security, just as much as for an Orthodox Jew. I go even further. I care for his living a Jewish life as I care for anyone belonging to an Orthodox synagogue, because I don't believe that Judaism was given to Orthodox Jews only. It is the common heritage of all of us.
>
> What I cannot accept is that there shall be pronouncements made which, ostensibly, speak on behalf of a Judaism which I must endorse as being legitimate and authentic when I know it has caused grievous damage not just to the unity of the Jewish people but to our most sacred beliefs ... Things have recently been said publicly in the name of Judaism which, to me, were obscene, a degradation of Jewish values relating to the life of the family, the preciousness of the marriage bond.
>
> When this happens, it grieves me deeply. I am bound to stand up and proclaim what I believe to be the genuine teachings of a faith recognised by a majority of our community, to distinguish what is genuine and what of recent vintage'.[1]

Jakobovits had in mind the pronouncements of Rabbi Julia Neuberger, of the South London Liberal Synagogue, who – as he put it – 'comes along and says that "the Chief Rabbi does not represent us", that she regarded pregnancy as a loathsome burden and loathed every minute of being pregnant, that she had had herself sterilised and if she wanted more children would be perfectly willing to have any further children through wombhire, a surrogate mother. This is not merely an obscene perversion of Jewish values, but something which borders on a *chillul hashem* [desecration of God's name].'[2]

In the run-up to this exchange, the climate had frozen to such a degree – 'of growing hostility towards our section of the community'[3] – as to provoke an unprecedented threat to the Chief Rabbi from the Council of Reform and Liberal Rabbis. 'How can anyone who is so publicly opposed to us still represent us?' asked its chairman, Tony Bayfield. 'How can we tolerate an increasing number of public statements with which we disagree [and] about which we have had no opportunity for prior consultation or discussion? I am now under considerable pressure to write to *The Times* and the BBC publicly stating that you no longer represent our section of the Jewish community.'

Similar sentiments were expressed in a leading article in the Reform journal, *Manna*:

> If he [the Chief Rabbi] still claims to represent those of us in the Reform and Liberal movements and our independent friends, then he must cease to lambast us as 'dissidents' or 'priests of an alien religion'. If he is to demand our acceptance of his office, he must not interfere with our right to talk Torah with open-minded men and women from all sections of the community.
>
> If he wishes to speak for us, then he must have some regard for our conscience and our sincere interpretation of Judaism. If he continues to choose to do the opposite, then the delicately balanced edifice at whose pinnacle he now stands will assuredly collapse.
>
> That need not necessarily frighten anybody. Facing reality is the first step towards robust communal health. We are prepared to represent ourselves. We are strong enough to face the challenge, and from that position of strength we shall continue to build bridges.
>
> Is Sir Immanuel[4] and his United Synagogue able to respond? Does the Chief Rabbi in name wish to remain Chief Rabbi in reality?[5]

Jakobovits replied to Bayfield:

> My most effective response to your astonishing threat would be to ignore it and to let you act as you wish. But since I do not share your apparent indifference to the interests of Anglo-Jewry, let me say this: I never knew I had, or required, your mandate to speak for the whole community. I believe the proportion of my support among the entire community is larger than the Prime Minister's among the people she represents.
>
> Nor has anyone asked you to 'tolerate' anything I state. Any public statements I make on behalf of the community I do my best to ensure represent all sections. But in statements on Judaism, I claim no communal endorsement, and I am accountable only to my conscience – and certainly not to you, so long as we subscribe to fundamentally opposed beliefs and practices. My stand has remained consistent for the past eighteen years, and you can be sure it will so continue.[6]

Concerned about the long-term repercussions, and anxious to activate the Consultative Committee with a view to diffusing the situation, Bayfield sought to 'arrive at an effective agreement to try to eradicate generalised abuse and gratuitous insults from sermons, letters and public statements on both sides'. He asked of Jakobovits: 'How can we discuss, debate and work together as rabbis without compromising each other's positions? How do we deal with the issue of consultation and the public expression of diverse Jewish points of view?'[7]

From the West London Synagogue, Hugo Gryn lent his support for a meeting of the committee, expressing the hope that 'subsequent get-togethers will have the effect of improving that part of the climate which it is in our power to improve', and that 'my role as a "dove" may result in actual and refreshing oil, and not just in mouthing a symbolic branch'.[8] Not only did the Consultative Committee agree to become involved, but it was instrumental in launching the Unterman Committee on its mission, aimed at 'agreeing to disagree amicably on differences of doctrine'.[9] The first step was a formula, drawn up by Unterman with the 'one hundred per cent agreement'[10] of Rayner, incoming chairman of the Council of Reform and Liberal Rabbis, to the effect that

> a 'moratorium' on statements of a recriminatory or discourteous nature should be observed by the leadership of the Orthodox and Progressive communities, and efforts made internally by each community for the exercise of a discipline of propriety, on the widest possible scale; that a spirit of fellowship between the leadership at several levels be inaugurated for the friendly discussion of such differences as may occur from time to time, whereby problems may be resolved or else left as matters upon which 'we agree to disagree' amicably; and that, to avoid a further recurrence of the confrontation of misunderstanding, each community should appoint an ecclesiastical liaison to monitor jointly the progress and conduct of the improved relationship.[11]

The formula was adopted at a meeting of the Council's executive committee, with a crucial amendment (proposed by Bayfield) reflected in a conciliatory message from Rayner to Jakobovits. 'What is needed', he wrote,

> is a little more than just 'monitoring' – namely, a small committee which will, in the course of time, explore and define in some detail what are the rules we must observe so that we may, on occasion, publicly discuss divergent views without provoking a crisis; and what possibilities there are of joint activities which would allow us to co-operate without raising the spectre of reciprocal 'recognition'.

> What is envisaged is a committee of four (two from each 'side'), or at the most six, and if this is agreeable to you, you may wish to give some thought to its membership, which I hope would include yourself as well as the chairman of the Council of Reform and Liberal Rabbis.
>
> I certainly hope that this will help to bring about a new period of communal peace, not only in the sense of a 'non-aggression' pact but of *shalom* in a positive sense. It is good to know, as I do, that you share that hope.[12]

So it was that the Unterman Committee was born, and for ten years it carried out its duties in an atmosphere of secrecy.[13] Only after Jakobovits had left office were its activities – indeed, its existence – revealed:

> A closed-door 'liaison committee' of prominent Orthodox and Progressive Jews this week decided to shed an eight-year-old veil of secrecy in a bid to encourage 'respect and tolerance' across doctrinal divides.
>
> A co-founder of the group – Rabbi Maurice Unterman, emeritus minister of the Marble Arch (United) Synagogue – said that wider communication was essential. 'Human beings who don't speak will always quarrel', he declared. 'There is too much collective position-taking in Anglo-Jewry and not enough respect, sympathy and communication among individuals.'
>
> The committee, which also includes prominent members of the Masorti, Reform and Liberal movements, was set up with the aim of 'agreeing to disagree amicably' on differences of doctrine, while trying to work for compromise solutions to other problems. 'We are present in individual, not organisational, capacities', said Jonathan Lew, the United Synagogue's chief executive. 'What has made the arrangement work is the honesty and trust that exist among all of us.'
>
> The main focus of the group – which began in 1985 as an informal response to a series of perceived attacks by a Progressive rabbi on the then Chief Rabbi, Sir Immanuel Jakobovits – has been to take the 'personal sting' out of relations between the various religious groups, one member said. 'We've had successes, partial successes, and failures', said Rabbi Tony Bayfield, the chief executive-designate of the Reform movement. 'But the attempt has always been to address the real issues without posturing.'
>
> The nine-member group, whose other founder was Liberal Rabbi John Rayner, is chaired by Lionel Swift, QC, of the United Synagogue, and also includes Progressive Rabbis Hugo Gryn and Charles Middleburgh; Reform movement executive director Raymond

Goldman; former Union of Liberal and Progressive Synagogues chairman David Lipman; and Mrs Eleanor Lind, of the New London (Masorti) Synagogue.[14]

\* \* \*    \* \* \*    \* \* \*

In the same week as the Unterman Committee was launched in 1985, Jakobovits received a letter (one of a series) from a close friend, American Reform rabbi and scholar Jakob J. Petuchowski, who, like him, had reached British shores as a child refugee from Nazi oppression. Berlin-born Petuchowski, the grandson of an Orthodox rabbi and the nephew of a mohel, had studied at Glasgow yeshivah before entering University College, London and, concurrently, teaching at the West London Synagogue. He later settled in the United States and was ordained at Hebrew Union College in Cincinnati, becoming an expert on Reform liturgy and history.[15]

Jakobovits and he were long-standing correspondents, and at the time of the letter – in the shadow of this latest dispute between the Chief Rabbi and the Progressives – had been discussing 'the recent and unfortunate polarisation'. Commiserating with his friend, Petuchowski wrote:

> I can only say that I am impressed by the fairness of your position. Some of the carryings-on of the Liberal brethren (and sisters!) shock me no less than they shock you ...
>
> You mention the harsh words of the late Chief Rabbi Hertz. No doubt you are referring to his *New Paths – Whither Do They Lead?* and you are right in insisting that nothing of that acrimony ever crossed your lips. But Hertz directed that tirade against the Liberals, not against the (British) Reform movement. It was, in fact, Hertz's policy to woo away the Reform people from too close an embrace with the Liberals and, in his time, he succeeded to a considerable extent ...
>
> I would argue that this policy ceased under your immediate predecessor, and that the lumping together (in condemnation) of the Liberals and Reformers by the British Orthodox Chief Rabbinate was – at least in part – responsible for bringing those two dissident movements ever more closely together, to the point where, today, they can even think of 'merging'. A different policy by the Chief Rabbinate might have succeeded in implementing a policy of 'divide and conquer'.[16]

\* \* \*    \* \* \*    \* \* \*

Early in 1975, a joint Progressive and Orthodox approach to conversions was advocated by Dow Marmur, vice-chairman of the Council of Reform and Liberal Rabbis and minister of the North-Western Reform Synagogue. Citing the opinion of two leading American rabbis – Eliezer Berkovits (Orthodox) and Theodore Friedman (Conservative) – that non-Orthodox conversion procedures could be acceptable to Orthodox Jews, since 'differences in interpretation of the halachah are not permitted to rupture the unity of the Jewish people', Marmur declared: 'We appeal to the leaders of British Orthodoxy to heed this principle, lest the unity of our people be ruptured. In view of the recent conciliatory and eminently sensible comments about the separation of politics and religion made by the Chief Rabbi, is it not reasonable to expect Dr Jakobovits to take a leaf out of Dr Berkovits' book and give a lead to Anglo-Jewry?'

Commenting on the suggestion, the Chief Rabbi's Office stated:

> At a time like this, far from accentuating and perpetuating our differences, we ought to be making a supreme effort to narrow and eliminate them. If only to find strength and comfort through unity, can we not now draw closer to our common heritage and repair the tragic rifts in our ranks whereby we cannot worship together, we cannot eat in each other's homes, and sometimes not even marry each other's children?
>
> Whether the arguments advanced by Dr Berkovits are tenable, and whether they bear the construction placed upon them, is open to debate. The Chief Rabbi has always favoured continued research and consultation on all matters concerned with conversion, including sociological and contemporary aspects, as well as historical and religious implications. He has been particularly concerned to avoid family tragedies resulting from the present divisions and the estrangement from traditional practices.[17]

The Reform and Liberal rabbinical authorities followed Marmur's lead by approving a dialogue with their Orthodox counterparts, 'in an attempt to heal the sectarian schism within Anglo-Jewry, especially in the field of conversion, marriage and divorce'.[18] Their initiative was received positively by Jakobovits and, acting in his capacity as chairman of the Reform and Liberal rabbis, Brichto invited him, the Haham and the Federation of Synagogues to 'immediate and joint discussions'. This move followed exploratory talks between Jakobovits and representatives of the Reform movement concerned mainly with matters of personal status in Jewish law and with 'the effects of sectarian divisions on communal unity'.

In attempting to formulate a joint approach to conversion, however, Jakobovits faced opposition from his own Beth Din to his dialogue with the Progressives. Dayan Swift stated that,

> in my view, there can be no possibility of any discussions with the Reform on the question of conversion.
>
> The Reform and, in many ways, the Conservatives have rejected the divine revelation of the Torah, the Written and the Oral Law. The admission into the Jewish faith of a convert by religious procedure, even if it includes *tevilah*, is not sufficient. The convert must accept completely that the Torah was divinely revealed.[19]

Notwithstanding Swift's opposition, the Chief Rabbi agreed to pursue the discussions. They were, in fact, expanded in scope and conducted, with great discretion (as he put it), 'in a sense of responsibility on all sides for what was at stake'.[20] From the meetings, there emerged a two-tier system of recommended procedures, one relating to long-term objectives. In a position paper, Jakobovits spelled out to the Reform and Liberal side 'what should, and could, be achieved in the light of our discussions':

*Principal Objectives*

We should seek to reach agreements designed, above all,

(a) to restore and preserve the unity of the Jewish people now gravely and increasingly imperilled by the consequences of diverse norms in the attitudes to marriage, divorce and conversion whereby admissibility to Jewish status and/or Jewish marriage is disputed for a large and ever-growing number of people who are recognised as Jews and/or eligible for marriage in the eyes of some congregations and denied such recognition by the rest; and

(b) to avert the personal tragedies often inflicted on individuals, or their descendants for all future times, arising from their disputed status, in the event they or their children should ever seek acceptance, or the right to marry, within the traditional community.

*Long-term Solutions*

Ideally, our problem would be solved by adopting the pattern which prevailed in German-Jewish *Grossgemeinden*. While Orthodox and Reform congregations naturally differed widely on religious services and other observances – perhaps even more widely than they do here – and despite the Orthodox often being in a minority, both sections were united under a common community administration and jointly submitted to the jurisdiction of an Orthodox Beth Din in matters normally within its purview, such as kashrut and shechitah, as well as divorce and conversion . . .

Any agreement on such lines to be eventually reached here could not be retroactive, and existing marriages or conversions of doubtful halachic validity would remain unaffected. But at least we would prevent any new cases being added to the grievous toll of communal bitterness, personal tragedies and national disunity afflicting our people today.

Pending such admittedly drastic restructuring of our inter-communal relations and organisation, it should prove possible progressively to introduce a number of measures aimed at the above objectives in the spirit of our discussions . . .

Accordingly, we believe that the following proposals would substantially advance the cause which has united us in our deliberations:

1. For members of Orthodox synagogues, the exclusive jurisdiction of Orthodox rabbis should be upheld. Such members, or parties applying for conversion with a view to marriage to such members, should under no circumstances be admitted for remarriage or conversion if such acts would not be sanctioned by Orthodox authorities. Progressive synagogues should never be used as a haven for 'rejects' of the Orthodox community.

2. Non-Orthodox divorcees applying for remarriage should also be advised that they must first obtain a *get* universally accepted by all rabbinic authorities, so as to preserve the unity of the Jewish people and to prevent the tragic disabilities of any children who may be born within the second marriage. Should efforts to obtain such a *get* prove unavailing, such exceptional cases should not be further considered until the lapse of at least two years.

3. Similarly, all applications for conversions should in the first instance be referred to Orthodox batei din, so as to give them unquestioned validity, and not be entertained for acceptance under non-Orthodox auspices for at least two years following the original application. The strictest enforcement of these provisions would substantially reduce, if not altogether eliminate, the incidence of *mamzerut* and the admission of persons whose Jewish status would be in dispute. It would also remove the principal cause of bitterness and dissension between our respective communities.

4. On the Orthodox side, undertakings should be given to deal with all applications with the utmost dispatch, courtesy and sympathy. Appeal procedures should be set up to take effective action on any complaints of undue delay, alleged lack of civility, etc. Representatives of the Progressive ministry should be entitled to pursue such complaints on behalf of their members.

'As in 1969', Jakobovits reported later, 'so again in 1976, our efforts proved abortive. On both occasions, the extended discussions had to be abandoned as the proposals were in the end not acceptable to the Progressives.'[21]

Despite a continued frostiness in the communal climate, Brichto spent much of the next decade working on an acceptable formula and, by 1987, was ready – however speculatively – to float his ideas. 'It would be an act of abhorrent and unforgivable self-destruction', he wrote,

> were we not to find the means of agreeing on a unified halachah in those areas which divide Jew from Jew and lead to enmity and internecine strife.
>
> In view of the seriousness of the situation, the time has come to put forward a solution – which will, however, in the present climate, most likely be rejected by both the Progressives and the Orthodox. Yet I do this now because now is the time for responsible Jews to have the courage to go out on a limb. When the future of the Jewish people is at stake, organisational and personal considerations are of secondary importance.

And his solution? 'For the preservation of *Klal Yisrael*', he conceded,

> I am prepared to entrust the halachah to the Orthodox. Why? Because there is no one else.
>
> Because the Orthodox have retained the structure of halachah for the sake of *Klal Yisrael*, I am prepared to accord them the responsibility of finding the means to enable *all* religious sections to achieve a standard practice in the important areas of Jewish status, marriage and divorce. They must appreciate, however, that we Liberals and Progressives have a great interest in the matter.
>
> Orthodox rabbis entrusted by us to administer the halachah must do so with humility, compassion, ingenuity, creativity and, above all, a love for *Klal Yisrael*. The areas requiring their immediate consideration are conversion, *get*, Jewish remarriage when a *get* is difficult to obtain, and *mamzerut*.
>
> On the question of conversion, the rabbis will need to reconsider the demands they make on applicants before acceptance for a course of instruction, and the length and intensity of that course. A more lenient attitude, as shown by many Orthodox rabbis throughout the world, would mean more Orthodox converts, since many apply to Progressive synagogues following the impossible demands made not only on the applicants, but on the entire family of the applicant's Jewish spouse.

As to those who, in principle, wish to embrace Progressive Judaism, there could be two alternatives, one or both of which might be acceptable to the Orthodox and the Progressives.

Brichto proposed either that candidates be instructed and accepted as Jews by three Progressive rabbis and later formally accepted by an Orthodox Beth Din 'according to its requirements', or that the Beth Din would be the only accepting body. 'In either situation, the Orthodox Beth Din could demand only knowledge of Orthodox practice and not its observance. If this appears as an unacceptable compromise of principle, let the dayanim consider that their sole responsibility is to inform the candidate of the mitzvot and not to pursue the matter'. On the question of divorce, where both Progressive partners with a civil decree were willing to give and receive a *get*, 'Progressive rabbis should require them to do so from an Orthodox Beth Din'. When a *get* could not be obtained, said Brichto,

> this would require ingenuity and creativeness. The Orthodox Beth Din would have to find loopholes to nullify the marriage – for example, that the witnesses to the marriage were not sufficiently observant, or that the ring did not belong to the groom and was not valid for the purposes of *kiddushin* (though I understand that there have been times when the Orthodox authorities have nullified marriages for no other reason than to ameliorate personal hardship).
>
> On *mamzerut*, the same ingenuity would be required to remove this offensive stigma from an individual: the 'pre-adulterous' marriage would need to be nullified. The Orthodox should also consider the fact that tradition clearly forbids investigations which would reveal the identity of *mamzerim*.
>
> Those Orthodox authorities who are really concerned over the deep divisions within our community could even consider guaranteeing that every Jewish wedding allows for a technical basis for annulment. And before anyone attacks me for cynicism or deviousness, let him consider that my motive is to preserve the unity of our people and the abatement of human suffering.[22]

That the Chief Rabbi – and, indeed, the Progressive movement – dismissed the proposals out of hand came as no surprise. In a personal letter to Brichto twenty months earlier,[23] Jakobovits had referred to a comment made by the Liberal rabbi in the *Jewish Chronicle*[24] to the effect that 'we would recommend that our converts undergo mikveh and the further acceptance of an Orthodox Beth Din, so long as they were not required to be hypocritical in the affirmation of the Orthodox *kabbalat mitzvot*' (acceptance of the mitzvot).

It was, wrote Jakobovits then,

> precisely because we object to such hypocritical acts as much as you do that your formula is so unacceptable to us. After all, how can an Orthodox Beth Din validate a conversion without *kabbalat mitzvot*? That in itself would be hypocritical, since it would flout the essence of a conversion as we understand it.
>
> So long as this gulf remains, and thousands will be declared as Jews (or as divorced) by some of our people and as non-Jews (or married) by the rest, I cannot see that the growing havoc inevitably created by these divisions can be eliminated, whatever the public declarations of unity and good will.[25]

Twenty months on, in a public lecture in London, the Chief Rabbi gave a similar response to Brichto's 'solution':

> What has recently been described as an 'unprecedented and revolutionary offer' – to place all these matters under Orthodox jurisdiction – contains among other conditions in the rather small print (or strings attached) the following: 'The Orthodox Beth Din could demand only knowledge of Orthodox practice and not its observance.' Now this is just not on.
>
> It is one thing for those who have abandoned our traditions not to believe in them, and therefore to require only a knowledge of them. But as traditional Jews, as Orthodox rabbis who are bound by conscience, and by the terms of the trust reposed in us, to uphold the Shulchan Aruch, we cannot make hypocrites of ourselves telling converts, 'All you have to do is to know what is expected of you, but you do not have to observe it'. This would turn us into hypocrites, never mind the convert.
>
> Any non-Jew could know all there is to know about Judaism. There are plenty of very learned non-Jews, but that does not make them into Jews. You do not become a Jew by having knowledge of Judaism. Therefore any such proposal is too laughable even to be referred for serious consideration.
>
> The last thing we can do is to sell our consciences, and make a mockery of our convictions, by subscribing to the idea of separating between knowing what is right and carrying it out.
>
> Similarly we are told: 'The Orthodox Beth Din would have to find loopholes to nullify the marriage' when it cannot proceed to a proper dissolution by *get*. No Beth Din can be told, 'You must find loopholes'. If they do not exist, you cannot invent them. Once again, these

are suggestions which are simply non-starters, to put it mildly.

Jakobovits then turned to the question of 'common denominators, how to narrow the gap, trying to redress the enormous damage, the havoc wrought in Jewish ranks and now threatening a major schism in the very oneness of our people'. It would not be advanced, he said,

> by public-relations exercises, by publicity forays playing to the gallery. This can be done only by quiet, delicate, discreet exploration.
> Any hope of success requires, in the first instance, a mandate given to those who will deal with this very highly complex area, at least to the extent that, when faced afterwards with having to give an account and securing the support of the constituency on whose behalf they purport to speak, they will not be rebuffed and disowned, as happened with the recent 'initiative'.
> Therefore, the absolute need here is to approach this with the utmost sense of responsibility, and not with the desire to obtain any form of public acclaim. Obviously, the points to be considered are complicated and of the utmost gravity. They cannot be argued out in public forums which are not exactly all dedicated to the same reverence for the ideals that should unite us.

Dealing, finally, with what he described as the latest trend in the Progressive break from traditional Judaism – the touchstone of his clash with Neuberger – the Chief Rabbi stated:

> There were three phases in the development of Reform and Liberal dissent. The first was ritual – the ceremonial part.
> The second, quite distinct, was the intervention in laws on personal status. The involvement in this area was relatively late and to this day is still left intact by such major Jewish units as the State of Israel, on the one hand, and the Reconstructionists, on the other. The third phase affects neither ritual nor personal status, but the wider field of the Jewish commitment to the moral law.
> It grieves me deeply that of late, in very recent times, the focus of the attack on our traditional values is no longer limited to the ritual, nor even to the inter-personal status and relations, but also challenges the moral commitments that we thought would unite us and would not be a matter of dissent, certainly not in public.
> Now, alas, the break in our ranks is threatening to sever the last ideological bonds of commitment that bound us together. And I say this with deepest grief and regret in the hope that we can reverse this current trend.[26]

# Broken Bridges

\* \* \*   \* \* \*   \* \* \*

Little seemed left of the bridges of understanding that the Chief Rabbi and Progressives had begun to build in the heady days of 1967. But more strife was yet to come, and as the Jakobovits era drew to a close, the bridges finally collapsed, with a declaration from the Liberals that destroyed any last bricks in the weakened structure of their troubled relationship:

> In view of the procedure now being implemented to appoint a successor to the present Chief Rabbi, we feel it important to clarify our own relationship to the Office of the Chief Rabbi.
>
> The Chief Rabbi of the United Hebrew Congregations of the British Commonwealth is elected by a committee appointed by the officers and council of the *United Synagogue*. All members of the committee are members of constituents of the *United Synagogue* and associated synagogues. No other synagogue body is formally consulted in the election of the Chief Rabbi.
>
> Accordingly, it is appropriate for us to say on behalf of the Union of Liberal and Progressive Synagogues that the Chief Rabbi to be elected has no authority over our own rabbis or lay people, nor does he represent us or speak on our behalf. Our community appoints its own rabbinic and lay representatives and spokespersons.
>
> This statement does not seek to detract from the status of the Chief Rabbi of the United Hebrew Congregations or his authority over his constituents, but only to reaffirm that the Jewish community is not monolithic but pluralistic in nature. In Judaism, as in other faiths, there is much diversity of belief and practice, even though the common ground far exceeds the differences.
>
> We make this statement before the forthcoming appointment to make it clear that our relationship to the Office of the Chief Rabbi is not dependent on the person who fills it. We will respect the view of the new appointee and seek to co-operate with him in our mutual efforts towards the strengthening of the Jewish community.
>
> We hope that he, too, will respect the differences between his views and ours, and that those differences will not be allowed to diminish co-operative endeavour in areas of common interests and objectives.[27]

While allowing for possible new bridges with the next incumbent, the Jakobovits-Liberal edifice was damaged beyond repair. An abbreviated version of the statement was blazoned across the front page of *The Times*[28] and, in a letter to Brichto following its publication, the Chief Rabbi wrote: 'I really think we should call it a day if hypocrisy is not to become a basic feature of communal and personal relations.'[29] For his part, Brichto commented: 'I have always admired your conviction and dedication to promoting Judaism. Your desire to represent all of Anglo-Jewry, however, has been in conflict with your deep, and not surprising, loyalty to the small but increasing band of the very Orthodox whom you believe will provide the sole basis for Judaism. I think this has been the reason for the increased differences between us over the last few years.'[30]

Board of Deputies president Lionel Kopelowitz described the Liberals' statement as 'ill-conceived and badly timed'. The Chief Rabbi, he told the Board, 'is recognised, both within and without the Jewish community, as the public religious representative of the whole of the British Jewish community. It is not in the communal interest for any group to take up a hard position.'[31]

Reform, meanwhile, dissociated itself from the Liberals' action. Weeks earlier, it had been approached by Brichto with a draft statement on the Chief Rabbinate which the Progressives had proposed should be endorsed by the Reform, Liberal and Masorti movements.[32] The Reformers, however, took the view that 'to issue a declaration which stated only what everyone already knows would be interpreted as unnecessarily divisive and would tend to alienate those in the centre of the community who are concerned for its unity, and those who support us within the Board of Deputies and in other forums, and that nothing was to be gained by an unprovoked declaration of this kind.'[33]

When the Liberal statement was published, the Reform Synagogues of Great Britain were quick to react, asserting that

> The report in *The Times* of 16 December, under the heading 'Liberal Jews Will Not Back the Chief Rabbi', has perhaps tended to create confusion where none existed. The statement issued by the ULPS seemed to us to proclaim what was already self-evident and, as a result, more has been read into it than we believe was intended.
>
> The authority of the Chief Rabbi of the United Hebrew Congregations of the British Commonwealth, to give him his full title, extends to those Orthodox congregations, forming a substantial majority in the community, who are 'United' for the purpose of appointing a chief rabbi as their principal rabbinic authority.
>
> There are differences in ideological interpretation and religious practice within Judaism, and Reform synagogues are guided in religious matters by their own Assembly of Rabbis. Similarly, there are smaller Orthodox groupings who appoint their own independent rabbinic authorities.

> There are many areas of common interest and concern to all Jews in which the Chief Rabbi is seen as a leading spokesman for British Jewry. Rather like the Archbishop of Canterbury, the Chief Rabbi, when making statements, speaks with the standing that derives from his Office. No one perceives the authority of the Archbishop as extending to the Free Churches or to other sectors of the Church.
>
> Similarly, to our knowledge, the Chief Rabbi has never claimed to speak for all Jews. There are many contemporary issues where opinions differ within the Jewish community, on which it is accepted there is room for open and courteous debate.
>
> Despite doctrinal differences with the Reform and Liberal movements, Lord Jakobovits has sought in a number of ways to foster greater unity or, as he has put it, 'to build bridges' in the community; for this he has sometimes been criticised.
>
> We trust that, whoever is appointed the next Chief Rabbi, he will have the courage to advance the work started by Lord Jakobovits and will help to bring greater harmony and sense of common purpose to the whole of British Jewry.[34]

Between themselves, the Reform and Liberal leaders sought to patch up their differences and to construct a common approach to the Chief Rabbinate. But, as the conflicting nature of their private and public correspondence made clear, that desire seemed unlikely to materialise. Liberal chairman Harold Sanderson wrote to his Reform counterpart, Marcus Bower:

> The ULPS made the statement out of the conviction that it was stating a truth that needed to be stated. We respected your reasons for not joining us, and we trust that you respect our reasons for going ahead.
>
> Now I hope we can go forward together to educate Anglo-Jewry and, indeed, members of our own community to understand that we have our own rabbinic and lay leaders who act as our spokespeople and representatives, and that on political matters in the wider community it should be the president of the Board of Deputies who represents us.[35]

Bower replied that, while they took 'different views on the value of press publicity and public controversy ... this should not inhibit discussions between us on harmonising our stance wherever this is possible, and I should be very happy to explore with you how this can be best achieved'.[36]

The movements' public declarations, however, told a different story. In a letter to the *Jewish Chronicle*, Bower wrote:

> There are many areas of common interest and concern to all Jews in which the Chief Rabbi, by virtue of his office and of his own personal standing, is seen as holding a unique position within British Jewry.
>
> Statements made by the Chief Rabbi are rightly treated with respect both inside and outside the community, but the Chief Rabbi has never claimed to speak for all Jews. On many issues, it is accepted that there is room for debate. On this basis, our movement has endeavoured to work closely and harmoniously with Lord Jakobovits and we would hope to be able to do so with his successor as Chief Rabbi.[37]

But the Liberals' Rosita Rosenberg was – not without reason – far less sanguine. She stated:

> The wisdom of expressing just where we stand was amply borne out when we read the reported words of Rabbi Jonathan Sacks.
>
> If Rabbi Sacks, a leading candidate for Chief Rabbi, known as a moderate, can reject the possibility of a pluralistic religious Jewish society (one which exists satisfactorily in the USA, in the absence of a Chief Rabbi), how can anyone claim that there is a likelihood the new holder of the post could or would wish to speak satisfactorily for Progressive Jews?[38]

Rosenberg's reference was to a lecture Sacks had given days earlier,[39] in which – asserting that 'Jewish unity cannot be achieved quickly' and that 'there is a terribly widespread belief that unity lies just within our grasp' – he had proclaimed his position as potential Chief Rabbi:

> Divisions that have lasted for almost two centuries are not going to be healed overnight. It is a mistake to see the Orthodox–Reform divide as the single problem confronting Jewry: other deep divisions beset the Jewish world, and false expectations of finding quick solutions are bound to lead to frustration and disappointment.
>
> Each of us wants Jewish unity, but each of us wants it on our own terms. That is why the search for unity doesn't resolve the tensions in the Jewish world, but instead merely reproduces them. In fact, it does worse, because it leads us to believe that there is some resolution in sight, and that all it needs is good will, tolerance and dialogue to achieve it.
>
> Now, manifestly, that is not so. What divides Jews today is not misunderstanding but a deep, substantive set of conflicts about what it is to be a Jew. Instead, the art is to know where we are going and to move forward, if necessary, an inch at a time.
>
> Pluralism is not an answer. Pluralism supposes that, somehow, all

the different and conflicting things that Jews believe today can be accommodated within one universe. They can't. If pluralism means that we should grant equal legitimacy to every interpretation of Judaism, it is not there to be granted. Orthodox rabbis cannot be called on to legitimate non-halachic forms of Judaism.

There can be no dialogue if that means the kind of public, staged confrontation between Jews of different beliefs, because that kind of dialogue never moved anyone an inch closer together. Instead, all Jews should engage in a personal dialogue with Torah and the totality of Jewish history in critical self-questioning.[40]

Brichto, however, had grounds for greater optimism. Two months after this lecture, the future Chief Rabbi – elected to the post that very week – wrote to him:

As you know (or, it occurs to me, perhaps you don't), as soon as I read your article, 'Halachah with Humility', I called it publicly 'the most courageous statement by a non-Orthodox Jew this century'. I felt it was a genuine way forward. Others turned out not to share my view.

It will be a while – eighteen months – before I take up office. But I believe we can still explore that way forward together. For if we do not move forward, I fear greatly for our community and for *Am Yisrael*.[41]

\* \* \*    \* \* \*    \* \* \*

Reflecting in 1992, a year after his retirement, on the vicissitudes of his Chief Rabbinate, Jakobovits wrote of his efforts to close the gaps within Anglo-Jewry:

I realise all too painfully that I had my great disappointments and setbacks. But my own assessment of crisis and failure does not necessarily correspond to public or press perceptions.

For instance, I deeply regretted my inability to move the community to greater self-esteem, away from its proneness to self-denigration. How much more could be achieved, and how many more talented younger people could be recruited to leadership, if Anglo-Jewry were more confident in its future and took greater pride in its enormous achievements, with less inclination to highlight petty squabbles and passing scandals?

Also futile was an effort to secure some real Jewish unity when I convened, and engaged in, intensive parleys with Progressive leaders, seeking an agreement on marriage, divorce and conversion to which all sections could subscribe.

Such an agreement would have removed the calamitous rift whereby members of one community could not marry those of another, and whereby persons deemed non-Jewish by some were accepted as Jews by others. This sad rupture distressed me endlessly.

Another objective which eluded me was to help eliminate, or reduce, the polarisation of our people into ever-more extremist groups, widening the gap between the religious and the secular, the Orthodox and the 'ultra-Orthodox', and even the political divide. The trend is global, and less pronounced in Britain, with its more mellow tradition, than in Israel and America.

But for me, committed as I am by nurture and conviction to *Torah im derech eretz*, in a setting of tolerance and moderation without sacrifice of principle, the process was, and remains, profoundly disturbing.

On communal and public policies, I have always tried to be guided by my sainted father's motto: 'One enemy is too many, a hundred friends are too few.' My efforts to cultivate friendships have, I believe, proved rewarding to the community and to the Jewish people no less than to me.

I have never yielded to the temptation to resort to mere gimmicks. In public utterances, I avoided expressing views with which all would agree – the convinced need no persuasion from anyone. After all, the task of a rabbi is to speak for Judaism and not necessarily for Jews.[42]

Distressed as he appeared to be at his failure to achieve unity, Jakobovits later admitted, however, that he had never supported the view that

> the unity theme will determine the future strength of the Orthodoxy community – or, indeed, of any part of the Jewish people. Our capacity to survive as Jews will not depend on whether we sit round the same table, or publicly debate our differences, or pursue a search for common ideals where none exist.
>
> While I was Chief Rabbi, I cared greatly about communal harmony and tolerance. In all areas on which religious difference did not impinge, I encouraged working together, and I formed a consultative committee which met regularly at my home, under a Reform or Liberal chairman, to discuss such common concerns as Jewish-Christian relations, Israel, Soviet Jewry, anti-Semitism, and threats to amicable relationships within the community.
>
> Happily, during my incumbency, we never experienced the vitriol

such as occurred at the time of the Jacobs Affair which spilt over into the national press. Nor did we witness public denunciations of the 'new paths' of the Liberals and the Reformers comparable to the vehemence of the widely circulated attacks under that title by the late Chief Rabbi Joseph Herman Hertz.

[But] promoting good will within the community – however desirable – was never my top priority. I had no illusions that, simply by talking with the dissidents, we would heal the rift of their defection; or save a single Jew from the prospect of marrying out; or make our youth more observant, our university students more committed to Jewish values, and our professionals more Jewish in the practice of their vocation.

For those objectives, we need not tolerance but learning and commitment. I was, and remain, convinced that the key to the religious stability and growth of Anglo-Jewry lies in intensive Jewish education, not in debating chambers and declarations of good will.[43]

Twenty-five years earlier, the incoming Chief Rabbi had told his divisive flock: 'I will encourage friendliness in our relations ... I will do my best to serve and unite all sections of the community ... It will be my privilege and my duty to do all within my power and authority to close the gaps within our people ... to befriend those who dissent and to work with them in Jewish and general causes unaffected by our religious differences.'[44]

But looking back on his Chief Rabbinate, he was forced to concede: 'The obsession with communal unity is a peculiarly Anglo-Jewish trait. It does not feature in such a form among American or European Jews – and certainly not in Israel. It is time we shifted our concern from form to substance: how to live as fuller and better Jews, rather than how to gloss over differences and proclaim a unity which turns out to be a mirage.'[45]

Epilogue

## Change or Die

'If it be the object of Divine Worship', wrote Nathan Marcus Adler in 1847,

> that man appear in the presence of his Creator with pious humility; that he give utterance to the sentiments of love and veneration which he entertains towards the Author of his being, and express his gratitude for His mercies, which are 'new every morning'; if it be the object of *Public Worship* that the Israelite, by praying in communion with his fellow believers, be the more powerfully roused to devotion; that he be encouraged and incited, by the holy word of the Law, to the performance of pious and noble actions; that the bond which links the individual to the community be strengthened and fortified by the sacred language in which he prays in common with his brethren; if such be the holy ends of Public Worship, then, whatever tends to counteract or to defeat these ends, ought to be strictly avoided.
>
> The Synagogue should not be deserted during the performance of the daily morning and evening service. Whatever either infringes upon the dignity of Divine worship, or occasions any bitterness of feeling, ought to be banished, and remain excluded from the House of God. The Israelite must prove by his conduct *before, during* and *after* service that Divine worship is to him at once a sacred and a pleasing duty, and that he delights in the benign influence of the House of Worship.[1]

With these solemn words, the recently installed Chief Rabbi of the United Congregations of Jews of the British Empire laid before his scattered and disunited flock the 'laws and regulations' through which he hoped to fill the empty pews of the houses of worship under his jurisdiction. Yet many remained empty in the ensuing decades, a source of continuing sorrow and distress to the Chief Rabbis who followed him, and to the ministers and chazanim charged with projecting the 'voice of prayer and praise' throughout the land.

At various times during the 160 years since those words were written, Adler's successors sought, by word and deed, to strengthen the bond between the absentee worshipper and the Author of his being. As we have seen, one of the first acts of Adler's son and heir, Hermann Adler – following the resolution of the United Synagogue council in 1891 that 'the question of Synagogue Ritual and Practice may be solved to the benefit and advancement of the religious well-being of the entire Community, and consistently with the maintenance of the traditional observances of our ancient faith'[2] – was to draw up a series of 'Modifications in the Ritual of your Synagogue' in conjunction with Moses Friedländer, the principal of Jews' College, 'calculated to enhance the impressiveness of your services, and to rouse and preserve the devotion of your worshippers'.[3]

That these 'modifications' appeared to fail in their purpose was manifest in the foundation of the Jewish Religious Union some ten years later, which led to the younger Adler's impassioned 'Old Paths' sermon against the 'novel features, or rather drastic innovations',[4] of the offending movement. At around the same time, the Chief Rabbi sanctioned the publication of a 'handbook of synagogue music for congregational singing', so that 'when the voice of prayer and praise is uplifted in their synagogue, "young men and maidens also, old men and children together, shall laud the Name of the Eternal"'.[5] But this, too, failed to draw in the old men, let alone the maidens.

Discussing the role of the United Synagogue in the sixty years since its establishment, Chief Rabbi Joseph Herman Hertz told an anniversary gathering in 1931:

> A new era opened in London Jewry when in 1870, after many years of effort on the part of Sir Anthony de Rothschild and Lionel Louis Cohen, the three City synagogues and their offshoots, the Central and Bayswater Synagogues, became incorporated as the United Synagogue. Under God's blessing, those five houses of worship have now become thirty-three constituent and associate synagogues. And its wonderful growth in power and numbers has been accompanied by an ever-widening outlook in regard to its sphere of labour.
>
> In addition to building houses of worship in new centres of the metropolitan Jewish population, and maintaining the various ecclesiastical and communal institutions of a world kehillah, it has organised a wonderful network of social welfare activities that extend far beyond the metropolis, such as helping the helpless by visitation of hospitals, prisons and reformatories; taking charge of the burials of the friendless poor, and coming to the rescue of the discharged prisoner; and, by means of its renowned arbitration court in connection with the Beth Din, fulfilling in a striking manner the sublime duty of 'bringing peace between man and his fellow'.

And to these widely ramified services in the realm of worship and loving-kindness, it has in recent years added a new enthusiasm for Torah, liberally subventioning Jewish religious education, higher and elementary, both within and without its affiliated synagogues. Moreover, the United Synagogue has given its distinctive character to English Judaism. By its example and influence, it has made Progressive Conservatism – i.e., religious advance without loss of traditional Jewish values and without estrangement from the collective consciousness of the House of Israel – the Anglo-Jewish position in theology.[6]

Surveying those productive golden years, Hertz's successor, Israel Brodie – speaking at the centenary service of the Bayswater Synagogue in 1963 – invoked the words of Hermann Adler, its one-time minister, in relation to the role of the preacher: 'He must show that the law of God is needed for all the various stages of human development ... And it is the preacher's duty to explain and expound the various ordinances of our faith. He must seek to excite in his hearers' minds *chibuv mitzvah*, the love and desire faithfully to obey these precepts by showing that their object is to keep alive in our minds the thought of God.'[7]

More than at any other time [continued Brodie] it is necessary for our contemporary religious teachers to impress upon congregations what and why they should observe, and not what they needn't observe nor believe of the Torah, Written and Oral. The famous literary critic and author Walter Pater once wrote: 'We have little patience with these clergy who dwell on nothing else than the difficulties of faith and the propriety of concession to the opposite force.'

While we sing the praises of this synagogue and evoke its past glories and achievements, spiritual and communal, we ought to be able to sing in confident anticipation the glories of tomorrow. The Hallel we recite on festivals and the New Moon summons us as servants of the Lord to praise Him for the marvellous things wrought for us in the past. It calls on us to praise Him for the cup of salvation which will be ours in the future. It is then fitting that on this occasion we should think of the possibilities and hopes of tomorrow.

Many changes have occurred in recent years which have had an impact upon this community; they have posed to leaders and members problems and challenges which will demand thought, vision, courage, humanity and prayer. One thing, however, is absolutely clear: an overwhelming consciousness in all deliberations and discussions that whatever is planned, the sacred purposes and needs of a synagogue must be prominently in the foreground.

More than the future destiny of a building which, of course, must occupy thought and attention, the future spiritual and moral character of the men, women and children who constitute the *kehillah* must have precedence. When our ancestors in the wilderness were called upon to contribute to the erection of the tabernacle, it was that God should dwell in their midst (Exodus 25:8).[8]

Seven years earlier, however – before a schism of equal proportions threatened to overwhelm him – Brodie had referred in different terms to the problems and challenges faced by the post-Hirschellian selection committee, and its successful candidate, in the wake of the Great Secession. 'The new era', he had commented, 'called for a spiritual leader who was a master and authority of Jewish law and, at the same time, was versed in the literary expressions of world culture. He had to understand his generation and be understood by them: hence to be able to communicate with them through the vehicle of the language which they employed daily and directly. To maintain and consolidate the communal entity and stay the evils of dissidence, one could employ persuasive methods other than by the threatened invocation and penalties of a *cherem*.'[9]

Nor was Brodie's successor, Immanuel Jakobovits, blind to the challenges that faced his increasingly deserted synagogues as he strove, a decade on, to alert his clergy and community to

> the grimmest crisis in all our long history ... of staggering losses by defections, by assimilation and by intermarriage ... Those who form the bulk of our rising generation are aliens to our synagogue services. They find them uninspiring and unintelligible, our classes often unattractive, our schools dilapidated, and our methods hopelessly outdated. Recruitment of first-class ministers and teachers is today almost nil. For the first time in our history, there is today a real fear for Jewish survival.
>
> Even in the Middle Ages, when the total number of Jews all over the world was only about one million, no one ever worried about the survival of the Jewish people and of Judaism. Today, with all the freedom and affluence we enjoy, we have become alarmed concerning our survival as a community of faith, destined to assume the heritage of our prophets, of our patriarchs, our sages and our martyrs. This is the threat and this is the challenge which face us. The challenge is at least as great, and potentially at least as disastrous, as that which confronted the two and a half million Jews in the land of Israel last June [1967].
>
> Shall it be said that the United Synagogue fiddled with bulky

accounts and antiquated bye-laws while Judaism was burning? Shall the United Synagogue council devote hours to discussing some choir expenditure here or the cost of a few trees on a cemetery there, to concern itself with other trifles, while every year thousands of sons and daughters of United Synagogue members opt out of traditional Judaism altogether?

We need an awareness of the state of crisis. After all, what helped to rescue Israel last summer was that Jews throughout the world began to be alarmed by the danger, and that aroused Anglo-Jewry as well as other Jewries in the diaspora. Let no one write off the latent enthusiasm and commitment of our young people. Give them a chance and they will rise to it. Convince them we are in danger – they will meet the danger and defeat it.

So first we have to create a 'crisis mentality', a realisation of the emergency that is upon us. Once we realise that, and we are driven by the awareness of that pressure day and night; once we are concerned and have sleepless nights as a result, then we will be able to mobilise the resources at our disposal.

We need today a new mentality and a new outlook. Tradition can be a wonderful thing if you live up to it. But in the administration of institutions, it can also be an oppressive thing if it makes you a prisoner of the past. We have to disabuse ourselves of the narrow lines of thinking conditioned by hidebound tradition and precedents. We have to clear away the cobwebs of convention which prevent us from exploring with bold imagination the pathways of the future.

Instead of looking back and searching for formal precedents, we have to look forward and search for challenges and new responses. We must not be afraid of setting new precedents and of ignoring those of the past which are irrelevant to the twentieth century and the 1960s.

Of course, the religious ideals for which we aim are supreme and eternal, but the methods of achieving them have to be changed. We cannot afford to wage a war of survival in this sophisticated age with bows and arrows. We require the latest, most up-to-date methods to break through the straitjacket of an oppressive set of constitutional rules and bye-laws.

Conceding that a fundamental overhaul was also required in the framework and functioning of the Chief Rabbinate, Jakobovits added:

> I am fully aware that in the process of adjustment to an entirely new society, to a new era which is breaking upon us – the scientific age, the atomic age, the age of moral permissiveness – enabling Jewish

thinking to bear an influence on the shape of things to come, my own office will also have to undergo some radical changes of outlook and methods. I realise that living as we do in a democratic age, my power as Chief Rabbi does not lie mainly in the authority of the office. What is the use of making rulings, of giving instructions, of issuing edicts, if they are not going to be accepted by popular support and understanding?

I am quite adjusted to the idea that my strength will lie not in the exercise of authority, but in the exercise of persuasion. If I do not carry the public with me, convince them that the ideals I advocate are worth struggling for, then all the authority vested in my office will be of no avail.[10]

Of the United Synagogue philosophy, the Chief Rabbi declared in 1970, at a service to mark the organisation's centenary:

More than any other group of congregations, the United Synagogue has relied for its stability on a commodity which is fast disappearing from our new society. Unlike other synagogue groups, whether to the right or to the left of us, which attract their members primarily through some ideological Torah commitment or non-commitment, our synagogues have depended in the main on a sense of reverence for tradition, on filial loyalty, on sons expecting to take the place of their fathers.

All this is no more. We no longer have a hereditary nobility in which parents automatically bequeath their titles and their obligations to their children. We have only life peerages, and must now induce our children to earn their own elevation to the House of Israel if we expect them to wear the crown of Torah-living after us.

Secondly, the United Synagogue is founded not only on the stability of tradition, but on a 'middle-of-road' philosophy. But in this 'either-or' age, compromise and half-commitment are no longer the better part of religious virtue, and one recalls the remark of the Chafetz Chaim: 'In the middle of the road, only horses walk'.[11]

We must recognise that we live in an increasingly polarised community, and once again, the United Synagogue will be the principal sufferer from this development. We are caught between two grinding millstones threatening to pulverise us.

The upper millstone will squeeze out of our ranks the finest of our synagogue family, the young religious intellectuals, the idealistic youth who will be drawn to the better day-schools, the yeshivot and girls' seminaries, gravitating from there either to Israel or to congregations more fervent than ours. And the bottom millstone will be littered with the chaff of the indifferent, the drop-outs of our classes and congregations who in their disenchantment with us will sever their last bonds with traditional Judaism.

For let us be under no illusion: the United Synagogue as it is today, our organisation, our education, our services, our leadership and our whole philosophy simply do not attract either element. It will reclaim neither the creative grain nor the wind-tossed chaff, and we will be left with the thinning ranks of the old faithfuls who are too stagnant to break with the past or to rally to the future.[12]

\* \* \*   \* \* \*   \* \* \*

Responding to the United Synagogue crisis uncovered by the Review he initiated after Jakobovits stepped down, Stanley Kalms was forthright in his analysis and prognosis. Without, of course, referring to the changes that had spurred the Reform secession and its Liberal aftermath, he reaffirmed unequivocally that change was needed if the United Synagogue was to regain its former glory.

In 'Hope for the Future', the concluding chapter of *A Time For Change*,[13] Kalms set out his vision, acknowledging in this quotation from Machiavelli the many obstacles that might lie ahead: 'There is nothing more difficult to execute, nor more dubious of success, nor more dangerous to administer than to introduce a new system of things: for he who introduces it has all those who profit from the old system as his enemies, and he has only lukewarm allies in all those who might profit from the new system.'

> The United Synagogue [wrote Kalms] was once a great institution. It shaped the religious character of Anglo-Jewry. It provided a spiritual home for the vast majority of London's Jews. It fostered the growth of new congregations. It supported the institutions – most obviously, the Chief Rabbinate – which guided the development of provincial and Commonwealth Jewry as well. It represented a Jewish ethos that combined loyalty to halachah with tolerance, inclusivism and an openness to the challenges of the modern world. Such an ethos, and such an organisation, is badly needed in today's Jewish world. The United Synagogue was once a great institution. Our belief is that it can be one again.
>
> We cannot hide the seriousness of our findings. They are based on a process of consultation, professional investigation, research and academic scrutiny quite possibly unprecedented in Anglo-Jewry. They reveal an organisation in financial crisis. This fact alone, we believe, is

sufficient to precipitate rapid and radical change. For if the financial predicament is not addressed with utmost urgency, the very survival of the institution will be in doubt.

But the financial problem is a symptom, not a cause. As long ago as 1976, concluding his history of the United Synagogue, Professor Aubrey Newman wrote: 'Emerging features would seem to indicate that the organisation was in danger of losing its way and failing to respond to the developing needs of the wider community.'[14] We believe that diagnosis to be correct, even more so now than then.

The United Synagogue is losing members, far more rapidly than any other synagogue organisation. Twenty-five years ago, it represented three-quarters of affiliated Jews, today little more than half. The high age-profile of its members indicates that it is failing to attract the young. Our market research has uncovered widespread dissatisfaction with what is seen as a remote and profligate head office, cold and unwelcoming communities, and a drift away from the United Synagogue's traditional tolerant religious ethos.

These are signals of an organisation that has lost its way.

It is our belief that the United Synagogue lost its way with the best of intentions. As the leading religious organisation in Anglo-Jewry, it has undertaken responsibilities on behalf of the whole community – responsibilities which, it is now clear, it could not afford, not least because the United Synagogue is no longer the whole community.

We believe that many of these responsibilities must now be handed back to the community, either locally to congregations or centrally in the form of new trusts or coalitions. Difficult though this process will initially be, we believe that it will release new funds, energies and leadership and will, in the fullness of time, reinvigorate the whole of our communal life.

But over the past few years something else, critical to our diagnosis, has occurred. As centrally funded projects grew in scope and scale, a shift took place in the balance of the organisation. Financially, administratively and professionally, its centre of gravity moved from the individual congregation to Woburn House. Instead of the centre existing to serve local communities, it began to seem as if the local communities existed to serve the centre. Once this took place, it was inevitable that the fundamental purpose or mission of the United Synagogue would be obscured.

Its mission, we believe, is to create communities to include Jews. If individual congregations are failing to attract or involve members; if they are failing to create dynamic, welcoming and multifaceted communities; if they are not reaching out to the unaffiliated – then the United Synagogue is failing in its task. Once the United Synagogue fails to be, and to be seen as, the natural home for the majority of Jews, its mission, authority and place in Anglo-Jewry will be lost. On this single issue all else depends.

Every proposal we have recommended has been designed to refocus the organisation to this one overriding priority. It will require significant changes in the structure of the United Synagogue. It will require no less significant changes in attitude on the part of lay and rabbinic leadership at all levels. All these changes flow, however, from one fundamental proposition: that membership and involvement are created locally, not centrally. It is in on the strength of its individual communities that the strength of the United Synagogue depends.

Machiavelli, in the quotation with which this chapter begins, reminds us how difficult it is to secure a consensus for change. What is old is familiar. What is new is untried, unsettling and uncertain. All the more so does this apply to the United Synagogue, whose stability seems to depend on its changelessness and whose very image has been of an unshakeable rock in a world of change.

Consensus for change will not be easy to achieve, but, given the seriousness of the present situation, achieve it we must. Institutions either change or die. Rarely do they die suddenly. Rather, they drift into a slow decline marked by a failure to attract the young, to recruit the best available talents as leaders, or to seem relevant to the problems of the age. These are all early warning signs of an establishment in danger, and, if not responded to in time, they become progressively harder to reverse. The single most critical test of whether an institution has the will to live is whether it has the will to change.

Three things have convinced us that in the case of the United Synagogue change is not only necessary but also possible.

The first is the remarkable creativity individual communities have shown in recent years wherever local energies have been allowed to flourish. We have encountered one example after another of dormant congregations that have been revived, of outer suburban communities full of activity and youth, and of more established congregations creating the internal diversity needed to attract and involve a wider membership. These facts have persuaded us that once resources and responsibility are handed back from the centre to the local congregation, the United Synagogue can recover its leading position in Anglo-Jewry.

The second is the equally remarkable loyalty we have discovered to the fundamental aims of the United Synagogue. Underlying the dissatisfaction, our research reveals a widespread commitment to the organisation and to what it once represented. The strongest consensus to have emerged is that there is a belief that the United Synagogue must change, that it has lost its way and must recover it again.

The strength of that consensus will be tested to the full in the months ahead. We can foresee some of the responses to this report. There will be those who damn it with faint praise. There will be others who promise to examine it with enthusiasm, with an eventual pigeon-hole in mind. Some will declare it to be unworkable. Others will try to sentence it to the slow death of further committees and working parties. It will meet with overt or covert resistance from those whose reputations and positions are at stake. All this is predictable.

But neither sentiment nor vested interest can be allowed to stand in the way of change, because this time the stakes are too high. It will be in the hands of the ordinary members of the council and of the management and membership of the congregations themselves, as much as of the present leadership of the United Synagogue, to see to it that this moment of opportunity is grasped and translated into action before it is too late.

This report has been concerned with structures: with management, governance and finance. But it has been a report about a religious institution, and in the end it has been driven by a religious faith. Our final reason for confidence in the possibility of change is an item of faith. It is simply this: that the true strength of the Jewish people throughout the ages has been its unique will to survive and its adaptability to change in pursuit of timeless values. The United Synagogue, we believe, will not allow itself to be an exception to this rule.

The first words of this Review were those of Chief Rabbi Dr Jonathan Sacks, so it is fitting to leave him the last thought as well: 'The miracle of almost four thousand years of Jewish continuity has depended on a stunning ability to create renewal in the midst of crisis.'

May the United Synagogue continue in that tradition.

\* \* \*  \* \* \*  \* \* \*

In his own response to *A Time For Change*, Sacks concluded by remarking that the Review represented

> a momentous challenge to the rabbinate. It is clear from both the research and recommendations that what is needed is more rabbinic

leadership, not less. Equally clear is that the rabbinate – and in this I include myself – could go further in the key tasks of 'creating a strong sense of community', 'being receptive to new ideas', and 'bringing the less involved into the community'. I have committed myself to working in the closest possible partnership with the rabbinate to plan and implement a programme for rabbinic development. The stature of the rabbinate depends on the stature of its individual rabbis, and we must take the report as an impetus to improvement.

All of us who care for the United Synagogue should recognise that the publication of the report represents a unique opportunity for renewal. It was the biblical Joseph who used a recession – seven years of famine – to restructure an economy. We must use our present economic difficulties to reshape our communal life to the benefit of our children and their children. Nothing would be more irresponsible or more lacking in spiritual depth than to take the report as an occasion for doom-laden rhetoric. God sends us not crises but challenges, and we are tested by the depth of our response ...

We look for moral signposts that do not blow down in the hurricane of change. We turn to values that are not at the mercy of speculation. Such moments are unique opportunities for spiritual renewal. For at such moments we remember what we should never have forgotten: that the most precious thing we have as Jews is our spiritual heritage, Torah, and its rich gifts: spirituality, ethics, family, community and continuity. Now is a time for religious leadership if ever there was one; and we must not be found wanting.[15]

# Notes

## PREFACE

1. *A Few Words Addressed to the Committee for the Election of a Chief Rabbi of England, and to the Electors at Large,* by A Friend of Truth (London: Brain and Payne, 1844), pp.1–15.
2. *Voice of Jacob,* 26 November 1841, p.35.
3. Ibid., p.36.
4. Jonathan Sacks, *Community of Faith* (London: Peter Halban, 1995), p.9.
5. Ibid., pp.88–9.
6. Ibid., pp.98–9.
7. *A Time For Change: A Report on the Role of the United Synagogue in the Years Ahead* (London: Stanley Kalms Foundation, 1992).
8. Ibid., pp.1–2.
9. Ibid., p.220.
10. Ibid., p.240.
11. Jonathan Sacks, *A Time For Renewal: A Rabbinic Response to the Kalms Report, 'A Time For Change'* (London: Office of the Chief Rabbi, 1992), pp.6–7.
12. Rona Hart and Edward Kafka, *Trends in British Synagogue Membership 1990–2005/06* (London: Board of Deputies of British Jews, 2006), pp.19–23. For earlier statistics of synagogue affiliation, see Appendix III.
13. Male membership of the United Synagogue fell 12.1 per cent from 22,761 in 1992 to 20,004 in 2006, though this was offset by a rise in female members from 16,851 to 19,907, bringing the respective totals to 39,612 and 39,911 (Research and Development Executive, United Synagogue Community Division, 2007).
14. The study and practice of Judaism alongside secular knowledge and pursuits.
15. 'The Evolution of the British Rabbinate Since 1845: Its Past Impact and Future Challenges,' in Immanuel Jakobovits, *The Timely and The Timeless* (London and Portland, OR: Vallentine Mitchell, 1977), p.269.
16. Chaim Bermant, 'The Rabbi's Rabbi,' *Jewish Chronicle,* 5 November 1999, pp.34–5. The remarks are from an appreciation, published following the Emeritus Chief Rabbi's death, written by Bermant some months before his own sudden demise in January 1998. The JC columnist and feature writer was the author of *Lord Jakobovits: The Authorized Biography of the Chief Rabbi* (London: Weidenfeld and Nicolson, 1990).
17. London: Vallentine Mitchell, 1957. Jacobs acknowledges his friend Ian Gordon as the originator of the title. On an earlier use, see chapter 5, note 26, and chapter 15 for details of later editions of the book.
18. Doreen Berger, *The Jewish Victorian: Genealogical Information from the Jewish Newspapers, 1871–1880* (Witney: Robert Boyd Publications, 1999).
19. Meir Persoff, 'Learning lessons from our history,' *Jewish Chronicle,* 28 January 2000, p.27.
20. *Jewish Chronicle,* 4 February 2000, p.20.
21. See reference following Bibliography.
22. Ibid.
23. Ibid.
24. Ibid.

## INTRODUCTION

1. Resolution 13, 'Matters Relating to the Office of the Chief Rabbi, passed at Meetings of the Several Metropolitan and Provincial Congregations, the Great Synagogue, London, 19 and 21 February, 1843,' *Voice of Jacob,* 3 March 1843, p.122.
2. Redcliffe N. Salaman, *Whither Lucien Wolf's Anglo-Jewish Community? – The Lucien Wolf Memorial Lecture, 1953* (London: Jewish Historical Society of England, 1954), p.7.

## PROLOGUE

1. *Jewish Chronicle,* 24 January 1890, p.6.
2. Marcus Nathan Adler does not name the ancestor, but a genealogy of the Adler family printed in his account of its history (see note 3) suggests Salman Kayn Hacohen (Wedel zur Zange, died 1648) as a possibility.
3. Josef Unna, 'Nathan Hacohen Adler', in *Guardians of our Heritage,* Leo Jung (ed.) (New York: Bloch Publishing House, 1958), pp.169–71; M. Friedländer, 'The Late Chief Rabbi Dr N.M. Adler', in *Jewish Quarterly Review,*

II (London, July 1890), pp.368–71; Marcus N. Adler, *The Adler Family* (London: Office of the Jewish Chronicle, 1909), pp.10–15.
4. H.D. Schmidt, 'Chief Rabbi Nathan Marcus Adler: Jewish Educator from Germany', in *Leo Baeck Institute Year Book*, VII (London: East and West Library, 1962), p.290.
5. Friedländer, 'The Late Chief Rabbi', p.372. Dr Michael Friedländer (1833–1910), born at Jutroschin in German Poland, was principal of Jews' College, London, from 1865 to 1907. See Isidore Harris, *Jews' College Jubilee Volume* (London: Luzac, 1906), pp.xxxi–clxxxii; Albert M. Hyamson, *Jews' College, London, 1855–1955* (London: Jews' College, 1955), pp.33–84; and Israel Cohen, 'Michael Friedländer', in Leo Jung (ed.), *Men of the Spirit*, (New York: Kymson, 1964), pp.469–76.
6. Eugene C. Black, 'The Anglicization of Orthodoxy: The Adlers', in *Profiles in Diversity*, Frances Malino and David Sorkin (eds), (Detroit, MI: Wayne State University Press, 1998), p.296.
7. Proponents of the Hebrew Enlightenment (*Haskalah*) movement – social, spiritual and literary – that developed in Germany in the late eighteenth century and spread to Austria, Poland and Russia. Its followers urged Jews to reform their schools, learn the vernacular, study secular subjects, and adopt native customs. The movement was fiercely challenged by the leaders of Orthodoxy, who regarded such innovations as a threat to Jewish tradition.
8. Friedländer, 'The Late Chief Rabbi', p.372; Schmidt, 'Chief Rabbi Nathan Marcus Adler', pp.290–1; Eliyahu Meir Klugman, *Rabbi Samson Raphael Hirsch* (New York: Mesorah Publications, 1996), pp.39–40.
9. Schmidt, 'Chief Rabbi Nathan Marcus Adler', p.292.
10. Noah H. Rosenbloom, *Tradition in an Age of Reform* (Philadelphia, PA: Jewish Publication Society of America, 1976), p.64.
11. Leo Trepp, *Die Oldenburger Jüdenschaft* (Oldenburg: Heinz Holzberg Verlag, 1973), p.85.
12. Ibid., p.87.
13. Black, 'The Anglicization of Orthodoxy', p.297.
14. Schmidt, 'Chief Rabbi Nathan Marcus Adler', p.294; Friedländer, 'The Late Chief Rabbi', p.374.
15. Michael A. Meyer, *German-Jewish History in Modern Times* (New York: Columbia University Press, 1977), p.54.
16. Schmidt, 'Chief Rabbi Nathan Marcus Adler', p.295.
17. Quoted in the *Jewish Chronicle*, 24 January 1890, p.7.
18. Mordechai Breuer, *Modernity Within Tradition: The Social History of Orthodox Jewry in Imperial Germany*, trans. Elizabeth Petuchowski (New York: Columbia University Press, 1992), p.ix.
19. Elkan Nathan Adler, *London* (Philadelphia, PA: Jewish Publication Society of America, 1930), pp.169–70. Initially, the manifesto – published in Hebrew and German – was signed by seventy-seven Orthodox rabbis. 'The second name subscribed (alphabetically) is that of our own newly appointed Chief Rabbi, Dr N.M. Adler', wrote the *Jewish Chronicle* (11 April 1845, p.136) in a preface to its published English translation. 'Among the rest, we see the names of Rabbis S.R. Hirsch and B[enjamin] Auerbach, two others of the admitted candidates for our [Chief] Rabbinical chair.' The signatories declared that the Brunswick *Rabbiner Versammlung* (Rabbinical Association) had come 'unanimously to the resolution of attacking the citadel of our holy religion, of removing its bulwarks, and of destroying its fortifications, so as to expose it to easy demolition ... We were not prepared to see such pernicious doctrines as those promulgated in a printed protocol which they issued; – doctrines which had only for their object the leading of the house of Israel astray, and the removal of it from our holy law; doctrines calculated to excite contempt against the law of the Almighty, to destroy our holy inheritance, to break down its fences, to tear asunder its cords, and to overstep the landmarks which our pious ancestors (among whom were the Great Synod) had established.' In their manifesto, the Orthodox rabbis urged their flocks – 'brethren, house of Israel' – not to 'hearken to, nor have any regard for, the voice of those who diverge from the path of truth; stand apart, and keep your children afar from them and their devices, by which they wish to ensnare you, and embrace all means in your power, consistent with reason and justice, to defeat their counsels and frustrate their designs' (Ibid., 11 April 1845, pp.136–7; 25 April 1845, pp.142–3).
20. Friedländer, 'The Late Chief Rabbi', p.375.
21. *Jewish Chronicle*, 24 January 1890, p.7.
22. Klugman, *Rabbi Samson Raphael Hirsch*, p.86.
23. See references in Preface and later in this chapter.
24. Isidor Grunfeld, *Three Generations: The Influence of Samson Raphael Hirsch on Jewish Life and Thought* (London: Jewish Post Publications, 1958), p.36. Born in Tauberettersheim, Bavaria, Grunfeld (1900–1975) settled in Britain in 1933 and served first as registrar and, from 1939, as dayan on the London Beth Din (see chapters 13 and 15). He wrote extensively on Samson Raphael Hirsch and translated many of his works.
25. Ibid., p.37.
26. Ibid., p.94.
27. Immanuel Jakobovits, 'Fragments From An Unpublished Autobiography', in Meir Persoff, *Immanuel Jakobovits: a Prophet in Israel* (London and Portland, OR: Vallentine Mitchell, 2002), p.6. The 'fragments' were discovered, collated and edited by the author after Jakobovits' death.
28. Immanuel Jakobovits, *Rabbinical Tasks in the Present Era*, Amsterdam, 5 November 1957 (London: Conference of European Rabbis, 1958), pp.1, 7–8.

29. Todd M. Endelman, *The Jews of Georgian England 1714–1830: Tradition and Change in a Liberal Society* (Ann Arbor, MI: University of Michigan Press, 1999), p.122.
30. Nathan Marcus Adler's grand-uncle, known as the 'Chief Rabbi of London'.
31. Endelman, *The Jews of Georgian England*, p.143.
32. Todd M. Endelman, *The Jews of Britain 1656 to 2000* (Berkeley, Los Angeles, CA, London: University of California Press, 2002), p.52.
33. Geoffrey Alderman, *Modern British Jewry* (Oxford: Clarendon Press, 1998), rev. edn, p.41.
34. Arthur Cohen, 'The Structure of Anglo-Jewry Today', in *Three Centuries of Anglo-Jewish History*, V.D. Lipman (ed.) (Cambridge: W. Heffer and Sons, for the Jewish Historical Society of England, 1961), p.177.
35. Eugene C. Black, *The Social Politics of Anglo-Jewry 1880–1920* (Oxford: Blackwell, 1988), p.26.
36. Norman Cohen, 'Non-Religious Factors in the Emergence of the Chief Rabbinate', in *Transactions of the Jewish Historical Society of England*, XXI (London: Jewish Historical Society of England, 1968), p.310.
37. Geoffrey Alderman, 'The British Chief Rabbinate: A Most Peculiar Practice', *European Judaism*, 23, 2 (Autumn 1990), p.46.
38. Ibid., pp.46–7. Of the Chief Rabbi's authority, Jonathan Sacks (holder of the post since 1991) writes: 'Solomon Hirschell, who took up office in 1802, was already known in non-Jewish circles as the "High Priest" of British Jews, and his authority extended as far as Australia, New Zealand and South Africa. By the time Nathan Marcus Adler became Chief Rabbi in 1845, the prestige of the office was already well established.' *Community of Faith* (London: Peter Halban, 1995), pp.80–1.
39. Albert M. Hyamson, *The Sephardim of England* (London: Spanish and Portuguese Jews' Congregation, 1951), p.269.
40. James Picciotto, *Sketches of Anglo-Jewish History*, Israel Finestein (rev. and ed.) (London: Soncino Press, 1955), p.367. Italics in text are in the original unless otherwise indicated.
41. Introduction to *Forms of Prayer, used in the West London Synagogue of British Jews, with an English Translation. Volume I – Daily and Sabbath Prayers*, D.W. Marks (ed.) (London: Wertheimer, 1841). The second and subsequent editions were co-edited with Marks' assistant, Albert Löwy. The prayer book revision committee comprised Francis (later Sir Francis) Goldsmid, Abraham Mocatta, Moses Mocatta, and Marks. 'Mr [later Sir] John Simon, then a student for the Bar, constantly worked with Mr Marks over the Prayer book and, to use the words of the reverend gentleman, "frequently turned night into day"' (*Jewish Chronicle*, 22 January 1892, p.18). Citing the Minute Book of the West London Synagogue of British Jews, 8 May 1840, 14 October 1840, and 2 March 1841, Kershen notes: 'The first Reform prayer book was drawn up by David Woolf Marks in consultation with Professor H. Hurwitz, holder of the first chair in Hebrew Studies at University College London, and the Rev. Dr Morris Jacob Raphall, the distinguished Orthodox rabbi from Birmingham. The trio followed the guidelines and directives of the Founders.' Anne J. Kershen and Jonathan A. Romain, *Tradition and Change: A History of Reform Judaism in Britain, 1840–1995* (London and Portland, OR: Vallentine Mitchell, 1995), p.17. In essence, the changes were mainly those of abbreviation, particularly in the *musaf amidah*; the omission of such sections as *yekum purkan* and *barneh madlikin*; and the substitution of Hebrew for Aramaic in, most notably, the *kaddish*. The basis for the revised liturgy, the editor pointed out, was still the traditional ritual. David Woolf Marks (1811–1909) had been secretary and reader of the 'Orthodox but progressive' Liverpool Congregation (Kershen and Romain, p.15), one of the largest outside London, and was 'a gentleman who had acquired no small degree of fame in those days in consequence of his singular gifts of speech, combined with qualities which marked him out as a young man of considerable ability. He was, moreover, well known to be an enthusiastic sympathiser of reform projects' (*Jewish Chronicle*, 22 January 1892, p.18). Moravian-born Albert Löwy (1816–1908) was appointed as second minister some six months after Marks, also in 1842. 'His assistance was a valuable accession to the infant congregation, for he had come to England two years earlier fresh from the University of Vienna, where he had established a reputation for sound German and Hebrew scholarship. His special aptitude as a man of learning was of much importance in the new congregation' (Ibid., p.19).
42. Moses Margoliouth, *The History of the Jews in Great Britain*, Vol. III (London: Richard Bentley, 1851), p.86. A Jewish-born cleric and theologian, Margoliouth (1820–1881) emigrated from his native Poland to Liverpool in 1837 and was baptised the following year. After becoming a curate in 1844, he held several ecclesiastical posts and launched a Hebrew-Christian monthly, *The Star of Jacob*. His many other works – all published in London – included *A Pilgrimage to the Land of My Fathers* (1858) and *The Poetry of the Hebrew Pentateuch* (1871). His three-part *History* was described by London rabbi and scholar Goodman Lipkind as 'a work of some merit in the last two volumes'. *The Jewish Encyclopedia*, Vol. VIII (New York: Funk and Wagnalls, 1925), p.330.
43. Margoliouth, *The History of the Jews in Great Britain*, pp.78–85.
44. *Voice of Jacob*, 4 February 1842, p.76.
45. Letter from the Western's wardens, John Salmon and S.K. Salaman, to Montefiore, 19 Shevat 5602, in Arthur Barnett, *The Western Synagogue Through Two Centuries, 1761–1961* (London: Vallentine Mitchell, 1961), pp.181–2. Barnett was minister of the congregation from 1924 to 1954, when he was succeeded by Bernard Casper.
46. Lionel D. Barnett, *El Libro de los Acuerdos* (Oxford: Oxford University Press, 1931), p.3.

47. Neville Laski, *The Laws and Charities of the Spanish and Portuguese Jews' Congregation of London* (London: Cresset Press, 1952), pp.32–3. Laski, who charts the progress of the law to modern times, points out that by 1850 the reference to Charles II had disappeared, and the wording ran: ' ... duly considering how important and beneficial has been the Union of our Congregation, since our settlement in this country in the year 5416 – 1656, and impressed with the conviction that the preservation of this nation is essential, not only to our present, but to our future welfare' (p.34). He adds: 'The gist of the prohibition is maintained, as is the provision for expansion.' Earlier he notes: 'The first *Ascama* is one which has cast its shadow over the history of the *Kahal* for two centuries. Its enforcement led to the institution of the Reform Congregation' (p.3). A vice-president of the Sephardi Elders, Laski was a son-in-law of Haham Moses Gaster.
48. Hyman A. Simons, *Forty Years a Chief Rabbi: The Life and Times of Solomon Hirschell* (London: Robson Books, 1980), pp.94–5.
49. Meeting in London in February 1843, representatives of the synagogues responsible for the election to, and maintenance of, the Chief Rabbinate unanimously passed a resolution – one of twenty-three – 'That he [the Chief Rabbi] shall on no account denounce *cherem* (anathema) against any person; neither shall he deprive any member of his religious rights in the Synagogue, without the consent of the Committee of the Congregation to which such person shall belong.' Resolution 20, 'Matters Relating to the Office of the Chief Rabbi, passed at Meetings of the Several Metropolitan and Provincial Congregations, the Great Synagogue, London, 19 and 21 February, 1843' (*Voice of Jacob*, 3 March 1843), p.122.
50. Ibid., 18 February 1842, pp.81–2. For amplification of this issue, see chapter 1.

CHAPTER 1

1. The document, in Hebrew, was formulated by M.S. Keyser 'to the satisfaction of the [Chief Rabbinical] executive committee, by whom severally it was attested in the usual way' (*Voice of Jacob*, 14 February 1845, p.97). Well before this letter appeared, the paper commented (20 December 1844, p.62), 'The circumstances that our Chief Rabbi is a Cohen – a lineal descendant of Aaron and of the order of the priesthood – will be regarded by many who have manifested an interest in this election as one of its most interesting features. The Holy Scriptures make direct and important reference to the vocation of the Cohen, in times of doubt or difficulty. See Deuteronomy xvii:8, and especially Malachi ii:7' – the quotation included by Keyser in the invitation to Adler.
2. On Ellis, see note 4.
3. *Jewish Chronicle and Working Man's Friend*, 6 December 1844, p.43.
4. Adler's reply, in Hebrew with English translation, and dated 22 Shevat 5605 A.M. (19 January 1845), was published and circulated as a two-page pamphlet by the Committee Appointed for the Selection of Candidates for the Office of Chief Rabbi (London, 1845). It was translated by Louis Cohen at the behest of Ellis, the Committee's chairman. Cohen, a nephew and confidant of Sir Moses Montefiore, was the father of Lionel Louis Cohen, the principal co-founder – with Sir Anthony de Rothschild – of the United Synagogue.
5. On Moses Montefiore (1784–1885), see S. and V.D. Lipman (eds), *The Century of Moses Montefiore* (London and Oxford: Litmann Library of Jewish Civilization, Jewish Historical Society of England, and Oxford University Press, 1985); L. Loewe (ed.), *Diaries of Sir Moses and Lady Montefiore* (London, 1890), facsimile edition, introduced by Raphael Loewe (London: Litmann Library of Jewish Civilization, Jewish Historical Society of England and Jewish Museum, London, 1983); Israel Finestein, 'Sir Moses Montefiore: A Modern Appreciation', in *Scenes and Personalities in Anglo-Jewry, 1800–2000* (London and Portland, OR: Vallentine Mitchell, 2002), pp.164–77; *Jewish Chronicle*, Supplement, 31 July 1885.
6. *Voice of Jacob*, 18 July 1845, p.198.
7. Ibid., p.199. Sir Moses was accompanied by Sir A. de Rothschild, S.H. Ellis, I. Foligno, H. de Castro, I.I. Brandon, H. Hyams, I.M. Montefiore, H. Guedalla, I. Barned, H.H. Cohen, J. Salmon, J. Levy, S. Cohen, L. Cohen, and I.H. Helbert.
8. Ibid. Five years later, at the third public examination of the Western Jewish Girls' Free School, the Duke of Cambridge, as a patron of the institution and chairman of the meeting, declared of Adler (also a patron): 'I must especially thank the Rev. the Chief Rabbi. I have had the pleasure of knowing that gentleman, I may almost say, from his childhood, and was instrumental in promoting him to his former position; and I am very happy to see him now occupy so distinguished a position in this country' (*Jewish Chronicle*, 19 April 1850, p.218).
9. The *Voice of Jacob* published a lengthy summary of the sermon in the course of a four-page supplement 'in honour of the installation ... furnishing so exact a record of its interesting details'. The text of the address was subsequently published in English translation alongside the German original. N.M. Adler, translated by Barnard van Oven, *Sermon Delivered at the Great Synagogue on the Occasion of His Installation into Office as Chief Rabbi of Great Britain* (London: Longman, Brown, Green and Longmans, 1845) pp.1–22.
10. N.M. Adler, *Sermon*, pp.8–9.
11. Ibid., pp.10–12.
12. Ibid., p.18.

Notes 395

13. Ibid., pp.16–17.
14. D.W. Marks, 'Discourse Delivered at the Consecration of the West London Synagogue of British Jews, Thursday, 27 January, 5602 [1842]', in *Sermons Preached on Various Occasions at the West London Synagogue of British Jews* (London: R. Groombridge and Sons, 1851), p.4.
15. Ibid., pp.5–6.
16. Ibid., p.7.
17. Ibid., pp.22–3.
18. N.M. Adler, *The Jewish Faith* (London: Effingham Wilson, 5608 – 1848), pp.1–19. The sermon was preached at the Great Synagogue, Duke's Place, on Sabbath, 24 Shevat 5608 (29 January 1848).
19. Psalms 62:11.
20. *The Jewish Faith*, pp.12–13. In *The Bonds of Brotherhood* (London: J. Wertheimer, 1849), a sermon delivered at the Synagogue of the Spanish and Portuguese Congregation, London, on 11 Shevat 5609 (3 February 1849), Adler described the Written Law and the Oral Law as 'twins of the same birth' (pp.7–8).
21. For the chronology of the move to abolish the second day of the festivals, see Anne J. Kershen and Jonathan A. Romain, *Tradition and Change: A History of Reform Judaism in Britain, 1840–1995* (London and Portland, OR: Vallentine Mitchell, 1995), pp.15–16. Picciotto remarks of the manifesto of 15 April 1840, 'not a word is here said respecting instrumental music in Synagogues or the abolition of the second days of Festivals, the two points most objectionable to those who call themselves strict Jews', in *Sketches of Anglo-Jewish History*, Israel Finestein (rev. and ed.) (London: Soncino Press, 1955), p.367.
22. On the background to ritual and liturgical reform, see Todd M. Endelman, *The Jews of Britain, 1656 to 2000* (Berkeley, CA: University of California Press, 2002), pp.110–17; David Englander, 'Anglicised not Anglican: Jews and Judaism in Victorian Britain', in Gerald Parsons (ed.), *Religion in Victorian Britain – I. Traditions* (Manchester: Manchester University Press and the Open University, 1988), pp.253–60; Michael A. Meyer, 'Jewish Religious Reform in Germany and Britain,' in Michael Brenner, Rainer Liedtke and David Rechter (eds), *Two Nations: British and German Jews in Comparative Perspective* (Tübingen: Mohr Siebeck, 1999), pp.67–74. An account based on earlier research is in David Philipson, *The Reform Movement in Judaism* (New York: Macmillan, 1907; rev. edn, 1931), pp.90–106.
23. *Jewish Chronicle and Working Man's Friend* (21 March 1845), pp.120–4. In publishing the letter as an advertisement, the Editor observed, 'a Journal limited to eight small pages cannot possibly allot more than a proportionate amount of space within its general columns to any one question, however important that may be to a portion of the public. Our sense of impartiality dictates the admission of controversial papers on religious questions arising within our body, before the tribunal of our readers; but should such contributions be more copious than is compatible with our sense of justice towards other matters of no less weight, they will have to appear in Supplements, to be paid for as advertisements.' Elkin was described in this introduction as 'a member of the Burton-street Congregation (whose integrity and philanthropy are admitted and respected even by those most violently opposed to his religious views)'.
24. *Jewish Chronicle*, 14 January 1848, p.390.
25. Ibid., pp.391–2.
26. On Sir Anthony de Rothschild, see note 4.
27. Discussed further in the following chapter.
28. *Jewish Chronicle*, 7 January 1848, p.387.
29. *Voice of Jacob*, 18 February 1842, pp.82–3.
30. *Jewish Chronicle*, 9 January 1846, pp.54–5.
31. This assertion resulted in a protracted altercation between the two papers which continued well after the affair had died down – until, indeed, the *Voice*'s closure on 1 September 1848.
32. *Voice of Jacob*, 16 January 1846, p.59.
33. *The Appeal of the Congregation of the West London Synagogue of British Jews to their Brother Israelites Throughout the United Kingdom*, *Jewish Chronicle*, 20 February 1846, pp.80–6. The opening pages constituted a summary of the events – as viewed by the reformers – leading to the establishment of the Congregation and the institution of the *cherem*; thereafter, the document concentrated on questions to Adler relating to the solemnisation of marriages, and an appeal to 'our brethren in this land' to 'judge for yourselves whether the faith of Israel, or that of a strange religion, animates the souls of those congregated within the sacred precincts of our Synagogue!'
34. *Jewish Chronicle*, 23 January 1846, p.67. Adler had met Sir Isaac's son, Francis H. Goldsmid, the West London's junior warden, on 22 December 1845, but the meeting – in the latter's view – had produced 'no satisfactory result', in that a written response from the Chief Rabbi to Jane Angel's account had not been forthcoming. In a letter to Francis Goldsmid two days later, Adler had written: 'so long as the union which I so anxiously desire has not been effected amongst us, I do not feel myself justified in engaging in any official correspondence on the subject in question'.
35. *Voice of Jacob*, 13 March 1846, pp.95–6.
36. Ibid., 27 March 1846, p.103; *Jewish Chronicle*, 27 March 1846, p.105.
37. *Jewish Chronicle*, 21 August 1846, p.201. A possible justification for Adler's solemnising the Henriques–Josephs union was contained in a letter to the paper from Samuel S. Oppenheim (ibid., 28

December 1855, p.430) commenting on another marriage performed by the Chief Rabbi, nine years later, between the granddaughter of Baron Goldsmid, 'a member of the Reform Synagogue', and Mr Lucas, of the New Synagogue. 'Dr Adler', wrote Oppenheim from Cincinnati, quoting his father (Simeon Oppenheim, secretary of the Great Synagogue) in London, 'considers her [the bride], by marrying a member of the New Synagogue [and] being married by him, as virtually leaving the Reformers. What she does afterwards, he has made no conditions about, nor can he control her, but it is not likely that she will attend one synagogue, and the husband another.'

38. Ibid., 18 September 1846, p.219.
39. Gaster, *History of the Ancient Synagogue of the Spanish and Portuguese Jews* (London: privately published, 1901), p.178. An Ashkenazi by birth and a native of Romania, Moses Gaster (1856–1939) studied at Bucharest and Leipzig Universities before attending the Rabbinical Seminary at Breslau. On arriving in Britain in 1885, he taught Graeco-Slavonic literature at Oxford University, and was appointed Haham in 1887.
40. *Address of the Wardens of the Sephardi Synagogue to their Elders*, 16 May 1841, in Picciotto, *Sketches of Anglo-Jewish History*, p.368.
41. *Voice of Jacob*, 29 August 1845, p.229.
42. Picciotto, *Sketches of Anglo-Jewish History*, pp.376–7.
43. *Jewish Chronicle*, 16 April 1847, p.117.
44. Ibid., 5 November 1847, p.300.
45. A reference to the Psalmist's 'Therefore my heart is glad, and my glory rejoiceth; my flesh also shall rest in hope' (Psalms 16:9).
46. *Jewish Chronicle*, 12 November 1847, pp.308–9.
47. Ibid., 19 November 1847, p.317.
48. Ibid., 28 January 1848, p.407.
49. Ibid.
50. 'The Modern Farce, Entitled "Excommunication"', ibid., 25 February 1848, p.441.
51. 'Repeal of an Obnoxious Law,' ibid., p.445.
52. The resolution was seconded by Moses Haim Picciotto (the father of James), who delivered 'a lucid and erudite speech, in the course of which he quoted several extracts from the Shulchan Aruch, Yoreh Deah, Section Halachoth Nedarim, in confirmation of his views of the question' (reproduced extensively). It was Picciotto's recitation of these quotations that was largely responsible for the 'much sensation' mentioned in the report (ibid.).
53. Picciotto, *Sketches of Anglo-Jewish History*, pp.378–9. Confirmation of the 'purge' was contained in a letter from Hananel de Castro to Moses Mocatta, dated 9 March 1849: 'I acknowledge, with much pleasure, your letters addressed to myself and Mr Guedalla, containing the signatures of yourself and thirteen other parties thereto; and, according to our promise, we placed ourselves in communication with the ecclesiastical authorities, and have the satisfaction to state that the *cherem* incurred by the disregard of *Ascama* No. 1, which was put in force against you, has been fully and finally abolished this day against each and all the parties signing that letter (as far as *Ascama* No. 1 of *Kaal* is concerned), in the presence of myself and Mr H. Guedalla. Let us trust the good that will result does not stop here' (*Jewish Chronicle*, 27 April 1849, p.231).
54. For a comprehensive account of the history and implementation of the *cherem*, and its revocation, by the Sephardi dayanim and mahamad, see Isidore Epstein's 'The story of *Ascama* I of the Spanish and Portuguese Jewish Congregation of London, with special reference to responsa material', in *Studies and Essays in Honor of Abraham A. Neuman* (Philadelphia: Dropsie College, 1962); reprinted in Isidore Epstein *Jewish Faith in Action*, ed. Philip Ginsbury (London: Jews' College Publications, 1995), pp.163–83.

CHAPTER 2

1. *Jewish Chronicle*, 30 March 1849, pp.197–8.
2. Moses Margoliouth, *The History of the Jews in Great Britain*, Vol. III (London: Richard Bentley, 1851), pp.99–101.
3. *Jewish Chronicle*, 23 March 1849, pp.189–90.
4. Ibid., 20 April 1849, p.221.
5. Ibid., 22 August 1845, p.221; *Voice of Jacob*, 15 August 1845, pp.217–18.
6. *Laws and Regulations for all the Synagogues in the British Empire* (London: John Wertheimer, London, 5607 – 1847), pp.i–iv, 1–23.
7. Bernard Susser, 'Statistical Accounts of all the Congregations in the British Empire, 5606 – 1845', in Aubrey Newman (ed.), *Provincial Jewry in Victorian Britain* (London: Jewish Historical Society of England, 1975).
8. As early as 1812, John King, of Bevis Marks, had repeatedly petitioned the wardens to improve decorum, stating that his absence from synagogue for many years was because 'it was not a place of devotion, and prayers could be better said in the closet'. He observed 'with grief and astonishment how little the syn-

agogue was attended [and] how indecent was the conduct of those that did attend.' James Picciotto, *Sketches of Anglo-Jewish History*, Israel Finestein (rev. and ed.) (London: Soncino Press, 1955) pp.294–5. Some modifications were adopted following a report of the Committee for the Promotion of Religious Worship, established by the congregation in 1828, including shortening the service 'as far as practicable'; abstention from conversation; the attendance of 'the wardens themselves ... as often as possible'; and 'sermons and proclamations in the English language' (Ibid., pp.318–19). In 1824, the Great Synagogue introduced changes in the mode of reading the service, without, however, any resultant improvement in decorum; and in 1832, the Hambro' abolished the sale of mitzvot but declined to sanction the abrogation of the misheberach. On pioneering attempts at religious reform, see Todd M. Endelman, *The Jews of Georgian England, 1714–1830* (Ann Arbor, MI: University of Michigan Press, 1999), pp.159–65.

9. *Laws and Regulations*, Section I, pp.5–6. The Ashkenazi ecclesiastical authority of the Board of Deputies was, in any event, the Chief Rabbi.
10. Ibid., Section IV, p.17.
11. Ibid., Section V, p.19.
12. Ibid., Section V, p.20.
13. *Jewish Chronicle*, 13 November 1846, p.21.
14. Ibid., p.22.
15. Ibid., 27 November 1846, p.29.
16. Ibid., 22 October 1847, p.278.
17. 'On the Revelation at Sinai, and the Perpetuity and Immutability of the Mosaic Law', in D.W. Marks, *Sermons Preached on Various Occasions at the West London Synagogue of British Jews*, Vol. I (London: R. Groombridge and Sons, 5611 – 1851), pp.276–90. The sermon was delivered on Shavuot 5607 (21 May 1847).
18. Malachi 4:4.
19. 'The Law of Moses, the Great End of Revelation', in D.W. Marks, *Sermons Preached on Various Occasions at the West London Synagogue of British Jews, Margaret Street, Cavendish Square*, Vol. II (London: A.W. Bennett, P. Valentine, 5622 – 1862), pp.16–27. The sermon was delivered in Manchester, whither Marks had been invited by the new congregation's Committee of Founders, on Shabbat Hagadol 5618 (25 March 1858).
20. N.M. Adler, *The Second Days of the Festivals* (London: Trübner, 5628 – 1868), pp.1-19. The sermon was delivered at the New Synagogue, Great St Helen's, on the second day of Pesach 5628 (8 April 1868).
21. *The Second Days*, pp.4–5.
22. Ibid., pp.7–9.
23. Leviticus 23:14, 21, 31, 41.
24. *The Second Days*, pp.9–10.
25. Deuteronomy 4:2.
26. *The Second Days*, pp.13–15.
27. Ibid., pp.15–17.
28. Todd M. Endelman writes that, '[u]rged on by Moses Montefiore, a bitter, intransigent opponent of Reform, Chief Rabbi Hirschell drew up an indictment of the reformers in late summer 1841, charging them with rejecting the authority of the Oral Law and banning them from participation in the religious life of the community' (*The Jews of Britain*, p.113).
29. L. Loewe (ed.), *Diaries of Sir Moses and Lady Montefiore*, Vol. I, facsimile edition, introduced by Raphael Loewe, Litmann Library of Jewish Civilization (London: Jewish Historical Society of England and the Jewish Museum, 1890), pp.301–2.
30. *Jewish Chronicle*, 29 January 1892, p.19. The correspondence between Goldsmid and Montefiore is included in a six-page supplement marking the fiftieth anniversary of the West London Synagogue and the commemorative service held at Upper Berkeley Street on 27 January 1892.
31. Later Sir John Simon, Serjeant-at-Law. See Prologue, note 41, and Anne J. Kershen and Jonathan A. Romain, *Tradition and Change: A History of Reform Judaism in Britain, 1840–1995* (London and Portland, OR, 1995), pp.15–16.
32. *Jewish Chronicle*, 29 January 1892, p.19. The *Voice of Jacob* questioned the legality of this procedure – 'the lawfulness of Mr M. [Marks], an unregistered officer, performing the act that is advertised as having been done by him in an unregistered building – viz., solemnised a marriage. The 39th clause of the Act of Parliament is apparently that upon which the question hinges; and upon the construction which legal minds shall put upon it depends whether – seeing that Mr M. has not contravened the spirit of the law (inasmuch that the parties were already made legally man and wife) before he performed any ceremony whatever – the calling of such ceremony "the solemnisation of a marriage" can involve that literal violation of the law which constitutes the felony.'
33. Kershen and Romain, *Tradition and Change*, pp.40–1.
34. David Philipson, *The Reform Movement in Judaism* (New York: Macmillan, 1931), p.450.
35. On Louis Cohen, see chapter 1, note 4.
36. *Jewish Chronicle*, 6 July 1855, p.226.
37. Ibid., 29 January 1892, p.19.

38. *Public General Statutes passed in the Fourth Session of the Sixteenth Parliament of the United Kingdom of Great Britain and Ireland.* 19 & 20 *Victoria,* 1856, Chapter CXIX (London: George Edward Eyre and William Spottiswoode, 1856), pp.793–806.
39. *Jewish Chronicle and Hebrew Observer,* 1 August 1856, p.676.
40. *Jewish Chronicle,* 8 June 1849, p.282.
41. On Salomon's attitude to Reform, see Chaim Bermant, *The Cousinhood: The Anglo-Jewish Gentry* (London: Eyre and Spottiswoode, 1971), pp.96–7. On his role in the Board of Deputies' controversy over the admission of Reform representatives, see Israel Finestein, 'The Anglo-Jewish Revolt of 1853', in *Jewish Quarterly,* 26 (1978–79), pp.103–13; reprinted in Finestein, *Jewish Society in Victorian England* (London and Portland, OR: Vallentine Mitchell, 1993), pp.104–29.
42. 'Report of the Royal Commission on the Laws of Marriage', in *Reports from Commissioners,* Vol. XXXII, Session 19, November 1867–31 July 1868 (London: George E. Eyre and William Spottiswoode, 1868).
43. Ibid., Session 16, 31 July 1865, Appendix, pp.10–11.
44. Ibid., Appendix, pp.83–7. The examination, held on 7 March 1866, was chaired by Chelmsford and attended by Lords Lyveden and Naas, Vice-Chancellor Sir W. Page Wood, Dr (later Sir) Travers Twiss (Regius Professor of Civil Law at Oxford), and Alexander Murray Dunlop, MP.
45. Following Adler's submission, these passages are recorded: Genesis 24:60: 'And they blessed Rebekah and said unto her: "Thou art our sister, be thou the mother of thousands of millions, and let thy seed possess the gate of them which hate them."' Ruth 4:11–12: 'The Lord make the woman that is come into thy house like Rachel, and like Leah, which two did build the house of Israel; and do thou worthily in Ephratah, and be famous in Bethlehem. And let thy house be like the house of Pharez, whom Tamar bare unto Judah, of the seed which the Lord shall give thee of this young woman.' Tobit 7:13–14: 'Then he called his daughter Sara, and she came to her father, and he took her by the hand, and gave her to be wife to Tobias, saying: "Behold, take her after the law of Moses, and lead her away to thy father." And he blessed them, and called Edna his wife, and did write an instrument of covenants, and sealed it.'
46. Ibid., Session 41, 30 April 1866, Appendix, pp.45–6.
47. 'Report of the Royal Commission', *Reports from Commissions,* pp.xxxvi–vii.
48. Kershen and Romain, *Tradition and Change,* p.41; Israel Finestein, 'The Jews and English Marriage Law', in the *Jewish Journal of Sociology,* 8 (1964), pp.3–21, reprinted in *Jewish Society in Victorian England,* pp.72–7. In 1959, Parliament extended this recognition to the Liberal Synagogue (see chapter 13).
49. Finestein, 'The Anglo-Jewish Revolt of 1853', *Jewish Society in Victorian England,* pp.104–29. This essay gives a broad outline of the background, evolution, development and ramifications of the episode, not least in relation to the wider issue of political emancipation.

CHAPTER 3

1. Charles H.L. Emanuel, *A Century and a Half of Jewish History: Extracted from the Minute Books of the London Committee of Deputies of the British Jews* (London: George Routledge and Sons, 1910), p.44. The entry for 1845 welcomes the appointment of Adler as successor to Hirschell, whom it describes as 'a firm friend of the Board' (p.52). Emanuel, a solicitor, was secretary of the Board.
2. Israel Finestein, 'The Anglo-Jewish Revolt of 1853', in *Jewish Society in Victorian England* (London and Portland, OR: Vallentine Mitchell, 1993), pp.109–11.
3. Ibid., pp.113–14.
4. Anne J. Kershen and Jonathan A. Romain, *Tradition and Change: A History of Reform Judaism in Britain, 1840–1995,* (London and Portland, OR: Vallentine Mitchell), p.43.
5. Finestein, 'The Anglo-Jewish Revolt of 1853', p.121.
6. Emanuel, *A Century and a Half of Jewish History,* p.65.
7. *Jewish Chronicle,* 9 September 1853, p.396. Jonassohn made these statements in a letter to Montefiore explaining, inter alia, how he became, and why he continued to be, a member of the West London Synagogue. D.W. Marks officiated in Sunderland at the marriage of Jonassohn's daughter, Henrietta, to George Bazett Colvin Leverson, a West London member, on 11 February 1851. Arnold Levy, *History of the Sunderland Jewish Community, 1755–1955* (London: Macdonald, 1956), pp.44–5.
8. Finestein, 'The Anglo-Jewish Revolt of 1853', p.105.
9. 15 May 1853.
10. Lucien Wolf, 'The Queen's Jewry, 1837–1897', in *Young Israel* (June and July 1897); reprinted in *Essays in Jewish History,* Cecil Roth (ed.), (London: Jewish Historical Society of England, 1934), p.335.
11. The election of the following candidates stood adjourned: Chatham – Samuel Ellis; Norwich – Elias Davis; Portsea/Portsmouth – Jacob L. Elkin; Sunderland – David Jonassohn; Sheerness – L.S. Magnus. That of Magnus, unlike of the previous four, 'stood adjourned to enable the resuscitated congregation to carry out certain requirements of the Chief Rabbi previous to his certifying. These conditions, we understand, are being fully carried out by the synagogue authorities' (*Jewish Chronicle,* 26 August 1853, p.372).
12. Ibid.
13. Ibid., 2 September 1853, p.380.

14. Ibid., p.381. Each of the letters from the three men listed eight reasons for opposing the resolution and concluded: 'I give notice to, and formally warn, the Deputies that if it should be carried, and any of the members of the Board should, in consequence thereof, be prevented from taking part in the business to be transacted, the remaining members (having excluded some of their colleagues, nominated by congregations of Jews in Great Britain) will thenceforth cease to be a body, described in the Act of Parliament relating to marriages, as the London Committee of Deputies of the British Jews, and all their subsequent proceedings, until the admission of such excluded members, will be irregular and invalid.'
15. *Jewish Chronicle*, 2 September 1853, pp.380–1.
16. 'The Crisis', ibid., 'Complementary Number', 5 September 1853, p.1; reprinted in ibid., 9 September 1853, p.385. The paper had taken the unusual step of publishing an extra edition on the Monday 'in the pleasing anticipation that the remarks and exhortations which we might deem it our duty to make would be listened to, and that the leaders among us, possessing the requisite power, authority and influence, would step forth, and throw consoling oil on the troubled waters. We have yet to see what effect the few words we have given utterance to have had, for at the time we write (Wednesday evening, 7 September) there is yet time for a peaceful solution of the crisis. We therefore refrain at the present moment from further comment, lest one unguarded sentence, expression or word on our part might mar the good work we have so sincerely at heart, and for which we have so anxiously desired and laboured – the union of all sections of our community in the holy bond of peace, fraternity and unity' (ibid., 9 September 1853, p.385).
17. Ibid., 15 September 1853, pp.400–3.
18. Ibid., 30 September 1853, p.423.
19. Ibid., 25 November 1853, pp.62–3.
20. Ibid., 9 December 1853, pp.79–82.
21. *For the amendment* (23): Bevis Marks – Judah Aloof, Isaac Foligno, M.H. Picciotto, Joseph Sebag, Solomon Sequerra; Great – Louis Cohen; Hambro' – Solomon Cohen, Moses Engel, Judah Jacobs, Jonah Levy; Maiden Lane – Nathan Defries, Henry Harris; Canterbury – Haim Guedalla; Edinburgh – Charles Ashenheim; Falmouth – Abraham Woolf; Ipswich – David Hyam; Jersey – Alfred A. Jones; Liverpool Old – Israel Barned; Liverpool New – Daniel Myers; Nottingham – Morris Van Praagh; Penzance – Samuel Solomon; Plymouth – Abraham Joseph; Yarmouth – A. de Pass. *Against the amendment* (23): Bevis Marks – Nathaneel Lindo; Great – Joshua Alexander, Lewis Jacobs, Samuel Moses, B.S. Phillips, Baron Lionel de Rothschild, MP; New – Lawrence Myers, David Salomons; Western – L.H. Braham, Henry L. Keeling; Birmingham Old – David Barnett, Jacob Phillips; Birmingham New – H.T. Louis; Bristol – Joseph Abraham; Cardiff – Michael Samuel; Dover – Judah Hart; Glasgow – David Davis; Hull – Meyer Meyer; Liverpool New – B.L. Joseph; Manchester – David Hesse, H.L. Micholls; North Shields – Isaac Levitt; Sheerness – L.S. Magnus. *Casting vote for the amendment*: Sir Moses Montefiore, Bart. *Absent from the division* (9): Great – Sir Anthony de Rothschild, Bart. (in Paris); New – Lawrence Levy, Lewis Levy (indisposed); Manchester – J.M. Isaac (indisposed); Cheltenham – E. Alex (declined to vote); Dublin – John Dyte (indisposed); Exeter – J. Lazarus (protested against); Sheffield – Josiah Solomon. *Unseated by amendment* (4) – Chatham – Samuel Ellis; Norwich – Elias Davis; Portsea/Portsmouth – Jacob L. Elkin; Sunderland – David Jonassohn.
22. 'The case submitted to Sir Frederick Thesinger, QC, and Mr [Edward] Badeley, and their opinion thereon', circulated to deputies on the day following the meeting, appeared in the *Jewish Chronicle*, 9 December 1853, pp.81–2.
23. Ibid., 16 December 1853, pp.90–1.
24. Ibid., p.90.
25. Ibid., 13 January 1854, p.130.
26. Ibid., 16 December 1853, p.87.
27. Ibid., 23 December 1853, p.99.
28. N.M. Adler, *Solomon's Judgment: A Picture of Israel* (London: Wertheimer, 1854), pp.1–15. The sermon was delivered at the Great Synagogue, London, on 31 December 1853.
29. I Kings 3:16–28.
30. *Solomon's Judgment*, pp.8–9.
31. Ibid., pp.9–10.
32. Ibid., pp.13–14.
33. *Jewish Chronicle*, 6 January 1854, p.126, and 20 January 1854, p.141. On the *cherem* and the emergence of Reform in Manchester, see Bill Williams, *The Making of Manchester Jewry, 1740–1875* (Manchester: Manchester University Press, 1976), pp.221–67.
34. See letters in the *Jewish Chronicle*, 3 February 1854, pp.157–8, and 14 April 1848, p.501.

CHAPTER 4

1. *Jewish Chronicle*, 9 December 1853, p.81.
2. Ibid.

3. Ibid., 8 August 1845, p.27, and 12 December 1845, p.41.
4. Albert M. Hyamson, *The Sephardim of England* (London: Spanish and Portuguese Jews' Congregation, 1951), p.286.
5. Adler's ambivalence is discussed in Steven Singer, 'Orthodox Judaism in Early Victorian London, 1840–1858' (Ph.D. diss., Bernard Revel Graduate School, Yeshiva University, New York, 1981), pp.267–75.
6. H.D. Schmidt, 'Chief Rabbi Nathan Marcus Adler: Jewish Educator from Germany', in *Leo Baeck Institute Year Book*, VII (London: East and West Library, 1962), p.295.
7. Ibid., pp.299, 301.
8. Eugene C. Black, 'The Anglicization of Orthodoxy: The Adlers', in *Profiles in Diversity: Jews in a Changing Europe*, Frances Malino and David Sorkin (eds) (Detroit, MI: Wayne State University Press, 1998), p.297.
9. Solomon Sofer (ed.), *Sefer Iggerot Soferim* (Vienna: Joseph Schlesinger, 1929), p.82. These remarks are contained in a letter from Solomon Eger (1786–1852), a noted Polish rabbi and passionate opponent of Reform, to his brother, Abraham, in which he described a visit to Altona (near Hamburg) and to Adler in London. The moneyed Jews, Eger wrote, were 'not Orthodox in practice but subscribed to Orthodoxy in a nominal manner'. He gave this as a reason for Adler's reluctance 'to fight publicly with the wealthy'.
10. Sir Moses was succeeded as president by his nephew, Joseph Mayer Montefiore, who had twice acted for him in that capacity. Six years later, the presidency went to another nephew, Arthur Cohen QC, MP, who held the post until 1895.
11. *Jewish Chronicle*, 30 January 1874, p.733.
12. Ibid., 20 February 1874, p.785.
13. Ibid., 6 March 1874, p.816. The *Jewish Chronicle* was refused admission to the 'conclave' and declined to publish a report of the proceedings, 'placed at our disposal by the courtesy of a gentleman present, since we cannot vouch for its accuracy and impartiality'.
14. Ibid., 13 March 1874, p.827. A vigorous refutation of these views was contained in a letter the following week (20 March 1847, p.844) from Alfred Henriques, who discussed in great detail the applicability of clauses 1, 6 and 24 of the Board's constitution and their references to the ecclesiastical authorities.
15. Ibid., leading article, 27 March 1874, pp.864–5.
16. Lucien Wolf, 'The Queen's Jewry, 1837–1897', in *Young Israel* (June and July, 1897); reprinted in *Essays in Jewish History*, Cecil Roth (ed.) (London: Jewish Historical Society of England, 1934), p.350.
17. *Jewish Chronicle*, 3 April 1874, p.885.
18. Todd M. Endelman points out that 'The organisation of the Board of Deputies well illustrates the deferential foundation on which the rule of the notables rested. In theory, every major congregation in Britain elected a deputy to the Board. In practice, most deputies had little connection with the synagogues that they ostensibly represented. Provincial synagogues regularly elected wealthy Londoners with the leisure to attend the Board's meetings, which were always held in the metropolis. This allowed the communal oligarchy to place its younger members on the Board by arranging their election as provincial representatives ... This system of rotten borough and "aristocratic" patronage continued until after the First World War.' 'Communal Solidarity Among the Jewish Elite of Victorian London', *Victorian Studies*, 28, 3 (2002), p.497.
19. *Jewish Chronicle*, 13 March 1874, p.827.
20. Wolf, 'The Queen's Jewry', p.350.
21. *Jewish Chronicle*, 20 July 1883, p.12.
22. Montefiore died on 28 July 1885, aged 100. In its seven-page obituary, published in a commemorative supplement (31 July 1885), the *Jewish Chronicle* referred to his leadership of the Board of Deputies – and, indeed, of the community – in a mere eleven lines: 'The years which followed [his 1840 mission to the Levant] were the most debatable of Sir Moses' public life. Holding deeply rooted Orthodox opinions, he opposed with great bitterness the Reform party, who, led by the Goldsmids and some members of his own family, formed the congregation of British Jews and now have a synagogue in Berkeley Street. While he always professed himself a Conservative, Sir Moses advocated progress among backward communities of Jews, as in Palestine and Poland. He always, however, urged gradual reform and respect to constituted authorities; sudden changes he feared and deprecated. The English schism of 1841 seemed to him the result of desiring too great and sudden a change in public worship. In this, he differed from many good men.'
23. *Jewish Chronicle*, 23 October 1885, p.12.
24. The meeting was held only hours before Montefiore's death.
25. At the first meeting of the newly elected Board, held at Bevis Marks on 15 June 1886, Goldsmid indicated that he would be sitting for the West London Synagogue (*Jewish Chronicle*, 18 June 1886, p.7).
26. *Annual Report*, Board of Deputies, London, 1887, p.12.
27. *Jewish Chronicle*, 14 May 1886, p.5.
28. Bill Williams, *The Making of Manchester Jewry 1740–1875* (Manchester: Manchester University Press, 1976), p.184; Geoffrey Alderman, *Modern British Jewry* (Oxford: Clarendon Press, 1992), p.28; Raphael Loewe, 'Solomon Marcus Schiller-Szinessy, 1820–1890', *Transactions of the Jewish Historical Society of England*, XXI,

(1962–1967), p.163; Michael Leigh, 'Reform Judaism in Britain, 1840–1970', in Dow Marmur (ed.), *Reform Judaism* (London: Reform Synagogues of Great Britain, 1973), p.36.
29. Leigh, ibid., p.37.
30. Ibid., pp.37–8.
31. Alderman, *Modern British Jewry*, p.44.
32. Aubrey Newman, 'The Chief Rabbinate and the Provinces, 1840–1914', in *Tradition and Transition: Essays Presented to Chief Rabbi Sir Immanuel Jakobovits to Celebrate Twenty Years in Office*, Jonathan Sacks (ed.) (London: Jews' College Publications, 1986), pp.222–3.
33. Alderman, *Modern British Jewry*, p.84.
34. Albert M. Hyamson, *The London Board for Shechita, 1804–1954* (London: Henry F. Thompson, for the London Board for Shechita, 1954), pp.29–30.
35. Leigh, 'Reform Judaism in Britain', p.33.
36. Arthur Barnett, *The Western Synagogue Through Two Centuries, 1761–1961* (London: Vallentine Mitchell, 1961), p.208.
37. Adler to the wardens of the Western Synagogue, 14 November 5644 (1883), London Metropolitan Archives, LMA ACC/2805/2/1/46.
38. *Jewish Chronicle*, 29 January 1892, pp.21–2.
39. Ibid., p.20.
40. Ibid., p.9.
41. Raymond Apple, *The Hampstead Synagogue 1892–1967* (London: Vallentine Mitchell, 1967), p.10.
42. *Jewish Chronicle*, 24 January 1890, p.8.
43. Ibid., p.9. The unsigned article is headed 'A Tribute to the Memory of the Venerable Chief Rabbi from a Member of the Berkeley Street Congregation'.
44. Aubrey Newman, in *Provincial Jewry in Victorian Britain: Papers for a Conference at University College, London, Convened by the Jewish Historical Society of England*, London, 6 July, sub-section on 'The Chief Rabbinate', p.3.
45. Cecil Roth, 'Britain's Three Chief Rabbis', in *Jewish Leaders (1750–1940)*, Leo Jung (ed.) (New York: Bloch, 5714 –1953), p.480.
46. Goodman Lipkin, 'Nathan Marcus Adler', in *The Jewish Encyclopedia*, Vol. I (New York and London: Funk and Wagnalls, 1925), p.198.
47. Elkan Nathan Adler, *London* (Philadelphia, PA: Jewish Publication Society of America, 1930), pp.169–70.
48. *Jewish Chronicle*, 24 January 1890, pp.13–14.
49. Schmidt writes that 'Dr Adler knew very well on whose help his work in England would depend, and many of his addresses and prayers were composed for a Rothschild or a Montefiore occasion. He accepted their influence willingly.' 'Chief Rabbi Nathan Marcus Adler', p.298.
50. *Jewish Chronicle*, 24 January 1890, p.8.
51. Williams, *The Making of Manchester Jewry*, p.193.
52. Stephen Sharot, 'Reform and Liberal Judaism in London, 1840–1940', in *Jewish Social Studies*, Vol. XLI (New York: Conference on Jewish Social Studies, 1979), p.214.
53. Michael A. Meyer, *Response to Modernity: A History of the Reform Movement in Judaism* (Oxford and New York: Oxford University Press, 1988), p.179. Robert Liberles asserts: 'It was the president of the Board of Deputies ... who led the opposition to the reformers ... The personalities involved in the conflict were F[rancis] H[enry] Goldsmid as warden of the West London Synagogue, and Moses Montefiore as president of the Board of Deputies.' Liberles ascribes the origins of this conflict to differences of opinion and approach 'over the emancipation struggle', with Goldsmid's father, Sir Isaac Lyon Goldsmid, using the West London as 'an alternative political structure' to the Board, 'not merely as a religious alternative to the established services at Bevis Marks and the Great Synagogue ... The primary objective of the Goldsmids was not to secede from the Great Synagogue, nor to inaugurate a Reform service, but to secede from the Board of Deputies. The Sephardim, however, demanded the introduction of reforms, while ... they were sympathetic to the Goldsmid cause.' Liberles argues that the religious changes adopted by the Reform congregation 'were introduced by the reformers as a significant factor in the emancipation strategy of the segment of British Jewry that believed the established community was moving too feebly in the struggle for equality'. 'The Origins of the Jewish Reform Movement in England', in *AJSreview*, Vol. I (Cambridge, MA: Association for Jewish Studies, 1976), pp.128–9, 133–5, 143.
54. Black, 'The Anglicization of Orthodoxy', pp.298, 303, 305, 309.
55. David Feldman, *Englishmen and Jews: Social Relations and Political Culture, 1840–1914* (New Haven, CT and London: Yale University Press, 1994), p.49.
56. Meyer, *Response to Modernity*, p.176.
57. Todd M. Endelman, 'The Englishness of Jewish Modernity in England', in *Toward Modernity: The European Jewish Model*, Jacob Katz (ed.) (New Brunswick, NJ and Oxford: Transaction Books, 1987), p. 236.
58. Feldman, *Englishmen and Jews*, p.66.
59. Endelman, 'The Englishness of Jewish Modernity in England', p.235; Sharot, 'Reform and Liberal Judaism in London', p.213. For a full discussion of this topic, see Endelman, *The Jews of Georgian England, 1714–1830: Tradition and Change in a Liberal Society* (Ann Arbor, MI: University of Michigan Press, 1999), pp.118–65.

60. Sharot, 'Reform and Liberal Judaism in London', p.222; Singer, 'Orthodox Judaism in Early Victorian London', pp.206–47.
61. Williams, *The Making of Manchester Jewry*, pp.247–63.
62. See especially *Jewish Chronicle* Supplement, 29 January 1892, p.21.
63. Meyer, *Response to Modernity*, p.179.
64. Ibid., p.173.
65. Leigh, 'Reform Judaism in Britain', pp.31, 39.
66. Hugh McLeod, 'Why Did Orthodoxy Remain Dominant in Britain?' in *Two Nations: British and German Jews in Comparative Perspective*, Michael Brenner, Rainer Liedtke, David Rechter (eds) (Tübingen: Mohr Siebeck, 1999), pp.85–9.
67. Endelman, *The Jews of Georgian England*, p.290.
68. David Englander, 'Anglicised not Anglican: Jews and Judaism in Victorian Britain', in *Religion in Victorian Britain*, Vol. I – *Traditions* (Manchester: Manchester University Press, 1988), p.254.
69. Henry Mayhew, *London Labour and the London Poor*, Vol. II (London: Griffin, Bohn, 1861–1862), p.124.
70. Stephen Sharot, 'Secularisation, Judaism and Anglo-Jewry', in *A Sociological Yearbook of Religion in Britain*, IV, M. Hill (ed.) (London: SCM Press, 1971), pp.121–40.
71. *Jewish Chronicle*, 4 January 1850, p.101.
72. Sharot, 'Secularisation, Judaism and Anglo-Jewry', p.133.
73. Englander, 'Anglicised not Anglican', p.258.
74. Endelman, 'Communal Solidarity', p.503.
75. Singer, 'Orthodox Judaism in Early Victorian London', p.8.
76. Englander, 'Anglicised not Anglican', p.260.
77. David Philipson, *The Reform Movement in Judaism* (New York: Macmillan, 1907; rev. edn 1931), p.94. The first edition of this book was published in 1907, following a series of articles in the *Jewish Quarterly Review*.
78. Ibid., p.106.

CHAPTER 5

1. Clauses 2, 3 and 4 of a report of the executive committee, signed by Lionel L. Cohen, chairman, presented to, and approved by, a meeting of the United Synagogue council, Central Synagogue Chambers, London, 4 November 1879. This followed receipt of a letter (13 October 5640 – 1879) from the Chief Rabbi, in which he referred to his failing health and added: 'I shall endeavour, God willing, to direct and to supervise, as heretofore, the spiritual affairs of the congregations under my charge, and specially to decide all questions connected with our religious observances ... But I shall no longer be able to attend at my office regularly throughout the year to take charge of matters of detail requiring immediate consideration.'
2. Letter to the wardens and board of management of the Bayswater Synagogue, London, 5 June 1891. Hermann Adler was appointed 'Lecturer' at Bayswater in 1864 at the age of 25 – his duties being to preach and to supervise the Hebrew classes – and occupied its pulpit for twenty-seven years. 'This was by no means a key to leisure, as his honorary officers had agreed from the start that his services were to be at the disposal of the whole metropolitan area. He was already a Chief Rabbi in the making.' Olga Somech Phillips and Hyman A. Simons, *The History of the Bayswater Synagogue 1863–1963* (London: privately published, 1963), p.17.
3. 'The Ideal Jewish Pastor: An Installation Sermon', preached at the Great Synagogue, London, 23 June 1891, in Hermann Adler, *Anglo-Jewish Memories and Other Sermons* (London: George Routledge and Sons, 1909), p.80.
4. A. Schischa, 'Hermann Adler, Yeshivah Bachur, Prague, 1860–1862', in *Remember the Days: Essays in Honour of Cecil Roth*, John M. Shaftesley (ed.) (London: Jewish Historical Society of England, 1966), p.258.
5. Raymond Apple, 'Hermann Adler: Chief Rabbi', in *Noblesse Oblige: Essays in Honour of David Kessler, OBE*, Alan D. Crown (ed.) (London and Portland, OR: Vallentine Mitchell, 1998), p.128.
6. Apple, ibid.
7. Born in Warsaw in 1831, Abrahams graduated from University College London and succeeded Louis Loewe as principal (then known as headmaster) of Jews' College in 1858, combining the post with those of dayan and acting Haham. He died only five years later, leaving a widow and six young children, many of whom were to attain prominence in the community.
8. Kalisch held this post from 1848 to 1853, before being engaged as tutor and literary adviser to the Rothschild family. Born in Treptow, Pomerania, in 1828, he died in Derbyshire, England, in 1885.
9. At the invitation of a wealthy relative, Asher, a German educationist and philosopher (1818–1890), spent some years in London, where he studied English at a private school and subsequently taught. He later held positions in the Jewish community and became tutor to Nathan Adler's children. On returning to Germany, he gained his doctorate of philosophy at Berlin University and thereafter wrote voluminously.
10. Apple, 'Hermann Adler: Chief Rabbi', p.128. Schischa writes: 'These good and dedicated men imparted to the young and very bright scholar not just a mechanical, dry knowledge of Jewish lore. They implanted in

him a love for "learning"; they imbued him with the enjoyment of the *"Blatt Gemoreh"* [page of Talmud]. This love for learning which Hermann Adler showed as a youngster he fully enjoyed until his last days.' He adds: 'This information is based on a typescript biographical sketch compiled after his death, I think, by his daughter Miss Nettie [Henrietta] Adler', though Apple ascribes it to 'some notes he [Adler] compiled about himself, probably at the time of his election as Chief Rabbi.' 'Hermann Adler, Yeshivah Bachur', p.241.
11. These included the presidency of Aria College and the Jewish Historical Society of England, and the vice-presidency of the Jewish Religious Education Board and the Anglo-Jewish Association.
12. Eugene C. Black, 'The Anglicization of Orthodoxy: The Adlers', in *Profiles in Diversity: Jews in a Changing Europe*, Frances Malino and David Sorkin (eds) (Detroit, MI: Wayne State University Press, 1998), p.312.
13. Black, ibid.
14. The synagogues represented were Bayswater, Borough, Central, East London, Great, New, New West End, North London, and St John's Wood.
15. *Jewish Chronicle*, 8 September 1882, p.2.
16. Raymond Apple, *The Hampstead Synagogue 1892–1967* (London: Vallentine Mitchell, 1967), p.10.
17. Orach Chayim, I:5, the first part of the code of Jewish law, *Arbaah Turim*, by Rabbi Jacob ben Asher (1270–c.1343), dealing with daily conduct, prayers, Sabbaths and holy days. The code also includes Yoreh Deah (dietary laws), Even Ha'ezer (personal and family matters), and Choshen Mishpat (civil law and administration).
18. Letter from Nathan Marcus Adler to Ernest D. Löwy, London: Office of the Chief Rabbi, 24 October 5650 – 1889.
19. In 1863, eight years after the College's founding, Morris Joseph was the recipient of the first Montefiore stipend, presented by Sir Moses in memory of his wife, Judith, who had died the previous year. The endowment, from 'that well-tried friend of the institution' (Isidore Harris, *Jews' College Jubilee Volume*, (London: Luzac, 1906), pp.xxiv–xxv), was tenable for three years at an annual rate of £100 and followed an examination conducted by Barnett Abrahams and Joseph Zedner, assistant librarian at the British Museum's department of Oriental printed books and manuscripts. Joseph taught homiletics at Jews' College from 1887 to 1893, combining the post for the last three years with his ministry of the Hampstead Sabbath afternoon services.
20. Morris Joseph, *Judaism as Creed and Life* (London: Macmillan, 1903), p.vii.
21. Deuteronomy 4:39.
22. Cordova-born Moses ben Maimon, the Rambam (1135–1204), was the foremost Jewish philosopher and halachist of the Middle Ages, author of the *Mishneh Torah*, *Moreh Nevuchim* (*Guide for the Perplexed*), and other commentaries.
23. Rabbi Chasdai ben Abraham Crescas (1340–c.1412), Barcelona-born theologian whose *Or Adonai* (*Light of the Lord*) was a refutation of Maimonides' views, seeking to vindicate Orthodoxy against what he regarded as the 'liberalism' of his earlier compatriot.
24. Rabbi Solomon ben Simeon Duran, the Rashbash (c.1400–1467). Born in Algiers, he became a dayan and yeshivah head and wrote *Milchemet Chovah*, a defence of the Talmud against the attacks of the convert Geronimo de Santa Fé (Joshua Lorki), who participated in the Disputation of Tortosa in 1413/14. Forced upon Spain's Jews by the anti-pope Benedict XIII, the disputation was an attempt to prove the truth of Christianity from the Talmud and other Hebrew works.
25. Born in Monreal, Aragon, in the fifteenth century, Joseph Albo is known chiefly as the author of *Ikkarim* (*Principles*), on the fundamentals of Judaism. First published at Soncino in 1485, it reduces the Jewish faith to three central dogmas: God's existence, Divine Revelation (*Torah min hashamayim*), and reward and punishment. A pupil of Chasdai Crescas, Albo debated against de Santa Fé in the Tortosa disputation.
26. The phrase, quoted as one of the two epigraphs for this book, was to achieve prominence in a later Anglo-Jewish challenge to Orthodox belief, principally to the doctrine of Divine Revelation (see chapter 15).
27. *Judaism as Creed and Life*, pp.39–42.
28. Hermann Gollancz, 'Jews' College – Then and Now', address delivered at the distribution of prizes on 31 October 1915, in *Sermons and Addresses Setting Forth the Teachings and Spirit of Judaism*, Second Series (London: Chapman and Hall, 1916), pp.292–3. Born in Bremen – where his father, Marcus, was a rabbi before moving to the Hambro' Synagogue in London – Gollancz (1852–1930) studied at Jews' College and University College, serving later as professor of Hebrew. He succeeded Hermann Adler at Bayswater in 1892, after ministering to the St John's Wood, New, South Manchester and Dalston Synagogues. He received his rabbinical diploma in 1897 and his doctorate of literature two years later, was president of the Jewish Historical Society of England (1905/06), and was knighted in 1923 for services to inter-faith relations, the first rabbi to be so honoured. For other honours, see chapter 19, note 4.
29. *Jewish Chronicle*, 20 December 1889, p.17. The paper reported that 'the Rev. Morris Joseph has promised to officiate regularly, and occasional addresses will be delivered by Mr Israel Abrahams, MA, Mr Claude G. Montefiore, MA, Mr Oswald J. Simon, and others'. Oswald John Simon was an amateur theologian who broke away from the Hampstead Synagogue project when many of its original proposals for ritual reform were rejected by Adler.

30. *Sefer Tefilat Minchah L'Shabbat*: Order of Prayer as Used at the Sabbath Afternoon Services at Hampstead, with an English Paraphrase of the Hebrew Text, Arranged and Written by the Rev. Morris Joseph (London: Gillingham and Henry, 5650 – 1890), p.9.
31. Ibid., p.ii.
32. *Jewish Chronicle*, 28 February 1890, p.16.
33. Ibid., 11 April 1890, p.5.
34. Ibid., 2 May 1890, p.14.
35. Ibid., 23 May 1890, p.8.
36. Ibid., 28 February 1890, p.7.
37. 'Yet Another Minister of the United Synagogue', ibid., 14 March 1890, p.7.
38. 'A Fourth Minister of the United Synagogue', ibid., 21 March 1890, p.6.
39. Preface to *The Ideal in Judaism and Other Sermons by the Rev. Morris Joseph Preached During 1890–91–92* (London: David Nutt, 1893), p.ix.
40. Talmud, tractate Chulin, 6b.
41. Ibid., tractate Menachot, 99b.
42. 'The Sacrificial Rite', in *The Ideal in Judaism*, pp.40–9.
43. Of this episode, Lucien Wolf commented: 'When, in January 1892, the Reformers celebrated their jubilee, all the lay heads and many of the ministers of the Orthodox Synagogues attended the special commemoration service held in the Berkeley Street Synagogue. The two Orthodox Chief Rabbis, Dr Adler and Dr Gaster, however, remained away. The fiction that the Reformers do not constitute a Jewish congregation is still maintained, although the Orthodox synagogues have taken several long strides in the wake of the heretics. Fortunately, this assumption of disunion is purely artificial. In all essentials, the Anglo-Jewish community is absolutely united.' 'The Queen's Jewry, 1837–1897', *Young Israel* (June and July 1897), reprinted in *Essays in Jewish History*, Cecil Roth (ed.) (London: Jewish Historical Society of England, 1934), pp.361–2. Earlier Wolf wrote: 'The Reform congregation is now as integral a part of the machinery of the Anglo-Jewish community as the Portuguese congregation, with the single difference that it is not officially recognised as a Jewish body by the ecclesiastical heads of either the German or Portuguese sections of the community. This is, however, a factitious technicality, for Mr F.D. Mocatta and several other Sephardi members of the Reform Synagogues were readmitted to their rights as *yehidim* of Bevis Marks without test or condition, and there are no Jews in the country with whom the Chief Rabbi delights more to co-operate, or whose loyalty and devotion to Judaism he holds in higher esteem, than the chiefs of the heretical fane in Upper Berkeley Street.' Ibid., pp.350–1.
44. *Jewish Chronicle*, 18 March 1892, p.10.
45. Ibid., 20 May 1892, p.9.
46. Apple, *The Hampstead Synagogue 1892–1967*, pp.24–5.
47. *Jewish Chronicle*, 3 June 1892, p.6.
48. A report of the sermon (ibid., 4 March 1892, p.19) is reproduced as Appendix I.
49. The affair provoked a lively correspondence in the press and a theological debate of some note between Oswald John Simon and the Rev. (later Dayan) Moses Hyamson, on 'the function and scope of ecclesiastical authority and the formulation of dogmas'. See 'Authority and Dogma in Judaism', in *Jewish Quarterly Review*, 5, I. Abrahams and C.G. Montefiore (eds) (London: D. Nutt, 1893), pp.231–43, 469–82, 715.
50. Joseph was appointed senior minister in July 1893 by a majority (forty-five to twenty) of the synagogue council, following the rejection of an offer to Simeon Singer (1848–1906), minister of the New West End Synagogue. Anne J. Kershen and Jonathan A. Romain, *Tradition and Change: A History of Reform Judaism in Britain, 1840–1995* (London and Portland, OR: Vallentine Mitchell, 1995), p.114. Of Singer's loyalty to the New West End, Israel Abrahams, his son-in-law, writes: 'Such was Singer's feelings towards his congregation, it is easy to understand that all attempts to lure him away were futile … What was, from the personal side, the most momentous of his decisions of this nature was taken in 1893, when he felt bound to refuse Sir Julian Goldsmid's urgent invitation to accept nomination for the ministry of Berkeley Street Synagogue. He replied that it was indeed one of the dearest wishes of his heart to bring about a "complete fraternal understanding and religious fellowship" between all sections of Jewry. But, he added, "so far as practical service in the interest of our common Judaism is concerned, I believe I can be of more use by not quitting my post in that section of the community where men are needed to testify fearlessly against narrowness and intolerance of every kind." But his first reason was the personal tie between himself and his own congregation. He had been for fourteen years their minister; perfect mutual confidence existed between them and him. "I have been permitted to exercise over my congregants such religious influences as I could legitimately claim, having regard to our ecclesiastical régime."' *The Literary Remains of the Rev. Simeon Singer*, Vol. I – *Sermons*, selected and edited with a memoir by Israel Abrahams (London: George Routledge and Sons, 1908), pp.xvii–xix.
51. *Jewish Chronicle*, 29 July 1911, p.17. On the attendance of Hermann Adler, his dayanim and other Orthodox dignitaries at the burial and memorial service of David Woolf Marks, two years earlier, see chapter 7.
52. Ibid., 25 April 1930, p.11.
53. Hermann Adler, *The Ritual: The Reply of the Chief Rabbi* (London: Wertheimer, Lea, 1892), p.2. The reply, dated

# Notes

23 June 5652 (1892), was addressed to the wardens of the Central, New West End, Borough and Hampstead Synagogues.
54. Ibid., p.12.
55. Ibid., pp.5–6.

## CHAPTER 6

1. *The Authorised Daily Prayer Book of the United Hebrew Congregations of the British Empire*, with a new translation by the Rev. S. Singer, published under the sanction of Chief Rabbi Nathan Marcus Adler (London: Wertheimer, Lea, 5650 – 1890), p.viii.
2. Ibid., second edition (London: Wertheimer, Lea, 5651–1891), p.viii. The new preface was written days after Hermann Adler's installation as Chief Rabbi – on 23 June 1891 – and refers to him as such in Singer's acknowledgements. The 'careful revision' was completed, however, during the Chief Rabbinical interregnum.
3. Born in London on 5 November 1846, Simeon Singer was one of the first pupils at Jews' College School, studied – and later taught – at the College (where he was the first to gain the £30-per-annum Barnett Meyers Scholarship), and served as minister of the Borough New Synagogue from 1867 until his appointment at the New West End twelve years later.
4. The youngest of the four children of Nathaniel Montefiore and his wife, Emma (the fifth daughter of Sir Isaac Lyon Goldsmid), Claude Montefiore was born in 1858 into a family with strong Reform connections. Educated at Balliol College, Oxford, and the Hochschule für Wissenschaft des Judentums in Berlin, he co-founded the *Jewish Quarterly Review* in 1887, was president of the Anglo-Jewish Association (1895), the Jewish Historical Society of England (1899–1900), and the World Union of Progressive Judaism (1926), and served on the councils of Jews' College, the Jewish Religious Education Board, and the Jewish Colonization Association. He died in London in 1938.
5. Claude G. Montefiore, *The Old Testament and After* (London: Macmillan, 1923), p.589.
6. A social worker and magistrate, Lilian Helen (Lily) Montagu was born in London in 1873, one of ten children of Samuel Montagu – originally Montagu Samuel – and his wife, Ellen (née Cohen). Lily founded the West Central Girls' Club when she was 20, and, with Claude Montefiore, established the World Union for Progressive Judaism in 1926. She died in London in 1963.
7. 'Where the Adlers and the United Synagogue proved ineffective, Sir Samuel Montagu, later first Baron Swaythling, retrieved the situation. Arguing that the Rothschild-Adler conception of West End missionary enterprise to the East End was conceptually wrong and misdirected, he created what he called the Federation of Minor Synagogues, which became the Federation of Synagogues. Although not part of the United Synagogue, the Federation acknowledged the authority of the Chief Rabbi while attempting to remain culturally closer to the traditionalist immigrants. Through a judicious use of carrots and sticks, Montagu drew newcomers into the acculturating network of Anglo-Jewish social and religious institutions. Being himself highly observant, politically sensitive and immensely wealthy, he did much to cover Hermann Adler's vulnerable flank.' Eugene C. Black, 'The Anglicization of Orthodoxy: The Adlers', in Frances Malino and David Sorkin (eds), *Profiles in Diversity: Jews in a Changing Europe*, (Detroit, MI: Wayne State University Press, 1998), p.318.
8. Lily H. Montagu, *Samuel Montagu, First Baron Swaythling* (London: Truslove and Hanson, n.d. [1913]), ('For Private Circulation Only'), pp.22–3.
9. Lily H. Montagu, 'The Spiritual Possibilities in Judaism Today', in *Jewish Quarterly Review*, XI (January 1899), I. Abrahams and C.G. Montefiore (eds) (New York: Macmillan, 1899), pp.216–31.
10. *Jewish Chronicle*, 6 June 1902, p.11.
11. Ibid.
12. David Philipson, *The Reform Movement in Judaism*, (New York: Macmillan, 1907; rev. edn 1931), p.408.
13. Lawrence Rigal and Rosita Rosenberg, *Liberal Judaism: The First Hundred Years* (London: Union of Liberal and Progressive Synagogues, 2004), p.21.
14. *A Selection of Prayers, Psalms and Other Scriptural Passages and Hymns for Use at the Services of the Jewish Religious Union*, London; 2nd, rev. edn (London: Wertheimer, Lea, 5664 – 1903).
15. Alice Lucas, wife of the senior vice-president of the United Synagogue, daughter of Nathaniel and Emma Montefiore, and sister of Claude G. Montefiore. The involvement of Emma and Alice in prayer books of such contrasting hues vividly illustrates the extent of religious pluralism among the upper-class families of Anglo-Jewry (see note 21). Alice enriched Jewish literature by her translations of the Hebrew poets, notably her *Songs of Zion* and *The Jewish Year*. She translated *Cassel's Manual of Jewish History* and collaborated with Israel Abrahams in a handbook on teaching Hebrew.
16. Yehudah Halevi (c.1075–1141), Spanish poet and religious philosopher, author of the *Kuzari* (written originally in Arabic and translated into Hebrew), describing a disputation conducted before the king of the heathen Khazars – who converted with his people to Judaism – by a rabbi, a Christian, a Moslem and an Aristotelian philosopher.

17. *A Selection of Prayers*, p.3. The contents of the 122-page book are listed as Prayers (pp.7–34); Ten Commandments (35–7); Scripture Verses (38–43); Psalms (44–98); Hymns (99–122). The bulk of the service is in English.
18. *Jewish Chronicle*, 24 October 1902, pp.10–11.
19. Ibid., p.9.
20. Ibid., pp.9–10.
21. Acknowledged in the preface to the first and subsequent editions of the *Authorised Daily Prayer Book* as Mrs Nathaniel [Emma] Montefiore – the mother, no less, of the very Claude G. Montefiore who was the subject of Adler's condemnation – through whose 'generosity and public spirit ... the entire cost of production has been defrayed. It is, therefore, now possible for all who can afford the outlay of ONE SHILLING to obtain a book which could not otherwise have been offered to the public except at a far higher price.'
22. Hermann Adler, *The Old Paths*, preached at the St John's Wood Synagogue, London, on 6 December 5663 – 1902 (London: Wertheimer, Lea, 1902), pp.1–14.
23. Israel Abrahams, 'An Open Letter to the Chief Rabbi', *Jewish Chronicle*, 9 January 1903, pp.11–12.
24. Rigal and Rosenberg, *Liberal Judaism*, p.27.
25. 'The Rev. J.F. Stern and the Jewish Religious Union', *Jewish Chronicle*, 16 January 1903, p.14. Of Stern's departure from the Union, Israel Finestein writes: 'Stern's association with the Union was a divisive matter in East London. All shades of Orthodox opinion, so far as they took account of that side of his public life, were dismayed by his friendships. His position in the Union was a contentious issue within his own congregation. To the large mass of the Jewish population of East London, these were remote matters, save that, to those who were conscious of communal trends, the citadel in Rectory Square [where Stern's East London Synagogue was situated] became yet more graphically an outpost of another world in the midst of the East End.' 'Joseph Frederick Stern, 1865–1934: Aspects of a Gifted Anomaly', in Aubrey Newman, (ed.), *The Jewish East End, 1840–1939* (London: Jewish Historical Society of England, 1981); reprinted in Finestein, *Jewish Society in Victorian England* (London and Portland, OR: Vallentine Mitchell, 1993), p.337.
26. 'Defence and Construction', preached at the New West End Synagogue, London, on 26 December 1891, in *The Literary Remains of the Rev. Simeon Singer*, Vol. I – *Sermons*, selected and edited with a memoir by Israel Abrahams (London: George Routledge and Sons, 1908), pp.268–9.
27. See Abrahams on Singer's attitude to 'the ecclesiastical régime', chapter 5, note 50. Abrahams also points out (*The Literary Remains*, p.xviii) that 'in 1890 [Singer] obtained the rabbinical diploma from Lector [Isaac Hirsch] Weiss, of Vienna, but he declined persistently to accept nomination as a dayan, although he did occasionally sit as a member of the Beth Din. "When the late Chief Rabbi [Nathan Adler] died, in that same year, there was a party among the more advanced section of the community who were in favour of dividing the [Chief] Rabbinate into two offices and appointing Mr Singer Chief Rabbi of the West End Jews. Mr Singer, however, gave no countenance to any such suggestions" (*Jewish Chronicle*, 24 August, 1906 [p.12])'. Nor, in deference to Adlerian fiat, did he use the title 'Rabbi', remaining 'the Rev.' throughout his ministerial career.
28. 'Religious Enthusiasm', preached at the Manchester Congregation of British Jews on 18 November 1893, in *The Literary Remains*, p.13. Seven years later, Singer occupied the same pulpit to deliver a eulogy for the congregation's minister, the Rev. Lawrence Simmons, who, he said, had had 'the respect and the affection of every school of religious thought and practice in Anglo-Jewry' ('God's Witnesses and Servants', preached on Shabbat, 20 October 1900, ibid., pp.142–50). Abrahams notes, in his memoir of Singer: 'That he was unable to throw his own pulpit open to Reform ministers was a matter of grief to him; but he invited the Rev. L.M. Simmons, of the Manchester Congregation, to preside at the annual prize distribution at the New West End Synagogue religion classes' (ibid., p.xxi). A.J. Kershen and J.A. Romain write of Simmons: 'He was Orthodox, conservative, tolerant and liberal-minded ... He was not afraid to exhibit his support for the Chief Rabbi if he felt the issue or occasion warranted it, and his middle path of Judaism enabled him to narrow the divide between the two Manchester Jewish communities. On Simmons' death, Chief Rabbi Hermann Adler stated that not only Reform Judaism had suffered a loss, but that "entire Anglo-Jewry" had "reason to mourn his removal from our midst."' *Tradition and Change: A History of Reform Judaism in Britain, 1840–1995* (London and Portland, OR: Vallentine Mitchell, 1995), p.70.
29. Simeon Singer, 'Personal Religion', preached on 25 October 1902, in *Jewish Addresses Delivered at the Services of the Jewish Religious Union During the First Session, 1902–3* (London and Edinburgh: Brimley Johnson, 1904), pp.16–26.
30. Joshua 5:13.
31. 'Art Thou For Us Or For Our Adversaries?', preached at the New West End Synagogue, 12 April 1903, *The Literary Remains*, pp.172–9.
32. *Jewish Chronicle*, 24 April 1903, p.20. This letter, and Singer's immediate response below it, appeared under the heading 'The Jewish Religious Union. Impending Withdrawal of the Rev. S. Singer'.
33. Comments on this episode from two of Singer's and Montagu's close relatives are revealing. Abrahams notes: 'When the Jewish Religious Union was founded in 1902, he [Singer] was one of its warm supporters; he joined its committee, and read once and preached once from its pulpit. He did not personally approve of

all the methods of the Union, and he would have decidedly opposed any attempt to introduce some of its reforms into the ordinary service of the synagogue. But he saw that many were drifting entirely from Judaism, partly because of the difficulty of Sabbath observance, partly because of religious opinions. He saw in the Union the only practical scheme for staying these evils ... [a]nd therefore it was that he associated himself with [it]. Though his action gave offence to some of his best friends, he was too convinced of the righteousness of his course to consent to abandon it. When, however, Sir Samuel Montagu asked him to withdraw from the Union ... Singer replied on the same day (15 April, 1903), consenting "with sincere regret" to accede to the step required of him ... Singer deeply appreciated the considerate and generous manner in which his devoted friend (now Lord Swaythling) approached him in the matter.' *The Literary Remains*, pp.xvi–xvii.

Of the same period, Lily Montagu writes: 'When the late Mr Singer showed practical sympathy with the work of the Jewish Religious Union, Samuel Montagu's complete confidence in his friend was unaffected. He believed that Mr Singer held the same point of view as himself, and was allowing certain *additions* to Orthodoxy in order that the weak-kneed might be beguiled to worship on the ancient sites, by the attractive appearance of the outer courts. So when other and less rigidly Orthodox Jews stormed with indignation, and quaked with alarm, Samuel Montagu merely waited the development of events, and only interfered with a gentle appeal when he found that his friend's position was being misunderstood, and therefore might influence his own congregation in a baneful manner. But after the retirement of Mr Singer from the movement, Samuel Montagu still regarded it with an easy tolerance. He did not think it would endure or succeed in its avowed object of recovering lives to the community, but he was quite satisfied to let it fizzle out, and even showed a little sympathy with those who would grieve over its certain decadence. At last one of his relatives – a peace-loving man – showed him some short addresses made by liberal leaders at a certain religious symposium. Then, for the first time, apparently, Samuel Montagu had to recognise the existence of a new and disturbing thought in the community.' *Samuel Montagu, First Baron Swaythling*, pp.25–6.

34. Hermann Adler, *Anglo-Jewish Memories and Other Sermons* (London: George Routledge and Sons, 1909), p.viii.
35. 'Faith', preached at the New West End Synagogue, London, on 30 May 1906, in *The Literary Remains*, pp.279–86.
36. Of Singer and his philosophy, the Rev. Ephraim Levine, who occupied the New West End pulpit from 1916 to 1954, writes: 'Simeon Singer is still regarded as the ideal of an Anglo-Jewish minister ... His religious standpoint was conservative and progressive at the same time. By training and by practice, he was conservative: he loved to maintain traditional Jewish custom; his intimate knowledge of the liturgy and its history served to keep alive his natural love for the old form of service and the traditional prayerbook. He was progressive, too, in that he recognised the ever-changing needs of the rising generation, and all his efforts were directed to fostering the love of the synagogue in the hearts of the young. At the same time, he never allowed them to lose sight of the fact that a healthy Jewish religious life must have its roots deep in tradition. He welcomed change where signs of life were evident; he espoused any cause that promised to strengthen Jewish allegiance; he even ran the risk of being misunderstood if he believed in a cause and its ultimate Jewish possibilities. His was a broad and catholic Judaism which won adherents from representatives of all shades of opinion. The man himself was true, and men put their trust in him.' *The History of the New West End Synagogue, 1879–1929* (Aldershot: John Drew, 1929), pp.18–19.
37. Meeting of the United Synagogue council, held on 13 January 1903, at Jews' College, Queen Square House, Guilford Street, London. Reported in the *Jewish Chronicle*, 16 January 1903, pp.10–14.
38. On L.J. Greenberg and his role and that of his paper in the affairs of the community, see David Cesarani, *The Jewish Chronicle and Anglo-Jewry, 1841–1991* (Cambridge: Cambridge University Press, 1994), pp.103–41, and Cecil Roth, *The Jewish Chronicle 1841–1941: A Century of Newspaper History* (London: Jewish Chronicle, 1949), pp.124–40.
39. Jessel was joint vice-president of the United Synagogue from 1899 to 1917, sharing the post with Henry Lucas until 1910, then with Felix A. Davis (treasurer 1896–1911) until 1916.
40. Before proceeding to the debate, Jessel said that as he was affected personally by one of the resolutions, 'although there is apparently no imputation upon my conduct in the chair', it was perhaps desirable that he should ask Henry Lucas to preside while that resolution was being discussed. His suggestion was greeted with cries of 'No, no', and he deferred to the wishes of the meeting by remaining in the chair.
41. Office of the Chief Rabbi, Finsbury Square, London, 12 December 5663 [1902]. Jessel told the meeting that the letter would be entered on the minutes, and that 'at the proper time it will be open for any member of the council to deal with the matter at large'.
42. Those supporting the resolution were reported as L.J. Greenberg, J. Jacobs, S.S. Oppenheim, and Nelson Samuel. A majority of the honorary officers not affected by the motion – including Lucas, the senior vice-president – abstained.

CHAPTER 7

1. This view of the Reform stance was subsequently reflected in letters to the *Jewish Chronicle* when Montefiore's 'manifesto' of Liberal Judaism was published in 1909 (see below).

2. Claude G. Montefiore, 'Religious Differences and Religious Agreements', in *Truth in Religion, and Other Sermons Delivered at the Services of the Jewish Religious Union* (New York: Macmillan, 1906), pp.283–6. On the flyleaf to the volume is printed the dedication: 'To the memory of Simeon Singer (born 1848: died 1906) this book is sorrowfully and affectionately inscribed.'
3. London-born Isidore Harris (1853–1925) was educated at Jews' College and its school, and at University College London. He was minister of the North London Synagogue (1874–1881) before becoming assistant minister to Albert Löwy, and then junior minister to Morris Joseph, at the West London Synagogue. Although serving that congregation for some four decades, he 'never left the Orthodox community; he remained with us all the time. One can say without fear of contradiction that ... the Judaism he preached was conservative, and very far removed from the type known as "Liberal" Judaism.' Rev. Isaac Livingstone, minister of the Golders Green [United] Synagogue, *Jewish Chronicle*, 24 July 1925, p.10. A scholarly writer, Harris edited the *Jewish Year Book* and was responsible for the *Jews' College Jubilee Volume* in 1906.
4. The original all-male choir was augmented by female voices in 1858, coinciding with the installation of an organ in the Margaret Street Synagogue, the forerunner to Berkeley Street. On United Synagogue mixed choirs, see Stephen Sharot, 'Religious Change in Native Orthodoxy in London, 1870–1914: The Synagogue Service', in *Jewish Journal of Sociology*, XV, 1 (June 1973); Raymond Apple, *The Hampstead Synagogue, 1892–1967* (London: Vallentine Mitchell, 1967), pp.22–3; Israel Finestein, *Anglo-Jewry in Changing Times* (London and Portland, OR: Vallentine Mitchell, 1999), pp.231–3.
5. *Jewish Chronicle*, 20 January 1905, p.19.
6. Ibid., 7 May 1909, p.19.
7. 'To the Very Rev. the Chief Rabbi from D.W. Marks', Belmont House, Belmont, near Maidenhead, 14 April 1909.
8. 'Rev. Professor D.W. Marks', preached at the Bayswater Synagogue, London, 8 May 1909, in Sir Hermann Gollancz, *Fifty Years After: Sermons and Addresses Setting Forth the Teachings and Spirit of Judaism*, Third Series (London: Humphrey Milford, Oxford University Press, 1924), pp.255–6.
9. Claude G. Montefiore, 'The Jewish Religious Union: Its Principles and its Future', in *Jewish Chronicle*, 15 October 1909, pp.19–22. An annotated text of the 'manifesto' appears in Lawrence Rigal and Rosita Rosenberg, *Liberal Judaism: The First Hundred Years* (London: Union of Liberal and Progressive Synagogues, 2004), pp.314–29, highlighting the alterations made in the restructured version of 1918.
10. *Jewish Chronicle*, 1 October 1909, p.6.
11. Ibid., 8 October 1909, p.16. Among others who resigned from the committee at this period were Morris Joseph and Oswald J. Simon. Joseph left the Union over the establishment of a separate synagogue, having ceased to preach at its services at the request of the West London Synagogue council (Rigal and Rosenberg, *Liberal Judaism*, pp.32, 43). In 1903, in accordance with his congregation's bye-laws, he had sought – and received – its approval to participate in the Union's activities and had supported the scheme (subsequently rejected by the Union as being 'subversive of its principles') to place the West London's premises at its disposal, 'anxious that his synagogue perform an act of religious liberality ... [and] anxious that the Union be stamped as Jewish in the eyes of the community'. David Philipson, *The Reform Movement in Judaism*, (New York: Macmillan, 1907; rev. edn, 1931), p.414.
12. Hermann Adler, 'A Menace to Judaism', preached at the Bayswater Synagogue, London, on 2 October 1909, in *Jewish Chronicle*, 8 October 1909, pp.15–16.
13. Ibid., pp.5–6.
14. Following its earlier dismissal of Adler's Sukkot sermon, the *Jewish Chronicle*'s denunciation of the manifesto was, in contrast, loud and clear: 'The attitude of the Jewish Religious Union has changed momentously. Originally the Union was declared to be intended primarily to provide a Sabbath service at a time when it could best be attended by those Jews who could not or would not abstain from their ordinary avocations on the Sabbath day. As such, it had the support of many earnest Orthodox Jews – clerics as well as laymen. It now stands forth as the pioneer of a new religion, and the symbol of a great cleavage. When those who are of the "people of the Book" substitute for the supreme authority of the Bible the authority of personal reason and conscience, they have left *terra firma*. They are, whatever may be their objects, launched on the rapids of disintegration and assimilation' (ibid., 15 October 1909, pp.5–6).
15. Hermann Adler, 'It is Time to Work for the Lord', preached at the New West End Synagogue, 30 October 1909, in *Jewish Chronicle*, 5 November 1909, pp.18–19.
16. Ibid., 12 November 1909, p.20. The full text of the letter is reproduced as Appendix II.
17. 'Religious Neglect and Apostasy: The Other Side of the Picture', preached at the Bayswater Synagogue, London, 2 May 1908, in Hermann Gollancz, *Sermons and Addresses* (London: Myers, 1909), p.202.
18. *Jewish Chronicle*, 31 December 1909, p.30.
19. Ibid., pp.30–1.
20. Ibid., 31 December 1909, p.54.
21. Ibid., 9 September 1910, p.7.
22. *To the Members of the West London Synagogue*, 26 October 1910, reprinted in the *Jewish Chronicle*, 4 November 1910, pp.8–9.

23. London-born Philip Magnus (1842–1933) served as an assistant minister at the West London Synagogue from 1866 to 1880, when he left the clergy to become organising secretary and director of the City and Guilds of London Institute. He was MP for the University of London from 1906 to 1922, was knighted in 1886, and became a baronet in 1917.
24. *Jewish Chronicle*, 2 December 1910, p.17.
25. Ibid., 3 February 1911, p.18.
26. The United Synagogue's Willesden cemetery, in Beaconsfield Road, London NW10, opened in 1873 – since then the last resting place of Britain's Chief Rabbis (apart from Lord Jakobovits, who was buried, in 1999, on the Mount of Olives in Jerusalem).
27. Ibid., 21 July 1911, p.18.
28. 'While he [Hermann Adler] worked assiduously in the East End, he had, at best, an ambiguous relation to, and view of, foreign Jews. He feared that they endangered the work of generations of British Jews. They were given to ecclesiastical indiscipline. Well they might be, for Adler's Orthodoxy seemed almost incomprehensible to their traditionalist sensibilities. These newcomers threatened British Jewry's harmonious world view.' Eugene C. Black, 'The Anglicization of Orthodoxy: The Adlers', in Frances Malino and David Sorkin (eds), *Profiles in Diversity: Jews in a Changing Europe* (Detroit, MI: Wayne State University Press, 1998), p.318.
29. In his installation address as dayan, Moses Hyamson also appealed to the 'the East' to work towards unity: 'The men of light and leading in the East End, they who stand out prominently by reason of their knowledge, energy and initiative, are earnestly implored not to retire to their tents, or build every one a high place for himself, but to accord the valued assistance of their loyalty and good will. Combination is better than competition. The latter, though certainly stimulating energy, involves enormous waste of force; the former secures the same results with a maximum of efficiency and economy. I ask you to aid in the worthy task of welding the community into one harmonious whole.' 'Installation into the Office of Dayan', preached at the Great Synagogue, London, 13 May 1902, in the Rev. M. Hyamson, *The Oral Law and Other Sermons* (London: David Nutt, 1910), p.139.
30. 'The Ideal Jewish Pastor: An Installation Sermon', preached at the Great Synagogue, London, 23 June 1891, in Hermann Adler, *Anglo-Jewish Memories and Other Sermons* (London: George Routledge and Sons, 1909), pp.91–2.
31. The printed text in the *Jewish Chronicle* (21 July 1911, p.18) appears as 'and who may lead them in and bring them out'.
32. Extract from a letter from Hermann Adler to his family, dated erev Rosh Chodesh Adar, 29 Shevat 5671 (27 February 1911). Reproducing the extract, the *Jewish Chronicle* commented that it was 'remarkable that the Chief Rabbi based the Communal Charge, which was written in February, upon a text [Numbers 27:16–17] from the *sidrah* [Torah portion, *Pinchas*] for last Shabbat'.
33. The passage appeared (as we have seen) not in Adler's will – which was published in full in the *Jewish Chronicle* a month later (18 August 1911, pp.8–9) – but in the letter quoted above.
34. *Jewish Chronicle*, 4 August 1911, p.15.
35. The Machzike Hadath emerged from a revolt by strictly religious Central and East European immigrants against the perceived tolerant and easy-going traditionalism of the United Synagogue's 'inclusive Orthodoxy', to use V.D. Lipman's term in *A History of the Jews in Britain Since 1858* (New York: Holmes and Meier, 1990), p.94. The catalyst for their secessionist movement was Hermann Adler's refusal to respond to requests for more stringent supervision of butchers licensed by the London Board for Shechita; as a result, a group of East Enders, supported by mainly German-born followers of Samson Raphael Hirsch, founded the Machzike Hadath, which eventually acquired its own rabbi – Abraham Aba Werner – and synagogue, Talmud Torah and kashrut infrastructure. In 1926, it formed a loose alliance with the Adath Yisroel Synagogue to form the Union of Orthodox Hebrew Congregations, under the leadership of Rabbi Victor Schonfeld. On the founding of the Machzike Hadath, see Bernard Homa, *A Fortress in Anglo-Jewry: The Story of the Machzike Hadath* (London: Shapiro, Vallentine, 5713 – 1953), pp.5–46: 'Dr Hermann Adler was a lesser scholar and authority [than his father] and was far less able to withstand the growing encroachments on traditional Jewish practice that were constantly being demanded and made. There can be no doubt that Anglo-Jewry was fast moving towards religious decadence when it was sharply awakened from its spiritual somnolence by the influx of thousands of Jewish refugees from Russia, Poland and Romania which began about 1880' (p.6). Homa was Abraham Werner's grandson. See also, Albert M. Hyamson, *The London Board for Shechita, 1804–1954* (London: Henry F. Thompson, for the London Board for Shechita, 1954), pp.45–8.
36. C. Russell and H.S. Lewis, *The Jew in London: A Study of Racial Character and Present-Day Conditions* (New York: Thomas Y. Cromwell, 1901), p.97, cited in Todd M. Endelman, *The Jews in Britain, 1656–2000* (Berkeley, CA: University of California Press, 2002), p.176; and in Stephen Sharot, 'Native Jewry and the Religious Anglicisation of Immigrants in London, 1870–1905', *Jewish Journal of Sociology*, XVI, 1 (June 1974) p.47.
37. *Jewish Chronicle*, 21 July 1911, pp.23–4.
38. Ibid., p.24.

39. Anne J. Kershen and Jonathan A. Romain, *A History of Reform Judaism in Britain, 1840–1995* (London and Portland, OR: Vallentine Mitchell, 1995), pp.99–100.
40. Philipson, *The Reform Movement*, p.402. This widely held view was strongly disputed some years earlier by Morris Joseph in a letter to the *Jewish Chronicle*, following the death of David Woolf Marks: 'To assert that the synagogue has lost much of its energy ... is to ignore facts. Since the establishment of the synagogue, important changes have been made in the service. Prayers are no longer offered for the restoration of the sacrificial rite; the Law is read in a triennial cycle; the Prophets are recited in English – changes introduced just twenty-one years ago. It is quite true that there is still, after the lapse of seventy years, only one Reform synagogue in London. But there are two in the provinces [Manchester and Bradford]; and if the parent congregation has hitherto been disinclined to use its opportunities – and they have been tempting ones, as I can certify from my own personal knowledge – of promoting the establishment of other Reform places of worship in the metropolis, it is not for want of energy or of faith in Reform principles, but simply from a dread – in my humble judgment, a needless dread – of widening the breach in the community' (*Jewish Chronicle*, 14 May 1909, p.12).
41. Rabbi Dr Israel Isidor Mattuck, a young Lithuanian-born minister serving the Reform congregation of Far Rockaway, Long Island, was recommended to Claude Montefiore and Charles Singer (Simeon Singer's son and an influential figure in the Liberal movement) during a visit they paid to the United States. Mattuck was invited to preach at the Hill Street Synagogue on 17 June 1911, and to address the members the next day. Shortly afterwards, he was offered the pulpit, and took up the post the following January.
42. Claude G. Montefiore, *Outlines of Liberal Judaism for the Use of Parents and Teachers* (London: Macmillan, 1912; 2nd edn, 1923), pp.vii–ix.
43. Abraham Geiger (1810–1874) launched his rabbinical career in Wiesbaden, where he reformed the synagogue services and published the *Wissenschaftliche Zeitschrift für jüdische Theologie*. In 1837, he convened the first gathering of Reform rabbis, subsequently participating in a number of similar synods. His last positions were in Frankfurt and Berlin, where he was instrumental in founding the Hochschule für Wissenschaft des Judentums.
44. Born in Steingrub, Bohemia, Isaac Mayer Wise (1819–1900) emigrated to the United States in 1846, serving as a rabbi first at Albany's Congregation Beth El and then in Cincinnati. He compiled a Reform prayer book, *Minhag America*, and was a leading figure in the establishment of Hebrew Union College in 1875, the Union of American Hebrew Congregations in 1873, and the Central Conference of American Rabbis in 1889.
45. *Jewish Chronicle*, 7 April 1911, p.22.
46. Ibid., 14 July 1911, p.20.
47. Shabbetai Zevi (1626–1676), Turkish scholar and pseudo-Messiah; Polish-born mystic Jacob Frank (1726–1791), regarded as a successor to Zevi and excommunicated, with his followers the Frankists, in 1756; Bessarabian missionary Joseph Rabbinowich (1837–1899), a member of the Hibbat Zion movement before founding the Children of Israel of the New Testament sect and converting to Protestantism.
48. See chapter 8, note 5.

CHAPTER 8

1. On Hertz's early years and education, see Miri J. Freud-Kandel, *Orthodox Judaism in Britain Since 1913* (London and Portland, OR: Vallentine Mitchell, 2006), pp.23–32; Harvey Meirovich, *A Vindication of Judaism: The Polemics of the Hertz Pentateuch* (New York and Jerusalem: Jewish Theological Seminary of America, 1998), pp.1–18; Sefton Temkin, 'Orthodoxy With Moderation: A Sketch of Joseph Herman Hertz', in *Judaism*, 24, 3 (Summer 1975), pp.278–95 (on Temkin, see note 10); Aubrey Newman, *Chief Rabbi Dr Joseph H. Hertz*, lecture delivered at the Adolph Tuck Hall, Woburn House, London, 25 September 1972 (London: United Synagogue, 1972), pp.1–26.
2. In the spirit of the age, Rabbi Ezriel Hildesheimer (1820–1899) championed *Wissenschaft des Judentums*, the academic study of Jewish sources, and in 1873 founded the Berlin Rabbiner-Seminar, the first modern Orthodox rabbinical seminary in Germany. There the critical study of Jewish sources was combined with an allegiance to the principle of *Torah min hashamayim* – that the Law, both Written and Oral, was divinely revealed 'from the mouth of the Almighty'. A master *posek* (Jewish legal authority), Hildesheimer issued hundreds of responsa during his lifetime. On his life and achievements, see David Ellenson, *Rabbi Ezriel Hildesheimer and the Creation of a Modern Jewish Orthodoxy* (Tuscaloosa, AL and London: University of Alabama Press, 1990).
3. Rabbi Sabato Morais, the Seminary's driving force, quoted in Hasia Diner, 'Like the Antelope and the Badger', in *Tradition Renewed: A History of the Jewish Theological Seminary*, Vol. I, Jack Wertheimer (ed.) (New York: Jewish Theological Seminary of America, 1997), p.11. Morais (1823–1897), born in Leghorn (Livorno), was briefly assistant chazan, and then teacher, of London's Spanish and Portuguese Congregation before occupying the pulpit of the Mikve Israel Synagogue in Philadelphia. 'Though his ministry covered the period of greatest activity in the adaptation of Judaism in America to changed conditions, he, as the advocate of Orthodox Judaism, withstood every appeal in behalf of ritualistic innovations and departures from

traditional practice, winning the esteem of his opponents in consistency and integrity.' Cyrus L. Sulzberger, *Jewish Encyclopedia*, Vol. VIII (New York: Funk and Wagnalls, 1925), p.680. Hertz was to say of Morais: 'All around him [in America] were so-called rabbis who were fanatically advocating the tearing up of Jewish life by the roots. To all this treason and revolution in religion, Sabato Morais was the life-long foe. Like Elijah, he for a long time stood alone; but he never lost courage. He at last succeeded in rallying all the forces that stood for historic continuity of Jewish life in America and called into existence the Jewish Theological Seminary. There, under his faithful guidance, and later under the guidance of Solomon Schechter, hundreds of Jewish teachers of religion have been trained who have definitely stemmed the advance of religious radicalism in American congregations.' J.H. Hertz, 'Divided Counsels', in *Sermons, Addresses and Studies*, Vol. I (London: Soncino Press, 1938), pp.224–5. Following the establishment of the Seminary, Morais was appointed president of the faculty and professor of Bible, holding both posts until his death.

4. Joseph Herman Hertz, in 'Graduation Address', delivered at the Jewish Theological Seminary, New York, 14 June 1894, in J.H. Hertz, *Early and Late: Addresses, Messages and Papers* (Hindhead, Surrey: Soncino Press, 1943), pp.122–5.

5. See previous chapter. In the 'Pittsburgh Platform' of the 1885 Pittsburgh Conference, eight principles were formulated that were to dominate American Reform for half a century. 'They concentrated on the prophetic tradition within Judaism and placed greater emphasis on personal conduct than on ritual observances. The platform stressed the spiritual and ethical in the Jewish message, and gave priority to the moral demands of Judaism. The right to initiate was fundamental, and Judaism was viewed as a "progressive religion ever striving to be in accord with the postulates of reason". There was no hesitation in discarding the legalisms of the past and maintaining "only such ceremonies as elevate and sanctify our lives, but reject all such as are not adapted to the views and habits of modern civilisation". The Jewish people were regarded not as a racial group but as a religious community, and all notions of returning to the Land of Israel were renounced. The ultimate task of Jews was to work for the reign of justice, truth, righteousness and peace. The Pittsburgh Platform was replaced in 1937 by the Columbus Platform, which expressed greater attachment to tradition, the Land of Israel, and historical precedents.' Anne J. Kershen and Jonathan A. Romain, *A History of Reform Judaism in Britain, 1840–1995*, (London and Portland, OR: Vallentine Mitchell, 1995), p.135. For the background to the Pittsburgh Conference, and full text of its declaration of principles – 'the most succinct expression of the theology of the Reform movement that has ever been published to the world' – see David Philipson, *The Reform Movement in Judaism* (New York: Macmillan, 1907; rev. edn 1931), pp.355–7.

6. Hertz was to employ this phrase many times, most notably during the acrimonious debates in London over the interpretation of 'Traditional Judaism'. See, for example, the first of his 'New Paths' sermons, referred to in chapter 11.

7. Philip Cowen, *Memories of an American Jew* (New York: International Press, 1932), p.402. Cowen, publisher of *The American Hebrew*, acted as an intermediary with the Witwatersrand Old Hebrew Congregation in its search for a rabbi in 1898, having carried an advertisement for the post in his paper (see notes 8 and 9).

8. *The American Hebrew*, XXIII, 17 June 1898, p.198.

9. This advertisement had earlier appeared in the *Jewish Chronicle* (London), 18 March 1898, p.3, where it specified a salary of £750 per annum, a free house, and life assurance for £1,000. An additional reference to 'congregation Orthodox but mixed choir' took into account the limits of toleration under Hermann Adler.

10. Temkin, 'Orthodoxy With Moderation', p.284. Sefton David Temkin (1917–1996) was born and educated in England and graduated from Liverpool University in law and modern history. He practised as a barrister, writing for legal periodicals and for *Halsbury's Laws of England*, and was later to serve as professor of Jewish history at the State University of New York in Albany. A prolific contributor to the international Jewish press throughout his working life, Temkin was secretary of the Anglo-Jewish Association in London while Hertz was on its council. In the article cited here, he recalls several encounters with the Chief Rabbi during which he 'had occasion to learn more about his personality and the struggles in which he was involved'.

11. *Standard and Diggers' News*, Johannesburg, 23 September 1898. The report read: 'Although the incumbents of the Johannesburg New Hebrew Congregation and Modern Hebrew Congregation were conspicuous by their absence, the priesthood of other denominations thought the occasion worthy of their presence.' The burgeoning attempt to introduce Reform Judaism to Johannesburg at this time was short-lived; the Rand Modern Hebrew Congregation, opened in the year of Hertz's arrival, dissolved after a few months. The joint proprietor (with Robert Stewart Scott) of the *Standard and Diggers' News* was Emmanuel Mendelssohn, JP (1850–1910), son of Itsich and Caroline Mendelssohn, of Berlin. Emmanuel was president of the Witwatersrand Hebrew Congregation before it added the prefix 'Old' in 1891 when two groups – one of Russian origin, the other Anglo-German-Polish – seceded to form the Beth Hamidrash and Johannesburg (New) Hebrew Congregation, respectively. The lengthy and prominent report in the local paper is so studded with Hebrew expressions, and so obviously familiar with the nature of the occasion, as to make it likely that it was written – or at the very least influenced – by Mendelssohn himself.

12. In an introductory statement read out by the synagogue secretary, E.M. Davis Marks: 'We hope that your devotion to the religion and race of Israel may mark you as a type of all that is noble and best in the Jewish priesthood, a true exponent of the Rabbinical traditions, and one worthy of the great rabbis who ordained you to the service of Israel and sent you in response to our call.' The president, S. Goldreich, followed this with the plea: 'Rabbi – be courageous and intrepid in the battle for Right and Truth, even as the Macabbeans.'
13. Joseph Herman Hertz, 'Installation Address', preached at the Witwatersrand Old Hebrew Congregation, Johannesburg, 22 September 1898, in *Souvenir of the Decennial Celebration of the Witwatersrand Old Hebrew Congregation and of the Public Reception of the Rev. Dr Joseph Herman Hertz, 16 November, 1898* (Johannesburg: M.J. Wood, for the Council of the Congregation, 1898), pp.17–19.
14. Ibid., p.20.
15. Hertz's 1898 address, *The Jew as a Patriot: a Plea for the Removal of the Civil Disabilities of the Jews in the Transvaal*, was reprinted and widely distributed.
16. The intervening period was spent in the United States, with brief visits to Britain en route.
17. Hertz served on the consultative committee of the British High Commissioner, Sir Alfred (later Lord) Milner; was professor of philosophy at the newly established Transvaal University College (1906–1908); helped found the South African Jewish Board of Deputies, the Hebrew School, and the Jewish Orphanage; and was vice-president of the South African Zionist Federation (1899–1904).
18. *Jewish Chronicle*, 7 April 1911, p.22.
19. 'Inaugural Sermon', preached at the Congregation Orach Chayim, New York, 13 January 1912, in J.H. Hertz, *Early and Late*, pp.126–33.
20. The details first appeared in an interview Hertz gave to the *Jewish Morning Journal*, New York, and subsequently reported in the *Jewish Chronicle*, 16 August 1912, p.11.
21. Ibid., 3 May 1912, p.23.
22. *On the Sanctification and Desecration of God's Name* (based on Leviticus 22:32 in the weekly Torah portion), preached at the Great Synagogue, London, 4 May 1912.
23. 'Rabbi Dr Hertz at the Bayswater Synagogue', *Jewish Chronicle*, 17 May 1912, p.19. Referring to Hermann Adler's former occupancy of the Bayswater pulpit and comparing the 'pulpitry' of the two rabbis, the paper's special correspondent found that 'they bore scarcely the slightest likeness. The late Chief Rabbi always carefully wrote out his sermons and read them with great deliberation. Dr Hertz preaches extempore with sharp, staccato diction, with nothing of the clergyman's manners. Dr Adler's delivery was not clear, but his voice was deep and sonorous. Dr Hertz can be readily heard ... Never does he seem lost for a word, a quotation, or an illustration, and somehow when he ended his sermon, which occupied just about half an hour in delivery, one felt that he had by no means exhausted either his subject or himself, and that he could without much effort straightaway have delivered another sermon of equal length from the same text without repeating himself. When Dr Adler ended his discourse, he gave one the impression that he had said all he had to say on the topic under his consideration, that he had told, as it were, the whole story. Dr Adler kept rigidly to his text. When he gave it out, he gave the key to his whole discourse so far as the subjects upon which he intended to speak were concerned. Dr Hertz took as his text the institution of the Jubilee. Who could have guessed that he would have taken his hearers into questions of the relative value to Judaism of the Ghetto Jew and the emancipated Israelite, of the relative progress in civilisation of the Congo Negro astride his bicycle, and the Americanised son of Jacob ensconced in his sixty-horsepower motor? No two preachers that can be thought of present for comparison so many actual pulpit opposites as Dr Hertz and the late Chief Rabbi.'
24. Leviticus 25:10.
25. *Jewish Chronicle*, 17 May 1912, p.19.
26. On Hyamson's appeal for the 'East' to work more closely with the 'West', see chapter 7, note 29.
27. On the events leading up to this contest, see Freud-Kandel *Orthodox Judaism*, pp.42–51, and Meirovich, *A Vindication of Judaism*, pp.17–18.
28. 'Message from the Chief Rabbi-Elect', by cable, *Jewish Chronicle*, 21 February 1913, p.24.
29. Ibid., 21 February 1913, p.34.
30. Ibid.
31. Ibid., 18 April 1913, p.26.
32. *The Installation Sermon of The Very Rev. Dr Joseph Herman Hertz, Chief Rabbi of the United Hebrew Congregations of the British Empire*, preached at the Great Synagogue, London, 14 April 5673 – 1913 (London: United Synagogue, 1913), pp.1–22. The quotation at the end of the sermon is from Hermann Adler's address at the inauguration of Queen's Square House, the new premises of Jews' College, on 6 May 1900, reprinted in Isidore Harris, *Jews' College Jubilee Volume*, (London: Luzac, 1906), p.cxxxii.
33. Temkin, 'Orthodoxy With Moderation', p.286. In 1913, Hyamson was appointed 'Rabbi for Life' at Orach Chayim. Two years later, despite acknowledging the institution's obvious Conservative bias (at one point, he declared that 'if, God forbid, the presidency of the Seminary should be offered to me, I could not accept it'), he assumed the professorship of codes at the Jewish Theological Seminary – 'perhaps the most Orthodox member of the Seminary faculty' according to Ira Robinson, in *Tradition Renewed: A History of the*

*Jewish Theological Seminary of America*, Vol. I, Jack Wertheimer (ed.), (New York: Jewish Theological Seminary of America, 1997), pp.124–5. Hyamson held the position until becoming professor emeritus in 1940, nine years before his death. A vice-president of the Union of Orthodox Jewish Congregations of America, Hyamson translated *Hovot Halevavot* (*Duties of the Heart*), by the eleventh-century Spanish philosopher, Bahya ibn Pakuda, and *Sefer Hamadah* from Maimonides' *Mishneh Torah*.

34. Hochman's appointment was made in October 1907, more than a year after Singer's death. For further details, see chapter 9.
35. The photograph of Hochman in Ephraim Levine, *The History of the New West End Synagogue, 1879–1929* (Aldershot: John Drew, 1929), presents him in a barrister's wig and gown. The history ignores the controversial circumstances of his ministry – devoting two paragraphs to his appointment and one sentence to his tenure of office, concluding with the blunt statement that 'he retired from the ministry in the summer of 1915' (33–4). A brief account of Hochman's more colourful activities is included in Elkan Levy, *The New West End Synagogue, 1879–2004*, delivered at the synagogue on 11 July 2004, as part of its 125th-anniversary celebrations. Levy, himself a graduate of Jews' College, is a past president of the United Synagogue and son of Raphael Levy (1916–1985), chazan of the New West End from 1946 to 1984.

CHAPTER 9

1. Isidore Harris, *Jews' College Jubilee Volume* (London: Luzac, 1906), pp.cxciii–iv. Hochman won the Sir Moses Montefiore Studentship – founded by the College council in Sir Moses' memory, out of an endowment received from the trustees of the Judith Lady Montefiore College – in 1905. His first two awards were the Michael Samuel Scholarship (1902), valued at £15; and £30 per annum, tenable for three years, from the Resident Scholarship Endowment Fund (1903), presented by an anonymous donor. He also gained the Hollier Scholarship at University College London in 1902 (*Jewish Chronicle*, 17 April 1942, p.6).
2. Ibid., 14 April 1939, p.10. Aaron Hochman's obituary notes the birth of two children by his second wife, and the Rev. Ephraim Frank, of Boston, formerly chazan at the Borough and Western Synagogues, London, as one of his sons-in-law.
3. Hochman entered Jews' College in 1901 and graduated from London University in 1905. He spent three semesters at Berlin University and went on to study at the Rabbiner-Seminar and at Heidelberg, where he gained his doctorate of philosophy. On his return to Britain, he founded a number of friendly and literary societies in the East End, reputedly 'much esteemed as a speaker' (ibid., 11 October 1907, p.6), and received training in chazanut under the Rev. E. Spero.
4. At the time of Hochman's appointment, the unflinchingly Orthodox Samuel Montagu was still a commanding figure at the New West End. The *Jewish Chronicle*'s obituary of the subsequently elevated Lord Swaythling noted that 'to the very last, he [Montagu] continued to take a keen interest in the fortunes of his place of worship, having been specially concerned in the appointment of Dr J. Hochman as minister' (17 January 1911, p.18). The other members of the selection committee were Dr Alfred Wolff, A.E. Franklin, H. Landau, Herbert P. Marsden, I. Rosenberg, Selim Samuel, Sir Stuart Samuel, MP, and Jacob Schwarzschild. Elkan Levy states that Hertz had expressed interest in the congregation in a letter to Hermann Adler, who had 'told him not to come', possibly because he had his only son, the Rev. Solomon Alfred Adler – then minister at Hammersmith – in mind for the position. (Levy, 'The New West End Synagogue, 1879–2004', lecture delivered at the New West End Synagogue, London, 11 July 2004.) The son was regarded by many as a potential third Adlerian Chief Rabbi, but was in failing health, resigned his Hammersmith post in 1908, and died in November 1910, aged 34. He had previously served in Dublin, Reading and Liverpool (*Jewish Chronicle*, 2 December 1910, p.8).
5. Many years later, Rabbi Harris Cohen (1869–1949), a grandson of Dayan Jacob Reinowitz and a student at Jews' College from 1882 to 1887, wrote of Bender and Hochman: 'When the pulpit of the New West End Synagogue became vacant after the death of Simeon Singer, the board of management had difficulty in finding a suitable successor. A. Bender, of Cape Town, was brought over, but Bender was proud and haughty and would not submit to all the laws and regulations of the United Synagogue. The young Joseph Hochman was tried, and he was appointed. When he heard this, Dr Hirsch said: "Bender was not elected because he was a Hochman, so Hochman was elected because he was a 'bender.'" Hirsch, 'At Jews' College Sixty Years Ago', *Jewish Chronicle*, (8 October 1948), p.13. Samuel Abraham Hirsch (1843–1923) was Cohen's theological tutor at Jews' College.
6. 'The board of management of the New West End Synagogue, in conjunction with a special advisory committee, have resolved that the election of a preacher and reader is inadvisable at the present juncture. They have therefore temporarily engaged Dr J. Hochman, BA, in that capacity for a period of one year from 1 November, 1907' (*Jewish Chronicle*, 11 October 1907, p.6). The temporary nature of the appointment was strongly criticised in the press, but was not reconsidered until February 1909, after the synagogue announced that its board of management had been 'empowered to invite applications for the position. As no other suitable candidate was forthcoming, the board decided to curtail the further probationary period and to proceed to an election' (ibid., 26 February 1909, p.8).

7. 'The Anglo-Jewish Ministry and the United Synagogue', preached at the New West End Synagogue on Sabbath, 16 April 1910, on a text from II Kings 4:40 (ibid., 22 April 1910, p.16).
8. The *Jewish Review*, launched in April 1910 and published by George Routledge and Sons. Hochman's co-editor was Norman (de Mattos) Bentwich (1883–1971), a noted Cambridge graduate, lawyer and Zionist, and a son of Herbert Bentwich (1856–1932), one of the earliest followers of Theodor Herzl in England and a founder of the British Zionist Federation (1899).
9. *Jewish Review*, I, 1 (April 1910), Norman Bentwich and Joseph Hochman (eds), pp.3–7.
10. Based on Isaiah 54:4–5 and delivered at the New West End Synagogue on 18 September 1910, the sermon was extensively reported the following week under the headline, 'Orthodoxy and the Knowledge of God', and described as 'an outspoken sermon on the relations of Orthodox observance and true religion' (*Jewish Chronicle*, 23 September 1910, pp.15–16).
11. Ibid., 7 October 1910, p.25.
12. *Orthodoxy and Religious Observance*, delivered at the New West End Synagogue, 4 October 1910, 'Printed by Request' (London: George Young, 1910), pp.1–15. The repercussions of the printed sermon are discussed in this chapter.
13. The quotation featured significantly in an interview Hochman gave five years later on his resignation from the New West End (*Jewish Chronicle*, 20 August 1915, pp.12–13), reproduced below.
14. *Orthodoxy and Religious Observance*, pp.6–7, 11–12.
15. *Jewish Chronicle*, 14 October 1910, p.6.
16. Adler to Schlesinger, 7 October 1910, London Metropolitan Archives, LMA ACC2805/1/1/71.
17. Adler to Hochman, 9 October 1910, ibid. A similar memorandum was addressed to Schlesinger (ibid.).
18. *Jewish Chronicle*, 13 February 1920, p.15.
19. Adler to Hochman, 2 November 1910, London Metropolitan Archives, LMA ACC2805/1/1/71.
20. *Orthodoxy and Religious Observance*, p.1.
21. *Jewish Chronicle*, 24 March 1911, p.10.
22. Ibid., 12 May 1911, p.25.
23. The United Synagogue council, meeting the following March, 'sanctioned the appointment of the Rev. Dr J. Hochman being made permanent' (ibid., 8 March 1912, p.34).
24. Ibid., 28 July 1911, p.19. Immediately beneath this extract, there appeared a contrasting tribute to Hermann Adler from Morris Joseph's pulpit at the West London Synagogue: 'When we try to estimate the manifold responsibilities of an English Chief Rabbi under existing conditions, it is amazing that one man, single-handedly, should have discharged them thus ably for so many years. He did the work of half-a-dozen men, upborne by his high-souled devotion and by his overmastering sense of duty.'
25. *Report on the Sabbath Reading of the Scriptures in a Triennial Cycle*, New West End Synagogue, London (London: Wertheimer, Lea, 1913), pp.1–20. The resolution was adopted at a meeting of seat-holders held on 19 May 1912.
26. Ibid., p.2.
27. The members of the committee were Meyer A. Spielmann (chairman), Herbert M. Adler, Ernest L. Franklin, Delissa Joseph, Jerrold N. Joseph, Arthur L. Lazarus, Ernest Lesser, Robert B. Pyke, James Rossdale, Selim Samuel, James H. Solomon and Henry Van den Bergh. Those who gave evidence and replied to questions were Dr Adolph Büchler, Dayan Moses Hyamson, Rev. Michael Adler, Rev. Dr Joseph Hochman, Rev. A.A. Green and Elkan N. Adler. Additional evidence was supplied by Dr J. Elbogen (of Berlin), Rev. Morris Joseph and Rev. S. Levy.
28. *Report on the Sabbath Reading*, pp.18–20.
29. Ephraim Levine, *The History of the New West End Synagogue, 1879–1929* (Aldershot: John Drew, 1929), pp.26–7.
30. *Jewish Chronicle*, 28 February 1913, p.13.
31. 'The Chief Rabbinate', in *Jewish Review*, III, 17 (January 1913), Norman Bentwich and Joseph Hochman (eds), p.382.
32. Ibid., III, 18 (March 1913), pp.465–6.
33. Told to John M. Shaftesley, a former editor of the *Jewish Chronicle*, by congregants of Hochman's and related in 'Religious Controversies', in Salmond S. Levin (ed.), *A Century of Anglo-Jewish Life, 1870–1970* (London: United Synagogue, 1971), pp.107–8.
34. 'The Chief Rabbi and the Ministry', in *Jewish Review*, IV, 23 (January–February 1914), Norman Bentwich and Joseph Hochman (eds), pp.381–4.
35. 'The Opportunity of the Synagogue', ibid., p.380.
36. Hochman had anglicised his name after becoming involved in a number of non-ministerial activities, most notably women's suffrage (both politically and within the synagogue), though he continued to use the original spelling in the *Jewish Review*. He was president of the West End Jewish Literary Society, deputy chairman of the Order of Ancient Maccabeans, and founder of the Notting Hill Jewish Lads' Clubs. His published writings included *An Ancient Hebrew Inscription at Oppenheim* (1906) and *Jerusalem Temple Festivities* (1908).
37. *Jewish Chronicle*, 13 August 1915, p.6.
38. Ibid., 10 September 1910, p.8.

Notes 415

39. The Rev. Dr Joshua Abelson (born Merthyr Tydfil, 1873; died Leeds, 1940), a graduate of Jews' College and University College London, was headmaster of the Bristol Hebrew School before becoming minister to that city's Hebrew Congregation in 1899. Eight years on, he was appointed principal of Aria College in Portsmouth, a theological institution established in 1874 with an endowment bequeathed by Lewis Aria. Later, he served in Cardiff (1919) and at the Great Synagogue, Leeds (1920–1938). Following Hockman's resignation, the pulpit of the New West End Synagogue remained vacant until March 1916, when Ephraim Levine, then one of the ministers of the St John's Wood Synagogue, was invited to fill the post.
40. *Jewish Chronicle*, 20 August 1915, pp.12–13.
41. German historian and biblical scholar Heinrich Graetz (1817–1891) was an early disciple of Samson Raphael Hirsch, from whom he later became estranged, allying himself with the historical approach of Zechariah Frankel (1801–1873), the founder of Conservative Judaism.
42. 'The end of my days', Hockman's last words in the interview, came on 5 April 1942, with his death, in Richmond, Surrey, at the age of 59 (*Jewish Chronicle*, 17 April 1942, p.6).
43. 'Lord Rothschild', eulogy delivered at the Great Synagogue, London, on 19 April 1915, in J.H. Hertz, *Sermons, Addresses and Studies*, Vol. I (London: Soncino Press, 1938), p.79.
44. Immediately after resigning from the New West End Synagogue, Hockman enlisted as a trooper in the City of London Yeomanry Corps, eventually obtaining a commission in the Royal Artillery. After the war, he took up legal studies and was called to the Bar (Inner Temple) in 1920, having passed the final examination of the Council of Legal Education (*Jewish Chronicle*, 23 January 1920, p.19). Eight years later, from his chambers at Paper Buildings, he was appointed legal adviser to the King of Siam, where he spent a number of years (ibid., 17 April 1942, p.6). He subsequently returned to Britain, taking up membership of his former congregation. Louis Jacobs, *Helping With Inquiries: An Autobiography*, (London and Portland, OR: Vallentine Mitchell, 1989), p.106.

CHAPTER 10

1. Lawrence Rigal and Rosita Rosenberg, *Liberal Judaism: The First Hundred Years* (London: Liberal Judaism – Union of Liberal and Progressive Synagogues, 2004), p.45, citing Leonard Montefiore in the *West London Synagogue Review*, XXVIII, 9 (May 1954) p.278.
2. 'The "Strange Fire" of Schism', preached at the Lauderdale Road Sephardi Congregation, London, 26 April 1914, in *Sermons, Addresses and Studies*, Vol. I (London: Soncino Press, 1938), pp.309–10. Based on Leviticus 10:1–2, 'And Nadab and Abihu, the sons of Aaron, took each of them his censer, and put fire therein, and laid incense thereon, and offered strange fire before the Lord, which He had not commanded them. And there came forth fire from before the Lord, and devoured them, and they died before the Lord.'
3. 'Cohesion or Decadence', preached at the Bayswater Synagogue, London, 8 July 1916, in Herman Gollancz, *Fifty Years After: Sermons And Addresses Setting Forth The Teachings and Spirit of Judaism*, Third Series (London: Oxford University Press, 1924), pp.66–72; *Jewish Chronicle*, 21 July 1916, pp.10–11.
4. 'Reconstruction', based on I Kings 6:7 and preached at the Singer's Hill Synagogue, Birmingham, 8 February 1919, in *Sermons, Addresses and Studies*, Vol. I (London: Soncino Press, 1938), pp.313–14.
5. Robert Waley Cohen (1877–1952), son of Nathaniel Cohen (a pioneer of labour exchanges and university appointment boards) and Julia Waley, and nephew of Lionel Louis Cohen, the United Synagogue's principal founder, was managing director of the Shell Transport and Trading Company; chairman of the Palestine Corporation and the Economic Board for Palestine; treasurer (1913–1918), vice-president (1918–1942), and president (1942–1952) of the United Synagogue; and a founder (1942) of the Council of Christians and Jews. He was knighted in 1920. See Robert Henriques, *Sir Robert Waley Cohen, 1877–1952* (London: Secker and Warburg, 1966).
6. Louis Samuel Montagu (1869–1927) was elected to the presidency of the Federation of Synagogues on Swaythling's death in 1911, when he also assumed the baronage as the eldest son. He shared neither his father's religious outlook nor his Zionism, which he regarded as 'a profound danger to the safety and standing of the Anglo-Jewish community'. Geoffrey Alderman, *The Federation of Synagogues, 1887–1987* (London: Federation of Synagogues, 1987), p.42. Louis Montagu married Gladys Goldsmid, daughter of Colonel A.E.W. Goldsmid; their second son, Ewen Edward Samuel Montagu (1901–1985), was president of the United Synagogue (1954–1962) during a particularly sensitive period in the organisation's history (see chapter 15).
7. F.C. Stern, OBE, MC – later Sir Frederick Stern, a noted City banker and horticulturist – had served as a major in Egypt and Palestine and mixed with young Jewish soldiers who had complained of a lack of rabbis. He told Jews' College council that in Gallipoli he had never encountered a rabbi and that in Palestine he had seen three, 'but never in the front-line trenches'. He had returned home 'with the conclusion that I ought to do something', and had found in Waley Cohen a man of similar views. The Jewish War Memorial Scheme was born out of their discussions and survives to this day as the Jewish Memorial Council.
8. *Jewish Chronicle*, 9 May 1919, pp.15–17, and 16 May 1919, p.17.

9. Ibid., 13 June 1919, pp.8–9. Regarding the naming of the Memorial, Israel Zangwill wrote: 'Without pronouncing any opinion on this scheme, may I suggest that it would be a *chillul Hashem* to revitalise Jewish life in connection with a "War" Memorial? Even in my little Sussex village [East Preston], I have secured the recognition that our commemoration of the local dead ought to take the form not of a "War" but of a "Peace Memorial" – a memorial of the peace they died to secure ... [A] war memorial to foster a religion whose essential aspiration is the peace of mankind would be peculiarly grotesque.' *Jewish Chronicle*, 30 May 1919, p.12.
10. Ibid., 19 September 1919, p.18.
11. J.H. Hertz, *Traditional Judaism: An Appeal for the Jewish War Memorial*, preached at the New West End Synagogue, London, 18 October 1919 (London: Williams, Lea, 1919), pp.3–14; reprinted (abridged and amended) as 'Religion and Life', in *Sermons, Addresses and Studies*, Vol. I (London: Soncino Press, 1938), pp.288–93.
12. *Jewish Chronicle*, 14 November 1919, pp.14–15.
13. Ibid., 19 December 1919, p.30.
14. The sermon was based on the text in Genesis (33:12–14), 'and I will journey on gently, according to the pace of the cattle that are before me, and according to the pace of the children, until I come unto my Lord unto Seir'.
15. *Jewish Chronicle*, 19 December 1919, p.31.
16. An editorial in the *Jewish Chronicle* noted: 'We have reason to believe that the invitation to preach was not extended to him [Mattuck] by the Ministers of the Congregation, and that the assent of these gentlemen was not asked until after the invitation was given, when courtesy would, of course, have prevented a refusal.' 'An Inconsistent Invitation', 23 January 1920, p.7.
17. The reference is to Lionel Jacobs, described as 'one of the foremost of "Liberal" Jews and, if we mistake not, one of the founders of Rabbi Mattuck's Congregation'. The issue was widely covered in the *Jewish Chronicle* (leading article, 9 January 1920, p.10, and 'Are "Liberal" Jews Jews?', pp.21–2, reprinted from the *Jewish World*).
18. Ibid.
19. Ibid., 6 February 1920, p.21.
20. Ibid., p.22.
21. Ibid., 13 February 1920, pp.15–16.
22. Waley Cohen to Hertz, 20 October 1921, London Metropolitan Archives, LMA ACC/2805/4/1/22.
23. Waley Cohen to Hertz, 7 November 1921, ibid.
24. *Jewish Chronicle*, 20 January 1922, pp.14–15, 21.
25. Ibid., 27 January 1922, pp.17–20.
26. Ibid., 10 March 1922, p.17. The charge was levelled by the conference chairman and movement founder, Woolf Wachman, who declared that 'Orthodox Judaism does not permit of any compromise', and that upon the results of their deliberations 'depends the future of Orthodox Judaism in this country'. The conference was held at the Monnickendam Rooms, Great Alie Street, Aldgate, on 5 March 1920.
27. Born in Lomza, Poland, Herzog (1888–1959) was 9 when his father, Rabbi Joel Herzog, emigrated to Britain and settled in Leeds. Isaac Herzog served as rabbi in Belfast before becoming Chief Rabbi of the Irish Free State (forerunner of the Republic of Ireland) in 1921. In 1937, he succeeded Abraham Isaac Kook (1865–1935) as Ashkenazi Chief Rabbi of Palestine, and later of Israel.
28. The Organisation's terms for co-operating with the War Memorial Scheme, and its agreement 'that immediate steps must be taken to counteract the activities of the work undertaken by the Liberal Jews in the East End', were outlined at a conference held in London on 1 February 1920 (ibid., 6 February 1920, pp.21–2), and reinforced in a letter from Wachman to the *Jewish Chronicle* (13 February 1920, p.16).
29. Ibid., 19 December 1919, p.31.
30. Hertz to de Rothschild, 6 March 1922, LMA ACC/2805/4/1/22.
31. 'Mentor' was the paper's joint owner and managing editor, Leopold Greenberg.
32. 'In The Communal Armchair: From My Note Book', *Jewish Chronicle*, 7 April 1922, p.9.
33. Albert M. Hyamson, *Jews' College, London, 1855–1955* (London: Jews' College, 1955), p.102.
34. This sum was later increased to £2,000 a year for the maintenance of the College. J.H. Hertz, opening address at the Conference of Anglo-Jewish Preachers, Jews' College, 12 July 1927, in *Sermons, Addresses and Studies*, Vol. II, (London: Soncino Press, 1938), p.166.
35. For an account of this episode, see Henriques, *Sir Robert Waley Cohen*, pp.333–4.

CHAPTER 11

1. Hertz to Aaron Blashki, a potential backer for his commentary on the Chumash, in Harvey Meirovich, *A Vindication of Judaism: The Polemics of the Hertz Pentateuch* (New York and Jerusalem: Jewish Theological Seminary of America, 1998), p.23.
2. Prefatory note to J.H. Hertz, *Affirmations of Judaism* (London: Oxford University Press, 1927), p.7.
3. A reference to Zipporah's circumcision of her son, Exodus 4:25–6.
4. *The New Paths: Whither Do They Lead* – I, preached at the New West End Synagogue, London, on the first day

# Notes 417

of Chanukkah, 12 December 1925, based on Psalm 119:126, 'It is time to act for the Lord; they have made void Thy Law.' Annotated texts of this and the subsequent two sermons are reprinted in *Affirmations of Judaism*, pp.149–85.
5. *The New Paths: Whither Do They Lead* – II, preached at the Hampstead Synagogue, London, on the eighth day of Chanukkah, 19 December 1925, based on Jeremiah 6:16, 'Thus saith the Lord: Stand ye in the ways and see, and ask for the old paths where is the good way, and walk therein, and ye shall find rest for your souls.'
6. Published and circulated by the Jewish Religious Union for the Advancement of Liberal Judaism, London, and reproduced in the *Jewish Chronicle*, 8 January 1926, pp.16, 18.
7. *The New Paths: Whither Do They Lead* – III, preached at the St John's Wood Synagogue, London, on Shabbat Shirah, 30 January 1926, based on Isaiah 58:1, 'Cry aloud, spare not; lift up thy voice like a trumpet, and declare unto My people their rebellion.'
8. Leading article, *Jewish Chronicle*, 25 December 1925, p.7.
9. Ibid.
10. Exodus 15:2.
11. Published together, with *The New Paths*, I-III, as *Affirmations of Judaism*, they were delivered at the Brondesbury, Bayswater, Dalston, New, Stoke Newington, East London and New West End Synagogues between 30 March 1926 and 29 January 1927. One of the two addresses on Jewish religious education, at Leeds on 6 July 1924, opened the conference of the Central Committee of Jewish Education.
12. 'The Unity of God', in *Affirmations of Judaism*, pp.17, 19–20.
13. 'The Revelation at Mount Sinai', ibid., pp.27–8.
14. Mishneh Torah, Teshuvah, 3:11.
15. Ethics of the Fathers, 1:17.
16. 'The Brotherhood of Israel', in *Affirmations of Judaism*, pp.124–8.
17. Waley Cohen to Hertz, 20 April 1926, in Aubrey Newman, *Chief Rabbi Dr Joseph H. Hertz, CH*, lecture delivered at Woburn House, London, 25 September 1972, to mark the centenary of Hertz's birth (London: United Synagogue, 1972), pp.15–16. The address was given in the presence of Chief Rabbi Dr Immanuel Jakobovits and Emeritus Chief Rabbi Sir Israel Brodie.
18. Robert Henriques, *Sir Robert Waley Cohen, 1877–1952* (London: Secker and Warburg, 1966), p.344.
19. Ibid., Hertz to Waley Cohen, 22 September 1924.
20. 'The Brotherhood of Israel', in *Affirmations of Judaism*, pp.126–7.
21. Michael Leigh, 'Reform Judaism in Britain, 1840–1970', in *Reform Judaism*, Dow Marmur (ed.) (London: Reform Synagogues of Great Britain, 1973), p.36; Anne J. Kershen and Jonathan A. Romain, *Tradition and Change: A History of Reform Judaism in Britain, 1840–1995* (London and Portland, OR: Vallentine Mitchell, 1995), p.97; and Lawrence Rigal and Rosita Rosenberg, *Liberal Judaism: The First Hundred Years* (London: Union of Liberal and Progressive Synagogues, 2004), pp.60–2.
22. *Jewish Chronicle*, 23 July 1926, p.5.

CHAPTER 12

1. *Jewish Chronicle*, 2 April 1926, p.15.
2. Unsigned obituary, ibid., 28 October 1927, p.12.
3. Ibid., 2 April 1926, p.15, reporting the annual meeting of the West London Synagogue.
4. Ibid., 23 April 1926, p.13.
5. Ibid., 9 July 1926, p.21.
6. See Prologue.
7. *Jewish Chronicle*, 9 July 1926, p.20.
8. Opening address at the Conference of Anglo-Jewish Preachers, Jews' College, 12 July 1927, in *Sermons, Addresses and Studies*, Vol. II (London: Soncino Press, 1938), pp.152–3.
9. This correspondence spanned the first fortnight of 1928, culminating in Waley Cohen's letter to Hertz on 19 January, quoted in Robert Henriques, *Sir Robert Waley Cohen, 1877–1952* (London: Secker and Warburg, 1966), pp.340, 345–7.
10. *Jewish Chronicle*, 26 March, 1915, p.18.
11. Hertz's memorial sermon was announced in the *Jewish Chronicle*, 21 December 1917, p.6.
12. Ibid., 28 October 1927, p.12.
13. *West London Synagogue Magazine*, March 1925, p.2.
14. *Jewish Chronicle*, 6 March 1925, p.16. The lecture, to the West London Synagogue Association on 26 February 1925, was entitled 'The Oldest Code of Laws in the World' [the Hammurabi Code].
15. Hertz was to address the West London Synagogue Association again ten years later when, having been 'enthusiastically received', he spoke in the communal hall on 'Ideals of Free Government in Israel'. Waley presided, and Simmonds and Harold Reinhart (see note 17) took part in the discussion (ibid., 22 November 1935, p.37).
16. Sub-heading to the report, ibid., 1 June 1934, p.10.

17. Born in Portland, Oregon, Harold Frederick Reinhart (1891–1969) was ordained at Hebrew Union College, Cincinnati, and served a number of American congregations before his appointment to the West London Synagogue in 1929. A year after taking office, he published his definition of Reform Judaism (*West London Synagogue Magazine*, February 1930, p.83), both as a personal declaration of faith and as a manifesto for his ministry to West London and beyond:

    THIS IS REFORM

    To be Jewish enough to have faith in the inner resources of the Jewish people, and its capacity for universal ideals and human service; and so to identify Jewish destiny with broad and progressive paths.
    To be Jewish enough to believe that truth is the seal of God, and so to allow the light of reason to play upon our past, our present and our future, and to pursue that light with confidence and with courage.
    To be Jewish enough to feel that man is the partner of God in the work of creation, and that it is our task to build the kingdom of heaven here on earth through the perception and fulfilment of God's living will progressively revealed through human history.
    To be Jewish enough to seek to love the Lord our God, not with formula and ritual, but with heart and soul and might, and to strive after that true and simple spiritual exercise which releases and nourishes the divine within us.

    THIS IS REFORM

    In 1957, Reinhart and a group of congregational supporters left the West London and established the independent Westminster Synagogue in Knightsbridge. 'His departure was due to disputes over internal synagogue policy and the direction of the congregation, with Reinhart feeling that elements who lacked spirituality and vision were taking over; while many members considered that Reinhart was becoming increasingly autocratic and out of touch with their needs.' Anne J. Kershen and Jonathan A. Romain, *Tradition and Change: A History of Reform Judaism in Britain, 1840–1995* (London and Portland, OR: Vallentine Mitchell, 1995), pp.137, 217. See also *Jewish Chronicle*, 22 August 1969, p.31.
18. 'Burying the Hatchet', ibid., 1 June 1934, pp.7–8.
19. Reference to the rise of Nazism in Europe, dealt with at length in Hertz's opening addresses to the Conference of Anglo-Jewish Preachers, Woburn House, London, 10 May 1932, and 28 May 1935.
20. 'Union of Orthodox Hebrew Congregations', letter from D. Melnick, secretary of the UOHC, *Jewish Chronicle*, 15 June 1934, p.14. See also Schonfeld to Ornstein, note 39 below.
21. Reference to the battle fought during 1931/2 to exempt shechitah from the scope of a Slaughter of Animals Bill which sought to enforce prior stunning, in contravention of Jewish law. With the concurrence of the Chief Rabbinate and the Board of Deputies, a clause was formulated to the effect that only shochetim holding a licence from the Chief Rabbi would be allowed to operate. The Union of Orthodox Hebrew Congregations saw this as an attack on religious liberty and as an attempt by the Chief Rabbinate to enforce its authority over the entire community by means of an Act of Parliament. The matter was resolved through the establishment of a Rabbinical Commission – comprising ten rabbis from across the Orthodox community – to license shochetim; its composition was set out in a schedule to the Act. See Bernard Homa, *Orthodoxy in Anglo-Jewry, 1880–1940* (London: Jewish Historical Society of England, 1969), pp.28–30.
22. 'The Chief Rabbi at Berkeley Street', letter from Rabbi Dr Samuel Daiches, *Jewish Chronicle*, 22 June 1934, p.24.
23. Waley Cohen to Hertz, 18 June 1934, London Metropolitan Archives, LMA ACC/2805/4/1/47.
24. Hertz to Waley Cohen, 4 July 1937, LMA ACC/2805/4/1/22.
25. Waley Cohen to Hertz, 6 July 1934, LMA ACC/2805/4/1/47.
26. Hertz to Laski, January 1935, in Homa, *Orthodoxy in Anglo-Jewry*, pp.34–5. The Chief Rabbi's ruling applied specifically to the Liberal Jewish Synagogue, St John's Wood. Two years later, he granted similar certification to the Liverpool Liberal Jewish Synagogue, but a fiercer battle was to follow after his death in relation to other Liberal congregations (see chapter 13).
27. *Jewish Chronicle*, 14 May 1937, p.24, 'a striking feature of ... a great united service', noted the paper. In the wardens' box were Waley Cohen and Frank Samuel, representing the United Synagogue; Israel Feldman, warden, Great Synagogue; Claude Montefiore, Liberal Jewish Synagogue; Gershom Delgado, Spanish and Portuguese Synagogue; Julian G. Lousada, West London Synagogue.
28. Mattuck to Hertz, 11 March 1937, LMA ACC/2805/4/1/20.
29. Mattuck to Hertz, 21 April 1937, ibid.
30. Lily Montagu's sister, Henrietta (Netta).
31. J.C. Stobart (for director of programmes, BBC) to Hertz, 15 May 1929, LMA ACC/2805/4/1/13.
32. Hertz to Stobart, 20 May 1929, ibid.
33. J.W. Welch (Broadcasting House, Bristol) to Hertz, 4 December 1939, ibid.
34. Welch to Hertz, 14 December 1939, ibid.
35. Aaron Sorasky, 'The Life and Times of Rabbenu Yechezkel Abramsky', in *Emunah: Pathways in Contemporary Jewish Thought*, 2 (January 1990) (Israel: Kollel Tal Torah, Tel Ganim), p.9.

36. Yechiel Michal ben Aaron Isaac Halevy Epstein (1829–1908), a disciple of Rabbi Isaac of Volozhin, was the author of the *Aruch HaShulchan*, consisting of novellae and halachic rulings on the four sections of the Shulchan Aruch. Having received semichah from Rabbi Elijah Goldberg in his native town of Bobruisk, Belorussia, he ministered at Novosybkov before becoming the rabbi of Novaradok, where he remained until his death.
37. Abramsky's contract, signed after protracted negotiations, included a special clause – at his insistence – 'that he would never be called upon to do anything which was contrary to the laws and regulations of the Shulchan Aruch' (*Jewish Chronicle*, 24 September 1976, p.22).
38. Ibid., 28 June 1935, p.16.
39. Ibid., p.18. Two decades earlier, Schonfeld had criticised the standards of the London Beth Din regarding the 'various features' to which the Union of Orthodox Hebrew Congregations yet again took exception and which remained 'unaltered'. 'In consequence of its constitution', he wrote to United Synagogue secretary Philip Ornstein (15 March 1917), 'and more so as an outcome of its – no doubt well-meant – endeavours to satisfy also the non-observant sections of the community, the Beth Din appears frequently not quite free from worldly influences. The result is often a compromise which not only thousands of strictly observant Jews find unsatisfactory but, we are convinced, must also be repugnant to members of the Beth Din itself' (Hertz Papers, MS 175, Hartley Library, Southampton University). Thus it was that, at an Adath-sponsored conference held six months before Abramsky's appointment, the chairman, Bernard Homa, announced that 'efforts are being made to establish an independent Orthodox Beth Din in London which shall satisfy, and minister to, the requirements of all Orthodox Jews in the metropolis' (*Jewish Chronicle*, 4 January 1935, p.10).
40. 'The New Dayan', letter from 'East-Ender', ibid., 28 June 1935, pp.19–20.
41. Ibid., p.19.
42. Isaiah 49:17.
43. Aaron Sorasky, *Melech Beyofyo [A King In His Glory]*, Vol. I (published privately, Jerusalem, 2004), p.393. Subtitled *The Life, Work and Holy Path of the Gaon Rabbi Yechezkel Abramsky, Author of Chazon Yechezkel*, the two-volume biography, in Hebrew, was written with the co-operation of the dayan's youngest son, Menachem Ezra Abramsky, who died in November 2006. On Abramsky's years in Britain, see also Cyril Domb, 'Dayan Yechezkel Abramsky: A Centenary Tribute', in *L'Eylah*, 23 (Pesach 5747) (London: Office of the Chief Rabbi and Jews' College, April 1987), pp.54–6.
44. Twenty-one-year-old Solomon Schonfeld had succeeded his father in 1933 as head of the Union of Orthodox Hebrew Congregations, three years after the latter's death at the age of 49. In January 1940, he married Judith Hertz, the eldest of the Chief Rabbi's three daughters.
45. Aubrey Newman, *The United Synagogue, 1870–1970* (London: Routledge and Kegan Paul, 1976), p.157. The remark is said to have been made to Dayan Harris Lazarus (Lazarus to United Synagogue honorary officers, 1944, memorandum 2206, United Synagogue archives, LMA).
46. Letter from Hertz to United Synagogue secretary Philip Goldberg, *Jewish Chronicle*, 12 February 1943, p.5.
47. Newman, *The United Synagogue*, pp.156–7.
48. Cohen to Reinhart, 6 October 1938; Beuno de Mesquita to Reinhart, 28 October 1938, Reinhart Papers, MS 171, Hartley Library, Southampton University.
49. On Edgar, see chapter 13, note 49.
50. Homa, *Orthodoxy in Anglo-Jewry*, p.46.
51. On Brodie, see chapter 13.
52. Newman, *The United Synagogue*, pp.107, 133–4; Kershen and Romain, *Tradition and Change*, pp.165–6.
53. Kershen and Romain, ibid., p.168.
54. *West London Synagogue Review*, June 1942, p.170.
55. Kershen and Romain, *Tradition and Change*, p.170.
56. *Jewish Chronicle*, 28 June 1940, p.1.
57. Ibid., 2 August 1940, pp.1, 11.
58. 'Recall to the Synagogue', I, delivered at the United Synagogue Conference, Woburn House, London, 25 July 1940, in J.H. Hertz, *Early and Late: Addresses, Messages, and Papers* (Hindhead, Surrey: Soncino Press, 1943), pp.153–9.
59. Cyrus Adler (1863–1940) was president of the Jewish Theological Seminary of America and of Dropsie College, and served as editor of the *Jewish Quarterly Review*.
60. 'Recall to the Synagogue', II, delivered at the Hampstead Synagogue, London, 17 August 1940, in *Early and Late*, pp.160–5.

CHAPTER 13

1. Aubrey Newman, *The United Synagogue, 1870–1970* (London: Routledge and Kegan Paul, 1976), p.156.
2. *Jewish Chronicle*, 9 May 1941, p.5.
3. Ibid., 16 May 1941, p.18.
4. Ibid., 23 May 1941, p.13.

5. Harold Reinhart to Leonard G. Montefiore, 31 May 1943, Reinhart Papers, MS 171, Hartley Library, Southampton University.
6. Note to a meeting of United Synagogue honorary officers, 6 May 1943, Goldberg Papers, MS 148, Hartley Library, Southampton University.
7. The action was brought in the High Court by the Rev. Maximilian Fried against Abram Isaac Bard. Fried complained that during a service on 13 October 1941 [Shemini Atseret], which he was conducting in his capacity as paid chazan, Bard, one of the wardens, said, 'You are reading the wrong prayer, shut up', and that, after the service, Bard said, 'You are suspended. You are not minister any longer.' The defence was a denial of the allegations, and alternative pleas of privilege and justification. Giving his reserved judgment, Mr Justice Atkinson said that, with regard to the dispute as to whether Psalm 27 should be read on the day in question, strict following of Jewish law required it to be read throughout the festival, although it was a local custom not to read it on the last day. There was nothing improper in Fried's reading it, said the judge, and he was satisfied that Bard had made use of the words attributed to him. Judgment for £400 and costs was entered against Bard, who was granted a stay of execution. *Jewish Chronicle*, 13 November 1942, p.14.
8. Honorary officers of the United Synagogue to Hertz, 14 March 1945, Hertz Papers, MS 175, Hartley Library, Southampton University.
9. Dayanim of the Chief Rabbi's Court to the honorary officers of the United Synagogue, 11 April 1945, Hertz Papers; *Jewish Chronicle*, 18 January 1946, p.14.
10. 'Crisis at United Synagogue: Grave Threat to Basis of Institution', *Jewish Chronicle*, 15 June 1945, pp.1, 5.
11. Ibid., 20 July 1945, pp.1, 13.
12. Hertz to honorary officers of the United Synagogue, 9 April 1945, Hertz Papers, MS 175.
13. *Jewish Chronicle*, 18 January 1946, p.1.
14. J.H. Hertz, preface to the first edition, *The Pentateuch and Haftorahs* (Oxford: Oxford University Press, 1936), p.vii.
15. Newman, *Chief Rabbi Dr Joseph H. Hertz*, lecture delivered at the Adolph Tuck Hall, Woburn House, London, 25 September 1972 (London: United Synagogue, 1972), pp.20–2.
16. *Jewish Chronicle*, 18 January 1946, p.15.
17. S.M. Lehrman, 'A Spiritual Warrior', in Wolf Gottlieb (ed.), *Essays and Addresses in Memory of the Very Rev. Dr Joseph Herman Hertz* (London: Mizrachi Federation of Great Britain and Ireland, 1947), pp.33–5.
18. Geoffrey Alderman, *Modern British Jewry* (Oxford: Clarendon Press, 1992), p.360.
19. Aaron Sorasky, *Melech Beyofyo [A King In His Glory]*, Vol. I (Jerusalem: privately published, 2004), p.393.
20. If a man refuses the obligation of *yibbum* (levirate marriage) to his widowed and childless sister-in-law, he is required to undergo the ceremony of *chalitzah*, during which she removes his shoe and spits in front of him, thereby freeing herself to marry someone else (Deuteronomy 25:5–10).
21. Yechezkel Abramsky, 'Who Represents Judaism?', in Sorasky, *Melech Beyofyo*, Vol. I, pp.394–6.
22. The letter, written in Hebrew and dated Rosh Chodesh Nisan 5705 (15 March 1945), was also signed by Dayanim Lazarus and Grunfeld.
23. 'Facing the Plague of Mixed Marriages', in Sorasky, *Melech Beyofyo*, Vol. I, pp.400–3.
24. *Jewish Chronicle*, 20 December 1946, p.6.
25. *Psak din* from Harris M. Lazarus (Deputy for the Chief Rabbi), I. Abramsky, I. Grunfeld, J. Jakobovits, and M. Swift to A.G. Brotman (secretary, Board of Deputies), 23 December 1946 – 5707, in ibid., 17 January 1947, p.5.
26. Dayanim to all members of the Board of Deputies, 8 January 1947 – 5707, in ibid., pp.1, 5. The penalty referred to in the letter, as laid down in Leviticus 20:10, is death. 'Marriage is not merely a "contract"; it is consecration, and adultery is far more than merely an offence against one of the parties to a contract. It is an offence against the Divine Commandment proclaimed at Sinai, and constitutes the annihilation of holiness in marriage.' Z. Frankel, quoted in J.H. Hertz, *The Pentateuch and Haftorahs*, 2nd edn, (London: Soncino Press, 1960), p.507.
27. *Jewish Chronicle*, 17 January 1947, p.5. The assembly was convened at the office of the Beth Din, in Creechurch Place, Aldgate, on 13 January 1947, and presided over by Lazarus.
28. Mattuck to Gluckstein, 12 January 1947, ibid., 24 January 1947, p.11.
29. 'The Beth Din's Reply to Dr Mattuck', letter from Lazarus, Abramsky, Grunfeld, Jakobovits, Swift, ibid., 31 January 1947, p.5.
30. 'Letter – and Spirit – of the Law', letter from Mattuck, ibid., 7 February 1947, p.5.
31. Cecil Roth, 'The Collapse of English Jewry', in *The Jewish Monthly*, 4, (July 1947) (London: Anglo-Jewish Association), pp.11–17.
32. *Jewish Chronicle*, 18 January 1946, p.10.
33. Philip Goldberg in a memorandum to the honorary officers, 1947, Goldberg Papers, MS 148, Hartley Library, Southampton University.
34. Newman, *The United Synagogue, 1870–1970*, p.182.
35. For a detailed account of the election process, see Miri J. Freud-Kandel, *Orthodox Judaism in Britain Since 1913* (London and Portland, OR: Vallentine Mitchell, 2006), pp.95–101; and, in relation to earlier elections,

# Notes

'The British Chief Rabbinate' ('By a Special Correspondent') in *The Jewish Monthly*, 2, 2 (May 1947), pp.23–33.
36. Newman, *The United Synagogue*, p.182. On Brodie's election, see Arthur Saul Super, 'Israel Brodie – Chief Rabbi', in *The Jewish Monthly*, 2, 3 (June 1948), pp.134–40.
37. John M. Shaftesley, 'Israel Brodie, Chief Rabbi: A Biographical Sketch', in *Essays Presented to Chief Rabbi Israel Brodie on the Occasion of his Seventieth Birthday*, H.J. Zimmels, J. Rabbinowitz, I. Finestein (eds), Jews' College Publications, NS 3 (London: Soncino Press, 1967), p.xxix.
38. Newman, *The United Synagogue*, p.183.
39. Israel Brodie, *Installation Sermon as Chief Rabbi of the United Hebrew Congregations of the British Commonwealth of Nations*, delivered at the New Synagogue, London, 28 June 1948, 21 Sivan 5708 (London: United Synagogue, 1948), pp.1–8.
40. Jonathan A. Romain, 'The Establishment of the Reform Beth Din in 1948: A Barometer of Religious Trends in Anglo-Jewry', paper presented to the Jewish Historical Society of England, 20 May 1993, in *Jewish Historical Studies*, XXXIII (1992–1994) (London: Jewish Historical Society of England, 1995), pp.249–63. For a detailed study of the subject, see Jonathan A. Romain, 'The Reform Beth Din: The Formation and Development of the Rabbinical Court of the Reform Synagogues of Great Britain, 1935–1965' (PhD diss., University of Leicester, 1990), upon which are based, in part, the Orthodox reactions to the Reform Beth Din's establishment as examined in the next chapter. Romain, a leading figure in the British Reform movement, is the rabbi of the Maidenhead Synagogue, Berkshire.
41. *Jewish Chronicle*, 25 March 1949, pp.1, 5.
42. Ibid., 29 April 1949, pp.1, 19.
43. Ibid., 20 May 1949, p.19.
44. Ibid., 3 June 1949, p.5.
45. Ibid., 13 May 1949, p.6; 3 June 1949, p.5.
46. Isaac Levy, *Historic Judaism Versus Liberal Judaism*, sermon preached at the Hampstead Synagogue, London, 7 May 1949 (London: United Synagogue, 1949), pp.1–7.
47. On the Union (later Conference) of Anglo-Jewish Preachers, see I. Livingstone, *The Union of Anglo-Jewish Preachers: A Retrospect* (London: Union of Anglo-Jewish Preachers, 1949).
48. *Jewish Chronicle*, 13 May 1949, pp.1, 5.
49. Mattuck was succeeded as senior minister earlier that year by Leslie I. Edgar.
50. I.I. Mattuck, 'Liberal Jews and Marriage', *Jewish Chronicle*, 2 December 1949, p.13.
51. Proverbs 14:12.
52. I. Grunfeld, 'Whither Anglo-Jewry' – I, ibid., 30 December 1949, p.13; – II, ibid., 6 January 1950, pp.13, 19.
53. Israel Brodie, 'Opening Address', in *Addresses given at the Ninth Conference of Anglo-Jewish Preachers* (London: Standing Committee, 1951), p.14. The conference was held at the Golders Green Synagogue, London, 14–17 May 1951.
54. I. Grunfeld, 'Problems of Modern Jewish Marriage and Family Life', in *Addresses given at the Tenth Conference of Anglo-Jewish Preachers* (London: Standing Committee, 1953), pp.29–44. The conference was held at the Golders Green Synagogue, London, 4–7 May 1953.
55. On Redcliffe Nathan Salaman, see *Jewish Chronicle*, 17 June 1955, p.12; James W. Parkes, 'Redcliffe Nathan Salaman', memorial address delivered before the Jewish Historical Society of England, 26 October 1955, in *Transactions of the Jewish Historical Society of England*, XVIII (1953–1955), pp.296–8; George H. Fried, *Encyclopaedia Judaica*, Vol. 14 (Jerusalem: Keter, 1972), pp.670–1.
56. Under the biblical laws of mixed species (Leviticus 19:19, Deuteronomy 22:11) the wearing of cloth made from wool and linen threads (*shaatnez*) is prohibited.
57. Redcliffe N. Salaman, *Whither Lucien Wolf's Anglo-Jewish Community?* The Lucien Wolf Memorial Lecture, 1953 (London: Jewish Historical Society of England, 1954).
58. *Jewish Chronicle*, 22 May 1953, p.12.
59. Ibid.
60. Ibid. A detailed account of this incident, its background and its place in the communal history of the period is contained in Todd M. Endelman, 'Practices of a Low Anthropologic Level: A Shechitah Controversy of the 1950s', in Anne J. Kershen (ed.) *Food in the Migrant Experience*, (Aldershot and Burlington, VT: Ashgate Publishing, 2002), pp.77–97.
61. *Jewish Chronicle*, 20 February 1959, p.5.
62. Sefton D. Temkin, 'An Old Controversy', in ibid.

## CHAPTER 14

1. Minutes of the Assembly of Ministers, 1 August 1956, in Jonathan A. Romain, 'The Reform Beth Din: The Formation and Development of the Rabbinical Court of the Reform Synagogues of Great Britain, 1935–1965' (Ph.D. diss., University of Leicester, 1990), p.155. Further points were later added to these conditions, providing for a smooth administrative process and ensuring that all cases were fully documented (ibid., pp.157–8). The duration of tuition leading to conversions was the subject of exten-

sive debate, with the Assembly of Ministers declaring at one stage (30 January 1957), 'The period of "nine months to a year" is mentioned only because the experience of the majority of ministers has shown that that is, in fact, the usual minimum. As stated also, however, many cases take fifteen months or even longer' (ibid., p.164).
2. Ibid., p.170.
3. On Swift, see chapter 15, note 24.
4. *Jewish Chronicle*, 6 March 1959, p.8.
5. Anne J. Kershen and Jonathan A. Romain, *Tradition and Change: A History of Reform Judaism in Britain, 1840–1995* (London and Portland, OR: Vallentine Mitchell, 1995), p.158.
6. Dayan Mark Gollop to the Rev. Vivian Simmons, 30 October 1930. Reinhart Papers, MS 171, Hartley Library, Southampton University.
7. In 1955, the number of proselytes successfully admitted by the London Beth Din was 23, out of 237 applications (Dayan Meyer Steinberg, *Jewish Chronicle*, 1 April 1960, p.12).
8. Romain, 'The Reform Beth Din', p.182.
9. *Annual Report of the Reform Beth Din*, 1962, p.2.
10. Israel Brodie, Opening Address, First Conference of European Rabbis, Amsterdam, 4 November 1957, in *The Strength of My Heart* (London: G.J. George, 1969), p.180.
11. Rabbi Chaim Cohen, of Amsterdam, *Jewish Chronicle*, 1 April 1960, p.12.
12. The Hungarian Rabbi Moses Sofer (1762–1839), who forbade the introduction of anything new into Judaism to preserve its traditional values. His vehement opposition to the Reform movement is continued to this day by his descendants and their disciples.
13. An excerpt of this pronouncement appeared in the *Jewish Chronicle*, 25 March 1960, p.8. It was reprinted in full – in Hebrew and English – in Morris Swift, *Jewish Marriage and Divorce*, Publication No. 9 (London: Beth Din, 1962 – 5722), pp.16–17. The declaration, dated Kislev 5720 (December 1959), was signed by the Chief Rabbi and Dayanim I. Grossnass, A. Rapoport, M. Lew, M. Steinberg and M. Swift.
14. Israel Brodie, Opening Address, Second Conference of European Rabbis, Westcliff, 22 March 1960, in *Jewish Chronicle*, 25 March 1960, p.8.
15. Romain, 'The Reform Beth Din', pp.206–7.
16. *Jewish Chronicle*, 23 March 1962, p.8. The ban, on the direct orders of the Chief Rabbi, came into operation at the end of 1961, with synagogue secretaries being notified of the revised hiring regulations. In effect, it applied only to Reform and Liberal celebrants and also, in the case of weddings, to those not married in a synagogue. Members of the Federation of Synagogues, which accepted the Chief Rabbi's authority, and of the Union of Orthodox Hebrew Congregations were not affected by the ban.
17. The second/third-century Babylonian talmudic sage Mar Samuel was the head of the academy at Nehardea and, with his colleague Rav, was instrumental in making Babylonia the main centre of Torah studies. His halachic expertise was in the field of civil law, and the dictum *dina demalchuta dina* ('the law of the land is law') – cited in these pages – emanated from him.
18. Israel Brodie, foreword to Swift, *Jewish Marriage and Divorce*, p.3.
19. Ibid., pp.12–15.
20. Romain, 'The Reform Beth Din', p.210.
21. Statement by the Assembly of Ministers, 21 March 1962, in ibid., pp.285–6.
22. Ibid., pp.210–12, citing the minutes of the West London Synagogue council, 18 October 1962, and of the Assembly of Ministers, 31 October 1962.
23. Jonathan A. Romain, 'The Establishment of the Reform Beth Din in 1948: A Barometer of Religious Trends in Anglo-Jewry', in *Jewish Historical Studies*, XXXIII (1992–1994) (London: Jewish Historical Society of England, 1995), p.261.
24. 'Our Beth Din', undated manuscript in the Reform Beth Din archives, cited in Romain, ibid.
25. Born in Philadelphia in 1936, and ordained as a rabbi in New York City, Brichto moved to Britain in the 1960s and became the first executive director of the Union of Liberal and Progressive Synagogues.
26. An *agunah* is a 'chained wife' or 'tied woman' whose husband has disappeared with no evidence of his death, or whose husband has deserted her and refuses to give her a *get*, leaving her unable to remarry.
27. Sidney Brichto, 'Validity of Liberal Marriages', *Jewish Chronicle*, 3 December 1965, p.8.
28. *Jewish Chronicle*, 17 December 1965, p.1.
29. Ibid., p.14.
30. Ibid.
31. Sermon at the Hampstead Synagogue, London, 18 December 1965. Ibid.
32. Sermon at the Western Synagogue, London, 18 December 1965. Ibid.
33. Saturday-night meal marking the departure of the Sabbath, traditionally depicted as a 'queen'.
34. *Jewish Chronicle*, 24 December 1965, p.12.
35. *Jewish Review*, December 1965, quoted in *Jewish Chronicle*, 31 December 1965, p.1.
36. *Jewish Chronicle*, ibid.
37. Ibid., p.12.
38. Ibid.

## CHAPTER 15

1. Louis Jacobs, *We Have Reason to Believe* (London: Vallentine Mitchell, 1957), p.61.
2. Ibid., p.62.
3. Ibid., p.63.
4. Ibid., pp.65–6.
5. Ibid., p.67.
6. Ibid., p.68, quoting J. Abelson's translation of Maimonides, *Jewish Quarterly Review*, OS XIX (1907), p.24ff.
7. The Documentary Hypothesis: 'that there are four documents of diverse ages to be detected in the Pentateuch, put together by a series of redactors ... The conclusion that the Pentateuch is, in part at least, post-Mosaic, and that it is a composite work, is accepted by every Bible scholar of note today who "plays the game" – that is, who does not dismiss the scholarly enterprise itself as erroneous. This is based on the strongest evidence and is extremely unlikely to be overthrown.' Louis Jacobs, 'Reflections on a Controversy', in *Quest*, 1 (September 1965), Jonathan Stone (ed.), (London: Paul Hamlyn), p.5.
8. *We Have Reason to Believe*, pp.69–70.
9. Ibid., p.71.
10. The italics are Jacobs'.
11. *We Have Reason to Believe*, pp.73–4.
12. Ibid., pp.77–8. Jacobs here extensively quotes examples from the talmudic and rabbinic writings over the centuries.
13. Ibid., pp.81–2.
14. From the Epilogue to the third edition of *We Have Reason to Believe* (London: Vallentine Mitchell, 1965, p.139), in which, writes Jacobs in a 'Retrospect' to the fifth edition, 'I essayed to provide an elaboration and defence of my views' (2004, p.viii).
15. *Jewish Chronicle*, 11 May 1962, p.10. This statement was made to the paper by the joint treasurers of the College, Laurence Jacobs and Felix Levy.
16. Louis Jacobs, *Helping With Inquiries: An Autobiography* (London and Portland, OR: Vallentine Mitchell, 1989), p.49.
17. Dessler (1891–1954), born in Homel, Russia, was a follower and exponent of the *musar* (ethicist) movement of Rabbi Israel Lipkin Salanter. In 1929, he settled in London, where he ministered and became the supervisor of a large Talmud Torah. In 1941, he co-founded the Gateshead kolel with the Rev. David Dryan, and five years later accepted an invitation to become the spiritual supervisor of the Ponevezh yeshivah in Bene Brak, Israel. He was the author of the posthumously published three-volume *Michtav Me-Eliyahu* (1955–1964).
18. *Helping With Inquiries*, p.59.
19. Ibid., p.54.
20. Ibid., p.69. See also Jacobs' 'Four Rabbinic Positions in Anglo-Jewry', in *The Jewish Year Book 2000*, Stephen W. Massil (ed.), (London and Portland, OR: Vallentine Mitchell in association with the *Jewish Chronicle*, 2000), pp.76–7.
21. Jacobs was Stein's only undergraduate student at the time and was later to be supervised by him for his PhD thesis on 'The Business Life of the Jews in Babylon, 200–500 CE'.
22. *Helping With Inquiries*, p.76.
23. This episode is described in some detail, ibid., pp.100–3.
24. Liverpool-born Morris Swift (1907–1983) studied at the yeshivot of his native city and Manchester, Ponevezh, Radun and Mir, from many of whose sages he received semichah. After junior posts, he served as minister of the Brondesbury Synagogue and part-time dayan on the London Beth Din from 1945, moved to the Johannesburg Beth Din in 1949, and then to the Young Israel congregation of Los Angeles. He returned to Britain in 1956 as principal rabbi of the Federation of Synagogues and, after barely a year, rejoined the London Beth Din, of which he later became senior dayan (*Jewish Chronicle*, 23 September 1983, p.18).
25. Swift to Abramsky, 8 Nisan 5722 (12 April 1962), in Aaron Sorasky, *Melech Beyofyo* [*A King In His Glory*], Vol. II (Jerusalem: privately published, 2004), p.686. The letter is in Hebrew.
26. *Helping With Inquiries*, p.102.
27. See 'Four Rabbinic Positions', pp.77–9.
28. Ibid., pp.79–80.
29. Louis Jacobs, *Induction Sermon at the New West End Synagogue, London*, 13 February 1954 (London: Henry G. Morris, for the New West End Synagogue, 1954), p.1.
30. *New West End Synagogue Newsletter*, 7 (March 1954 – II Adar 5714), p.2. In a significant message to his congregants in the same newsletter, Jacobs wrote: 'It is indeed a high honour to be called upon to serve and interpret Judaism to a body of men and women who are serving the Jewish community, the State of Israel, our beloved country and the whole world with such distinction in so many fields ... It is hardly necessary for me to say that I intend taking a keen interest in all the activities of the congregation and have plans for one or two more ... [see note 33]. With your help, we can accomplish great things for

Judaism, and the future of the synagogue can be worthy of its inspiring past' (*Newsletter*, p.1). Under the heading 'Dates to Note', the newsletter includes details of Jacobs' planned address, entitled 'Judaism in the Future' – in a series at the New West End communal centre on 'The Jewish Contribution to Civilisation' – scheduled for 9 May 1954 (*Newsletter*, p.2).
31. Jacobs, *Induction Sermon*, pp.1–4.
32. The induction merited a twenty-eight-line report in the *Jewish Chronicle* (18 February 1954, p.6), with two sentences devoted to the sermon (including one paying tribute to Jacobs' predecessors), and seven lines to the kiddush.
33. The significance of Jacobs' early reference (note 30) to 'one or two more' activities becomes evident here.
34. *Helping With Inquiries*, p.118.
35. 'Jews' College Centenary', sermon preached at the St John's Wood Synagogue, London, 16 November 1955, in Israel Brodie, *A Word in Season: Addresses and Sermons, 1948–1958* (London: Vallentine Mitchell, 1959), pp.123–4.
36. 'Historical Judaism: Challenge To Our Times', preached at the Hampstead Synagogue, London, 1 December 1951, ibid., pp.184–5.
37. In his lecture, devoted to the principles of the Pharisees, Jacobs noted 'their emphasis on the participation of all the people of Israel in the heritage of the Torah – a democratic idea which opposed the concept of the teaching of the Torah as the exclusive preserve of a chosen few' (*Jewish Chronicle*, 13 March 1959, p.10).
38. Ibid.
39. Ibid., 12 June 1959, p.10.
40. Louis Jacobs, *Montefiore and Loewe on the Rabbis*, eleventh annual Claude Montefiore Lecture, delivered at the Liberal Jewish Synagogue, London, 15 November 1962 (London: Liberal Jewish Synagogue, 1962), pp.26–7.
41. *Jewish Chronicle*, 7 August 1959, p.7. On the timing of the appointment, Norman Cohen writes: 'Dr [Isidore] Epstein was scheduled to retire as principal of Jews' College in 1959 and Dr Brodie's term of office was to end in 1965. Dr Jacobs was brought into Jews' College as a tutor shortly before Dr Epstein's retirement date. The appointment was made against Dr Epstein's wishes, and Dr Brodie's concurrence was given most unwillingly. (I was told by Sefton Temkin, now in the USA but then a columnist of the *Jewish Chronicle* and a strong Jacobs supporter, that the Chief Rabbi was threatened that, unless the appointment was made, Dr Jacobs would follow Dr Alexander Altmann, at Brandeis since 1959, on the "brain drain" to the United States and he [Brodie] would then have to account to an outraged public opinion for the loss, in quick succession, of two of the leading clergymen under his jurisdiction. Dr Brodie must have had ample opportunity in the following years to regret the weakness which he demonstrated in this instance and which involved him in the embarrassing dilemma of having to explain why Jacobs was *kasher* as a tutor, but *treifah* as a principal.) The appointment led to immediate hostility on the part of the Orthodox, and some of the Jews' College students showed an inclination to boycott the new tutor's lectures. Dr Epstein made no secret of his annoyance, and the student body petitioned for his period of office to be extended. The council agreed on an extension of two years, but with such bad grace that they never even informed Dr Epstein, who learned of it from a press report (he told me this himself).' 'The Religious Crisis in Anglo-Jewry', *Tradition*, 8, 2 (Summer 1966), Walter S. Wurzburger (ed.), (New York: Rabbinical Council of America, 1966), pp.49–50.
42. *Jewish Chronicle*, 22 January 1960, p.12.
43. Ibid., 15 December 1961, p.12.
44. Ibid., 22 December 1961, p.10. The letter was dated 14 November 1961, and was read to the council at a meeting held on 18 December 1961.
45. Ibid.
46. The honorary officers subsequently announced that they would not stand for re-election at the annual meeting in May 1962.
47. *Jewish Chronicle*, 5 January 1962, p.8.
48. Ibid., 26 January 1962, p.8.
49. Ibid., 2 February 1962, p.8.
50. Ibid.
51. Ibid., 11 May 1962, p.10.
52. The undercurrents of the Jacobs Affair are fully explored in Elliot J. Cosgrove, 'The Road Not Taken: The Iconoclastic Theology of Rabbi Louis Jacobs' (PhD diss., University of Chicago, 2008) and in Miri J. Freud-Kandel, *Orthodox Judaism in Britain Since 1913* (London and Portland, OR: Vallentine Mitchell, 2006), pp.123–57. A Conservative viewpoint is supplied by Sefton Temkin, 'A Crisis in Anglo-Jewry', in *Conservative Judaism*, XVIII, 1 (Fall 1963), Samuel H. Dresner (ed.) (New York: Rabbinical Assembly, 1963), pp.18–34; an Orthodox perspective by Norman Cohen, 'The Religious Crisis in Anglo-Jewry', pp.40–57, and a Reform overview by Ignaz Maybaum, 'The Jacobs Affair', in *Quest* 1, pp.80–83. Jacobs provides detailed discussions in 'Reflections on a Controversy', ibid., pp.4–5; the Epilogue to *We Have Reason to Believe*, third edition (1965), pp.138–51; the 'Retrospect' to the fifth edition (2004), pp.viii–xvi; *Helping*

*With Inquiries: An Autobiography* (London and Portland, OR: Vallentine Mitchell, 1989), pp.134–222; and *Beyond Reasonable Doubt*, (London: Littman Library of Jewish Civilization, 1999) pp.1–30. On the twenty-fifth anniversary of the Jews' College controversy, he examined 'its contemporary relevance and long-term repercussions' in 'For the Sake of Heaven', *Jewish Chronicle*, 19 December 1986, pp.22–3. A *Jewish Chronicle* insider's view is William Frankel, *Tea With Einstein And Other Memories* (London: Halban in association with the European Jewish Publication Society, 2006), pp.157–71.
53. *Jewish Chronicle*, 8 June 1962, p.12.
54. William Frankel, editor of the *Jewish Chronicle* from 1958 to 1976 and a former honorary officer of the New West End Synagogue, died in Washington DC on 18 April 2008, aged 91.
55. *Helping With Inquiries*, pp.136–7.

CHAPTER 16

1. Among the members of the sponsoring committee were Ephraim Levine, Jacobs' predecessor at the New West End, and Isaac Levy, of Hampstead Synagogue.
2. Louis Jacobs, *Helping With Inquiries: An Autobiography* (London and Portland, OR: Vallentine Mitchell, 1989), p.144.
3. *Creative Judaism: Some Aims And Objects* (London: Society for the Study of Jewish Theology, 1963), pp.1–4.
4. *Helping With Inquiries*, p.157.
5. Liverpool-born Dr Chaim Pearl (1919–1995) had succeeded Jacobs at the New West End in 1960, but his leftist tendencies beckoned him to the Conservative Synagogue in Riverdale, New York, where he ministered for twenty years before retiring to Jerusalem. Educated at the Universities of Birmingham and London, he also attended Liverpool Yeshivah, later serving the Birmingham Hebrew Congregation, Singer's Hill, as assistant minister (1945–1949) and chief minister (1950–1960). Among his many books were a translation of *Sefer Ha-Aggadah*, *A Guide to Jewish Knowledge*, and *The Medieval Jewish Mind: Studies in the Religious Philosophy of Isaac Arama*, as well as two volumes on Rashi. Writing from the United States in 1967, Pearl provided some insights into his decision to leave the New West End: 'In the eighty synagogues of the United Synagogue, the Orthodox Ashkenazi ritual is jealously guarded and discipline is accepted without question. Officially, one does not omit a single line of a *yekum purkan* paragraph of the Sabbath service. Restless rabbis in the United Synagogue are unknown. They just get out ... There are Jews in London who sigh for the greater tolerance of an earlier age when the United Synagogue professed an enlightened Orthodoxy which, they say, attracted Jews of all shades of religious loyalty under its wing. Today, they complain, the rigorous, unbending Orthodoxy of the Beth Din has alienated the middle-of-the-road Jew. This Jew doesn't want Reform, yet he cannot accept the fundamentalist legalism of the present-day leaders of the Establishment. He must find another way, and the New London Synagogue, and what it represents, may be his answer. As a whole, the British Jewish community is still loyal to the office of Chief Rabbi. It wants its religious life organised and disciplined by central control and leadership. But it is a community of highly educated people who will not be browbeaten by an ecclesiastical authority with a medieval outlook on Judaism. It is still essentially Orthodox, but there are many members who believe that Orthodoxy can be harmonised to a tolerant outlook and to freedom of inquiry. It is not unreasonable to suppose that this number will increase in the years ahead. Everyone wishes for unity – but uniformity is on the way out. There is today an insistent call for a more enlightened Orthodoxy which will take account of new knowledge in Bible studies and of new historical insights into the development of halachah. The call is made for a fresh and dynamic approach to the synagogue and to such issues as frequently erupt over the edicts of the London Beth Din. The time when the Beth Din can simply decree without the courtesy of a reasonable explanation is over for many people, and the new Chief Rabbi may have to take a different attitude from that of his predecessor's Beth Din. The English Jewish community needs reawakening to the meaning of Judaism as a spiritual power for the individual, the Jewish group and for society as a whole. It stands in need of a great teacher who will interpret Judaism for them in a way which will make it the meaningful heritage we claim it is. This is particularly necessary for the youth, most of whom are today on the periphery of Judaism.' Chaim Pearl, 'About "Chief Rabbis,"', *Jewish Spectator*, January 1967 (New York) pp.21–3.
6. Brodie's refusal was contained in an exchange with Alfred H. Silverman, secretary of the United Synagogue, who had written to him on 17 January 1964 regarding the vacancy: 'The above post having been advertised, the ministerial appointments committee met last evening. I was directed by the committee to write to you to ascertain whether your certificate is still in being in respect of Rabbi Dr Louis Jacobs, and if not whether a certificate will be forthcoming for him in respect of the above vacancy'. Brodie replied (23 January 1964): ' ... I have to inform you that my certificate is not in being for Dr L. Jacobs in respect of the New West End Synagogue. It is with the deepest possible regret that I am compelled, owing to the views which Dr Jacobs has expressed publicly both by written and spoken word, to answer your second question by stating that my certificate will not be forthcoming for him for the above vacancy.' In *Statement by the President of the United Synagogue*, special meeting of the United Synagogue council, 23 April 1964, pp.2–3.
7. Oscar B. Davis (warden), Bernard Spears (financial representative) and fourteen members of the board of management to Sir Isaac Wolfson, 17 February 1964. Two members of the board, Frank H. Levine

(warden) and Frank A. Rossdale (vice-president of the United Synagogue, chairman of its ministerial appointments committee, and past warden) wrote to the members of the congregation (27 February 1964) dissociating themselves from the views expressed in that letter.
8. Wolfson to Davis and others, 21 February 1964.
9. *Statement by the President*, pp.9–11.
10. *Statement by the Very Rev. the Chief Rabbi, Dr Israel Brodie*, meeting of rabbis and ministers of the Anglo-Jewish community, Adolph Tuck Hall, London, 5 May 1964 (London: United Synagogue, 1964), pp.2–8.
11. A pre-Chief Rabbinical view on Revelation and on Jacobs' interpretation of it was provided by Jonathan Sacks, then principal of Jews' College, in 'The Origin of Torah', a review of Jacobs' *A Tree of Life: Diversity, Flexibility, and Creativity in Jewish Law* (Oxford: Oxford University Press for the Littman Library of Jewish Civilization, 1984) in the *Jewish Chronicle*, 2 November 1984, pp.24–5. The article was described as 'a rabbinical response to the non-fundamentalist views of Rabbi Louis Jacobs, for the first time in these columns since the Jacobs Affair broke twenty years ago'. Jacobs replied to the review in the issue of 16 November 1984, p.25, and the two articles led to a prolonged and scholarly correspondence spanning several weeks. See also chapter 15, note 52, on Jacobs' twenty-fifth anniversary retrospect of the Jews' College controversy; Jonathan Sacks, 'Fundamentalism Reconsidered', in *L'Eylah*, 28 (September 1989), Philip Ginsbury (ed.) (London: Office of the Chief Rabbi and Jews' College, 1989), pp.8–12; and, on an earlier encounter between Jacobs and Sacks, chapter 17, note 64. In response to a lecture delivered by Rabbi Yitzchak Schochet at London's Mill Hill Synagogue on 8 February 1995, Jacobs engaged in an exchange of views on theological issues and challenged the Chief Rabbi 'to state clearly and unambiguously that he believes Moses to have written every word of the Chumash at the dictation of God and that he rejects totally all modern biblical scholarship, not only the Documentary Hypothesis.' Jacobs, *Masortimatters*, (March 1995) (London: Masorti Publications, 1995), pp.1–4.
12. *Jewish Chronicle*, 15 May 1964, p.13.
13. *Helping With Inquiries*, p.172.
14. Ibid.
15. The building, purchased by property developer Alec Coleman, was resold first to Louis Mintz and then on to the New London Synagogue. For details of the transaction, see William Frankel, *Tea With Einstein and Other Memories* (London: Halban in association with the European Jewish Publication Society, 2006), pp.170–1.
16. Louis Jacobs, 'Four Rabbinic Positions in Anglo-Jewry', in *The Jewish Year Book 2000*, Stephen W. Massil (ed.) (London and Portland, OR: Vallentine Mitchell in association with the *Jewish Chronicle*, 2000), p.80.
17. *Helping With Inquiries*, p.180.
18. 'Four Rabbinic Positions', p.80.
19. Louis Jacobs, *What We Stand For*, preached at the New London Synagogue, 7 September 1964, first day Rosh Hashanah 5625 (London: Blackfriars Press for New London Synagogue, 1964), pp.1–5.
20. *Helping With Inquiries*, p.137.
21. Louis Jacobs, 'Reflections on a Controversy', in *Quest*, 1 (September 1965), Jonathan Stone (ed.) (London: Paul Hamlyn, 1965), p.5.
22. *Helping With Inquiries*, p.142.
23. Ibid., pp.142–3.
24. See chapter 17.
25. *Helping With Inquiries*, pp.199–200.
26. *Jewish Chronicle*, 24 December 1965, p.12.
27. Ibid., 19 January 1962, p.20. Five weeks earlier (10 December 1961), Jakobovits had written to Jacobs: 'I hear with interest from several quarters that we may look forward to a visit from you in the none too distant future, on an American lecture tour. From my own experience, I can assure you that this will prove a most thrilling and stimulating, albeit also exacting, enterprise, and I shall personally be extremely happy to welcome you.' Jacobs Papers, London.
28. *Jewish Review*, 8 February 1962, p.1.
29. S.J. Goldsmith in *Congress Bi-Weekly*, 22 January 1962.
30. Ibid., 5 February 1962, quoted in Immanuel Jakobovits, *Journal of a Rabbi* (New York: Living Books, 1966), pp.458–60.

CHAPTER 17

1. Yechezkel Abramsky, *Address at the Installation of Rabbi I. Jakobovits*, Great Synagogue, London, 6 October 1947 (London: United Synagogue, 1947), pp.3–6.
2. Immanuel Jakobovits, 'Fragments From An Unpublished Autobiography', in Meir Persoff, *Immanuel Jakobovits: a Prophet in Israel* (London and Portland, OR: Vallentine Mitchell, 2002), p.90. The allusion is to Fifth Avenue's ladies' gallery, unusual for a Manhattan synagogue, and to the absence of political symbolism, either verbal (from the pulpit) or ornamental (through the draping of national flags).
3. Ibid., p.112.
4. Ibid., pp.113–14.

# Notes

5. Ibid., p.115.
6. *Jewish Chronicle*, 12 June 1964, pp.1, 14.
7. Yaacov (Jacob) Herzog (1921–1972) was an Israeli attorney and doctor of international law, diplomat, ordained rabbi, and translator and commentator of the Mishnah. A former adviser to Israeli Prime Minister David Ben-Gurion, he had served as Minister Plenipotentiary in Washington, Ambassador to Canada, and assistant director-general of the Ministry of Foreign Affairs.
8. *Jewish Chronicle*, 13 November 1964, p.13.
9. Ibid., 21 May 1965, p.14.
10. An unsigned insight into 'The Making of a Chief Rabbi' is in *the jew: Quest* 2 (London: Cornmarket Press, 1967), pp.10–17.
11. *Jewish Chronicle*, 21 May 1965, p.1.
12. Ibid., 28 May 1965, p.15.
13. Ibid., p.1.
14. Ibid., p.18.
15. Ibid., p.7.
16. Sidney Brichto to Yaacov Herzog on his appointment as Chief Rabbi, 1 June 1965, Brichto Papers, London.
17. Herzog to Brichto, June 1965, ibid.
18. *Religious Reorganisation in Anglo-Jewry* (unsigned), (London: Union of Liberal and Progressive Synagogues, 1965), Brichto Papers, London.
19. Sunderland-born Goldberg (1918–1981) studied at London University and Jews' College. He was briefly minister of the Kingsbury (United) Synagogue, London, before joining the Manchester Congregation of British Jews (Reform) in 1940, serving there for thirty-four years. He later ministered to the Beth Israel Congregation in Hot Springs, National Park, Arkansas.
20. Goldberg cites as examples the Tercentenary Service of Dedication (Bevis Marks, London, 22 March 1956), when, he writes, 'backdoor methods had to be used in order to have two non-Orthodox rabbis included among those who were in the procession' (Goldberg, *Three Hundred Years* [London: Vallentine Mitchell, 1957], pp.69–72); annual Israel Independence Day services, and the presence of Orthodox ministers in non-Orthodox synagogues, and vice versa.
21. P. Selvin Goldberg, *The Reform Synagogues of Great Britain and its future relationship with the Anglo-Jewish community*, July 1965, pp.1–4, Brichto Papers, London.
22. *Jewish Chronicle*, 27 August 1965, pp.1, 13.
23. Ibid., 10 September 1965, pp.1, 15. Reporting on Herzog's withdrawal, *The Times'* Tel Aviv correspondent wrote that 'while the rabbi's illness was patently not diplomatic, religious circles here believe that it was not the only reason for his decision. He has expressed qualms about his competence to handle the touchy situation of British Jewry' (*The Times*, 8 September 1965, p.1). Of Herzog's appointment as Chief Rabbi, Jakobovits commented: 'Surprising as it was, I thought it might restore respect for the office after the denigration it had suffered for many years. Even in retrospect, I felt that his acceptance helped to break the back of the pro-Jacobs campaign. I was later to be the beneficiary of this, but meanwhile was relieved that his appointment had taken the pressure and the focus of attention off me' (Meir Persoff, *Immanuel Jakobovits: a Prophet in Israel*, p.116).
24. A detailed account of this episode is in Persoff, ibid., pp.94–111.
25. Ibid., p.118.
26. Jakobovits to Herzog, 1 July 1966, Jakobovits Papers, London.
27. Herzog to Jakobovits, 7 July 1966, ibid.
28. Herzog to Jakobovits, 17 July 1966, ibid.
29. Herzog to Jakobovits, 27 September 1966, Jakobovits Papers, London.
30. *Jewish Chronicle*, 16 September 1966, pp.1, 14.
31. Wolfson to Jakobovits, 23 September 1966, Jakobovits Papers, London.
32. Rabbi Maurice Rose to Jakobovits, 4 November 1996, ibid.
33. See Prologue.
34. Jakobovits to Grunfeld, 3 July 1966, Jakobovits Papers, London.
35. *Jewish Chronicle*, 28 May 1965, p.15.
36. Ibid., 27 August 1965, p.13.
37. Ibid., 4 June 1965, p.6. John Shaftesley, a former editor of the *Jewish Chronicle*, wrote of this passage: 'There are ironic echoes in the farewell comment of some of his [Brodie's] fiercest critics'; and of the reference to 'a raging conflict which tore the community asunder': '... the hyperbole in this statement ... may be disregarded.' 'Israel Brodie, Chief Rabbi: A Biographical Sketch', in *Essays Presented to Chief Rabbi Israel Brodie on the Occasion of his Seventieth Birthday*, H.J. Zimmels, J. Rabbinowitz, I. Finestein (eds), Jews' College Publications, NS 3, (London: Soncino Press, 1967), p.xxxviii.
38. Israel Brodie, *Induction Address*, installation of Dr Immanuel Jakobovits, St John's Wood Synagogue, London, Rosh Chodesh Nisan 5727 – 11 April 1967 (London: United Synagogue, 1967), pp.3–4.

39. Immanuel Jakobovits, *Installation Address as Chief Rabbi of the United Hebrew Congregations of the British Commonwealth of Nations*, St John's Wood Synagogue, London, 1 Nisan, 5727 – 11 April 1967 (London: Office of the Chief Rabbi, 1967), p.7.
40. Ibid., pp.7–9.
41. Memorandum submitted to Sir Isaac Wolfson and the Chief Rabbinate Committee, London, July 1966, in Immanuel Jakobovits, *Prelude to Service* (London: Office of the Chief Rabbi, April 1967), pp.4–5.
42. Goldberg to Jakobovits, 22 July 1966, Jakobovits Papers, London.
43. Memorandum by Dr P. Selvin Goldberg and Rabbi Sidney Brichto, 2 November 1965, Brichto Papers, London.
44. Immanuel Jakobovits, 'The major tasks ahead', letter to the *Jewish Chronicle*, 16 December 1966, p.6.
45. Ibid., 13 January 1967, p.6. The letter was signed by Lord Cohen of Walmer, Rabbi Sidney Brichto, Rabbi Dr P. Selvin Goldberg, Sir Louis Gluckstein, Sir Seymour Karminski, Rabbi Jacob Kokotek, Rabbi John D. Rayner, S.G. Schwab, Malcolm Slowe, and Rabbi Dr Werner Van der Zyl.
46. Jakobovits to Slowe, 23 January 1967, Brichto Papers, London.
47. Brichto told Jakobovits that he had inadvertently omitted the phrase 'which could just as well have taken place in an Orthodox synagogue' from his original letter to the *Jewish Chronicle* (Brichto Papers, London).
48. *Jewish Chronicle*, 29 December 1967, p.15.
49. Rogosnitzky to Jakobovits, 15 January 1968, Jakobovits Papers, London.
50. Jakobovits to Brichto, 28 February 1967, Brichto Papers, London.
51. Brichto to Jakobovits, 6 March 1967, ibid.
52. Jakobovits to Brichto, 9 March 1967, ibid.
53. Louis Jacobs, *Helping With Inquiries*, p.186.
54. Lithuanian-born Moshe Feinstein (1895–1986) was world-renowned for his expertise in halachah and was the de facto supreme rabbinic authority for Orthodox Jewry of North America. Joseph Ber Soloveitchik (1903–1993) born in Pruzhany, Russia, was named earlier (though speculatively) as one of the 'also-rans' in the British Chief Rabbinical race.
55. Louis Jacobs, *Record of conversations and impressions of the visit of Rabbi Dr Jakobovits insofar as they concern the New London Synagogue*, signed and witnessed 3 August 1966, Jacobs Papers, London.
56. In his introductory remarks to the above record, Jacobs describes the 'cloak-and-dagger' moves that preceded his meeting with Jakobovits: 'Thursday, 28 July, 1966 – At around 7 p.m. there was a telephone call from Captain Myers, Sir Isaac Wolfson's secretary, to say that Rabbi Dr Jakobovits would like to meet me. I said that I would be glad to see Rabbi Jakobovits and we fixed as the time for the meeting Monday, 1 August, at 11 a.m. When Captain Myers asked where the meeting should take place, I replied that I would be delighted to see Rabbi Jakobovits at my home, and this was agreed.

'Friday, 29 July, 1966 – At around 10 a.m. there was a further telephone call from Captain Myers to say that Rabbi Jakobovits had many engagements on Monday and found it impossible to come to my home. It was suggested that instead I meet him at the same time as originally arranged but at his hotel, the Hilton. I said that I would be prepared to see Rabbi Jakobovits at any time suitable to him, but I had to insist that the meeting took place at my home. Captain Myers then said that he would pursue the matter further.

'At around 11.30 a.m. Captain Myers telephoned again to ask if I would agree to meet Rabbi Jakobovits at the Tottenham Court Road offices of Sir Isaac Wolfson. In any event, he said, Sir Isaac would like me to come to see him because we had not met for some time. I replied that I was always glad to see Sir Isaac, but that this had nothing to do with my meeting with Rabbi Jakobovits, which I felt ought to take place at my home since if I visited New York, I, as the visiting rabbi, would naturally call on Rabbi Jakobovits if I wished to see him. Captain Myers then put the call through to Sir Isaac himself, who repeated the request that I meet Rabbi Jakobovits at his offices (as Sir Isaac put it) "to shake hands with him." I repeated that it seemed to me to be wrong to have the meeting arranged in this way and that I would be glad to welcome Rabbi Jakobovits to my home. Sir Isaac asked me to leave the matter with him for further consideration.

'Monday, 1 August, 1966 – At 9.30 a.m. Rabbi Cyril Shine, rabbi of the Central Synagogue (Sir Isaac's congregation) telephoned to say that Rabbi Jakobovits, a contemporary of Rabbi Shine at Jews' College, was to have tea with him on Tuesday, 2 August, and Rabbi Shine invited me to come along and meet Rabbi Jakobovits. I had to repeat that I did not think that a meeting of this kind should be arranged in this way and that I would be glad to welcome Rabbi Jakobovits to my home. Rabbi Shine thought that I was being unreasonable. When I said that in my opinion it was Rabbi Jakobovits who was being unreasonable, Rabbi Shine said that this may be true but that I should be "big enough" not to insist on any rights in this matter. I replied that it seemed wrong for me, with the prestige of the New London Synagogue to be considered, to agree to Rabbi Shine's suggestion.

'Rabbi Dr Solomon Goldman, of the St. John's Wood Synagogue, telephoned to the New London Synagogue office to speak to me at around 10.30 a.m. Rabbi Goldman said that Rabbi Shine had acquainted him with the situation and he, Rabbi Goldman, begged me in my own interests to meet Rabbi Jakobovits at Rabbi Goldman's home. I had to repeat again that I did not consider this the correct way of arranging the meeting.

'Rabbi Jakobovits telephoned me at 1.30 p.m. to say that he had heard that matters were getting out of hand and that he saw the difficulty about my coming to see him but that there were difficulties in his coming to see me. He suggested that we meet on neutral ground, and I suggested a meeting at the Commonwealth Institute in Kensington on 2 August at 11 a.m. Rabbi Jakobovits agreed.

'Tuesday, 2 August, 1966 – At 11 a.m. I met Rabbi Jakobovits at the Commonwealth Institute, Kensington. It being a fine morning, we decided to walk in nearby Holland Park ... ' (ibid.).

57. Louis Jacobs, *Helping With Inquiries*, pp.186–7.
58. Jacobs to Brichto, 27 October 1965, Brichto Papers, London.
59. Brichto to Jacobs, 24 December 1965, ibid.
60. Louis Jacobs, 'Where the Chief Rabbi Stands', in *Glasgow Jewish Echo*, 21 April 1967.
61. *Jewish Chronicle*, 31 March 1967, p.12. Invited to enlarge on this comment, Jakobovits told the JC that 'he did not wish to do so then, as he intended to deal with "the broader issues involved in communal relationships" in his address after his induction as Chief Rabbi'.
62. Ibid., 7 April 1967, p.6.
63. Ibid., 14 April 1967, p.6.
64. Ibid., 21 April 1967, p.6. Several months after this exchange, Jacobs encountered another budding Chief Rabbi during a visit to the Cambridge University Jewish Society, where he addressed the inaugural meeting of its discussion group. 'I think that the meeting was a great success', wrote Jonathan Sacks, the Society's external secretary, in a letter of thanks to Jacobs (6 November 1967), 'for it precisely set out what is to be our task, and validated its appropriateness. Everyone I have spoken to enjoyed the meeting very much, and it has served to stimulate interest in the group's future activities ... We hope that it will not be the last time that you honour Cambridge with your presence.' Jacobs Papers, London.
65. *Jewish Chronicle*, 29 November 1968, p.21.
66. Ibid., 12 July 1968, p.16.
67. Immanuel Jakobovits, *Moving Ahead: A Review and a Preview* (London: Office of the Chief Rabbi, Ellul 5728 – September 1968), pp.16–17.
68. Louis Jacobs, *Helping With Inquiries*, p.185.
69. See chapter 18 for Jakobovits' reference to this event in his New Year message, *Moving Ahead: A Review and a Preview*.
70. Minutes of meeting of the Board of Deputies of British Jews, London, item seven, 2 July 1967, London Metropolitan Archives, LMA ACC/3121/A042; Lionel Kopelowitz, member of the Chief Rabbinate Council, 1968–1977, and president of the Board of Deputies, 1985–1991, to the author, 22 March 2007. Similar certificates were later granted to other Masorti synagogues, with the St Albans congregation, for example, receiving authorisation from Chief Rabbi Jonathan Sacks on 11 January 1994 (Sandra Clark, administrative director, Board of Deputies, to the author, 9 May 2007).
71. Minutes of meeting of the Chief Rabbinate Council, London, 17 July 1977, p.3, in response to a statement from Kopelowitz.
72. Rabbi Dr Julian Shindler (Office of the London Beth Din) to the author, 21 and 22 March 2007.
73. Louis Jacobs, *Helping With Inquiries*, pp.214–15.
74. Louis Jacobs, 'Questions of Personal Status', in *New London Forum*, I, 2 (September 1983) (London: New London Synagogue, 1983), pp.1–3.
75. Marcus Carr, clerk to the London Beth Din, *Jewish Chronicle*, 30 September 1983, p.1.
76. Ibid.
77. Nathan Goldbenberg, ibid., 21 October 1983, p.18.
78. Ibid., 16 June 1972, pp.1, 6.
79. Ibid., p.6.
80. *Jewish Review*, 9 August 1972, p.2. The report was prefaced: 'In view of the unauthorised publication in the *Jewish Chronicle* of some arbitrary extracts from the Chief Rabbi's newsletter addressed to his colleagues and marked "Not for Publication", we have requested and received permission for parts significantly omitted in the JC report, in that the general public has the possibility of knowing the full facts.'
81. Immanuel Jakobovits, 'Eulogy to Sir Israel Brodie', Willesden Cemetery, London, 14 February 1979, *L'Eylah*, I, 7 (Spring 5739 – 1979), A. Melinek (ed.) (London: Office of the Chief Rabbi), pp.1–3.
82. In a *Jewish Chronicle* readers' poll, attracting two thousand entries and aimed at nominating 'Britain's greatest Jew' since the readmission in 1656 under Oliver Cromwell, Jacobs received nearly double the number of votes of the second-placed Sir Moses Montefiore (1784–1885). Reform rabbi Hugo Gryn (1928–1996) was third, penicillin pioneer Professor Sir Ernst Boris Chain (1906–1979) fourth, and DNA and double-helix researcher Professor Rosalind Elsie Franklin (1920–1958) fifth. Told of his success, Jacobs is reported to have said: 'I feel both embarrassed and daft' (*Jewish Chronicle*, 30 December 2005, p.1).
83. 'Louis Jacobs' Legacy', leading article, ibid., 7 July 2006, p.30.
84. Louis Jacobs, *Beyond Reasonable Doubt* (London: Littman Library of Jewish Civilization, 1999), p.12.

CHAPTER 18

1. P. Selvin Goldberg to Sigmund Schwab, chairman of the Reform Synagogues of Great Britain, 14 February 1967, Brichto Papers, London.
2. Immanuel Jakobovits, 'My Plea to Progressive Jews', in *Prelude to Service* (London: Office of the Chief Rabbi, April 1967), p.25.
3. Malcolm Slowe to Schwab, 24 April 1967, Brichto Papers, London.
4. Berlin-born Rayner (né Hans Sigismund Rahmer, 1924–2005) studied at Cambridge University and was ordained by Israel Mattuck in 1953. He was minister of the South London Liberal Synagogue (1953–1957) before serving the Liberal Jewish Synagogue, St John's Wood, as associate minister (1957–1961) and senior minister, retiring in 1989. He was a vice-president of the Leo Baeck College, chairman of the Council of Reform and Liberal Rabbis, and honorary life president of the Union of Liberal and Progressive Synagogues.
5. Rayner to Slowe, 6 February 1967, Brichto Papers, London.
6. *Jewish Chronicle*, 12 April 1968, p.19.
7. Ibid.
8. John D. Rayner, 'Anglo-Jewish Unity', sermon delivered at the Liberal Jewish Synagogue, St John's Wood, London, 18 May 1968, Brichto Papers, London.
9. Jakobovits to Rayner, 21 June 1968, Brichto Papers, London.
10. Rayner to Jakobovits, 2 August 1968, ibid.
11. *Moving Ahead: A Review and a Preview*, Ellul 5728 – September 1968 (London: Office of the Chief Rabbi, 1968) pp.15–18.
12. Rose to Brichto, 7 July 1969, Brichto Papers, London.
13. Brichto to Jakobovits, 9 July 1969, ibid.
14. Brichto to Jakobovits, 20 July 1970, ibid.
15. Jakobovits to Brichto, 23 July 1970, ibid.
16. On Gryn, see chapter 19, note 13.
17. *Jewish Chronicle*, 2 October 1970, p.20.
18. Ibid., 23 October 1970, p.1.
19. Ibid., pp.1, 36.
20. Ibid.
21. *The Times*, 20 September 1969. The letter, wrote Jakobovits, was one of 'some half-a-dozen from me [to the paper] in defence of Israel, seeking [in this case] to temper the Islamic frenzy raised by the Al Aksa fire.' *If Only My People: Zionism in My Life* (London: Weidenfeld and Nicolson, 1984), p.189.
22. Lawrence Rigal and Rosita Rosenberg, *Liberal Judaism: The First Hundred Years* (London: Liberal Judaism, 2004), p.165. See also Anne J. Kershen and Jonathan A. Romain, *Tradition and Change: A History of Reform Judaism in Britain, 1840–1995* (London and Portland, OR: Vallentine Mitchell, 1995), pp.279–80, and Harold S. Langdon, 'The Place of Reform in Anglo-Jewry Today', in Dow Marmur (ed.), *A Genuine Search*, (London: Reform Synagogues of Great Britain, 1979), pp.239–61.
23. King-Hamilton to Jakobovits, 29 December 1969, Jakobovits Papers, London.
24. Rose to King-Hamilton, 13 January 1970, ibid.
25. King-Hamilton to Jakobovits, 6 February 1970, ibid. Rose replied: 'While there is nothing I can add at this stage to my previous letter on the subject, the Chief Rabbi will certainly bear your further representations in mind in future discussions' (18 February 1970, ibid.).
26. Quoted in *Living Judaism* (November 1972) (London: Reform Synagogues of Great Britain, 1972), in connection with Jakobovits' refusal to read a psalm, alongside Gryn, at a Board of Deputies memorial service for the Israeli victims of the Munich Olympics massacre.
27. Immanuel Jakobovits, 'Division and Diversion', in *Jewish Chronicle*, 26 February 1971, p.23.
28. Langdon, 'The Place of Reform in Anglo-Jewry Today', p.247.
29. Jakobovits, 'Division and Diversion', p.23.
30. *Jewish Chronicle*, 28 May 1971, p.17.
31. Langdon, 'The Place of Reform in Anglo-Jewry Today', p.250.
32. Jakobovits to Homa, 24 August 1971, in Abba Bornstein and Bernard Homa, *Tell It In Gath: British Jewry and Clause 43. The Inside Story* (London: privately published, 1972), pp.30–1.
33. Ibid., pp.54–5.
34. Minutes of meeting of the Chief Rabbinate Council, London, 19 December 1971, p.7.
35. Figures for synagogue affiliation and attendances during the period covered by this book, and their relationship to marriage statistics, are given in Appendix III.
36. Langdon, 'The Place of Reform in Anglo-Jewry Today', p.252.
37. *Jewish Chronicle*, 21 December 1984, p.4.
38. Rigal and Rosenberg, *Liberal Judaism*, p.171.
39. Kershen and Romain, *Tradition and Change*, p.345.
40. For a discussion of this issue, see Jack Wolkind, *London and its Jewish Community*, annual West Central Lecture

delivered at University College, London, 13 June 1985 (London: West Central Counselling and Community Research, 1985), pp.1–26.
41. The committee's terms of reference were '(a) To receive all communications addressed by the Council of Christians and Jews to the Anglo-Jewish community as such, to discuss attitudes, and direct policy in regard to same; (b) generally to discuss policy in regard to Jewish/non-Jewish relations and to ascertain whether joint or separate action should be taken, and to inform groups concerned accordingly; (c) in such cases where individuals or organisations within the group have been approached on matters of common interest, including parliamentary legislation, to bring such matters to the attention of the group.' The formation of this Consultative Committee was, the Chief Rabbi said, in accordance with his often stated principle, affirming co-operation with the non-Orthodox segments of the community in all matters of common concern which did not impinge on their religious differences' (minutes of meeting of the Chief Rabbinate Council, London, 16 June 1974, p.7).
42. Minutes of meeting of the Consultative Committee, Adler House, London, 2 May, 1974, Jakobovits Papers, London.
43. Rosita Rosenberg in Rigal and Rosenberg, *Liberal Judaism*, p.169.
44. 'David Nathan talks with Chief Rabbi Jakobovits', *Jewish Chronicle*, 6 January 1978, p.17.
45. Ibid., 6 April 1979, p.1.
46. Immanuel Jakobovits, 'The Quiet Revolution', reproduced with an article by Israel Finestein as a two-part feature on 'The Changing Face of Anglo-Jewry', *Jewish Chronicle*, 9 November 1984, pp.24–5.
47. Minutes of meeting of the Chief Rabbinate Council, London, 19 December 1982, p.5.
48. The 'certain events' alluded to involved Dr Alan Unterman, minister of the Yeshurun Synagogue, Gatley, and lecturer in comparative religion at the University of Manchester, who was on the editorial board of, and a contributor to, *Manna*, the quarterly journal of the Reform movement's newly opened Sternberg Centre for Judaism. See Chaim Bermant, *Lord Jakobovits: The Authorized Biography of the Chief Rabbi* (London: Weidenfeld and Nicolson, 1990), pp.186–7. Bermant writes: 'Nothing he [Unterman] wrote in the magazine could have been construed as non-kosher, and his sin, if any, lay not in what he said but where he said it, and in keeping non-kosher company. It was an unfortunate episode, for Unterman's transgression – if it may be called that – was noticed by a colleague, who, instead of remonstrating on the matter with Unterman himself, went behind his back and brought it to the attention of the Chief Rabbi.' On 2 January 1985 Jakobovits' office instructed the United Synagogue Council of Ministers by letter not to associate with the Sternberg Centre so as to avoid conferring 'legitimation' upon it or 'providing a *hechsher* for teachings and organisations which violate our most fundamental beliefs and practices'.
49. 'Avoiding the collision', *Jewish Chronicle*, 8 February 1985, pp.18–19.

CHAPTER 19

1. 'Avoiding the collision', *Jewish Chronicle*, 8 February 1985, pp.18–19.
2. Letter to *The Times*, 14 January 1985, reported in *Jewish Chronicle*, 18 January 1985, p.7.
3. Bayfeld to Jakobovits, 7 January 1985, Jakobovits and Brichto Papers, London.
4. Jakobovits was knighted in the 1981 Queen's Birthday Honours. In the 1988 New Year Honours, he became the first Chief Rabbi to be elevated to the peerage – a unique tribute, wrote the *Jewish Chronicle*, to his 'spiritual leadership of the overwhelming majority of Anglo-Jewry, and particularly to his personal contribution to the national debates on the great moral and ethical issues of the day' (JC, 8 January 1988, p.22). Hermann Adler was appointed a Commander of the Royal Victorian Order in June 1909, marking his jubilee in the ministry and his seventieth birthday. In the 1943 New Year Honours, Hertz became a Companion of Honour, while Brodie was appointed a Knight Commander of the British Empire in January 1969 for services to British Jewry.
5. Leading article in *Manna* (Winter 1985) (London: Reform Synagogues of Great Britain), p.1.
6. Jakobovits to Bayfield, 10 January 1985, Brichto Papers, London.
7. Bayfield to Jakobovits, 15 January 1985, ibid.
8. Gryn to Jakobovits, 15 January 1985, Jakobovits Papers, London. Proposals to diffuse the controversy were outlined in letters from Bayfield and Brichto to the *Jewish Chronicle*, 15 February 1985, p.18.
9. *Jewish Chronicle*, 19 March 1993, p.1.
10. Unterman to Jakobovits, 18 February 1985, Jakobovits Papers, London.
11. Ibid.
12. Rayner to Jakobovits, 27 February 1985, ibid.
13. The Consultative and Liaison Committees were disbanded in 1997 'when disgust over the actions of Rabbi Jakobovits' successor [Jonathan Sacks], following the death of Rabbi Hugo Gryn, caused the Liberal and Reform members to withdraw'. Lawrence Rigal and Rosita Rosenberg, *Liberal Judaism: The First Hundred Years* (London: Liberal Judaism, 2004), p.170. The reference is to a letter written by Sacks on 12 Shevat 5757 (20 January 1997) – marked 'Not for Publication' – to Dayan Chenoch Padwa, spiritual head of the Union of Orthodox Hebrew Congregations, explaining his participation in a memorial

service for Gryn organised by the Board of Deputies and the Council of Christians and Jews, having declined the previous August to attend Gryn's funeral. See 'Right-wing tells Sacks: snub Gryn memorial', *Jewish Chronicle*, 17 January 1997, p.1; 'Chief Rabbi focuses on Reform leader's Holocaust experience', ibid., 28 February 1997, p.13; 'Sacks: my pain at having to praise "Rabbi" Gryn', ibid., 14 March 1997, p.1. Auschwitz survivor Gryn (1930–1996) was born in Berehovo, Czechoslovakia, and studied at Cambridge and London Universities before being persuaded by Leo Baeck and Lily Montagu to continue at Hebrew Union College, where he was ordained in 1957. He was director of the World Union of Progressive Judaism (1962–1964), assistant minister (1964–1968) and senior minister of the West London Synagogue, and president of the Reform Synagogues of Great Britain (1990) until his death (ibid., 23 August 1996, p.14). On the successor to the Consultative Committee, see note 41.
14. *Jewish Chronicle*, 19 March 1993, p.1.
15. Petuchowski (1925–1991) was a communal rabbi in Texas and West Virginia before becoming professor of rabbinics and Jewish thought, and later of Judaeo-Christian studies, at Hebrew Union College. He was the author of numerous books, including *Ever Since Sinai: A Modern View of the Torah, Prayer-Book Reform in Europe: The Liturgy of European Liberal and Reform Judaism, Understanding Jewish Prayer, When Jews and Christians Meet, The Lord's Prayer and Jewish Liturgy*, and *Zion Reconsidered*. At the time of writing to Jakobovits, he was at Harvard University's Centre for the Study of World Religions.
16. Petuchowski to Jakobovits, 26 February 1985, Jakobovits Papers, London.
17. *Jewish Chronicle*, 7 February 1975, p.6.
18. Ibid., 28 February 1975, p.6.
19. Ibid.
20. Immanuel Jakobovits, *Preserving The Oneness Of The Jewish People: Orthodox-Progressive divisions and discussions on marriage, divorce and conversion – can a permanent schism be averted?* Lecture to the Jewish Marriage Council, Royal Society of Medicine, London, 14 December 1987 (London: Office of the Chief Rabbi, 1988), p.13.
21. Ibid., pp.13–15.
22. Sidney Brichto, 'Halachah with Humility', *Jewish Chronicle*, 2 October 1987, p.29.
23. Jakobovits to Brichto, 26 February 1986, Brichto Papers, London.
24. *Jewish Chronicle*, 21 February 1986, p.20.
25. To this letter, Brichto replied: 'I do appreciate your points about conversion, though I do know that the degree of acceptance of *kabbalat mitzvot* has been differently interpreted during our history. This, however, is not the essential matter. It is the maintenance of tolerance between the two communities which you and I had fostered when you became Chief Rabbi, and the positive results of which I see disappearing' (3 March 1986, Brichto Papers, London).
26. See note 20.
27. Harold Sanderson and Rosita Rosenberg, 'Statement on the Appointment of the Chief Rabbi of the United Hebrew Congregation' (London: Union of Liberal and Progressive Synagogues [ULPS], 14 December 1989), Brichto Papers, London. Sanderson was the chairman, and Rosenberg the director, of the ULPS.
28. Clifford Longley, religious affairs editor of *The Times*, reported: 'Leaders of the liberal Jewish community in Britain have decided to stop treating the office of Chief Rabbi as the titular head of all Britain's 300,000 Jews. After the retirement of Lord Jakobovits as Chief Rabbi next spring, the Union of Liberal and Progressive Synagogues says it will regard his successor as the leader only of Orthodox Jews. They will describe him as "Chief Rabbi of the United Hebrew Congregation," the main Orthodox organisation'. After quoting the statement's assertion that 'our relationship to the office of Chief Rabbi is not dependent on the person who fills it', Longley wrote: 'Leading members [of the ULPS] were saying privately that Lord Jakobovits had caused tension between Progressive and Orthodox Jews because of his claim that "Thatcherism" was in line with Jewish principles, and because he had taken an over-rigid view on sexual morality.' Longley also noted: 'Before making its decision, the ULPS wrote to the council of the United Synagogue, the governing body of the United Hebrew Congregation, asking whether there was any intention to consult Progressive Jewish bodies and were told there was not' (*The Times*, 16 December 1989, p.1).
29. Jakobovits to Brichto, 19 December 1989, Brichto Papers, London.
30. Brichto to Jakobovits, 17 January 1990, ibid.
31. *Jewish Chronicle*, 22 December 1989, p.40.
32. 'ULPS Statement on the Chief Rabbinate', Raymond M. Goldman, executive director of the Reform Synagogues of Great Britain, to 'all rabbis and synagogue chairmen', 28 December 1989, Brichto Papers, London.
33. Ibid.
34. 'Press statement', Raymond M. Goldman, 19 December 1989. An amended text was addressed to *The Times*, signed by Marcus Bower, chairman of the Reform Synagogues of Great Britain, and Rabbi Simon Franses, chairman of the RSGB Assembly of Rabbis. Brichto Papers, London.
35. Sanderson to Bower, 27 December 1989, ibid.

# Notes

36. Bower to Sanderson, 2 January 1990, ibid.
37. *Jewish Chronicle*, 5 January 1990, p.21.
38. Ibid., 12 January 1990, p.22.
39. The event – sponsored by the British Friends of Bar-Ilan University and Bamah (the Forum for Jewish Dialogue) – was in memory of Louis Mintz, on whom see chapter 16, note 15.
40. *Jewish Chronicle*, 29 December 1989, p.5.
41. Sacks to Brichto, 4 March 1990, Brichto Papers, London. In 1998, in the wake of the Sacks/Gryn controversy (see note 13), the so-called 'Stanmore Accords' – signed by the lay leaders of the United, Reform, Liberal and Masorti Synagogues – drew up guidelines 'to bring about a more harmonious and productive relationship between the several sections of the community'. Ten years on, concern was expressed that the quarterly forum set up to further this aim 'has made too little progress in the way of practical co-operation' (*Jewish Chronicle*, 11 January 2008, p.7). The Masorti chairman, Michael Burman, stated that 'the outcomes are frustrating as far as we are concerned', while Reform chairman Michael Grabiner declared: 'I don't think we have engaged with really substantive issues.'
42. Immanuel Jakobovits, 'Trouble and Tradition', *Jewish Chronicle*, 25 September 1992, pp.24, 26.
43. Immanuel Jakobovits, 'Putting Stability Before "Mirage" Of Unity', ibid., 10 January 1997, p.23.
44. Immanuel Jakobovits, *Installation Address as Chief Rabbi of the United Hebrew Congregations of the British Commonwealth of Nations*, St John's Wood Synagogue, London, 1 Nisan 5727 – 11 April 1967 (London: Office of the Chief Rabbi, 1967), pp.5, 8, 9.
45. Jakobovits, 'Putting Stability Before "Mirage" Of Unity', p.23.

## EPILOGUE

1. N.M. Adler, *Laws and Regulations for all the Synagogues in the British Empire* (London: John Wertheimer, 5607 – 1847), pp.iii–iv.
2. Hermann Adler, *The Ritual: The Reply of the Chief Rabbi* (London: Wertheimer, Lea, 1892), p.5.
3. Ibid., p.4.
4. Hermann Adler, *The Old Paths: A Sermon Preached at the St John's Wood Synagogue, 6 December, 5663 – 1902* (London: Wertheimer, Lea, 1902), p.7.
5. Francis L. Cohen and David M. Davis, *The Voice of Prayer & Praise* (London: United Synagogue, 1899); 3rd edn, with Supplement arranged and edited by Samuel Alman (1933), p.viii.
6. J.H. Hertz, 'The Chief Rabbi's Sermon', in *Joint Celebration of the Seventy-Fifth Anniversary of Jews' College; the Seventieth Anniversary of the Jewish Religious Education Board; and the Sixtieth Anniversary of the United Synagogue* (London: Oxford University Press, 1931), p.11.
7. Hermann Adler, 'Functions of the Jewish Pulpit' (1892), quoted in Israel Brodie, *The Strength of My Heart* (London: G.J. George, for the Israel Brodie Publications Committee, 1969), p.34.
8. Israel Brodie, ibid., pp.34–5.
9. Israel Brodie, 'The Chief Rabbinate', *Jewish Chronicle Tercentenary Supplement*, 27 January 1956, p.9; reproduced as 'The Chief Rabbis of England', in Brodie, *The Strength of My Heart*, pp.396–8.
10. Immanuel Jakobovits, *Looking Ahead*, Sermon given at the United Synagogue, London, 26 November 1967 (London: United Synagogue, 1967), pp.4–7.
11. Known as the 'Chafetz Chaim' – the title of his best-known book, on the sins of gossip and slander – the Polish halachist Israel Meir Hacohen Poupko (1838–1933) was a follower of Israel Lipkin Salanter's *musar* (ethicist) movement, the organiser of the Radun yeshivah, and the author of guides for Jewish soldiers in the Russian army, and Jewish migrants to the United States.
12. Immanuel Jakobovits, *Milestones and Millstones*, United Synagogue, London, 19 July 1970 (London: Office of the Chief Rabbi, 1970), p.9.
13. *A Time For Change: A Report on the Role of the United Synagogue in the Years Ahead* (London: Stanley Kalms Foundation, 1992), pp.97–9.
14. Aubrey Newman, *The United Synagogue, 1870–1970* (London: Routledge and Kegan Paul, 1977), p.203.
15. Jonathan Sacks, *A Time For Renewal: A Rabbinic Response to the Kalms Report, 'A Time For Change'* (London: Office of the Chief Rabbi, 1992), pp.19–21.

# Appendix I

THE PRESENT POSITION OF JUDAISM IN ENGLAND

*An address delivered at the Kilburn Town Hall, on Sabbath afternoon, 20 February 1892, by the Rev. Morris Joseph.*
(Jewish Chronicle, 4 March 1892, p.19)

Today marks the beginning of the third year of our movement. Let us lift our hearts in gratitude to Almighty God for the help He has vouchsafed to us thus far, for the courage that has sustained us under the difficulties with which we have been confronted – above all, for the blessings that have visited our souls as a result of our prayers. We thank Thee, O Heavenly Father, for these, Thy mercies. Be with us henceforth as Thou hast been with us hitherto. Make our worship of Thee yet more fruitful. May it bind us to Thee in a still deeper love, a yet more willing service! May it impel other hearts to seek Thy face, to draw near to Thy footstool in prayerful aspiration and in purity of life! Amen.

Two years ago, when inaugurating these services, I pointed out that our movement had a twofold character. I said that it aimed at providing a form of worship acceptable to those Jews who were spiritually out of touch with the ordinary synagogue service, but that it was also designed to illustrate the possibility of harmonising Judaism with modern ideas.

The second object, indeed, is the logical corollary of the first. You cannot consistently shut up religious progress within the covers of the prayer-book. You cannot let liberal tendencies have full play in the service and keep them out of the pulpit. Nay, it is clear that to touch the prayer-book is inevitably to touch the religion. For every exponent of conservative Judaism will tell you that there can be no such thing as change – even in the liturgy. Its form has been fixed by Jewish law, and that law, like those of the Medes and Persians, is immutable.

Well, as soon as we lay a finger on the prayer-book, we proclaim our rejection of this theory, and this apart from the significance of the particular modification we effect. We declare by the most emphatic of all methods that the sanctity with which prescription has hedged round the ancient ordinances is purely artificial, to be invaded if the interests of religion, of the higher life, demand it; that, in the conflict between the old and the new, between institutions and ideas, it is the old and not the new that must give way. The past is entitled to our utmost veneration, but only in so far as it is capable of constituting the inspiration of the present. It must be wings, not fetters to the spirit; it must add, not impede, the soul's flight to God.

This is what we have proclaimed in establishing these services. We are helping to furnish a new presentment of Judaism. Can we doubt that the task is needed? Look at the position of Judaism in this country at the present moment. The community is split up into two parties, one strenuously demanding, the other as resolutely resisting, the revision of the liturgy. Beneath the ostensible points in dispute is a marked divergence of religious thought. On the one hand, Judaism is conceived of as essentially a rigid system, for which change portends enfeeblement, disruption, death; on the other hand, it is viewed as an organism, capable of, and destined to, constant, almost unlimited growth.

Never have the two great parties in English Judaism been more sharply divided, or more feverishly active. The conservative section, reinforced by numerous fugitives from Russian oppression, who have brought with them the old religious ideas, is confronted by the more modern party, who are feeling to an unparalleled degree the influence of the intellectual forces that dominate the age. Thus far, victory outwardly remains with the conservatives. We know it from personal experience. The service we are holding in this hall would this very day have been transferred to an Orthodox synagogue but for the triumph – a temporary one, I believe – of the view that progress is treachery to the religion, and that to widen the confines of the synagogue is to threaten its stability. I do not doubt for a single moment the sincerity of the men who adopt this view. I simply record the fact that such opinions prevail, and ask you to note its significance and its consequences.

Think of it! Judaism – for this is what it amounts to – is not strong enough to breathe the rarefied atmosphere of modern ideas. Liberal exposition of ancient doctrine, a denial to sacrifices of a place in the ideal worship which is to glorify God in the Golden Age, even a removal of the antiquated symbols which betoken the spiritual inferiority of women – these cannot be tolerated, for they would be fatal to the faith. How melancholy all this seems to us – this insistence upon minor points when the most tremendous of issues – the maintenance of religion itself against the assaults of latter-day infidelity – is at stake. But, as I have said, to what a state of decrepitude must Judaism have been reduced in the opinion of its Orthodox defenders when the slightest onward movement threatens to overthrow it.

My brethren, you and I do not share these fears, for to share them would be to despair of our religion. We cannot believe that it is fated ever to stand still, for that would be equivalent to believing that it is fated to perish. If Judaism is organised stagnation, then when the sun of knowledge waxes hot and floods the whole earth, it must vanish, as did the neglected manna of old. We refuse to take this view, and in so refusing, claim to be the true champions of our ancestral faith. We refuse to admit that the time will come when Judaism will have lost its life as the inevitable consequence of having lost all meaning for the spiritual life. We think of it retaining its vitality by virtue of changing its shape through all the coming days. We think of it keeping step with the human mind in its onward march, leaving ever further behind it the mist-covered plains of imperfect knowledge, and climbing one by one those sunny peaks where dwells the larger truth.

And surely it is this conception, and not that which depicts Judaism remaining for ever unmoved, unquickened, by the spiritual activities that play about it, which is destined to be realised. Reason declares it; history declares it. Change is not only the essential condition of the survival of a religion; it is the story of Judaism throughout its long life. There has scarcely ever been a time when Israel has not felt the ferment of new spiritual ideas. Moses, the Prophets, the Talmud, the philosophical rabbins of Spain, Mendelssohn, the apostles of German Reform – each and all represent successive links in that long chain of religious inquiry which constitutes the history of Judaism.

The opponents of change, then, with whom we have to reckon at the present moment, forget the life story of the very religion they would preserve. They make a claim for Judaism which it has never made for itself. Today, according to their view, it is to do what it has hardly ever done before, and never done save to its own hurt – stand still, and refuse as unholy the alliance proffered to it by the intellect and the soul. They have as their type of Judaism that form of it which corresponds to the ideas of victims of Russian bondage, physical and mental, and they would insist upon English Jews adopting it. The attempt would be tyrannical were it not utterly vain. All it accomplishes is the securing of outward uniformity; but spiritually the old diversity continues. For a man's Judaism is not what others would have it be; it is what his own soul has fashioned for him after the pattern he has seen on the Mount.

If this be not so, then our religion has fallen on evil days. If the hundreds of our brethren whose religious ideas are the sparks evolved from the clash of English life and Jewish feeling – if they have not got Judaism, then woe to it! They are ready to bring to it all the strength that intellectuality can lend it; but their precious gifts are refused. The synagogue, they are told, has no place for independent thought, for the latest truths won by scientific research, by literary criticism, by the comparative study of religions. Above its portals there has been written the legend, 'Abandon all hope of intellectual satisfaction ye who enter here.' And so the flower of Israel's army is rejected, and, reversing the old ordinance, only the fearful and faint-hearted are retained. The slow defection goes on which deprives us of some of our best comrades. There is no open revolt, but what is far worse, because more insidious, passive dissatisfaction and gradual desertion. But one day the community wakes up from its sleep and finds that its poverty has come upon it like an armed man. It is appalled at the number of those who have left it, at the thought that each might have been a force helping to mould a happy future for the race.

Nor is this the whole extent of the evil. There are those who do not desert, but who yet are estranged. There are children growing up about us – children already drawing in the influences of the age with the very air they breathe. What sort of hold will medieval conceptions of religion have on their minds when they have reached man's estate? What sort of foundation is being laid for Judaism in their hearts now? Can we wonder that there is dissatisfaction? Orthodoxy admits its existence, but disclaims all responsibility for it. The discontented conservative apologists say, have their remedy: they can form synagogues for themselves. 'We do not', it is urged, 'deny them a place in the Jewish communion; all we say is that they are not Orthodox.' But there are those who refuse to accept this left-handed fellowship. 'If this religion is so narrow that it can offer me no resting-place, save on some debatable land outside its recognised boundaries, I will have none of it.'

So argue some. Others, happily, are more patient, more logical. They deny the fundamental assumption of so-called Orthodoxy. They deny its right to the possession of the only true Judaism. There is no reason, they contend, why Rabbinism, itself a modern product compared with the religion of the Bible, should claim to be the authoritative standard of Jewish belief and practice. No system – no, not even nineteenth-century Reform – dare make this claim. Judaism must change from age to age if it is to live; and to declare of any one of its many developments, 'This is Israel's religion for all time', is unhistorical, unphilosophical. This is the view that is gaining ground among us at the present moment, and its prevalence is one of the healthiest features in the existing situation. This sturdy independence of thought, conjoined to sincere love for the ancestral faith, contains the promise and potency of its future vitality. Judaism is not going to perish of dry rot – of indifference on the one hand, or stagnation on the other. A vigorous party is growing up, imbued with modern ideas and yet full of religious enthusiasm. A new spiritual life is being generated within us – the beginning of a real hunger and thirst for the living God.

It is for those who claim to be the leaders of Jewish thought to satisfy these higher cravings – satisfy them by instituting a more spiritual worship, by teaching enlightened doctrine, by intelligently explaining old institutions. We have begun the work; it is for others to help in completing it. I advocate no revolutionary movement. If here and there we have to pull down, it is only that we may more securely build up again. There is no need to reject the old materials, if only the new spirit animates the builders. There must be a revival in the synagogue, to match the revival that has begun in the individual soul.

But, more than this, we must get rid once for all of those irritating terms 'Orthodoxy' and 'Reform', with all the arbitrary, the unrighteous distinctions of which they are the symbols. All Israel must be one – one despite the differences that exist within its confines. The synagogue must be wide enough, catholic enough, to embrace every school of Jewish thought. Liberty must be the watchword of Judaism in the coming days. The Jew who, though he lives in England, has not yet thrown off the heavy yoke of Russian life and ideas must be free to worship and to serve God in the manner dictated to him by his conscience; but his English brother, who has long breathed the free air of the West that emancipates both mind and spirit, must enjoy the same liberty. Each is a human soul whose salvation is precious in the eyes of the Eternal, and shall it be lightly esteemed by any man? Mutual tolerance – that is what we have more diligently to cultivate: a recognition of each other's need, the everlasting need of humanity to be at one with the Highest, and of each other's right to satisfy that need in the only way possible to him.

Let us work for this, and Judaism will be saved, and by her salvation shall save many souls. I look into the future and I see the synagogue established on the surest of all foundations – the loyalty and love of all the House of Israel. I see it the rallying-point of all the forces that are mightily working in our midst and which, triumphing over all our disputes, make us truly united: the desire to vindicate our common Judaism in the estimation of the world; the desire to live the higher life and, by so glorious an example, help others to live it too. May God put His spirit upon us, so that this vision may be fulfilled speedily in our days! Amen.

# Appendix II

THE JEWISH RELIGIOUS UNION

Mr Claude G. Montefiore's Reply to the Chief Rabbi
(Jewish Chronicle, 12 November 1909, pp.19–20)

SIR, – I was rather disappointed to observe that, in his second sermon, Dr Adler did not see his way to withdrawing the assumption on which his first sermon seemed to be based – that the Jewish Religious Union contemplated the transference of the Sabbath to Sunday. In my pamphlet, which forms the text of the second sermon, I had made it perfectly clear that we have resolutely set our face against any such step. Of this emphatic passage, Dr Adler has scarcely taken adequate notice.

The second sermon is difficult to answer, because it hardly grapples with the real problem at issue. Dr Adler, however, allows that I understand the Orthodox and the traditional position. He does not suggest for a moment that I have incorrectly stated it, for example when, in my last letter, I said: 'In a certain code book, the will of God is contained for all time, perfect, immutable and divine. Whatever, in other words, is in the Pentateuch is perfect and flawless, because it is there. Because it is there, it is the infallible, absolute and undiluted word of God.'

I, then, have understood the Orthodox position. Has Dr Adler understood mine? I would ask Dr Adler a simple question. He is, of course, aware that many students of the Bible have arrived at certain new conclusions as to its compilation, and he knows that these conclusions are so widely accepted in their general outlines that they are taught in the vast majority of the universities of Europe and America, and are presupposed in numerous places of worship belonging to all creeds. These conclusions are incompatible with the old attitude towards the Bible. What follows? Either we must reject the new conclusions or we must change the old attitude. But we cannot reject the new conclusions, for we are firmly convinced that they are true. Will Dr Adler tell us how we are to retain the old attitude? This is a fundamental difficulty, and this the sermon has altogether ignored. Yet it is to us perhaps the most serious of all the problems connected with the Bible and its authority at the present day.

On our side, we are trying to deal with the problem, for unless it can be somehow solved, the outlook for Judaism seems to us perilous. For we see around us that worst form of demoralisation in which verbal homage is paid to a code which is violated in practice.

The law, supposed theoretically to be binding, is in fact defied. Many of the so-called Orthodox are each of them a law unto himself. In *practice*, you may pick and choose in your observance of the Law; you may, for instance, smoke and kindle fire on Sabbath, but observe the Passover; you may let your children work on Saturdays, but fast on the Day of Atonement; you may neglect the enactment against wearing garments made of mixed cloths, but retain the fringed *tallit*; you may eat meat and milk together, but reject the shot pheasant; or you may eat the pheasant, but refuse the shrimp. Each man allows his conscience or his convenience to decide. What is this but putting some other authority between themselves and the Law? This is what many do; but they stop short of admitting what their course of action implies. I seem to see why Orthodoxy apparently prefers this chaotic condition to our frank resolve to make theory square with fact. 'We recognise', I have said, 'no binding authority between us and God, whether in a man or in a book, whether in a church or in a code, whether in a tradition or in a ritual.' I said it, I repeat it, and the offence is in the saying. Your life may proclaim it, and no offence is taken; nay, you are admitted to offices which must not be held by such as I.

Let us be done with these inconsistencies. And as for those who do not observe the whole Law, and who also do not believe with intense sincerity in its being the absolutely flawless and undiluted word of God, written down at God's dictation to Moses – let not these venture to throw a stone at my colleagues and at me.

Now, a word or two about the question of 'bondage'. The word is first used by me on page twelve of the pamphlet: 'To free ourselves from the heavy bondage of the rabbinical law and of the Shulchan Aruch may be, and indeed is, desirable and necessary.' Well, as I have pointed out in my 'Hibberts' [lectures delivered by Montefiore at Oxford in 1892 on 'The Origin and Growth of Religion as Illustrated by the Religion of the Ancient Hebrews'] and often elsewhere, if you believe that the rabbinic law, and all the ordinances of the Shulchan Aruch, are divine, that it is the perfect God who has ordered you to obey them, then obedience to them constitutes liberty. But *only then*. That, without this belief, they constitute a heavy bondage is perhaps clear from the number of excellent persons – in high places, on many committees, councils and boards – who notoriously and flagrantly disobey them. I quite admit, on second thoughts, that the Rabbinical law, as many of Dr Adler's supporters observe it, is in no sense a bondage!

So much, then, for my first use of the word 'bondage'. I go on to say: 'But the bondage of the written law of the Pentateuch, or the view that the Bible, and the Bible alone, is the religion of Judaism, may be even heavier, or at all events more fossilising, than the Bible plus the interpretations and additions of Tradition.' Dr Adler is right in saying that this view, which I here condemn, is the Karaite view. And I do not think that he will hold that I am so very wrong in saying that this form of Karaitism – the religion of 'the Bible, and the Bible alone' – is a fossilising variety of Judaism. And if we were to fulfil the Law today, here in England, as Karaites bid us observe it (among other things, sitting in absolute darkness throughout the eve and night of Fridays), I think most people – unless cheered by the Karaite faith – would find it a tolerably 'heavy bondage'. But the strange thing is that even among the Orthodox today, there is a tendency to forget, or comfortably to ignore, the divinity of the Oral Law – a tendency, for instance, to divide Jews into 'biblical Jews' and ' non-biblical Jews'.

To pass, however, from the practice to the theory. Here, all depends upon our faith. Believe that the Law of the Pentateuch is the absolute, flawless word of God, then to obey its laws to the very letter may mean the truest freedom. But if we do not so believe, our religious liberty cannot be derived from an unquestioned obedience to a code from every law, letter and line, of which we can no longer hear the perfect and absolute word of God.

But I do not think, even though we seek our highest and most binding authority elsewhere, that therefore we are bound to become libertines, as Dr Adler's arguments would seem to suggest to be likely.

For we too bow before a divine authority which is not ourselves though in ourselves. We hear its voice. And this is the 'final authority', as I have said in the pamphlet. The odd thing is that I believe it is the 'final authority' even to Dr Adler himself! For if Dr Adler did not believe that the Pentateuch contained – for 'today and tomorrow' (by which I meant, of course, the present and the future) – the perfect, flawless and immutable word of God, would he think it right to accept all its dicta as true and to obey all its behests? Surely for him, too, there must be a voice, on the validity of which he depends, justifying the faith that is in him. That voice speaks to me, too, though, as far as the Bible is concerned, in somewhat different language.

God is the Source of righteousness, and of truth, and from what I, as the heir of the ages, hold to be true and good, I dare not turn away in rebellion. Only in obedience to the moral law and the intellectual law – to righteousness and truth – can I win my freedom. If I transgress – as, of course, I often do – if I do what I believe to be wrong, if I juggle with what

I believe to be true, then I am in bondage, and I feel and recognise the chain.

Once more then: 'We recognise no binding authority between us and God, whether in a man or in a book', and 'We accept nothing which does not seem to us good.' 'The final authority is within.' But this does *not* mean that we follow mere personal desires or inclinations. What we obey is the inward call of an authority which originates in the moral ideal itself. This authority *asserts* itself within us, but it is not *originated* within us. Its Source is the same Lawgiver whom Dr Adler and I both worship and adore – each in his different way – for its Source is God.

Dr Adler summarises another section of the pamphlet as arguing thus: 'We readily accept the moral law of the Bible, but not because it is in the book, but because it is good, because our reason and conscience approve it.' This argument he calls a grave fallacy. He calls it grotesque. Let me examine it therefore a little closely.

To begin with, I believe that Dr Adler himself accepts the Pentateuch as the undiluted word of God, invested in all its injunctions with equal divine authority, because such a faith commends itself to his conscience and reason. Unless he attributes his own faith to the accident of birth, what is it but reason and conscience that impel him to accept as divine the Pentateuch, and reject from that category the Gospel of the Christians and the Koran of the Mohammedans? I cannot conceive that he bases on anything but conscience and reason his belief in the one, and his disbelief in the other two documents. There is, however, a difference between him and me, though not, I submit, in the ultimate 'authority'. For – his reason and conscience being convinced, and telling him in no uncertain voice that the whole Pentateuch is the word of God – he has no longer to test each separate enactment. All the laws must be equally divine and perfect because the whole Pentateuch is perfect and divine. We, on the other hand, to whom conscience and reason do not declare that the whole Pentateuch is divine, what higher test of divinity can we find for its parts than goodness and truth? Where is the fallacy?

I do not deny that the Pentateuch has, along with other portions of the Bible and with many other agencies, 'guided our reason and educated our conscience throughout the ages'. But it is not on this ground that, here and now, we individually recognise many moral laws of the code as true, and willingly obey them. I will not, however, on this occasion, elaborate this statement farther, because Dr Adler's next sentence is more important, and brings me to my real answer on this point. The grotesque argument, worthy of the 'boor', is said to be this: 'Because reason and conscience tell us that the moral code is good, we are free to reject the authority of the book and the code.' This is, indeed, a 'grotesque' and 'boorish' argument, but then – I never used it!

Note the double use of the word 'code' in Dr Adler's argument. First we have the 'moral code', then the 'code'. Now the Pentateuch does not contain only 'moral laws'. You cannot jump from the 'moral laws' to the authority of all the ritual laws. You cannot have the moral code in one half of your sentence, and then drop the adjective in the other half. As I have said in my pamphlet, 'the inward moral law ... may and does recognise as the words of God the moral laws of a code'. And in a real sense, it is the Bible itself which helps us to the distinction between what may be recognised as the word of God and what does not seem to us to belong to that category. The highest in its pages is the touchstone which reveals the flaws in the lowest.

Why did Maimonides 'allegorise' away the human expressions used in Scripture with regard to God? Partly, at least, because he had derived from the Bible itself a conception of God with which the anthropomorphisms of the Bible were inconsistent. So with us; our inward moral law is confirmed by, though not derived from, the moral law of the code, and the two harmonise in a principle of selection which not only satisfies and justifies both forms of authority, but enables us to continue to use a very great deal of the Bible as our guide and support. It is indeed bewildering to us to be told that we are parting from the Bible when, following what Dr L. Blau assures us was the ancient Jewish practice, we are thinking of including not merely the Pentateuch but the Prophets and the Hagiographa in the Ark of our proposed new synagogue, though we shall naturally only use a lectionary in public worship. [Hungarian scholar Ludwig Lajos Blau (1861–1936) was a prolific writer on Bible and Talmud and a professor at the Jewish Theological Seminary of Budapest, of which he became director in 1914.]

Dr Adler goes on to argue that morality will be harmed if men no longer believe as he does. We cannot trust 'conscience and reason alone to curb man's wayward will'. If by this is meant that were men no longer to believe that conscience and reason are the gifts of God, and that God is the ultimate source of morality, then morality would suffer, I am inclined to agree with him. But if Dr Adler means merely that the 'inward moral law deprived of the authority of the Book will not suffice to fortify the human heart against the assaults of temptation', and if this authority means the old Orthodox belief in the verbal inspiration of Scripture, and the belief that the Pentateuch is the perfect word of God, then I think he takes far too gloomy a view of the situation.

He has, I venture to think, misapplied the story of the boor who thought more highly of the moon than of the sun. The great source of moral light is the intrinsic worth of the moral law itself. It is this that has been influencing for good millions of people to whom the Pentateuch was and is unknown. The Pentateuch itself is but a manifestation, or rather a series of manifestations, of this ultimate source of morality. It is the Pentateuch which is the real moon (or one of the moons) reflecting the light of the great Sun of Righteousness. Those who rank the Pentateuch higher than the moral law seem to think more of the moon than of the sun. Dr Adler's sad augury for the future has been made again and again, and again and again disproved at similar critical moments in the past. On the whole, the morality of the so-called 'Ages of Faith' was probably inferior to our own. We know how it was argued by Christians that morality could not survive disbelief in hell and eternal punishment and verbal inspiration. It has, however, survived them all, and so far as the Jews are concerned, I think their morality will survive a disbelief in the absolute perfection and divine authority of every enactment of the Law.

One personal word before I reach my conclusion. Neither in this nor in my former letter have I made any apologia. I stand by every thought and opinion expressed in the pamphlet, though the latter nevertheless takes something for granted. It presupposes some knowledge of my book on Liberal Judaism, and some acquaintance with my sermons during several years past. In this sense, I allow that the pamphlet is more likely to be fully grasped by our own members than by the general public.

And now for my conclusion. Those who attack the pamphlet and the Union – the Chief Rabbi among them – seem studiously to ignore the big wave of liberalism and modernism which is passing over all religions at the present time. They seem to ignore the fact that the same causes which are creating a number of modernists and liberals in every phase and section of Christianity are creating them in Judaism as well. They forget that we – the Jewish modernists and liberals – are part of a great movement which cannot possibly be combated, checked and destroyed by scholastic arguments or medieval denunciations. The movement will not easily be arrested. As Father Tyrrell says of one particular part of it, it is no longer confined to the study. It 'has reached the street and the railway bookstall'. The only question is whether – so far as the Jewish modernists are concerned – it can be kept within Jewish channels.

We think – I and my friends – that it can. We think that Judaism is in better case, for instance, than the religion of which Father Tyrrell was so distinguished an advocate and so noble an ornament. [Irish-born George Tyrrell was one of a new generation of 'liberal' Catholics who, in the late nineteenth century, raised questions of a theologically critical kind and became part of the loose network of liberal thinkers known as Modernists. He first clearly indicated his heterodoxy in 1899 with an attack on hell and eternal punishment.] Be that, however, as it may, it is only we, and such as we, who can keep those Jews who are infected with the modernist spirit within the religion of Judaism. Of that we are assured. And even as Liberal Judaism has been the salvation of Judaism for thousands in America – and is rapidly becoming again the hope and salvation of many in Germany – so do we believe that it may become the salvation of hundreds of Jews and Jewesses in England. At all events, we mean to have a try. Have our Orthodox brethren of the House of Israel no word of Godspeed for us?

# Appendix III

### SYNAGOGUE AND MARRIAGE STATISTICS

The fluctuations in synagogue affiliation during the period covered by this book, and their relationship to marriage ceremonies, have formed a major plank of the work of the Board of Deputies' statistical and demographic unit over several decades. Well before that work commenced, the first published account of synagogue attendances – indeed, 'the first scientific attempt in the history of this country to discover the number of those who attend places of worship in the Metropolis' – appeared in Richard Mudie-Smith, *The Religious Life of London* (London: Hodder and Stoughton, 1904), with a report of the *Daily News* census carried out between November 1902 and November 1903. During the day on which the synagogue census was conducted – the first day of Pesach – the following attendances (men/women/children) were among those recorded in the sixty-four congregations covered: Brick Lane (Spitalfields) – 1,217/89/438; Sandys Row (Spitalfields) – 310/40/121; Cannon Street Road – 547/36/503; Great Garden Street – 409/188/219; Great Alie Street – 172/14/80; East London (Stepney Green) – 649/92/236; Hambro' (Union Street) – 214/53/62; Great Synagogue – 1,021/155/427; Spanish and Portuguese (Bevis Marks) – 544/43/226; New Synagogue (Great St Helens) – 754/261/55; West End Lane (Hampstead) – 361/317/220; St Alban's Place – 155/34/187; Maiden Lane – 26/18/25; Upper Berkeley Street – 627/320/164; Central – 525/210/307; St John's Wood – 236/233/153; Lauderdale Road – 156/113/62; St Petersburgh Place – 328/304/105; Forest Gate (West Ham) – 42/1/25. The synagogue census recorded a grand total of 26,612, comprising 15,157 men, 4,375 women, and 7,080 children. Mudie-Smith noted: 'We must bear in mind that a very much larger proportion of the middle-class in East London – namely, the shopkeepers, clerks, etc. – attend a place of worship than the working-class proper' (24). One of the enumerators, Charles T. Bateman, reported: 'With respect to the Jews, Dr H. Adler, Chief Rabbi of the United Hebrew Congregations, informs me that in nearly all the synagogues in London – as well as in the large provincial congregations – services are held every day, both morning and evening ... The attendance is not large in the West End, as people have a long distance to go to their place of business, but in the East End attendance is fair' (310).

Of later figures, S.J. Prais writes: 'There were some 150 synagogues at the beginning of the [twentieth] century, and the growth in the subsequent half-century parallels in an approximate way what is known of the growth of the Jewish population ... Between 1947 and 1971, the net decline of some fifty synagogues consisted of 140 synagogues that were closed, offset by some ninety new synagogues ... In London, the trends in the community are mirrored by some twenty or so new Right-wing Orthodox synagogues (mostly in the Stamford Hill area, and generally small), five new Sephardi synagogues, eleven Reform, and eight Liberal. But the community is still dominated by its traditional Ashkenazi-Central-Orthodox complexion, as is shown by the establishment of twenty new United synagogues (mainly in the Outer London area) and nine new Federation synagogues (partly in North-West London, and partly in Outer London).' Prais, 'Synagogue Statistics and the Jewish Population of Great Britain, 1900–1970', *Jewish Journal of Sociology*, XIV, 2 (December 1972), pp.226–7.

In 1977, synagogue membership in Britain (London/provinces) was divided as follows: Right-wing Orthodox – 2,327/556; Central Orthodox – 38,663/22,476; Sephardi – 1,853/375; Reform – 7,577/3,286; Liberal – 5,074/811 (Barry A. Kosmin and Deborah de Lange, *Synagogue Affiliation in the United Kingdom, 1977*, Research Unit, Board of Deputies, London, 1978, p.6). The comparable figures for 1983 were: Right-wing Orthodox – 2,837/645; Central Orthodox – 35,228/20,378; Sephardi – 1,752/368; Reform – 8,794/3,286; Liberal – 4,748/913 (Barry A. Kosmin and Caren Levy, *Synagogue Membership in the United Kingdom, 1983*, Research Unit, Board of Deputies, London, 1984, p.6). In 1990, the 356 synagogues in Britain comprised (Greater London/provinces): Right-wing Orthodox – 51/18; Central Orthodox – 94/113; Sephardi – 10/3; Reform – 15/26; Liberal – 13/13 (Marlena Schmool and Frances Cohen, *British Synagogue Membership in 1990*, Community Research Unit, Board of Deputies, London, 1991, p.8).

The changing pattern of male membership by synagogue grouping, in percentage terms, was reflected as follows: Right-wing Orthodox: 1970, 2.6; 1977, 4.2; 1983, 5.3; 1990, 8.8 (numerical change 1983-1990, +1,599). Central Orthodox: 1970, 72.3; 1977, 69.7; 1983, 66.0; 1990, 58.2 (numerical change, 1983–1990, -5,939). Sephardi: 1970, 4.5; 1977, 3.3; 1983, 3.3; 1990, 3.7 (numerical change, 1983–1990, +100). Reform: 1970, 11.9; 1977, 13.7; 1983, 16.5; 1990, 18.0 (numerical change, 1983–1990, +251). Liberal: 1970, 8.7; 1977, 9.1; 1983, 8.9;

1990, 11.3 (numerical change, 1983–1990, +935) (ibid., p.25).

In numerical terms, national synagogue groupings were as follows: Union of Orthodox: 1990, 5,805; 1996, 6,622 (net change 1990–1996, +817: +14.1 per cent). Mainstream Orthodox: 1990, 68,704; 1996, 56,895 (net change 1990–1996, -10,396: -15.1 per cent). Sephardi: 1990, 3,208; 1996, 3,169 (net change 1990–1996, -39: -1.2 per cent). Masorti: 1996, 1,413. Reform: 1990, 17,169; 1996, 17,614 (net change 1990–1996, +445: +2.6 per cent). Liberal: 1990, 7,258; 1996, 7,971 (net change 1990-1996, +713: +9.8 per cent) (Marlena Schmool and Frances Cohen, *British Synagogue Membership in 1996*, Community Unit, Board of Deputies, London, 1997, p.8).

The average number of synagogue marriages per annum (Orthodox/Reform/Liberal) in the first half of the twentieth century was as follows: 1901–1910: 2,020/23/0; 1911–1920: 2,071/22/7; 1921–1930: 2,306/32/22; 1931–1940: 2,658/56/55; 1941–1950: 2,660/130/86; 1951–1955: 1,925/163/107; 1956-1960: 1,676/173/131 (S.J. Prais and Marlena Schmool, 'Statistics of Jewish Marriages in Great Britain, 1901–1965', *Jewish Journal of Sociology*, IX, 1 (1967), p.154).

Of the annual average of 1,823 synagogue marriages between 1961 and 1965, 1,373 were Central Orthodox, 39 Right-wing Orthodox, 64 Sephardi, 192 Reform, and 155 Liberal. Comparable figures for the 1966–68 annual average of 1,829 synagogue marriages were: 1,381, 55, 64, 195, and 134 (S.J. Prais and Marlena Schmool, 'Synagogue Marriages in Great Britain, 1966–1968', *Jewish Journal of Sociology*, XII, 1 (June 1970), pp.21–8). Later figures were: 1976–1980 (annual averages): 899, 98, 43, 190, 80; 1990: 722, 103, 48, 167, 58; 2000: 571, 215, 39, 144, 48 (Research Unit, Board of Deputies, London, 1981, 1991, 2001).

# Bibliography

A Friend of Truth. *A Few Words Addressed to the Committee for the Election of a Chief Rabbi of England, and to the Electors at Large*. London: Brain and Payne, 1844.

*A Selection of Prayers, Psalms and Other Scriptural Passages and Hymns for Use at the Services of the Jewish Religious Union, London*. Second, revised edition. London: Wertheimer, Lea, 5664 – 1903.

A Special Correspondent. 'The British Chief Rabbinate'. *The Jewish Monthly* 2 (May 1947). London: Anglo-Jewish Association.

*A Time For Change: A Report on the Role of the United Synagogue in the Years Ahead*. London: Stanley Kalms Foundation, 1992.

Abramsky, Yechezkel. *Address at the Installation of Rabbi I. Jakobovits*. London: United Synagogue, 1947.

*Act for confirming a Scheme of the Charity Commissioners for the Jewish United Synagogues* [33 & 34 Vict., Ch. cxvi]. 14 July 1870.

*Addresses Delivered at the Services of the Jewish Religious Union During the First Session, 1902–3*. London: Brimley Johnson, 1904.

Adler, Elkan Nathan. *London*. Philadelphia, PA: Jewish Publication Society of America, 1930.

Adler, Hermann. 'The Chief Rabbis of England'. In *Papers Read at the Anglo-Jewish Historical Exhibition, Royal Albert Hall, London, 1887*. London: Office of the Jewish Chronicle, 1888.

— *The Ritual: The Reply of the Chief Rabbi*. London: Wertheimer, Lea, 1892.

— *The Jews During the Victorian Era*. London: Alfred J. Isaacs and Sons, 5657 – 1897.

— *The Old Paths*. London: Wertheimer, Lea, 1902.

— 'In Memory of the Late Sir Moses Montefiore'. In *Anglo-Jewish Memories and Other Sermons*. London: George Routledge and Sons, 1909.

— 'The Ideal Jewish Pastor: An Installation Sermon'. The Great Synagogue, London, 23 June 1891. In *Anglo-Jewish Memories and Other Sermons*. 1909.

— 'The Passing of the Late Chief Rabbi, Nathan Adler'. In *Anglo-Jewish Memories and Other Sermons*. 1909.

— *Anglo-Jewish Memories and Other Sermons*. London: George Routledge and Sons, 1909.

— 'A Menace to Judaism'. *Jewish Chronicle*, 8 October 1909.

— 'It is Time to Work for the Lord'. *Jewish Chronicle*, 5 November 1909.

Adler, Marcus N. *The Adler Family*. London: Office of the Jewish Chronicle, 1909. Reprinted, expanded and translated into Hebrew by Yitzhak Kaufmann. Israel: Bnei Berak, 1993.

Adler, N.M. 'The Reciprocal Duties of a Pastor and his Flock', 1829. In *'Antrittsrede in Oldenburg,' Sulamith* VII (1824–1833). David Frankel (ed.). Dessau, 1833.

— *Abschiedspredight in Hannover*. Hanover, 1845.

— *Sermon Delivered at the Great Synagogue on the Occasion of His Installation into Office as Chief Rabbi of Great Britain*. Translated by Barnard van Oven. London: Longman, Brown, Green and Longmans, 1845.

— *Laws and Regulations for all the Synagogues in the British Empire*. London: John Wertheimer, 5607 – 1847.

— *The Jewish Faith*. London: Effingham Wilson, 5608 – 1848.

— *The Bonds of Brotherhood*. London: J. Wertheimer, 1849.

— *Solomon's Judgment: A Picture of Israel*. London: Wertheimer, 1854.

— *The Second Days of the Festivals*. London: Trübner, 5628 – 1868.
— 'Traditional Will'. In *Ethical Wills: A Modern Jewish Treasury*. Jack Riemer and Nathaniel Stampfer (eds). New York: Schocken Books, 1983.
Alderman, Geoffrey. *The Jewish Community in British Politics*. Oxford: Clarendon Press, 1983.
— *The Federation of Synagogues, 1887–1987*. London: Federation of Synagogues, 1987.
— *London Jewry and London Politics, 1889–1986*. London: Routledge, 1989.
— *Anglo-Jewry: A Suitable Case for Treatment*. Egham: Royal Holloway and Bedford New College, 1990.
— 'The British Chief Rabbinate: A Most Peculiar Practice'. *European Judaism* 23:2 (Autumn 1990).
— 'Power, Authority and Status in British Jewry: The Chief Rabbinate and Shechita'. In G. Alderman and C. Holmes (eds). *Outsiders and Outcasts: Essays in Honour of William J. Fishman*. London: Duckworth, 1993.
— 'The defence of shechita: Anglo-Jewry and the "humane conditions" regulations of 1990'. In *new community* 21:1 (January 1995).
— *British Jewry: Religious Pluralism and Public Identity*. Judentum und Moderne in Frankreich und Italien Internationaler Kongress. Universität Münster, 1996.
— *Modern British Jewry*. Oxford: Clarendon Press, 1992; rev. edn, 1998.
Apple, Raymond. *The Hampstead Synagogue 1892–1967*. London: Vallentine Mitchell, 1967.
— *In Farewell to Hampstead*. London: Hampstead Synagogue, 1972.
— 'Hermann Adler: Chief Rabbi'. In *Noblesse Oblige: Essays in Honour of David Kessler, OBE*, Alan D. Crown (ed.). London and Portland, OR: Vallentine Mitchell, 1998.
Asaria, Zwi. 'Samson Raphael Hirsch's Wirken im Lande Niedersachsens'. In *Udim: Zeitschrift der Rabbinerkonferenz in der Bundesrepublik Deutschland*. Frankfurt: Heft I, 5731 – 1970.
Barnett, Arthur. *The Western Synagogue Through Two Centuries, 1761–1961*. London: Vallentine Mitchell, 1961.
Barnett, Lionel D. *El Libro de los Acuerdos*. Oxford: Oxford University Press, 1931.
Bayme, Steven. 'Claude Montefiore, Lily Montagu and the Origins of the Jewish Religious Union'. *Transactions of the Jewish Historical Society of England* XXVII (1978–1980).
Bentwich, Norman. *Claude Montefiore and His Tutor in Rabbinics: Founders of Liberal and Conservative Judaism*. Southampton: University of Southampton, 1966.
Berger, Doreen. *The Jewish Victorian: Genealogical Information from the Jewish Newspapers, 1871–1880*. Witney: Robert Boyd Publications, 1999.
— *The Jewish Victorian: Genealogical Information from the Jewish Newspapers, 1861–1870*. Witney: Robert Boyd Publications, 2004.
Bermant, Chaim. *Troubled Eden: An Anatomy of British Jewry*. New York: Basic Books, 1970.
— *The Cousinhood: The Anglo-Jewish Gentry*. London: Eyre and Spottiswoode, 1971.
— *London's East End: Point of Arrival*. New York: Macmillan, 1975.
— *Lord Jakobovits: The Authorized Biography of the Chief Rabbi*. London: Weidenfeld and Nicolson, 1990.
— 'The Rabbi's Rabbi'. *Jewish Chronicle*, 5 November 1999.
Black, Eugene C. *The Social Politics of Anglo-Jewry 1880–1920*. Oxford: Blackwell, 1988.
—'The Anglicization of Orthodoxy: The Adlers'. Frances Malino and David Sorkin (eds). *Profiles in Diversity*. Detroit, MI: Wayne State University Press, 1998.
Blank, Joseph E. *The Minutes of the Federation of Synagogues: A Twenty-Five Years' Review*. London: E.W. Rabbinowicz, 5673 – 1912.
Bornstein, Abba, and Bernard Homa. *Tell It In Gath: British Jewry and Clause 43. The Inside Story*. London: privately published, 1972.
Brenner, Michael, Rainer Liedtke and David Rechter, (eds). *Two Nations: British and German Jews in Comparative Perspective*. Tübingen: Mohr Siebeck, 1999.

Breuer, Isaac. 'Samson Raphael Hirsch'. In *Jewish Leaders, 1750–1940*. Leo Jung (ed.). New York: Bloch, 5714 – 1953.
Breuer, Mordechai. 'Samson Raphael Hirsch'. In *Guardians of our Heritage, 1724–1953*. Leo Jung (ed.). New York: Bloch,1958.
— *Modernity Within Tradition: The Social History of Orthodox Jewry in Imperial Germany*. Translated by Elizabeth Petuchowski. New York: Columbia University Press, 1992.
Brichto, Sidney. 'What is wrong with the Chief Rabbinate?' *Liberal Jewish Monthly* (May 1965). London: Union of Liberal and Progressive Judaism, 1965.
— 'Halachah with Humility'. *Jewish Chronicle*, 2 October 1987.
Brodie, Israel. *Installation Sermon as Chief Rabbi of the United Hebrew Congregations of the British Commonwealth of Nations*. London: United Synagogue, 1948.
— 'Opening Address'. In *Addresses Given at the Ninth Conference of Anglo-Jewish Preachers*. London: Standing Committee, 1951.
— 'The Chief Rabbinate'. In *Jewish Chronicle Tercentenary Supplement*, 27 January 1956.
— 'Historical Judaism: Challenge To Our Time'. In *A Word in Season*, 1959.
— 'Jews' College Centenary'. In *A Word in Season*. 1959.
— *A Word in Season: Addresses and Sermons, 1948–1958*. London: Vallentine Mitchell, 1959.
— *Statement by the Very Rev. the Chief Rabbi, Dr Israel Brodie*. London: United Synagogue, 1964.
— *Induction Address, Installation of Dr Immanuel Jakobovits*, St John's Wood Synagogue, London. London: United Synagogue, 1967.
— 'Opening Address, First Conference of European Rabbis'. In *The Strength of My Heart*. 1969.
— *The Strength of My Heart: Sermons and Addresses 1948–1965*. London: G.J. George, for the Israel Brodie Publications Committee, 1969.
Brook, Stephen. *The Club: The Jews of Modern Britain*. London: Constable, 1989.
*Bye-Laws of the Constituent Synagogues*. London: United Synagogue, 1881.
*Bye-Laws of the Constituent Synagogues*. London: United Synagogue, 1936.
Carlebach, Julius. 'The Impact of German Jews on Anglo-Jewry – Orthodoxy, 1850-1950'. In Werner E. Mosse, Julius Carlebach, Gerhard Hirschfeld, Aubrey Newman, Arnold Paucker, Peter Pulzer, J.C.B. Mohr (eds). *Second Chance: Two Centuries of German-Speaking Jews in the United Kingdom*. Tübingen: Paul Siebeck, 1991.
Cesarani, David. 'The Transformation of Communal Authority in Anglo-Jewry, 1914–1940'. In *The Making of Modern Anglo-Jewry*. David Cesarani (ed.). Oxford: Basil Blackwell, 1990.
— *The Jewish Chronicle and Anglo-Jewry, 1841–1991*. Cambridge: Cambridge University Press, 1994.
Cohen, Arthur A., and Paul Mendes-Flohr (eds). *Contemporary Jewish Religious Thought*. New York and London: The Free Press and Collier Macmillan, 1988.
Cohen, Arthur. 'The Structure of Anglo-Jewry Today'. In V.D. Lipman (ed.). *Three Centuries of Anglo-Jewish History*. Cambridge: W. Heffer and Sons, for the Jewish Historical Society of England, 1961.
Cohen, Francis L., and David M. Davis (eds). *The Voice of Prayer & Praise: A Handbook of Synagogue Music for Congregational Singing*. London: Office of the United Synagogue, 1899. Third edition, with Supplement arranged and edited by Samuel Alman, 5693 – 1933.
Cohen, Israel. 'Michael Friedländer'. In Leo Jung (ed.). *Men of the Spirit*. New York: Kymson, 1964.
Cohen, Jeffrey M. (ed.). *Dear Chief Rabbi: From the Correspondence of Chief Rabbi Immanuel Jakobovits on Matters of Jewish Law, Ethics and Contemporary Issues, 1980–1990*. New Jersey: Ktav, 1995.
— *Issues of the Day: A Modern-Orthodox View*. Stanmore: Gnesia Publications, 1999.

Cohen, Norman. 'The Religious Crisis in Anglo-Jewry'. *Tradition* 8:2. Walter S. Wurzburger (ed.). New York: Rabbinical Council of America, 1966.
— 'Non-Religious Factors in the Emergence of the Chief Rabbinate'. *Transactions of the Jewish Historical Society of England* XXI (1968).
Cohen, Stuart A. *English Zionists and British Jews: The Communal Politics of Anglo-Jewry, 1895–1920*. Princeton, NJ: Princeton University Press, 1982.
Cosgrove, Elliot J. 'The Road Not Taken: The Iconoclastic Theology of Rabbi Louis Jacobs'. PhD dissertation. University of Chicago, 2008.
Cowen, Anne (ed.) *New London Synagogue: The First Twenty Years*. London: New London Synagogue, 1984.
Cowen, Philip. *Memories of an American Jew*. New York: International Press, 1932.
*Creative Judaism: Some Aims And Objects*. London: Society for the Study of Jewish Theology, 1963.
*Death of Sir Moses Montefiore: Supplement to the Jewish Chronicle*, 31 July 1885.
Diner, Hasia. 'Like the Antelope and the Badger'. *Tradition Renewed: A History of the Jewish Theological Seminary*. Vol. I. Jack Wertheimer (ed.). New York: Jewish Theological Seminary of America, 1997.
Domb, Cyril. 'Dayan Yechezkel Abramsky: A Centenary Tribute'. *L'Eylah* 23 (Pesach 5747). London: Office of the Chief Rabbi and Jews' College, April 1987.
Duschinsky, Charles. *The Rabbinate of the Great Synagogue, London, 1756–1842*, London: Oxford University Press, 1921.
Ehrmann, Salomon. 'Rabbi S.R. Hirsch as a Pioneer of Judaism in Eretz Yisroel and in the Diaspora'. In *Ateret Zvi: Rabbi Dr Isaac Breuer Jubilee Volume*. New York: Feldheim, 1962.
Ellenson, David. *Rabbi Ezriel Hildesheimer and the Creation of a Modern Jewish Orthodoxy*. Tuscaloosa, AL and London: University of Alabama Press, 1990.
— *After Emancipation: Jewish Religious Responses to Modernity*. Cincinnati: Hebrew Union College Press, 2004.
Elton, Benjamin J. 'Did the Chief Rabbinate move to the right? A case study – the mixed choirs controversies, 1880–1986'. *Jewish Historical Studies* 39 (2004).
— 'Britain's Chief Rabbis: The Jewish response to modernity and the remoulding of tradition'. PhD dissertation. University of London, 2007.
Emanuel, Charles H.L. *A Century and a Half of Jewish History: Extracted from the Minute Books of the London Committee of Deputies of the British Jews*. London: George Routledge and Sons, 1910.
Endelman, Todd M. 'The Englishness of Jewish Modernity in England'. In *Toward Modernity: The European Jewish Model*. Jacob Katz (ed.). New Brunswick, NJ and Oxford: Transaction Books, 1987.
— *Radical Assimilation in English Jewish History, 1656–1945*. Bloomington, Indianapolis, IN: Indiana University Press, 1990.
— *The Jews of Georgian England 1714–1830: Tradition and Change in a Liberal Society*. Ann Arbor, MI: University of Michigan Press, 1999.
— 'Communal Solidarity Among the Jewish Elite of Victorian London'. *Victorian Studies* 28:3 (2002).
— 'Practices of a Low Anthropologic Level: A Shechitah Controversy of the 1950s'. In Anne J. Kershen (ed.). *Food in the Migrant Experience*. Aldershot and Burlington, VT: Ashgate Publishing, 2002.
— *The Jews of Britain 1656 to 2000*. Berkeley, Los Angeles, CA and London: University of California Press, 2002.
Englander, David. 'Anglicised not Anglican: Jews and Judaism in Victorian Britain'. In Gerald Parsons (ed.). *Religion in Victorian Britain – I. Traditions*. Manchester: Manchester

University Press and the Open University, 1988.
— (ed.). *The Jewish Enigma: An Enduring People*. London: Open University in association with Peter Halban and the Spiro Institute, 1992.
— (ed.) *A Documentary History of Jewish Immigrants in Britain, 1840–1920*. Leicester: Leicester University Press, 1994.
Epstein, Isidore. *Jewish Faith in Action*. Philip Ginsbury (ed.). London: Jews' College Publications, 1995.
*Facts and Fallacies about Liberal Judaism*. London: Union of Liberal and Progressive Synagogues, 1961; revised and reprinted, 1972.
Feldman, David. *Englishmen and Jews: Social Relations and Political Culture, 1840–1914*. New Haven and London: Yale University Press, 1994.
Finestein, Israel. *A Short History of Anglo-Jewry*. London: Lincolns-Prager for the World Jewish Congress British Section, 1957.
— 'The Jews and English Marriage Law'. *Jewish Journal of Sociology* 8 (1964). Reprinted in *Jewish Society in Victorian England*, 1993.
— 'The Anglo-Jewish Revolt of 1853'. *Jewish Quarterly* 26 (1978–79). Reprinted in *Jewish Society in Victorian England*. 1993.
— 'Joseph Frederick Stern, 1865–1934: Aspects of a Gifted Anomaly'. In *The Jewish East End, 1840–1939*. Aubrey Newman, (ed.). London: Jewish Historical Society of England, 1981. Reprinted in *Jewish Society in Victorian England*, 1993.
— *Jewish Society in Victorian England*. London and Portland, OR: Vallentine Mitchell, 1993.
— *Anglo-Jewry in Changing Times*. London and Portland, OR: Vallentine Mitchell, 1999.
— 'Sir Moses Montefiore: A Modern Appreciation'. In *Scenes and Personalities in Anglo-Jewry, 1800–2000*, 2002.
— *Scenes and Personalities in Anglo-Jewry, 1800–2000*. London and Portland, OR: Vallentine Mitchell, 2002.
Fishman, William J. *East End Jewish Radicals, 1875–1914*. London: Duckworth, 1975.
— *East End 1888*. London: Duckworth, 1988.
Frankel, Jonathan, and Steven J. Zipperstein, (eds). *Assimilation and Community: The Jews in Nineteenth-Century Europe*. Cambridge: Cambridge University Press, 1992.
Frankel, William. *Tea With Einstein And Other Memories*. London: Halban, in association with the European Jewish Publication Society, 2006.
Freedman, Maurice (ed.). *A Minority in Britain: Social Studies of the Anglo-Jewish Community*. London: Vallentine Mitchell, 1955.
Freud-Kandel, Miri J. *Orthodox Judaism in Britain Since 1913*. London and Portland, OR: Vallentine Mitchell, 2006.
Friedländer, M. 'The Late Chief Rabbi Dr N.M. Adler'. *Jewish Quarterly Review* II (July 1890): 368–71.
Frosh, Sidney. 'Clause 74 And All That'. *Hamesilah* [*The Path*] (Pesach 5745). London: United Synagogue, 1985.
Gaon, Solomon. 'The Contribution of the English Sephardim to Anglo-Jewry'. In Dov Noy and Issachar Ben-Ami (eds). *Studies in the Cultural Life of the Jews in England*. Jerusalem: Hebrew University Magnes Press, 1975.
Gartner, Lloyd P. *The Jewish Immigrant in England, 1870–1914*. London: George Allen and Unwin, 1960.
Gaster, Moses. *History of the Ancient Synagogue of the Spanish and Portuguese Jews*. London: privately published, 1901.
Gavron, Daniel. 'Montefiore: Man or Myth?' *Jewish Chronicle*, 13 October 1989.
Goldberg, David J., and Edward Kessler (eds). *Aspects of Liberal Judaism*. London and Portland, OR: Vallentine Mitchell, 2004.
Goldschmidt-Lehmann, Ruth P. 'Nathan Marcus Adler: A Bibliography'. In *Studies in Judaica,*

*Karaitica and Islamica: Presented to Leon Nemoy on his Eightieth Birthday*. Ramat Gan: Bar-Ilan University Press, 1982.

Gollancz, Hermann. 'Religious Neglect and Apostasy: The Other Side of the Picture'. In *Sermons and Addresses*. London: Myers, 1909.

— 'Halt!'. In *Sermons and Addresses*, 1916.

— 'Jews' College – Then and Now'. Address, 31 October 1915. In *Sermons and Addresses*, 1916.

— 'The Moderate Jew'. In *Sermons and Addresses*, 1916.

— *Sermons and Addresses Setting Forth the Teachings and Spirit of Judaism*. Second Series. London: Chapman and Hall, 1916.

— 'Cohesion or Decadence'. In *Fifty Years After*, 1924.

— 'Rev. Professor D.W. Marks'. In *Fifty Years After*, 1924.

— *Fifty Years After: Sermons and Addresses Setting Forth the Teachings and Spirit of Judaism*. Third Series. London: Humphrey Milford and Oxford University Press, 1924.

Gould, Julius, and Shaul Esh, (eds). *Jewish Life in Modern Britain*. London: Routledge and Kegan Paul, 1964.

Green, A.A. *Sermons*. London: Martin Hopkinson, 1935.

Grunfeld, Isidor. 'Problems of Modern Jewish Marriage and Family Life'. In *Addresses Given at the Tenth Conference of Anglo-Jewish Preachers*. London: Standing Committee, 1953.

— *Three Generations: The Influence of Samson Raphael Hirsch on Jewish Life and Thought*. London: Jewish Post Publications, 1958.

Gutwein, Daniel. *The Divided Elite: Economics, Politics and Anglo-Jewry, 1882–1917*. Leiden: E.J. Brill, 1992.

Harris, Isidore. *Jews' College Jubilee Volume*. London: Luzac, 1906.

Hart, Rona, and Edward Kafka. *Trends in British Synagogue Membership 1990–2005/06*. London: Board of Deputies of British Jews, 2006.

Heinemann, Isaac. 'Supplementary Remarks'. *Historia Judaica* X:2. Guido Kisch (ed.). New York, 1948.

— 'Samson Raphael Hirsch: The Formative Years of the Leader of Modern Orthodoxy'. *Historia Judaica*, XIII:1. Guido Kisch (ed.). New York, 1951.

Henriques, Robert. *Sir Robert Waley Cohen, 1877–1952*. London: Secker and Warburg, 1966.

Hertz, J.H. 'Installation Address'. In *Souvenir of the Decennial Celebration of the Witwatersrand Old Hebrew Congregation and of the Public Reception of the Rev. Dr Joseph Herman Hertz, 16 November, 1898*. Johannesburg: M.J. Wood, for the Council of the Congregation, 1898.

— *The Jew as a Patriot: a Plea for the Removal of the Civil Disabilities of the Jews in the Transvaal*. Johannesburg: M.J. Wood, 1898.

— 'Inaugural Sermon'. Congregation Orach Chayim, New York, 13 January 1912. In *Early and Late*, 1943.

— *The Installation Sermon of The Very Rev. Dr Joseph Herman Hertz, Chief Rabbi of the United Hebrew Congregations of the British Empire*. London: United Synagogue, 1913.

— *Traditional Judaism: An Appeal for the Jewish War Memorial*. London: Williams, Lea, 1919. Reprinted (abridged and amended) as 'Religion and Life'. In *Sermons, Addresses and Studies*, Vol. I, 1938.

— 'The Holiness of Home'. In *Affirmations of Judaism*, 1927.

— 'The New Paths: Whither Do They Lead'. In *Affirmations of Judaism*, 1927.

— *Affirmations of Judaism*, London: Oxford University Press, 1927. Reprinted, London: Edward Goldston, 1946.

— *The Pentateuch and Haftorahs*. Oxford: Oxford University Press, 1936.

— 'Opening address at the Conference of Anglo-Jewish Preachers'. In *Sermons, Addresses and Studies*, Vol. II, 1938.

# Bibliography

—— 'Reconstruction' In *Sermons, Addresses and Studies*, Vol. I, 1938.
—— 'The "Strange Fire" of Schism'. In *Sermons, Addresses and Studies*, Vol. I, 1938.
—— 'Divided Counsels'. In *Sermons, Addresses and Studies*, Vol. I, 1938.
—— 'The Coronation'. In *Sermons, Addresses and Studies*, Vol. I, 1938.
—— 'The First Pastoral Tour to the Jewish Communities of the British Overseas Dominions.' In *Sermons, Addresses and Studies*, Vol. II, 1938.
—— *Sermons, Addresses and Studies*. Three vols. London: Soncino Press, 1938.
—— 'Recall to the Synagogue', I and II. In *Early and Late*, 1943.
—— 'Graduation Address'. In *Early and Late*, 1943.
—— *Early and Late: Addresses, Messages, and Papers*. Hindhead, Surrey: Soncino Press, 1943.
Hirsch, Henriette (née Hildesheimer). 'Memories of My Youth'. In *Jewish Life in Germany: Memoirs From Three Centuries*. Monika Richarz (ed.). Bloomington and Indianapolis, IN: Indiana University Press, 1991.
Hirsch, S.A. 'Jewish Philosophy of Religion and Samson Raphael Hirsch'. *Jewish Quarterly Review*, London, January 1890.
Hochman, Joseph. *Jewish Separatism and Human Progress*. London: George Young, 1910.
—— *Orthodoxy and Religious Observance*. London: George Young, 1910.
—— 'The Chief Rabbi and the Ministry'. *Jewish Review* IV: 23 (January–February 1914). Norman Bentwich and Joseph Hochman (eds). London: George Routledge and Sons, 1914.
—— 'The Chief Rabbinate'. *Jewish Review* III:17 (January 1913). Norman Bentwich and Joseph Hochman (eds). London: George Routledge and Sons, 1913.
Holmes, Colin. *Anti-Semitism in British Society, 1876–1939*. London: Edward Arnold, 1979.
Homa, Bernard. *A Fortress in Anglo-Jewry: The Story of the Machzike Hadath*. London: Shapiro, Vallentine, 5713 – 1953.
—— *Orthodoxy in Anglo-Jewry, 1880–1940*. London: Jewish Historical Society of England, 1969.
—— *Footprints on the Sands of Time*. Charfield: Beaver Press, 1990.
Hyamson, Albert M. *The Sephardim of England*. London: Spanish and Portuguese Jews' Congregation, 1951.
—— *The London Board for Shechita, 1804–1954*. London: Henry F. Thompson, for the London Board for Shechita, 1954.
—— *Jews' College, London, 1855–1955*. London: Jews' College, 1955.
Hyamson, Moses, and Oswald John Simon. 'Authority and Dogma in Judaism'. *Jewish Quarterly Review* 5. I. Abrahams and C.G. Montefiore (eds). London: D. Nutt, 1893.
Hyamson, Moses. 'Installation into the Office of Dayan'. In *The Oral Law and Other Sermons*. London: David Nutt, 1910.
*Installation of Chief Rabbi: Supplement to the Jewish Chronicle*, 26 June 1891.
Jacobs, Louis. *Induction Sermon, New West End Synagogue*. London: Henry G. Morris, for the New West End Synagogue, 1954.
—— *We Have Reason to Believe*. London: Vallentine Mitchell, 1957; second edition, 1962; third edition, 1965; fourth revised edition, 1995; fifth edition, with a new Introduction by William Frankel, and a new Retrospect by the author, 2004.
—— *Montefiore and Loewe on the Rabbis*. London: Liberal Jewish Synagogue, 1962.
—— *Principles of the Jewish Faith: An Analytical Study*. London: Vallentine Mitchell, 1964.
—— *What We Stand For*. London: Blackfriars Press for New London Synagogue, 1964.
—— 'Reflections on a Controversy'. *Quest* 1. Jonathan Stone (ed.). London: Paul Hamlyn, 1965.
—— *A Tree of Life: Diversity, Flexibility, and Creativity in Jewish Law*. Oxford: Oxford University Press for the Littman Library of Jewish Civilization, 1984.
—— 'For the Sake of Heaven'. *Jewish Chronicle*, 19 December 1986.
—— *Helping With Inquiries: An Autobiography*. London and Portland, OR: Vallentine Mitchell, 1989.

— *The Jewish Religion: A Companion*. Oxford: Oxford University Press, 1995.
— *Beyond Reasonable Doubt*. London: Littman Library of Jewish Civilization, 1999.
— 'Four Rabbinic Positions in Anglo-Jewry'. In Stephen W. Massil (ed.). *The Jewish Year Book 2000*. London and Portland, OR: Vallentine Mitchell, in association with the *Jewish Chronicle*, 2000.
Jakobovits, Immanuel. 'The Influence of the Yeshivah on the Jewish Public'. In *HaChaim*. London: Tree of Life College, 1940.
— (ed.) *Irish-Jewish Year Book, 5712 (1951 – 1952)*. Dublin: Jewish Representative Council of Ireland, 1951.
— *Rabbinical Tasks in the Present Era*. London: Conference of European Rabbis, 1958.
— *Journal of a Rabbi*. New York: Living Books, 1966.
— *Installation Address as Chief Rabbi of the United Hebrew Congregations of the British Commonwealth of Nations*. London: Office of the Chief Rabbi, 1967.
— *Prelude to Service*. London: Office of the Chief Rabbi, 1967.
— *Looking Ahead*. London: United Synagogue, 1967; 2nd edn, 1968.
— *Moving Ahead: A Review and a Preview – A New Year Message from the Chief Rabbi to the Leadership of Anglo-Jewry*. Ellul 5728 – September 1968. London: Office of the Chief Rabbi, 1968.
— *Milestones and Millstones: Centenary of the United Synagogue*. 15 Tammuz 5730 – 19 July 1970. London: Office of the Chief Rabbi, 1970.
— *Driving Forward*. United Synagogue, London, 26 Ellul 5730 – 27 September 1970. London: Office of the Chief Rabbi, 1970.
— 'Division and Diversion'. *Jewish Chronicle*, 26 February 1971.
— *Memorandum on Synagogue Services*. London: Office of the Chief Rabbi, June 1971.
— *Samson Raphael Hirsch: A Reappraisal of his Teachings and Influence in the Light of our Times*. London: Office of the Chief Rabbi, 1971.
— *The Timely and The Timeless*. London and Portland, OR: Vallentine Mitchell, 1977.
— 'The Evolution of the British Rabbinate Since 1845: Its Past Impact and Future Challenges'. In *The Timely and The Timeless*. 1977.
— *If Only My People: Zionism in My Life*. London: Weidenfeld and Nicolson, 1984.
— 'The Changing Face of British Jewry: The Quiet Revolution'. *Jewish Chronicle*, 9 November 1984.
— 'Who is a Jew? New Questions, New Passions'. *Jewish Chronicle*, 7 December 1984.
— 'Torah im Derech Eretz Today'. *L'Eylah*, New Year issue (5746 – 1985). London: Office of the Chief Rabbi and Jews' College, 1985.
— 'Avoiding the Collision'. *Jewish Chronicle*, 8 February 1985.
— 'SOS: The Way We Live Now'. *Jewish Chronicle*, 10 October 1986.
— *Preserving The Oneness Of The Jewish People: Orthodox-Progressive divisions and discussions on marriage, divorce and conversion – can a permanent schism be averted?* London: Office of the Chief Rabbi, 1988.
— *New Priorities on the Orthodox Agenda*. London: Office of the Chief Rabbi, 1989.
— *A Collection of Essays and Articles by the Chief Rabbi, Prepared for the Traditional Alternatives Symposium*. London: Jews' College, 1989.
— 'Modern Trends in Orthodoxy'. In *Encounter: Essays on Torah and Modern Life*. H. Chaim Schimmel and Aryeh Carmell (eds). London, Feldheim, Jerusalem and New York: Association of Orthodox Jewish Scientists 1989.
— *Address Delivered at the Installation of Rabbi Dr Jonathan Sacks as Chief Rabbi of the United Hebrew Congregations of the Commonwealth*, 1 September 1991. London: Office of the Chief Rabbi, 1991.
— 'Trouble and Tradition'. *Jewish Chronicle*, 25 September 1992.
— 'Fragments From An Unpublished Autobiography'. In Meir Persoff, *Immanuel Jakobovits:*

*a Prophet in Israel*. London and Portland, OR: Vallentine Mitchell, 2002.

Japhet, Saemy. 'The Secession from the Frankfurt Jewish Community Under Samson Raphael Hirsch'. *Historia Judaica*, X:2. Guido Kisch (ed.). New York, 1948.

*Joint Celebration of the Seventy-Fifth Anniversary of Jews' College; the Seventieth Anniversary of the Jewish Religious Education Board; and the Sixtieth Anniversary of the United Synagogue, 23–24 March, 1931*. London: Oxford University Press, 1931.

*Joseph Herman Hertz, 1872–1946: In Memoriam*. London: Soncino Press, 1947.

Joseph, Morris. *Sefer Tefilat Minchah L'Shabbat: Order of Prayer as Used at the Sabbath Afternoon Services at Hampstead*. London: Gillingham and Henry, 5650 – 1890.

— *The Ideal in Judaism and Other Sermons by the Rev. Morris Joseph Preached During 1890–91–92*. London: David Nutt, 1893.

— *Judaism as Creed and Life*. London: Macmillan, 1903.

— *The Message of Judaism*. London: Routledge, 1907.

— *The Spirit of Judaism*. London: Routledge, 1930.

*Jubilee of the Reform Congregation: Supplement to the Jewish Chronicle*, 29 January, 1892.

Jung, Julius. 'Rabbi Dr Mayer Lerner', 'Rabbi Meir Tsevi Jung' and 'Samuel Montagu'. In *Champions of Orthodoxy*, London, 1974.

Karp, Abraham J. *New York Chooses a Chief Rabbi*. Publication of the American Jewish Historical Society XLIV:3 (March 1955).

Katz, David S. *The Jews in the History of England, 1485–1850*. Oxford: Clarendon Press, 1994.

Katz, Jacob. *A House Divided*. Hanover, NJ and London: Brandeis University Press, 1998.

— *Out of the Ghetto: The Social Background of Jewish Emancipation, 1770–1870*. Syracuse, NY: Syracuse University Press, 1973.

Katz, Steven T. (ed.). *Interpreters of Judaism in the Late Twentieth Century*. Washington: B'nai B'rith, 1993.

Kershen, Anne J., and Jonathan A. Romain. *Tradition and Change: A History of Reform Judaism in Britain, 1840–1995*. London and Portland, OR: Vallentine Mitchell, 1995.

Kessler, Edward. 'Claude Montefiore: Defender of Rabbinic Judaism'. *Jewish Historical Studies* XXXV (1996–1998). London: Jewish Historical Society of England, 2000.

— *A Reader of Early Liberal Judaism*. London and Portland, OR: Vallentine Mitchell, 2004.

— *An English Jew: The Life and Writings of Claude Montefiore*. London and Portland, OR: Vallentine Mitchell, 2002.

Klugman, Eliyahu Meir. *Rabbi Samson Raphael Hirsch*. New York: Mesorah Publications, 1996.

Kosmin, Barry A. 'Localism and Pluralism in British Jewry, 1900–80'. *Transactions of the Jewish Historical Society of England* XXVIII (1982).

Kosmin, Barry A., and Deborah de Lange. *Synagogue Affiliation in the United Kingdom, 1977*. London: Research Unit, Board of Deputies, 1978.

Kurzweil, Zvi E. 'Samson Raphael Hirsch: Educationist and Thinker'. *Tradition* II:2. Norman Lamm (ed.). New York: Rabbinical Council of America, 1960.

Kushner, Tony (ed.). *The Jewish Heritage in British History: Englishness and Jewishness*. London: Frank Cass, 1992.

Langdon, Harold S. 'The Place of Reform in Anglo-Jewry Today'. In Dow Marmur (ed.). *A Genuine Search*. London: Reform Synagogues of Great Britain, 1979.

Langton, Daniel R. *Claude Montefiore: His Life and Thought*. London and Portland, OR: Vallentine Mitchell, 2002.

Laski, Neville. *The Laws and Charities of the Spanish and Portuguese Jews' Congregation of London*. London: Cresset Press, 1952.

*Laws of the Congregation of the Great Synagogue, Duke's Place, London*. London: Wertheimer, 5623 – 1863.

Lehmann, Ruth P. 'Hermann Adler: A Bibliography of his Published Works'. In *Studies in the Cultural Life of the Jews in England*. Dov Noy and Issachar Ben-Ami (eds). Jerusalem: Hebrew University Magnes Press, 1975.

Lehrman, S.M. 'A Spiritual Warrior'. In Wolf Gottlieb (ed.). *Essays and Addresses in Memory of the Very Rev. Dr Joseph Herman Hertz*. London: Mizrachi Federation of Great Britain and Ireland, 1947.

Leigh, Michael. 'Reform Judaism in Britain, 1840–1970'. In Dow Marmur (ed.). *Reform Judaism*. London: Reform Synagogues of Great Britain, 1973.

Lerner, Isaac. 'The Attitude to Halachah of the Progressive Movements: Can they be considered a *kehillah kedoshah?*' *L'Eylah* I:10 (Autumn 5741). A. Melinek (ed.). London: Office of the Chief Rabbi, 1981.

Levin, Salmond S. (ed.). *A Century of Anglo-Jewish Life, 1870–1970*. London: United Synagogue, 1971.

Levine, Ephraim. *The History of the New West End Synagogue, 1879–1929*. Aldershot: John Drew, 1929.

Levine, Howard I. 'Enduring and Transitory Elements in the Philosophy of Samson Raphael Hirsch'. *Tradition* 5: 2. Walter S. Wurzburger (ed.). New York: Rabbinical Council of America, 1963.

Levy, Arnold. *The Story of Gateshead Yeshivah*. Taunton: Wessex Press, 1952.

— *History of the Sunderland Jewish Community, 1755–1955*. London: Macdonald, 1956.

Levy, Elkan. *The New West End Synagogue, 1879–2004*. London: New West End Synagogue, 2004.

Levy, Isaac. *Historic Judaism Versus Liberal Judaism*. London: United Synagogue, 1949.

Liberles, Robert. 'The Origins of the Jewish Reform Movement in England'. *AJSreview* I. Cambridge, MA: Association for Jewish Studies, 1976.

— *Religious Conflict in Social Context*. Westport, CT: Greenwood Press, 1985.

Lipkin, Goodman. 'Nathan Marcus Adler'. In *The Jewish Encyclopedia*. Vol. I. New York and London: Funk and Wagnalls, 1925.

Lipman, Sonia L. 'Judith Montefiore – First Lady of Anglo-Jewry'. *Transactions of the Jewish Historical Society of England* XXI (1968).

Lipman, Sonia L., and Vivian D. Lipman. *Jewish Life in Britain, 1962–1977*. New York: H.G. Saur, 1981.

— (eds). *The Century of Moses Montefiore*. London and Oxford: Litmann Library of Jewish Civilization, Jewish Historical Society of England and Oxford University Press, 1985.

Lipman, Vivian. D. *Social History of the Jews in England, 1850–1950*. London: Watts, 1954.

— *A Century of Social Service, 1859–1959*. London: Routledge and Kegan Paul, 1959.

— *Three Centuries of Anglo-Jewish History*. London: W. Heffer and Sons for the Jewish Historical Society of England, 1961.

— 'The Anglo-Jewish Community in Victorian Society'. In *Studies in the Cultural Life of the Jews in England*. Dov Noy and Issachar Ben-Ami (eds). Jerusalem: Hebrew University Magnes Press, 1975.

— *A History of the Jews in Britain Since 1858*. New York: Holmes and Meier, 1990.

Livingstone, I. *The Union of Anglo-Jewish Preachers: A Retrospect*. London: Union of Anglo-Jewish Preachers, 1949.

Loewe, L. (ed.). *Diaries of Sir Moses and Lady Montefiore*. London, 1890. Facsimile edition, introduced by Raphael Loewe. London: Litmann Library of Jewish Civilization, Jewish Historical Society of England, and Jewish Museum, 1983.

Loewe, Raphael. 'Solomon Marcus Schiller-Szinessy, 1820–1890'. *Transactions of the Jewish Historical Society of England* XXI (1962–1967).

Lowenstein, Steven M. *The Berlin Jewish Community: Enlightenment, Family, and Crisis, 1770–1830*. Oxford: Oxford University Press, 1994.

Malino, Frances, and David Sorkin (eds). *Profiles in Diversity: Jews in a Changing Europe, 1750–1870*. Detroit, MI: Wayne State University Press, 1998.
Margoliouth, Moses. *The History of the Jews in Great Britain*. London: Richard Bentley, 1851.
Marks, D.W. (ed.) *Forms of Prayer, used in the West London Synagogue of British Jews, with an English Translation. Volume I – Daily and Sabbath Prayers*. London: Wertheimer, 1841.
— 'Discourse Delivered at the Consecration of the West London Synagogue of British Jews, Thursday, 27 January, 5602 [1842]'. In *Sermons Preached on Various Occasions at the West London Synagogue of British Jews*. Vol. I. London: R. Groombridge and Sons, 1851.
— 'On the Revelation at Sinai, and the Perpetuity and Immutability of the Mosaic Law'. In *Sermons Preached on Various Occasions*. Vol. I, 5611 – 1851.
— 'The Law of Moses, the Great End of Revelation'. In *Sermons Preached on Various Occasions at the West London Synagogue of British Jews, Margaret Street, Cavendish Square*. Vol. II. London: A.W. Bennett, P. Valentine, 5622 – 1862.
— 'The Synagogue and the Organ'. In *Sermons Preached on Various Occasions*. Vol. II, 5622 – 1862.
Marmur, Dow (ed.). *A Genuine Search: God, Torah, Israel – A Reform Perspective*. London: Reform Synagogues of Great Britain, 1979.
— *Reform Judaism*. London: Reform Synagogues of Great Britain, 1973.
Maybaum, Ignaz. 'The Jacobs Affair'. *Quest* 1. Jonathan Stone (ed.). London: Paul Hamlyn, 1965.
— *The Office of a Chief Rabbi*. Judaism Today. A Series Edited by Rabbi Dr Ignaz Maybaum. London: Reform Synagogues of Great Britain, 1964.
Mayhew, Henry. *London Labour and the London Poor*. Vol. II. London: Griffin, Bohn, 1862.
McLeod, Hugh. 'Why Did Orthodoxy Remain Dominant in Britain?'. In *Two Nations: British and German Jews in Comparative Perspective*. Michael Brenner, Rainer Liedtke, David Rechter, (eds). Tübingen: Mohr Siebeck, 1999.
Meirovich, Harvey. *A Vindication of Judaism: The Polemics of the Hertz Pentateuch*. New York and Jerusalem: Jewish Theological Seminary of America, 1998.
Meyer, Michael A. *German-Jewish History in Modern Times*. New York: Columbia University Press, 1977.
— *Response to Modernity: A History of the Reform Movement in Judaism*. New York and Oxford: Oxford University Press, 1988.
— 'Jewish Religious Reform in Germany and Britain'. In Michael Brenner, Rainer Liedtke and David Rechter (eds). *Two Nations: British and German Jews in Comparative Perspective*. Tübingen: Mohr Siebeck, 1999.
Mills, John. *The British Jews*. London: Houlston and Stoneman, 1853.
Montagu, Lily H. 'The Spiritual Possibilities in Judaism Today'. *Jewish Quarterly Review* XI (January 1899). I. Abrahams and C.G. Montefiore (eds). New York: Macmillan, 1899.
— *Samuel Montagu, First Baron Swaythling*. London: Truslove and Hanson, n.d. [1913].
Montefiore, Claude G. *Truth in Religion and Other Sermons*. London: Macmillan, 1906.
— 'Religious Differences and Religious Agreements'. In *Truth in Religion, and Other Sermons Delivered at the Services of the Jewish Religious Union*. New York: Macmillan, 1906.
— 'The Jewish Religious Union: Its Principles and its Future'. *Jewish Chronicle*, 15 October 1909.
— *The Synoptic Gospels*. London: Macmillan, 1910.
— *Is There a Middle Way?* London: Jewish Religious Union, 1920.
— *Outlines of Liberal Judaism for the Use of Parents and Teachers*. London: Macmillan, 1912; second edn, 1923.
— *The Old Testament and After*. London: Macmillan, 1923.
Moor, James R. (ed.). *Religion in Victorian Britain – III. Sources*. Manchester: Manchester University Press and the Open University, 1988.

Mudie-Smith, Richard. *The Religious Life of London*. London: Hodder and Stoughton, 1904.
Nathan, David. 'David Nathan Talks with Chief Rabbi Jakobovits'. *Jewish Chronicle*, 6 January 1978.
— 'The Mystique of Survival: Interview with Chief Rabbi Sir Immanuel Jakobovits'. *Jewish Chronicle*, 17 April 1987.
Newman, Aubrey (rapporteur). *Migration and Settlement: Proceedings of the Anglo-American Jewish Historical Conference*. London: Jewish Historical Society of England, 1971.
— *Chief Rabbi Dr Joseph H. Hertz*. London: United Synagogue, 1972.
— (ed.). *Provincial Jewry in Victorian Britain: Papers for a Conference at University College, London, Convened by the Jewish Historical Society of England*. London, 6 July 1975.
— 'The Chief Rabbinate'. In *Provincial Jewry in Victorian Britain*. London: Jewish Historical Society of England, 1975.
— *The United Synagogue, 1870–1970*. London: Routledge and Kegan Paul, 1976.
— 'The Chief Rabbinate and the Provinces, 1840–1914'. In Jonathan Sacks (ed.). *Tradition and Transition: Essays Presented to Chief Rabbi Sir Immanuel Jakobovits to Celebrate Twenty Years in Office*. London: Jews' College Publications, 1986.
— *The Board of Deputies of British Jews, 1760–1985*. London and Portland, OR: Vallentine Mitchell, 1987.
Paneth, Philip. *Guardian of the Law: The Chief Rabbi, Dr J.H. Hertz*. London: Allied Book Club, 1940.
Parkes, James W. 'Redcliffe Nathan Salaman'. *Transactions of the Jewish Historical Society of England* XVIII (1953–1955).
Parsons, Gerald (ed.). *Religion in Victorian Britain – I. Traditions*. Manchester: Manchester University Press and the Open University, 1988.
Pearl, Chaim. 'About "Chief Rabbis"'. *Jewish Spectator* (January 1967).
Persoff, Meir. 'When yesterday meets tomorrow'. Interview with Chief Rabbi Dr Immanuel Jakobovits. *Jewish Chronicle*, 21 July 1967.
— 'Stubborn resistance to change'. Interview with Chief Rabbi Dr Immanuel Jakobovits. *Jewish Chronicle*, 27 June 1969.
— 'Keep politics out of Jews' College'. Interview with Rabbi Dr Nachum Rabinovitch. *Jewish Chronicle*, 21 November 1969.
— 'Wolfson overrules Chief Rabbi'. *Jewish Chronicle*, 14 August 1970.
— 'Communal history was born in a succah'. *Jewish Chronicle*, 11 September 1970.
— 'Anti-Jacobs society to disband'. *Jewish Chronicle*, 19 March 1971.
— 'The kind of rabbi we need now'. Interviews with Rabbi Dr Nachum Rabinovitch and Salmond S. Levin. *Jewish Chronicle*, 16 March 1973.
— 'Conflict and Conciliation: Religious Pluralism and the British Chief Rabbinate, 1840–1940'. MA dissertation. University of London, 1994.
— 'Learning lessons from our history'. *Jewish Chronicle*, 28 January 2000.
— *Immanuel Jakobovits: a Prophet in Israel*. London and Portland, OR: Vallentine Mitchell, 2002.
Petuchowski, Jakob J. *Points of View*. London: Reform Synagogues of Great Britain, 1970.
Philipson, David. *The Reform Movement in Judaism*. New York: Macmillan, 1907; rev. edn, 1931.
Phillips, Olga Somech, and Hyman A. Simons. *The History of the Bayswater Synagogue 1863–1963*. London: privately published, 1963.
Picciotto, James. *Sketches of Anglo-Jewish History*. Revised and edited by Israel Finestein. London: Soncino Press, 1955.
Pollins, Harold. *Economic History of the Jews in England*. London: Littman Library of Jewish Civilization, 1982.
Prais, S.J., and Marlena Schmool. 'Statistics of Jewish Marriages in Great Britain, 1901–1965'.

# Bibliography 461

*Jewish Journal of Sociology* IX: 1 (1967).
— 'Synagogue Marriages in Great Britain, 1966–1968'. *Jewish Journal of Sociology* XII:1 (June 1970).
Prais, S.J. 'Synagogue Statistics and the Jewish Population of Great Britain, 1900–1970'. *Jewish Journal of Sociology* XIV:2 (December 1972).
*Public General Statutes passed in the Fourth Session of the Sixteenth Parliament of the United Kingdom of Great Britain and Ireland. 19 & 20 Victoria, 1856.* London: George Edward Eyre and William Spottiswoode, 1856.
Rabinowitz, Louis. 'The Status of the Ministry'. *The Jewish Monthly* 4: 9 (December 1950).
Rapaport-Albert, Ada, and Steven J. Zipperstein (eds). *Jewish History: Essays in Honour of Chimen Abramsky.* London: Peter Halban, 1988.
*Recorded Minutes of the First Meeting of Elected Members of the Vestry of the United Synagogue,* London, 11 January, 1871; and *Deed of Foundation and Trust,* signed, sealed and delivered by Sir Anthony de Rothschild, Baronet; Lionel Louis Cohen; Sampson Lucas; Solomon Schloss; and Assur Henry Moses, in the presence of Algernon E. Sydney, Solicitor, 46 Finsbury Circus, London, EC, 13 January, 1871.
Reif, Stefan C. *Judaism and Hebrew Prayer: New Perspectives on Jewish Liturgical History.* Cambridge: Cambridge University Press, 1993.
*Report of the Committee Appointed for the Selection of Candidates for the Office of Chief Rabbi, With an Appendix Containing Abstracts of Testimonials, Etc.* London: John Wertheimer, 1844.
'Report of the Royal Commission on the Laws of Marriage'. In *Reports from Commissioners* XXXII, Session 19 (November 1867–31 July 1868). London: George E. Eyre and William Spottiswoode, 1868.
*Report on the Sabbath Reading of the Scriptures in a Triennial Cycle.* London: New West End Synagogue, Wertheimer Lea, 1913.
Rigal, Lawrence, and Rosita Rosenberg. *Liberal Judaism: The First Hundred Years.* London: Union of Liberal and Progressive Synagogues, 2004.
Romain, Jonathan A. 'The Reform Beth Din: The Formation and Development of the Rabbinical Court of the Reform Synagogues of Great Britain, 1935–1965'. PhD dissertation. University of Leicester, 1990.
— *Faith & Practice: A Guide to Reform Judaism Today.* London: Reform Synagogues of Great Britain, 1991.
— 'The Establishment of the Reform Beth Din in 1948: A Barometer of Religious Trends in Anglo-Jewry. *Jewish Historical Studies* XXXIII (1992–1994). London: Jewish Historical Society of England, 1995.
Rosenbloom, Noah H. *Tradition in an Age of Reform.* Philadelphia, PA: Jewish Publication Society of America, 1976.
Rosenheim, Jacob. 'The Historical Significance'. *Historia Judaica* X:2. Guido Kisch (ed.). New York, 1948.
Roth, Cecil. *Archives of the United Synagogue: Report and Catalogue.* London: United Synagogue, 1930.
— *Records of the Western Synagogue, 1761–1932.* London: Edward Goldston, 1932.
— *The Federation of Synagogues, 1912–1937.* London, 5698 – 1937.
— 'The Collapse of English Jewry'. *The Jewish Monthly* 4 (1947).
— *The Jewish Chronicle 1841–1941: A Century of Newspaper History.* London: Jewish Chronicle, 1949.
— *History of the Great Synagogue, 1690–1940.* London: Edward Goldston and Son, 1950.
— *The Rise of Provincial Jewry. The Jewish Monthly* (1950).
— 'Britain's Three Chief Rabbis'. In *Jewish Leaders (1750–1940).* Leo Jung (ed.). New York: Bloch, 5714 – 1953.

— *A History of the Jews in England*. London: Oxford University Press, 1941. Repr. London: John Trotter, 1989.

Rubinstein, W.D. *A History of the Jews in the English-Speaking World: Great Britain*. Basingstoke: Macmillan, 1996.

Russell, C. and H.S. Lewis. *The Jew in London: A Study of Racial Character and Present-Day Conditions*. New York: Thomas Y. Cromwell, 1901.

Sacks, Jonathan (ed.). *Tradition and Transition: Essays Presented to Chief Rabbi Sir Immanuel Jakobovits to Celebrate Twenty Years in Office*. London: Jews' College Publications, 1986.

— *Tradition in an Untraditional Age: Essays on Modern Jewish Thought*. London and Portland, OR: Vallentine Mitchell, 1990.

— *Orthodoxy Confronts Modernity*. London and New Jersey: Ktav in association with Jews' College, 1991.

— *A Decade of Jewish Renewal: Installation Address as Chief Rabbi of the United Hebrew Congregations of the Commonwealth*. 1 September 1991. London: Office of the Chief Rabbi, 1991.

— *A Time For Renewal: A Rabbinic Response to the Kalms Report, 'A Time For Change'*. London: Office of the Chief Rabbi, 1992.

— *One People? Tradition, Modernity, and Jewish Unity*. London: Littman Library of Jewish Civilization, 1993.

— *Community of Faith*. London: Peter Halban, 1995.

— *Traditional Alternatives: Orthodoxy and the Future of the Jewish People*. London: Jews' College Publications, 1989. Published in the United States as *Arguments for the Sake of Heaven*. New Jersey: Jason Aronson, 1995.

Salaman, Redcliffe N. *Whither Lucien Wolf's Anglo-Jewish Community?* The Lucien Wolf Memorial Lecture, 1953. London: Jewish Historical Society of England, 1954.

Salbstein, M.C.N. *The Emancipation of the Jews in Britain*. London: Littman Library of Jewish Civilization, 1982.

Salomon, Sidney. *The Jews of Britain*. London: Hutchinson, 1938.

Schimmel, H. Chaim, and Aryeh Carmell (eds). *Encounter: Essays on Torah and Modern Life*. New York: Association of Orthodox Jewish Scientists, 1989.

Schischa, A. 'Hermann Adler, Yeshivah Bachur, Prague, 1860–1862'. In *Remember the Days: Essays in Honour of Cecil Roth*. John M. Shaftesley (ed.). London: Jewish Historical Society of England, 1966.

Schmidt, H.D. 'Chief Rabbi Nathan Marcus Adler: Jewish Educator from Germany'. *Leo Baeck Institute Year Book* VII. London: East and West Library, 1962.

Schmool, Marlena, and Frances Cohen. *British Synagogue Membership in 1990*. London: Community Research Unit, Board of Deputies, 1991.

— *British Synagogue Membership in 1996*. London: Community Research Unit, Board of Deputies, 1997.

Schwab, Hermann. 'A Champion of Orthodoxy (ii)'. *The Jewish Monthly* IV:3 (June 1950).

— *The History of Orthodox Jewry in Germany*. London: Mitre Press, 1950.

Seltzer, Robert M. *Jewish People, Jewish Thought*. London: Macmillan, 1980.

Shaftesley, John M. (ed.). *Remember the Days: Essays in Honour of Cecil Roth*. London: Jewish Historical Society of England, 1966.

— 'Israel Brodie, Chief Rabbi: A Biographical Sketch'. In H.J. Zimmels, J. Rabbinowitz, I. Finestein (eds). *Essays Presented to Chief Rabbi Israel Brodie on the Occasion of his Seventieth Birthday*. Jews' College Publications NS 3. London: Soncino Press, 1967.

— 'Religious Controversies'. In Salmond S. Levin (ed.). *A Century of Anglo-Jewish Life, 1870–1970*. London: United Synagogue, 1971.

Sharot, Stephen. 'Secularisation, Judaism and Anglo-Jewry'. *A Sociological Yearbook of Religion in Britain* IV. M. Hill (ed.). London: SCM Press, 1971.

— 'Religious Change in Native Orthodoxy in London, 1870–1914: The Synagogue Service'. *Jewish Journal of Sociology* XV:1 (June 1973).
— 'Native Jewry and the Religious Anglicisation of Immigrants in London, 1870–1905'. *Jewish Journal of Sociology* XVI:1 (June 1974).
— *Judaism: A Sociology*. New York: Holmes and Meier, 1976.
— 'Reform and Liberal Judaism in London, 1840–1940'. *Jewish Social Studies* XLI. New York: Conference on Jewish Social Studies, 1979.
Shashar, Michael. *Lord Jakobovits in Conversation*. London and Portland, OR: Vallentine Mitchell, 2000.
Shewzik, B. *A Grievous Mourning: A sermon in memory of the late Chief Rabbi, Rev. Dr Nathan M. Adler*. London: E.W. Rabbinowicz, 5650 – 1890.
Shisler, Geoffrey L. *The Life of the Rev. Simeon Singer*. London: New West End Synagogue, 2004.
Simmons, Vivian G. 'Claude Goldsmid Montefiore'. *Transactions of the Jewish Historical Society of England* XIV (1935–1939). London: Edward Goldston, 1940.
— *The Path of Life: A Study of the Background, Faith and Practice of Liberal Judaism*. London: Vallentine Mitchell, 1961.
Simon, Maurice. *Jewish Religious Conflicts*. London: Hutchinson, 1950.
Simons, Hyman A. *Forty Years a Chief Rabbi: The Life and Times of Solomon Hirschell*. London: Robson Books, 1980.
Singer, Simeon (ed.). *The Authorised Daily Prayer Book of the United Hebrew Congregations of the British Empire*. London: Wertheimer, Lea, 5650 – 1890, 5651 – 1891.
— 'Personal Religion'. In *Jewish Addresses Delivered at the Services of the Jewish Religious Union During the First Session, 1902–3*. London and Edinburgh: Brimley Johnson, 1904.
— *The Literary Remains of the Rev. Simeon Singer*. Vol. I – *Sermons*. Selected and edited with a memoir by Israel Abrahams. London: George Routledge and Sons, 1908.
Singer, Steven. 'Chief Rabbi Nathan Marcus Adler: Major Problems in His Career'. MA dissertation. Bernard Revel Graduate School, Yeshiva University, New York, 1974.
— 'Orthodox Judaism in Early Victorian London, 1840–1858'. PhD dissertation. Bernard Revel Graduate School, Yeshiva University, New York, 1981.
Sofer, Solomon (ed.). *Sefer Iggerot Soferim* Vienna: Joseph Schlesinger, 1929.
Sorasky, Aaron. 'The Life and Times of Rabbenu Yechezkel Abramsky'. In *Emunah: Pathways in Contemporary Jewish Thought* 2 (January 1990). Tel Ganim, Israel: Kollel Tal Torah.
— *Melech Beyofyo* [*A King In His Glory*]. Two vols. Jerusalem: privately published, 2004.
Super, Arthur Saul. 'Israel Brodie – Chief Rabbi'. *The Jewish Monthly* 2:3 (June 1948).
Susser, Bernard. 'Statistical Accounts of all the Congregations in the British Empire, 5606 – 1845'. In Aubrey Newman (ed.). *Provincial Jewry in Victorian Britain*. London: Jewish Historical Society of England, 1975.
Swift, Morris. *Jewish Marriage and Divorce*. London: Beth Din, 1962 – 5722.
Taylor, Derek. *British Chief Rabbis, 1664–2006*. London and Portland, OR: Vallentine Mitchell, 2006.
Temkin, Sefton. 'A Crisis in Anglo-Jewry'. *Conservative Judaism* XVIII:1. Samuel H. Dresner (ed.). New York: Rabbinical Assembly, 1963.
— 'Orthodoxy With Moderation: A Sketch of Joseph Herman Hertz'. *Judaism* 24:3 (1975).
Tessler, Gloria. *Amélie: The Story of Lady Jakobovits*. London and Portland, OR: Vallentine Mitchell, 1999.
*The Celebration of the Chief Rabbi's Silver Jubilee*. London: Chief Rabbi Presentation Committee, 1938.
Trepp, Leo. *Die Oldenburger Jüdenschaft*. Oldenburg: Heinz Holzberg Verlag, 1973.
Unna, Josef. 'Nathan Hacohen Adler'. In Leo Jung (ed.). *Guardians of our Heritage*. New York: Bloch Publishing House, 1958.

Waterman, Stanley, and Barry Kosmin. *British Jewry in the Eighties*. London: Board of Deputies of British Jews, 1986.
Webber, Jonathan (ed.). *Jewish Identities in the New Europe*. London: Littman Library of Jewish Civilization, 1994.
Wertheimer, Jack (ed.). *The American Synagogue: A Sanctuary Transformed*. Hanover, NJ and London: Brandeis University Press, 1995.
Wertheimer, Jack (ed.). *Tradition Renewed: A History of the Jewish Theological Seminary of America*. New York: Jewish Theological Seminary of America, 1997.
Williams, Bill. *The Making of Manchester Jewry, 1740–1875*. London: Manchester University Press, 1976.
Wolf, Lucien. 'The Queen's Jewry, 1837–1897'. *Young Israel* (June and July 1897). Reprinted in Cecil Roth (ed.). *Essays in Jewish History*. London: Jewish Historical Society of England, 1934.
—— *Essays in Jewish History*. London: Jewish Historical Society of England, 1934.
Wolfson, Isaac. *Statement by the President of the United Synagogue*. London: United Synagogue, 1964.
Wolkind, Jack. *London and its Jewish Community*. London: West Central Counselling and Community Research, 1985.
Zolti, Bezalel. 'The "Man Of Freedom" Of Our Generation'. In *Sefer Zikaron [Memorial Volume to Rabbi Yechezkel Abramsky]*. Joseph Buchsbaum, Abraham Halevy Sher (eds). Jerusalem: Moriah, 5738 – 1978.

The London Metropolitan Archives (40 Northampton Road, London EC1R 0HB) house the papers of, among other institutions, the Board of Deputies of British Jews (ACC/3121), United Synagogue (ACC/2712), Office of the Chief Rabbi (ACC/2805), London Beth Din (ACC/3400), Kashrus Commission (ACC/2980), Federation of Synagogues (ACC/2893), Western Synagogue (ACC/2911), Liberal Jewish Synagogue (ACC/3529), West London Synagogue (ACC/2886), Westminster Synagogue (LMA/4071), London School of Jewish Studies, formerly Jews' College (LMA/4180), Jewish Memorial Council (ACC/2999).

The Archive and Manuscript Collections of the Hartley Library, University of Southampton (Highfield, Southampton SO9 5NH), include the papers of C.J. Goldsmid-Montefiore (MS 108), Lord Swaythling (MS 117), Selig Brodetsky (MS 119), Michael Adler (MS 125), Laski family (MS 134), West London Synagogue (MS 140), Bernard Homa (MS 141), London Board of Shechita (MS 142), P. Goldberg (MS 148), New London Synagogue (MS 149), Machzike Hadath Congregation (MS 151), Cecil Roth (MS 156), Jewish Religious Education Board (MS 157), H.F. Reinhart (MS 171), J.H. Hertz (MS 175), Solomon Schonfeld (MS 183), Adolf Büchler (MS 186), Salis Daiches (MS 189), Victor Schonfeld (MS 192), Israel Brodie (MS 206), *Jewish Chronicle* (MS 225), J.M. Shaftesley (MS 230), V.D. Lipman (MS 245), Van der Zyl family (MS 297).

The Special Collections of the Mocatta Library at University College London (140 Hampstead Road, London NW1 2BX) include books, manuscripts and papers of Frederic David Mocatta, Hermann Gollancz, Israel Abrahams, Lucien Wolf

The Archives in the Special Collection of the Jewish Theological Seminary of America Library (3080 Broadway at 122nd Street, New York, NY 10027-4649) contain personal papers of Nathan Marcus Adler (boxes 5-1 to 5-4), Hermann Adler (3-1 to 3-3) and Marcus Nathan Adler (4-1). Earlier and later Adler material is in boxes 1 and 2; papers relating to Morris Joseph, Albert H. Jessel and Albert M. Hyamson are in box 3; to Moses Montefiore, Judith, Lady Montefiore, Claude G. Montefiore, Cecil Roth and Redcliffe Nathan Salaman, in box 4; to Isidore Spielmann, in box 5. Boxes 6 to 17 include a wealth of material from organisations across the Anglo-Jewish spectrum.

# Index

Abelson, Joshua, 183
Abraham, biblical, 273–4
Abrahams, Barnett, 100
Abrahams, Israel, 105, 113, 123
Abramsky, Yechezkel Alter, 237, 247, 252, 253, 276, 287; and Chief Rabbinate, 238–9; and Jakobovits, 318
Adath Yeshurun, Syracuse, 159, 160
*Adath Yisroel* (German Jewish Religious Society), 4, 5
Adler, Elkan Nathan, 3, 90
Adler, Felix, 157
Adler, Henrietta (née Worms), 2
Adler, Hermann, xix, 88, 109, 142–3; birth and early life, 100; death of, 151, 152, 154, 163, 207; as Delegate Chief Rabbi, 100; and Hochman, 176, 177; on Jewish Religious Union, 118, 120–1, 122–3, 145–6; 'Modifications in Synagogue Ritual', 381; 'Old Paths' sermon, 131, 381; personal qualities, 99; preaching, gift for, 101; on reforms, 104
Adler, Marcus Nathan, 1
Adler, Mordechai (Marcus Baer), 1
Adler, Nathan Hacohen, 1
Adler, Nathan Marcus (Chief Rabbi), xix, xxv, 41–2, 76; birth and early life, 1; and Board of Deputies' controversy (1853), 61, 64, 85; death of (1890), 89; on Divine Worship, 380; education/rabbinical ordination, 1–2; election as British Chief Rabbi, 3, 4, 8; and Hampstead Synagogue, 89; in Hanover, 3, 80; as Hirschell's successor, 8; impact of, 89–90, 99; Joseph as protégé, 103; *Laws and Regulations for all the Synagogues in the British Empire*, xxviii, 41, 42; on marriage ceremonies *see* marriage ceremonies; marriage of, 2; and Montefiore, 92, 93; in Oldenburg, 2–3, 80; 'Omens of Peace', 33, 34, 52; Orthodoxy of, 90; power, 93; and Reform Judaism, 48, 76, 85, 86, 101; Sabbath-eve liturgy, changes to, 42–3; and second festival day, 44–6; on West London Synagogue, 79–80
Aloof, Judah, 63, 66
American Reform, conservative school, 225
Angel, Daniel, 31
Angel, Jane, 31, 32, 52
Anglican Church of Ireland, disestablishment, xxviii
Anglo-Jewish Association, 293
Ansell, J.M., 149
*Ascamot*, 17
Asher, David, 100
Asher, Joseph, 156
Ashkenazi Jews, 11

Associated British Synagogues, 261
Auerbach, Benjamin, 19
Austria, Jewish religious life in, xxvii
*Authorised Daily Prayer Book* (Singer's), 116, 121, 123

B

Balkind, Reb Yonah, 286
Bamberger, Yitzchak Dov, 2
Barned, Israel, 73
Barnett, David, 65
Bayfield, Tony, 362, 363, 364
Bayswater Synagogue, 100
Bender, Alfred P., 171
Bentwich, Herbert, 109, 246
Bentwich, Norman, 286
Berger, Isaac, 339
Berkovits, Eliezer, 366
Bernays, Isaac, 2
Beth Din, 247, 248, 257, 338; on marriage ceremonies, 271; Reform, 261–2, 273; Sephardi, 35
*Beth Din Zedek* (Court of Righteousness), 272, 275, 277
Beth Hamidrash, North London, 5
Bevis Marks synagogue, 62, 65, 80, 83–4
Bible: Joseph on, 103; and Liberal Judaism, 216; and Orthodox Judaism, 117, 175
Biblical Criticism, 283
Bing, Abraham (Chief Rabbi of Würzburg), 2
Blau, Joel, 225, 226, 229
Bloch, Rabbi Isaac, 207
B'nai B'rith, 336
Board of Deputies, 54–5, 56; constitution, 81, 82, 84, 352, 353; controversy (1853), 61–78, 80, 85; elections, 62; key figures in dispute, 62; on marriage ceremonies, 256

Bower, Marcus, 375–6
brazen serpent, talmudic reference to, 108
Brichto, Sidney, 279, 328, 330–2, 334, 356; and Jakobovits, 348–9; and Liberals, 374; on Progressives, 344; 'solution', 371
Britain, voluntary nature of Jewish community membership, xxvii
British Broadcasting Corporation (BBC), 235–6
British School of Jewish Learning, proposals for, 192–3; and Hochman, 201–2; as 'The Great Communal Scheme', 196
Brodetsky, Selig, 263
Brodie, Israel, xix, xx, 116, 265, 269–70, 304, 382; birth and early life, 260; as Chief Rabbi, 261; Conference of European Rabbis, Amsterdam (1957), 273; death of, 341; and Jacobs, xxvi, 288, 298–9, 305, 309; on marriage and divorce, 276; retirement, 319, 325
Burton Street Place of Worship *see* West London Synagogue of British Jews

C

Carr, Marcus, 280, 281
Chaikin, Rabbi Moshe Avigdor, 113, 167–8
Chait, Rabbi Isaac, 335
Chelmsford, Lord, 52–3, 55
*cherem*, 18, 47, 78
Cherns, Godfrey, 254
Chief Rabbi, qualities required of, xiii–xiv
Chief Rabbinate, Britain: and Abramsky, 239; Adler, influence of, 89; birth of, xxix; evolution of,

8; opposition to moderate reformers, within United Synagogue, xxvi; recognition by Anglo-Jewry, xxix; and Reform leaders, 80; unique nature of, xxvii; and United Synagogue, 182
Christianity: and Liberal Judaism, 212, 216–17; Sabbath, 213
Citron, Yisrael Abba, 237
Cohen, Abraham, 239
Cohen, Arthur, 83
Cohen, Benjamin L., 108
Cohen, Julia, 229
Cohen, Lionel Louis, 241
Cohen, Lord, of Walmer, 270, 330–1
Cohen, Louis, 49; on Board of Deputies' controversy (1853), 63, 72, 73; on Reform Judaism, 79
Cohen, Neville D., 178
Conference of Anglo-Jewish Preachers, London, 265, 266
Conference of European Rabbis, Amsterdam (1957), 6, 273
Council of Reform and Liberal Rabbis, 352
Court of the Association of Synagogues of Great Britain, 272

### D

Daiches, Samuel, 231
D'Avigdor-Goldsmid, Osmond, 200
Davis, Elias, 62, 63, 67
Davis, Felix A., 118, 132–6; withdrawal from Jewish Religious Union, 141–2
de Castro, Hananel, 38, 39
de Mesquita, Bueno, 229, 235
de Rothschild, Lionel see Rothschild, Baron Lionel de
Defries, Nathan, 63
Dessler, Rabbi Eliyahu Eliezer, 286, 287
Diamond, A.S., 291
*dina d'malchuta dina* (law of the land is the law), 256, 257
Dissenters' Marriage Bill, 49, 50
Documentary Hypothesis, 284

### E

Edgar, Leslie, 240
Elkin, Benjamin, 26, 27, 62, 64
Elkin, Jacob Levi, and Board of Deputies' controversy (1853), 62, 63, 64, 67, 68, 69, 71
Ellis, Samuel Helbert, 19, 62, 63, 71
Emanuel, George Joseph, 148
Epstein, Isidore, 287
Ettlinger, Jacob, 2
Etz Chaim yeshivah, London, 6

### F

Federation of Synagogues, 237; Montagu as Orthodox founder of, 117; and Union of Orthodox Hebrew Congregations, 354; and United Synagogue Orthodoxy, 154
Feinstein, Rabbi Moshe, 333
Feldman, Dayan Asher, 113, 168, 169, 207
Fidler, Michael, 350
Fifth Avenue Synagogue, New York City, 8, 318
Finchley Synagogue, 247, 248
Finkelstein, Louis, 336
Fisher, Michael, 280
Foligno, Isaac, 49
*Forms of Prayer*, 13
France, Jewish religious life in, xxvii
Frankel, William, 301
Franklin, Ellis, 302
Frederick, Prince Adolphus (Duke of

Cambridge), 3
Freund, Rabbi Samuel, 100
Friedländer, Michael, 1
Friedländer, Moses, 381
Friedman, Theodore, 366
fundamentalism, 311

G

Gaster, Moses, 88, 89, 108, 139
*gedolei hador*, 333
Gee, George, 350
Geiger, Abraham, 212
Germany: Jewish religious life in, xxvii; reform in, 3
*get* (Jewish divorce), 277
Goldberg, P. Selvin, 322, 328
Goldberg, Philip, 247, 260
Golditch, Isaac, 280, 281
Goldsmid, Francis, 47, 48, 61, 80, 94; as President of Jews' Hospital and Jews' Free School, 79
Goldsmid, Sir Isaac Lyon, 116
Goldsmid, Sir Julian, 81, 82, 83, 85, 88; and Hermann Adler, 100
Gollancz, Hermann, 104, 140, 147–8, 190
Gollop, Mark, 240, 273
Goulston, Michael, 350
Great Sanhedrin, 45, 46
Great Secession/secessionists *see* secessionists
Great Synagogue, 28, 43, 167; communal service (1937), 235
Green, Aaron Asher, 118, 119
Green, Michael A., 141
Greenberg, Leopold J., 131, 132, 134
Grunfeld, Isidor, 300–1, 324, 325
Gryn, Hugo, 350, 356, 363
Gumprecht, J.J., 2

H

Habbakuk, verse on, 129
Hadarshan, Rabbi Shimon ('The Preacher'), 1
Hailsham, Baron, 349
ha-Levi, Jehuda, liturgical poems of, 119
Halsted, Dulcie, 350
Hampstead Synagogue, 89, 98, 112, 264; and Hertz, 243; and Joseph, 101, 110, 111; proposal, 108
Handler, Arieh, xxii
Harris, Cyril (South African Chief Rabbi), xx
Harris, Henry: on Board constitution, 84; on Board of Deputies' controversy (1853), 63, 65, 67, 68, 69, 70–1; on marriage ceremonies, 49
Harris, Isidore, 138, 166, 229; retirement as acting senior minister at Berkeley Street, 225; sermon, 197–8, 199
Hart, Judah, 65, 68
Hartog, Lady, 262
Hegel, Georg Wilhelm Friedrich, xxi
Hellenistic civilisation, 185, 211
Henriques, Alfred, 80, 81
Henriques, Cecil Q., 149
Henriques, D.Q., 33
Henriques, Henry S.Q., 149, 229
Hertz, Joseph Herman, xix, 5, 190, 232, 329, 379; 'Affirmations' sermon, 221, 222; and BBC, 235–6; and Bentwich (Norman), 286; birth and early life, 159; death of, 251–2; at Great Synagogue communal service, 235; at Hampstead, 243; and Hochman, 180, 181; inaugural sermon, 161–2, 165; induction, 167, 169; on Liberal Judaism, xxvi, 218, 219; London

visit, 156, 157, 159, 164; 'New Paths' sermon, 217, 218, 222; on Pittsburgh Conference, 160; on Reform Judaism, 157, 158, 159, 160; on religious indifference, 229–30; on sacred days, 212–13; on Sinai revelation, 220; and South Africa, 162, 163, 164, 203; on Traditional Judaism, 195, 211, 214, 219, 220; and United Synagogue, 228, 381; and Waley Cohen, xxx, 193, 203–5, 209, 222, 223, 228, 233–4, 241, 245
Hertz, Rose (née Freed), 251
Hertz, Simon, 159
Herzog, Isaac, 6, 226
Herzog, Yaacov, 320, 321
Hesse, David, 63
Hildesheimer, Ezriel, 159
Hirsch, Emil G., 212, 214
Hirsch, Samson Raphael, xix, 2, 19; as Chief Rabbi, 4; influence of, 5
Hirschell, Solomon (Chief Rabbi), xiii, xiv, 8; Burton Street synagogue, refusal to certify as synagogue, 61; 'Caution', 9; death of, 21; and secessionists, 12–13, 15, 16
Hirschfeld, Hirsch, 19
Hochman, Joseph Simon, xxvi; and Adler (Hermann), 176, 177; on attitudes to women, 184–5; birth and early life, 171; and British School of Jewish Learning, proposals for, 201–2; Chief Rabbis, conflict with, 170, 175–6, 177–8, 181; and Hertz, 180, 181; on Liberal Judaism, 172; as New West End Synagogue minister, 162, 171, 173, 176; resignation as minister of New West End, 170, 183–4; scholarship awards, 171; sermons on Orthodox observance, 173–4; on triennial reading of Torah, 179, 188; and United Synagogue, 172, 178, 179, 186, 188
Homa, Bernard, 240, 254, 353
Hungary, Jewish religious life in, xxvii
Hurwitz, Rabbi Hirsh, 207
Hyam, David, 68
Hyamson, Dayan Moses, 113, 165, 169
Hyman, Morrice, 31

I

intermarriage, 273; wartime conditions, 253–4
IRG (German Jewish Religious Society), 4, 5

J

Jacobs, Lawrence, 295
Jacobs, Louis, 63, 334–5; appointment as principal of Jews' College, blocking of, xxvi, 292–5; and Brodie, xxvi, 288, 298–9, 305, 309; at Jews' College, 286; as minister of Manchester's Central Synagogue, 287; as New West End Synagogue minister, 286, 305, 311; Orthodoxy of, 313; 'The Sanction for the Mitzvot' lecture, 306, 309; West London Synagogue, lecture at, 291
'Jacobs Affair', xx
Jakobovits, Immanuel, xix, xxvi; and Bayfield, 362; birth of, 5; and Board of Deputies, 358; and Brichto, 348–9; on Brodie, 341; as Chief Rabbi, 6, 318, 328, 329,

337, 383, 384–5; dialogue and reconciliation policy, 331; on gaps within Anglo-Jewry, 377–8; in Ireland, 6, 8; and Liberal Judaism, 330; 'New Year Message to the Leadership of Anglo-Jewry', 346; and Rayner, 344, 346, 363; on Reform Judaism, 6–7; religious education, 6
Jakobovits, Julius (Joel), 5–6, 318
Janner, Greville, 355–6
Jessel, Albert H., 118, 131, 132–4, 153; withdrawal from Jewish Religious Union, 141–2
*Jewish Chronicle*: on Abramsky, 238; on Adler (Nathan Marcus), 29, 33; on Board of Deputies' controversy (1853), 64–5; on Brodie, 325; on Elkin, 27–8; on Hermann Adler, 151; on Hertz, 224, 251, 259–60; on Jakobovits, 352; on Jewish Religious Union, 119–20, 124, 141; on Jews' College, 105; on marriage ceremonies, 51–2; on Nathan Marcus Adler, 90–3; on Reform and Orthodox relations, 88; on reforms, 114; on rift in Jewish community, 40; on Sabbath-eve liturgy, 42; on West London Council, 80–1
Jewish Religious Education Board, 166
Jewish Religious Union, 439–45; Adler (Hermann) on, 118, 120–1, 122–3, 145–6; foundation of, 381; inaugural service, 119; on Israel, 124; *Jewish Chronicle* on, 119–20, 124, 141; as Jewish Religious Union for the Advancement of Liberal Judaism, 172; lay resignations from, 131; and Liberal Judaism, establishment in Britain, 116; manifesto, 141, 143–5, 148;

Marylebone services, 137; Montefiore (Claude) as president, 118; naming of, 118; and Reform/Chief Rabbinate relations, 147; Sunday services, accusations of, 141, 142; on Ten Commandments, 123; types of service, 120; vicissitudes in fortunes of, 141; *see also* Liberal Judaism
*Jewish Review*, 172, 180
Jewish Theological Seminary, 159
Jewish War Memorial Scheme, 192, 196, 200, 202, 203, 205
Jews' College: and British School of Jewish Learning, proposals for, 192–3, 198; Conference of Anglo-Jewish Ministers at, 148; constitution, 194; Louis Jacobs, as principal, xxvi, 286; and Joseph, 103, 105, 194–5; *Jubilee Volume*, 171; and Orthodox Judaism, 208; and Reform 'Academy of Jewish Learning', 203; Singer at, 116; teaching staff, 105
Jonassohn, David, 62, 65, 68, 71
Joseph, Abraham, 66
Joseph, Morris, 109, 148, 168; on Hermann Adler's death, 154; on Bible, 103; on brazen serpent, 108; on conservative Jew, 107; cremation of, 113; 'dream', 110; and Hampstead Synagogue, 101, 110, 111; and Hertz, 166; and Jews' College, 103, 105, 194–5; as protégé of Nathan Adler, 103; 'revised services' of, 106; Sabbath afternoon services, 107, 108; as senior minister at West London Synagogue, 113
Joseph, Nathan S., 118
Joseph, Sir Keith, 270
Josephs, Walter, 33
Jowett, Benjamin, 117

Judaism: Blau on, 225; Hertz on, 162; Hochman on, 175; Jacobs on, 288–90; Liberal *see* Liberal Judaism; Montefiore (Claude) on, 137–8; present position, in England, 434–7; Reform *see* Reform Judaism; Singer on, 126; Traditional *see* Traditional Judaism; Waley Cohen on, 193

### K

Kahn, Augustus, 206
Kalisch, Marcus, 100
Kalms, Stanley, 386
*ketubah* (marriage certificate), 280
*kiddushin* (solemnisation of marriage), 278
King-Hamilton, Alan, 350–1
*Klal Yisrael*, concept, 320, 321, 369
kolel, Gateshead, 286, 287
Kopelowitz, Lionel, 374

### L

Lamentations, 173, 174
Landau, Frederick, 350
Langdon, Harold, 351, 356
Laski, Neville, 232, 234
Laub, Morris, 336
*Laws and Regulations for all the Synagogues in the British Empire*, xxviii, 41, 42
Lazarus, Dayan, 229
Lazarus, Harris, 252, 254
legitimacy of children, 274, 278
Lehrman, Simon, 251
Lerner, Isaac, 287
Levine, Ephraim, 180, 288
Levy, Felix, 295
Levy, Isaac, 264–5, 280
Levy, Jonas, 49, 52, 68
Lewis-Barned, Harry B., 149

Liaison Committee, 356
Liberal Judaism: on Abrahamic covenant, 216; beliefs, 137–8; on Bible, 216; and birth of Chief Rabbinate, xxix; on British School of Jewish Learning, proposals for, 196; and Christianity, 212, 216–17; Claude Montefiore lecture, Liberal Jewish Synagogue (1962), 292; growth of, in twentieth century, xxix; Hertz on, xxvi, 218, 219; Hochman on, 172; and Jewish Religious Union, 116; Liberal Jewish Synagogue, first AGM, 167; on marriage ceremonies, 262, 270; opposition of dayanim to, 258; Orthodox Judaism, similarities and differences, 197; roots of, 115; on Sabbath and Holy Days, 215–16; strengths of, 117; *see also* Jewish Religious Union
liturgical reform, 41
Loewe, Louis, 47
London: Beth Din, 247, 248, 257, 261, 338; conflict in Jewish press, xiv; Hertz's visit, 156, 157, 159, 164; and provincial communities, 86; unique nature of Jewry in, 97; *see also* West London Synagogue of British Jews
Löwry, Ernest, 102
Lucas, Henry, 131
Lucas, Victor, 293, 350
Lucien Wolf lecture, 268
Lyons, Frank, 109

### M

Machzike Hadath (Upholders of the Faith), 154, 237
Magnus, Laurie, 149, 150

Magnus, Philip, 84, 85, 149
Maimonides, 72, 284
*mamzerim*, 274
Manchester Congregation of British Jews, 44, 125
Manchester Jewry, 85
Manchester Reform movement, 82
*Manna* (Reform journal), 362
Margolies, Raphael, 287
Margoliouth (apostate), 39–40
Marks, David Woolf, 10–11, 24, 25; ambitions of, 41; death and funeral of, 138, 139; and Hampstead Synagogue, 89; and Montefiore (Moses), 29, 47, 50, 61; on Reform Judaism, 98; Sabbath sermons at Western Synagogue, invitation to preach at, 87; on secessionist reform, 44–5
Marmur, Dow, 366
Marriage (Secretaries of Synagogues) Bill (1959), 270
Marriage and Registration Acts, 53; Amendment (1856), 50, 51, 56–8, 82
marriage ceremonies: authorisation of marriage secretaries of Reform congregations, 60; Dissenters' Marriage Bill, 49, 50; *ketubah* (marriage certificate), 280; *kiddushin* (solemnisation of marriage), 278; and Liberal Judaism, 262, 270; Marriage and Registration Acts, 50, 51, 53, 56–8; post-Second World War, 254; Royal Commission on the Laws of Marriage, 52–3; Schiller-Szinessy on, 85; statistics, 446; *see also* intermarriage, wartime conditions
Marsden, Herbert, 132
Masorti (Conservative) movement, xvi
Mattuck, Israel, 155, 167, 168, 197, 229; criticism of, 257; at Great Synagogue communal service, 235; on marriage ceremonies, 256, 266; on opposition to Liberal Judaism, 258; at West London Synagogue, 199
Mayhew, Henry, 96
Melchior, Bent, 339, 340, 341
Melchior, Marcus, 336
Meldola, David, 39
Mendelssohn, Moses, 1
Mendes, Abraham Pereira, 100
Merthyr Tydfil synagogue, 83, 84, 85
Michaels, Maurice, 356
Micholls, Horatio, 52
Mishnah, 174
mixed seating, in synagogues, 160
Mocatta, Abraham, 94
Mocatta, B. Elkin, 149
Mocatta, Daniel, 69–70
Mocatta, Frederic David, 138–9
Mocatta, Moses, 47
Mocatta, Owen, 240
Mocatta, Sir Alan, 292, 295
Montagu, Ewen S., 295, 296, 298
Montagu, Lilian (Lily) Helen, 116, 117, 118, 224
Montagu, Samuel, 84, 117; and Singer, 127, 128
Montefiore, Claude G., 116, 120, 146–7, 167; *Jewish Chronicle* on, 143; as president of Jewish Religious Union, 118; on Reform Judaism, 138, 155; as speaker, 137
Montefiore, Horatio, 52
Montefiore, Leonard, 291
Montefiore, Sir Moses, 21, 47, 48; and Adler, 92, 93; and Board of Deputies' controversy (1853), 61, 63, 65, 68; as chairman, 72; and Claude Montefiore, 116; and Marks, 47, 50, 61; retirement as

Index 473

president of Board of Deputies,
80; and Salomons, 74; and secessionists, 15
Morais, Sabato, 165
Munk, Eliyahu, 287
Munk, Rabbi Ezra, 358
musar (ethical instruction), 287

N

Neuberger, Rabbi Julia, 361, 372
New London Synagogue, 336
New West End Synagogue, xxvi, 162,
171, 173, 176; Jacobs as minister,
286, 305, 311; resignation of
Hochman as minister, 170, 183–4
Ninth of Av, 213

O

'Omens of Peace', 33, 34, 52
Oppenheim, Samuel, 105
Orach Chayim Congregation, New
York, 156, 162, 163, 164
Oral Law, 77, 85, 306; authority and
validity, 25; and English
Reformers, 214; rejection by
secessionists, 10, 32
Orthodox Judaism: affiliation to tradition by non-Orthodox Jews,
96–7; Anglo-Jewish revolt (1853),
60; Bible, authority owed to, 117,
175; congregational life, reforms,
43; growth of, in twentieth century, xxix; and Jews' College, 208;
Liberal Judaism, similarities and
differences, 197

P

Palmer, Sir Roundell, 48
Palmerston, Lord, 50

Pearl, Chaim, 302
Pentateuch, 144, 306
Peter Fredrick (Grand Duke), 2
Petuchowski, Jakob J., 365
Phillips, B.S., 64, 73, 79
Picciotto, Moses Haim, 68
pluralism, 376–7
prayer, language of, 185
Progressives, 344, 347, 349, 352,
365, 370, 373
proselytes, 212, 216, 279
psak din (religious ruling), 255, 256

R

Rabbinic Conference, 348, 349
Rabbinowich, Joseph, 157
Rapoport, Rabbi Salomon Loeb, 100
Rayner, John D., 343, 345; and
Jakobovits, 344, 346, 363
Recall to the Synagogue movement,
243, 245
Reform Assembly of Ministers, 344
Reform Beth Din, 261–2, 273
Reform Judaism: and Adler, 48, 76,
85, 86, 101; American conserva-
tive school, 225; and birth of
Chief Rabbinate, xxix; British, 26;
condemnation of, 79; and German
contemporaries, 94, 95; growth
of, in twentieth century, xxix;
Hertz on, 157, 158, 159, 160;
Jakobovits on, 7; in Manchester,
82, 94; Montefiore (Claude) on,
138, 155; neo-Karaite structure,
97; rabbis, 157, 261; Reform
Synagogues of Great Britain, ministers' assembly, 281; religious
leaders, 278; on suicide, 158; and
United Synagogue, xvii; see also
secessionists
Reinhart, Harold, 261

religious observance, decline in, 95, 96, 229–30
Revised Prayer Book, 116
ritual, 41
Rivkin, Rabbi Moshe, 287
Rogosnitzky, Ber, 274, 331
Rose, Maurice, 340, 344, 351
Rosenberg, Rosita, 376
Roth, Cecil, 258
Rothschild, Baron Lionel de, 62, 63, 64, 66, 67, 88, 194; on ecclesiastical authorities, 73; and Hertz, 208; as United Synagogue president, 203, 241
Rothschild, Sir Anthony de, 29, 63, 241, 381
Royal Commission on the Laws of Marriage, 52–3

S

Sabbath-eve liturgy, changes to (by Adler), 42–3
Sacks, Jonathan (Chief Rabbi), 389–90; on United Synagogue, xv–xvi, xvii–xviii
sacred days, Jewish year, 212–13
sacrificial rite, 106–7, 175
Salaman, Redcliffe Nathan, xxx, 267–9, 270
Salmon, John, 31
Salomons, Sir David: on Board of Deputies, 56, 66, 67; and Cohen, 73; on ecclesiastical authorities, 75; on marriage ceremonies, 53–4, 55, 59, 60; and Montefiore, 74; on Orthodoxy, 66; resignation from Board of Deputies, 74–5; and Royal Commission on the Laws of Marriage, 58; on secessionists, 62
Samuel, Sampson, 50
Sanderson, Harold, 375
Sanhedrin, 45, 46
Schiff, David Tevele, 1, 8, 9
Schiller-Szinessy, Solomon, 85
Schlesinger, Leonard, 176
Schonfeld, Solomon, 5
Schonfeld, Victor, 227, 228; as executive director of Religious Emergency Council, 239; Union of Orthodox Hebrew Congregations, 5, 230–1
Schott, Moses, 86
Schreiber, Rabbi Simcha Bunim, 5
Scripture, as Word of God, 285
Sebag-Montefiore, Joseph, 84
secessionists *see* secessionists: declaration, 9–10; edict of excommunication against, 12–13, 14; letters by, 11, 14–15; Oral Law, rejection of, 10, 32; prayer book, 10; principles of, 11–12; reforms of, 94; Salomons on, 62; second festival day, abolition, 44–6
Sefer Torah, 214
Segal, Moshe Yitzhak, 287
*Selection of Prayers, Psalms and Hymns*, 119, 122
Sephardi Jews, 11
Shachter, Rabbi Jacob, 207
shochet, certificates of competence for, 86
Shulchan Aruch, 103, 185, 280
Simon, John, 47
Sinai revelation, 220
Singer, Simeon, 118–19, 120, 124; death of, 129; on faith, 129–30; Jewish Religious Union, sermon to, 125–6; at Jews' College, 116; and Montagu (Samuel), 127, 128; on nature of Judaism, 126
Sir Moses Montefiore Studentship, 171
Slowe, Malcolm, 343

Society for the Study of Jewish Theology, 302, 306
'Solomon's Judgment' (Chanukkah sermon), 76, 77
Spielmann, Isidore, 118, 141
St John's Wood Synagogue, 118, 120
Stamford Hill, Adath Yisroel congregation, 227
Stein, Siegfried, 287
Steinberg, Rabbi Baruch, 287
Stern, Frederick C., 193–4
Stern, Joseph F., 118, 124
suicide, 158
Sunday, as Sabbath of Jew, 213
Swift, Morris, 281, 287–8, 367
Swift, Harris, 280
synagogue membership, 1836 constitution, 61
synagogue statistics, 446–8

T

Talmud, 103, 174
Teff, Solomon, 337
Ten Commandments, 218
*A Time for Change* (United Synagogue's Review), xvi–xvii
Tisha b'Av, 213
Torah, 179, 188, 214, 284; as basis of Jewish existence, 306; as divine revelation, 286; lishmah (Torah for its own sake), 286; parts of as man-made, 306, 310
Traditional Judaism, 192–210; definition issues, 192, 195, 211; and Hertz, 195, 211, 214, 219, 220; and West London Synagogue, 199
Twiss, Travers, 56

U

Union of Liberal and Progressive Synagogues, 263–4, 321; ministers' conference, 280–1
Union of Orthodox Hebrew Congregations, 5, 230–1; and Federation of Synagogues, 354
United Synagogue: on Adler (Nathan Marcus), 99; Beth Din on, 247; and Chief Rabbi, 182; and Conservative movement, xvi; Deed of Foundation and Trust, 42, 118, 131, 228; and East End Jews, 132; establishment of (1870), xv, xxvi–xxvii; and Hertz, 228, 381; and Hochman, 172, 178, 179, 186, 188; membership, on self-identity, xvii; as 'merely' a house of prayer, 186; moderate reformers within, opposition from Chief Rabbinate, xxvi; and Reform Judaism, xvii; Review, xvi–xvii; Sacks on, xvii–xviii
United Synagogue of America, 275
Unterman Committee, 356, 364, 365

V

Van der Zyl, Werner, 277, 279, 350
'verbal' inspiration, doctrine of, 285
*Voice of Jacob*, 30, 32

W

Waley, Philip, 200, 229
Waley Cohen, Robert, xxvi; on Brodie, 260; as chairman of Jewish War Services Committee, 240; on creation of British School of Jewish Learning, proposals for, 193; and Hertz, xxx, 193, 203–5, 209, 222, 223, 228, 233–4, 241, 245; on Liberal Judaism, 225–6;

on Reform 'Academy of Jewish Learning', 203; and Reform Judaism, 200–1
Wessely, Naphtali Hartwig, 1
West London Synagogue of British Jews: and Adler (Hermann), 167; in Berkeley Street, 81, 84, 85, 87, 102; as Burton Street Place of Worship, 10, 32, 40–1; establishment of, 125; golden jubilee service (1892), 87; and Hertz, 166; Jacobs, lecture by, 291; Joseph as senior minister, 113; in Margaret Street, 40, 49, 67, 68, 69, 71; on marriage ceremonies, 48; marriage secretaries of Reform congregations, authorisation, 60; Mattuck at, 199; modifications introduced in, 102; philanthropic congregants, 79–80; refusal to certify as synagogue (Hirschell), 61; representation on Board of Deputies, 83; and Traditional Judaism, 199
Wise, I.M., 157
Wolf, A., 141
Wolfson, Sir Isaac, 302, 303, 319
women, synagogue's attitude to, 184–5
Woolf, Albert M., 229
Woolf, Alfred, 350
World Council of Synagogues, 336
World Union for Progressive Judaism, 224
Wright, Aaron, 247, 248

Y

*Yalkut Shimoni*, 1
Yom Kippur, 213

Z

Zechariah (prophet), 21
Zimmels, H.J., 294